SAINT JOSEPH'S COLLEGE

INDIANA

Involved For Life

LAW ENFORCEMENT

IN THE

UNITED STATES

James A. Conser, PhD, CPP

Deputy Director
Ohio Peace Officer Training Commission
London, Ohio

(On leave from the Criminal Justice Department
Youngstown State University
Youngstown, Ohio)

Gregory D. Russell, JD, PhD

Director
Washington State University
Criminal Justice Program
Pullman, Washington

AN ASPEN PUBLICATION®
Aspen Publishers, Inc.
Gaithersburg, Maryland
2000

THE LIBRARY
ST. JOSEPH'S COLLEGE
RENSSELAER, INDIANA 47978

HV
8138
.C6445
2000

Library of Congress Cataloging-in-Publication Data

Conser, James A. (James Andrew), 1948–
Law enforcement in the United States / James A. Conser, Gregory D. Russell.
p. cm.
Includes bibliographical references and index.
ISBN 0-8342-1724-4 (alk. paper)
1. Law enforcement—United States. 2. Police—United States. I. Russell, Gregory D. II. Title.

HV8138.C6445 2000
363.2′3″0973—dc21 99-045510
CIP

About Aspen Publishers • For more than 40 years, Aspen has been a leading professional publisher in a variety of disciplines. Aspen's vast information resources are available in both print and electronic formats. We are committed to providing the highest quality information available in the most appropriate format for our customers. Visit Aspen's Internet site for more information resources, directories, articles, and a searchable version of Aspen's full catalog, including the most recent publications: **www.aspenpublishers.com**
Aspen Publishers, Inc. • The hallmark of quality in publishing
Member of the worldwide Wolters Kluwer group.

Orders: (800) 638-8437
Customer Service: (800) 234-1660

Editorial Services: Lenda P. Hill
Library of Congress Catalog Card Number: 99-045510
ISBN: 0-8342-1724-4

Printed in the United States of America

1 2 3 4 5

Contents

Dedication

To my patient and understanding wife, Linda.

—Jim Conser

To my son, Fred.

—Greg Russell

Preface

The law enforcement field today is more demanding and complex than ever before and yet there are literally thousands of students studying to become officers or agents. There are also many non-students who desire and seek employment in this field. This trend is both positive and a negative. It is positive in that so many want to pursue careers in a very important field of work. Becoming an officer of the law is an extremely significant undertaking and is one where you can touch the lives of many people and serve the larger community. The negative side of this large number of job-seekers is that not all will be successful in pursuing a career in law enforcement. While the positions have many benefits and career mobility, there are a limited number of them. Yes, there are cycles of employment opportunities, and we are actually experiencing a time of high recruitment and hiring. But the motivations and quality of persons *wanting* to enter the field of policing may not match the *needs and demands* of the agencies. Some people seek law enforcement positions because of the perceived excitement and risk—a picture often envisioned from media highlights and "cop shows" on television. Others seek these positions because of the salary, benefits, and job-stability. Still others seek such policing jobs because of a deep-felt desire to help people in need. In reality, there is some of all these aspects and motivations in many job applicants. However, employers will be the first to tell you that they need applicants who can deal with people, have the ability to relate and communicate with others, and can handle the authority and decision-making that is part of the job. They must be able to write and operate computerized equipment, be able to work long hours on occasion, and be flexible. They must have a personality that can withstand being called names, being given a number of hand gestures, and having their actions publicly scrutinized. Moreover, potential candidates must accept the fact that they are officers of the Constitution of the United States, which they swear to uphold. As public servants, they enforce the law and help solve community problems, but they do not make policy. The rather tricky balancing this requires is not a task to enter into lightly.

As a society, we are blessed with a significantly large number of citizens who are law-abiding and pose no harm to others. On the other hand, the level of violence of those who are not so inclined appears to be increasing—not in numbers—in the *level of violence*. There are definitely dangerous persons "out there," and, if some sociologists and psychologists are correct, there are many in our elementary and secondary schools and the criminal justice system is expected to encounter them in the near future.

But it is possible to make a difference. It is possible to have a rewarding career in the field of law enforcement. "The power of one person," is underestimated today and there are too many people with the "I can't make a difference attitude." If you believe the latter, then the field of law enforcement is not for you. If you are open to the idea of making a difference, then read on. There are many opportunities in the field and this text just scratches the surface of them. Hopefully, you will continue to seek out additional information, to use this text as guide to other resources and references. To many, policing appears to suffer from a constant state of *confusion*. But to those of us who have worked the streets, prosecuted cases, and/or studied this field for the last several decades, we know that it is not a constant state of confusion; rather, it is a constant state of *change!* Knowing the difference and being able to cope with that constant change is an asset needed in the criminal justice community today.

Throughout the text, we have provided web sites or addresses for the World Wide Web. If you are a frequent user of the Internet, you already know that occasionally a web site changes addresses or is off-line for a while. If the web addresses cited in this text do not immediately work, try them another day or at a different time. If you still cannot successfully locate the site, use your search engine and try entering a few key words related to the topic of the original site. You may find the originally intended site or an alternate site that may serve the same purpose. Please do not become frustrated—there is a wealth of criminal justice information on the World Wide Web and more being added daily. It is a medium that is truly changing how textbooks are written, how courses are taught, and how students learn. It is a gateway to the future.

Of course, it is also the case that the study of law enforcement is important for student/citizens regardless of one's career interests. Policing agencies are the one institutional entity in America that are regularly authorized to use force against other citizens without prior approval. This is a serious power and, in a democracy, one that we must guard carefully. Much of the literature on community policing, whether by academics or practitioners, makes reference to the "distance between" police and community or the "isolation" the officers feel from the people they were intended to serve. If this observation is empirically true, it is as much a fault of law enforcement as it is of the people for failing to study this most significant institution in the preservation of a democracy. Moreover, the study of police organizations and officer behavior is a rich field of human behavior and tells us much about the society in which we live. It is unlikely that any institution, police or congresss, could survive long if it did not reflect the expectations of the people. Hence, law enforcement is an eye into the soul of the culture and the society. The fact that law enforcement feels pressure to reform now is stark evidence of this reality. The field of study is, therefore, suited to all citizens.

James A. Conser

Gregory D. Russell

Acknowledgments

The authors acknowledge Courtney Ballard (YSU graduate assistant) for her early editorial assistance on the manuscript, and Mary Dillingham (YSU secretary) for typing assistance.

The authors appreciate the many agencies that granted permission to use examples of their publications, operations, and structures. They also acknowledge the many law enforcement professionals with whom they have had the privilege of working and from whom much has been learned.

The Field Of Law Enforcement

New York City police officer Eric Perez patrols 139th Street in the Washington Heights neighborhood of New York. December 1998. (AP/ Wide World Photos)

THE BASIC CONCEPT OF LAW ENFORCEMENT

In a democratic society, as in all modern societies, the enforcement of the law is a vital function. Without some type of law enforcement, a society would eventually cease to exist. Generally speaking, the function called **law enforcement** is a society's formal attempt to obtain compliance with the established rules, regulations, and law of that society. Without law enforcement, our American society as we know it would probably succumb to social disorder and chaos.

The United States is a representative democracy that places great emphasis on the protection of individual freedoms and liberties. As such, its institutions must reflect those principles upon which the country was founded. Because the United States is predominately an open and free society, disagreements about how to enforce the law are common. Questioning the actions of law enforcement officials, as is commonly done in the mass media, is also a national characteristic. Historically, our country's citizens have often questioned the actions of government officials. As citizens, we may not always agree with what happens on the street, in police stations, in courtrooms, in jails, and in prisons.

However, people in the United States possess the liberty and freedom to criticize and protest governmental actions. It is actually a tribute to our criminal justice system that these liberties and freedoms exist—they do not exist in all countries!

Our purpose here is to assist you in becoming more informed about the field of law enforcement so that you have an understanding and appreciation for its activities. Such a background is necessary for you to develop informed opinions about the field, rather than opinions based on limited knowledge and experience. Everyone has opinions; some are more informed than others. "Educated persons" have informed opinions and can describe why they believe certain things. They have a foundation (facts and evidence) for their arguments and reasons for doing things, making choices, and advocating changes. Society needs informed, knowledgeable citizens who understand the field of law enforcement and its impact on social behavior.

Law Enforcement as Policing

Law enforcement is one means of formally supervising human behavior that insures that laws and regulations of a society are followed. The term **policing,** on the other hand, is a much broader term than law enforcement and refers to the process of regulating the general health, safety, welfare, and morals of society. The right to engage in the policing function stems from the legal concept of **police powers,** which is the government's lawful right to enact regulations and laws related to health, safety, welfare, and morals. The policing function in the United States is primarily observed through the operations of the criminal justice system in the prevention, detection, investigation, and prosecution of crime. However, the police powers carried out by governments include other activities such as the establishment and regulation of water and sewer systems, highway and transportation systems, fire protection, monetary regulatory systems, health and medical systems, park and recreation areas, general assistance to the economically deprived, and food processing.

The process of policing is a *formal* one sanctioned in American society by the people (voters) through their elected governmental bodies. Of the three branches of government in the United States, the policing function is the responsibility of the executive branch. Executive branch officials include the President of the United States at the federal level, governors at the state level, and mayors at the local level. These officials and their representatives use their governmental authority in selecting policing officials and establishing the philosophies and general policies under which they will operate. The other branches of government also affect the abilities of policing officials to perform their jobs. The legislative branch provides the statutory authority under which police operate. This authority includes the lawful right to use different levels of force to achieve law enforcement goals and objectives. It is the authorized use of force that sets policing officials apart from other occupations. Of course, the legislative branch is formally responsible for defining behavior which is to be considered criminal in a particular jurisdiction. The judicial branch of government reviews the actions of police officials according to the established rules of constitutional law, criminal procedure, and evidence. This review normally occurs during judicial proceedings such as initial hearings, preliminary hearings, suppression of evidence hearings, and trials. Table 1–1 summarizes the role of the three branches of government in the policing function of the United States.

Police Officials

The concept of law enforcement encompasses all levels (federal, state, and local) of the executive branch of government. It includes agencies that enforce administrative codes and regulations (rules of agencies) and criminal laws related to the health, safety, and welfare of the people. A broad spectrum of officials with titles such as officer, deputy, agent, trooper, inspector, auditor, investigator, ranger, marshal, constable, or compliance officer can be found in policing agencies. These officials may be employees of agencies that inspect the food supply (Department of Agriculture) or places of employment (Occupational Safety and Health Administration), investigate the causes of fires (State Fire Marshal), protect abused and neglected children (County Children's Services), investigate airplane accidents (Federal Aviation Administration), conduct audits of government expenditures (State Auditor's Office), investigate criminal complaints (federal, state, and local law enforcement), and/or apprehend offenders (any agency with arrest authority). The personnel affiliated with such agencies who are engaged in policing functions can be referred to as law enforcement personnel. However, in the United States, **police officials** are a special group of law enforcement officials by the fact that they are armed and are authorized to use coercive and physical force under certain conditions when carrying out their duties. This text's focus is on these police officials— nonmilitary, armed, governmental personnel who are granted the authority to prevent, detect, investigate, and prosecute criminal behavior and to apprehend alleged offenders. Some states, for the purpose of statutory references, use the phrase "peace officer" in lieu of the various titles used in the field (see Exhibit 1–1). Police officials take an **oath of office** to uphold and enforce the law (see Exhibit 1–2 for a sample oath of office).

As a student of the policing function, you should be aware that the terminology associated with police officials and their agency affiliation is important and occasionally confusing. Several terms (policing, law enforcement, and police officials) that have been used above may appear to be very similar, and they are. If you are going to be an informed person and possibly a future criminal justice professional, you should know that differences do exist and sometimes titles

Table 1–1 The Government's Involvement in Policing

BRANCH	*Legislative*	*Executive*	*Judicial*
OFFICES or TITLES	Congress Legislatures Boards Councils	President Governors Trustees Mayors	Courts Justices Judges Magistrates
POLICING ROLE	Enacts statutes, codes, ordinances, and resolutions Establishes policy	Enforces legislative enactments Operates law enforcement agencies Initiates criminal prosecutions Establishes agency procedures/rules	Reviews enforcement actions Adjudicates legal disputes Tries criminal cases Issues orders and sanctions

Exhibit 1–1   What's in a Name?

THE DEFINITION OF PEACE OFFICER IN OHIO

"Peace officer" includes . . . a sheriff; deputy sheriff; marshal; deputy marshal; member of the organized police department of any municipal corporation, including a member of the organized police department of a municipal corporation in an adjoining state serving in Ohio under a contract pursuant to section 737.04 of the Revised Code; member of a police force employed by a metropolitan housing authority . . .; member of a police force employed by a regional transit authority . . .; state university law enforcement officer . . .; enforcement agent of the department of public safety . . .; employee of the department of natural resources who is a natural resources law enforcement staff officer . . ., a forest officer . . ., a preserve officer . . ., a wildlife officer . . ., a park officer . . ., or a state watercraft officer . . .; veterans' home police officer . . .; police constable of any township; and police officer of a township or joint township police district; and, for purpose of arrests within those areas, and for purposes of Chapter 5503 of the Revised Code, and the filing of and service of process relating to those offenses witnessed or investigated by them, includes the superintendent and troopers of the state highway patrol.

Source: State of Ohio, §2935.01 *Ohio Revised Code.*

---

distinguish some police officials from others. At the federal level, police officials are usually referred to as "agents," although members of the U.S. Marshal's Office are called "deputy marshals." At the state level, police officials may be called "troopers," "state police officers," and/or "agents." At the local level, members of the county sheriff's office are "deputies" or "deputy sheriffs," and members of municipal and village police departments are called "police officers." The terms "constable" and "marshal" may be used in some jurisdictions at the local level. Members of federal and state forestry, park, or wildlife divisions may have the title of "ranger" or "warden." It can get confusing, but personnel in the law enforcement field do make these distinctions for reasons of courtesy, respect, and clarification of responsibilities. An analogy might be that most of us drive cars, but some insist on referring to their vehicles by name—Saturn, Cougar, Grand AM, Maxima, Corvette, Jetta, and so on. Not all cars are created equal, and some car owners want you to know that! In the same vein, all police officials are law enforcement officers, but not all law enforcement officers are called

Exhibit 1–2

SAMPLE OATH OF OFFICE FOR POLICE OFFICIALS

I, (*name*), do solemnly swear to uphold and defend the constitutions of the United States and the State of Michigan, all federal and state laws, and local ordinances, and that I will faithfully discharge the duties of my office according to the law and to the best of my ability, so help me God.

"police"! It is possible that you may encounter some police officials who are very sensitive about their titles. While they may not correct you if you wrongly state their title, you may see them wince occasionally.

Law enforcement personnel occupy unique positions in American society. They act with the authority of the state, meaning that they have been entrusted with the lawful right to enforce the law. Few people in the United States are given such authority along with the right to use coercive force to carry out that duty. Some of these officials are uniformed (and therefore easily visible); others are not. Regardless of the title or whether they wear a uniform, police officials in our society serve in a formal **social control** capacity. Social control is the process whereby a society encourages or enforces compliance with social norms, customs, and laws. There are various viewpoints regarding how limited or extensive this social control function should be. Let us examine in greater depth some of the aspects of the concept of social control.

LAW ENFORCEMENT AS SOCIAL CONTROL

Law enforcement is a societal function necessary for internal stability and security. Through the process of law enforcement, society exercises social control, which impacts the control of behavior, deviant or otherwise. Every society has social control mechanisms because they serve as a means of **socialization,** the process of teaching the culture and norms of the society to its members.

Social control mechanisms are either formal or informal. *Formal mechanisms* generally refer to the units of the governing authority of the country. Formal social control units in the United States include the executive, legislative, and judicial components of the governmental structure at all levels of government. *Informal mechanisms* include the family, peers, church, significant others, and so on. Figure 1–1 depicts a simplified version of selected social control mechanisms.

Social control mechanisms are not as simple to classify, however, as Figure 1–1 might indicate. For example, where should *education* be placed? The educational process can be considered a formal control mechanism because it is often supported through government (tax-supported) institutions. What you learn in school, however, is not simply the formal curriculum (principles of democracy, math, psychology, etc.), but many other things as well (social skills, teamwork, manners, customs, and so on). Thus, education could be classified equally well as an informal mechanism.

The social control mechanisms of a society do not exist in a vacuum. Social, economic, and political influences impact social control. These influences cause shifts in attitudes and values over time. They can cause a society to become more conservative or more liberal in its approach to controlling behavior. Social influences come mainly from the interaction between people and groups and include forces such as customs, values, and religion. Economic influences refer to resources (employment, income, and inflation) and the distribution of goods and services (transportation systems and businesses). Political factors refer to the policy-making process (elections, legislative actions, lobbying) and its related institutions (Congress, legislatures, city councils). As such, these factors relate to the quest for power and the right to influence others, which is one of the major objectives of politics. Exhibit 1–3 identifies a number of examples of these influences upon society.

As with the placement of formal and informal social control mechanisms, the influencing factors are not easily categorized into social, economic, or political ones. For example, the factor of "poverty" is purposely listed in all three categories. Is poverty a social condition? Is it an economic one? What influence do politics and public policy have on poverty? Persuasive arguments could be made for each of these three categories as the major influence on poverty, and there is some validity to each position.

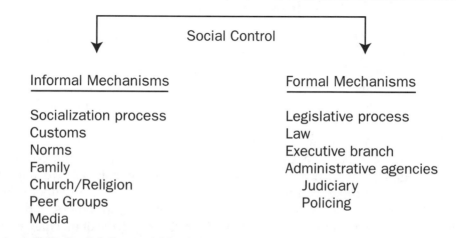

Figure 1–1 Social Control Mechanisms

Exhibit 1-3

INFLUENCES UPON SOCIAL CONTROL		
SOCIAL	**ECONOMIC**	**POLITICAL**
Fads/Trends	Inflation/Recession	Major Parties/Elections
Social Movements	Unemployment	Party in Power
Morality	Welfare	Wars/Conflicts
Religion	Interest Rates	Arms Race
Poverty	Poverty	Poverty
Homelessness	Energy Costs	Congress
Race Relations	Consumer Confidence	Patriotism
Abortion Debate	National Debt	Government Regulation
Crime	Crime Control Costs	Government Policy
Mass Media	Credit Rates	Foreign Relations
Entertainment	Advertising	Foreign Aid
	Imports/Exports	

The issues for law enforcement are several. How much of a role should policing have on the social control function in society? Should there be greater emphasis placed on formal control mechanisms—that is, the government's influence on controlling behavior? Or should the informal control mechanism be emphasized for guiding and influencing behavior? Ultimately, the question becomes one of how much influence the police should have on controlling people's behavior. Someone who believes that the police should not have much of a role in controlling societal behavior would probably believe that there should be greater emphasis placed on the informal mechanisms (e.g., family, church, peer group). One who believes the police should play an active role in controlling social behavior may emphasize tough police measures to control behavior and greater use of the courts and formal punishments to influence behavior. Let us examine four common perspectives (viewpoints) on social control and their impact on policing in the United States. These perspectives are important because they reflect the diversity of ideas and beliefs about how our government agencies should function. They reflect how citizens view crime and influence government policies related to preventing and controlling criminal behavior.

FOUR PERSPECTIVES TO LAW ENFORCEMENT

There are several ways to view the world in which we live. Some people take a narrow viewpoint of certain issues, while others take a broader approach in perceiving situations or issues. For example, in a verbal description about the design of a building, the architect has one mental perspective, the builder another, and the prospective resident another. The architect may be concerned about how the building "fits" into the landscape or with the surrounding buildings. The builder is possibly thinking about cost and what type of materials are to be used. The resident is concerned about the location of internal features, operational costs, and how soon it can be built. Each viewpoint is valid in and of itself, but the focus of the discussion can become very confusing if the three persons do not attempt to "see the other person's approach" to the building. In this example, a comprehensive set of blueprints and architectural drawings could help each person better perceive the others' concerns.

In the following discussion, various approaches to viewing the field of law enforcement are presented. If a person is an advocate of one of these approaches and is discussing law enforcement with someone who holds a different viewpoint, there could be confusion or heated debate over whose position is best. The purpose here is to increase your understanding of each approach to help you reduce confusion and conflict over issues in policing. Sometimes situations are improved when one can see the other person's point of view and compromises can be worked out (or at least there can be better communications about the topic or issue). These approaches are not totally independent of one another; occasionally some aspects overlap with other perspectives.

The Legal Perspective

One common approach to policing is that "the law is the law." **The legal perspective** is an approach that views behavior from a "rule-based" philosophy, in that the law is paramount and is the guide for behavior which everyone must follow. Strong advocates of crime control and severe punishment legislation often adopt this perspective. While there is merit in holding the law in high regard, one must be careful to evaluate a particular law's purpose and whether it is too restrictive. The legalistic approach is evident when someone says, "There should be a law against that." This person is implying that making the behavior a crime will stop people from doing it, or at least will allow the authorities to intervene.

Most people in American society obey the majority of laws. The two most likely reasons for this are: (1) the majority of laws are deemed appropriate, and/or (2) most people respect the law. But it is known that not everyone believes that all laws are appropriate. There also are different levels of "legality." For example, gambling is generally against the law, but certain types may not be (e.g bingo, horse racing, and lotteries), and some people believe that all forms of gambling should be legal. And while some people believe that crimes related to certain sexual behaviors (e.g., prostitution and adultery) should not be against the law, others believe that the law should enforce traditional sexual morality. As any society becomes more diverse in terms of ethnic (national origin), racial, religious, and social backgrounds, agreement diminishes on what should be legal and illegal regarding many behaviors. This lack of agreement leads to many problems for policy makers as well as law enforcement officials. Too many laws against too many behaviors can reduce respect for the law.

In this perspective, police officials are placed in awkward positions since they have sworn to enforce the laws of the nation and the state. They know that if they strictly enforce the law, many people will be arrested or given summonses. Therefore, they must evaluate behavior in terms of "the letter of the law" and "the spirit of the law." If the letter of the law is adhered to, then any violation of law results in official intervention by the police. If the spirit of the law is followed, degrees of seriousness may be considered. Some laws may not be enforced at all, and some people who non-flagrantly violate the law may be handled informally (e.g., verbal reprimand, warnings, or no intervention at all).

This evaluative process leads to the use of **discretion** and **selective enforcement.** Discretion is the process of making a choice among appropriate alternative courses of action. Although most state codes do not give police officers the lawful right to use discretion, it has been professionally and judicially acknowledged. The police simply cannot enforce every law that has been enacted. Selective enforcement refers to enforcing those laws deemed appropriate to the situation or related to the priorities of the agency and the community. The opposite of selective enforcement is **full enforcement,** which requires enforcing all laws all the time—and which, as we just said, is not possible. One major drawback of the legal perspective is the belief that most social control problems can be solved simply by passing and enforcing criminal laws.

The Public Policy Perspective

Public policy, broadly defined, is made up of the rules and regulations that legislative bodies and agencies choose to establish. For example, if spousal abuse or drug abuse requires regulation, a city council or state legislature may pass a law or an ordinance regarding domestic violence and drug dealing. At the same time, a bill might be passed to provide counseling for those charged with spousal abuse or drug use. Both of these actions are examples of public policy developed to address societal problems (Cochran and Malone 1995). This approach is similar to the legal approach just discussed; however, greater emphasis is placed on the political process and on internal agency operations in the public policy approach.

Policy also is established in administrative agencies such as law enforcement agencies. A departmental policy regarding citizen complaints might set out the procedure for reviewing a complaint and detail the possible alternative solutions. Policy can also be made simply by consistently doing something in a particular way. For example, some police departments may tend to avoid domestic violence arrests or ignore concealed weapons found on citizens who have no criminal record. In both cases, a policy has been constructed and followed, even if it is not written.

Using a public policy approach to study law enforcement is important for a number of reasons. First, as the field of law enforcement evolves and becomes more **proactive** in community problems, more policy will be made at the department level. (A proactive response to problems is one that anticipates potential problems and tries to prevent the worst consequences from occurring.) Second, law enforcement managers may need legislative assistance in enacting policy because of current legal restrictions or because they lack the proper authority to enact the needed policy. Therefore, it is important to understand the political nature of the policy-making process and the importance of defending or justifying a policy in an appropriate manner.

Formal policy making at the agency level is a function of the executive team. The chief of police, sheriff, or department head is generally the final authority on policy. Policy cannot be made without considering internal procedure and management, community expectations, and political influences. Internal management issues might include union reactions, current contract language, and officer morale or resistance. Community expectations might emanate from meetings held with civic groups or from public meetings on selected issues (e.g., curfew enforcement, treatment of juveniles, or rumors of a growing gang influence). Political influences can relate to local politics and the campaign promises of elected officials who have some influence over the department's budget. Other forces that impact policy development and evaluation include pending litigation over the actions taken by officers and severe fiscal problems that may cause layoffs or a cut in agency services (Gilmore and Halley 1994). Issues related to political concerns and their impact on law enforcement agencies are discussed in later chapters.

Establishing policy within an agency is a three-step process. The first step is the identification of needs for policy. This often becomes apparent when things do not function properly or serious problems have developed, such as an officer who used deadly force when not authorized to do so but thought he was. However, identification of policy needs also occurs during agency evaluations and review of existing policies when compared to model (or suggested) policy. The professional literature and associations often publish the experiences of other agencies in matters of policy.

The second step involves implementation, or putting the policy into action. Obviously, this relates to how the written word is put into practice by the persons authorized to enforce it: the policy must be properly interpreted, conveyed, and practiced by the agency's personnel. This often involves meetings and training sessions to explain the policy and its rationale and significance.

The third step in establishing policy is evaluation. In the current law enforcement environment, it is critical to evaluate the effectiveness of all law enforcement policies to ensure that improvements have actually occurred. Evaluations can be made through periodic assessment of officer performance, critical incidents, threatened litigation, selected agency measures, and current deficiencies. It should be noted that the evaluation process also leads to the identification of weaknesses and needs for future policy; therefore, the process becomes cyclical and permits continuous updating of policy. Thus, each aspect of policy making—identification, implementation, and evaluation—must be understood for an agency to function effectively (Fischer 1995). Figure 1–2 summarizes the policy-making process.

The Systems Perspective

Law enforcement can also be viewed from the perspective of **systems theory.** This approach encompasses the entire context in which an issue exists by analyzing all the forces or influences impacting it. In other words, the law enforcement field or a particular agency is perceived by analyzing all the influences upon it from the environment in which it operates. Systems theory is more easily grasped if one understands the concept of subsystems. As an example,

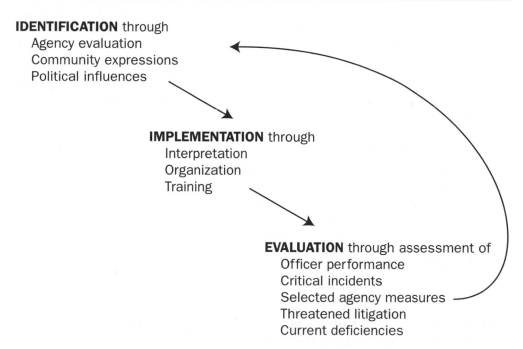

Figure 1–2 The Public Policy-making Process & Cycle

let us consider a person sitting at home in an air-conditioned room. If the focus of discussion is on the person's body, we could use systems theory to examine the situation this way. The body itself is made up of subsystems—the nervous subsystem, the respiratory subsystem, the cardiovascular subsystem, the skeletal subsystem, and the digestive subsystem. When all of the subsystems function properly, the body as a whole functions well. But if something affects one subsystem, it can impact the others. If this person is frightened by some external force—say, a bolt of lightning striking the tree outside the room—various subsystems can be affected. Fright causes the heart to beat faster, breathing to become shallow and rapid, digestive juices to be released by the nervous system, and the stomach possibly to become upset. The sudden jolt and noise may additionally cause the body to jump or swing around quickly, perhaps bumping into a table and breaking a bone, causing pain. Each of the subsystems is interconnected, and their functions impact the others.

In this example, the systems theory approach would describe the person's body and the immediate surroundings of the room and house as the "environment." This approach attempts to consider the forces or influences of the environment and their impact upon the entity or issue being considered. Taking a systems perspective to the earlier discussion of social control and its influences (Figure 1–1 and Exhibit 1–3) would mean viewing each factor as having a possible impact on the others as well as an impact on social control. In other words, the various types of social control and the different types of social, economic, and political forces that impact it are interrelated. The best symbol to illustrate the systems approach is that of the atom. The nucleus becomes the issue being considered (e.g., the concept of social control or the police agency as an organization). The orbiting electrons and their paths become the factors that influence the issue being discussed. So Figure 1–3 could be a systems approach illustration of the concept of social control, and Figure 1–4 is a systems representation of a police agency in today's society.

Viewing law enforcement from a systems perspective is important because it ensures that we consider the impact and influence of other environmental forces in our society. It assists in understanding the possible implications of decisions and to anticipate the impact of those decisions on other subsystems. We say that in a systems approach, "everything affects everything else." It is a view that makes one consider issues that otherwise might be overlooked. For example, what if a Neo-Nazi or Ku Klux Klan group seeks a permit to hold a rally in a city? City officials must consider all the implications (forces) and outcomes (effects) of the decision. These questions should be considered regarding this matter:

■ If denied, might the group have standing to sue the agency for a breach of constitutional rights of freedom of expression?
■ Is the city willing and financially capable of fighting the matter in court?

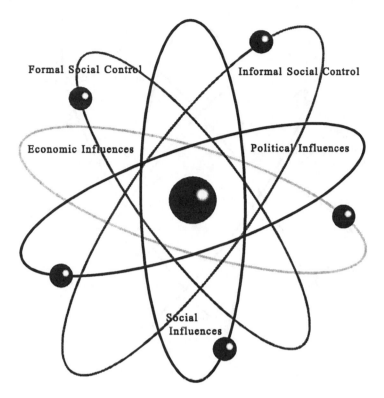

Figure 1–3 The Systems Theory Applied to Social Control

- If the permit is granted, will the rally be orderly or will there be opposition groups present seeking a confrontation?
- Might people get injured and need medical attention?
- Will your officers have to work overtime to provide necessary security?
- Will the budget of the department permit overtime to be used?
- Does your city policy require such groups to have insurance coverage for any damages that may be incurred as a direct result of the rally?
- Does the permit require the group to pay for officer overtime for providing security to the group?
- Will the group provide any security of its own?
- What are the public media ramifications?
- Who protects the rest of the city when most of your officers are protecting the rally?

In short, the systems approach assists in analyzing issues from a broader perspective, one in which the agency is just one entity (subsystem) among many in the total environment. In this example, the total environment includes several city officials such as the mayor, law director or prosecutor, council

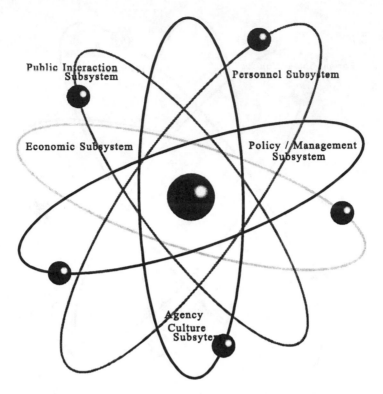

Figure 1–4 Systems Approach Applied to Law Enforcement Agencies

members, the fire department, ambulance/medical services, and the city services director.

The Global Perspective (or Extended Systems Approach)

The global perspective is an extension of the systems approach; in addition to recognizing the immediate environmental influences, it gives significant recognition to world events and international influences upon the agency. The instability of a government can cause problems for other countries. Many great societies and nations have risen and fallen during the last 3,000 years. During the twentieth century, for example, many government officials in powerful countries have lost their right to govern. Some lost that right as a result of war (e.g., World Wars I and II, the war in Vietnam), and some as a result of internal conflict and unrest (e.g., East Germany and the former Union of Soviet Socialist Republics during the early 1990s). Changes continue to occur in the trouble spots around the world. Daily events in countries of the Balkan Peninsula (of Europe), the Middle East, Africa, and East Asia are a constant threat to regional and even world peace. According to the National Defense Council Foundation, during 1995 there were 71 "little wars" across the globe, which was double the tally of 1989. According to the State Department, there are 1,649 U.S. law enforcement personnel permanently assigned overseas for crime fighting, intelligence, liaison, and training purposes. FBI agents were sent to assist with the investigation of the bombing of the U.S. Embassy in Tanzania in August of 1998, and it is estimated that by the year 2000, there will be nearly 100 agents assigned to about 37 overseas offices (Johnson 1999).

One may ask, "What do the events in other countries have to do with policing in the United States?" The answer is, "A great deal, depending on where you are." The United States, as a prosperous world leader, is often called upon to provide military and humanitarian aid to those in need. Although the country's success to date places it in this position, continuing this role in the future may become more challenging. The opportunity exists to assist many people in their struggles to survive and to relieve their pain and suffering. Realizing these goals, however, reduces the resources available for American needs of all types, including the enhancement of public safety. For example, whenever the National Guard is activated in the U.S., police departments are adversely affected, since officers are often members of the National Guard. Staffing of affected agencies is adversely impacted, as are services to the public in that jurisdiction.

The global approach is very similar to the systems perspective in that it views the situation in terms of outside forces and environmental impact. The major difference between the two is that the global approach has more focus on international influences as they impact the field of policing. While international issues are also considered under the systems approach, their influence on that perspective is much less. The federal law enforcement community, without doubt, is more involved and concerned with the global approach than are local police. However, this approach is important to all American law enforcement officials because they must be alert for possible trouble in the United States because of situations in foreign countries. Terrorist activities are no longer confined to other countries, as witnessed by the explosion of Pan Am flight 103 returning to the U.S. from Europe in 1988, resulting in 270 deaths, and the 1993 bombing of the World Trade Center in New York City that killed six and injured more than a thousand. In 1992, there were 1,911 bombings within the United States, a substantial increase over the 842 bombings that occurred in 1986.

These kinds of events have increased the cautionary measures that law enforcement must take to protect national security and local public safety. For example, during the fall of 1995, the airlines and the Federal Aviation Administration imposed extra precautions on travel during the trial of the Middle Easterners accused of the World Trade Center bombing in 1993 (they were convicted). Most airports in the United States are policed by local law enforcement agencies, so global incidents always impact their operations. Another example would be the precautions taken to prevent possible terrorist incidents at the

1996 Olympic Games in Atlanta, Georgia; these involved police at all government levels. No one wanted a repeat of the 1972 massacre of the Israeli athletes in the Olympic Village in Munich, Germany. Just two days before the opening of the Atlanta Olympics, the explosion of TWA Flight 800 from New York to Paris, killing all 230 aboard, heightened security concerns across the nation. A bomb explosion in Olympic Park did kill two people during the Olympics in Atlanta. (The investigation of the TWA Flight 800 explosion ruled out sabotage or terrorism, and the Atlanta bombing remains unsolved at the time of this writing.) Domestic terrorism also has become a concern in recent years, especially since the Oklahoma City Federal Building bombing in 1995. In July of 1999, tours of the FBI headquarters in Washington, D.C. were curtailed because of intelligence reports indicating it may be the target of a terrorist attack.

The global approach to social control realizes that law enforcement is a global challenge and is impacted by global events. While most police officers in the United States are probably not affected greatly by global events, more have been affected in the last decade than in previous decades since the world wars. However, the professional law enforcement officer understands the importance of world events and their possible impact on policing here. The accidental bombing of the Chinese Embassy in 1999 during the Kosovo/Yugoslavia conflict resulted in demonstrations against the U.S. in many foreign cities and in several larger ones at home.

Officers in the larger cities often have contact with persons possessing (and claiming to possess) **diplomatic immunity**, which means that such persons are immune from the laws of the United States and its political subdivisions. Persons with diplomatic immunity can (and do) get away with serious felonies in the U.S. because our laws are powerless against them. Of course, we must remember that American diplomats abroad also enjoy diplomatic immunity from the laws of other countries. It should be remembered that most diplomats enjoy their assignments in the United States and seldom are a problem for public law enforcement. Diplomats are not immune from their home country's laws, and generally do not want to be sent home for what is criminal behavior in this country.

THE APPROACH OF THIS TEXT

The field of law enforcement is one component of the process of social control. The focus of this text is on crime-related law enforcement services provided by those agencies commonly referred to as the police. The approach taken in our presentation is primarily the systems approach, which encompasses all the forces or influences in society that impact policing. Among those influences are issues related to politics, public policy, social trends, international events, and national issues. The text describes the background of the field of policing: where it has been, where it is now, and where the challenges of the future are. Basic elements of management and organizational principles are also included.

Our approach recognizes the significant involvement of government and public policy makers in setting goals and objectives for the law enforcement community. In selected sections, the text approaches policing from a policy viewpoint because entry-level officials (usually patrol officers or field agents) need to understand the power and influence of their office. They make policy-related decisions and/or carry out policy every day they are on duty. They affect the lives of people they encounter, and they possess some of the most powerful discretion of any person working in the criminal justice system. With the emphasis on community policing today, those officers are also leaders and resource persons in many communities.

SUMMARY

This chapter has introduced you to the field of law enforcement. It has described law enforcement as one of the formal processes of social control, which means that it is one of society's attempts to obtain compliance with the law. The common term "policing" is defined as one form of law enforcement that emphasizes the prevention, detection, investigation, and prosecution of crime as well as providing numerous services to society. Police officials are distinguished from other law enforcement officials by the fact that they are nonmilitary government personnel who are armed and may use coercive and physical force under certain conditions. Since policing is a form of social control, the differences between formal (government-sponsored) and informal control mechanisms have been presented here as well. Of particular concern are the many influences upon social control, which have been presented as social, economic, and political factors. Many of these factors influence the police function in every community.

The chapter also describes the various perspectives to law enforcement in a social control context. The four approaches—legal, public policy, systems theory, and global—have each been presented and applied to the field of law enforcement. The legal approach emphasizes the enforcement of the law; however, since full enforcement is not possible,

discretion and selected enforcement becomes prevalent. The public policy approach emphasizes the process of developing policy at the governmental and agency levels. This policy impacts the delivery of police services to the community. The systems theory and global approaches both recognize the importance of all the influences in society and in the international community on policing. The recognition and identification of these influences is vital to providing effective policing in a complex democratic society.

While there is some overlap among these approaches, the differences are significant. The legal approach recognizes the formal and informal influence of law and sanctions on members of society. The public policy approach emphasizes the systematic approach to policing (among other things) through the governmental policy-making process. The systems approach attempts to understand how the environmental forces of politics, law, community, economics, and community impact policing. The global perspective emphasizes the larger impact of world events on the law enforcement function. While each approach has merit, the focus of this text is primarily from a systems theory approach that, in essence, recognizes the impact and contribution of all the other approaches as they relate to one another.

QUESTIONS FOR REVIEW

1. Using the concepts described in this chapter, what does the statement "All police officials are law enforcement officials but not all law enforcement officials are police officials" mean?
2. How does policing relate to the concept of social control? Which is the broader concept?
3. Using the four perspectives of the police function presented in this chapter, identify the similarities and differences among them.
4. Using the systems theory approach to policing, what are two social factors, two economic factors, and two political factors that influence policing at the local level of government?

SUGGESTED ACTIVITIES

1. Using three different dictionaries, look up the definitions to the terms *law enforcement, policing,* and *discretion.* Write them down on three note cards and be sure to indicate the source used. In the classroom, share your definitions with two other members of the class. Compare the definitions and describe how they are similar or dissimilar to the descriptions used in this text.
2. Ask students who are not in your class to describe what contact they have had with police officers and what they thought of the experience. Listen closely to what terms they use to describe the officers and write down their version of the contact. Determine whether you consider the contact to be a positive or negative one and why; write down your reasons for your assessment.
3. Contact a local health inspector, fire inspector, fire (arson) investigator, or building inspector and ask them if they consider themselves a "law enforcement" official. After they answer, ask if they consider themselves a "police officer."
4. Using the Internet, conduct searches using three different search engines (e.g., Infoseek, Webcrawler, Yahoo, Hotbot, etc.) on the terms "law enforcement," "policing," and "police" (use quotation marks around the terms) and compare the total number of categories, pages, or sites found. Browse some of the sites.

CHAPTER GLOSSARY

discretion: the process of making a choice among appropriate alternative courses of action

full enforcement: enforcing all laws all the time

the global approach: an extension of the systems approach that, in addition to recognizing immediate environmental influences, gives significant recognition to world events and the international influences upon the agency

law enforcement: a society's formal attempt to obtain compliance with the established rules, regulations, and law of that society

the legal perspective: an approach that views behavior from a "rule-based" philosophy, in that the law is paramount and is the guide for behavior which everyone must follow

policing: refers to the process of regulating the general health, safety, welfare, and morals of society

police officials: a special group of nonmilitary law enforcement officials who are armed and authorized to use coercive and physical force under certain conditions when carrying out their duties to prevent, detect, investigate, and prosecute criminal behavior

police powers: the government's lawful right to enact regulations and laws related to health, safety, welfare, and morals

proactive: a response that anticipates the direction of problems and tries to prevent the worst consequences from occurring

public policy: the rules and regulations legislative bodies and agencies choose to establish

selective enforcement: refers to enforcing those laws deemed appropriate to the situation or related to the priorities of the agency and the community

social control: the processes whereby a society encourages or enforces compliance with social norms, customs, and law

socialization: the process of teaching the culture and norms of the society to its members

systems theory or **systems approach:** an approach that views the entire context (environment) in which an issue exists by analyzing all the forces or influences impacting it

---

REFERENCES

Cochran, Charles L. and Eloise F. Malone. 1995. *Public Policy: Perspectives and Choices.* New York: McGraw-Hill.

Fischer, Frank. 1995. *Evaluating Public Policy.* Chicago: Nelson-Hall.

Gilmour, Robert S. and Alexis A. Halley. 1994. *Who Makes Public Policy?* Chatham, N.J: Chatham House.

Johnson, Kevin. 1999. "FBI Takes on Expanding Role, Staff." *USA Today* (8 June).

A Brief History of Early Law Enforcement

The Dodge City peace commission of 1882 poses for a celebratory photo after putting the corrupt town marshall and his henchmen on a train out of town. Back row left to right: W. H. Harris, Luke Short and Bat Masterson. Front row, from left: Charles Bassett, Wyatt Earp, F. McClain and Neil Brown. (AP/ Wide World Photos)

The history and evolution of policing are important to an overall understanding of the law enforcement profession. Current trends and policies are often a reflection of historic occurrences. After studying this chapter, you should be able to.

1. State three reasons why the study of history is important to a professional in the criminal justice system.
2. Explain how responsibility for providing protection to a community has evolved and fluctuated throughout history.
3. Discuss the contributions of various civilizations and societies to the evolution of law enforcement.
4. Describe the significance of the establishment of the Vigiles in the Roman Empire under Augustus.
5. Identify the contributions to policing made by the French from the Middle Ages to the early 1800s.
6. Describe the social and economic background of the Metropolitan Police in England in 1829.

CHAPTER OUTLINE

THE SIGNIFICANCE OF HISTORY

This chapter focuses on the history and evolution of law enforcement and their impact on current policing practices. History is an interpretation of the significance or important events of a society. Since this chapter is a limited presentation, you are encouraged to consult additional sources regarding the history of policing, including those in the references at the end of this chapter and on selected sites on the Internet. Let us begin this section by discussing three reasons for studying history.

First, history provides the foundation for any present society; it is studied in order to better understand current times and our reactions to them. History consists of all the people and events that precede us; it is part of our heritage. Very recent history can be referred to as "current events"—those things that have just occurred. The "recent past" includes the past few years of our lives. For some, history is what occurred before they were born, and since it has not been experienced, it needs to be studied. To illustrate the significance of history, we need to look no further than the evening news and issues of constitutional controversies. The history and evolution of the United States is strongly tied to the Declaration of Independence and the Constitution. We cannot fully understand current controversies in public policy if we do not know the foundation upon which they are based. For example, think of the statement "We don't need another Vietnam." Unless you have an understanding of the "what," "how," and "why" of the Vietnam conflict (it was not an official "war"), you cannot appreciate the context, issues, or implications of what is being discussed. During the recent Kosovo/Yugoslavia conflict, analogies related to the Second World War and the Vietnam conflict were used. These statements meant little to those who did not know and understand history.

The second reason for studying history is to help us understand and identify the social, economic, and political forces that have shaped and continue to shape our society. It is important for law enforcement officers to be aware of the cultural background of the persons they serve. However, social, economic, and political events do not occur in a vacuum, and some of the events are affected by issues occurring beyond a country's borders. As you study the history of law enforcement, try to place yourself in the time period being discussed; think about what was occurring in society in terms of the economy, politics, and social concerns.

The third major reason for studying history is that criminal justice professionals need to understand the history of their field. "Knowing from whence you came" is part of being a professional. Only then can you make informed decisions based on the realization that others before you have made similar decisions. It is this frame of reference that gives meaning to George Santayana's (1905) famous quotation: "Those who cannot remember the past are condemned to repeat it." Many misquote this statement by saying that history repeats itself, which is not the true basis of the quote. History sometimes repeats itself because people fail to remember events and merely react according to human nature instead of acting with knowledge. Decisions can be made more effectively by drawing the proper analogy to previous events and by analyzing similar forces in the environment. Professionals in the criminal justice system must have an understanding and a "sense" of history so that they do not repeat mistakes. However, it should also be understood that sometimes it is desirable to repeat history. This is especially true when using past experience to plan future goals. We want our plans and programs to be successful. By reviewing history, we can identify practices and procedures that "worked," and attempt to repeat those successes. This is a primary reason for conducting and reviewing research in the criminal justice field.

THE FLUCTUATIONS OF SOCIAL CONTROL

The nature of the criminal justice system appears to be very dependent on the culture, country, or area under consideration. In other words, the events of one country or group of people cannot be generalized. They do not necessarily apply to another country or group, even though the same time period may be involved. The history of areas of Europe is not identical to the history of Asia, South America, or North America. Further, today, events can have a global impact. In earlier time periods, it was common to have events in one country occur in relative isolation from the events in other countries. Because of today's global interconnectedness, that is no longer the case. When there is turmoil in the Mideast or in the Balkan countries, it can affect events within countries elsewhere.

A country's criminal justice system and, more specifically, system of formal social control (internal policing) develop and evolve dynamically. It is not a straight line progression. Instead, the cycle fluctuates from individual responsibility to military control to state civilian responsibility or some combination of these (see Figure 2–1).

Fluctuations in the responsibility for and type of social control, from individual to group to military control and so on, depend on the social, economic, and political forces of the time period in any particular society (country) being studied. Figure 2–1 illustrates these types of social control. In a given society, as time progresses (from T^1 to T^2), the responsibility for social control may shift from individuals to the family. Families may join together in a small geographical area to form a community whose members watch over and protect each other (T^3). An outside army may invade the community, conquer it, and impose military control over its members (T^4). Because of changes in the social,

CONTROL TYPE	TIME PERIODS								
Military Control				*			*		
State (government)					*				*
Community			*						
Clan/Tribe						*			
Family		*						*	
Individual	*								
TIME PERIOD	T^1	T^2	T^3	T^4	T^5	T^6	T^7	T^8	T^9

Figure 2–1 Evolution and Fluctuation of Social Control

economic, and political situation of the area, a civilian (government) type of social control may be established (T⁵) either until it collapses (leading to T⁶) or
until another army conquers the region (T⁷). Following a period of chaos, during which time the family takes responsibility for social control (T⁸), the state
(after reorganization) again may implement social control responsibility (T⁹).
If the region happens to suffer a terrible natural or manmade disaster, social
control may become the responsibility of individuals or communities again.

Various areas of the globe experience different types of social control at the
same time. For example, the United States currently has a civilian governmental form of social control. In other parts of the world, wars and dictators create
a quite different form of social control, protection, and survival. In summary,
in order to understand the type of social control that exists in a society and the
reason that it exists at a particular time in history, one must review the social,
economic, and political forces at work in that society (and to some extent, in
the rest of the world). The focus of the remainder of this chapter is on selected
civilizations and the countries that have impacted the evolution of American
heritage.

SELECTED ANCIENT CIVILIZATIONS

Across the thousands of years of ancient civilizations, laws and methods of
enforcing laws were created. In this section, we briefly review the contributions of selected ancient civilizations. Of course, other ancient civilizations existed and thrived as well; the ones described here are generally considered the
most significant to policing in the United States.

The Babylonian and Egyptian Empires

Early civilizations that enjoyed lengthy existences, such as Egypt and Babylon, clearly had stable societies. Between 5000 and 2500 B.C., various city-state
or small kingdoms arose in the Middle Eastern area from the Tigris-Euphrates
River valley to the Nile valley, an area called the "cradle of civilization." The
head of each of these was the king, who was usually also the chief religious
leader. His power was absolute and complete, with all people being subject to
him. Not only was he the source of law and the dispenser of justice; he was
also the provider for the people's existence. Therefore, he was responsible for
hunting, raising crops, and providing shelter. When necessary, he would lead
his people into war. Kings ran their kingdoms through a system of authority
that included dividing land over which certain noblemen were placed in charge.
They held the land at the will of the king and, in return, paid him tribute and
military service. The nobility, in general, were the king's counselors, assistants
in government, governors, judges, and military officers. Society below the king
and the nobility consisted of the common people, the artisans and tradesmen,
and slaves. None of these groups played any role in government or public life.

Agriculture (farming) was the mainstay of the economy initially, with merchants later becoming more powerful as they collected wealth from trading and banking (Goodspeed 1904; Brandon 1970; and Grun 1991).

Life under Egyptian and Babylonian kings was dominated by a rule of law. Order, not chaos, was common. Social control during these times was probably a combined system of group responsibility (following the edicts of kings and pharaohs) and military control. In other words, the formal control mechanism (the military) and informal social control (tradition, custom, and fear of the King's power) influenced compliant behavior. The family was a recognized institution with great emphasis on respect and love for parents. The father was the head of the household; however, the mother was highly honored as well.

Religion played a predominant role in these early societies and was the foundation of social and political life. Priests served as judges, scribes, teachers, and authors; temples were fortresses, treasuries, and learning centers as well as places of worship. Religion affected and inspired their literature, science, and art. These ancient city-states had a rich culture that included libraries for collections of hymns, songs, and stories; public repositories for legal documents; and gardens. History also has documented the use of running water, wigs, cosmetics, musical instruments, and board games as part of the life scene in these early civilizations.

In the eighteenth century B.C., a united Babylonian Empire was founded by King Hammurabi, most noted for his extensive legal code. The **Code of Hammurabi** contained some 282 regulations and evidenced a sense of justice built on personal responsibility and accountability (refer to Exhibit 2–1). It is the oldest preserved code of ancient law. The code included forms of punishment, fines, or obligations for offenders, although fines were usually paid to the victims and not the state. The code was more advanced than tribal custom in that it recognized no blood feud, private retaliation, or marriage by capture. One of its main legal principles was **lex talionis,** or the law of retaliation—an "eye for an eye"— as sanctioned by the state. The death penalty was frequently imposed for offenses against the state and criminal negligence. The Code's provisions went far beyond offenses; they essentially addressed all aspects of family, social, and business life as well as property transactions (Gadd 1971).

The city states of ancient Egypt (the Nile River valley) were united into one dynasty under one king sometime between 3500 and 3200 B.C. Historians differ as to the identity of this unifier—Menes or Narmer. However, the first pharaoh to rule over a united Egypt is considered to be Hor-Aha. His reign is known as the first dynasty and occurred sometime between 3200 and 3000 B.C. (Trojan 1986, 15). Few written records of this time period exist, and those that do are carvings and etchings in stone or clay (papyrus did not come into use until about 2500 B.C.).

Obviously, trying to decipher the type of social control system during such time periods is difficult, so the "history of policing" in ancient times is left want-

Exhibit 2–1

HISTORICAL LEGAL CODES ON THE WORLD WIDE WEB

The principal source of the Code of Hammurabi is the stone monument made of black basalt stele on which the Code is inscribed. Part of the Code on the lower portion of the monument was erased by an Elamite king who captured the stele around 1200 B.C. The stone was discovered in 1901 and is preserved in the Louvre in Paris.

For a picture of the stone monument and an entire translation of the Codex Hammurabi, log on to The Law Museum Archives at **http://www.wwlia.org.** This site is maintained by the World Wide Legal Information Association. There are other major legal documents at this site worth reviewing. Another interesting web site is **http://www.common-law.com/index.html,** which is dedicated to legal history and philosophy. Additionally, **http://julen.net/ancient/Law_and_Philosophy/** contains links to many sites related to law and philosophy of the ancient world.

---

ing. According to Trojan (1986), there is some evidence that internal security officials known as "Judges Commandment of the Police" existed during the Fourth Dynasty (circa 2900 B.C.) and that Hur Moheb created an organized police force around 1340 B.C. to protect commerce and ensure safe navigation along the Nile. Trojan also states the following about policing in ancient Egypt:

> Ramses III (1198–1166 B.C.) invested the police with much authority in an effort to establish peace and security. He produced laws which dealt severely with criminals and punishment being awarded in public. The most important police units were those responsible for the security of the tombs, where valuables were placed with the dead. The Egyptians claim that they were the first to use dogs for police purposes, using them for guarding property. The police of ancient Egypt were also vested with judicial powers; they not only tried the cases, but they passed judgment and executed the sentences (Trojan 1986, 15).

The advanced civilizations that existed in the Middle East in ancient times had a tremendous influence on other empires that followed. Brandon states that the debt owed to Egypt by western Asia and eastern Europe is immense:

> The ancient Greeks, probably the most intelligent race that has ever lived, acknowledged this debt freely. From the time when their merchants began setting up trading posts in Egypt in the seventh and sixth centuries B.C. they were

fascinated by Egypt. . . . Archaic Greek art was clearly influenced by Egyptian sculpture, which at its best has few equals anywhere in the world. The Greeks copied Egyptian medicine and surgery and in many other fields of knowledge looked upon the Egyptian priests as their mentors (Brandon 1970, 127).

One practice of the Egyptian princes was the social control philosophy of **feudalism,** the practice of providing basic needs to those under a leader's control or subject to a leader's authority. The leader in such a situation has been known as king, prince, master, lord, and so on. The practice surfaced in different time periods throughout history and, generally, the leader was responsible for the safety and security of the people. This included apprehending offenders and rendering judgment on them at the local level.

It also is known that the ancient civilizations fell into decay and were overcome by both internal and external military forces. During these times, total military control replaced the existing social control mechanisms. The First Babylonian Empire perished about 1600 B.C., and the peaceful Egyptian dynasties declined between 1800 and 1600 B.C. Egypt would rise again and form a mighty empire during the sixteenth century B.C. and become the second major empire in the Middle East spreading its influence beyond the Nile River area.

The Hebrews

During the time period 1650–1300 B.C., groups of wandering tribes, the Hebrews (later known as Israelites), migrated toward and into Egypt. They claimed a common ancestor, Abraham, and shared a common religion. Eventually, they left Egypt under the leadership of Moses (about 1250 B.C.), wandered through the "wilderness" (the Sinai Desert) for forty years, crossed the Jordan River, and established a homeland in Palestine along the northern shores of the Dead Sea. The significance of this to the modern day world was the development of **Mosaic Law,** the law of Moses. Besides the biblical Ten Commandments, the Law of Moses is recorded in the Old Testament books of Exodus, Leviticus, Numbers, and Deuteronomy. At the heart of the Mosaic Law is the covenant between man and God. People live according to the law out of an obligation to a higher authority (God) and not to an earthly ruler. It is from this Hebrew foundation and its principles that Judaism and Christianity evolved. The impact of these religions throughout subsequent history and upon social customs, laws, and moral beliefs is referred to as the "Judeo-Christian influence." From about 1050 B.C. to 930 B.C., the Kingdom of Israel was a major power in the Middle East. King David established the national capital at Jerusalem, built up an army, and made Israel's influence felt throughout the region. Under King Solomon, alliances were established with other powers in the region, including Phoenicia and Egypt (Brandon 1970, 127).

The Greeks

The tribes of the Eastern Mediterranean area expanded their trade and commerce into other nearby regions, including that of Asia Minor (Turkey), the Aegean Sea, and the Balkan Peninsula. The advanced social systems of the Egyptians, the Assyrians, the Phoenicians, and the Hittites upon the Greeks allowed them to gain great power and influence of their own by 1500 B.C. The Greek conquest of the Aegean area occurred between 1500 and 1200 B.C. Their influence declined shortly thereafter because of invading groups (barbarians) from the north. Greeks migrated back toward their homelands where they prospered in limited geographical colonies called city-states (*poleis* or *polis* in Greek).

Each city-state was an independent, close-knit entity that formed its own political and social life. It was in these self-contained city-states that the principles of democracy, "the rule of the people," was born (Breasted 1916, 300). The early city-states were ruled originally by aristocrats who had accumulated great wealth and, therefore, were able to rule as a king would. As their influence grew weaker, they used unjust and despotic methods to maintain their positions. One of the major complaints of the people they ruled was that only the rulers knew all the laws. The people began demanding that the laws be written. According to Goodspeed (1904, 100), the Greek custom became one of commissioning "the best man in the state, to whom all power was given that he might prepare, publish and administer a code of law which should be binding upon the people." One such lawgiver, Draco, was appointed around 624 B.C. in Athens. He codified the oral law and customs of the land. Unfortunately, the law of Draco was considered very harsh and punitive, some saying it was "written in blood." Subsequently, another lawgiver, Solon, modified the law and was responsible for giving political power to all citizens of the state. Solon is known as the "Founder of the Athenian Democracy" (Goodspeed 1904, 109–110).

Interestingly, it was the age of tyrants, which originally meant a high office held by a ruler not of aristocratic lineage, that led to the development of a more democratic society. One such tyrant, Pisistratus of Athens, was known for looking after the rights of the people, curbing the nobles, giving great attention to public works like harbor improvements, state buildings, and temples, and cultivating art, music, and literature (Breasted 1916, 317). He expanded the basic principles of political rights of the masses established by Solon. It is also in this time period that Homer's poems were first written, and other cultural advances in the theater prospered.

During the early fifth century B.C., many of the larger Greek city-states banded together to successfully ward off invasions by the Persians. This led to a stronger Greek influence in the Aegean Sea area. Athens and Sparta became the more predominant city-states following the defeat of the Persians and began to rival each other. Sparta represented the tradition of military might and limited privileges to citizens, and Athens represented the seeds of democracy and culture (Breasted 1916, 347). Unfortunately, this rivalry and domination of other cities and lands brought some curtailments in democracy. Citizenship was no longer granted to foreigners, and people with legal disputes were forced to travel to Athens to present their case to the citizen juries; this was a great inconvenience to the people of the Athenian Empire. Meetings of representatives from all states of the Empire were discontinued also. Athens was viewed as more and more dictatorial and losing the favor of people outside her immediate borders.

By 404 B.C., following a 27-year war with Sparta, the Athenian Empire had crumbled. Democracy had failed to overcome the fragmented nature of the Empire and to unite the Greek world. In conquered lands, Sparta set up a form of government known as oligarchy (a term meaning "rule of a few") which consisted of the upper class or nobility supported by military force (Breasted 1916, 400–401). The Spartan rule of the area, however, came to an end with a military defeat in 371 B.C. As the Athenian Empire was crumbling, the Macedonians to the north were gaining power. Alexander of Macedonia was thirteen (around 343 B.C.) when he studied under the great philosopher Aristotle. Alexander was twenty when he became King of Macedonia. He believed that the Greeks should submit to his leadership, but they did not. He militarily conquered the major Greek city-states and small empires and set out to the east to establish his own empire. Persia, Phoenicia, and Egypt fell to Alexander's armies before he turned age 26. During the following six years (circa 323 B.C.), he conquered the lands of today's Iran, India, and parts of China. He died shortly thereafter at the age of 33. Although his empire was maintained for some time by his heirs, some communities in the region (e.g, the Greek city-states) were beginning to regain their identity and history, and others (e.g, the Romans) were gaining power and expanding their borders (Breasted 1916, 430–438).

The Romans

Rome, founded between 800–750 B.C., was first ruled by aristocratic kings. From 500 to 133 B.C., the government of Rome experienced great change. People gradually secured the right to have laws published, the power to elect magistrates, and the establishment of a republican form of government. Around 450 B.C., the **Laws of the Twelve Tables** became the foundation of the early Roman legal system. These laws were inscribed upon twelve tablets of brass set up for public inspection on the walls of the Temple of Jupiter. Although only fragmentary portions of the laws remain, it is known that they were a collection of Roman maxims of universal application from which formal law later developed. The Twelve Tables were like crude chapters of procedures of conduct (see Exhibit 2–2).

Exhibit 2–2

SELECTED SECTIONS OF THE LAWS OF THE TWELVE TABLES

Table I

1. If a man call another to law, he shall go. If he go not, they shall witness it; then he shall be seized.
2. If he flee or evade, lay hands on him as he goes.
6. If they settle the matter, let it be told.
7. If they settle not, they shall join issue in the assembly or in the Forum before midday, then they shall plead and prove, both being present.

Table II

3. He who needs a witness shall within three days go to his house and notify him.

Table VIII

2. If a man has broken the limb of another and does not settle with him, let there be retaliation.
3. If a man with fist or club breaks the bone of another, he is liable to penalty, of 300 (pence) if done to a free man, 150 if done to a slave.
12. If by night a man have done a theft, and (the owner) kills him, let him be (as if) killed by law.

Table X

1. A dead man you shall not bury or burn within the city.
4. Women shall not tear their faces, nor make excessive lamentation for the dead.

Later, during the reign of Augustus (28 B.C.–A.D. 14), a new system of government was instituted. The army was the key to Roman control and influence for defense both within its borders and to its frontiers, which extended to England (Brandon 1970, 127). Internal social control under Augustus, however, took on a new look. The city of Rome at this time had a population of over one-and-a-quarter million people, made up of large numbers of slaves and indentured servants from conquered lands. The city was built largely of wood and brick, and buildings were close to one another, causing major problems when fires broke out. There was a constant fear of insurrection because of social class distinction, limited civil rights for non-citizens, and discrimination against non-Romans. Crime in the streets was rampant. There was no efficient law enforcement agency or street lighting system; gangs controlled large areas of the city (Kelly 1973, 56–60).

Augustus established the **Praetorian Guards** as his personal bodyguards (the privileged corps) and the **Urban Cohort** as protectors of the peace throughout Rome. Both were military units and part of the regular army under the control of the emperor. Around 14 B.C., and in partial response to political opposition, he appointed a force of freedmen called **Vigiles,** or night watchers, to act as Rome's first fire-fighting unit. The Vigiles eventually numbered about 9,000 and were divided into seven cohorts (districts). Besides their fire-related duties, they were eventually assigned policing duties of making arrests for theft, burglary, and assault, capturing runaway slaves, and serving as guards at the public baths. Exhibit 2–3 lists terms associated with the Vigiles.

The Vigiles was the first large civilian unit in a metropolitan setting used for law enforcement and social control purposes. It was also the first known public safety unit appointed to serve both the fire-fighting and policing needs of a city. Because of Augustus' creation of the Vigiles, he is referred by some as the "Father of Policing." Some historians claim that policing did not see an

---

Exhibit 2–3

TERMS ASSOCIATED WITH THE VIGILES OF ROME

Excubitorem—the substation located in the districts; it housed the Vigiles and the equipment needed to fight fire. It also had cells for prisoners.

Karcerarius—the Vigil assigned to jailor duty.

Quae-stionarius—the interrogator and/or torturer.

Sebaciarii—believed to be the plainclothes men or early form of detective.

Saint Sebastian—Patron saint of the police; was an officer in the Vigiles.

Source: Adapted with permission from M. A. Kelly, The First Urban Policeman, *Journal of Police Science and Administration*, March 1973, pp. 58–59, © 1973, International Association of Chiefs of Police.

equivalent force in history until the establishment of city agencies in nineteenth-century Europe (Kelly 1973, 56 and 60).

As we conclude this section about social control in selected ancient civilizations, it may be appropriate to ask, "What caused great countries or empires to decline?" Of course, we must rely on researcher interpretation to answer such a question because of the expanse of time since they collapsed. One researcher's recent list of reasons includes several factors related to our discussion of social control. Black's (1994) book, *When Nations Die,* identifies ten warning signs of decline, according to his analysis of history:

1. A crisis in lawlessness
2. A loss of economic discipline
3. Rising bureaucracy
4. Declining level of education
5. Weakening of cultural foundations
6. Lack of respect for traditions
7. Increasing materialism
8. Rising immorality
9. Devaluing of human life
10. Decay of religious belief

When one reviews and reflects upon this list of warning signals, the relationship among social, economic, and political factors and their impact upon social control (and policing) becomes profound. The authors of this text are not claiming that Black's warning signs are totally accurate or that they agree with his interpretation. However, the warning signs do reflect a type of systems approach in viewing society and the concept of social control. Today, several of the warning signs are mentioned often in various forums debating issues such as crime, violence, morality, religion, and culture.

The French

After the fall of the Roman Empire, the next major developments in policing occurred in the Middle Ages in France. During the eighth century, the whole area of Gaul was united by Charlemagne, who consolidated power into a centralized government and required all free men to take an oath of fidelity to him. This oath is sometimes referred to as a **frankpledge**, which is a system of social control supported by oath to obey the law of the land. Charlemagne divided his staff of servants according to duties, one assignment was the position of **constable**, or count of the stable, an important position of trust (Seignobos 1932, 58–59). By the ninth century, the area of Gaul was again fragmented into large centers of authority, each consisting of a king and his subjects. Feudalism was established as a system of social life. Under this arrangement in

France, the king or lord had trusted agents in every village, known as mayors, who policed the village with the aid of armed **sergeants**. The mayors of towns, ... "exercised all the powers enjoyed by the town, dispensing justice, both civil and criminal, levying taxation, controlling public order, leading the militia composed of the burgesses, providing for the defense of the walls, and keeping the treasure, the archives and the keys to the town gates" (Seignobos 1932, 126). By the twelfth century, many towns had formed a mutual defense association known as **commune juree** in which a large number of men of equal status took an oath for the defense of a collective interest (Seignobos 1932, 103–126).

France's first efforts to establish a centralized police force occurred during the reign of Louis XIV. In 1666, he appointed a council under the direction of Jean-Baptiste Colbert to develop a plan for police organization and administration. The edicts of the council (1666–1667) established police powers and procedures, restricted the private ownership of arms, and created the **Lieutenant of Police** for the City of Paris. The Lieutenant of Police was granted seven distinct areas of authority by Louis XIV:

1. The security of Paris, including repression of civil disorders, making arrests, and surveillance of foreigners.
2. The cleaning and lighting of streets, fire fighting and prevention, and flood control.
3. Regulating and upgrading the moral behavior of the citizens.
4. Regulating social affairs in matters of abandoned children, unfaithful wives, organization of hospitals, and inspection of prisons and jails.
5. Assuring adequate food supplies for the city.
6. Protecting the city in times of epidemics and general maintenance of health conditions.
7. Regulating the economy, which included surveillance of worker's associations and policing the marketplace (Arnold 1979, 14–15).

Louis XIV later set up Lieutenants-General of Police in all the principal cities of France. The idea of a royal police continued for over 100 years until the French Revolution of 1789, the result of growing distrust among the people of France toward the monarchy and its government. Power was transferred from the king to the Assembly, which reorganized the government based on the uniformity of institutions and not obedience to the king (the monarchy, however, was retained, with Louis XVI on the throne). Every region became autonomous, having an elected administration with the powers to maintain order, police its own area, and even collect taxes. (This manner of decentralized power was adopted from the new government formed in the United States following its independence from England.) Conflict between the monarchy and the Assembly, however, led to the revolution of 1792 and years of civil strife. The Committee of General Security was responsible for police power, and centralization of the police became a primary issue. In 1796, the Ministry of General Police was established for the "execution of the laws relative to the police, security, and general tranquility of the Republic" (Arnold 1979, 23–24).

With Napoleon's rise to power in 1799, the police system of France became an integral part of his regime. His initial Minister of General Police was Joseph Fouche. Fouche maintained an elaborate intelligence system that kept the Emperor well informed (Arnold 1979, 33–35 and 161). Also during the reign of Napoleon, a former convict, Eugene Francois Vidocq, became the head of a small detective unit of the Paris police. He staffed his unit with former criminals, under the philosophy that "it takes a thief to catch a thief," and paid them according to their performance (see Exhibits 2–4 and 2–5 for additional information about Vidocq's legacy). Vidocq developed an elaborate system of

---

Exhibit 2–4

EUGENE FRANCOIS VIDOCQ

Historically, Eugene Francois Vidocq's legendary crime-solving reputation was lauded in Poe's *Murders in the Rue Morgue* and in Herman Melville's *Moby Dick*. The fugitive in Charles Dickens' *Great Expectations* is also inspired by Vidocq's real-life exploits. As a fugitive from French justice, he first offered his services as a police spy and informer, later becoming a master of disguise who was so successful at catching criminals that, in 1811, he was named the first chief of the Surete. In time he directed a force of 28 detectives, all of whom were also former criminals.

Eugene Francois Vidocq is considered by historians and those in law enforcement to be the father of modern criminal investigation. Vidocq's accomplishments and contributions to law enforcement were many. He introduced recordkeeping (i.e., a card index system) and criminalistics, introduced the science of ballistics, was the first to make plaster-of-Paris casts of foot/shoe impressions, was a master of disguise and surveillance, held patents on indelible ink and unalterable bond paper, and founded the first modern detective agency and credit bureau, Le Bureau des Renseignements. After resigning from the Surete, he published *Memoires de Vidocq* (1828), a book that became a best-seller in Europe and firmly established Eugene Francois Vidocq as the world's greatest detective.

Vidocq's regard for his fellow man also was legendary. He was a philanthropist who also helped the poor and abandoned of Paris; at the same time that he was pursuing the guilty, he was also freeing the innocent.

Source: Copyright © 1998, The Vidocq Society.

Exhibit 2–5

THE VIDOCQ SOCIETY

One of the most unusual crime-solving organizations in the world meets in the historic area of Philadelphia next to Independence Hall. The Vidocq Society is named in honor of Eugene Francois Vidocq, the brilliant 19th century French detective who founded the Surete. Vidocq Society Members ("V.S.M.s") and their guests draw upon years of forensic skills used each day at work to evaluate, investigate, and endeavor to solve unsolved crimes, particularly murder. When requested, members participate in the investigation and prosecution of the person or persons who are eventually charged with the murder. Members are motivated purely by public service. They are forensic professionals who eagerly donate centuries of deductive and scientific talent for the common good. The Vidocq Society credo is "Veritas Veritatum." The phrase, translated from Latin, means "Truth Begets Truth." The Vidocq Society was founded in Philadelphia in 1990 by world-renowned sculptor and forensic reconstructionist Frank Bender; internationally-known forensic psychologist and crime "profiler" Richard Walter, M.A.; and Bill Fleisher, a former Philadelphia Police Officer and then FBI Special Agent who later became the Assistant Special Agent in Charge of the U.S. Customs Service in Philadelphia.

Vidocq Society membership represents 17 states and 11 foreign countries. It is a rare privilege and has been bestowed upon fewer than 150 men and women; new members must be sponsored by existing members. Most members are employed in public service by federal, state, and local law enforcement—either behind badges or at prosecutors' tables. Some Vidocqians consult regularly with federal, state, or local law enforcement; attorneys in private practice and entrepreneurs are also members.

A long-unsolved homicide or disappearance is usually the centerpiece of each Vidocq Society meeting. The crime and its evidence are disclosed to members and invited guests, with an eye towards rekindling or refocusing the investigation. The presenter of a cold-case murder or disappearance at a Vidocq Society luncheon could be a law enforcement professional who has investigated the murder over the years and continues to carry it on his caseload, a Vidocq Society member, or a private investigator hired by the murder victim's family. The spirited,

(continues)

Exhibit 2–5 *(continued)*

> synergistic question-and-answer period that follows each formal case presentation becomes a collaborative effort that involves members and invited guests in the search for a solution to a previously unsolved crime. If substantial interest is shown by Vidocq Society members following the case presentation, a "working group" is assembled (an investigative team of Vidocq Society members and volunteers that is tailored to advance that specific investigation).
>
> Additional information about the Society can be found on the World Wide Web at: **http://www.vidocq.org.**
>
> *Source:* Copyright © 1998, The Vidocq Society.

informants and intelligence-gathering networks that became the established procedures for the entire criminal division (the **Surete**, which in 1913 became the **Police Judiciaire**) (Holden 1992, 26). France has undergone a number of changes in the form of governmental structure since Napoleon, but the centralization of the police has remained a major feature of most of these governmental reforms.

The British

Early History   As mentioned earlier, the Roman Empire once stretched to England, and by the beginning of the fifth century, London had a population of about 20,000. During much of its early history, parts of England were occupied by other groups as well. Social control in early England was an individual and group responsibility. Known as the **tything** (or **tithing**) **system**, it consisted of a group of ten families (normally an extended family) living in close proximity to each other to provide self-protection and security. If an infraction of the common law happened, members of the tything were expected to raise the "hue and cry" prompting others to come to their aid. A territory containing ten tythings was called a **hundred**, and several hundreds covered an area called a **shire.** (Using today's terms, a tything would be a village, a hundred a township, and a shire a county.) The chief law enforcement and magistrate of the shire was called a **reeve.** It was from this early terminology that the word "sheriff" (shire-reeve) originated (Lee 1971, 3–7).

The shire-reeve was responsible for conducting annual inspections of the tythings and court proceedings. By the end of the tenth century, **peace guilds** had become popular as a local means of social control. These guilds were private, voluntary associations, arranged in 10 groups under 10 headmen, one of whom acted as a chief and treasurer. The guilds were mutual assurance societies. The contributions made to them went toward apprehension of offenders.

Following the Norman conquest of 1066, some traditional titles of positions associated with the tything system changed. The headman of the tything became the **praepostus**, and the shire-reeve was replaced by **vicecomes**, who went from town to town to hold court (known as the police courts). The Normans also established a feudalistic form of social control. By the twelfth century, **Courts of Leet** (local police courts) had been instituted as a substitute for the sheriff's courts. They became so popular that the sheriff eventually "ceased to trouble the village communities with his annual visit of inspection" (Lee 1971, 6–17).

During the 1100s, kings of England continued judicial reforms, which did not appease a growing sense of injustice in the feudal society. In 1215, King John was forced to sign the **Magna Carta** (the great charter) which granted certain guarantees toward a fairer justice system and rights to the people and noblemen. Section 20 of the document rebukes the alleged abuses by officials in rendering justice and penalties: "We will not make men justiciaries, constables, sheriffs or bailiffs, unless they understand the law of the land, and are well disposed to observe it" (Lee 1971, 20).

Historian Melville Lee (1971, 20) observed that after 1215, the term "frankpledge" meant a recognition of the responsibility of every citizen to take his part in the duty of maintaining peace in the state, or the liability that all men share to render police services when called upon to do so. During the reign of Edward I, the **Statute of Winchester** (1285) was enacted, and it created a policing system that continued for nearly 500 years. Among other things, it provided for:

■ A "watch and ward" system of protection (a night watch system made up of all eligible males, who took turns serving on the watch)
■ A duty to inform others of offenses and offenders (the "hue and cry")
■ The arming of all males aged 15 to 60 to defend the kingdom and to maintain order
■ The removal of brush and most trees 200 feet on each side of the king's highway (to prevent surprise attacks from robbers) (Lee 1971, 24–28)

The 1700s and 1800s   The watch system served the English people well until the 1700s, when numerous social, economic, and political upheavals caused a need for reform. England was no longer an agrarian country. The advent of trade and commerce, the discovery of new lands, the expansion of the British Empire, the war with Spain and France, religious protests and reform, and civil war within its Empire created a social environment that unpaid, unskilled watchmen could not be expected to control. Along with the Industrial Revolution (which brought increased urbanization, hunger, child and women labor atrocities, sanitation problems, and increased crime), internal riots and disorders were becoming common. The Riots Acts of 1715 made rioting a felonious act and extended the powers of the Justices of the Peace. A 1736 act of Parliament allowed London's city Council to raise monies for all police purposes, and constables were empowered to make arrests (Lee 1971, 147–151).

In 1746, Henry Fielding, an English writer, was appointed magistrate of the Bow Street court in a part of London. He is noted for his research and insights into crime and police reform. He authored one of the first treatises on police reform in 1751, *Enquiry into the Causes of the Late Increase of Robbers*, which addressed the social context of crime. He established a police office (the Bow Street Police Office) as part of his court for the purpose of responding to criminal incidents and for apprehending known thieves. These officers were paid from the fines levied against wrongdoers. Fielding supported the idea of a 24-hour patrol by officers and even recommended horse patrols for the city. Some have called him the "Father of the Police of London." His brother, John Fielding, who succeeded him as magistrate of the Bow Street court, continued the police reform movement. Specific foot patrol officers were assigned in 1782, a horse patrol was added in 1805, and a dismounted horse patrol was established in 1821 (Tobias 1979, 44–52).

Patrick Colquhoun, a Middlesex magistrate, was another police reformer of this time. He published several works about policing, *Treatise On the Police of the Metropolis* in 1796, *The Commerce and Policing of the Thames River (1800)*, and *Treatise on the Functions and Duties of the Constable* in 1803 (Lee 1991, 177, 218–219). These reform efforts informed the public of alternatives to the antiquated watch and parish constable systems that served the city. Within the next two decades, police reform was to occur on a much larger scale.

The seeds of reform advocated by Fielding and Colquhoun were being applied by a young chief secretary for Ireland known as Robert Peel. From 1812 through 1818, Peel governed Ireland during civil disorders, increasing crime, and religious conflict. Shortly after passage of the Peace Preservation Act of 1814, he was able to establish a new form of policing that created the Royal Irish Constabulary. The Constabulary was a civil (as opposed to military) police force to assist in reducing crime and disorder (Stead 1985, 62). By the time Peel was selected Home Secretary of England in 1921, he already had experience with reforming the police. By the year 1829, five distinct classes of police officers existed in the London area:

1. Parochial Constables, elected annually in parish or townships, serving gratuitously
2. Their substitutes for deputies serving for a wage voluntarily paid by the principals
3. Salaried Bow Street Officers and patrols charged with the suppression of highwaymen and footpads (thieves who robbed pedestrians)

4. Stipendiary police constables attached to the public officers established under the "Middlesex Justices Act"
5. Stipendiary Water-Police attached to the Thames Office, as established by Act of Parliament in 1789 (Lee 1971, 177)

In 1829, Sir Robert Peel, in his role as home secretary, introduced a bill to create a "new police." **An Act for Improving the Police in and near the Metropolis** established a centralized police force for the metropolitan London area. The first co-commissioners were appointed, and over 1,000 officers started their duties. The first co-commissioners were Charles Rowan, a former military colonel, and Richard Mayne, an attorney. They reported to and conferred with Peel, recruited the necessary officers, structured the Metropolitan Police Force, and issued the *First Instructions* to the New Police. Other early decisions made about the force included:

■ The force would function on a 24-hour basis.
■ Officers would wear a uniform and a top hat.
■ Officers would carry no weapons beyond a truncheon.
■ Officers would carry a small staff with a crown on one end to symbolize the royal authority (Tobias 1979, 44–46).

Based on the *First Instructions* issued by Rowan and Mayne (and approved by Sir Robert Peel), historians have devised various listings of what is known as "Peel's Principles," or "Principles of Peelian Reform." Exhibit 2–6 shows two different lists derived from the many versions that exist. The wording has been modernized somewhat.

Conser and Frissora (1994) stress that any lists of "Peel's Principles" are interpretations and not reprints of any specific document from that time period. In fact, they analyzed a copy of the original *First Instructions* as they appeared in the *Times* (London newspaper) in September of 1829 and concluded that there were as many as seventy "principles" contained in the document (Conser and Frissora 1994). Appendix 2–1 of this chapter is the first publication of their findings. This is an example of how a revisitation to historical documents can yield some interesting findings. In the current era of community policing, many of the principles of the early British policing model are worthy of review.

The New Police force did not *replace* the existing classes of peace officers mentioned earlier; it was an addition to them. But by 1839, following a number of select committees to establish the English police system, especially in London, most of the other police forces in London had been "absorbed" into the New Police. Although the new force was not popular at first (because of the fear of centralized police authority), it eventually won wide public support and became one model of municipal police forces worldwide (Emsley 1991), especially in the United States. Peel's influence earned him recognition as "Father of Modern Municipal Policing."

Exhibit 2–6

PEEL'S PRINCIPLES OF POLICING

Version 1—General Principles

1. Prevention of crime is the basic mission of the police.
2. Police must have full respect of the citizenry.
3. A citizen's respect for the law develops respect for the police.
4. Cooperation of the public decreases as the use of force increases.
5. Police must render impartial enforcement of the law.
6. Physical force is used only as a last resort.
7. The police are the public and the public are the police.
8. Police represent the law.
9. The absence of crime and disorder is the test of police efficiency.

Version 2—Organizing Principles

1. Police must be stable, efficient, and organized along military lines.
2. Police must be under government control.
3. The efficiency of the police should be judged by the absence or presence of crime.
4. Distribution of crime information is essential.
5. The police should be deployed by time and area.
6. Qualities such as the command of temper, a quiet determined manner, and so on are indispensable to police officers.
7. Good appearance commands respect.
8. Efficiency is premised on securing and training the proper persons.
9. Public security demands that every police officer be given a number.
10. Police headquarters should be centrally located and easily accessible to the people.
11. Police officers should be hired on a probationary basis.
12. Police records are necessary to the correct distribution of police strength.

Source: Reprinted with permission from J. A. Conser and G. G. Frissora, *Peel's Principles Revisited*, Paper presented at the annual conference of the Midwestern Criminal Justice Association, Chicago, Ill., September 15, 1994, © 1994, Midwestern Justice Association.

SUMMARY

This chapter has presented an overview of nearly 3800 years of the history of policing. Its focus was from Babylon to the British Empire. It emphasizes that social control methods evolve and change. In most ancient civilizations, the policing function was carried out by the military and the elite forces of the aristocracy. In the history of the Roman Empire, law enforcement by civilians became an important feature of social control. In the seventeenth through nineteenth centuries, France and England developed the fundamentals of the policing systems that are in place today.

History is the study of past events and all the surrounding elements of those events. It provides the foundation for any present society; it is studied in order to better understand current times and our reactions to them. History can help us understand and identify the social, economic, and political forces that have shaped and are shaping our society. Criminal justice professionals need to understand the history of their field. "Knowing from whence you came" is part of being a professional person. Only then can you make informed decisions based on the realization that others have made similar decisions before you. It is this frame of reference that gives meaning to George Santayana's (1905) famous quotation: "Those who cannot remember the past are condemned to repeat it."

QUESTIONS FOR REVIEW

1. What are three reasons why the study of history is important to the field of criminal justice?
2. What are the types and levels of social control that may fluctuate throughout a country's history?
3. What was unique about the establishment of the Vigiles in ancient Rome? What social and political forces affected their creation?
4. What were the key contributions made by the French to the field of policing from the Middle Ages to the early 1800s?
5. What were the reasons for establishing the Metropolitan Police of London in 1829? Who were some of the early police reformers in England during the 1700s and 1800s?

SUGGESTED ACTIVITIES

1. Select a country or region of the world and research its history of social control. Identify, if possible, early forms of policing. Try to identify the social, political, and economic conditions of the period. Selected material can be found on the World Wide Web at **http://history.evansville.net/**.
2. Check your library's holdings (possibly on microfilm) of old newspapers of England (e.g., *The Times* of London) and find some of the debate in daily newspapers at the time of the introduction to create the "New Police" in London. Look for letters to the editor and editorials on the subject of the New Police.
3. Using the World Wide Web, check out the home page of the New Scotland Yard (London Metropolitan Police Department) at **http://www.met.police.uk/**. Click on the "History" icon and select "History A-Z," where you can read about the early years of the London policing.

CHAPTER GLOSSARY

Act for Improving the Police in and near the Metropolis: introduced and enacted during the term of Sir Robert Peel, Home Secretary of England, in 1829; established a centralized police force for the metropolitan London area

Code of Hammurabi: the legal code of ancient Babylon, about 1750 B.C.; codified under King Hammurabi; contained some 282 statutes and evidenced a sense of justice built on personal responsibility and accountability

commune juree: twelfth-century French mutual defense association where an oath formed a bond between a large number of men of equal status for the defense of a collective interest

constable: important position of trust in France during the Middle Ages; count of the stable

Courts of Leet (local police courts): instituted as a substitute for the sheriff's courts

feudalism: the practice of providing the living needs of those under a leader's control or subject to a leader's authority

frankpledge system: a form of social control where all free men took an oath of fidelity to the king; introduced in France during the reign of Charlemagne

hundred: a collection of ten tythings

Laws of the Twelve Tables: a set of twelve brass tablets describing proper conduct that became the foundation of the Roman Empire's legal system (about 450 B.C.)

lex talionis: the law of retaliation

Lieutenant of Police: established by the edicts of the council in France (1666–1667) for the City of Paris

Magna Carta: the great charter of England signed by King John in 1215; it granted certain guarantees toward a fairer justice system and rights to the people

Mosaic Law: the law of Moses as found in the Old Testament books of Exodus, Leviticus, Numbers, and Deuteronomy

peace guilds: tenth-century England; local means of social control; private and voluntary associations, arranged in 10 groups under 10 headmen; mutual assurance societies

praepostus: the title of the headman of the English tything following the Norman conquest of 1066

Praetorian Guards: personal bodyguards of Caesar Augustus; an elite military unit

reeve: the chief law enforcement and magistrate of the shire in the English tything system (known as the shire-reeve or, later, as the sheriff)

sergeant: armed police assistants to early French village mayors

shire: a geographical area roughly equivalent to a county

Statute of Winchester (1285): enacted during the reign of Edward I; it created a policing system that continued for nearly 500 years

Surete: the criminal division of the Paris Police (which in 1913 became the **Police Judiciaire**)

tything (or **tithing**) **system:** early English system of social control

Urban Cohort: Roman military units used as protectors of the peace throughout Rome

vicecomes: title change of the shire-reeve following the Norman conquest of 1066; responsible for going on the circuit to hold court (known as the police courts)

Vigiles: a civilian force of freedmen created by Emperor Augustus around 14 B.C. to act as night watchers; was the City's first fire-fighting unit and police unit

---

APPENDIX 2–1

PEEL'S PRINCIPLES BY CATEGORY

(Numbered by order of appearance in the *First Instructions*)

A. GENERAL PRINCIPLES

1. Rules and regulations cannot cover every type of incident police may encounter.
2. Discretion is necessary in police work.
8. The fundamental undergirding responsibility for police is crime prevention.
9. Crime rates are the best indicator of evaluating police efficiency.
46. Complaints against police should be signed.

48. Policing should be community oriented.
59. Members of the public may be called upon to assist an officer.
68. The police shall be under civilian control.
70. The public should be made aware of police duties and responsibilities.

B. ORGANIZATIONAL PRINCIPLES

11. Allocation of officers on a shift should be made according to special conditions and calls-for-service.
12. A community should have a number of centrally located police stations.
13. Officers should live in the area they serve.
14. Uniformed officers should be clearly identified with a badge number.
20. Departments should have formal written rules and regulations.
24. Weapons should be issued by and remain the property of the department.
31. A superior officer should remain on-station at all times.
36. The superintendent is not required to live in the district.
37. Ranking officers should reside within a designated area.
38. Ranking officers should not assume line functions.
45. An officer should be assigned the responsibility of accounting for evidence and property.
58. Police departments should have a pursuit policy.
62. Police departments should establish procedural regulations for arresting individuals.
63. Departmental procedures should be established for identifying individuals with particularity.
69. Police departments should have a paramilitary organizational design.

C. PERSONNEL MANAGEMENT PRINCIPLES

3. Testing for mental ability and reasoning is an appropriate entrance and promotional requirement.
4. Psychological testing should be part of the entrance exam process.
5. Officers should have control of their temper.
6. Officers must be literate.
7. Officers should have police training.
10. Officers should be rewarded for doing a good job.
15. Officers should pay for their own uniforms.
16. Officers should appear in complete uniform.
18. Regulations should be established that specify hair length and facial hair.
19. Officers should not be permitted outside employment.
22. The department may discipline officers for not paying personal debts.
51. Officers should receive training updates on the law and procedures.

D. SUPERVISORY PRINCIPLES

28. Officers should be inspected prior to going on duty.
29. Officers should be inspected immediately after going off duty.
30. Officers should be given written orders of their daily assignment.
39. Unannounced inspections and spot checks of officers, beats, and stations should be made.
40. All reports should be reviewed by a superior officer.
41. The chief should have the power of summary punishment in minor violations.
42. Supervisors should initiate immediate action and investigations into serious infractions by officers.
43. Ranking officers should become acquainted with talents and moral character of officers.

E. PRINCIPLES OF DUTY

17. Uniforms should be clean and well kept.
21. Officers should not accept gratuities.
23. Officers should keep a notebook of their activities.
25. Off-duty officers may be called to duty at any time.
26. Officers are on duty 24 hours a day.
27. Officers should have different arrest powers when on and off duty.
32. Officers must remain at their assignment until properly relieved.
33. A written report/log/turn sheet of shift activities should be made.
34. Police should always respond to fire calls.
35. Police should not drink alcoholic beverages while on duty.
44. Property and evidence should be signed for.
47. Officers should have a level of familiarity with one's beat.
49. Officers should not casually visit bars while on duty.
50. Officers should not leave the beat to see what is going on elsewhere.

52. Officers should not abuse their power.
53. Officers should treat prisoners with civility.
54. Officers should use only force as necessary to perform duties.
55. Officers may arrest upon probable cause of a felony.
56. Officers should not unnecessarily interfere with people.
57. Officers are charged with the duty of maintaining the public peace.
60. Officers should obtain an arrest warrant whenever possible.
61. Officers should be responsible for all warrants issued to them.
64. Officers should not abuse their powers by responding to taunts.
65. Officers should treat all persons with courtesy and respect.
66. Officers should not engage in idle chit-chat or gossip.
67. Officers should render aid and assistance whenever called upon.

Source: Reprinted with permission from J.A. Conser and G.G. Frissora, *Peel's Principles Revisited*, Paper presented at the annual conference of the Midwestern Criminal Justice Association, Chicago, Ill., September 15, 1994, © 1994, Midwestern Justice Association.

REFERENCES

Arnold, Eric A. Jr. 1979. *Fouche, Napoleon, and the General Police.* Washington D.C.: University Press of America.

Black, Jim. 1994. *When Nations Die.* Wheaton, IL: Tyndale House.

Brandon, S.G.F., ed. 1970. *Ancient Empires.* New York: Newsweek.

Breasted, James Henry. 1916. *The Conquest of Civilization.* New York: Harper & Brothers Publishers.

Conser, James A. and Gordon G. Frissora. 1994. Peel's Principles Revisited. Paper presented at the annual conference of the Midwestern Criminal Justice Association, September, Chicago, IL.

Cottrell, Leonare. 1970. *Gift of the Nile.* In *Ancient Empires,* edited by S.G.F. Brandon (New York: Newsweek, 13).

Emsley, Clive. 1991. *The English Police: A Political and Social History.* New York: St. Martin's Press.

Gadd, Cyril John. 1971. *Hammurabi, Code of.* In *Encyclopaedia Britannica* Chicago, IL: W. Benton Publishers, 11, 41–43).

Goodspeed, George S. 1904. *A History of the Ancient World.* New York: Charles Scribner's Sons.

Grun, Bernard. 1991. *The Timetables of History, The New Third Revised Edition.* New York: Simon & Schuster.

Holden, Richard N. 1992. *Law Enforcement: An Introduction.* Englewood Cliffs, NJ: Prentice Hall.

Kelly, Martin A. 1973. The First Urban Policeman. *Journal of Police Science and Administration* 1(1) (March): 56–60.

Kocourek, Albert and John H. Wigmore. 1915. *Sources of Ancient and Primitive Law.* Boston: Little, Brown, and Company.

Lee, W.L. Melville. *History of Police in England.* (1901; reprint, Montclair, NJ: Patterson Smith, 1971).

Santayana, George. 1905. *The Life of Reason.* Vol. 1. New York: Charles Scribner's Sons.

Seignobos, Charles. 1932. *The Evolution of the French People.* Translated by Catherine Alison Phillips. New York: Alfred A. Knopf.

Stead, Philip John. 1985. *The Police of Britain.* New York: Macmillan.

Times (London) 1829. New Police Instructions. (25 September): 3–4.

Tobias, J.J. 1979. *Crime and Police in England, 1700–1900.* New York: St. Martin's Press.

Trojan, Carol. 1986. Egypt: Evolution of a Modern Police State. *CJ International,* 2(1) (January-February): 15.

CHAPTER 3

The Evolution of Law Enforcement in the United States

Undercover Chicago police officers of the prohibition era pose with tommy guns next to an armored car that features bullet-proof windows, 1920s. (Popperfoto/ Archive Photos)

COLONIAL AMERICA

Policing in colonial America resembled law enforcement practices in England during the same period. Night watchmen and constables, appointed or elected in villages and cities, were assigned a number of duties. For example, Joshua Pratt, the constable in Plymouth, Massachusetts in 1634, was the sealer of weights and measures, surveyor of land, jailer, and an announcer of marriages (Whitehouse 1973, 88). County governments copied the English precedent of appointing sheriffs as their primary law enforcement officials. These sheriffs, like their British counterparts, were appointed through the political system (usually the colonial governor's office) and were not elected.

Night-Watch System

Service as a night watchman or constable was an obligation of the adult males of the community. Although some communities experimented with paid constables, most colonists relied on volunteers to staff their law enforcement offices well into the 1700s (Johnson 1981, 5). Some variations existed, however. For example, in New Amsterdam (later named New York when the British took over the city), a group of citizens equipped with rattles to warn of their watchful presence was referred to as the **rattlewatch**. In 1658, New Amsterdam appointed eight paid watchmen to replace the volunteers, but it was not until 1693 that the first uniformed police officer was appointed by the mayor.

During the 1700s, policing in most colonial cities changed little, although Johnson (1981, 6–7) notes that the reliance on volunteer watchmen was becoming strained:

> By the middle of the eighteenth century the colonists faced a dilemma which some residents felt they could no longer ignore. The towns had become large enough to need reliable police, but their best citizens habitually refused this duty and the men who did serve were not as effective as they needed to be. Circumstances, not incompetence, dictated this ineffectiveness. Watchmen who worked all day at other jobs could hardly stay awake, let alone maintain order at night. Some cities did pay their watchmen, but not enough to allow someone to earn his living by law enforcement. The idea of citizen participation in policing was breaking down, and something was needed to replace it.
>
> In 1749 the city of Philadelphia was permitted to levy a tax and appoint **wardens** with the authority to hire watchmen as needed. Only those interested in working on the watch for pay applied to the wardens, and watchmen could now be dismissed for inefficiency (Johnson 1981, 7).

The military presence of the British became an increasing factor as massive social and political discontent grew stronger toward the latter part of the 1700s. This presence extended to the frontier in the Ohio Valley and Lake Erie during the French and Indian War (1756–1763). From 1765 through the end of the Revolutionary War (1783), the colonies faced several riots and disturbances, economic depression, and an ever-increasingly restrictive imperial policy of Britain. The duties of public safety were given to military forces. Following the war, policing was turned back over to civilian authority (local government).

Some parts of the colonies had their own unique forms of policing. For example, southern governments enacted **slave patrol** legislation in the 1740s.

These laws protected people from runaway slaves, inhibited insurrection, and authorized recapture of slaves. The slave patrols had the right to visit every plantation and to search all "Negro-Houses for offensive weapons and ammunition." The infliction of corporal punishment was also permitted if any slave was found to have left his owner's property without permission (Wood 1984, 123–124). Some maintain that the slave patrols of the South were America's first modern-style police forces (Williams and Murphy 1990, 3). By 1837, the Charleston (South Carolina) slave patrol, about 100 officers, was possibly the country's largest single police force at that time (Wintersmith 1974, 19–21).

Policing did vary somewhat among the various regions of the United States. It is difficult to accurately reflect the history of early American policing in a single chapter. For this reason, the reader is encouraged to read the history of selected police departments as documented by those departments. A sample of such list of sites on the World Wide Web appears in Exhibit 3–1.

Appointment of Federal Marshals

On the national level, the British military had provided a certain level of social control and protection. Its emphasis was on the borders and in those areas where discontent, insurrection, and rebellious behavior were fermenting among the colonists. In 1789, following the war, the Congress of the newly formed United States began to take over this function. It was during this time that the first federal law enforcement position, the federal marshal, was created.

George Washington appointed the first marshals following authorization by the Judiciary Act of 1789. They were to support the federal courts and to carry out all lawful orders issued by judges, Congress, or the President. Marshals often met with local resistance, and sometimes their efforts were less than successful. Throughout their early years, they were assigned to enforce unpopular federal laws, which included collection of taxes on whiskey. A marshal served papers on distillers in western Pennsylvania in 1794. Before the incident ended, 13,000 state militiamen had to be summoned to put down what is known as the Whiskey Rebellion (Jackson 1989). Marshals enforced the law banning African slave trade following its passage in 1819 and later carried out the Fugitive Slave Law of 1850 (which required the return of runaway slaves to their owners). Before the Civil War, marshals tracked down counterfeiters (since the Secret Service did not exist until 1865). The U.S. Marshals may be best remembered for their efforts to bring some justice to the Wild West. Marshals pursued Billy the Kid, Jesse James, and Butch Cassidy. The Oklahoma Territory was patrolled by marshals such as Heck Thomas, Chris Madsen, and Uncle Billy Tilghman. Wyatt Earp is now thought to have had an overstated reputation and instead may have used the law as a way to make money and avenge his brother's murder (Jackson 1989). Today, as a part of the Department of Justice, marshals' responsibilities include: insuring federal court secu-

Exhibit 3–1

SELECTED HISTORIES OF LAW ENFORCEMENT AGENCIES FOUND ON THE WORLD WIDE WEB

By reviewing the histories of several law enforcement agencies you will be able to identify various similarities and differences:

Southern Region
New Orleans, LA P.D. 1805–1889
http://www.lsu.edu/guests/lsuprss/spr-sum-96/rousey.htm
http://www.gnofn.org/~nopl/inv/neh/nehtb.htm
Tallahassee, FL P.D.
http://www.state.fl.us/citytlh/tpd/history.html
Winston-Salem, NC P.D.
http://wsnetra.ci.winston-salem.nc.us/psc/history.html

Northeastern Region
New York City, NY P.D. 1845–1890
http://www.ci.nyc.ny.us/html/nypd/html/3100/retro.html
Westborough, MA P.D.
http://web.iquest.net/ust/history.htm

Midwestern Region
Pennsylvania State Police
http://www.state.pa.us/PA_Exec/State_Police/history/
    history.htm
Xenia, OH P.D.
http://www.erinet.com/xenmis/police/pdhistory.html
Detroit, MI P.D.
http://www.jimsweb.com/detroitpolice/01h.htm

Western Region
Bakersfield, CA P.D.
http://www.bakersfield.com/city/goodbad/bpdhistory.html
Maricopa County, AZ Sheriff's Office
http://www.mcso.org/

Also see **http://www.geocities.com/CapitolHill/7900/oth-musm.html**
for a page of sites covering police history around the world.

rity; protecting federal witnesses; transporting prisoners; executing court orders; capturing fugitives; and seizing, managing, and disposing of federally seized property (U.S. Marshals Service, 1994).

EARLY TO MID-1800S

Following the Revolutionary War there were many social and political uncertainties in the unsettled American society, such as economic depression, continued debates over slavery, waves of immigrants, Indian skirmishes on the frontier, vigilantism, anti-immigrant/anti-Catholic sentiment, racial disturbances, and the like. American cities were poised for police reform, and they began establishing police departments that extended beyond night watches.

Establishment of Police Departments

During the 1830s to 1860s, most larger cities established paid police forces. Many of these departments were structured, in part, after the Metropolitan Police of London that had been formed a few years earlier. Major American cities such as Philadelphia, Boston, and New York have interesting histories as to the emergence of a unified, 24-hour police operation. Each had a social, economic, or political situation that caused reorganization and reform in the police department. In Philadelphia, Stephen Girard, a wealthy philanthropist, left a large sum of money to the city to establish a competent police force. It became one of the first American police forces to offer an organized metropolitan service. It consisted of 24 day police officers and 120 night watchmen. In Boston, an assault on the publisher William Lloyd Garrison, because of his anti-slavery writings, and the Broad Street Riot of 1837 led to police reform. Marshal Francis Tukey was hired to establish a competent and efficient police force. In New York (1844), because of rivalries that existed among the three separate components of the police force, it was reorganized as a unified department modeled after the Metropolitan Police of London, England (LEAA 1976, 17–18).

Vigilantism and Private Detectives

Another form of policing, **vigilantism**, appeared more frequently during the late 1790s through the mid-1870s. Especially where law enforcement officials or agencies did not exist or were ineffective, citizens took control. Originally, the philosophy of vigilantism was based on self-preservation and self-protection. It was a form of vigilance, often encouraged and supported by the best of citizens. According to one source, vigilance committees were first organized to patrol towns in California by citizen volunteers. Most members were honest men who were forced to collective action to protect their communities (LEAA

1976, 19). Vigilance committees had different names (e.g., regulators, committees, and vigilantes) and spread to other states, particularly Arizona, Montana, Colorado, and Nevada. Such vigilance committees were common until formal policing methods and agencies developed in those areas (Bopp and Schultz 1972, 50–51).

Along with the vigilante movement, the private police (detective) field was forming. Private industry and the railroads needed to protect their assets from criminals and disgruntled employees and competitors. An early private protection agency was founded by Allan Pinkerton in 1855. Known as Pinkerton's North West Police Agency, its initial task was to investigate criminal activity against railroads. Earlier, in 1850, Henry Wells and William Fargo established the American Express Company, which was a freight service company. They had to provide their own protection as they transported goods and valuables, including payrolls. Their security personnel were known as "shotgun riders" (Green and Fisher 1987, 11). (Chapter 4 describes the private police movement in the United States in greater detail.)

THE CIVIL WAR AND ITS AFTERMATH

At the time of the Civil War in the United States, racism and discrimination were common in states beyond the South. Every new state admitted to the Union after 1819 restricted voting to whites only. Several northern and western states prohibited black testimony in court if whites were a party to the proceeding. Even where blacks were totally free, some states maintained **"Jim Crow" laws** and practices that separated the races. One eminent historian, C. Vann Woodward, has been cited by Williams and Murphy (1990, 5–6) regarding this practice: "One of the strangest things about Jim Crow was that the system was born in the North and reached an advanced age before moving South in force."

Following the Civil War and during the Reconstruction Period in the South, states began to enact laws that specifically spelled out the rights and responsibilities of the newly freed slaves. The laws, known as the **Black Codes**, were eventually enacted by every former Confederate state. According to Foner (1988, 203), the entire complex of Black Codes was enforced ". . . by a police apparatus and judicial system in which blacks enjoyed virtually no voice whatever. Whites staffed urban police forces as well as State militias, intended, as a Mississippi white put it in 1865, to 'keep good order and discipline amongst the Negro population.'" During this time period, whites victimized blacks with nearly total immunity. When whites were prosecuted, their sentences were less harsh than those for blacks who committed the same offense. After the Civil War, the federal government reacted by passing the Civil Rights Act of 1866, which specified the rights of citizens regardless of race. It also allowed for lawsuits against persons who deprived a citizen of a civil right. This law led

Congress to adopt the Fourteenth Amendment to the Constitution, which provided "equal protection" under the law. The Fifteenth Amendment, enacted shortly thereafter, addressed the voting rights of blacks. The Civil Rights Act of 1875 outlawed the exclusion of blacks from hotels, theaters, railroads, and other public accommodations (Williams and Murphy 1990, 7).

With the guarantee of the right to vote, blacks were courted by politicians. Elected officials responded by appointing blacks to police departments. Selma, Alabama hired black officers in 1867; Houston, Texas, in 1870; Galveston, Texas, in 1870; Jackson, Mississippi, in 1871; Chicago in 1872; Columbia and Charleston, South Carolina, in 1873; and Philadelphia in 1874. The City of New Orleans, by 1870, had 177 black officers, and three of the five police board members were black. Although agencies were appointing blacks, it did not mean that they were equal to their white counterparts. In many cities, blacks were restricted in making arrests and may not have been permitted to arrest whites. Some cities refused to put the officers in uniform, having them wear plain clothes instead. Other cities assigned them to black areas and even marked the cruisers "Negro Police" (Williams and Murphy 1990, 7).

The Supreme Court added to this disparity in treatment and authority by deciding **Plessy v. Ferguson** (1896), stating that the doctrine of "separate but equal" was constitutional and that states could enact laws that allowed segregation in public accommodations. Some cities began firing black officers after the court decision. Even New Orleans dropped to only 5 black officers by 1900 and did not appoint another black officer until 1950 (Williams and Murphy 1990, 9).

EARLY REFORMS AND REFORMERS, 1890S TO 1930S

Policing from the end of the Civil War to the early 1900s was dominated by politics. Appointments and terms of office for regular uniformed officers often were made annually by city council members (aldermen and ward representatives) and mayors. Officers and departments were often heavily influenced by politicians; "political machines" and corruption were ongoing problems.

Reform and the Progressive Movement

Efforts to initiate reform in policing coincided with the **Progressive Movement**. In the words of Fogelson (1977, 44):

This [Progressive] movement, which began at the turn of the century and thrived for the next two decades, sought to shore up the position of the upper middle and upper classes by reforming the courts, schools and other urban institutions. It attempted to reorganize their structure, upgrade their personnel, and redefine their function in ways that would . . . destroy the system of machine politics which had developed in the middle and late nineteenth century. Police reform subsequently gathered momentum as part of the so-called war on crime.

Well-known figures of the day took part in the movement, including Theodore Roosevelt, who became Police Commissioner of New York City (see Exhibit 3–2).

The Birth of Professional Associations

Reform also came from the police administrators themselves, who established the National Chiefs of Police Union in 1893. The National Chiefs of Police Union changed its name to the **International Association of Chiefs of Police** (IACP) in 1902. The original purpose of the association was to provide mutual assistance and cooperation in arresting and detaining persons known to have committed a crime. Some of the issues addressed in early meetings of the association would continue to be concerns for decades (see Exhibit 3–3).

Other issues such as civil service standards, arresting persons on the basis of telegrams, adopting a police telegraph code, and adopting a uniform system of identification of criminals were addressed by the group. These early reformers included Chief William S. Seavey of Omaha, Superintendent Robert McLaughrey of Chicago, Chief W.C. Davis of Memphis, Chief Roger O'Mara of Pittsburgh, Chief L. Harrigan of St. Louis, and Chief Harvey O. Carr of Grand Rapids (Dilworth 1976, 3–6). The IACP's annual conventions allowed police executives from

---

Exhibit 3–2

POLICE COMMISSIONER THEODORE ROOSEVELT

During his three years as police commissioner of New York City (1895–1897), Roosevelt gained international acclaim for his reforms. He pioneered a bicycle squad, a telephonic communications system, and training for new recruits. He routed out corrupt elements within the department and instituted promotion based on merit rather than on politics. Later, he enthusiastically supported the Pennsylvania State Constabulary (State Police) and, in 1908, as President, he organized the Bureau of Investigation in the Department of Justice, the forerunner of the FBI.

Source: Reprinted from Law Enforcement Assistance Administration (LEAA), *Two Hundred Years of American Criminal Justice,* p. 20, 1976, U.S. Department of Justice.

Exhibit 3–3

FLASHBACK TO 1905
THE "RIGHTS" WARNING

Chief Benjamin Murphy of Jersey City, New Jersey, addressed the 12th annual convention (1905) of the IACP about a system adopted in his department some TEN years earlier.

It is one of the standing rules of our force . . . we have what we term a statement. This statement is typewritten and is furnished to each station house. Just as soon as a person is arrested on the charge of having committed a felony, rape, robbery, burglary, murder, etc., it is the duty of the superior officer present to bring that defendant into a room. This statement is picked up and read to him in the presence of the arresting officer, and, if possible, some other witness. The statement reads in this way: "I am John Brown, a sergeant of police. I am going to ask you some questions concerning the crime for which you are arrested. You are arrested for _____ on _____ street a short time ago. You may answer these questions or not just as you please, but what you do say will be taken down in writing and used at your trial. It must be a free, voluntary statement. Do you understand that?

Source: Reprinted with permission from D. C. Dilworth, *The Blue and The Brass: American Policing 1890–1910,* p. 66, © 1976, International Association of Chiefs of Police.

---

across the country and around the world to exchange ideas and keep current on the latest technology and legal developments (see Appendix 3–2 for the evolution of criminal identification in the United States during this period).

Also during the early 1900s, the rise of big business and trade unionism and the accompanying labor strikes affected police forces. In 1915, two Pittsburgh patrol officers founded the **Fraternal Order of Police** as a social benevolent association that included all ranks in the police organization. In 1919, the Boston Police Strike had national ramifications (refer to Chapter 10 for discussion of the unionization movement) in that it curtailed police unionization efforts for nearly 40 years.

From 1905 to 1914, over 10.5 million immigrants from southern and eastern Europe entered the United States. Urbanization became a major problem; police departments were strained in their efforts to keep order. Society was turning to the police departments to assist in all types of issues emerging from a complex society. To assist with problems related to women and juveniles, women officers were needed. In 1910, **Alice Stebbins Wells** became the first policewoman with full police powers in the city of Los Angeles—and probably in the world. She became a national advocate of women in policing, and helped organize and was the first president of the International Association of Police-women in 1915 (today known as the **International Association of Women Police**). By the end of World War I, over 200 American cities had policewomen on their police forces, frequently operating out of separate "women's bureaus."

World War I added more tensions and strain to American society. Many police officers left their departments to serve in the war effort. In some parts of the country, women and older volunteers helped supplement the existing resources. When the "troops" returned, the number of women in policing actually decreased. However, other events such as the temperance movement and Prohibition (1919–1933), the granting of the right to vote to women in 1920, and concern for female victims of crime kept the issue of women police officers in the forefront of policing controversies.

During this era of early reform, August Vollmer (Chief of Berkeley, California from 1905–1932) and Superintendent Richard Sylvester (Washington, D.C. and President of IACP from 1901–1915) were staunch advocates of police professionalism. They encouraged greater use of science and technology and less political interference from elected and non-elected officials. (See Exhibit 3–4 for the major contributions of August Vollmer.)

The Wickersham Commission

One major involvement by the federal government also influenced the police community, although more subtly than directly. In the latter part of the 1920s, several state and local commissions began looking into police practices and the related issues of the administration of criminal justice. In 1929, President Hoover appointed Attorney General George W. Wickersham to chair the **National Commission on Law Observance and Enforcement** (commonly referred to as the Wickersham Commission). The country was facing a surging crime problem, private detectives and crime prevention activities were mounting, the public was fearful of lawlessness, and some people advocated a reduction in civil liberties in the name of safety (Fogelson 1977, 120). The Wickersham Commission undertook the first national study of the criminal justice system in the United States. Vollmer was placed in charge of surveying and reporting the findings regarding the police community. Publication Number 14, *Report on Police,* was released in 1931. Its ten major conclusions were as follows:

1. The corrupting influence of politics should be removed from the police organization.
2. The head of the department should be selected at large for competence, a leader, preferably a man of considerable police experience, and removable from office only after preferment of charges and a public hearing.

Exhibit 3–4

THE CONTRIBUTIONS OF AUGUST VOLLMER (B.1876–D.1955)

Recognition: "America's Greatest Cop"
"Father of Modern Police Science"
"Dean of American Law Enforcement"

August Vollmer served as Berkeley, California's chief law enforcement officer for 27 years, first being elected town marshal in 1905 and then as police chief until his retirement. In 1907, he was elected president of the California Police Chiefs Association, and by 1922 he had ascended to the presidency of the International Association of Chiefs of police.

He was a strong advocate of training and college education for police officers. He established one of the first police training schools in the U.S. and initiated the first college-level law enforcement courses at San Jose State College in 1916. He became a full professor of police administration at the University of Chicago (in 1929 while on leave from Berkeley P.D.) which was followed with an appointment as Professor of Police Administration at the University of California at Berkeley. He served as the Police Consultant to the National Law Observance and Enforcement Commission and was the primary author of its *Report on Police* (1929–1931). He was instrumental in many state and national professional associations. He acted as a consultant to over 75 police departments throughout the world during his career. He promoted police professionalism through his many writings which included books, articles, reports, and correspondence with academic and police leaders throughout the country.

Vollmer was an ardent innovator and advocate of the use of technology. He instituted bicycle patrols (1905), a red light recall system (1906), police records and modus operandi systems (1906), motorcycle patrol (1913), automobile patrol service (1914); installed a fingerprint system, handwriting system, and deception detection system (1921); and installed the first aluminum street signs (1924).

He believed in stringent recruitment standards, emphasized ethical conduct, and advocated freedom from political interference. At times his views were unpopular with contemporaries. He considered crime prevention a priority, opposed capital punishment, supported decriminalization of victimless crime, and advocated probation for first-time offenders.

(continues)

Exhibit 3–4 *(continued)*

Plagued by ill health in his later years, he ended his own life on 4 November 1955.

Source: Data from G. E. Carte and E. Carte, *Police Reform in the United States*, pp. 125–128, © 1975, University of California Press; D. E. J. MacNamara, August Vollmer, in *The Encyclopedia of Police Science*, Second Edition, W. Bailey, ed., © 1995, Garland Publishing, Inc.; and *Biographical Sketch*, August Vollmer Papers, BANC MSS C-B 403, © The Bancroft Library, University of California, Berkeley.

---

3. Patrolmen should be able to rate a "B" on the Alpha test, be able-bodied and of good character, weigh 150 pounds, measure 5 feet 9 inches tall, and be between 21 and 31 years of age. These requirements may be disregarded by the chief for good and sufficient reasons.
4. Salaries should permit decent living standards, adequate housing, eight hours of work, one day off weekly, annual vacation, fair sick leave with pay, just accident and death benefits when in performance of duty, and a reasonable pension provision on an actuarial basis.
5. Adequate training for recruits, officers, and those already on the roll is imperative.
6. The communication system should provide for call boxes, telephones, recall system, and (in appropriate circumstances) teletype and radio.
7. Records should be complete, adequate, but as simple as possible. They should be used to secure administrative control of investigations and of department units in the interest of efficiency.
8. A crime-prevention unit should be established if circumstances warrant this action, and qualified women police should be engaged to handle juvenile delinquents' and women's cases.
9. State police forces should be established in States where rural protection of this character is required.
10. State bureaus of criminal investigation and information should be established in every State (National Commission on Law Observance and Enforcement, 1931: 140).

Although these improvements were successful in some jurisdictions, social and political forces undermined national reform. America was in the midst of a depression; the political machines were stronger than originally thought. Municipal authority was more diffused than centralized, and the public did not believe that there would be any effect on the crime and morality problem of the day (and even less on their underlying causes) (Fogelson 1977, 134–136). The recommendations did set the groundwork for a later generation of reform efforts.

THE EVOLUTION OF STATE POLICE

The changing social environment of the early decades of the twentieth century in the United States included urbanization, industrialization, rising immigration, governmental regulation, and an increasing crime problem. State governments often found themselves with no agency to enforce state laws. Only Texas and Massachusetts had created state agencies prior to the twentieth century. The Texas Rangers were officially formed in 1835, originally to protect the frontier life of American settlers, primarily from Indian raids. Although Massachusetts created its first state agency in 1865 to focus on vice laws (which some concluded was directed toward Irish Catholics), the force was abolished in 1875 because of the lack of public acceptance (Johnson 1981, 157–158).

Pennsylvania led the reform efforts to create a modern state police force. Rural crime and violence in the industrial union movement (especially in the coal fields) led Governor Samuel Pennypacker to encourage legislative creation of the Pennsylvania Constabulary, which was modeled after the Philippine Constabulary (a paramilitary structure). Between 1908 and 1923, fourteen states (mostly in the northern industrial regions) established similar organizations. After the decline of labor strife and reduced immigration during the war years, state police turned more toward rural policing and traffic enforcement. During the 1930s, eight more states added "state police" forces, while eighteen established highway patrols whose authority was limited by law to traffic matters. State involvement in policing also included setting up communication systems and bureaus of criminal identification. By 1934, twenty-four states had bureaus of criminal identification. Also by the early 1930s, telephone systems and two-way radios were sufficiently developed to permit more modern police practices. State troopers generally enjoyed good reputations, and across America they became elite law enforcement officers (Johnson 1981, 158–164).

POST–WORLD WAR II DEVELOPMENTS

A Changing Society

Following the Second World War, policing in the United States turned toward a more professional approach. A new generation of reformers was better educated than earlier counterparts, had distinguished service records, held positions of public influence, and spoke out and debated issues. Some of these individuals were responsible for spearheading the movement for improved training and for creating police science and criminology programs in colleges and universities. They wrote books and articles about the police profession; they began to establish a systematic body of knowledge about the field. When the relatively tranquil 1950s turned into the tumultuous 1960s, people and political leaders were more inclined to listen and search for answers (conditions necessary for serious reform). It is not possible to list everyone who had some impact on this wave of reform efforts. Exhibit 3–5 identifies some major reformers; you may wish to seek out other sources that detail their accomplishments. Some of these individuals will be mentioned in other chapters of this text as well.

During the 1950s and early 1960s, policing in the United States evolved to placing officers in cruisers and sending them out to respond to calls for service. There were, of course, exceptions; some larger cities maintained foot and mounted patrols. Most small towns had few officers on duty at most times, but they were not pressured by the calls for service. The country, however, was changing. Rural America was mostly prosperous and peaceful (for non-minorities), while urban life was becoming more chaotic, fast-paced, and burdened with increasing racial/ethnic tensions. Migration of blacks from the rural South to northern cities increased, and immigrants came to the larger cities. Social institutions were unable to cope with this dramatic increase in urbanization and diverse population mix. Coupled with this was the ever-increasing involvement of the United States in foreign affairs (the Korean conflict, the "cold war," the Cuban missile crisis, and Vietnam). The baby-boom generation began questioning the country's social and political direction—questions that often went unanswered by government. People of all ages across the country began to engage in civil protest.

From the mid-1950s through the 1960s, racial unrest and the accompanying civil rights movement sparked incidents across the United States, with the most violent in the South. The police who attempted to control these incidents were often untrained to handle crowds, especially racially diverse ones. They often did not perform adequately. Nationally televised examples included the school desegregation incidents in Alabama, civil rights marches in several cities, and the "police riot" of the Democratic National convention in 1968.

Presidential Commissions and LEAA

Social unrest and crime conditions were so severe that, in 1965, President Johnson declared a "war on crime" and appointed the **President's Commission on Law Enforcement and Administration of Justice**. Officially charged to investigate the causes of crime, the commission was quite broad in its analysis. The summary report, *The Challenge of Crime in a Free Society*, was issued in 1967. Nine supplemental reports also were published: *The Police, The Courts, Corrections, Juvenile Delinquency and Youth Crime, Organized Crime, Assessment of Crime, Narcotics and Drug Abuse, Drunkenness*, and *Science and Technology*. These reports provide interesting reading, since each elaborates on the conditions found in the criminal justice system during the mid-1960s. Each report as well as the summary report contained numerous recommenda-

Exhibit 3–5

SELECTED REFORMERS OF THE 1950s–1970s

Orlando Winfield Wilson (1900–1972)

O.W. Wilson is best known for authoring several major texts in the police field, especially *Police Administration*, which was first published in 1950 and became the unofficial "bible" for police managers (and students). In 1921, he began his police career as a patrolman in Berkeley, California. He served as chief in Fullerton (CA) and later at Wichita (KS). He taught at Harvard and in 1939 became professor of police administration at the University of California at Berkeley, replacing the retired August Vollmer. He served with the military and also assisted in reorganizing the police forces in Europe following WWII. He served as Superintendent of the Chicago Police Department from 1960–1967.

Vivian Anderson Leonard (1898–1984)

V.A. Leonard joined the Berkeley Police Department in 1925. He went on to earn a BA and MA in colleges in Texas and a PhD from Ohio State (1949). He served as superintendent of the records and identification division of the Ft. Worth Police Department from 1934–1939. From 1941 to 1963, he was affiliated with the Washington State University and became a full professor of Police Science and Administration. He authored *Police Organization and Management* in 1950, as well as six other texts: *Police Communications Systems, Police Records Systems, The Police of the Twentieth Century, The Police, Police Personnel Administration, Criminal Investigation and Identification,* and *Police Crime Prevention.* He was active in several national organizations, was a founder of what later became the Academy of Criminal Justice Sciences, and was founder of Alpha Phi Sigma (the national criminal justice honor society).

John Edgar Hoover (1895–1972)

Born and educated in Washington, DC, Hoover spent his career there as well. During WWI, he worked as a special assistant on counterespionage activities to the U.S. Attorney General. In 1924, at age 29, he was appointed the director of the FBI following a major reorganization of it. He reformed the agency into a highly effective and efficient organization. By the 1930s, the agency was a modern crime-fighting organization that was aggressively pursuing major criminals throughout the

(continues)

Exhibit 3–5 *(continued)*

U.S. He adopted modern crime lab technology (in addition to finger-printing), detailed criminal records, statistics, and, later, computerization (the National Crime Information Center). The National Police Academy was established to help train state and local managers in the latest methods and techniques. Under Hoover's leadership, the FBI became one of the most effective and respected law enforcement agencies in the world. Unfortunately, some of Hoover's methods and constitutional rights abuses tarnished his latter years of service. He served as director until his death in 1972.

William H. Parker (1902–1966)

Parker is best known for his professional leadership of the Los Angeles Police Department from 1950 to 1966. During that time, he took the agency to national and international prominence by demanding excellence and efficiency, and by projecting a positive public image. He began his career in LA in 1927 and rose through the ranks. During WWII, he served in the U.S. Army and was highly decorated, receiving the American Purple Heart, the French Croix de Guerre with Silver Star, and the Italian Star of Solidarity. He served under Colonel O.W. Wilson and assisted in the reorganization of European police forces following the war. As Chief of LAPD, he demanded that highly qualified personnel be employed and that they receive only the best training. He reorganized the department and modernized the agency in terms of procedures, buildings, and equipment.

---

tions for improvement of the policing system, some of which have never been implemented or adopted as public policy.

After publication of the findings of the President's Crime Commission, Congress created the **Law Enforcement Assistance Administration** (LEAA) to assist government agencies at all levels of government to implement some of the recommendations set forth by the Commission. The enabling legislation was the **Omnibus Crime Control and Safe Streets Act of 1968**, commonly referred to as the "Safe Streets Act" or the "Crime Control Act" of 1968. LEAA provided billions of dollars of assistance to the criminal justice community until its funding was removed in 1980.

During the late 1960s and through the 1970s, other major commissions were established by various Presidents that focused on perceived serious problems or a specific series of incidents:

— Commission on Civil Disorders, 1968
— Commission on Causes and Prevention of Violence, 1969
— Commission on Campus Unrest, 1970
— Commission on Civil Rights, 1970
— Commission on Obscenity and Pornography, 1970
— Commission on Marihuana and Drug Abuse, 1972
— National Advisory Commission on Criminal Justice
  Standards and Goals, 1973
— Commission on Gambling, 1976
— Commission on Disorders and Terrorism, 1976
— Commission on Private Security, 1976
— Commission on Organized Crime, 1976

National Commissions have not been used much during the 1980s and 1990s for crime-related issues. They have become more popular on the state and municipal level, primarily to investigate allegations of police corruption and abuse. However, in 1997, Congress approved the formation of the National Gambling Impact Study Commission to study the social and economic impact of gambling in the United States. It was to make recommendations for potential legislation in 1999. Some of the recommendations will likely address law-enforcement issues related to gambling. Also in 1999, Attorney General Janet Reno was calling for a national commission on police integrity in the United States (see Chapter 15) and House Resolution 1659 in Congress was calling for a "National Police Training Commission" for the purpose of conducting a study of the effectiveness of training, recruiting, hiring, oversight, and funding policies and practices in law enforcement (U.S. Congress, 1999).

The 1980s and 1990s

Since the late 1970s, policing in the United States has continued to undergo reform and scrutiny. According to police historian Samuel Walker (1992, 26–28), the police have been "caught between old problems and new ideas." Old problems include the crime rate (down in the 1980s, then rising until the early 1990s when it started to decline) and varying types of crime (drug offenses, drive-by shootings, domestic violence, and juvenile crime) that upset the community. The new ideas have included problem-oriented policing, community policing, neighborhood crime prevention programming, and other enhanced community efforts. However, added to this puzzle are problems associated with police corruption and misconduct, rising fear of international and domestic terrorism, the application of military technology to civilian public safety and law enforcement, school violence, hate crime, and economic resources.

The many issues, debates, and trends in policing of the last two decades are incorporated throughout the rest of this text. They include role and style

(Chapter 7), strategies (Chapter 9), personnel selection and training (Chapters 10 and 11), legal restrictions (Chapter 12), technological applications (Chapter 13), police misconduct (Chapter 15), professionalism, accreditation (Chapter 15), and general challenges and future directions (Chapters 14 and 16). Each of the following chapters contains selected historical and current descriptions of the status of policing in the United States and the many challenges it faces.

SUMMARY

During the colonial period, policing was first carried out by volunteer watchmen. Gradually, the demands of law enforcement in cities required full-time, paid police forces. The position of federal marshal was created to enforce federal law. The vigilantism movement and private security agencies arose in areas where effective law enforcement was not in place. State police, first used in Texas, gradually evolved into highly professional state highway patrols and state investigative agencies.

Reforms for policing were part of the political Progressive Movement and were spearheaded by police leaders of the International Association of Chiefs of Police (IACP). Officer associations such as the Fraternal Order of Police and the International Association of Women Police also emerged to address concerns of the working officers. The Wickersham Commission issued the first national study of the criminal justice system in 1931. Its recommendations became the basis for future reform. Following the Second World War, changing societal developments and demands on law enforcement have resulted in the current police forces, which are at the same time more

professional and more scrutinized in the performance of their role. During the last two decades, the highlights of the history of policing in the United States have been focused on the changing strategies of policing, the integrity of law enforcement personnel, effectiveness, improved technology, and research efforts.

Policing in the United States has been constantly evolving and being shaped by the social forces of the day. Changes have occurred because of increasing urbanization and crime, general social disorder, racial and gender discrimination, changing technology, and the quest for professional status. For the most part, policing in this country has never been stagnant, and further change is inevitable. The field is becoming more professionalized, modernized, and at the same time more criticized. Its members must acknowledge their weaknesses and become determined to set a path toward developing more positive relationships with the community. The quality of law enforcement services is a continuous debate in many jurisdictions. That debate is a reflection of the ever-present impact of social, economic, and political forces in our society.

QUESTIONS FOR REVIEW

1. What was the night-watch system of protection during the colonial period, and what were its characteristics?
2. What historical development led to the creation of the position of federal marshal? What were the marshal's duties?
3. What were the legal and social customs in America prior to and following the Civil War, and how did they impact policing?
4. What was the "Progressive Movement," and how did it impact American policing in the early 1900s?
5. What were the names and contributions of at least three major American reformers of law enforcement during the period of the 1890s to the 1930s?
6. How did the functions of state police evolve?

7. What was the major commission that reviewed and reported on law enforcement

issues in the mid-1960s? What were its
findings?

SUGGESTED ACTIVITIES

1. Select a state in the United States and write a letter to its attorney general asking how law enforcement agencies at the state level are structured and organized. Conduct the same research on the World Wide Web using your Web browser and a search engine.
2. At your local library or police department, locate a history of the police department. Summarize your findings in class.
3. Secure a copy of one of the commission studies mentioned in this chapter and write a brief (3-page) summary of its major findings and recommendations as they relate to policing in the U.S.
4. On the World Wide Web, log on to the address **http://www.fbi.gov** and click on the "Your FBI" icon, then click on "90 years of FBI History." The site provides an interesting selection of photographs and insights about the agency.

CHAPTER GLOSSARY

Alice Stebbins Wells: first full-time, paid policewoman with full police powers, the city of Los Angeles (1910)

Black Codes: laws enacted in southern states after the Civil War that specifically spelled out the rights and responsibilities of the newly freed slaves

"Jim Crow" laws: practices and formal sanctions, established primarily in the northern states, that continued to separate the races (segregation)

International Association of Chiefs of Police (IACP): originally the National Chiefs of Police Union; established in 1893 to organize cooperative efforts among police departments

International Association of Women Police: originally organized as the International Association of Policewomen in 1915; it advocated and advanced the employment of more women in law enforcement

Law Enforcement Assistance Administration (LEAA): a federal agency created in 1968 to assist government agencies at all levels of government to implement some of the recommendations set forth by the President's Commission

National Commission on Law Observance and Enforcement: appointed by President Hoover in 1929 to survey the criminal jus-

tice system and causes of crime in the U.S.; commonly referred to as the Wickersham Commission

Omnibus Crime Control and Safe Streets Act of 1968: the enabling legislation for the LEAA; commonly referred to as the "Safe Streets Act" or the "Crime Control Act" of 1968

Plessy v. Ferguson: the Supreme Court decision in 1896 that sanctioned the doctrine of "separate but equal"; the decision focused on segregation in public accommodations

Progressive Movement: a movement in the U.S. beginning at the turn of the century and thriving for the next two decades that attempted to reform the courts, schools, and other urban institutions by reorganizing their structures, upgrading their personnel, and redefining their functions

President's Commission on Law Enforcement and Administration of Justice: commission appointed by President Johnson in 1965 to investigate the causes of crime and the condition of the criminal justice system

rattlewatch: in colonial New Amsterdam (New York City), a group of citizens equipped with rattles to warn of their watchful presence; a form of night-watch

slave patrols: early form of American police (1740s) for protecting persons from runaway slaves and to inhibit insurrection or other irregularities

vigilantism: a form of policing in America appearing during the late 1790s through the mid-1800s; originally, the philosophy of vigilantism was premised on self-preservation and self-protection

wardens: early supervisors of night watchmen, established in the city of Philadelphia in 1749

APPENDIX 3–1

MAJOR AMERICAN RIOTS, DISORDERS, AND SOCIAL TENSIONS

Law enforcement and social control are influenced by the social, political, economic, and cultural events of the day. Throughout American history, there have been a number of events and periods of social unrest that, in the final analysis, generally brought about changes in policing or in public policy. This is a reference of events that deserve recognition. They are provided to add perspective to the time periods discussed in this chapter.

1692—Salem witchcraft episodes

1765—Stamp Act riots in Boston and New York (taxes on legal documents, newspapers, almanacs, playing cards, and dice)

1767—The Regulators—South Carolina's "vigilante group"

1772—Burning of the *Gaspee,* a British patrol ship, off the coast of Rhode Island by colonists (the ship patrolled for smugglers)

1774—Resistance to the Boston Port Bill which required the Port to close until Boston paid restitution for the lost tea thrown overboard by colonists

1776–1783—American Revolutionary War

1784—Revolt against North Carolina—sections of the State claimed secession to form a separate state and to look to Spain for possible affiliation

1786—Shay's Rebellion—over 2,000 western Massachusetts farmers rose in armed rebellion over heavy taxation, high legal and court fees, and state government waste

1794—Whiskey Rebellion in Pennsylvania, over the federal tax on whiskey

1795—Demonstrations against the Jay Treaty with England

1798—Virginia and Kentucky Resolutions declared that certain Federal Government actions could be declared "unconstitutional" by state legislation—particularly directed toward the Alien and Sedition Acts (which were anti-immigrant in nature)

1799—Fries Rebellion—John Fries led mob to free two tax-evaders from prison

1819—Panic of 1819 followed by economic depression

1829–1850—Five major race riots in Philadelphia

1832—Tariff Nullification by South Carolina brought a national crisis in federal/state relationships and authority

1830s–1840s—Indian/Army skirmishes and small "wars"

1834—Boston convent burned as a result of anti-Catholic sentiment

1837—Irish immigrants clash with fire department—15,000 people involved

1842—Dorr Rebellion (over extension of suffrage to all males instead of property owners)

1844—Anti-Catholic riots in Philadelphia

1849—Astor Place riot in NYC; 31 killed, 150 wounded, 86 arrested (British actor, named Macready, insults the crowd, which was already upset because of the theatre's dress code)

1851—San Francisco Committee of Vigilance (vigilantism forces)

1850s—American Indians were "concentrated" to certain geographical areas (reservations); the struggle and debate continued for decades

1854—Struggle and dissent over slavery in Kansas' application for statehood

1855—German tavernkeepers' revolt in Chicago (also called the Lager Beer Riots); many killed, hundreds injured when tavern owners protested 500% increase in liquor license fees and prohibition of Sunday liquor sales

1859—John Brown's raid near Harper's Ferry, Virginia, where he led an armed group to seize a federal arsenal; he planned to establish a stronghold for escaped slaves and freed Blacks

1856—The Dred Scott decision by the Supreme Court—ruled that Blacks could not be entitled to federal citizenship and Congress did not have authority to regulate slavery in the territories, nor did the territorial legislatures

1861–1865—Civil War in the United States

1863—Conscription (Draft) Riots in Boston and NYC—many killed, hundreds injured

1865–1877—KKK activity—founded in Pulaski, Tennessee

1871—Anti-Chinese riot in Los Angeles; 23 Chinese killed

1871—Irish Catholics and Protestants clash (Orange Riots) in NYC; 33 killed, 91 wounded

1878s–1900s—Jim Crow laws (segregation of the races)

1877—Great labor strikes in West Virginia and Pittsburgh, PA; in two days, 16 soldiers and 50 strikers killed; 125 locomotives, 2,000 freight cars, and depot burned and destroyed; many killed and wounded in Chicago

1886—Haymarket Riots in Chicago—labor disputes fueled tensions, a bomb killed a police officer and six others

1914—Ludlow Massacre; more than 30 killed when company managers attempted to end a seven-month strike by mine workers in Colorado

1914—Berkeley P.D. becomes the first agency in the U.S. to have all patrol officers using automobiles

1915—The Ku Klux Klan officially organizes in Georgia (modeled after its predecessor) by William Joseph Simmons; lasted until WW II

1917—A bomb explodes at Milwaukee, WI, Police Department; nine officers are killed

1917–1919—World War I

1919—Chicago race riot; 38 killed, 537 injured

1921—Tulsa race riot; 30 killed, 700 injured

1929—Eliot Ness is picked to lead a group of federal agents nicknamed "The Untouchables."

1934—Union violence at the Republic Steel plant in Chicago; police shot and killed 10 pickets; also called Memorial Day Massacre

1930s—Nation of Islam (Black Nationalist) movement begins

1941–1945—World War II

1943—Detroit race riot; 34 killed, several hundred injured

1943—Zoot-Suit Riots in Los Angeles (anti-Mexican-American)

1950s-1960s—Battle over desegregation leads to school integration and social tension

Early 1950s—The third Klan movement was revived by Dr. Samuel Green, an Atlanta dentist.

1954—*Brown v. Board of Education of Topeka* (*Plessy v. Ferguson* reversed)—segregation ruled illegal

1955—Montgomery, Alabama; boycott over segregated bus system; precipitated by Rosa Parks' refusal to give up her bus seat to a white person

—Executive Order 10450 (Nov. 1) required the Attorney General of the U.S. to prepare a list of subversive or fascist groups in America

1955–56—Segregationist groups called White Citizens' Councils spread throughout the South.

1956—Racial violence in Clinton, Texas

1957—Little Rock, Arkansas—Eisenhower orders in Federal troops to enforce the desegregation of Central High School

1958—John Birch Society formed in Indianapolis by Robert H.W. Welch, Jr.

1960—Racial violence in New Orleans

1962—President John F. Kennedy sends troops to University of Mississippi, Oxford, MS, to protect James Meredith

1963—Racial confrontation with police in Birmingham, Alabama; President Kennedy denounces Governor George Wallace's stand on segregation

—Mississippi NAACP leader Medgar Evers assassinated

—Dr. Martin Luther King, Jr.'s, march on Washington and "I Have a Dream" speech

—November 21: President John Fitzgerald Kennedy assassinated in Dallas

1964—Race riots in NYC, Rochester, Philadelphia, Jersey City, Paterson, Elizabeth, and Chicago; 6 killed, 952 injured

—Civil Rights Act of 1964 passed; Title VII outlaws discrimination in employment on the basis of race, color, religion, national origin, or sex.

—October 1: The Free Speech Movement was born at Berkeley, California, led by Mario Savio and Joan Baez; the movement lasted about a year but received broad national attention and led to more "student movements"

1965—Los Angeles (Watts) race riot; 36 killed, 895 injured; violence spread to San Francisco where 200 were injured and 6 killed

—In February, Malcolm X assassinated by three gunmen as he began a speech in a Harlem ballroom; he was a major leader in the Nation of Islam movement

—Students for a Democratic Society (SDS) experienced phenomenal growth, basically as an anti-Vietnam movement; Tom Hayden a leader of the movement

1967—George Lincoln Rockwell, Commander of the American Nazi Party, was killed from ambush in front of a laundromat in Arlington, Virginia.

—The Youth International Party (YIPPIE) is formed; Abbie Hoffman, Jerry Rubin, and Paul Krassner were primary leaders.

—150 U.S. cities experience racial disturbances

1968—April 4: Assassination of Martin Luther King, Jr.; over 168 cities in the U.S experience demonstrations, riots, burnings, or protests

—June 4: Assassination of Robert F. Kennedy

—Black Panther Huey Newton convicted of voluntary manslaughter in killing of Oakland police officer

—August 18–29: National Democratic Convention in Chicago becomes a "Police Riot"; over 24 "protest" organizations were represented in the crowded streets and demonstrations outside the convention; 192 officers injured, 49 hospitalized; 425 civilians treated at hospitals, 200 treated on the spot, and over 400 given first aid for tear gas or mace; 81 police vehicles damaged; 668 persons arrested; much of the confrontation was televised nationwide; 49 newsmen reported being hit, assaulted, or having cameras/recorders damaged by officers

Mid 1960s—Vietnam War protest movement gains momentum—Flower Power—students for a Democratic Society (SDS)

1970—May 4: Four killed at Ohio's Kent State University; ROTC buildings burned

—Jackson State University violence, Jackson, Mississippi

1971—Anti-war march in Washington, D.C.; 12,000 arrested

—Voting age lowered to 18 (26th Amendment)

1972—Presidential candidate George Wallace shot in Laurel, MD

—Watergate

1973—U.S. involvement in Vietnam ends

1974—Symbionese Liberation Army kidnaps Patricia Hearst

—President Ford escapes two assassination attempts

—The single deadliest year in law enforcement history, with 268 officers killed

1979—Iranian militants seize U.S. Embassy and take hostages

1980—Racial disturbances in Miami

1981—President Reagan shot by John W. Hinckley, Jr.

1985—Police storm /firebomb home of radical group MOVE; fire spreads, killing 11 and leaving 200 homeless

1991—Rodney King beating incident in Los Angeles, California, leads to indictment of four officers

—The National Law Enforcement Officers Memorial is dedicated in Washington, D.C.

1992—On April 29, the officers charged in the King incident found not guilty of all but one charge against one officer; riots erupted and lasted for five days, resulting in more than 40 deaths, 2,382 injuries, over 5000 buildings destroyed or damaged, an estimated 40,000 jobs lost, and over $1 billion in property damage; 5,633 people arrested. The riots spread to other cities across the country.

1993—Two of the four officers indicted in the King incident were convicted in federal court on civil rights charges and sentenced to 30 months in prison.

—February 26: bombing of the World Trade Center in New York City; six killed and over 1,000 injured

—April 19: following a 51-day standoff at Waco, Texas, compound of the Branch Davidians religious cult, headed by David Koresh, burns to the ground after an assault by federal agents; 80 believed to have died in the incident, including women and children

1994—Nicole Simpson and Ronald Goldman murdered; O.J. Simpson accused but later found not criminally guilty

1995—April 19: bombing of the Murrah Federal Building in Oklahoma City, Oklahoma; 169 killed and over 800 injured

1996—National crime rate continues to drop, but juvenile violence increasing

—Bomb explodes at summer Olympics in Atlanta, Georgia, killing one

—Theodore Kaczynski, the alleged Unabomber, is arrested after 18 years of incidents

1997—Communications Decency Act ruled unconstitutional as an attempt to regulate the Internet

—Timothy McVeigh found guilty of the Oklahoma City Federal Building bombing

—Ramzi Ahmed Yousef and Eyad Ismoil were convicted of the NYC Trade Center Tower bombing

—O.J. Simpson found civilly responsible for the deaths of Nicole Simpson and Ronald Goldman

1998—A series of school violence incidents in several states where students and teachers were killed raises concerns about access to firearms by juveniles. Locations included Edinboro, Pennsylvania; Jonesboro, Arkansas; Springfield, Oregon; ages of the shooters range from 10–17.

—Theodore Kaczynski, the Unabomber, is sentenced to life in prison.

1999—Two students at Columbine High School in Littleton, Colorado, kill 13 and then themselves during an assault on the school

—Congress continues to debate gun control and regulation and juvenile violence in the U.S.

—The Kosovo/Yugoslavian conflict destabilizes the Balkan peninsula in Europe; NATO conducts airstrikes, and U.S. Reservists are called into action to assist

SELECTED PASSAGES DESCRIBING AMERICA'S RACIAL/ETHNIC TOLERANCE

"Between 1790 and 1900, vigilantism prospered in the settlements of the American Frontier. The instability of settlements made social control almost impossible. Counterfeiting for example, became prevalent on the frontier because law enforcement agencies were almost totally nonexistent. . . . Citizens saw vigilantism as a means of coping with social problems. They began to take the law into their own hands."

"The local law enforcement officer thus found that his methods of enforcing the law often conflicted with the mood of the community and the activities of the vigilantes. . . . Vigilantism, however, was not just a phenomenon of the frontier or rural settlements. Law enforcement officers and the courts in larger cities were also criticized for their ineffectiveness by citizens' groups, newspaper editors, and popular opinion. . . . When municipal law enforcement was ineffective, vigilante activities became commonplace."

"Rapid industrialization following the Civil War created new problems, especially for urban communities. Many conflicts existed between different socio-economic classes, as well as between races. Labor unions were still very weak and struggling to survive, and often violence erupted between labor and management."

— Trojanowicz, Trojanowicz, and Moss, pp. 76–78.

"Law and order means different things and yet the same thing—to an as yet undetermined number of the Black masses. It means historically the use of sadistic red-necked cops in the South to keep Blacks in their place, to keep them segregated, discriminated against, exploited, and brutalized. To Blacks it means police brutality, provocation and the epitome of all that is repressive in the history and operation of American Black-White relations."

— Nicholas Alex, p. xiii

"Mexican-Americans were perceived as vicious—they fought with lethal weapons such as knives, whereas other 'more acceptable ethnic groups' used their fists. This stereotyped perception of Mexican-Americans as lazy, dirty, and undesirable contributed to a feeling of relief of any moral obligation by the community toward the Mexican-Americans who were exploited."

"The Broad Street riot of June 11, 1837 erupted when firemen returning from an alarm clashed with an Irish funeral procession [requiring a cavalry regiment to restore order]. Irish immigrants created problems for the police, especially in large cities. The Irish lived in poverty and misery and were involved in many types of criminal activities."

"'The Chickesters,' 'Roach Guards,' 'Plug Uglies,' 'Short Tails,' and 'Dead Rabbits,' were the names of some of the more notorious gangs [late 1920s]. Many battles raged between the gangs, and long-standing feuds culminated with killing and maiming, or both. The police were called in to disperse gang activity but in larger disturbances, they almost always needed the assistance of the army."

"Time and again, lynching parties struck at Italians charged with murder. In 1891 a wild rumor that drunken Italian laborers had cut the throats of a whole American family in West Virginia set off further rumors of a pitched battle between the sheriff's posse and the assassins . . . The Italian immigrants not only had to bear the brunt of much hostility that was naturally directed at immigrants, they also had to 'live down' the stereotype of the Italian criminal that resulted from the problems police had with some immigrants from Sicily."

"Slavic and Polish immigrants were as exploited as any other ethnic group that ever set foot on this continent. Among other indignities, they were given the worst jobs, imprisoned for minor offenses, and forced to live like animals. Disturbances by Hungarian and Polish workers in the late 1800s were common."

"The Germans at one time were also recipients of much community hostility. In 1855 the arrest of saloon keepers touched off riots by Germans necessitating police intervention . . . Many Germans were injured in these confrontations, and increased hostility developed between the police and German immigrants because the police were perceived as agents of repression."

"Numerous complaints have been made in regard to the Hebrew immigrants who lounge about Battery Park, obstructing the walks and sitting on the chairs . . . The police have had many battles with these newcomers, who are determined to have their own way. Jewish women were involved in disturbances in 1906 because of rumors that physicians were cutting the throats of children in the east-side schools."

"Orientals, especially the Japanese during the second world war, were also recipients of community hostility and police force. The expression 'Yellow Peril' reflected the paranoiac feeling of many persons toward Asians."

— Trojanowicz and Dixon, pp. 84–94

APPENDIX 3–2

TIME LINE OF CRIMINAL IDENTIFICATION IN THE U.S., 1854–1939

1854–1859—Captain Lees of the San Francisco P.D. used a commercial photographer to make daguerreotypes (an early form of photograph using thin brass plate) of all arrested persons.

1858—New York City P.D. had collected over 450 photographs in its rogues' gallery.

1884—Chicago P.D. established its own police photograph gallery at police headquarters, believed to be the first city in the world to do so.

1888—Chicago P.D. became the first American city to adopt the Bertillon system of identification (which was developed by Alphonse Bertillon of the Paris Police in 1882—his "portrait parle" system was one that included a person's bodily measurements along with details about complexion, color of hair and eyes, shape of nose, ear and face, special marks and peculiarities, and photographs).

1894—The National Chiefs of Police Union (forerunner of the International Association of Chiefs of Police) petitioned Congress to establish a bureau of identification of criminals at the national level.

1896—The National Chiefs of Police Union created the National Bureau of Criminal Identification (on paper); it eventually opened in Chicago in 1897, staffed by George Porteous, an expert in the Bertillon system, as its superintendent. A single office could now receive and respond to police requests for "Identification Wanted."

1902—The National Bureau of Criminal Identification was relocated to the Washington, D.C. Police Department with Edward Evans as Superintendent.

1904—The World's Fair, held in St. Louis, MO, brought exhibitors from all over the world displaying and advocating criminal identification equipment and systems. Fingerprinting as a means of identification received great attention. The St. Louis P.D. began using the Henry Finger Print System.

—Mrs. Mary E. Holland, assistant editor of "The Detective," was trained in the Henry System and became competent to instruct on and install the system as an expert.

—The U.S. Army and Navy and federal prisons adopt the fingerprint system over the Bertillon system.

1906—The New York City P.D. inaugurated the use of the Henry Finger Print System.

1921—By this date, five state identification bureaus were in operation: California, Washington, Ohio, Wisconsin, and Iowa.

1923—Attorney General Harry M. Daugherty issued orders to transfer the IACP's National Bureau of Criminal Identification to the Justice Department's Division of Identification, which became statutorily official on July 1, 1924. State Bureaus numbered 23.

1935—Eye Retina Pattern identification scheme developed and offered as an adjunct to the fingerprint system.

1936—The American Dental Association in conjunction with the U.S. Department of Justice began developing a system of identification for recording dental peculiarities and records.

1939—Colonel H. Norman Schwarzkopf of the New Jersey State Police demonstrated the uses of motion pictures in making a permanent record of criminals.

1939—First color photographs were used in wanted circulars by the Indiana State Police.

Source: Reprinted with permission from D.C. Dilworth, *Identification Wanted: Development of the American Criminal Identification System, 1893–1943,* © 1997, International Association of Chiefs of Police.

REFERENCES

Alex, Nicholas. 1969. *Black in Blue: a Study of Negro Policemen.* New York: Appleton-Century Crofts.

Bopp, William J. and Donald O. Schultz. 1972. *Principles of American Law Enforcement and Criminal Justice.* Springfield, IL: Charles C. Thomas.

Dilworth, Donald C., ed. 1976. *The Blue and the Brass: American Policing 1890–1910.* Alexandria, VA: International Association of Chiefs of Police.

Eldefonso, Edward, Alan Coffey, and Richard Grace. 1982. *Principles of Law Enforcement.* 3d ed. New York: Wiley.

Fogelson, Robert M. 1977. *Big-City Police.* Cambridge, MA: Harvard University Press.

Foner, E.F. 1988. *Reconstruction: America's Unfinished Revolution, 1863–1877.* New York: Harper and Row.

Green, Gion and Robert Fisher. 1987. *Introduction to Security.* 4th ed. Boston: Butterworths.

Jackson, Donald Dale. 1989. "Take the oath, put on the badge and do the job." *Smithsonian,* Vol. 20, No. 1 (April): 114–25.

Johnson, David R. 1981. *American Law Enforcement: A History.* Saint Louis, MO: Forum Press.

Law Enforcement Assistance Administration. 1976. *Two Hundred Years of American Criminal Justice.* Washington, D.C.: U.S. Department of Justice.

National Commission on the Causes and Prevention of Violence. 1968. *Rights in Conflict: The Chicago Police Riot.* New York, NY: New American Library, Inc.

National Commission on Law Observance and Enforcement. 1931. *Report on Police.* Washington, D.C.: U.S. Government Printing Office.

Strecher, V.G. 1971. *The Environment of Law Enforcement: A Community Relations Guide.* Englewood Cliffs, New Jersey: Prentice Hall.

Thayer, George. 1967. *The Farther Shores of Politics: The American Political Fringe Today.* New York: Simon and Schuster.

Trojanowicz, Robert and Samuel Dixon. 1974. *Criminal Justice and The Community.* Englewood Cliffs, New Jersey: Prentice Hall.

Trojanowicz, R., Trojanowicz, J., and Moss, F. 1975. *Community Based Crime Prevention.* Englewood Cliffs, New Jersey: Prentice Hall.

U.S. Congress. House of Representatives. *Committee Amendment in the Nature of a Substitute to H.R. 1659.* 106th Congress, 1st sess.,1999. H.Rept.106–190.

U.S. Marshals Service. 1994. *The United States Marshals Service: Past and Present*. Publication Number 3 (May).

Whitehouse, Jack E. 1973. "Historical Perspectives on the Police Community Service Function," *Journal of Police Science and Administration* 1(1) (March):87–92.

Williams, Hubert and Patrick V. Murphy. 1990. The Evolving Strategy of Police: A Minority View. *Perspectives on Policing* 13. Washington, D.C.: National Institute of Justice and Harvard University.

Wintersmith, Robert F. 1974. *Police and the Black Community*. Lexington, MA: Lexington Books.

Wood, B. 1984. *Slavery in Colonial Georgia*. Athens, GA: University of Georgia Press.

LAW ENFORCEMENT AGENCIES IN THE UNITED STATES

A principal of a Miami aviation company is escorted by an unidentified DEA agent to federal prison after being arrested in Miami for conspiracy to distribute cocaine and marijuana. July 1999. (AP/ Wide World Photos)

LEARNING OBJECTIVES

In Chapter 3, you learned about the evolution of policing in the United States. This chapter presents the governmental framework for the authority and existence of law enforcement agencies. It also describes the type and number of agencies that operate in this country. After studying this chapter, you should be able to:

1. Understand how policing fits in the governmental structure of the United States.
2. Explain the basic principles of American government, such as federalism, checks and balances, three branches of government, implied powers doctrine, and judicial review.
3. Describe what is meant by "political subdivision."
4. Cite the approximate number of law enforcement agencies and the number of law enforcement personnel in the United States.
5. Distinguish between "specific police authority" and "general police authority" and be able to give examples of each.
6. List the major federal law enforcement agencies and their organizational placement in the federal government structure.
7. Summarize the purpose and extent of private policing in the United States.

THE U.S. GOVERNMENTAL FRAMEWORK APPLIED TO POLICING

The agencies responsible for criminal law enforcement in the United States vary significantly in size, scope of responsibility, and policing authority. The model of policing that has evolved in the United States can be referred to as a "fragmented system" since there is no "national police force." The country's law enforcement community is decentralized—made up of independently functioning agencies. In comparison, some countries (e.g., France and Italy) utilize a "centralized system" of policing, in which all agencies' policies and procedures are controlled by a national or governmental headquarters (Hunter 1990).

Basic Organizing Principles

A review of basic organizing principles of American government is appropriate in examining the authority of U.S. law enforcement agencies. By ratifying the Constitution, the states of the United States adopted a form of representative democracy known as **federalism**. This established a "dual system" of government made up of the federal and state systems. The authority, powers, and limitations of the federal government were framed in the Constitution and the Bill of Rights (reprinted in Appendix I for reference). The Tenth Amendment (also referred to as the "states' rights amendment") clearly indicated that there would be a sharing of power in the United States:

> The powers not delegated to the United States by the Constitution, nor prohibited by it to the states, are reserved to the states respectively, or to the people.

Thus, the states were permitted to establish their own governmental structures as long as they did not violate or interfere with the Federal Constitution. This permitted the formation of various state structures that could deviate somewhat from the federal system (see Figure 4–1).

When a conflict of laws (between state and federal law) exists, the federal judicial system may be asked to clarify and interpret the law in order to resolve the conflict. Such conflicts fall under the "supremacy clause" of Article IV of the United States Constitution, which states:

> This Constitution, and laws of the United States which shall be made in pursuance thereof . . . shall be the supreme law of the land; and the judges in every state shall be bound thereby, any thing in the constitution or laws of any state to the contrary notwithstanding.

Throughout the federal and state governments, there is a system of **checks and balances**. By establishing three branches of government—executive,

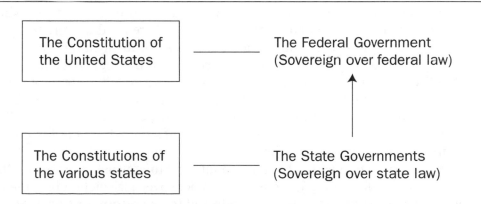

The federalism allowed by the United States Constitution has resulted in the creation of one federal system and 50 state systems, or 51 individual sovereignties.

Figure 4–1 The Federalism Concept in the United States

legislative, and judicial—the United States Constitution provided a mechanism to prevent any one branch from becoming too powerful. This principle is also referred to as **separation of powers**. Once the legislative branch enacts legislation, it is the responsibility of the executive branch to enforce it. The judiciary supervises judicial proceedings, including trials, and through the process of **judicial review**, rules on the constitutionality of laws enacted by the legislative branch and procedures used by the executive branch in enforcing laws.

While it may appear that the concepts of federalism and checks and balances create a clear structure of authority, the system leaves much room for debate. It is common to hear comments on the evening news or read articles in newspapers about the debates over controversial issues that involve the government's role in deciding matters concerning health care, education, farm subsidies, and criminal justice. The debate often centers around whether the federal government is overstepping its authority, thereby limiting the rights of the states to govern according to their preference. An example in policing includes the issue of the funding of local police officer positions. Since the mid-1990s, billions in federal funds have been provided to local agencies for community policing officers. Some argue that the money should be given to the states in the form of block grants and then the states should be permitted to decide how to allocate it.

Multiple Jurisdictions

The framework outlined above has led to many geographical jurisdictions, not just those of the federal and state governments. Although the federal level of government maintains a single national jurisdiction, the states have created **political subdivisions**. The most common names for these political subdivisions include: county, municipality or city, village, borough, and township. However, park districts, school districts, public colleges and universities, and port authorities can also be subdivisions of states. Political subdivisions may have the authority to establish police departments if the legislative body that created the subdivision granted such authority. As a result, often more than one police department can have jurisdiction over the same geographical territory. For example, township police officers have police authority within their township, but so may members of a county sheriff's department of the county wherein the township lies. In addition, it is possible that a state police force would have jurisdiction within both the county and the township. Based on this example, the possible complications and conflicts over jurisdiction become evident. When this situation exists, it is referred to as **concurrent** or **overlapping jurisdiction**. Usually, when agencies have overlapping jurisdiction there is an understanding (perhaps formal, but usually informal) as to which agency is the "primary" responding agency and which is the "secondary" or "supportive" agency.

However, if there is a breakdown in the relationships among or between agencies where concurrent jurisdiction exists, agencies may have open conflict between officers at crime scenes. Many jurisdictions have seen local news media reports about feuds that occurred at sites of crimes. The report usually describes a call for assistance from a citizen, such as after a robbery or shooting, to which officers from two different agencies (e.g., a city agency and a county sheriff's deputy) respond. Some accounts have reported on the verbal arguments that have occurred between the officer and the deputy about who will investigate the incident. Needless to say, such reports of unprofessional conduct are not well received by the public.

Executive Authority

Every law enforcement agency has a chief executive official. The most common title is "police chief." Other titles include "sheriff," "director," "superintendent," "colonel," "commissioner," "marshal," or "chief constable." Whatever the title of the chief executive, the position has the authority and responsibility to guide the organization and direct its members. Duties include establishing and enforcing policy, managing the budget, recommending personnel for employment and for dismissal, scheduling resources, addressing community concerns, and evaluating the overall daily performance of the agency. In addition to these responsibilities, the agency's chief executive official reports and is accountable to another jurisdictional official or board. The law normally describes how the chief executive is appointed. For example, in many large cities in the United States, the mayor appoints the police chief. In some cases, however, the chief is promoted from within the agency and occupies the position regardless of who is mayor. In some jurisdictions, a board of three or more members chooses the chief executive. Once appointed, the chief executive official may occupy the position until retirement, be removed by a new mayor for cause, or be removed at any time, depending on the appointment authority within the jurisdiction and the specific law related to removal or dismissal. (See Chapter 10 for additional information about personnel issues and civil service systems.)

The chief executive official derives his or her authority from several sources of law. There may be **statutory law** enacted by legislatures that specifically describes the rights of the executive in making decisions on the operation of the agency. The statutory law may be found in state codes under different sections, usually related to the type of jurisdiction involved. For example, the state code sections addressing the statutory law of municipalities may have sections specifically devoted to the authority of the police chief. Likewise, sections of the state code may address the authority of the sheriff, of the township chief constable, and so on. Secondly, there may be **administrative law** that describes the authority of the chief executive. Such law is derived from statutory law that gives an agency or board the power to establish its own rules and procedures. The agency or board may then promulgate the necessary provisions that describe the authority and duties of the chief executive of the law enforcement agency. A third source of executive authority may be **contract law** in the collectively bargained contract between a jurisdiction and a union. The negotiated contract may describe the specific authority and the limits placed upon the chief executive authority of the law enforcement agencies. A fourth source of executive authority is **constitutional law**, the body of law that concerns the interpretation of the U.S. and state Constitutions. Constitutional law usually does not specifically spell out the authority of chief executives; however, through interpretation and case law, it serves as a source of restrictions upon the chief executive. (Chapter 12 discusses the major sources of legal restrictions on law enforcement officials.)

STATISTICAL PROFILES AND FUNCTIONS PERFORMED AT THE LOCAL LEVEL

How many law enforcement agencies are there in the United States? Although this is a straightforward question, it is extremely difficult to answer. Because of the fragmented nature of the governmental system, no one agency or office is responsible for maintaining accurate lists of information about the American policing community. Also, the accuracy of state statistics regarding their agencies varies. Smaller agencies "come and go" at the deliberation of executive and legislative boards. An agency can be formed in one community and abolished in another during the same week. Central registries of this activity are rare, although some reliable data are maintained by state offices responsible for the training and certification of officers. Thus, any count of the number of law enforcement agencies is an estimate and not an exact figure.

Since 1987, the Bureau of Justice Statistics (BJS) in the Office of Justice Programs within the United States Department of Justice has been collecting data from law enforcement agencies under the Law Enforcement Management and Administrative Statistics (LEMAS) program. This program conducts surveys of the law enforcement community every three years. Because the survey consists of several thousand questionnaires and considerable data, there always is some time delay in reporting the results. The data reported in this chapter were the most recent available when the text was prepared, but Web sites of the Bureau of Justice Statistics, Office of Justice Programs (part of the U.S. Department of Justice) should be consulted as well.

Local Agencies

Table 4–1 summarizes the number of state and local law enforcement agencies, employees, and operating expenses at the various levels of government by type of agency (Reaves 1996a).

Table 4–1 Employment by State and Local Law Enforcement Agencies in the United States, 1993

Type of Agency	Number of Agencies	Number of Employees						
		Full-time			Part-time			
		Total	Sworn	Civilian	Total	Sworn	Civilian	
Local Police	12,361	474,072	373,554	100,518	58,146	28,186	29,960	
Sheriff	3,084	224,236	155,815	68,421	19,660	11,048	8,612	
State Police	49	76,972	51,874	25,098	845	228	617	
Special Police	1,626	53,156	41,670	11,485	9,224	3,428	5,796	
TOTAL	17,120	828,435	622,913	205,522	87,875	42,890	44,985	

Note: Consolidated police-sheriff agencies are included under the local police category. The special police category includes both state-level and local-level agencies. Data are for the pay period that included June 30, 1993.

Source: Adapted from B.A. Reaves, *Local Police Departments, 1993*, p. 1, 1996b, U.S. Department of Justice.

Obviously, of the 17,120 state and local agencies, the large majority (over 12,000) are the general policing agencies that include the municipal, village, town, and township departments in the United States. These agencies employ over 370,000 sworn officers and over 100,000 civilians. When the state and local agencies are combined, the totals are over 600,000 sworn officers and over 200,000 civilians in full-time positions. These numbers have been growing at a rate of about 3 percent every three years; therefore, in 1999 there should be about 660,000 sworn officers and 218,000 civilians at the state and local levels. According to data collected in 1997 (Reaves and Goldberg 1999, xii), the 10 largest local level police departments in the country, in terms of sworn personnel, are:

New York City	38,328	Detroit	4,070
Chicago	13,271	Washington, D.C.	3,618
Los Angeles	9,423	Baltimore	3,082
Philadelphia	6,782	Dallas	2,817
Houston	5,355	Boston	2,190

Source: Reprinted from B. A. Reaves and A. L. Goldberg, *Law Enforcement Management and Administrative Statistics, 1997: Data for Individual and Local Agencies with 100 or More Officers*, 1999, U.S. Department of Justice.

A more revealing finding from the LEMAS data is the relationship between the number of agencies and the size of agency in terms of sworn personnel. Table 4–2 lists the breakdown of local agencies by number of sworn person-

Table 4–2 Local Police Departments by Number of Sworn Personnel, 1993

Number of Sworn Personnel in Agency*	Agencies		Full-time Sworn Personnel	
	Number	Percent	Number	Percent
1,000 or more	38	0.3	118,460	31.7
500–999	38	0.3	27,351	7.3
250–499	86	0.7	29,344	7.9
100–249	326	2.6	46,983	12.6
50–99	692	5.6	45,779	12.3
25–49	1,443	11.7	45,160	12.1
10–24	3,361	27.2	40,913	11.0
5–9	2,940	23.8	13,906	3.7
2–4	2,587	20.9	5,065	1.2
1	851	6.9	594	0.2
TOTAL	12,361	100	373,554	100

*Includes both full-time and part-time employees.

Note: Detail may not add to total because of rounding.

Source: Adapted from B. A. Reaves, *Local Police Departments, 1993*, p. 2, 1996b, U.S. Department of Justice.

nel. Notice that 27.8 percent of the agencies have fewer than 5 sworn officers, 51.6 percent employ less than 10, and about 90.5 percent employ fewer than 50 officers. Notice that there are over 850 agencies that employ only one officer. Of all the local police departments in the United States, only 3.9 percent or 488 departments employ 100 or more officers. See Exhibit 4–1 for some "what if" statements regarding the impact of possible consolidation based on number of officers.

Although there are many small agencies in the United States employing low numbers of officers, 49.7 percent of the sworn officers at the local level are employed in agencies serving populations over 100,000 persons. These sworn officers are employed in only 231 agencies, or 1.9 percent of all local agencies. Table 4–3 shows the number of officers employed by size of jurisdiction. Combining Tables 4–2 and 4–3 reveals an inverse relationship between the number of agencies and the number of persons employed by those agencies, by size of population served. That is, of the over 12,000 agencies, the categories containing the largest number of agencies employ only a few officers each, while fewer than 50 agencies employ over 30 percent of all police officers in the United States. Another analysis reveals that about 10 percent of all the agencies in the country account for 70 percent of all sworn officers employed.

Local policing, the uniformed officer on the beat, is what most Americans observe on a daily basis. It is the local police who respond to general street crime and most of the traffic accidents. Authority of the local police is general in scope, which means they can enforce the general criminal code of the state plus appropriate county or city ordinances. They may be the first officers to initially investigate federal offenses, however, such situations are usually

Exhibit 4–1

WHAT IF WE CONSOLIDATE?

Based on current data, what if the United States undertook an agency consolidation effort? If the law were to require a minimum of 10 full-time officers in every agency, a minimum of 6,378 agencies would be affected (about half of all local agencies). If the law were to require a minimum of 25 full-time officers, 9,739 agencies would be affected (about 78 percent of all local agencies). If the law required a minimum of 50 full-time officers, 11,182 agencies would be affected (about 90 percent). Not all of the affected agencies would necessarily be eliminated; that would depend on whether they consolidated with other small agencies to form a larger one or whether they joined with a large agency.

Table 4–3 Local Police Departments and Full-Time Sworn Personnel by Size of Population Served, 1993

	Agencies		Full-time Sworn Personnel	
Population Served	Number	Percent	Number	Percent
1,000,000 or more	12	0.1	75,496	20.2
500,000–999,999	27	0.2	37,856	10.1
250,000–499,999	45	0.4	33,261	8.9
100,000–249,999	147	1.2	39.057	10.5
50,000–99,999	340	2.7	40,493	10.8
25,000–49,999	703	5.7	42,864	11.5
10,000–24,999	1,662	13.4	47,405	12.7
2,500–9,999	4,099	33.2	42,879	5.7
Under 2,500	5,327	43.1	14,243	3.8
ALL SIZES	12,361	100	373,554	100

Note: Detail may not add to total because of rounding.

Source: Adapted from B.A. Reaves, *Local Police Departments, 1993,* p. 2, 1996b, U.S. Department of Justice.

referred to federal authorities or investigated jointly. Nearly all local police departments have primary responsibility for investigating at least some types of crimes occurring in their jurisdiction. All departments in jurisdictions with a population of 250,000 or more have primary responsibility for investigating homicides and other violent crimes such as rape, robbery, or assault. Nearly all departments serving a population of 10,000 or more have primary responsibility for homicide investigation, but 11 percent of those serving a population of 2,500 to 9,999 and 30 percent of those serving fewer than 2,500 residents report that they do not have primary responsibility for such investigations. In jurisdictions under 2,500 in population, about 1 in 7 local police departments do not have primary responsibility for the investigation of any violent crimes. The size of agencies does have some relationship to their primary function and responsibilities. The major and minor functions carried out by local agencies are identified by population served in Table 4–4.

Sheriff's Departments

One unique type of local agency is the county sheriff's department. The LEMAS survey treats these departments as a separate category and as of 1993 had identified 3,084 such agencies. The sheriff's departments in the United States are predominantly operated by county governments, and most are small

Table 4–4 Percent of Local Police Agencies Having Responsibility for Functions, by Size of Population Served, 1993

Selected Functions	Population Served									
	1 million +	500,000–999,999	250,000–499,999	100,000–249,999	50,000–99,999	25,000–49,999	10,000–24,999	2,500–9,999	Under 2,500	All Sizes
Routine Patrol	100	100	100	100	100	99	99	98	95	97
Traffic Law Enforcement	100	100	100	100	100	99	100	99	99	99
Accident Investigation	100	100	100	99	100	99	99	99	97	98
Traffic Direction and Control	83	85	89	93	98	96	93	93	86	90
Homicide Investigations	100	100	100	99	97	96	95	89	70	83
Rape, Robbery, or Assault (violence)	100	100	100	99	97	98	98	98	86	93
Drug Enforcement	92	96	93	97	95	92	86	83	72	80
Property Crime (burglary/auto theft)	100	100	100	99	97	99	100	98	94	97
Arson	75	70	62	79	78	93	88	83	66	76
Vice Enforcement	100	96	93	99	92	82	75	53	33	51
Animal Control	8	11	22	30	52	52	57	48	47	49
Search and Rescue	67	33	38	29	26	32	31	31	37	33
Lockup Operations	83	63	38	36	46	70	57	30	6	26
Emergency Medical Services	8	15	0	10	20	20	23	21	20	20
Court Security	17	18	9	16	24	22	27	23	14	19
Environmental Crimes	8	15	13	12	13	13	21	13	13	14
Servicing Civil Process	15	13	2	5	5	11	4	8	16	11
Civil Defense	25	26	7	8	17	14	19	17	16	16
Fire Services	0	0	0	1	5	5	6	7	13	9

Source: Adapted from B.A. Reaves, *Local Police Departments, 1993*, pp. 9–13, 1996b, U.S. Department of Justice.

in terms of the number of employees. Nearly 60 percent of them employ fewer than 25 sworn officers each, and 31.1 percent (961 agencies) employ fewer than 10 officers (see Table 4–5). Of all the sheriff's departments, 67.2 percent of the sworn personnel work in the 444 agencies (or 14.3 percent of all sheriffs' departments) serving populations over 100,000 (see Table 4–6) (Reaves and Smith 1996).

Unlike local agencies, sheriff's departments often have primary responsibilities for jail operations and court-related duties. In the LEMAS study for 1993, 79 percent of the departments had jail operations responsibilities, 97 percent served the civil process of the court, and 93 percent provided court security. About 65 percent of the sheriff's departments participated in 911 emergency telephone systems. Table 4–7 identifies the primary functions and responsibilities of sheriff's departments according to population served.

Some counties (in Delaware, Georgia, Hawaii, Illinois, Maryland, Missouri, New York, Pennsylvania, and Virginia) have a county police department as well as a county sheriff's department. Where this occurs, the sheriff's department of that county usually has no police patrol or criminal investigation responsibilities. These police departments operate much like municipal police departments.

Table 4–5 Sheriff's Departments by Number of Sworn Personnel, 1993

Number of Sworn Personnel in Agency*	Agencies		Full-time Sworn Personnel	
	Number	Percent	Number	Percent
1,000 or more	17	0.6	32,045	20.6
500–999	24	0.8	15,010	9.6
250–499	77	2.5	26,775	17.2
100–249	199	6.4	29,022	18.6
50–99	307	10.0	18,735	12.0
25–49	564	18.3	16,596	10.7
10–24	936	30.4	12,782	8.2
5–9	602	19.5	3,811	2.4
2–4	340	11.0	1,028	0.7
1	19	0.6	10	—
TOTAL	3,084	100	155,815	100

*Includes both full-time and part-time employees.

—Less than 0.5%.

Note: Detail may not add to total because of rounding.

Source: Adapted from B.A. Reaves and P.Z. Smith, Sheriffs' Departments, 1993, p. 2, 1996, U.S. Department of Justice.

Table 4–6   Sheriff's Departments and Full-Time Sworn Personnel by Size of Population Served, 1993

Population Served	Agencies		Full-time Sworn Personnel	
	Number	Percent	Number	Percent
1,000,000 or more	25	0.8	31,266	20.1
500,000–999,999	63	2.0	24,483	15.7
250,000–499,999	96	3.1	21,504	13.8
100,000–249,999	260	8.4	27,442	17.6
50,000–99,999	376	12.2	19,144	12.3
25,000–49,999	616	20.0	15,244	9.8
10,000–24,999	916	29.7	12,146	7.8
Under 10,000	731	23.7	4,585	2.9
ALL SIZES	3,084	100	155,815	100

Note: Detail may not add to total because of rounding.

Source: Adapted from B.A. Reaves and P.Z. Smith, *Sheriffs' Departments, 1993*, p. 2, 1996, U.S. Department of Justice.

State Agencies

Every state except Hawaii has at least one state-level policing agency. Usually this major agency is known as the "state police," "state patrol," or "department of public safety." Other state agencies exist, however, and may have responsibilities for specific areas of enforcement, such as alcoholic beverage control, fish and wildlife protection, parks protection, health care fraud, and environmental crimes. As with other governmental levels, the jurisdiction and authority of state agencies depend on legislative mandate. The terms used to describe and distinguish police authority are **specific police authority** and **general police authority**. As the terms imply, agencies with limited or specifically stated responsibilities (such as highway patrols) possess specific police authority. Those with policing authority over a broad range of criminal offenses or those that can enforce any statutory laws possess general police authority (see Figure 4–2). For example, in Ohio the state highway patrol is authorized to exercise specific police authority to (1) enforce the traffic code on all roads and highways of the state, (2) enforce the criminal code on state property, (3) investigate accidents and incidents involving aircraft, and (4) protect the governor and other dignitaries. Therefore, the Ohio Highway Patrol does not have jurisdiction over common criminal offenses such as robbery, burglary, and murder unless committed on state property. Local or county agencies, which have general police authority, must investigate those of-

Table 4–7 Percent of Sheriff's Departments Having Responsibility For Functions, by Size of Population Served, 1993

Selected Functions	Population Served								
	1 million +	500,000–999,999	250,000–499,999	100,000–249,999	50,000–99,999	25,000–49,999	10,000–24,999	Under 10,000	All Sizes
Routine Patrol	83	53	73	79	86	92	90	90	88
Traffic Law Enforcement	70	49	65	67	80	75	77	84	77
Accident Investigation	56	43	50	54	62	71	69	81	69
Traffic Direction and Control	47	39	55	56	66	62	64	72	64
Homicide Investigations	75	51	71	75	90	90	96	91	89
Rape, Robbery, or Assault (violence)	75	58	72	79	89	93	96	94	91
Drug Enforcement	80	47	60	58	71	78	85	85	78
Property Crime (burglary/auto theft)	79	53	76	79	88	95	97	94	92
Arson	61	46	65	68	85	81	84	80	80
Vice Enforcement	56	47	56	57	56	56	45	41	49
Animal Control	9	4	11	16	26	29	29	38	28
Search and Rescue	51	44	57	64	64	59	67	73	65
Jail Operations	84	71	73	83	85	85	83	67	79
Dispatching Services	75	51	62	64	72	84	86	82	80
Court Security	68	88	91	93	96	95	94	91	93
Environmental Crimes	19	27	17	16	19	25	22	25	22
Servicing Civil Process	76	98	96	98	97	99	98	95	97
Civil Defense	14	14	11	15	21	15	22	34	22
Fire Services	0	2	2	3	8	6	9	13	8

Source: Adapted from B.A. Reaves and P.Z. Smith, Sheriffs' Departments, 1993, pp. 10–14, 1996, U.S. Department of Justice.

Agencies with Specific Police Authority	*Agencies with General Police Authority*
Highway Patrols	State Police
Environmental Enforcement Units	County Police
Bureau of Liquor Control	Municipal Police
Fish & Wildlife	County Sheriff's Depts. (most)
State Narcotics Units	Townships/Villages (most)

* The concept of Specific and General Police Authority applies to all levels of policing, not just state agencies.

Figure 4–2 Specific Versus General Police Authority*

fenses. In contrast, in Pennsylvania (and in most states with a "state police" agency), the state police are authorized to exercise general police authority to investigate any criminal offense anywhere in the state.

Table 4–8 lists each primary state agency in the United States and gives information about number of full-time employees, both sworn and civilian. The state population is also listed, as well as the number of sworn employees per 10,000 residents (Reaves and Goldberg 1999, 12). This last figure is used for comparison purposes; however, remember to consider the primary responsibility of the agency (e.g., designating traffic and/or general policing) when making such comparisons. For example, Ohio has one officer in the highway patrol per 10,000 population, while Pennsylvania has 3 officers in its state police per 10,000 population. The two are not directly comparable because of the difference in primary responsibilities.

Of the state policing agencies, 32 (65 percent) have 500 or more full-time officers; 15 (30.6 percent) have 1,000 or more officers. The percentage of full-time employees that are sworn officers ranged from a low of 42 (Texas) to a high of 100 (Mississippi). The percentage of officers assigned to respond to calls for service ranged from a low of 48 (New Jersey) to a high of 99 (Nevada and South Dakota). The ratio of full-time officers to 10,000 population ranged from 1 to 8, with 2 being the mode. The major functions performed by state policing agencies (from most prevalent to least) included the following:

■ Accident investigation and traffic enforcement
■ Patrol and first response
■ Communications and dispatch
■ Special Weapons and Tactics (SWAT)
■ Search/rescue operations

Table 4–8 Number of Full-Time Employees Per 10,000 Residents in Primary State Law Enforcement Agencies, 1997

| Name of Agency | Full-time Employees, 1997 | | | | | | State Population | Officers per 10,000 Residents |
| | Total | Sworn Officers | | Officers Assigned to Respond to Service Calls | | | | |
		Number	Percent	Number	Percent			
Alabama Department of Public Safety	1,340	716	53	382	53		4,287,178	2
Alaska State Troopers	679	321	47	173	54		604,966	5
Arizona Department of Public Safety	1,678	966	58	922	95		4,434,340	2
Arkansas State Police	735	505	69	375	74		2,506,293	2
California Highway Patrol	9,533	6,532	69	5,253	80		31,857,646	2
Colorado State Patrol	803	568	71	531	93		3,816,179	1
Connecticut State Police	1,459	945	65	871	92		3,267,293	3
Delaware State Police	763	561	74	330	59		723,475	8
Florida Highway Patrol	2,067	1,637	79	1,495	91		14,418,917	1
Georgia State Police	1,910	826	43	776	94		7,334,274	1
Idaho State Police	265	195	74	185	95		1,187,597	2
Illinois State Police	3,660	1,980	54	—	—		11,845,316	2
Indiana State Police	1,877	1,222	65	797	65		5,828,090	2
Iowa State Patrol	554	432	78	360	83		2,848,033	2
Kansas Highway Patrol	741	526	71	452	86		2,579,149	2
Kentucky State Police	1,606	918	57	578	63		3,882,071	2
Louisiana State Police	1,375	909	66	617	68		4,340,818	2
Maine State Police	475	337	71	320	95		1,238,566	3
Maryland State Police	2,202	1,516	69	1,014	67		5,060,296	3
Massachusetts State Police	2,588	2,270	88	1,300	57		6,085,395	4
Michigan State Police	2,950	2,054	70	1,185	58		9,730,925	2
Minnesota State Patrol	718	499	69	374	75		4,648,596	1
Mississippi Highway Safety Patrol	520	520	100	325	63		2,710,750	2

Table 4–8 (continued)   Number of Full-Time Employees Per 10,000 Residents in Primary State Law Enforcement Agencies, 1997

Missouri State Highway Patrol	2,056	1,056	51	733	69	5,363,669	2
Montana Highway Patrol	278	212	76	193	91	876,684	2
Nebraska State Patrol	624	466	75	230	49	1,648,696	3
Nevada Highway Patrol	547	375	69	365	97	1,600,810	2
New Hampshire State Police	393	289	74	237	82	1,160,213	2
New Jersey State Police	3,521	2,555	73	1,225	48	8,001,850	3
New Mexico State Police	592	435	73	324	74	1,711,256	3
New York State Police	4,681	3,979	85	2,558	64	18,134,226	2
North Carolina State Highway Patrol	1,719	1,298	76	1,090	84	7,309,055	2
North Dakota Highway Patrol	195	131	67	121	92	642,633	2
Ohio State Highway Patrol	2,382	1,354	57	1,218	90	11,162,797	1
Oklahoma Highway Patrol	1,290	747	58	712	95	3,295,315	2
Oregon State Police	1,339	853	64	514	60	3,196,313	3
Pennsylvania State Police	5,318	4,098	77	2,112	52	12,040,084	3
Rhode Island State Police	225	184	82	176	96	988,283	2
South Carolina Highway Patrol	1,110	891	80	736	83	3,716,645	2
South Dakota Highway Patrol	234	154	66	149	97	737,561	2
Tennessee Department of Safety	1,731	913	53	—	—	5,307,381	2
Texas Department of Public Safety	6,563	2,757	42	2,260	82	19,091,207	1
Utah Highway Patrol	421	389	92	335	86	2,017,573	2
Vermont Department of Public Safety	404	263	65	177	67	586,461	4
Virginia State Police	2,251	1,658	74	924	56	6,666,167	2
Washington State Patrol	2,016	935	46	736	79	5,519,525	2
West Virginia State Police	925	608	66	542	89	1,820,407	3
Wisconsin State Patrol	658	495	75	460	93	5,146,199	1
Wyoming Highway Patrol	290	156	54	143	92	480,011	3

Note: Personnel data for 1997 are for the pay period that included June 30, 1997. Population data are based on Bureau of Census figures for April 1, 1996.

—Data were not provided by an agency.

Source: Reprinted from B.A. Reaves and A.L. Goldberg, *Law Enforcement Management and Administrative Statistics, 1997: Data for Individual and Local Agencies with 100 or More Officers*, p. 261, 1999, U.S. Department of Justice.

■ Narcotics/vice enforcement and training academy operations
■ Fingerprint processing
■ Major crime investigation (violent and property crime)
■ Ballistics/laboratory testing

Special Police Agencies

The 1993 LEMAS survey identified 1,626 special police agencies at both the state and local agency levels. Such agencies employed 53,156 full-time personnel, of which over 41,670 were sworn officers (see Table 4–1, above). These special police agencies constitute about 9.4 percent of all local and state agencies in the United States. This category of agency is very difficult to describe because it contains a variety of agencies. Such agencies usually have names that describe their uniqueness, such as transit, park district, alcohol beverage control, metropolitan housing authority, campus, port authority, or airport police. Officers working in some special police agencies may possess general police authority, but only within the geographical limitations of their jurisdiction. Other special agencies possess specific police authority over a large geographical area (for example, a state liquor control agent has authority throughout a state, but only over liquor-related offenses and regulations).

Of the 1,626 special police agencies, 680 are campus law enforcement agencies. Table 4–9 summarizes the breakdown of these campuses by size of enrollment, authority to arrest, and armed status.

Table 4–9   Use of Officers with Arrest Authority and Armed Officers on 4-Year Campuses with 2,500 or More Students, by Size of Campus Enrollment, 1995

| | | Percent of Campuses Using Officers with | |
Campus Enrollment	Number of Campuses	Arrest Authority	Armed Officers on Patrol
30,000 or more	27	96	96
25,000–29,999	30	100	97
20,000–24,999	33	97	94
15,000–19,999	52	90	75
10,000–14,999	108	88	79
5,000–9,999	210	78	65
2,500–4,999	222	54	42
TOTAL	680	75	64

Source: Reprinted from B.A. Reaves, *Campus Law Enforcement Agencies, 1995.* Table 1, 1996a, U.S. Department of Justice..

The findings of the 1995 survey of campus police agencies clearly indicate that as size of campus enrollment decreases, the percentage of campuses using officers with arrest authority and on armed patrol also generally decreases. The survey also verified that sworn and armed officers were more likely to be found at institutions under public rather than private control. Overall, 93 percent of the agencies serving public institutions used sworn officers and 81 percent used armed patrol officers, compared to 43 percent and 34 percent respectively among private institutions. As of March 15, 1995, the 680 campus law enforcement agencies serving four-year campuses of 2,500 or more students employed approximately 20,000 persons full-time (Reaves 1996a).

THE FEDERAL AGENCIES AND THEIR RESPONSIBILITIES

Criminal law enforcement responsibility at the federal level in the United States is shared among approximately 60 agencies. These agencies have been created by Congress under the authority of the **implied powers doctrine** or the **necessary and proper clause** of Article I, Section 8 (Paragraph 18) of the United States Constitution, which states:

> Congress shall have authority . . . To make all laws which shall be necessary and proper for carrying into execution the foregoing powers, and all other powers vested by this Constitution in the Government of the United States, or in any Department or Officer thereof.

"Foregoing powers" refers to the powers of Congress specifically enumerated in the first 17 paragraphs of Section 8 (see Appendix A of this text). These powers include the right to lay and collect taxes and duties, provide for the general welfare, regulate commerce with foreign nations and among the states, establish a uniform rule of naturalization, coin money and provide for the punishment of counterfeiting, establish post offices and roads, declare war, and raise and support armies and a navy. These specific powers and others of the Constitution are important because they provide the federal authority under which law enforcement agencies are created and operated by the federal government. Generally, when Congress enacts a criminal offense or law enforcement responsibility, it specifically designates which agency is responsible for its enforcement. Exhibit 4–2 lists major federal agencies with some type of enforcement responsibility. They are listed according to the department in which they are found in the federal government's organizational structure.

It is evident from Exhibit 4–2 that the extent of federal law enforcement is very broad and diverse, with many opportunities existing for employment in the federal sector. As of June 1996, federal agencies employed about 74,500 full-time personnel authorized to make arrests and carry firearms, according to agency responses to a Bureau of Justice Statistics survey. In a comparison of 1996 data with those reported by the same agencies for December 1993,

Exhibit 4–2

MAJOR FEDERAL LAW ENFORCEMENT AGENCIES

Department of Agriculture
Forest Service *
Office of Inspector General *

Department of Commerce
Bureau of Export Admin., Office of Export Enforcement *
National Institute of Standards and Technology *
Nat'l. Oceanic & Atmospheric Admin., National Marine Fisheries Service,*
Office of Inspector General

Department of Defense
Criminal Investigation Command, Army *
Defense Investigative Service
Intelligence and Security Command, Army *
Military Police Corps, Army *
Naval Investigative Service, Navy *
Office of Security Police, Air Force *
Office of Special Investigations, Air Force *
Office of Inspector General *

Department of Education
Office of Inspector General *

Department of Health and Human Services
Food & Drug Administration, Office of Criminal Investigation *
National Institutes of Health, Police *
Office of Inspector General *

Department of Housing and Urban Development
Office of Inspector General

Department of Interior
Bureau of Land Management, Office of Enforcement *
Bureau of Reclamation *
Div. of Law Enforcement Services, Bureau of Indian Affairs *
Div. of Ranger Activities & Protection, National Park Police *
Office of Inspector General *
U.S. Fish and Wildlife Service *

Department of Justice
Bureau of Prisons *
Drug Enforcement Administration *
Federal Bureau of Investigation *
Immigration and Naturalization Service *
Office of Inspector General *
U.S. Marshal's Service *

Department of Labor
Office of Labor-Management Standards
Office of Inspector General *

Department of State
Bureau of Diplomatic Security *
Office of Inspector General *

Department of Transportation
Federal Aviation Administration Police
Federal Air Marshals *
U.S. Coast Guard, Intelligence & Law Enforcement Branch
Office of Inspector General *

Department of the Treasury
Bureau of Alcohol, Tobacco, and Firearms *
Criminal Investigation Division, Internal Revenue Service (IRS) *
Inspection Service, Internal Revenue Service
Office of Inspector General *
Bureau of Engraving and Printing, Police *
U.S. Secret Service *
U.S. Customs Service *
White House Police, Secret Service *

Department of Veterans Affairs
Office of Inspector General *
Veterans Health Administration *

Independent Agencies
Administrative Office of the U.S. Courts, Federal Corrections & Supervision Division *
Amtrak Police *
Civil Aeronautics Board
Environmental Protection Agency
Office of Inspector General *
Office of Criminal Enforcement *
Federal Communications Commission
Federal Maritime Commission
Federal Trade Commission
General Services Administration
Federal Protective Service *
Office of Inspector General *
Interstate Commerce Commission
Government Printing Office, Police *
Library of Congress, Police *
National Aeronautics and Space Administration
Office of Inspector General *
Office of Personnel Management
Compliance and Investigations Group
Office of Inspector General
Securities and Exchange Commission
Smithsonian Institution, National Zoological Park Police *
Social Security Admin., Office of Inspector General *
Tennessee Valley Authority, Public Safety Service *
U.S. Postal Service, Postal Inspection Service *
U.S. Capitol Police *
U.S. Supreme Court Police *

* Authority to carry firearms and make arrests.

Source: Data from D. A. Torres, *Handbook of Federal Police and Investigation Agencies,* © 1985, Greenwood Press; and B. A. Reaves, *Federal Law Enforcement Officers, 1996, 1998,* U.S. Department of Justice.

employment of such personnel was up about 6 percent. Of these employees, 32,000 perform duties related to criminal investigation and enforcement. The major federal agencies with primary criminal investigative responsibilities in terms of size (number of agents) are listed in Exhibit 4–3 (Reaves 1998). They are the most commonly thought-of agencies when one mentions federal agents with policing responsibilities. Of course the number of agents for each agency is constantly changing, and current figures are slightly larger than those listed. For example, in June of 1999, the FBI reported a staff of 11,431 agents, with almost 40 percent having less than five years of experience with the agency (Johnson 1999).

Federal employment is often a goal of many students pursuing criminal justice degrees. It is evident from Exhibit 4–3 that the number of agencies involved in the law enforcement function is considerably large. Many of the agencies with investigative and criminal responsibilities often require an applicant to have three years of full-time experience (not necessarily in policing) before being considered for an armed agent or investigative position. Persons graduating from college may want to consider seeking employment with one of the "lesser known" federal agencies and then transferring to one of the major policing agencies after gaining the necessary experience. Exhibit 4–4 describes one of the lesser known but very important federal agencies.

Exhibit 4–3

NUMBER OF FEDERAL OFFICERS WITH FIREARMS AUTHORITY, 1996

Agency	Officers/Agents
Immigration and Naturalization Service	12,403
U.S. Marshals Service	2,650
Federal Bureau of Prisons	11,329
Drug Enforcement Administration	2,946
Internal Revenue Service	3,784
Federal Bureau of Investigation	10,389
U.S. Postal Inspection Service	3,576
U.S. Customs Service	9,749
Bureau of Alcohol, Tobacco, and Firearms	1,869

Source: Reprinted from B. A. Reaves, *Federal Law Enforcement Officers, 1996,* 1998, U.S. Department of Justice.

Exhibit 4–4

WHY CONSIDER A CAREER WITH THE GSA?

The federal agency responsible for providing security for federal buildings and grounds nationwide is the General Services Administration (GSA). Its Federal Protective Services force designs security features and programs at federal facilities. Sixty-nine percent of its 732 officers provide police response and patrol services. The GSA also manages the contracts for security guards (over 4,923 positions) providing protection at many buildings.

The GSA is one of the three central management agencies in the federal government. (The Office of Personnel Management and the Office of Management and Budget are the others.) The mission of the agency is to provide managed space, supplies, services, and solutions, at the best value, to enable federal employees to accomplish their missions. In support of this mission, GSA provides workspace, security, furniture, equipment, supplies, tools, computers, and telephones. GSA also provides travel and transportation services, manages the federal motor vehicle fleet, oversees telecommuting centers and federal child care centers, preserves historic buildings, manages a fine arts program, and develops, advocates, and evaluates government-wide policy.

The GSA was established on July 1, 1949, by section 101 of the Federal Property and Administrative Services Act. It negotiates contracts that account for $40 billion of goods and services bought annually from the private sector. GSA employs about 15,000 people and has an annual budget of nearly $13 billion. Within the GSA is the Federal Protective Service (FPS), which manages GSA's nationwide physical security and law enforcement programs. FPS also conducts preliminary investigations of incidents and criminal complaints occurring on GSA-controlled property, coordinates the Occupant Emergency Program, conducts risk assessments of federal facilities, and provides expert advice on security systems.

In the aftermath of the bombing of the Alfred P. Murrah Federal Building in Oklahoma City on April 19, 1995, FPS has contended with a new level of threat from domestic terrorism by upgrading security in GSA buildings, nearly doubling its ranks of uniformed officers and developing new security standards. In FY 1996 and FY 1997, GSA obligated $233.8 million for security upgrades, including substantial capital improvements and equipment in each of four critical areas: perimeter, entry and interior security, and security planning. About 6,700 of the 7,930 recommended and approved security countermeasures identified in the post-Oklahoma City Vulnerability Assessment of Federal Facilities have been fully implemented. Ninety percent of the highest-priority recommendations—those for large, multi-tenant buildings—have been reported as complete.

Source: Reprinted from **http://www.gsa.gov/**, U.S. General Services Administration.

PRIVATE POLICING IN THE UNITED STATES

An interesting and often overlooked police-related field is the **private police/ security** profession. It does not have a single title—it has been referred to as "private security," "private policing," "loss prevention," "loss control," "assets protection," and even "risk management." The field encompasses dozens of job titles, extending from the uniformed guard at financial and retail establishments to corporate security directors of international companies. It includes private detectives, hospital security personnel, railroad police, nuclear power plant SWAT team members, armored car officers, computer security specialists, access control specialists, electronic technicians, occupational health/safety personnel, fire safety experts, contingency/disaster management planners, and security and crime prevention consultants.

According to research, private security is now clearly the nation's primary protective resource, outspending public law enforcement by 73 percent and employing two and a half times the workforce. The study estimated 1990 annual expenditures for private security at $52 billion and employment of 1.5 million persons. Public law enforcement in that year cost $30 billion and had a workforce of 600,000. In 1993, public policing efforts cost taxpayers about $42 billion while $65 billion was spent by citizens and businesses on private security guards, alarm systems, and locks. Although the spending and hiring in the public sector has risen some in the last six years, so has that in the private sector. According to the *Security Magazine* Industry Forecast, in 1998 about $80 billion was spent on the private security industry in the U.S. (Zalud 1999). Private security is a growth industry, with growth estimates ranging from 8 to 15 percent per year, depending on which aspect of the field is being considered. One of the fastest-growing components is the manufacture, distribution, and installation of security equipment and technology. Generally, the growth rate for private security services is double that of the public sector. By the year 2000, it is estimated that private security expenditures will reach $104 billion and 1.9 million persons will be employed in the field (Cunningham *et al.* 1991), which will mean that security personnel will outnumber public law enforcement officers by a ratio of three to one (Spencer 1997).

Authority of Private Police

The authority of private police is primarily dependent upon the law of the state in which the person is employed. Generally, they have no more authority than private citizens, although that varies from state to state. Many states have enacted specific statutes regulating and delimiting the authority of private persons employed in a security or protective capacity. A recent study identified 43 states as having statutes regulating security guards, with the other 7 not doing so. The study only addressed provisions that related to employees of security agencies (Maahs and Hemmens 1998, 124). States may permit the carrying of weapons, the right to detain and arrest, and the right to search persons. State law may address actions ranging from the arrest of shoplifters (in mercantile statutes) to the use of deadly force.

The focus of most state regulation is to license certain types of security-related activity, such as the carrying of a firearm, private detective services, security guard services, and alarm installation services (see Exhibit 4–5). The trend to regulate such services has led to the formation of the National Association of Security and Investigative Regulators (NASIR), which has a membership of 34 states and 2 Canadian provinces. NASIR began its operation in the spring of 1993 with an initial group of fifteen state licensing regulators. It is made up of representatives who license the private security and investigative industries. In order to accomplish its mission, NASIR established these goals (NASIR 1999):

- Enhanced applicant processing and records management
- Expedient background investigation and fingerprint processing
- Dissemination of information on insurance/bonds
- Keeping abreast of, and sharing information about, new licensing technology
- The promotion of effective state regulation and enforcement
- Assisting in education and training standards
- Eliminating unlicensed activity
- Developing harmony between law enforcement and the regulated industries
- Influencing federal legislation
- Formulating model laws and regulations
- Assisting states in developing and enforcing laws and regulations
- Encouraging reciprocity between states
- Providing training and education opportunities for state regulators

NASIR has become an influential organization. It monitors national legislation in an effort to ensure the continued growth and professionalism of the private security and private investigative industries (NASIR 1999).

Besides state regulatory agencies, certain segments of the security industry regulate themselves by advancing and adhering to a code of ethics, as illustrated in Exhibit 4–6.

In addition to state regulation and self-regulation, the authority of security personnel and the limits of liability are interpreted through case law. Often it is the courts that have to determine how the law applies to private police. For example, in *Bowman v. State* (1983), an Indiana court ruled that *Miranda* warnings (informing those arrested of their rights) did not have to be given by private police, since they were not involved in "state action" (Hess and Wrobleski 1992, 100). Generally, U.S. Constitutional protections only apply to governmental actions, not those of private citizens. In 1921, the United States Supreme

Exhibit 4–5

WHAT DO STATES REGULATE IN THE SECURITY FIELD?

Based on recent research, at least 47 states regulate some aspect of private security services:

- 33 states regulate private investigators
- 47 states regulate contract security and guard services
  — 32 states disqualify the hiring of felons
  — only 2 states have a minimum educational level (8th grade)
- 19 states set the minimum age for employment at age 18, 7 states set it at age 21, 1 at age 22, and 7 at 25
- 16 states require a minimal level of training for armed personnel in security
- 8 states regulate alarm system contractors

Sources: Data from C. Buikema and F. Horvath, Security Regulation—A State-by-State Update, *Security Management*, January 1984; and J.R. Maahs and C. Hemmens, Guarding the Public: A Statutory Analysis of State Regulation of Security Guards, *Journal of Crime and Justice*, © 1998.

Court clearly stated in *Burdeau v. McDowell* (1921) that the Fourth Amendment gives protection against unlawful searches and seizures conducted by governmental agencies. The Court held that the Constitution does not protect persons against arrests, searches, and seizures conducted by private parties (including private security personnel). However, the courts also have indicated that if there is a close relationship or a state connection to the actions of the security officer, a review based upon Constitutional considerations may be required. In other words, if private security personnel are acting at the request of governmental agents, their actions may be governed by Constitutional restrictions (*People v. Selinski,* 1979; Euller 1980).

Public and Private Police Relationships

Both the public and private police fields exist for specific purposes or reasons. Public law enforcement is usually responsible for an array of safety services and the enforcement of criminal prohibitions by responding to citizen calls for service, investigating crime and apprehending offenders. As such, it is reactive in nature and usually responds upon receiving a complaint from a citizen or company. Private policing, on the other hand, has traditionally been focused on

Exhibit 4–6

AMERICAN SOCIETY FOR INDUSTRIAL SECURITY— CODE OF ETHICS

PREAMBLE

Aware that the quality of professional security activity ultimately depends upon the willingness of practitioners to observe special standards of conduct and to manifest good faith in professional relationships, the American Society for Industrial Security adopts the following Code of Ethics and mandates its conscientious observance as a binding condition of membership in or affiliation with the Society.

CODE OF ETHICS

I. A member shall perform professional duties in accordance with the law and highest moral principles.
II. A member shall observe the precepts of truthfulness, honesty and integrity.
III. A member shall be faithful and diligent in discharging professional responsibilities.
IV. A member shall be competent in discharging professional responsibilities.
V. A member shall safeguard confidential information and exercise due care to prevent its improper disclosure.
VI. A member shall not maliciously injure the professional reputation or practice of colleagues.

Source: Copyright © American Society for Industrial Security.

---

prevention of crime, accidents, injuries, and loss of resources; and the detection of crime or emergency situations. Private security extends beyond crime and policing and into areas of loss reduction, safety, hygiene, and risk management.

There are areas of obvious conflict and concern in which it appears that public and private police are responsible for the same thing, such as protecting areas open to the public (e.g., supermarkets, banks, bus terminals). When uniformed private officers are involved, they are "supplementing" the public agency's responsibility. Public agencies do not have enough personnel to permanently assign officers to private establishments to provide protection. Private officers also "complement" public agency responsibility in that the public officers have limited authority on totally private property and may not even provide the services that the private officers perform. These services include private employment background checks, armored car services, private detective work, alarm installation and monitoring, initially investigating suspected financial crimes, and protecting trade secrets or sensitive corporate information and data.

The general relationship between private and public officers varies from place to place. Some communities have worked hard to promote a clear understanding of the roles of each entity. In other places, visible conflict exists. This may be the case even though some estimates categorize 20 percent of the security personnel in the United States as off-duty public officers working a second job. In fact, both groups are needed. The public cannot afford to employ all the security personnel at its expense, and clearly much of what private security involves is not a public responsibility.

SUMMARY

The public law enforcement community of the United States consists of nearly 17,000 separate agencies employing over 800,000 personnel. Those agencies are found throughout the political subdivisions of each state and of the federal government. Consequently, the law enforcement system of the United States is fragmented and nonstandardized. Each agency operates within its own jurisdiction, each agency has its own chief executive official, and each agency operates within its own rules and regulations. Some of these agencies possess general police authority, while others are restricted to specific police authority such as offenses related to the traffic code, fish and wildlife, or narcotics. Public law enforcement in the United States is an expenditure of over $41 billion each year (Lindgren 1997, 6).

Private policing, estimated to be a $80 billion industry employing over 1.5 million persons, is considered a growing industry. Although the authority of private police is usually the same as private individuals, they serve the private sector by supplementing and complementing local public policing efforts. They provide protection for private property that cannot be provided by local public police. The major focus of private policing is on the prevention and detection of crime rather than the investigation of crime and the apprehension of offenders.

QUESTIONS FOR REVIEW

1. In what branch of the U.S. governmental structure is policing found? Why is this the case?
2. Define the following terms or principles of government: federalism, checks and balances, three branches of government, implied powers doctrine, and judicial review.
3. What is meant by a "political subdivision" of a state? Name at least four.
4. Approximately how many law enforcement agencies are there in the United States? How many persons do they employ?
5. Compare and contrast "specific police authority" and "general police authority."
6. Identify the major federal law enforcement agencies with investigative and criminal responsibilities and their organizational placement (major department) in the federal government structure.
7. Explain the purpose and extent of private policing in the United States.

SUGGESTED ACTIVITIES

1. Obtain accurate figures regarding how many sworn police officers your state has. You may want to log on to the Bureau of Justice Statistics at **http://www.ojp.usdoj.gov/bjs/** to review additional data, analyses, and graphs about law enforcement and criminal justice issues in the United States. The site also contains the latest available reports and statistics. Additionally, agency-specific Web sites often list current statistics regarding their personnel.
2. Identify the various law enforcement agencies in your state or a neighboring state. Based on information in this chapter, determine whether they possess specific or general police authority.
3. Select one local, state, and federal agency and search the World Wide Web for sites that contain information about each one. Compile a short three-page report on what you found.
4. Check your state laws on the regulation and licensing of private security and private investigators. You may need to call or write to a licensing board for the criteria and requirements for licensing. Check the World Wide Web for such information as well.
5. Using the World Wide Web, log on to **http://www.asisonline.org**, and **http://www.sec-mag.com/** and navigate the site to review the scope of the private security and loss prevention field. Also, use a search engine and conduct selected searches on terms such as "private security," "security alarms," and "safety."

CHAPTER GLOSSARY

administrative law: derived from statutory law and gives an agency or board the power to establish it own rules and procedures; the purpose of administrative law is to guide administrative officers in government agencies and guard against arbitrary decisions

checks and balances (or **separation of powers**): a mechanism for preventing any one branch of government (executive, legislative, or judicial) from becoming too powerful

concurrent or **overlapping jurisdiction:** when two or more law enforcement agencies, often from different levels of government, have jurisdiction (the right and authority) to respond to and investigate criminal complaint in a given geographical area

constitutional law: the body of law that concerns the interpretation of the U.S. and state Constitutions

contract law: provisions that have been negotiated between parties and often committed to writing

federalism: a form of representative democracy establishing a "dual system" of government made up of the federal and state systems

general police authority: police responsibility that extends to most any criminal offense committed within the jurisdiction

implied powers doctrine (or the **necessary and proper clause**): Article I, Section 8 (Paragraph 18) of the United States Constitution, which grants Congress the right to enact laws in order to properly carry out the specific rights of Congress enumerated in the Constitution

judicial review: the authority of the courts to review cases from lower courts and rule on constitutionality of laws

political subdivisions: jurisdictions or entities created by the state that possess authority and control over local matters; the most common names for these political subdivisions include: county, municipality or city, village, borough, and township

private police/security: a policing-related field found in the private sector that is referred to as "private security," "private policing," "loss prevention," "loss control," "assets protection," and even "risk management"; the field emphasizes prevention and detection of crime and safety hazards

specific police authority: police responsibility and the right to investigate that is limited by law to certain matters

statutory law: a statute (code) created by legislative authority

REFERENCES

Buikema, Charles and Frank Horvath. 1984. Security Regulation—A State-by-State Update. *Security Management.* 28(1)(January): 39–43.

Burdeau v. McDowell, 256 U.S. 475 (1921).

Cunningham, William C., John J. Struchs, and Clifford W. Van Meter. 1991. *Private Security: Patterns and Trends.* Washington, D.C.: National Institute of Justice.

Euller, Stephen. 1980. Private Security in the Courtroom: The Exclusionary Rule Applies. *Security Management.* 24(3)(March): 38–40.

Hess, Karen M. and Henry M. Wrobleski. 1992. *Introduction to Private Security.* 3d ed. St. Paul, Minnesota: West Publishing Co.

Hunter, Ronald D. 1990. Three Models of Policing. *Police Studies 13*, no. 3 (Fall): 118–123.

Johnson, Kevin. 1999. "FBI Takes on Expanding Role, Staff." *USA Today* (8 June).

Lindgren, Sue A. 1997. *Justice Expenditures and Employment Extracts, 1992: Data from the Annual General Finance and Employment Surveys.* Washington, D.C.: U.S. Department of Justice.

Maahs, Jeffrey R. and Craig Hemmens. 1998. Guarding the Public: A Statutory Analysis of State Regulation of Security Guards, *Journal of Crime and Justice XXI,* no. 1.: 119–134.

National Association of Security and Investigative Regulators. May 1999. **http://www.nasir.org/History.htm**.

People v. Zelinski, 594 P.2d 1000 (1979).

Reaves, Brian A. and Pheny Z. Smith. 1995. *Law Enforcement Management and Administrative Statistics, 1993: Data for Individual State and Local Agencies with 100 or More Officers.* Washington, D.C.: U.S. Department of Justice.

Reaves, Brian and Pheny Z. Smith. 1996. *Sheriffs' Departments, 1993.* Washington, D.C.: U.S. Department of Justice.

Reaves, Brian A. 1996a. *Campus Law Enforcement Agencies, 1995.* Washington, D.C.: U.S. Department of Justice.

Reaves, Brian. 1996b. *Local Police Departments, 1993.* Washington, D.C.: U.S. Department of Justice.

Reaves, Brian A. 1998. *Federal Law Enforcement Officers, 1996.* Washington, D.C.: U.S. Department of Justice.

Reaves, Brian A. and Andrew L. Goldberg. 1999. *Law Enforcement Management and Administrative Statistics, 1997: Data for Individual and Local Agencies with 100 or More Officers.* Washington, D.C.: U.S. Department of Justice.

Spencer, Suzy. 1997. Private Security. **http://www.onpatrol.com/cs.privsec.html**. Accessed May 16, 1999.

Zalud, Bill. 1998. Whose Advantage? **http://www.sdmmag.com/98stats.htm**. Accessed May 16, 1999.

Zalud, Bill. 1999. Security Spending, Budgets Grow; Upgrades, Services Hot. *Security* 36(1) (January): 30–32.

Crime in the United States

A Los Angeles police officer holds a shotgun on two looting suspects as a California state police officer handcuffs them during the 1992 riots following the acquittal of officers accused of beating black motorist Rodney King. (AP/Wide World Photos)

Policing officials need to understand the basic aspects of crime causation and victimization. Police officers need to understand how crime impacts the local community and national policy. This chapter's focus is on crime in the U.S. After studying this chapter, you should be able to:

1. Describe the role of patrol officers in gathering and interpreting information.
2. Identify the major methods by which we count and track crime.
3. Describe the impacts of crime on communities and policy making.
4. Define the major theories of crime causation.
5. Identify the trends in five major areas of crime that may impact future discussions of crime causation theory.

CHAPTER OUTLINE

I. The Need to Understand Crime
   A. Counting Crime
   B. Reported Crime
   C. Victim Studies
   D. Impact of Crime
   E. Changing Patterns of Crime
II. Causes of Crime—Overview
III. Individual Level Theories of Crime
IV. Causes of Crime—Social Level Theories
   A. Classical Schools
   B. Differential Association
   C. Labeling
   D. Social Control
V. Emerging Issues in Crime Causation
   A. Drugs
   B. Hate Crime
   C. Computer Crime
   D. Gangs
   E. Domestic Violence
VI. Summary

THE NEED TO UNDERSTAND CRIME

Why must a patrol officer or field agent understand the causes of crime or how it is measured? Why should these same officers concern themselves with emerging trends in crime? Because patrol officers are the front line in the continuing struggle to control antisocial activity, and because they are the eyes and ears of law enforcement management. Patrol officers are the primary sources of community information. In order for managers to properly plan, they need to understand developing trends. Contemporary law enforcement management techniques require patrol officers to gather information and assist in its interpretation. Information on individual offenders is also important for sentencing, probation, parole, and corrections assessment. Finally, policy makers in legislative and administrative agencies rely upon data and information collected by officers to project trends and develop policy.

Often, patrol officers do not even realize they perform an information-gathering role outside of investigations. They may give statements in court or write various reports (e.g., investigative reports, supplemental reports, administrative reports, or offense reports) but usually do not think of themselves as "researchers."

Officers may be the subject of opinion surveys or observation by academic researchers, and they may give policy testimony before legislative, policy-making, or other investigative boards. Finally, they may serve on a departmental team or task force reporting to the command staff on community problems and likely solutions. In each of these cases, information either gathered by officers or interpreted by officers goes beyond investigations of an individual case and can be of the utmost importance to the department and other policy-making actors.

Understanding the various theories of crime causation is one task of the professional law enforcement official. Data on crime may not match the personal experience of each officer in a given jurisdiction, nor may crime in that jurisdiction fully reflect accepted explanations of the causes of crime. General theories and approaches are just that—general. They give us a view of how things seem *overall*. We expect locations to differ slightly, or even in major ways, from the general trend of data. But that, too, is important for patrol officers to know. If other jurisdictions seem to have one general sort of experience, why, based upon their own experience, is their jurisdiction different? Do trends in criminal behavior in that jurisdiction differ in ways that might give officers a better understanding of the causes of criminality in their community? These questions are important and set the tone for emerging expectations of the contemporary law enforcement officer.

Counting Crime

There are three primary sources of data on the amount of crime in the United States.

Self-Reported Crime. The first source of crime data is self-reporting of criminal activity by offenders. This is obviously problematic and not very reliable in many instances, though it may be useful for academic research. It is also limited in scope, as it captures only a picture of one type of offense, some characteristics of some types of offenders, or types of offenders in one area. An example is data that is collected on drug and alcohol use by offenders in some cities (see Table 5–1). This sort of data is important for theory building, but it has less significance for community problem solving. Therefore, we tend to rely upon other sources of major crime data.

Reported Crime. The second and most commonly known data source is taken from offenses reported to police and is counted at the level of the local law enforcement agency. Collected and presented in the **Uniform Crime Report** or **UCR**, it is published annually by the FBI under the title *Crime in the United States.* Participating law enforcement agencies keep monthly records of offenses reported to or discovered by police. Monthly totals are then forwarded to the Federal Bureau of Investigation. Monthly reports have two parts. **Part 1 Offenses** are called **Index Crimes** and are those from which the FBI tracks

Table 5–1 Drug Use by Adult Arrestees in 23 U.S. Cities, by Type of Drug and Sex, 1996

	(Percent Testing Positive)				
City	Any Drug*	Marijuana	Cocaine	Opiates	Multiple Drugs
Male					
Atlanta, GA	80%	37%	59%	3%	20%
Birmingham, AL	70	44	43	4	22
Chicago, IL	82	47	52	20	35
Cleveland, OH	67	37	41	3	18
Dallas, TX	63	44	32	5	20
Denver, CO	71	42	44	5	24
Detroit, MI	66	46	27	7	15
Ft. Lauderdale, FL	67	38	44	2	19
Houston, TX	64	33	39	8	29
Indianapolis, IN	74	51	42	3	24
Los Angeles, CA	64	30	44	6	20
Manhattan, NY	78	38	56	17	35
Miami, FL	67	34	52	1	22
New Orleans, LA	67	40	46	7	26
Omaha, NE	63	52	24	1	18
Philadelphia, PA	69	39	40	11	27
Phoenix, AZ	59	28	32	9	22
Portland, OR	66	35	34	13	25
St. Louis, MO	75	52	43	10	29
San Antonio, TX	57	39	28	10	21
San Diego, CA	71	40	27	9	31
San Jose, CA	48	27	16	5	15
Washington, DC	66	40	33	9	17

(continues)

the "Crime Index," which it reports to the nation through the media (see Exhibit 5–1). If you read or hear a story in the media that crime was reported going up or down, it is likely based upon this data. These offenses are used to gauge the crime "index," or its rate of decrease or increase.

Table 5–2 shows the total reported numbers of Index offenses for the past two decades. In 1995, the year for which the most complete data are available, there were 13,867,100 Index (Part 1) offenses reported to law enforcement agencies. Of that, 1,798 million were violent offenses. This is expressed, however, as

Table 5–1 Continued

City	Any Drug*	Marijuana	Cocaine	Opiates	Multiple Drugs
		(Percent Testing Positive)			
Female					
Atlanta, GA	77%	26%	63%	3%	18%
Birmingham, AL	59	22	39	6	21
Chicago, IL					
Cleveland, OH	70	22	52	6	13
Dallas, TX	58	27	36	10	21
Denver, CO	69	27	53	5	17
Detroit, MI	69	19	53	18	21
Ft. Lauderdale, FL	66	24	52	3	19
Houston, TX	54	26	34	4	16
Indianapolis, IN	72	31	52	3	23
Los Angeles, CA	74	20	49	12	24
Manhattan, NY	83	19	69	27	37
Miami, FL					
New Orleans, LA	35	13	26	3	10
Omaha, NE	51	33	28	3	16
Philadelphia, PA	81	21	69	16	34
Phoenix, AZ	65	22	42	13	27
Portland, OR	74	26	46	26	33
St. Louis, MO	73	29	55	7	20
San Antonio, TX	44	19	23	13	20
San Diego, CA	62	23	22	10	25
San Jose, CA	53	19	21	9	23
Washington, DC	58	23	40	11	17

Note: These data are from the Drug Use Forecasting (DUF) program sponsored by the National Institute of Justice. DUF data are collected in booking facilities in participating cities throughout the United States. Each quarter, trained local DUF staff obtain voluntary and anonymous urine specimens and interviews from a sample of arrestees. Chicago and Miami did not test or interview female arrestees.

*Includes cocaine, opiates, marijuana, phencyclidine (PCP), methadone, benzodiazepines, methaqualone, propoxyphene, barbiturates, and amphetamines.

Source: Reprinted from *Sourcebook of Criminal Justice Statistics, 1996,* K. Maguire and A.L. Pastore, eds., p. 409, 1997, U.S. Department of Justice, Bureau of Justice Statistics, citing *1996 Drug Use Forecasting Annual Report on Adult and Juvenile Arrestees,* NCJ-165691 (U.S. Government Printing Office), pp. 24–46, 1997, U.S. Department of Justice, National Institute of Justice.

Exhibit 5–1

PART ONE OFFENSES / INDEX CRIMES

arson
assault
burglary
forcible rape
larceny-theft
motor vehicle theft
murder & non-negligent manslaughter
robbery

Source: Federal Bureau of Investigation.

---

the rate of Index offenses per 100,000 people. We express it as a rate in order to compare periods and take into consideration population growth. The index is shown for the past two decades in Table 5–3 (Maguire and Pastore 1997). The 1993 Crime Index fell 3 percent from 1992, with similar drops through 1995. The crime rate has been falling since 1991, and early figures for 1997 show similar trends downward.

There are some problems with this method of counting, however. First, it covers only crime reported to law enforcement, and much of the crime committed in the United States is not reported. Hence, if victims change their behavior and report more crimes, the result may leave the impression that crime is increasing, which may not be true. This is a significant problem. Second, if law enforcement agencies become more effective in discovering crimes, the rate will seem to increase because more crime was discovered. Third, the definitions of crimes are not the same from state to state and, in some cases, from year to year. For example, an offense such as entering an outbuilding (storage shed) might be a criminal trespass in Ohio, but a burglary in Georgia. One is a minor offense, while the other is serious. A fourth problem with the UCR is that it does not account for **victimless crime**, which is behavior defined as criminal but engaged in by many who think it should not be. Generally, this includes prostitution, gambling, drug abuse, pornography, and others. The fifth problem with the UCR is that it relies on victims to report crimes. If victims do not trust police or the criminal justice system, or fear retaliation or humiliation, they may never report victimization. For all of these reasons and more, the UCR alone is not sufficient for us to grasp the true rate of crime. Exhibit 5–2 summarizes the problems with the UCR discussed here.

Table 5–2 Estimated Number of Offenses Known to Police, 1976–1995

Number of Offenses For Year	Total Crime Index	Violent Crime	Property Crime	Murder and Non-negligent Manslaughter	Forcible Rape	Robbery	Aggravated Assault	Burglary	Larceny-Theft	Motor Vehicle Theft
1976	11,349,700	1,004,210	10,345,500	18,780	57,080	427,810	500,530	3,108,700	6,270,800	966,000
1977	10,984,500	1,029,580	9,955,000	19,120	63,500	412,610	534,350	3,071,500	5,905,700	977,700
1978	11,209,000	1,085,550	10,123,400	19,560	67,610	426,930	571,460	3,128,300	5,991,000	1,004,100
1979	12,249,500	1,208,030	11,401,500	21,460	76,390	480,700	629,480	3,327,700	6,601,000	1,112,800
1980	13,408,300	1,344,520	12,063,700	23,040	82,990	565,840	672,650	3,795,200	7,136,900	1,131,700
1981	13,423,800	1,361,820	12,061,900	22,520	82,500	592,910	663,900	3,779,700	7,194,400	1,087,800
1982	12,974,400	1,322,390	11,652,000	21,010	78,770	553,130	669,480	3,447,100	7,142,500	1,062,400
1983	12,108,600	1,258,090	10,850,500	19,310	78,920	506,570	653,290	3,129,900	6,712,800	1,007,900
1984	11,881,800	1,273,280	10,608,500	18,960	84,230	485,010	685,350	2,984,400	6,591,900	1,032,200
1985	12,431,400	1,328,800	11,102,600	18,980	88,670	497,870	723,250	3,073,300	6,926,400	1,102,900
1986	13,211,900	1,489,170	11,722,700	20,610	91,460	542,780	834,320	3,241,400	7,257,200	1,224,100
1987	13,508,700	1,484,000	12,024,700	20,100	91,110	517,700	855,090	3,236,200	7,499,900	1,288,700
1988	13,923,100	1,566,220	12,236,900	20,680	92,490	542,970	910,090	3,218,100	7,705,900	1,432,900
1989	14,251,400	1,646,040	12,605,400	21,500	94,500	578,330	951,710	3,168,200	7,872,400	1,564,800
1990	14,475,600	1,820,130	12,655,500	23,440	102,560	639,270	1,054,860	3,073,900	7,945,700	5,635,900
1991	14,872,900	1,911,770	12,961,100	24,700	106,590	687,730	1,092,740	3,157,200	8,142,200	1,661,700
1992	14,438,200	1,932,270	12,505,900	23,760	109,060	672,480	1,126,970	2,979,900	7,915,200	1,610,800
1993	14,141,800	1,926,020	12,218,800	24,530	106,010	649,870	1,135,610	2,834,800	7,820,900	1,563,100
1994	13,989,500	1,857,670	12,131,900	23,330	102,220	618,950	1,113,180	2,712,800	7,879,800	1,539,300
1995	13,867,100	1,798,790	12,068,400	21,600	97,460	580,550	1,099,180	2,595,000	8,000,600	1,472,700

Source: Reprinted from *Sourcebook of Criminal Justice Statistics, 1996*, K. Maguire and A. L. Pastore, eds., p. 306, 1997, U.S. Department of Justice, Bureau of Justice Statistics, citing *Crime in the United States, 1975*, p. 49 and *Crime in the United States, 1995*, p. 58, U.S. Department of Justice, Federal Bureau of Investigation.

Table 5-3 Estimated Rate Per 100,000 Inhabitants of Offenses Known to Police, 1976–1995

Rate per 100,000 Inhabitants	Total Crime Index	Violent Crime	Property Crime	Murder and Non-negligent Manslaughter	Forcible Rape	Robbery	Aggravated Assault	Burglary	Larceny-Theft	Motor Vehicle Theft
1976	5,287.3	467.8	4,819.5	8.8	26.6	199.3	233.2	1,448.2	2,921.3	450.0
1977	5,077.6	475.9	4,601.7	8.8	29.4	190.7	240.0	1,419.8	2,729.9	451.9
1978	5,140.3	497.8	4,642.6	9.0	31.0	195.8	262.1	1,434.6	2,747.4	460.5
1979	5,565.5	548.9	5,016.6	9.7	34.7	218.4	286.0	1,511.9	2,999.1	505.6
1980	5,950.0	596.6	5,353.3	10.2	36.8	251.1	298.5	1,684.1	3,167.0	502.2
1981	5,858.2	594.3	5,263.9	9.8	36.0	258.7	289.7	1,649.5	3,139.7	474.7
1982	5,603.6	571.1	5,032.5	9.1	34.0	238.9	289.2	1,488.8	3,084.8	458.8
1983	5,175.0	537.7	4,637.4	8.3	33.7	216.5	279.2	1,337.7	2,868.9	430.8
1984	5,031.3	539.2	4,492.1	7.9	35.7	205.4	290.2	1,263.7	2,791.3	437.1
1985	5,207.1	556.6	4,650.5	7.9	37.1	208.5	302.9	1,287.3	2,901.2	462.0
1986	5,480.4	617.7	4,862.6	8.6	37.9	225.1	346.1	1,344.6	3,010.3	507.8
1987	5,550.0	609.7	4,940.3	8.3	37.4	212.7	351.3	1,329.6	3,081.3	529.4
1988	5,664.2	637.2	5,027.1	8.4	37.6	220.9	370.2	1,309.2	3,134.9	582.9
1989	5,741.0	663.7	5,077.9	8.7	38.1	233.0	383.4	1,276.3	3,171.3	630.4
1990	5,820.3	731.8	5,088.5	9.4	41.2	257.0	424.1	1,235.9	3,194.8	657.8
1991	5,897.8	758.1	5,139.7	9.8	42.3	272.7	433.3	1,252.0	3,228.8	659.0
1992	5,660.2	757.5	4,902.7	9.3	42.8	263.6	441.8	1,168.2	3,103.0	631.5
1993	5,484.4	746.8	4,373.6	9.5	41.1	255.9	440.3	1,099.2	3,032.4	606.1
1994	5,373.5	713.6	4,660.0	9.0	39.3	237.7	427.6	1,042.0	3,026.7	591.3
1995	5,277.6	684.6	4,593.0	8.2	37.1	220.9	418.3	987.6	3,044.9	560.5

Source: Reprinted from *Sourcebook of Criminal Justice Statistics, 1996*, K. Maguire and A. L. Pastore, eds., p. 306, 1997, U.S. Department of Justice, Bureau of Justice Statistics, citing *Crime in the United States, 1975*, p. 49 and *Crime in the United States, 1995*, p. 58, U.S. Department of Justice, Federal Bureau of Investigation.

Exhibit 5–2

PROBLEMS WITH UCR DATA

- Crime increases in Index may reflect changed enforcement, not crime
- Only includes crimes actually reported to law enforcement agencies
- Same actions are given different names in different states
- Cannot provide accurate count for victimless crimes
- Depends largely upon victim reporting behavior

Victim Studies

A third means of measuring crime derives from the **National Crime Victimization Survey (NCVS)**. This is a survey of thousands of households conducted for the Bureau of Justice Statistics (U.S. Department of Justice) by the Federal Bureau of the Census. Essentially, this survey measures crimes that were committed against households, residents, and businesses. In conducting the survey, people are asked if they have been the victim of a crime in the past year and, if so, to describe it. Detailed information is acquired for each victimization. On the basis of this broad survey, estimates are generated for the nation as a whole. As Table 5–3 and Table 5–4 illustrate, the NCVS provides interesting information. First, the rate of victimization is generally going down, not up. However, it is also clear that as much as 65 percent of all crime is not reported. For example, of the 167,550 rapes that were estimated to have occurred in 1994, only 102,100 were reported to police.

Still, victimization surveys are limited. Self-reported recollections, as noted above, are not reliable, and each respondent is going to interpret events from his or her own perspective. She or he may see a situation as an assault when it was not. Another limitation of the NCVS, like that of the UCR, is its inability to capture information regarding white-collar crime and fraud, or information about crimes in which the respondent may have been involved. Respondents must be relied upon to report offender characteristics, and frequently this information is not known to the victim at all. Information from the NCVS is important, but it is limited as well, and we need to keep that in mind while interpreting it.

Impact of Crime

The rate of crime and the impression it leaves have very clear effects in society. First, this can affect policy decisions. In late 1993, Congress passed a

| | Victimization rates (per 1,000 persons age 12 or older or per 1,000 households) | | | | | Percent change | | | |
Type of crime	1993	1994	1995	1996	1997	1993-97	1994-97	1995-97	1996-97
Personal crimes[a]	52.2	54.1	48.5	43.5	40.8	-21.8%*	-24.6%*	-15.9%*	-6.2%*
Crimes of violence	49.9	51.8	46.6	42.0	39.2	-21.4*	-24.3*	-15.9*	-6.7*
Completed violence	15.0	15.4	13.8	12.4	12.2	-18.7*	-20.8*	-11.6*	-1.6
Attempted/threatened violence	34.9	36.4	32.8	29.6	27.0	-22.6*	-25.8*	-17.7*	-8.8*
Rape/Sexual assault	2.5	2.1	1.7	1.4	1.4	-44.0*	-33.3*	-17.6	0
Rape/attempted rape	1.6	1.4	1.2	0.9	0.9	-43.8*	-35.7*	-25.0‡	0
Rape	1.0	0.7	0.7	0.4	0.5	-50.0*	-28.6	-28.6	25.0
Attempted rape	0.7	0.7	0.5	0.5	0.4	-42.9*	-42.9*	-20.0	-20.0
Sexual assault	0.8	0.6	0.5	0.5	0.5	-37.5‡	-16.7	0	0
Robbery	6.0	6.3	5.4	5.2	4.3	-28.3*	-31.7*	-20.4*	-17.3*
Completed/property taken	3.8	4.0	3.5	3.5	2.8	-26.3*	-30.0*	-20.0*	-20.0*
With injury	1.3	1.4	1.0	1.1	1.1	-15.4	-21.4	10.0	0
Without injury	2.5	2.6	2.5	2.3	1.7	-32.0*	-34.6*	-32.0*	-26.1*
Attempted to take property	2.2	2.3	1.9	1.7	1.5	-31.8*	-34.8*	-21.1‡	-11.8
With injury	0.4	0.6	0.4	0.4	0.3	-25.0	-50.0*	-25.0	-25.0
Without injury	1.8	1.7	1.6	1.4	1.2	-33.3*	-29.4*	-25.0*	-14.3
Assault	41.4	43.3	39.5	35.4	33.5	-19.1*	-22.6*	-15.2*	-5.4
Aggravated	12.0	11.9	9.5	8.8	8.6	-28.3*	-27.7*	-9.5	-2.3
With injury	3.4	3.3	2.5	2.4	2.7	-20.6‡	-18.2‡	8.0	12.5
Threatened with weapon	8.6	8.6	7.1	6.4	5.9	-31.4*	-31.4*	-16.9*	-7.8
Simple	29.4	31.5	29.9	26.6	24.9	-15.3*	-21.0*	-16.7*	-6.4‡
With minor injury	6.1	6.8	6.6	5.7	5.7	-6.6	-16.2*	-13.6‡	0
Without injury	23.3	24.7	23.3	20.9	19.2	-17.6*	-22.3*	-17.6*	-8.1‡
Personal theft[b]	2.3	2.4	1.9	1.5	1.6	-30.4*	-33.3*	-15.8	6.7
Property crimes	318.9	310.2	290.5	266.3	248.3	-22.1%*	-20.0%*	-14.5%*	-6.8%*
Household burglary	58.2	56.3	49.3	47.2	44.6	-23.4*	-20.8*	-9.5*	-5.5
Completed	47.2	46.1	41.7	39.5	37.4	-20.8*	-18.9*	-10.3*	-5.3
Forcible entry	18.1	16.9	15.5	14.7	14.4	-20.4*	-14.8*	-7.1	-2.0
Unlawful entry without force	29.1	29.2	26.2	24.8	23.0	-21.0*	-21.2*	-12.2*	-6.9
Attempted forcible entry	10.9	10.2	7.6	7.7	7.1	-34.9*	-30.4*	-6.6	-7.8
Motor vehicle theft	19.0	18.8	16.9	13.5	13.8	-27.4*	-26.6*	-18.3*	2.2
Completed	12.4	12.5	11.5	9.1	9.7	-21.8*	-22.4*	-15.7*	6.6
Attempted	6.6	6.3	5.5	4.4	4.1	-37.9*	-34.9*	-25.5*	-6.8
Theft	241.7	235.1	224.3	205.7	189.9	-21.4*	-19.2*	-15.3*	-7.7*
Completed[c]	230.1	224.3	215.3	197.7	182.3	-20.8*	-18.7*	-15.3*	-7.8*
Less than $50	98.7	93.5	85.2	73.8	69.4	-29.7*	-25.8*	-18.5*	-6.0‡
$50-$249	76.1	77.0	76.0	71.8	64.2	-15.6*	-16.6*	-15.5*	-10.6*
$250 or more	41.6	41.8	42.1	41.1	38.0	-8.7‡	-9.1*	-9.7*	-7.5‡
Attempted	11.6	10.8	9.0	8.0	7.6	-34.5*	-29.6*	-15.6*	-5.0

Note: Victimization rates may differ from those reported previously because the estimates
are now based on data collected in each calendar year rather than data about events
within a calendar year. (See *Survey methodology* on page 10.) Completed violent crimes
include rape, sexual assault, robbery with or without injury, aggravated assault with injury,
and simple assault with minor injury. See the note on table 1, page 3, for the population counts, 1993-97.
*The difference from 1996 to 1997 is significant at the 95% confidence level.
‡The difference from 1996 to 1997 is significant at the 90% confidence level.
[a]The NCVS is based on interviews with victims and therefore cannot measure murder.
[b]Includes pocket picking, purse snatching, and attempted purse snatching not shown separately.
[c]Includes thefts with unknown losses.

Source: Reprinted from M. Rand, Criminal Victimization 1997: Changes 1996–97 with Trends 1993–97,
National Crime Victimization Survey, p. 9, 1998, Bureau of Justice Statistics.

Figure 5–1 Rates of Criminal victimization and percent change, 1993–97

crime bill that, among other things, provided for the addition of 100,000 police officers on the streets of the United States. This major policy shift resulted from the perception of increased crime. But was crime increasing? As Figures 5–1 and 5–2 above demonstrate, general victimization rates were falling overall, and, while violent crime increased in the period from 1990 to 1994, it decreased in 1995. Violence, of course, is what most people fear, and people believe violence is increasing. In 1991, 55 percent of the respondents in a national Harris opinion survey thought crime was increasing (Maguire, Pastore, and Flanagan 1993). Table 5–4 presents the estimated number, percent distribution, and rate of personal and property victimization for 1994.

Because the National Crime Victimization Survey relies on a sample of households, the rates and numbers from it are estimates and are not exact.

The figure shows trends in the violent victimization rate: Each bar shows the range within which the true victimization rate is likely to fall for the indicated year, and the line represents the best estimate, the most likely value for the rate in each year, which is the published number. There is a greater likelihood that the true rate will fall near the best estimate, and the bars reflect that likelihood: The darker the bar segment, the greater the likelihood.

Because the estimates are based on samples, their precision depends on the sample size: The larger the sample, the better the estimate and the smaller the range bars. Some year-to-year changes are so large that contiguous bars do not touch (1980-81, 1982-83, 1990-91, 1994-95, and 1995-96), suggesting statistically significant increases and decreases. Where there is a lot of overlap

The best estimate and range of estimates

Violent victimizations per
1,000 population age 12 or over

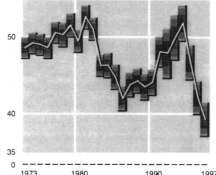

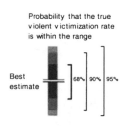

Probability that the true violent victimization rate is within the range

Note: Because of changes made to the victimization survey, data prior to 1992 are adjusted to make them comparable to data collected under the redesigned methodology.

Source: National Crime Victimization Survey, 1973-97.

(1973-76 and 1986-90), the year-to-year changes may be too small to be statistically significant.

Even though the victimization rates have a range of possible values, general trends are readily apparent. Violent crime rates increased from the early 1970's to the early 1980's, then fell until around 1986. For several

years in the late 1980's, violent crime rates were stable, but increased in the early 1990's and fell after 1994 through 1997.

For more explanation of this graph, see the BJS Technical Report *Displaying Violent Crime Trends Using Estimates from the National Crime Victimization Survey*, NCJ 167881.

Source: Reprinted from M. Rand, Criminal Victimization 1997: Changes 1996–97 with Trends 1993–97, *National Crime Victimization Survey*, p. 10, 1998, Bureau of Justice Statistics.

Figure 5–2 Trends in violent victimization, 1973–97

The sense of increasing crime produced demands, beginning in the 1980s, for stiffer penalties and longer sentences, and for a greater portion of the sentence to actually be served. Hence, while victimization studies consistently showed a general decrease in offenses against persons and households between 1980 and 1995, the rate of imprisonment increased dramatically. As Table 5–5 demonstrates, the rate at which people were placed in prison escalated quickly between 1980 and 1995—a rate of increase far greater than the drop in the crime rate over the same period.

Other impacts can be less immediate but no less clear. There are social and economic costs associated with each offense, including loss of income and property, as well as increased medical costs and insurance. Families of both victim and perpetrator are damaged, and there are costs to society as well (see Exhibit 5–3). Policing, prosecution, and incarceration costs, loss of productivity, and distribution of medical costs by way of insurance premiums or taxes are only some of these costs. **Lost opportunity costs** are also tangible. These losses represent the things that society and victims *could have done* with the

Table 5–4 Estimated Number, Percent Distribution, and Rate of Personal and Property Victimization by Type of Crime*

Type of Crime	Number of Victimizations	Percent of All Victimizations**	Rate per 1,000 Persons or Households
All crimes	42,361,840	100%	NA
Personal crimes	11,349,640	26.8	53.1
Crimes of violence	10,860,630	25.6	50.8
Completed violence	3,205,410	7.6	15.0
Attempted/threatened violence	7,655,220	18.1	35.8
Rape/sexual assault	432,750	1.0	2.0
Rape/attempted rape	316,160	0.7	1.5
Rape	167,550	0.4	0.8
Attempted rape***	148,610	0.4	0.7
Sexual assault****	116,590	0.3	0.5
Robbery	1,298,750	3.1	6.1
Completed/property taken	795,130	1.9	3.7
With injury	287,620	0.7	1.3
Without injury	507,510	1.2	2.4
Attempted to take property	503,620	1.2	2.4
With injury	121,790	0.3	0.6
Without injury	381,830	0.9	1.8
Assault	9,129,120	21.6	42.7
Aggravated	2,478,150	5.8	11.6
With injury	678,580	1.6	3.2
Threatened with weapon	1,799,570	4.2	8.4
Simple	6,650,970	15.7	31.1
With minor injury	1,466,060	3.5	6.9
With injury	5,184,900	12.2	24.3
Purse snatching/pocket picking	489,010	1.2	2.3
Completed purse snatching	90,160	0.2	0.4
Attempted purse snatching	23,160	0.1	0.1
Pocket picking	375,690	0.9	1.8
Total population age 12 and older	213,747,270	X	X

(continues)

money otherwise wasted on crime. Other losses are community pride and attractiveness. In the wake of the riots associated with the Rodney King case, community groups tried to rebuild South-Central Los Angeles, but they found few investors who wanted to risk their money in an area that was thought to be crime- and gang-ridden. The net result is a general and steady decline in the standard of living in the area. This affects the social fabric of the community, the schools, and overall patterns of crime. In effect, it is a spiral of decline.

Table 5–4 Continued

Type of Crime	Number of Victimizations	Percent of All Victimizations**	Rate per 1,000 Persons or Households
Property crimes	31,012,200	73.2	307.6
Household burglary	5,482,720	12.9	54.4
Completed	4,572,900	10.8	45.4
Forcible entry	1,725,540	4.1	17.1
Unlawful entry without force	2,847,360	6.7	28.2
Attempted forcible entry	909,820	2.1	9.0
Motor vehicle theft	1,763,690	4.2	17.5
Completed	1,172,300	2.8	11.6
Attempted	591,390	1.4	5.9
Theft*****	23,765,790	56.1	235.8
Completed	22,743,840	53.7	225.6
Less than $50	9,377,150	22.1	93.0
$50 to $249	7,874,230	18.6	78.1
$250 or more	4,251,340	10.0	42.2
Amount not available	1,241,130	2.9	12.3
Attempted	1,021,950	2.4	10.1
Total number of households	100,807,650	X	X

Note: The National Crime Victimization Survey (NCVS) is conducted annually for the U.S. Department of Justice, Bureau of Justice Statistics by the U.S. Bureau of the Census. These estimates are based on data derived from a continuous survey of a representative sample of housing units in the United States. For the 1994 survey, approximately 90,000 residents in 48,000 housing units were interviewed about the crimes they had experienced in the previous 6 months. Response rates were 96% of eligible housing units and 92% of individuals in interviewed households. Readers should note that murder is not measured by the NCVS because of the inability to question the victim. The NCVS has undergone a redesign and all data presented are based on the redesigned survey. The redesign was implemented during 1993 and data based on the redesign are not comparable to data prior to 1993.

*Detail may not add to total because of rounding.
**Percent distribution is based on unrounded figures.
***Includes verbal threats of rape.
****Includes threats.
*****Includes crimes previously classified as "personal larceny without contact" and "household larceny."

Source: Reprinted from *Sourcebook of Criminal Justice Statistics, 1996*, K. Maguire and A. L. Pastore, eds., p. 208, 1997, U.S. Department of Justice, Bureau of Justice Statistics, citing *Criminal Victimization in the United States, 1994*, NCJ-162126 (U.S. Government Printing Office), Table 1, 1997, U.S. Department of Justice, Bureau of Justice Statistics.

Table 5–5 Adults on Probation, in Jail or Prison, and on Parole, 1980–1995

Year	Total Estimated Correctional Population[a]	Probation	Jail[b]	Prison[c]	Parole
1980	1,840,400	1,118,097	182,288	319,598	220,438
1981	2,006,600	1,225,934	195,085	360,029	225,539
1982	2,192,600	1,357,264	207,853	402,914	224,604
1983	2,475,100	1,582,947	221,815	423,898	246,440
1984	2,589,200	1,740,948	233,018	448,264	266,992
1985	3,011,500	1,968,712	254,986	487,593	300,203
1986	3,239,400	2,114,621	272,735	526,436	325,638
1987	3,459,600	2,247,158	294,092	562,814	355,505
1988	3,714,100	2,356,483	341,893	607,766	407,977
1989	4,055,600	2,522,125	393,303	683,367	456,803
1990	4,348,000	2,670,234	403,019	743,382	531,407
1991	4,535,600	2,728,472	424,129	792,535	590,442
1992	4,762,600	2,811,611	441,781	850,566	658,601
1993	4,944,000	2,903,061	455,500	909,381	676,100
1994	5,141,300	2,981,022	479,800	990,147	690,371
1995	5,374,500	3,096,529	499,300	1,078,545	700,174
Percent change					
1994 to 1995	4.5%	3.9%	4.1%	8.9%	1.4%
1985 to 1995	78.5	57.3	95.8	121.2	133.2

Note: Counts for probation, prison, and parole population are for December 31 of each year; jail population counts are for June 30 of each year. Counts of adults held in jail facilities for 1993–96 were estimated and rounded to the nearest 100.

[a] A small number of individuals may have multiple correctional statuses; consequently, the total number of persons under correctional supervision is an overestimate.
[b] The jail population counts exclude persons supervised outside jail facilities for 1980, 1981, 1994, and 1995.
[c] Includes only prisoners under custody.

Source: Reprinted from *Sourcebook of Criminal Justice Statistics, 1996,* K. Maguire and A. L. Pastore, eds., p. 502, 1997, U.S. Department of Justice, Bureau of Justice Statistics, citing *Correctional Populations in the United States, 1994,* NCJ-160091 (U.S. Government Printing Office), Table 1.1, U.S. Department of Justice, Bureau of Justice Statistics.

Exhibit 5–3

THE COSTS OF CRIME

community pride and attractiveness
families damaged
incarceration costs
increased medical costs
increased insurance costs
loss and damage to property
loss of income
loss of productivity
lost opportunity costs
policing
prosecution
tax revenue loss

Research has consistently demonstrated that if people in an area feel safe, they behave differently. Investing, spending, and communicating increase, even if the crime rate is stable. Therefore, one of the major impacts of crime prevention and community policing programs has been the elevation of a sense of community security (Skogan 1990).

Changing Patterns of Crime

In the latest edition of his book *Sense and Nonsense about Crime and Drugs*, Samuel Walker argues that the patterns of crime have changed in the past decade for several reasons. First, he argues that the get-tough policies of the 1980s generally failed. Not that they failed in getting tough—rather, the whole idea of getting tougher did not produce the expected dramatic reduction in crime. Second, the appearance of crack cocaine altered the crime problem by changing the manner in which drugs were marketed. Crack was cheaper, more easily transported, and offered a higher profit potential than other drugs, including other forms of cocaine. The latter fact invited widespread violence as gangs fought over "turf" and market share. In behavior reminiscent of the bootleg days of the 1920s, murder escalated in the major cities of the United States.

A third change was also the result of drugs. In the 1980s, a new war on drugs emerged as middle-class white America brought political pressure to do something about drug use in the country. The result was a rapid tripling of the prison population nationwide, much of this coming in the form of drug convictions (Walker 1998). As prisons became overcrowded, conditions deteriorated and rehabilitation took a back seat. The crush of cases also inundated the criminal justice system generally. Law enforcement allocated tremendous resources to this crime type, and the courts were overwhelmed by the increased case loads. This left less prison space for violent offenders and fewer law enforcement resources for other areas, such as violent crime investigation and patrol activities. Coupled with budget cuts, law enforcement was left more overworked than before. Limited community services that might have helped many who could turn themselves around were further reduced. Despite clear evidence that most offenders can be directed away from crime without the potentially harmful effects of incarceration, incarceration rates increased. Those convicted of nonviolent offenses (e.g., drug offenses) were given priority, thereby pushing more violent offenders onto probation and parole (Irwin 1994). During the late 1980s and continuing through the late 1990s, we also have experienced a serious increase in the violence of juveniles, despite an overall decline in violent crime in the late 1990s.

For patrol officers in major cities, these changes meant an increased level of danger associated with the job. While the number of American police officers killed each year declined between 1980 and 1995 (104 to 74), the number assaulted remained relatively stable (57,847 to 56,686), despite a jump to more than 81,000 in 1992 (see Table 5–6). These conditions are bad enough to keep the level of stress for patrol officers high and reduce the degree of positive interaction with citizens, thereby hampering efforts to reduce crime.

These conditions also significantly altered the social conditions in cities. Earlier, we noted that crime was decreasing rather than increasing. Based upon victimization studies as opposed to crime indexes, this trend was relatively consistent for the 15 years preceding 1995. However, violent crime increased in some major cities in that same period. Drug arrests, which also dramatically increased, tended to cluster in the major cities. Hence, while the average American was *less likely* to be a victim of crime in 1995 than in 1978, the average poor citizen and the average African-American citizen were *more likely* to be a crime victim than had been the case only a decade earlier. The decreased level of safety felt by citizens, mixed with law enforcement's increased sense of community hostility and the clustering of arrests in particular areas in the cities, resulted in increased community resentment and fear. Patrol officers became less connected to the population, more reactive, more aggressive, and more hostile. These pervasive feelings contributed to the Rodney King incident. These same conditions ushered in the advent of Community Policing as a major initiative in law enforcement to reconnect law enforcement to the community it served. In many ways, changing crime patterns produced changes in community responses toward law enforcement and in law enforcement's approach to communities.

Table 5-6 Assaults on Law Enforcement Officers and Percent Receiving Personal Injury—By Type of Weapon Used, 1980–95

		Type of Weapon Used			
	Total Victims	Firearm	Personal Weapon	Knife or Cutting Instrument	Other Dangerous Weapon
Total					
1980	57,847	3,295	47,484	1,653	5,415
1981	57,174	3,334	47,304	1,733	4,803
1982	55,775	2,642	46,802	1,452	4,879
1983	62,324	3,067	51,901	1,829	5,527
1984	60,153	2,654	50,689	1,662	5,148
1985	61,724	2,793	51,953	1,715	5,263
1986	64,259	2,852	54,072	1,614	5,721
1987	63,842	2,789	53,807	1,561	5,685
1988	58,752	2,759	49,053	1,367	5,573
1989	62,172	3,154	51,861	1,379	5,778
1990	71,794	3,662	59,101	1,641	7,390
1991	62,852	3,532	50,813	1,493	7,014
1992	81,252	4,455	66,098	2,095	8,604
1993	66,975	4,002	53,848	1,574	7,551
1994	64,912	3,168	53,021	1,513	7,210
1995	56,686	2,238	46,848	1,301	6,299

(continues)

Table 5–6 Continued

Type of Weapon Used

	Total Victims	Firearm	Personal Weapon	Knife or Cutting Instrument	Other Dangerous Weapon
Percent receiving personal injury					
1980	37.2%	22.5%	38.2%	34.4%	38.0%
1981	35.5	18.3	36.2	34.3	40.6
1982	30.7	16.4	30.7	27.0	39.1
1983	33.4	21.8	33.4	31.4	40.2
1984	33.6	20.1	33.5	30.0	42.2
1985	33.7	20.8	33.9	27.4	41.1
1986	33.7	22.3	33.9	29.9	38.3
1987	33.3	21.7	33.5	30.7	38.4
1988	35.8	27.3	35.6	32.3	42.1
1989	35.2	30.2	35.0	30.5	40.8
1990	36.3	29.4	36.1	29.4	42.5
1991	37.6	30.8	37.5	30.6	43.5
1992	36.5	25.5	36.9	30.4	40.9
1993	35.9	27.4	36.6	31.0	36.3
1994	35.7	26.3	36.3	29.4	36.7
1995	28.5	15.2	29.2	21.7	29.6

Note: These data are based on agencies reporting assaults to the Uniform Crime Reporting Program during the particular year. Number of agencies reporting and percent of total population represented vary from year to year. Data for 1995 are based on 8,938 agencies covering approximately 74% of the total population. Data for previous years are from agencies covering from 76% to 85% of the total population.

Source: Reprinted from *Sourcebook of Criminal Justice Statistics, 1996,* K. Maguire and A. L. Pastore, eds., p. 359, 1997, U.S. Department of Justice, Bureau of Justice Statistics, citing *Law Enforcement Officers Killed and Assaulted, 1989,* p. 55, and *Law Enforcement Officers Killed and Assaulted, 1995,* p. 71, U.S. Department of Justice, Federal Bureau of Investigation, and FBI Uniform Crime Reports.

The lessons are clear for patrol officers. They must learn to see past the immediate incident, avoid stereotyping, and look for larger trends revealed by the *big picture.* Many of the problems encountered by patrol officers in cities are the result of a bad mix of poverty, drugs, and despair. Intervention in and interaction with the community are necessary both to reduce opportunities for crime and to reduce tensions. Crime prevention approaches are as important as arrests. In order to make **Drug Abuse Resistance Education (DARE)**, Neighborhood Watch, or other community involvement approaches work, patrol officers must know the community and become connected to it. They are the eyes and the ears of policy creation and implementation.

CAUSES OF CRIME—OVERVIEW

Public policy is the sum total of what the government decides to do. Public policy is made by elected officials in a democracy and is carried out by administrative agents in executive agencies such as law enforcement agencies. Patrol officers are, in effect, administrative agents or **street-level bureaucrats** with a tremendous amount of discretion (Lipsky 1980). Though they cannot decide what the law is, they can and do decide when to use the law. Policy makers identify problems in society and create public policy (law) in an attempt to respond to observed problems. In the area of crime and criminal justice, public policy initiatives are usually a response to the believed causes of crime.

Religious-based assumptions about crime (*sin* in church law) date to the dawn of civilized society. Typically, the rules based upon such principles sought to punish *evil* or influence from the devil. More recently, theorists and researchers focused rigorously on finding a **cause of crime** rooted in human behavior and environment. Modern efforts in this direction can be traced to at least the late 1700s. Jeremy Bentham (1748–1832), an English philosopher, suggested that the **utilitarian principle** of seeking pleasure and avoiding pain should guide policy responses to crime. Similarly, Cesare Beccaria (1738–1794) held that people will always seek to maximize their pleasure and minimize their pain. In their view, legal institutions could control conduct by increasing one or the other, with pain discouraging crime. These theorists believed that if an act is deemed illegal by society, then the society should only increase the "pain" of committing the act in order to prevent its occurrence. This **pleasure-pain principle** lies at the heart of early crime control ideas (McShane and Williams 1988).

The age in which these theories developed was very much caught up in **rationalism**, and this period produced another rational theory—capitalism. Bentham's early model of **deterrence** reasoning formed a basic set of theoretical principles around which much of our early criminal justice system evolved. However, despite the fact that England used the death penalty for nearly 200 offenses, including picking pockets, crime did not decrease. The simplicity of the pleasure-pain principle did not fully explain the causes of crime. Others tried different techniques, thought to be *scientific* approaches, for finding causes of crime. These included notions such as counting the bumps on the heads of those convicted of offenses (McShane and Williams 1988). Obviously, this and other similar methods left much to be desired in terms of science.

In the twentieth century, social sciences including criminology, sociology, psychology, and anthropology improved society's ability to both accumulate and analyze evidence concerning crime causation. In the past 40 years or so, the social sciences have compiled an impressive array of partial explanations for the causes of crime. They are categorized here for discussion purposes into two groups. Some theories focus on the individual offender while others focus on society as a whole. This is an important distinction for the patrol officer to consider.

Persons associated with law enforcement frequently ask why a given defendant committed a particular crime. Usually, in any such discussion, several theories are commonly advanced. These theories tend to focus on background, family, and prior life experiences (drug use, child abuse, etc.). When a defendant is found guilty and a court contemplates the level of punishment, these same issues surface in the sentencing process. In both cases, the focus is on individual actions and history. Policy makers, however, look at large numbers of offenders in a given period of time and determine whether there are events in the society at large that explain some crime. Without debating the point, assume that drugs cause crime. If this were true, then a policy directed at limiting the availability of drugs would seem prudent if it could be achieved. Here we are not concerned with the individual. Rather, our focus is on social causes of crime. We assume that certain social conditions produce increased or decreased risks of crime. Both individual focused theory and societal level explanations are useful for patrol officers to know and understand.

Individual-based theories may assist officers in solving a crime or in structuring a plausible motive. Social theories of crime call upon officers to be alert to changes in their environment that may signal changes in the nature and kind of crime they might expect. Some aspects of the theory of community policing address exactly these issues. If officers are alert, proper community intervention may actually prevent crime from occurring.

INDIVIDUAL LEVEL THEORIES OF CRIME CAUSATION

While early theorists focused upon offender physical attributes (by counting bumps on the head or measuring body types, for example), others took note of obvious profiles of offenders. They found that offenders tended to be young males with relatively poor intellectual skills. This did not mean, of course, that youth, gender, or lack of intellect caused crime. Rather, it suggested that there might be things about society that influenced young, poorly educated males to commit crimes. Specifically, gender roles might influence males to become more aggressive. Similarly, young people tend to be less cautious and are more easily influenced by peers. Finally, poor educational experiences may cause a person to believe that legal approaches to success are not possible (or will not produce benefits). Poor education also precludes the skills development necessary to see future value to lawful pursuits. In a complex theory reminiscent of the pleasure-pain theory, James Q. Wilson and Richard J. Hernstein argued that much of the explanation for crime lies in the relationship between (1) human needs, (2) the anticipation that these needs will be fulfilled by lawful conduct, and (3) internalized prohibitions against unlawful conduct to fulfill those needs (Wilson and Hernstein 1985). In this view, criminals typically fail to learn internal controls that would prevent needs satisfaction by illegal conduct. Wilson and Hernstein maintain that offenders cannot see how lawful conduct will fulfill those needs.

Similarly, the idea of internalization of norms or values suggests that those who experience very dysfunctional childhoods will internalize either the wrong norms or no norms at all. On the one hand, if children are exposed to alcohol, drug abuse, or violence, their norms may be very abnormal and at odds with those of society. Children may **associate** or **learn** approaches to satisfying their needs that are wholly illegal. **Differential association**, originally proposed by Donald Sutherland in 1939, suggests that criminal behavior results when one is exposed to the "patterns" or "definitions" of others which are favorable to, or supportive of, antisocial behavior (Akers 1997, 61). This theory was expanded by Akers and others to include the notion of rewarding or punishing those definitions. This is frequently referred to as "learning theory" (Akers 1997; Gorman and White 1995; Braithwaite 1989, 34–38). This may seem like "deterrence" theory combined with "hanging around with the wrong crowd," but it is not. These theories are complex suggestions about how we respond to examples in our environment and, as a general theory of deviance, apply to us all and to all forms of deviance, even police deviance. If neighborhoods and families present "definitions" to children that are contrary to social standards of lawfulness, but these children are rewarded for accepting those definitions, we should not be surprised at the result.

On the other hand, if families, neighborhoods, and peers assist in internalizing proper values (including supporting educational performance) and teaching the value of future lawful rewards, crime as a path of conduct will be less likely for that person. Both of these observations offer value for patrol officers. In one sense, officers can assume there is a good probability that offenders are young and male. It is not a good assumption, however, that all young males are likely offenders (see Table 5–7). A small number commit most Index offenses. While 30 percent to 40 percent of all males will be arrested once before their 18th birthday, only 6 percent of all young males account for 50 percent of the arrests (Greenwood 1995). However, this information also suggests a focus of patrol information-gathering and departmental intervention. Most juvenile

Table 5–7 Percent Distribution of Total U.S. Population and Persons Arrested for All Offenses by Age Group, United States, 1995

Age	U.S. Resident Population	Persons Arrested
Age 12 and younger	19.0%	1.7%
13 to 15	4.3	8.2
16 to 18	4.1	12.9
19 to 21	4.1	11.6
22 to 24	4.2	10.0
25 to 29	7.2	14.5
30 to 34	8.3	14.3
35 to 39	8.5	11.5
40 to 44	7.7	7.1
45 to 49	6.6	4.0
50 to 54	5.2	2.0
55 to 59	4.2	1.0
60 to 64	3.8	0.6
Age 65 and older	12.8	0.7

Note: This table presents data from all law enforcement agencies submitting complete reports for 12 months in 1995 (source, U.S. Department of Justice, p. 371). Because of rounding, percents may not add to 100.

Source: Reprinted from *Sourcebook of Criminal Justice Statistics, 1996*, K. Maguire and A. L. Pastore, eds., p. 371, 1997, U.S. Department of Justice, Bureau of Justice Statistics, citing *Crime in the United States, 1995*, p. 218–219, 1996, U.S. Department of Justice, Federal Bureau of Investigation; and *U.S. Population Estimates by Age, Sex, Race and Hispanic Origin: 1990 to 1996*, March 1997, Table 1, U.S. Department of Commerce, Bureau of the Census.

offenders can clearly be pointed in positive directions. For example, pursuing the possibility that a child has been abused or neglected, an officer may have a hand in preventing, possibly even reversing, damaging lessons. Participation in school activities such as sports programs, tutoring, DARE, police athletic leagues, and camp sponsorships can provide positive role models and experiences. In part, officers become role models as a big brother/big sister for children at risk.

CAUSES OF CRIME—SOCIAL LEVEL THEORIES

While some theories focus on the specific attributes of individual offenders, learning environments to which they were exposed, and personal experiences they have had, social level theories choose a much broader perspective. These theories suggest that social structure impacts the prevention or creation of crime. Some of these theories attempt to bridge the distance between individual explanations and social explanations. These theories examine how individuals are exposed to the process of a social system. Hence, individual behavior is more or less directly influenced by social conditions. Not all people respond in the same way to the same social conditions, but overall, we can predict how many will behave. Hence, alteration of social conditions will also predictably have an effect, according to these theories.

Classical Schools

The **Chicago** or **Ecological School** examined the conditions in which people grow, live, and develop for an explanation of crime. These theorists argued that as an area of a city deteriorates, certain processes take place. A new culture develops with its own norms and values. These may and probably will differ from the norms of the larger society. For example, gangs may form as social support mechanisms. Gangs represent a local cultural response to conditions of conflict with other cultures. While gangs may turn to the manufacture and sale of drugs, or fencing stolen property, the reason for gang emergence is a sense of belonging, replacing structures that are missing in their lives (such as a stable family or strong scholastic support). In this respect, the law society seeks to enforce is not *theirs* because it is not from *their culture.* If law enforcement officers have difficulty accepting this interpretation, it is understandable. But studies of gangs and the Mafia substantiate the claim that conflict over culture plays a large role in crime creation. Cultures are based upon values that are transmitted to members of that culture. The idea of **subculture** is based upon this theory. Conflict between the main culture, which creates the law, and the culture of a given group or neighborhood (subculture) generates violations of norms from the main culture.

In many cultures, bribing and gambling are accepted, lawful behaviors. In ours, they are illegal. Some Native American tribes claim the right to use some parts of natural plants in their religious ceremonies, but society calls them drugs and bans them. In the 1800s, fist-fighting in streets and bars rarely led to arrest and prosecution. In short, crime is very value-laden. Of course, as we will discuss later, some actions strike us as patently wrong (robbery, murder, assault, and rape, to name a few) and it is difficult to imagine a culture in which such conduct would be accepted conduct.

Differential Association

Closely related to the above is the theory of differential association (briefly discussed above). This theory holds that crime is learned from close personal contacts with others, and, accordingly, it bridges individual and social level theories . Hence, close contact with a given cultural perspective would lead one to learn those cultural values and act on them even though these actions were contrary to established law. Because this theory focuses on the process of "learning," it can be thought of as social theory, as well as an individually focused theory.

For law enforcement, these theories suggest that mere reaction to criminal events is insufficient to stop crime. Rather, breaking down cultural barriers seems to be a more responsive strategy to prevent crime. Reactive behavior assumes that crime is generated by a rational actor—that is, someone who thinks about the consequences of criminal acts. As discussed earlier, that rational model holds that if offenders know they will get caught and punished, they will not do the crime. But if crime is partially created by culture, then rational models do not apply. For example, when Prohibition came into being, very honest, dedicated citizens found themselves on the other side of the law because in their culture drinking was not only permitted, it was part of everyday life. This was particularly true for those of European descent.

In the same respect, today's problems of drugs, gambling, sex crimes, gang-related violence, and theft suggest that some of the problem is more cultural than individual. To curb crime, then, law enforcement would need to address community concerns, listen to community interests, and develop a more positive, less conflict-oriented image in the community. These results are achieved by intervention in the culture and neighborhoods, not by traditional enforcement methods alone. Such intervention approaches do not mean lower levels of law enforcement. Rather, they mean more complex methods of enforcement and prevention mixed together. Law enforcement becomes not merely the response to criminal actions. It must involve the whole environment of the community, including schools, community services, citizen organizations, and alternative outlets. In this respect, modern policing is partially concerned with introducing and positively reinforcing new values. This, in essence, is what community policing means.

Labeling

Other explanations for crime attempted to bridge the gap between theories that focused on the individual and those that focused on the social structure. These theories focused on the processes by which people were exposed to different forces in society. **Labeling** theory was one prominent notion. There are a number of different perspectives in this approach, but essentially they argue that when an individual is "labeled" deviant, that person is more likely to continue *being* deviant. For some, this might seem either obvious or not very informative. However, this theory is supported by evidence that juveniles who are subjected to high levels of labeling (that is, repeatedly labeled from one event) are more likely to continue deviant patterns (Braithwaite 1989). Table 5–8 reveals the formal reasons for which many juveniles are institutionalized.

Evidence from a number of perspectives and studies suggests that non-Index crime offenders, particularly juveniles, who pass through the criminal justice system display an increased rate of offending as a result of formal charge processing. In other words, for many offenders, arresting, charging, and formally

Table 5–8 Juveniles Held in Public Juvenile Facilities by Sex and Reason Held, United States, 1991

Reason held	Total	Male	Female
Total Juveniles	57,661	51,282	6,379
Delinquent offenses[a]	95%	97.3%	80.7%
Offenses against persons			
Violent[b]	19	20.5	10.3
Other[c]	12	12.1	9.4
Property offense			
Serious[d]	24	24.4	17.1
Other[e]	12	12.5	12.9
Alcohol offenses	1	1.0	1.0
Drug-related offenses	10	10.4	5.3
Public-order offense[f]	4	4.4	5.4
Probation/parole violations	8	7.2	12.9
Other	5	4.8	6.4
Nondelinquent reasons			
Status offenses[g]	3	1.8	12.9
Nonoffenders[h]	1	0.7	4.2
Voluntary commitments	1	0.2	2.2

[a] Offenses that would be criminal if committed by adults
[b] Includes murder, non-negligent manslaughter, forcible rape, robbery, and aggravated assault.
[c] Includes negligent manslaughter, simple assault, and sexual assault.
[d] Includes burglary, arson, larceny/theft, and motor vehicle theft.
[e] Includes vandalism, forgery, counterfeiting, fraud, stolen property, and unauthorized vehicle use.
[f] Includes weapons offenses, prostitution, commercialized vice, disorderly conduct, minor traffic offense, curfew or loitering law offenses, and offenses against morals and decency and the like.
[g] Offenses that would not be considered crimes if committed by adults.
[h] Dependency, neglect, abuse, emotional disturbance, retardation, and other.

Source: Reprinted from Office of Juvenile Justice and Delinquency Prevention, *Comprehensive Strategy for Serious, Violent, and Chronic Juvenile Offenders: Program Summary*, p. 3, 1993, U.S. Department of Justice, p. 3.

pursuing a charge caused them to become more likely to offend (Ludman 1993). This discovery led to the creation of large diversion programs for first offenders who committed relatively minor offenses. While recent research has called labeling theory into question, prior evidence of this effect has not been fully refuted.

For law enforcement, labeling theory suggests that the use of guided discretion in making arrests is effective in crime prevention. This system cannot work like that of the early days of this century, however, where unlimited discretion was typical. This approach requires departments to develop (in consultation with the prosecutorial function) a set of policy guidelines on the appropriate use of such methods. It also suggests that crime prevention will result from the application of carefully defined procedures for diversion. Patrol officers need to understand the theory behind this approach.

Social Control

A final theoretical approach attempts to pull all of these diverse perspectives together. **Social control** theory suggests that internal controls (learned values) and restraining controls from other significant influences (family, peers, etc.) dramatically influence behavior . A breakdown of the appropriate controls is caused by, among other things, surrounding culture and life experiences.

Socialization is the process by which we learn the norms of society. The family, as the primary socializing agent of good effect, is central to developing internal restraints in individuals (also see social control discussions in Chapter 1). The breakdown of families makes this more difficult to achieve, though not impossible. Similarly, the breakdown of traditional neighborhoods reduces the reinforcing effects of other socializing agents such as extended families, schools, neighbors, and social organizations. Gangs play a role in replacing all of these missing agents of socialization.

This approach was echoed in one recent effort to create a "general theory of crime" (Gottfredson and Hirschi 1993). The authors of this theory argue that the absence of self-control (internal control) and the presence of opportunity account for most criminal behavior that is either violent or theft-related. In this view, people with low self-control are likely to commit antisocial behavior given the opportunity. Self-control, in this theory, is developed early in childhood from all of the contacts that children experience. This theory may seem abstract and unrelated to the day-to-day activities on the streets and in the station houses, but closer examination may yield some benefits for law enforcement organizations. Other similar efforts to develop a "general theory" of crime attempt to integrate multiple theories but are complex enough to justify exploration in a course devoted to criminology (Tittle 1995; Braithwaite 1989).

Because young males produce much of the serious crime in the United States, a focus on youth is important. Preschool care for children, schools in general, sports (both scholastic and community organized), and family units are important socializing agents. In a similar fashion, the neighborhood is a powerful influence. By looking at these particular socializing agents, some general approaches for addressing the problem of crime can be sketched. For law enforcement officers specifically, this theory offers some obvious strategies that deviate from the reactive response model typical to law enforcement until recently.

Volatile patterns of youth crime make crime predictions difficult. For example, Cook and Laub (1998) note that homicide arrests for youth in the 10–17 age range peaked in 1993, but by 1995 they had declined by 23 percent (Cook and Laub 1998, 28). Still, they argue, it is generally true that youth arrests in 1994 for violent crime were about the average for the previous 30 years (Cook and Laub 1998, 35). Hence, the notion that there has been an "epidemic" of youth crime is not borne out by the evidence. Still, it is true that violent and property crime is committed disproportionately by young males, and this pattern is one that continues (Miethe and McCorkle 1998, 233–234).

The evidence is clear that most juvenile offenders will stop offending relatively early in their lives. Therefore, law enforcement officers should look at youthful offenders not as lifetime troublemakers. Rather, officers should see them as people who are capable of being properly directed. This does not mean going easy on offenders. On the contrary, it means paying close attention to them but with the approach that help is being offered. Officers must show offenders that they do care about them as people. No one says this is easy or enjoyable, but one can be tough with offenders and still offer the human touch that may be, and most likely is, missing in their lives. Stopping by their homes, talking to friends and families, going out of the way to find them work, or assisting programs to redirect the energies of offenders are all means to the same end: crime prevention. These approaches are also part of community policing. The community is not merely juveniles who are in school, or citizens who have not violated the law; the community is everyone.

Patrol officers must understand that they are the closest and most important law enforcement contacts with the community. They represent, in most respects, not just law enforcement, but the government and society in general. Messages sent by patrol officers are sent on behalf of the whole society. Patrol officers, therefore, are central to the prevention of crime by finding ways to draw young offenders away from offending patterns. This may be by arrest, patrol, and inquiry, or intervention in the schools, neighborhoods, or families. *Patrol officers are the key to successful crime prevention and law enforcement.*

Routine Activities Theory (or RAT theory to some) suggests that much violence and property crime is the result of an interaction between motivated offenders, attractive targets, and levels of guardianship (Cohen and Felson 1979). Implications of this theory for law enforcement are significant. Guardianship can be conceived of in many ways. However, in its most broad conception, it would involve neighborhood groups providing surveillance, target-hardening efforts to make property less attractive (e.g., window locks), and police-community interactions to provide other means to increase guardianship and reduce target availability. In theory, community interventions should be able to succeed in reducing some patterns of crime. This theory has many critics (including your authors) and has not successfully been supported by research (Miethe and McCorkle 1998, 29). Like all theories, however, it is important to test theory against the real world in order to improve our understanding of human behavior as it relates to crime and, in doing so, revise our theories to give policy better direction. Law enforcement is essential in this effort.

EMERGING ISSUES IN CRIME CAUSATION

Drugs

Surely one of the most significant changes in crime in the United States during the past two decades has been related to the use, importation, sale, and manufacture of drugs. While general discussion in the nation focused on the relationship between drugs and crime, those either working in the field or studying the subject examined the complex impact that drugs seemed to have. It must be noted that there are several different kinds of drugs in ready supply, each of which differs in several ways. Physical effects, profit potential, ease of transport, sources, and demand all differ from drug to drug. Complicating this is the way in which a legal drug, alcohol, impacts crime and general drug use.

A good place to start is by looking at the usage of drugs. By far the most widely used drugs are alcohol, marijuana, and cocaine (crack form or crystal powder form). Information consistently shows that drug use is high among those arrested for criminal offenses, running as high as 50 percent on average (see Table 5–9). The rate of drug use depends on the age and gender of the offender, as well as location and nature of the offense. Rates of drug use run as high as 78 percent and as low as 30 percent among offenders. Incidence of drug use is closely linked with incidence of violent crime, though drugs are not necessarily a cause of that violence (D.O.J. 1992). It is just as likely that both violence and drug use are related to a set of conditions which are the core causative agents for both.

Interestingly, drug use rates have declined in the past decade except for marijuana, which increased from 1992 to 1996 after a sharp decline from high levels of usage in the mid-1980s (see Tables 5–10 and 5–11) (Walker 1998). The rates among the young are particularly important, as early use is highly related to their likelihood to be involved in crime generally. Because the rate of drug use among the young seems to be declining (except for marijuana) and because the young commit most offenses, it is no surprise that crime rates are

Table 5–9 Reported Drug Use by Convicted Prison and Jail Inmates

Drug Type	Percent Who Used Drugs at the Time of the Offense		Percent Who Used Drugs in the Month Before the Offense	
	1989 Jail Inmates	*1991 Prison Inmates*	*1989 Jail Inmates*	*1991 Prison Inmates*
Any drug	27%	31%	44%	50%
Marijuana	9	11	28	32
Cocaine/crack	14	14	24	25
Heroin/opiates	5	6	7	10

Source: Reprinted from Bureau of Justice Statistics, *Drugs and Crime Facts*, p. 5, 1994, U.S. Department of Justice.

Table 5–10 Percent of Inmates Who Committed Their Offenses for Money to Buy Drugs

Most Serous Current Offense	Federal Prison Inmates, 1991	State Prison Inmates, 1991	Jail Inmates, 1991
All offenses	10%	17%	13%
Violent offenses	18	12	12
Homicide[a]	3	5	3
Sexual assault[b]	0	2	2
Robbery	27	27	32
Assault	2	6	3
Property offenses	9	26	24
Burglary	32	30	31
Larceny/theft	13	31	28
Motor vehicle theft	—	—	7
Drug offenses	9	22	14
Possession	7	16	10
Trafficking	10	25	19
Public-order offenses	6	5	3

[a] Includes murder, nonnegligent manslaughter, and negligent manslaughter.
[b] Includes rape.
— Not reported

Source: Reprinted from Bureau of Justice Statistics, *Drugs and Crime Facts*, p. 5, 1994, U.S. Department of Justice.

Table 5–11 Drug-Related Homicides

Year	Number of Homicides	Percent Drug-related
1986	19,257	3.9
1987	17,963	4.9
1988	17,971	5.6
1989	18,954	7.4
1990	20,273	6.7
1991	21,676	6.2
1992	22,716	5.7
1993	23,271	5.5

Source: Reprinted from Bureau of Justice Statistics, *Drugs and Crime Facts*, 1994, U.S. Department of Justice.

declining slightly. However, as was noted earlier, violent crime is increasing, thereby suggesting that overall drug use is not a primary cause of most violent crime (if by "cause" we mean that doing drugs produces criminals). It is more reasonable to observe that doing drugs conditionally adds to the probability of criminal activity. Over the long term, drug use has remained relatively stable, as has that of alcohol ,and has not fluctuated as widely as crime rates. This suggests a more conditional relationship.

Still, the increase in the rate of violent crime more or less coincides with the appearance of crack cocaine. This drug is easy to manufacture and transport and offers a large profit margin. But there seems to be a declining market for this and other drugs. The result appears to be a concentrated market in which violence is both a product of the use of the drug and of competition over "turf" to sell the drug. While general use declines, use and sales becomes more concentrated in the central city. Much of the increase in violence may therefore be specifically related to the crack market. While there is widespread belief about this, there is currently insufficient evidence to be certain.

Hate Crimes

Because it is difficult to determine if a crime was motivated by racial, religious, ethnic, or gender status hatred, there is very little data on the subject of hate crimes. However, the impression of most people in law enforcement is that crimes motivated by such attitudes are, in fact, on the increase. Hate crimes pose a particular problem for law enforcement since they tend to be random and spontaneous crimes, thereby leaving few traces of evidence from which to proceed.

Enforcement is made more difficult by the fact that merely saying hateful things or making hateful signs is insufficient to overcome the constitutional protection of free speech. In 1992, the United States Supreme Court declared unconstitutional a municipal ordinance that made it a crime to convey hateful messages (see Exhibit 5–4). The ordinance in question made the content of the message illegal. The Court refused to permit this infringement of what it called "protected speech" (R.A.V. v. Minneapolis, 505 U.S. 377). This decision leaves very little room for the prosecution of hate crimes by other than traditional means: prosecuting the action (assault, arson, criminal damaging, etc.). The issue will no doubt occupy a good deal of litigation as we define what the limits might be for language that is not protected but is, rather, "fighting words" that can be prosecuted. In April of 1990, Congress passed the Hate Crime Statistics Act and mandated the collection of data on crimes motivated by religious, ethnic, racial, or sexual-orientation prejudices. Over time, this data will enhance our knowledge of the prevalence of such offenses. In most respects, the causes of these sorts of crimes are also found in the socialization of the perpetrators. This type of crime can be reduced by proper education and socialization of children in the community.

Computer Crime

One area of crime for which data is virtually nonexistent is computer crime. Once the domain of only federal law enforcement concerns, this complex and virtually transparent crime is now the concern of local enforcement. Recently, a computer consultant was arrested for intentionally implanting a virus (a program that kills stored information) in a computer sold to a customer. The consultant threatened to activate the virus if he did not receive full payment for his work. The proliferation of thousands of electronic bulletin board services (BBS) and World Wide Web (WWW) pages opened avenues for illegal distribution of pornography, anonymous messages related to drug deals, and theft of software and other intellectual property (including company trade secrets). These crimes are in addition to embezzlement, illegal fund transfers, data alteration, and simple extensions of existing crime syndicates.

There is no national accounting of such crime, and the numbers of unreported (and undiscovered) events is no doubt very large. Accurate figures are difficult to obtain, as businesses may choose not to report them. While many might think that law enforcement agencies must react by creating special units to deal with such crime, for most departments this is not an option. Instead, it is clear that law enforcement as a whole must become computer literate quickly. There are already substantial resources at the command of law enforcement for information retrieval about suspects, criminal histories, and fingerprints (see also Chapter 13).

The causes of this form of crime seem to be rooted in two areas. The traditional causes such as greed or anger (related to the social control models and

Exhibit 5–4

R.A.V. V. ST. PAUL, 505 U.S. 377 (1992)
Decided June 22, 1992

JUSTICE SCALIA delivered the opinion of the Court.

In the predawn hours of June 21, 1990, petitioner and several other teenagers allegedly assembled a crudely made cross by taping together broken chair legs. They then allegedly burned the cross inside the fenced yard of a black family that lived across the street from the house where petitioner was staying. Although this conduct could have been punished under any of a number of laws,[fn1] one of the two provisions under which respondent city of St. Paul chose to charge petitioner (then a juvenile) was the St. Paul Bias-Motivated Crime Ordinance, St. Paul, Minn. Legis. Code § 292.02 (1990), which provides:

> *Whoever places on public or private property a symbol, object, appellation, characterization or graffiti, including, but not limited to, a burning cross or Nazi swastika, which one knows or has reasonable grounds to know arouses anger, alarm or resentment in others on the basis of race, color, creed, religion or gender commits disorderly conduct and shall be guilty of a misdemeanor.*

. . . [W]e conclude that, even as narrowly construed by the Minnesota Supreme Court, the ordinance is facially unconstitutional. Although the phrase in the ordinance, "arouses anger, alarm or resentment in others," has been limited by the Minnesota Supreme Court's construction to reach only those symbols or displays that amount to "fighting words," the remaining, unmodified terms make clear that the ordinance applies only to "fighting words" that insult, or provoke violence, "on the basis of race, color, creed, religion or gender." *Displays containing abusive invective, no matter how vicious or severe, are permissible unless they are addressed to one of the specified disfavored topics. Those who wish to use "fighting words" in connection with other ideas—to express hostility, for example, on the basis of political affiliation, union membership, or homosexuality—are not covered. The First Amendment does not permit St. Paul to impose special prohibitions on those speakers who express views on disfavored subjects.*

(continues)

Exhibit 5–4 *(continued)*

In its practical operation, moreover, the ordinance goes even beyond mere content discrimination to actual viewpoint discrimination. Displays containing some words—odious racial epithets, for example—would be prohibited to proponents of all views. But "fighting words" that do not themselves invoke race, color, creed, religion, or gender—aspersions upon a person's mother, for example—would seemingly be usable ad libitum in the placards of those arguing in favor of racial, color, etc. tolerance and equality, but could not be used by that speaker's opponents. One could hold up a sign saying, for example, that all "anti-Catholic bigots" are misbegotten; but not that all "papists" are, for that would insult and provoke violence "on the basis of religion." St. Paul has no such authority to license one side of a debate to fight freestyle, while requiring the other to follow Marquis of Queensbury Rules.

One must wholeheartedly agree with the Minnesota Supreme Court that "[i]t is the responsibility, even the obligation, of diverse communities to confront such notions in whatever form they appear," ibid., but the manner of that confrontation cannot consist of selective limitations upon speech. St. Paul's brief asserts that a general "fighting words" law would not meet the city's needs, because only a content-specific measure can communicate to minority groups that the "group hatred" aspect of such speech "is not condoned by the majority."The point of the First Amendment is that majority preferences must be expressed in some fashion other than silencing speech on the basis of its content.

... [T]he reason why fighting words are categorically excluded from the protection of the First Amendment is not that their content communicates any particular idea, but that their content embodies a particularly intolerable (and socially unnecessary) mode of expressing whatever idea the speaker wishes to convey. St. Paul has not singled out an especially offensive mode of expression. Rather, it has proscribed fighting words of whatever manner that communicate messages of racial, gender, or religious intolerance. Selectivity of this sort creates the possibility that the city is seeking to handicap the expression of particular ideas.

Let there be no mistake about our belief that burning a cross in someone's front yard is reprehensible. But St. Paul has sufficient means at its disposal to prevent such behavior without adding the First Amendment to the fire.

The judgment of the Minnesota Supreme Court is reversed, and the case is remanded for proceedings not inconsistent with this opinion.

It is so ordered.

socialization) are certainly one realm. However, there is also a new characteristic not common in any crime-committing group. Some computer-based crime is committed by highly capable specialists who commit the offenses solely as a test of their skills against government agencies or businesses. Those who engage in such criminal invasions of computers via phone lines or Internet connections are commonly referred to in the media as **hackers**. The types of computer-based crime are identified in Exhibit 5–5.

Gangs

An area of increasing concern to law enforcement is the continuing influence of youth and street gangs. The impression of most people in and out of law enforcement is that gangs are becoming more prevalent, more violent, and more involved in drugs. Research on gangs is relatively substantial, but one major problem that hampers good policy research is the definition of a gang. There is no generally accepted definition from which research, whether government or private, has proceeded. The result is a wide variation in results (Ball and Curry 1995; Winfree *et al.* 1992).

However, we can say that gangs seem to operate in the manner suggested earlier, as a social mechanism that replaces lost or dysfunctional family and community structures. As such, there is a long history, because we can find references to gang activity in England as early as the 1600s—or earlier, should we choose to include the legend of Robin Hood. A reading of the Charles Dickens classic *Oliver Twist,* for example, details the exploits of Oliver Twist as a member of a young gang of orphaned thieves in 19th-century London.

This evidence of a long-term presence of gangs is useful, however, because it indicates that gangs appear to grow more active during times of social upheavals and instability. The evidence suggests that there has been a wide variation of gang activity in the United States over the past 30 years. It has not been

---

Exhibit 5–5

TYPES OF COMPUTER-BASED CRIME
• Information Theft
• Illegal Fund Transfers
• Information Destruction
• Fund Transfers to Assist Other Crimes

constant, and seems to vary according to the year and the region. Overall, there is no real evidence of an increase in gang size or participation. In many specific areas, however, gang activity has reached the critical stage. These suggestions contradict the commonly held view that gangs are rampant everywhere. Part of this seeming contradiction is the difference between the highly organized gang and mere delinquent groups (so called *wanna be* groups).

We do know that those who engage in gang membership tend to have a much higher rate of offending and much higher rates of violence than do non–gang members (Esbensen and Huizinga 1993). As a general rule, it is clear that gang member crime patterns are more violent now than at any time in the past, but they are not consistent. However, this behavior does not persist if the member leaves a gang, which suggests the strong social influence of the group (Spergel 1990). For example, in Los Angeles 25.2 percent of the murders were gang-related in 1987, but in Chicago in the same year, only 6.9 percent were related to gangs. Moreover, despite contrary public views, there is no strong, clear relationship between gangs, drug use, drug sales, and the commission of violent crimes (Klein, Maxson, and Cunningham 1991).

While the growth of crack sales in the 1980s was quite significant, street gang member involvement was low both in New York and Los Angeles. Gang members did not play a predominant role in crack distribution. Nor did they seem to elevate the level of violence and organization related to distribution (Thornberry, Krohn *et al.* 1993). The sharp rise in 1993 of crack-related shootings in cities altered this perception, but there is no reason to believe that this level of violence will persist or that it is related to gang activity as opposed to temporary groups of delinquents.

For patrol officers, this evidence provides both useful and disturbing information. The increase in drive-by shootings suggests that extreme caution is needed regarding occupied vehicles. It also suggests that understanding the role of gang-related activity in a neighborhood is essential to understanding the community. In a way, gang activity becomes a barometer of the condition of the community. A perceived increase should send signals that the community itself is suffering. Community involvement and intervention play a large role in controlling and reducing gang influence in a community that is declining and destabilizing. The fact that members of gangs who leave gangs will return to low levels of criminality offers incentive for officer involvement in community programs to reduce gang influence and provide alternatives for juveniles. The evidence is strong that gangs form when there are insufficient community and family structures to properly socialize young people.

Domestic Violence

While juvenile problems frequently relate to family problems, another family-centered problem of concern to law enforcement is the area of domestic violence. Sometimes referred to as spousal abuse, this area has taken on a larger meaning as the number of households involving unmarried couples has grown. Moreover, because of the levels of violence surrounding couples who are separated or divorced, the concept must include even those loosely connected to another person in a way that suggests a spousal type of relationship. One effect of the O.J. Simpson trial was to refocus attention on spousal abuse between separated or divorced adults.

Estimates of spousal abuse range greatly, from 2.1 million to more than 8 million per year, and there is a lifetime probability, according to some studies, that 25 to 30 percent of all couples will experience a violent incident (Hirschel *et al.* 1992a). It is a generally accepted estimate that only about one-half of those who are abused will report an incident to the police. But for patrol officers it is important to understand that the events that are likely to be reported are not typical of the events that occur. Victimization surveys demonstrated that those who do report events of violence are more likely to be poor and uneducated. Non-white lower income females are almost twice as likely to report an incident than other females. Moreover, the calls are more likely to involve more severe violence. Hence, calls that are made are not representative of all offenses that do occur (Hirschel *et al.* 1992a).

The traditional law enforcement response to such calls was to attempt to separate the parties and restore order. While there were many reasons advanced for this approach, that approach changed when an experiment addressed alternate approaches. The Minneapolis experiment seemed to suggest that arrest of the alleged offender was the most effective means of deterring subsequent events. The National Institute of Justice sought to conduct more controlled experiments using this approach to assess the effectiveness of arrest as a deterrent. The first two of these studies found that arrest may not be the most effective. Generally, three possible results were (1) arrest, (2) citation by the officer, or (3) separation and advice. In fact, there was no difference in the rate of **recidivism** (re-offending) regardless of which approach was used. Even more significant were findings from follow-up surveys that the true rates of reoffending were very high, though most subsequent violent events were not reported. Repeat incidents were the rule, not the exception, but were no less frequent for those arrested the first time (Hirschel *et al.* 1992b). Therefore, the actions of responding officers were not related to subsequent violence.

There could be many reasons for these results. In one study, most of the offenders had criminal records and came from relationships in which abuse was common. Hence, it was likely to happen again, and a few hours in jail was not very significant to the outcome. Some studies suggest that as few as 10 percent of calls for domestic violence result in arrest despite the fact that as many as 50 percent of such cases have sufficient evidence for making arrests (Hirschel *et al.* 1992b). Because of the shortage of available jail and prison space, it is unlikely that priorities on incarceration will change in the near future. This may help explain, but not justify, the low arrest rate. Even if arrest does occur, past experience suggests that few will be convicted unless the criminal justice system as a whole alters the manner in which domestic violence is addressed. In one study, only 35 percent of the cases produced a finding of guilty, and in only 1 percent of the cases was any jail time actually served (Gondolf and McFerron 1989). Clearly, research must continue in order to assist law enforcement and the courts in controlling and preventing domestic violence. Still, while there is no evidence that arrest prevents future events of violence, it may be inferred that arrest prevents escalation of current violence.

The evidence to date suggests some approaches for the patrol officer. First, it is likely that a domestic violence incident event is not the first such event in the household. Second, it is more likely to be a serious violent event. Third, a records check is in order where independent evidence of violence seems clear. Fourth, officers should assume that the likelihood of a subsequent offense is great and should endeavor to build trust with the victim in order to establish bridges rather than destroy communications. Fifth, examine the event in light of the neighborhood, and determine if there are any approaches that might be used to involve other services to interdict the situation. Last, a determination to arrest or not should be based upon the question of probable cause and legal authority to arrest since *there is no social science evidence that arrest does harm* to the situation.

SUMMARY

In this chapter, we examined many suggested causes of crime (Exhibit 5–6 summarizes these). In nearly every case, the theories are based upon the conditions of the community (or environment) in which people live, grow, learn, and work. People's families (or lack thereof), relationships, and experiences all influence behavior both criminal and non-criminal. Understanding the behavior of people is the key. It is related to determining who has committed an offense, as well as who might commit an offense and what might be done to prevent future crime. Understanding begins by identifying the underlying causal forces of crime. This very cursory view is intended only as an introduction to the more detailed aspects of criminological theory.

Similarly, this chapter addressed several emerging areas in which particular types of crime pose significant challenges for law enforcement and for patrol officers in particular. Because we are only now learning about many of these kinds of problems in sufficient detail to address corrective approaches, the new patrol officer must commit himself or herself to learning about these as knowledge develops. They will form some of the most significant crime challenges of the next decade.

QUESTIONS FOR REVIEW

1. What are the underlying problems with UCR data?
2. What are the advantages of NCVS data over UCR data?
3. Compare individual theories of crime to social theories of crime. Which theories offer us more direction in what law enforcement should do? Why?
4. Define, in one or two sentences, each of the major theories of crime.
5. What are the two primary motives of those who commit computer-based crime?
6. What is meant by lost opportunity costs of crime?

Exhibit 5–6

CAUSES OF CRIME

Individual Causes

    Pleasure-Pain Principle

    Internal Control Deficiency

    Poor Education

    Dysfunctional Childhood

Social Causes

    Ecological Conditions

    Differential Association and Learning Labeling

    Social Control and Socialization

Emerging Possible Causes

    Drugs

    Technological Ease

    Discriminatory Attitudes

    Gang Organization

    Domestic Dysfunction

SUGGESTED ACTIVITIES

1. At the library, look up UCR data for your city, county, and state. How does it compare to other cities, counties, and states? To the national data?
2. Divide into teams. Prepare a debate concerning the usefulness of crime causation theory in policy making. What policies seem to be most suited to reducing crime?
3. Explain each of the major theories of crime. For each theory, list the kinds of data or information needed to test the theory. Examples might include the divorce rate, single parenthood rate, child abuse rate, unemployment rate, and the number of hours children watch television as opposed to spending time with parents.
4. With the data you developed in exercise #3, test each theory by comparingf predictions to known outcomes.
5. Go to the home page of the National Criminal Justice Reference Service (NCJRS) and locate at least one article and one graph depicting trends in crime patterns. **(http://www.ncjrs.org)**

CHAPTER GLOSSARY

associate: to learn certain traits, norms, or behaviors by close connections with others who act the same way

cause: a temporal relationship between two or more conditions, in this sense, each theory of the cause of crime states that if the conditions outlined in the theory occur, crime will follow

Chicago School: the group of theorists who believed that one's surroundings account for subsequent behavior

deterrence: a theory that suggests that people are rational and if threatened with potential punishment for doing certain things, they will not commit the acts

differential association: a theory that holds that close contact with another culture will cause the subject to adopt that culture

Drug Abuse Resistance Education (DARE): a national educational program that places police officers in the elementary classrooms to teach children about drugs and the negative aspects of drug use

Ecological School: see Chicago School

hackers: common title used by the media to refer to computer specialists who seek ways to access other computers and bypass computer security systems

Index Crimes or Crime Index: the number of Index crimes committed in each year per 100,000 population; the eight major crimes counted by the UCR

labeling: a theory that suggests that juveniles who are repeatedly described as delinquent will come to act in exactly that manner

learn: acquire norms or attitudes by observing others with whom there is some close connection

lost opportunity cost: money that is lost due to crime and thus cannot be used for other, more beneficial things in society or individually

National Crime Victimization Study (NCVS): a survey of thousands of households and businesses regarding victimization during the last year; conducted for the Bureau of Justice Statistics (U.S. Department of Justice) by the Bureau of the Census

Part 1 Offenses: see Index Crimes

pleasure-pain principle: the central aspect of utilitarian theory, which holds that people will always seek to maximize their pleasure and minimize their pain

public policy: anything that the government chooses to do or to not do

rationalism: the school of thought associated with utilitarianism that held that people make decisions after weighing the costs and benefits, choosing the course of action most likely to benefit them

recidivism: committing crimes after once being punished

social control: a theory that holds that family and other similar groups teach people Internal controls (self-control) and exercise direct control over their behavior, thereby preventing antisocial actions

socialization: the process of learning one's culture

street-level bureaucrats: term used to apply to government employees, including police, who make street-level decisions that affect people's lives

subculture: a set of norms and beliefs that are separate from the main culture and represent the beliefs of a comparatively small number of people

Uniform Crime Report (UCR): reports made by participating law enforcement agencies that keep exact monthly records of offenses reported to them; monthly totals are given to the FBI

utilitarian principle: people attempt to maximize their self-interest (seek pleasure) and will avoid penalties (pain); if the cost of doing something exceeds the value of doing it, then the action will be avoided

victimless crime: behavior defined as criminal but engaged in by many who think it should not be

REFERENCES

Akers, R. L. 1997. *Criminological Theories: Introduction and Evaluation.* Los Angeles, CA: Roxbury Publishing.

Ball, R. A. and G. David Curry. 1995. The Logic of Definition in Criminology: Purposes and Methods for Defining 'Gangs.' *Criminology* 33(2): 225–245.

Barlow, H. D., ed. 1995. *Crime and Public Policy: Putting Theory to Work.* Boulder, CO: Westview Press.

Bureau of Justice Statistics. 1994. *Drugs and Crime Facts.* Washington, D.C.: U.S. Department of Justice.

Cohen, Lawrence E. and Marcus Felson. 1979. Social Change and Crime Rate Trends: A Routine Activity Approach. *American Sociological Review* 44:588–608.

Cook, Philip J. and John H. Laub. 1998. The Unprecedented Epidemic in Youth Violence. In *Youth Violence,* edited by Michael Tonry and Mark H. Moore. Vol. 24 of *Crime and Justice: A Review of Research.* Chicago, IL: University of Chicago Press.

Esbensen, F.A. and David Huizinga. 1993. Gangs, Drugs, and Delinquency in a Survey of Urban Youth. *Criminology* 31(4): 565–586.

Gondolf, E. W. and J. Richard McFerron. 1989. Handling Battering Men: Police Action in Wife Abuse Cases. *Criminal Justice and Behavior* 16(4) (December): 429–439.

Gottfredson, M. and Travis Hirschi. 1990. *A General Theory of Crime.* Palo Alto, CA: Stanford University Press.

Grasmick, H., Charles Tittle, Robert Bursik, and Bruce Arneklev. 1993. Testing the Core Empirical Implications of Gottfredson and Hirschi's General Theory of Crime. *Journal of Research in Crime and Delinquency* 30(1) (February): 5–29.

Greenwood, P. 1995. Juvenile Crime and Juvenile Justice. In *Crime,* edited by James Q. Wilson and Joan Petersilia. San Francisco: ICS Press.

Hirschel, J. D., Ira W. Hutchinson, Charles W. Dean, and Anne-Marie Mills. 1992a. Review Essay on the Law Enforcement Response to Spouse Abuse: Past, Present and Future. *Justice Quarterly* 9(2) (June): 247–283.

Hirschel, J. D., Ira W. Hutchison, Charles W. Dean, and Anne-Marie Mills. 1992b. The Failure of Arrest to Deter Spouse Abuse. *Journal of Research in Crime and Delinquency* 29(1) (February): 7–33.

Irwin, J. 1994. *It's About Time: America's Imprisonment Binge.* Belmont, CA: Wadsworth Publishing.

Klein, M. W., Cheryl L. Maxson, and Lea C. Cunningham. 1991. Crack, Street Gangs and Violence. *Criminology* 29(4): 623–650.

Lipsky, M. 1980. *Street-Level Bureaucracy: Dilemmas of the Individual in Public Service.* Newbury, CA: Russell Sage Foundation.

Ludman, R. J. 1993. *Prevention and Control of Juvenile Delinquency.* New York: Oxford University Press.

Maguire, K., Ann L. Pastore, and Timothy J. Flanagan. 1993. *Sourcebook of Criminal Justice Statistics, 1992.* Washington, D.C.: U. S. Department of Justice.

Maguire, K. and Ann L. Pastore, eds. 1997. *Sourcebook of Criminal Justice Statistics: 1996.* Washington, D.C.: U.S. Department of Justice.

Miethe, Terance D. and Richard McCorkle. 1998. *Crime Profiles: The Anatomy of Dangerous Persons, Places and Situations.* Los Angeles, CA.: Roxbury Publishing.

Skogan, W. G. 1990. *Disorder and Decline: Crime and the Spiral of Decay in American Neighborhoods.* New York: Free Press.

Spergel, I. A. 1990. Youth Gangs: Continuity and Change. In *Crime and Justice: A Review of the Research, Vol. 12,* edited by Michael Tonry and Norval Morris. Chicago: University of Chicago Press.

Tittle, C. R. 1995. *Control Balance: Toward a General Theory of Deviance.* Boulder, CO: Westview Press.

U.S. Department of Justice. Office of Juvenile Justice and Delinquency Prevention. 1993. *Comprehensive Strategy for Serious, Violent, and Chronic Juvenile Offenders: Program Summary.* Washington, D.C.: U.S. Department of Justice.

Walker, Samuel. 1998. *Sense and Nonsense About Crime and Drugs.* 4th ed. Belmont, CA: Wadsworth Publishing Co.

Williams, F. P. and Marilyn D. McShane. 1988. *Criminological Theory.* Englewood Cliffs, NJ: Prentice Hall.

Wilson, James Q. and Richard J. Hernstein. 1985. *Crime and Human Nature: The Definitive Study of the Causes of Crime.* New York: Touchstone/Simon and Schuster.

Winfree, L. T., Kathy Fuller, Teresa Vigil, and G. Larry Mays. 1992. The Definitions and Measurement of "Gang Status": Policy Implications for Juvenile Justice. *Juvenile and Family Court Journal* 43(1): 29–38.

Wolfgang, M. R. M. F. and Thorsten Sellin. 1972. *Delinquency in a Birth Cohort.* Chicago: University of Chicago Press.

VALUES IN LAW ENFORCEMENT

Police officer Peter Davis of the NYPD K-9 unit stands with Apollo, who is wearing a velcro-fastened bulletproof vest designed to protect K-9 dogs searching buildings for dangerous suspects. February 1997 (AP/Wide World Photos)

THE IMPORTANCE OF VALUES

Law enforcement officials do what their name implies, but they do much more as well. What law enforcement officers and policing officials do and how they perform those duties frequently requires choices between competing social values. This chapter explores those values, the sources thereof, and the implications for policing. Some of these values are obvious and stem from the need for social order. Enforcing the law and keeping social order are reasons why many choose lifelong careers in policing. Other values are less clear but are the basis of the process of policing in a democracy. Still other values involve personal judgment between competing values that are never very clear, even to objective researchers.

What decisions do officers make in performing their job? Is a minor arrest so important if in the process of making it, one violates constitutional principles that the courts have made clear? Would officers do it if they knew they could get away with it? Do feelings about the issue change if the stakes are higher? How far can officers go in undercover operations before they are part of the problem? Can everyone agree that a bribe to destroy evidence is wrong? If so, why do some officers have such a hard time ignoring (and refusing) offers of free food or other day-to-day items that merchants attempt to shower on law enforcement officers? Are officers embattled by the community, or are they part of it?

Does one's perspective alter the answers to these ethical and value-referenced questions? Answers to these ethical questions are not offered or claimed in this chapter. Rather, the purpose here is to suggest that there are competing demands about values and ethics that present themselves to law enforcement officers. Readers are asked to think about them and defend their answers in an ethical and reasoned manner in light of the values of policing.

What Are Values?

One formal definition states that **values** are "something for which one has an enduring preference; an enduring belief that a specific mode of conduct or end-state of existence is personally or socially preferable to an opposite or inverse mode of conduct or end-state existence" (Rokeach 1973). In his 1992 article, then Chief Cornelius J. Behan of the Baltimore County (MD) Police Department put it this way: "Values are not a set of rules, but rather beliefs held so strongly that they affect the way we think and act." In essence, then, values are strongly held beliefs that help guide our actions. Values assist in setting priorities. Mentally, one can ask, "What are my priorities? What do I value?" In policing, the same question is asked as well as another: "What are my agency's priorities? What does it value?" These questions are what this chapter explores.

Values are not the same as ethics. However, they are related. Ethics refers to the decision-making process of choosing a course of action. Values and what one deems important (strongly held beliefs) impact the decision made. Therefore, when faced with an ethical question, values play a role in the decision (Chapter 15 also discusses ethics in light of the quest for professionalism).

It is important for the student of policing to explore the nature of the values that are discussed here and how balancing those values is central to a democratic society. The content of these values and the means by which we manage their balancing are the substance of public administrative morality and ethics. While the questions are sometimes more pronounced for law enforcement officers, the implications for the society are the same. All law enforcement agencies have an **organizational culture**, which essentially provides the "basic philosophy and beliefs of the agency." This culture helps guide officer behavior and decisions. It is important that an agency develop a positive culture that insures the proper behavior of its personnel. This is enhanced by developing a set of values. Exhibit 6–1 identifies the many purposes that values serve.

Exhibit 6–1

THE PURPOSES OF AGENCY VALUES

An understanding of the agency's values can serve the following purposes:

- They set forth the agency's philosophy of policing.
- They state in clear terms what an agency believes.
- They articulate in broad terms the overall goals of the agency.
- They reflect the community's expectations.
- They serve as a basis for developing policies and procedures.
- They serve as the parameters for organizational flexibility.
- They provide the basis for operational strategies.
- They provide the framework for officer performance.
- They provide criteria with which the department can be evaluated.

The characteristics of values help to explain why many emphasize their importance in organizational culture. According to Whisenand (1981, 40–53), these characteristics include the following:

- They are at the center of our lives—they serve as priorities in our decision making and activities.
- They function as "standards" of behavior—values act as informal guidelines or rules for our actions. As such, they are forces within us that help cause us to obey and behave appropriately.
- They serve as conflict resolvers—values can help us determine a course of action when confronted with conflicting issues or situations.
- They are stimuli for thinking—reflecting on values helps stimulate thought and contemplation about matters of importance.
- They strongly influence one's emotional state of mind—values impact our emotions and can assist us in keeping our composure or allowing us to become upset.
- They can act as motivators—deep-rooted beliefs (values) affect our drives to perform or act; they impact self-motivation.
- They are stable, relatively unchanging but can change over time or because of a "significant emotional event"—although stable and somewhat resistant to change, they can change slowly over time or more rapidly because of significant emotional events that occur in our lives (such as becoming a victim, losing a loved one to illness, or because of a sudden accident or suicide).

Values can be articulated into an agency's culture by establishing them in writing and disseminating them to agency personnel. An example of this is the core values statement of the Ohio State Highway Patrol illustrated in Exhibit 6–2.

Exhibit 6–2

CORE VALUES OF THE OHIO STATE HIGHWAY PATROL

These "core values" are what make an Ohio State trooper what he or she is. They are simple, yet very important, and are the foundation upon which a new trooper can become a consummate public servant. The core values of the Highway Patrol are:

Honesty—The single most reliable mark of a trooper's value is to be able to admit when he/she is wrong and go forward.

Sense of Urgency—Troopers realize the importance of prompt response to crashes and other calls for service.

Attention to Detail—If it is worth doing, it's worth doing thoroughly. Attention to detail is the mark of a good public servant.

Team Oriented—Members of the Patrol, and members of the law enforcement community in general, are a team, of which the individual components are not as valuable as the whole.

Professionalism—Being professional means being punctual, courteous, prepared, and well-groomed. It also means having and showing respect for every person a trooper encounters.

Adaptability—Troopers must maintain flexibility with a high degree of performance. A trooper's job is never the same from one day to the next— s/he must be able to make changes and still perform the job to the highest degree.

Self-Discipline—Or stated another way, Accountability. Every trooper must recognize what job needs to be done, and then do that job well. Law enforcement officers have a responsibility to those they serve to be accountable for their actions.

Performance Driven—Being performance driven means working hard. Troopers are driven to perform because success is measured in both quantity and quality. We are constantly reminded of our department mission . . . to save lives, reduce injuries and economic losses on the streets and highways of Ohio.

Officer Safety—This is the final core value that we instill in our troopers. They must maintain a high level of awareness in every situation.

Courtesy of Ohio State Highway Patrol, Columbus, Ohio.

Mission Statements as Values

Not all police agencies have a formal stated values statement. Many have incorporated basic values into a formal **mission statement.** An agency's mission is usually stated in very broad terms and concepts; it says something about the overall purpose or philosophy of the agency. Review the mission statements contained in Exhibits 6–3 and 6–4 for basic values that are expected to be part of the agencies' standards.

MODELS OF THE CRIMINAL JUSTICE SYSTEM

There are different ideas about the role of the criminal justice system in general and law enforcement in particular. Some efforts have been made over the years to articulate these in systems, or **models,** that place differing views in contrast to each other. A model is an estimate or representation of how major concepts or processes are thought to interrelate in the real world. Herbert Packer (1968) offered two opposing views of the criminal justice system in his book *The Limits of the Criminal Sanction.* He argued that there were two very different views of how the criminal justice system operated or should operate. One of these views he called the **crime control model** the other, the **due process model.** Each model is based upon certain values, or principles, that frame the meaning of each.

While the two models embody differing views and values, some values are held in common. For example, both models attempt to achieve a sense of justice, and both argue that the use of power by the state against an individual must be severely restricted. Still, despite certain similarities, Packer contended that the two models are very different in terms of very important values.

The Crime Control Model

Modern debates over crime and justice echo the claim of the crime control model. In this model, the most important principle of the criminal justice system is the suppression of crime. The second most important principle is a demand for efficiency in the process of screening suspects, determining guilt, and assessing penalties. The faster this is done, and the more certain the end, the better the system is working. To maintain efficiency, the system depends upon informality and the elimination of challenges (hearings and trials). Success is judged by ensuring that those who are truly innocent are rejected at the beginning while those who are clearly guilty meet swift conviction. Lastly, and most profoundly, a "presumption of guilt" is attached to those who are charged. Hence, Packer concluded, the two expected and preferred outcomes were either exoneration or quick guilty pleas.

Exhibit 6–3

THE HONOLULU POLICE DEPARTMENT MISSION STATEMENT

In late 1994, then Chief Michael Nakamura brought together a group of employees from all facets of the department. He charged them with the task of formulating a mission statement which would guide our department into the future. These sworn officers and civilian employees turned to their roots as members of our community, and examined their experiences living in this special place we call Hawaii. What they developed represents our mission and values of the Honolulu Police Department. It speaks for itself:

MISSION STATEMENT

We, the men and women of the Honolulu Police Department, are dedicated to providing excellent service through partnerships that build trust, reduce crime, create a safe environment, and enhance the quality of life in our community. We are committed to these principles:

INTEGRITY

We have integrity. We adhere to the highest moral and ethical standards. We are honest and sincere in dealing with each other and the community. We have the courage to uphold these principles and are proud that they guide us in all we do.

RESPECT

We show respect. We recognize the value of our unique cultural diversity and treat all people with kindness, tolerance, and dignity. We cherish and protect the rights, liberties, and freedoms of all as granted by the constitutions and laws of the United States and the State of Hawaii.

FAIRNESS

We act with fairness. Objective, impartial decisions and policies are the foundation of our interactions. We are consistent in our treatment of all persons. Our actions are tempered with reason and equity.

. . . in the spirit of Aloha.

Courtesy of Honolulu Police Department, Honolulu, Hawaii.

Exhibit 6–4

ARIZONA DEPARTMENT OF PUBLIC SAFETY

Employee Empowerment, Mission and Vision Statements

EMPLOYEE EMPOWERMENT

When faced with a decision, ask yourself:

- *Is it the right thing for the public and the state's citizens?*

- *Is it the right thing for the Arizona Department of Public Safety?*

- *Is it ethical?*

- *Is it legal?*

- *When practical, have those being impacted by the decision been considered and consulted?*

- *Is it something you are willing to be accountable for?*

If the answer is YES to all of these questions, then go ahead and make the decision.

MISSION STATEMENT

To enforce state laws, deter criminal activity, assure highway and public safety, and provide vital scientific, technical and operational support to other criminal justice agencies in furtherance of the protection of human life and property.

VISION STATEMENT

The Arizona Department of Public Safety is a statewide law enforcement agency committed to providing professional quality police and support services to the public and to the criminal justice community while fostering a caring and supportive environment for our employees.

Through dedication to total quality concepts and innovative leadership, the Arizona Department of Public Safety will capitalize on its resources to provide the highest quality service now and into the 21st century.

Courtesy of The Arizona Department of Public Safety, Phoenix, Arizona.

The Due Process Model

While Packer saw the crime control model as an assembly line in a factory, the due process model is more akin to an obstacle course. This model rejects the premise that police and the prosecution can obtain an accurate account of a criminal event via the informal process of investigation. Moreover, adherents to this model expect that all possible errors in guilt determination should be eliminated. Hence, it does not focus on just **factual guilt** (the defendant committed the crime). Rather, it focuses on **legal guilt,** which is the ability of the system to obtain a finding of guilt that is free of procedural or factual errors. In this model, Packer views the criminal justice system as so powerful that it needs to be controlled, and any doubts about the goals sought by this power should be resolved against the state. Figure 6–1 summarizes the competing values and priorities of Packer's models.

CRIME CONTROL MODEL	DUE PROCESS MODEL
Repression of criminal conduct is the paramount function of the criminal process.	Justice is achieved according to prescribed formal procedures of the law.
Criminal conduct is seen as a breakdown of public order and threat to a person's liberty.	It emphasizes eliminating mistakes which could convict innocent persons.
The criminal process is to insure social freedom by controlling crime.	The criminal process is to ensure individual rights and protections.
Efficiency of operation is highly valued, which expects a high rate of apprehensions and convictions.	Emphasis is on establishing legal guilt through adherence to rules of evidence and constitutional safeguards.
There is a presumption of guilt as a prediction of outcome.	There is a presumption of innocence as a guide to treating the accused.
It is assembly line justice based on factual guilt and many guilty pleas.	It is obstacle course justice based on factual guilt plus legal guilt.
Authority of the system is validated through the legislature.	Authority of the system is validated through the judiciary.

Source: Adapted with permission from H. L. Packer. Two Models of the Criminal Process, *The University of Pennsylvania Law Review,* Vol. 11, pp. 1–23, © 1964, University of Pennsylvania Law Review.

Figure 6–1 Competing Values in Packer's Models of Criminal Justice

Conflicting Values

In a sense, these two models represent the polar opposites of demands made upon law enforcement today. These demands are encountered more profoundly by patrol and investigations than at other levels of law enforcement. Officers are expected to solve crimes and get the responsible party, but they are blamed when their efforts result in events that lead to the suppression of evidence or tainted confessions. The expectation for quick and efficient resolution of crimes leads to sidestepping some of the same protections that the public also demands. When this happens, police abuse of authority is likely, as exemplified in Exhibit 6–5.

This conflict of values is clear, but difficult to resolve. Hence, from these two models we see two distinct sets of values from which law enforcement draws. It is interesting, and problematic, that the law enforcement culture identifies more with the crime control model than with the due process model. This creates tremendous organizational and managerial problems. As we will note later, reliance on the crime control model and its values is incompatible with implementation of community policing.

Recent calls for civilian review boards to watch and judge police actions is similarly focused on the need for civilian intervention in law enforcement agencies (Hensley 1988). While the use of civilian review boards is not yet common practice in the United States, it seems to represent a rising demand for more accountability from law enforcement. This is a genuine concern for patrol and supervisory officers, since it is likely to be actions at the line level that spark discussions and investigations of department policy.

Balancing Values

What is the patrol or supervisory officer to make of such issues? Are not these issues settled by command personnel, senior management, courts, and legislators? In a manner of speaking, patrol officers and their supervisors cannot directly impact the range of values from which they select when making decisions. The selection is done by the political process, which involves courts, legislators, and political executives such as mayors and governors. The problem, of course, is that these decision makers select all of these values. One can see from early analysis that these values are in conflict. Patrol and supervisory officers are left the problem of balancing these competing demands on the streets of the United States.

The act of balancing these competing demands is guided by regulations and training. Therefore, patrol and supervisory personnel must understand the competing demands while at the same time accept regulations as achieving the purpose of value enforcement. Understanding comes from training that is value-related. Training must, therefore, make clear the values at issue and set out the acceptable limits of each value. This must be reinforced by the training of field

Exhibit 6–5

NEW YORK CITY'S "DIRTY 30" SCANDAL NETS ITS FIRST SUPERVISORS

An additional 14 police officers assigned to a New York City precinct battered by an ongoing drug-corruption scandal were arrested recently on charges that included stealing and selling drugs, extortion, tampering with evidence, and perjury.

The arrests, which occurred Sept. 28, brought the total number of officers implicated in the scandal to 29 so far this year—nearly one-sixth of the personnel assigned to the 191-officer 30th Precinct in Harlem.

And, for the first time since arrests began in March, two sergeants—11-year veteran Richard J. McGauley, 36, and 10-year veteran Kevin P. Nannery—were charged with crimes, making this the most sweeping corruption scandal involving a single precinct in the history of the 31,000-officer Police Department.

Nannery is alleged to have led a crew of at least six officers—known as "Nannery's Raiders"—who broke down apartment doors to steal drugs, guns and cash in incidents that investigators said occurred throughout 1992 and 1993. The officers allegedly faked police radio and 911 emergency calls to make their raids on narcotics dealers, most of them Dominican immigrants.

"These officers not only committed crimes and then lied about it, they also manipulated the system for their own gain," said Manhattan District Attorney Robert M. Morgenthau, whose agency spearheaded the probe. Morgenthau said the repeated acts of perjury committed by some of the accused officers already had caused the dismissal of 11 criminal cases, with another 50 expected to be thrown out in the next few months.

Five of the officers from the "Dirty 30"—as the precinct has been dubbed—immediately pleaded guilty and agreed to cooperate with state and Federal prosecutors against their fellow officers. Charges against one of the 29 officers have been dropped, while seven others have been on modified duty since the spring, pending completion of the investigation.

Source: Reprinted with permission from *Law Enforcement News,* Vol. 20, No. 411, p. 7, © 1994, John Jay College of Criminal Justice.

---

training officers (FTOs; see Chapter 11 for a further discussion of training). The value conflicts must also be reflected in the training and supervision of both probationary and permanent employees. Finally, officers must be encouraged to enforce the regulations and support values established by the political authority. It is critical in a democracy that public employees understand that they are not policy makers; they are public servants. Servant status requires adherence to values established outside the process of administration.

This is a key aspect of recruitment, training, promotion, and retention, as well as discipline and leadership. Patrol and supervisory officers are the front line in values-adherence by law enforcement. If these levels of the organization do not accept and apply certain values, the department will continue to violate laws, constitutional provisions, regulations, or standards.

The problem for both patrol and supervisory personnel is that the two models of the criminal justice system discussed so far give very little assistance in finding a means to balance the two conflicting sets of values. Yet a balance is necessary. A balancing approach can be established by management if the values of the organization (set by management and political authority) are integrated into the administrative systems and organizational culture of the department (Wasserman and Moore 1988). Where does management get these values, and what sort of outside influences are important for patrol and supervisory officers to understand? Let us examine some efforts at defining values for public servants in and out of law enforcement and gain an understanding of how they might apply to patrol and supervision officers.

SOURCES OF VALUES

If we want officers to make ethical and value-based decisions, two steps must be taken. First, values must be identified and articulated. Second, those values must be reinforced at every stage of the organizational process through rules, training, policy, and discipline. But where do we look for these values? A number of sources can be identified.

The Two Models

Regarding the first step, we have already identified some of the values underlying the entire criminal justice process: (1) Those values related to the need to efficiently determine the perpetrators of crimes (crime control model), and (2) the desire to protect the individual rights of the defendant (due process model). At their polar opposites, these values are not consistent. In reality, each is altered and integrated into a process that more or less approaches the intentions of the two sets of value systems. Pure efficiency is sacrificed for fundamental fairness, while the demand for absolute and unbending rules for actions like search and seizure give way to a more enlightened acknowledgment of the complexity of normal human affairs. Therefore, the faster approach of searching without a warrant is not favored. However, the many exceptions to the "warrant requirement" suggest that the warrant requirement is not an immutable rule (see Chapter 12 for a discussion about these exceptions).

Search and seizure are not the only considerations, of course. In other portions of this text the authors have addressed other concerns that stem from values that require certain adherence by law enforcement. One of these is the use of unnecessary force. Concern for this issue tends to stem from the potential civil and criminal legal implications for officers who step over the boundaries. However, it should also stem from a concern for fellow human beings and citizens. For example, some in law enforcement defended the actions of officers in the Rodney King case largely due to King's criminal record. But at the time of the officer's actions, that information was not known to them. Based on what they knew, they acted without justification. Worse, knowing more would not have justified their actions. An underlying value for law enforcement, therefore, must be the preservation of life and the avoidance of unnecessary violence. These commands come from the Fifth and Eighth Amendments to the Constitution of the United States, which guarantee, respectively, due process before the deprivation of life, liberty, or property and the prohibition of cruel and unusual punishment (see the Bill of Rights in Appendix I).

Agencies Themselves

With the advent of the accreditation process (see Chapter 15), many law enforcement agencies have prepared their own statement of values. Exhibits 6–2, 6–3, and 6–4 above exemplify some of the agencies that have incorporated values into their formalized statements. Another example of this is found in Exhibit 6–6.

Wasserman and Moore (1988) warn about the problems associated with agency values:

> Police departments are powerfully influenced by their values. The problem is that police departments, like many organizations, are guided by **implicit values** that are often at odds with **explicit values**. This breeds confusion, distrust, and cynicism rather than clarity, commitment, and high morale.

They are saying that implied, informal (implicit) values of the agency can conflict with the formal, publicly (explicitly) stated values. Unless this conflict is resolved toward the explicit values (which are usually preferred), the agency and its personnel probably will not reflect the appropriate professional standards of behavior (Kleinig and Shang 1993). One of the many challenges for administrators and managers is to ensure that explicitly stated values take precedence over contrary implicit values.

Other Government Sources

While recognizing that each department must develop its own set of values, the Community Relations Service of the U.S. Department of Justice (1987) has compiled a set of generic "values for good policing":

1. The police department must preserve and advance the principles of democracy.

Exhibit 6–6

JACKSONVILLE SHERIFF'S OFFICE CORE VALUES

COMMUNITY FOCUSED

The community is our customer. As such, it is the community who must define quality service. We will form partnerships with our citizens and listen to them. We will stay close. We will remember that every contact between a member of the community and any part of the Sheriff's Office is where community opinion is formed.

ALWAYS IMPROVING

Our business is service. The only way we can improve our business is to improve our service. We are constantly in a learning mode. We are willing to examine what we do and make changes to improve.

WORTHY OF TRUST

The Jacksonville Sheriff's Office has achieved its reputation as a premier law enforcement agency because it has earned the trust of the community. We will safeguard that trust. We will keep our promises. Whether on or off duty, we will behave according to the highest set of ethical standards. We will protect the rights of all citizens.

RESPECT FOR EACH OTHER

Employees deserve a decent working environment, one in which relationships are characterized by mutual respect. We will listen actively, talk straight and act fairly. We will encourage each other and every employee to contribute and grow to his/her fullest potential. We will work together as a TEAM and appreciate the contributions of all.

Courtesy of Jacksonville, Florida Sheriff's Department, Jacksonville, Florida.

---

2. The police department places its highest value on the preservation of human life.
3. The police department believes that the prevention of crime is its number one operational priority.
4. The police department will involve the community in the delivery of its services.

5. The police department believes it must be accountable to the community it serves.
6. The police department is committed to professionalism in all aspects of its operations.
7. The police department will maintain the highest standards of integrity.

This list forms an excellent basis for developing agency values that can be incorporated into policy, training material, supervisory operations, and standards of behavior.

The documents that form the basis of the United States government are a source of fundamental values to be echoed by law enforcement agencies. The Declaration of Independence, the Constitution, the Bill of Rights, and the subsequent Amendments to the U.S. Constitution provide the principles that guide our governmental system. Since the police function is, in part, one mechanism to assure the maintenance of the country, the values expressed in its founding documents must be given high priority. These documents establish a number of principles that must be valued and respected by all public officials:

1. FEDERALISM: A dual system of governmental power; the sharing or dividing of power between state and national government, each with its own sphere of influence.
2. SEPARATION OF POWERS: The concept of dividing power among the various "branches of government."
3. CHECKS AND BALANCES SYSTEM: The complex process of allocating powers and responsibilities to each branch of government. Each branch can then "watch" the other branch and attempt to "counter" out any actions deemed inappropriate or undesired.
4. RULE OF LAW: Government of laws, not of men; authority derived from the people (as opposed to a dictatorship, noble class, etc.); it is the law that grants the authority to act.
5. INDIVIDUAL RIGHTS AND RESPONSIBILITIES: Our system of government strongly believes in individual rights, especially as they relate to the criminal justice process. These "rights" refer to proper authority and legitimacy while "responsibility" refers to the obligation owed to another.
6. ADVERSARY SYSTEM OF JUSTICE: Two sides compete against the other according to prescribed rules to determine guilt. Our system pits the "state" against the accused, the "defendant."
7. ACCUSATORY SYSTEM: A system in which the government must prove suspicion and guilt. The burden of proof is on the state.
8. DUE PROCESS OF LAW: Doctrine requiring government to proceed against individuals according to the prescribed rules and constitutional protections; the application of law in its established, fair, and regular manner; the proper and normal course of the law.

9. PROBABLE CAUSE: A legal standard for initiating certain action against a person, such as arrest and obtaining a search warrant. Often defined as the facts and circumstances that would lead a reasonable person to believe that a crime has been, is being, or will be committed and that a specific person is responsible.
10. PROOF BEYOND A REASONABLE DOUBT: Standard of guilt in criminal law that means there needs to be a very substantial amount of evidence of guilt before convicting a person; it is not absolute proof; it is not proof beyond a shadow of a doubt.
11. FACTUAL GUILT plus LEGAL GUILT: Factual guilt means that the accused did in fact commit the crime or the act in question. Legal guilt means that the accused was properly brought to trial, provided due process, and given proper procedural rights.
12. TRIAL BY JURY: A fundamental belief from English common law that protects the accused from arbitrary, dictatorial decisions by government.
13. FAIRNESS and EQUALITY UNDER THE LAW: Equal treatment of the accused regardless of race, color, creed, sex, national origin, status, or socio-economic level.

It should be remembered that law enforcement officials (like most elected officials) take an oath "to uphold the Constitution of the United States." One can ask, "How can a person take such an oath if he or she does not know what the Constitution says or represents?" If a person cannot accept the principles and values expressed in the U.S. Constitution and other founding documents, that person should NOT consider a career in the criminal justice system.

Professional Associations

The police function has been the focus of study and review for professional associations interested in the criminal justice system. In the early 1970s, the American Bar Association published *The Urban Police Function*, which identified 11 distinct functions of policing. Some discuss these in the context of the police role (Chapter 7). However, the functions are identified in Exhibit 6–7 because they also serve as underlying values of policing.

In contrast, the International Association of Chiefs of Police (IACP) has not identified a specific set of policing values. However, it has compiled a series of statements related to police behavior from which values can be inferred. They include a Police Code of Ethics, a Police Code of Conduct, and Canons of Police Ethics, all of which are discussed and reprinted in Chapter 15.

Theories of Policing

Another set of sources for values are new theories of law enforcement, such as community policing. This approach to policing is not old; it is genuinely new.

Exhibit 6–7

MAJOR RESPONSIBILITIES OF THE POLICE

1. To identify criminal offenders and criminal activity and, where appropriate, to apprehend offenders and participate in later court proceedings;
2. To reduce the opportunities for the commission of some crimes through preventive patrol and other measures;
3. To aid individuals who are in danger of physical harm;
4. To protect constitutional guarantees;
5. To facilitate the movement of people and vehicles;
6. To help those who cannot care for themselves;
7. To resolve conflict;
8. To identify potentially serious law enforcement or governmental problems;
9. To create and maintain a feeling of security in the community;
10. To promote and preserve civil order; and
11. To provide other services on an emergency basis.

Source: Major Responsibilities of the Police, *ABA Standards for Criminal Justice—Urban Police Function*, p. 53, © 1972, ABA Publishing. Reprinted by Permission.

It requires departments to work closely with "law-abiding people in the community, allowing them a greater voice in setting local police priorities and involving them in efforts to improve the overall quality of life in their neighborhoods. It shifts the focus of police work from handling random calls to solving community problems" (Trojanowicz and Bucqueroux 1990). Such an approach implies a shift of focus from police-defined activities to community-defined activities. This philosophical shift in values is further described in Exhibit 6–8.

APPROACHES TO GOVERNMENT

The mix of values so far discussed includes efficiency, individual rights, and community input and control. These values reflect those that dominate most of the discussions about values in the field of public management (or public administration) generally. It might be helpful, therefore, for law enforcement officers to understand how other public officers respond to the examination of values. While each area of public management is likely to see itself as very

Exhibit 6–8

THE PHILOSOPHICAL SHIFT TO COMMUNITY POLICING

Philosophy/Strategy/Tactic—Though a semantic debate about whether a new concept is a philosophy, a strategy, or merely a tactic may sound like quibbling, experience shows that a failure to understand how broadly a new concept must be applied can doom a promising new idea before it has a chance to demonstrate what it can do. In this context, a *philosophy* is defined as what you think and believe, a *strategy* is how you put the philosophy into practice, and a *tactic* is one method that can be used to achieve a narrowly defined goal.

To understand the distinctions, for the sake of argument, suppose that you have decided to adopt a personal philosophy based on *brotherly love*. The next step is for you to develop a coherent strategy to express that philosophy in your behavior. This might require making a personal commitment that all future personal interactions must be based on honesty, respect, compassion, courtesy, and sensitivity to the other person's needs. One tactic you might choose to employ would be to make a habit of saying *please* and *thank you*. Another might be to mark a calendar with all your friends' birthdays, so that you never forget to send a card or make a call.

As this illustrates, a philosophical change must find its expression in a coherent strategy—just believing in brotherly love is not enough if it does not alter your behavior. A tactic plays a far more limited role—after all, people can say *please* and *thank you* without having any commitment to brotherly love.

This helps explain why it is crucial to understand that Community Policing is a new philosophy that offers a coherent strategy that departments can use to guide them in making the structural changes that allow the concept to become real. Community Policing is not just a tactic that can be applied to solve a particular problem, one that can be abandoned once the goal is achieved. It implies a profound difference in the way the police view their role. Just adopting one or more tactics associated with Community Policing is not enough. Conversely, departments that embrace Community Policing must not only change the way they think, but the way they act.

Source: Reprinted with permission from R. Trojanowicz and B. Bucqueroux, *Community Policing: A Contemporary Perspective,* p. 5, © 1990, Anderson Publishing Co.

different from every other area, the values that dominate the daily activities of any agency are very similar.

David Rosenbloom (1993) of American University in Washington, DC, argues that there are three major competing "approaches" to public management. These are drawn from the history of government in the United States and the efforts to reform and change government covering two hundred years of American history. While the approaches are continually evolving, they offer much to students of government and practitioners alike (Zhiyong and Rosenbloom 1992). Essentially, the three *approaches* are really *traditions* and parallel much of the public discussion about government. Law enforcement officers will note that these approaches also parallel much of the discussion about the criminal justice community in general and law enforcement in particular. They are traditions because the roots of each approach to managing are deep in American political culture and history. They could also be thought of as "models of public management" since each represents a particular focus or manner of managing the public's business: managerial, political, and legal. The idea of models of public management is important for both patrol and supervisory officers, since the task of enforcing laws falls primarily upon them and is clearly a part of the public's business. Each of these models is discussed in the following sections.

Managerial Model

The model of managing the public's business that most resembles the crime control model of Packer is the **managerial model** of public management. In its own way, law enforcement had a large hand to play in the development of this perspective. In the aftermath of the American Revolution of 1776, government was run by the elite few. These were primarily white males with education and property, most importantly the latter. By the 1820s, the view that government was "out of touch" with the common person was very strong, resulting in the election of Andrew Jackson as President in 1828. There were also changes in many state constitutions creating "long ballots," which essentially guaranteed that most public offices would be elected, not appointed. If you look at your state government, for example, you will note that your attorney general, secretary of state, and treasurer are elected. At the federal level, they are appointed. Jackson won on the proposition, among others, that he should be permitted to hire whomever did the job for him. Then, if the people were dissatisfied with the production of government, they could vote in a new President who would replace the government with new people. It was a simple and, many thought, democratic model.

What happened, of course, was that **political machines** were formed. Some were Democratic, others Republican (after 1860), but the effect was the same. In virtually every state or city, one party controlled the government, and if you wanted a job with the government, you needed to "pay" for it both with loyalty to the party and, frequently, with cash (see Exhibit 6–9). Sometimes this was a prepayment and usually involved a portion of each paycheck.

Exhibit 6–9

THE PRICE MUST BE RIGHT

. . . Despite regulations requiring that recruits pass physical, medical, and literacy tests and have no criminal record or outstanding debts, the real requirement for a recruit was a political sponsor from the machine. The payment to the machine for a job was either made in political loyalty or money or both. In the 1890s, patrolmen had to pay $300 for their jobs in New York City and $400 in San Francisco. With the correct political support, all the requirements for the recruit would be forthcoming: syphilitics would pass medical exam; criminals and illiterates joined the force as easily.

As valuable as the patrolman's job was, appointment to higher positions in the department cost the applicant even more. The going rate in New York City was a payment to the party machine of $1,600 for a sergeant's job, and upwards of $12,000 for a captaincy.

How could policemen pay the party organization more for a captain's job than the job would pay in salary? The answer was that the captain was normally expected to make more money from graft than the $12,000 he had to pay the ward boss for the job. Here again, the connection with the local vice operations was all-important, for "the police did not suppress vice; they licensed it"—for a fee. The license to operate a den of sin came with a payoff, either directly to the machine or, more normally, to a low-level police "bag man" who took his share then passed it up the police hierarchy to the local political boss, each taking a larger share. This practice applied to burglary rings as well as prostitution or gambling operations.

Source: J. H. Knott and G. J. Miller, *Reforming Bureaucracy: The Politics of Institutional Choice*, © 1987. Reprinted by permission of Prentice-Hall,Inc., Upper Saddle River, NJ.

Obviously, this sort of arrangement had its problems. First, justice was distributed not by equal treatment but by party affiliation. Second, people were not hired for their skill or professionalism, such as it was then, but rather for their ability to get out the vote. This sort of problem existed at every level of government. Pressure built for more changes in government, and in the 1890s the revolt called the Progressive Reform Movement was given life (also see Chapter 3).

The Progressive Reform Movement had many facets, but the one that interests us most is the focus on how government was managed. A young government professor, fresh from earning his Ph.D. at Johns Hopkins University, noted in an 1887 essay that it was time for government to be run *more like a business* by separating politics from the administration of the public's business (Wilson 1887). One of the solutions this future President proposed was the use of a civil service system so that hiring would be on merit alone, and job performance assessment would be based upon the professional skill needed for the work. Political decisions were to be excluded from the management of government. Woodrow Wilson began a monumental debate concerning the role of merit versus political control of administration, a debate that has raged for nearly 110 years.

The values that this approach to management embraced were efficiency and effectiveness as well as an attempt at economizing in the delivery of services. Of course, the only way to manage such a system was to have a hierarchy of authority based upon continually improving skill. Finally, personal preference was excluded from all government decisions in this approach. Individuals were treated as if they were "cogs in a machine." In other words, people were interchangeable because of training and their attainment of position by merit.

In the current context of law enforcement, this model is still very much alive. Hiring is primarily by civil service, and promotion follows via the same route. The overriding ethic is to clear as many cases as possible and get convictions, and do so with the least expenditure of time and other resources. Individuals are trained for specific tasks and are generally assigned on the basis of that training. The organizational structure of most law enforcement organizations represents a true **hierarchy** designed along the **military model** (rank, uniforms, orders, etc.). Also, individuality is sacrificed for the "good of the department." True, the notion of a "brotherhood" is strong in the profession, leading to traditions like the **code of silence**. However, it comes more from a need to defend the organization (and profession) than from a need to defend the individual. Any officer who has ever testified against another knows that in most cases, the action is not well received by others in the department. The recent television show *NYPD Blue* highlighted the degree to which Internal Affairs Divisions are looked upon with disdain. Clearly, the individual is not important in this approach. Problems associated with the code of silence (secrecy) are identified in Exhibit 6–10.

There are, of course, problems with the managerial approach. First, and most importantly, values that are inconsistent with defense of the hierarchy and the pursuit of efficiency and effectiveness are rejected. This deficiency is problematic since the Constitution of the United States and each of the state constitutions limit the authority of government agents such as law enforcement officers. Moreover, government agents can be prosecuted criminally or sued civilly for actions that step over the boundaries of these limitations. Second,

Exhibit 6–10

CODE OF SILENCE

The passion for secrecy—the lust to conceal actions behind a blue veil among police who want to commit acts of corruption or brutality—amounts to a desire to draw police work away from the constraints of law and policy and into the domain of the unenforceable. Once accomplished, bad police can behave without integrity, a will and with impunity. The intimidation of otherwise decent officers is but an instrument of this passion for secrecy, and where it succeeds, it confirms the insistence of Lord Acton, the 19th-century British historian, that "everything secret degenerates, even the administration of justice; nothing is safe that does not show it can bear discussion and publicity." Secrecy, as Lord Acton knew, is far different from legitimate confidentiality.

If bad cops cannot drive out or destroy good cops, they will be content to corrupt them by entanglement in a web of secrecy, whether it is woven of fear and a related willingness to go along to get along, or supported by cynicism about the department itself and by feelings of contempt for the general public.

Source: Reprinted with permission from What Is This Noble (and Elusive) Concept We Call Integrity? *Law Enforcement News,* Vol. 21, No. 427, p. 8, © 1995, John Jay College of Criminal Justice.

the structure of a hierarchical system has built-in limitations in its ability to manage (see Chapter 8). Third, the need for individual participation in management decisions is a key aspect of newer management theories and community policing. Hence, the values inherent in the military model may be quite disadvantaged in dealing with emerging problems that law enforcement faces (Franz and Jones 1987).

Political Model

As the discussion above indicates, there has long been a close connection between law enforcement and politics. There are several reasons for this. First, at least in recent times, crime is one of the three major issues that dominates the personal agendas of most voters and, therefore, most politicians. Second, most law enforcing is done at the local level by patrol officers and their immediate superiors. It is closer to the people and to politics than most other units of government. Finally, because law enforcement is generally a concern of local government, it is much easier to control at the local level. It offers opportunities for political interference that other segments of the government do not offer. A parallel can be drawn with school boards, another sector of government that is deeply scrutinized and frequently politicized.

In the **political model**, there is no reason to distinguish between law enforcement and other public agencies. While the kind of direct political interference typical of the 1880s has disappeared in an era of professional policing, there are still efforts to use values typical of the political model. These values argue that government should reflect and truly represent the people it serves. Further, government should be responsive to the needs of the people. Government should be politically accountable to the legislative policy makers and the ultimate policy makers, the public.

While progressive reform efforts and intense professionalism have managed to reduce political influence in the 100 years since the passage of the first civil service act, there are many efforts to reassert that political control. Many officers can recall phone conversations with city council persons about their *very special constituent* or other limited efforts at affecting the actions of law enforcement. But *organized* efforts to interfere with the decision process of law enforcement are rather recent.

One example is the use of civilian review boards. The board members may be appointed by political authority such as the mayor or county executive, they may be elected, or they may hold a seat on the board by reason of their position in another agency or organization. The makeup of such boards varies quite radically, and the purpose and authority of the boards may be dissimilar as well. The basic functions of these boards include taking and investigating citizen complaints, reviewing complaints already reviewed by the department, holding hearings on complaints, actually ordering organizational actions in response, generally reviewing department actions on its own initiative, and even participating in hiring. While this is merely a sampling of the activities in which such boards may engage, the idea is clear. This is political influence in the management of law enforcement agencies.

Another form of the reappearance of politics in management would be demand for affirmative action hiring (see Chapter 10). While parts of this demand stem from legal notions of equal protection, another body of theory found in public management calls for the democratization of bureaucracy in order to make it more responsive. The central idea behind this demand is that government operates more effectively if it represents and reflects those that it serves. This is a variation on the Jacksonian theme of 1828, and is not new to American politics.

Still other forms of political influence have been invited by law enforcement itself. Some strategies for hiring and promotion, for example, use members of the community to sit in judgment of those seeking advancement in law enforcement. While the rules and approaches to this process are relatively constrained, and the appointing authority is most usually a chief of police, it is still an invitation to political influence. Of course, political influence is not a stranger to law enforcement, since sheriffs in most counties in the United States are elected.

The biggest and most widely accepted form of political involvement in policing is the shift towards community policing. A portion of the idea of community policing is to bring the community and law enforcement together in order to address the concerns of citizens and enlist citizen assistance in crime prevention. This may take the form of community volunteers assisting law enforcement at public events or assignment of community service officers to specific community concerns not typically considered to be law enforcement. This is a mission change due to community input—and that is political action.

Law enforcement should not resent or feel negatively towards efforts to bring some political intervention back into law enforcement. Rather, law enforcement must recognize its role in a democratic society and learn to adapt to demands for improvement. In most respects, the demands for intervention would not occur but for citizen unhappiness in performance. A casual perusal of literature on law enforcement might suggest that it is no better than any other organized bureaucracy at preventing actions that citizens consider unprofessional or worse. The focus on themes such as **total quality management** and **reinventing government** is strong and growing. Law enforcement officers, particularly at the service delivery level of patrol and supervision, must be aware that they will not be overlooked as politicians, at the urging of the public, pursue the continual improvement of service. This quest is exemplified by the Code of Ethics of the American Society for Public Administration, reprinted in Exhibit 6-11.

There are, of course, problems with the political model. Unchecked, political interference in management and service delivery can be misused or diverted for personal reasons or reasons of group interest. The danger is that the result will be one of benefit to special interests and not necessarily to the public at large. One fear that the founding generation had was of a government run purely by transient public opinion. They designed a Constitution that was very stable, slow, and deliberate in its process. At the local level, once political participation is permitted in the management of an agency, the risk of momentary public opinion directing policy decisions is great. This can run in a number of directions that are troubling. For example, organized crime groups would no longer need to corrupt officers. They could influence public opinion through propaganda and then public opinion would influence public policy. Further, certain problems or areas might receive greater attention at the risk of ignoring other, more significant problems or other areas in need of intervention. Similarly, the public might demand actions that are patently illegal, unconstitutional, or unprofessional. Minority interests and viewpoints would receive little attention.

Exhibit 6–11

AMERICAN SOCIETY FOR PUBLIC ADMINISTRATION — CODE OF ETHICS

The American Society for Public Administration (ASPA) exists to advance the science, processes, and art of public administration. The Society affirms its responsibility to develop the spirit of professionalism within its membership, and to increase public awareness of ethical principles in public service by its example. To this end, we, the members of the Society, commit ourselves to the following principles:

I Serve the Public Interest

Serve the public, beyond serving oneself.

ASPA members are committed to:

1. Exercise discretionary authority to promote the public interest.
2. Oppose all forms of discrimination and harassment, and promote affirmative action.
3. Recognize and support the public's right to know the public's business.
4. Involve citizens in policy decision-making.
5. Exercise compassion, benevolence, fairness and optimism.
6. Respond to the public in ways that are complete, clear, and easy to understand.
7. Assist citizens in their dealings with government.
8. Be prepared to make decisions that may not be popular.

II Respect the Constitution and the Law

Respect, support, and study government constitutions and laws that define responsibilities of public agencies, employees, and all citizens.

ASPA members are committed to:

1. Understand and apply legislation and regulations relevant to their professional role.
2. Work to improve and change laws and policies that are counter-productive or obsolete.
3. Eliminate unlawful discrimination.

4. Prevent all forms of mismanagement of public funds by establishing and maintaining strong fiscal and management controls, and by supporting audits and investigative activities.
5. Respect and protect privileged information.
6. Encourage and facilitate legitimate dissent activities in government and protect the whistleblowing rights of public employees.
7. Promote constitutional principles of equality, fairness, representativeness, responsiveness and due process in protecting citizens' rights.

III Demonstrate Personal Integrity

Demonstrate the highest standards in all activities to inspire public confidence and trust in public service.

ASPA members are committed to:

1. Maintain truthfulness and honesty and to not compromise them for advancement, honor, or personal gain.
2. Ensure that others receive credit for their work and contributions.
3. Zealously guard against conflict of interest or its appearance: e.g., nepotism, improper outside employment, misuse of public resources or the acceptance of gifts.
4. Respect superiors, subordinates, colleagues and the public.
5. Take responsibility for their own errors.
6. Conduct official acts without partisanship.

(continues)

Exhibit 6-11 *(continued)*

IV Promote Ethical Organizations

Strengthen organizational capabilities to apply ethics, efficiency and effectiveness in serving the public.

ASPA members are committed to:

1. Enhance organizational capacity for open communication, creativity, and dedication.
2. Subordinate institutional loyalties to the public good.
3. Establish procedures that promote ethical behavior and hold individuals and organizations accountable for their conduct.
4. Provide organization members with an administrative means for dissent, assurance of due process and safeguards against reprisal.
5. Promote merit principles that protect against arbitrary and capricious actions.
6. Promote organizational accountability through appropriate controls and procedures.
7. Encourage organizations to adopt, distribute, and periodically review a code of ethics as a living document.

V Strive for Professional Excellence

Strengthen individual capabilities and encourage the professional development of others.

ASPA members are committed to:

1. Provide support and encouragement to upgrade competence.
2. Accept as a personal duty the responsibility to keep up to date on emerging issues and potential problems.
3. Encourage others, throughout their careers, to participate in professional activities and associations.
4. Allocate time to meet with students and provide a bridge between classroom studies and the realities of public service.

Enforcement of the Code of Ethics shall be conducted in accordance with Article I, Section 4 of ASPA's Bylaws. In 1981 the American Society for Public Administration's National Council adopted a set of moral principles. Three years later in 1984, the Council approved a Code of Ethics for ASPA members. In 1994 the Code was revised.

Source: Copyright © American Society for Public Administration.

The topic of political input into a law enforcement agency, therefore, is not simple to address. Law enforcement cannot and should not avoid political input into its decision process. At the same time, the method and means by which this is done must be moderated in order to preserve professional and constitutional concerns relating to the abuse of power and the effective enforcement of law. Patrol and supervisory personnel must be alert and sensitive to the competing demands for professional service and citizen control of the process.

Legal Intervention Model

Those who study public agencies in general also examine the impact of the legal system on public management. While this subject is treated in a purely legal context in Chapter 12, we need to examine its management impact, particularly for the values it implies for patrol officers and supervisors. The values that underlie public management must include those that flow from the Constitution of the United States and the various state constitutions. The impact of these values increased dramatically in the 1940s through the 1960s, as more and more court decisions focused on *how* government did its job. One of the most visible impacts was on law enforcement. The rules courts set out for search and seizure and interrogation, to name but two areas, had an immediate impact on day-to-day operations. But much of the discussion about legal rights can be summarized in a few basic value statements. Officers can and must learn the specific limitations on their actions as public servants. They ignore the underlying value system at their own risk. It is difficult to remember dozens, even hundreds of specific rules. It is easier, safer, and more responsible to understand the underlying values at issue and act in the most cautious manner in making decisions that impact those values.

The central legal values are due process and equal protection. For the purposes of state and local officials, including law enforcement, the legal source for these principles comes from the Fourteenth Amendment to the Constitution of the United States (see Appendix I). This was one of the post–Civil War amendments and was intended to make certain that the states did not violate rights that were considered clear relative to the federal government. States had in fact treated people differently and regularly denied basic rights to citizens. The intention of this amendment was to end that practice. During the 120 years since its passage, the Fourteenth Amendment has undergone significant interpretations by the courts.

Due process is not very clear as terms go, and legal scholars and justices on the Supreme Court have struggled to define the concept in ways to avoid case-by-case determinations. Due process protections, in essence, are the "fundamental principles of liberty and justice which lie at the base of all our civil and political institutions," or which are "basic in our system of jurisprudence" (Gunther 1991, 422). This general notion holds for criminal and civil cases, as well as for administrative procedure (including officer disciplinary or promotion procedures).

Similarly, the idea of equal protection is not terribly clear, though the words seem to imply equality to most people. Actually, pure equality is not logically possible. For example, we make distinctions all the time. Employees' work performances differ in most organizations and are evaluated against certain standards. All employees do not receive the same evaluative ratings—most do not perform equally well in all job functions. But all employees are to be treated fairly and evaluated using the same process. Equal protection is a valued principle, not a claim that all persons perform (or behave) equally.

The two central questions concerning equal protection are these: (1) Is everyone judged by the same standard, and (2) Is the standard "reasonable"? The second question is more difficult to answer than the first. Over the past one hundred years, the courts have developed a set of complex approaches to interpret the second question (Gunther 1991, 601–608). We can summarize them as a matter of basic values. First when reviewing a prohibition, we must ask whether the state is restricting a fundamental right or if a racial or other "invidious" distinction is being made. If it is doing the latter, the state (or law enforcement officer or department) must show a very compelling interest to do so. For example, you generally cannot prevent unpopular speeches (free speech is a fundamental right) from being made or targeting a racial group (racial distinctions evoke anger and are invidious). To restrict such rights would require a very powerful reason, and there are not many (refer to Exhibit 6–12).

Exhibit 6–12

FUNDAMENTAL RIGHTS AND INVIDIOUS DISCRIMINATION

What Are Fundamental Rights?

- Freedom of Speech
- Freedom of Press
- Freedom of Religion
- All other Rights Specifically Mentioned in the Bill of Rights

Numerous other rights NOT listed in the Bill of Rights including:

- The right to marry
- The right to interstate travel
- The right to retain citizenship
- The right to associate with others
- The right to choose a profession
- The right to attend and report on criminal trials and numerous other rights

What is Invidious Discrimination?

The Supreme Court of the United States has developed a set of standards for judging both laws and actions of government servants regarding the notion of equal protection. Only distinctions that are racially made are considered truly invidious. Any such distinction is inherently assumed to be unconstitutional. However, the court has also defined some distinctions or *classifications* that are considered *suspect* or that deserve *close scrutiny*. These include gender, status as an alien, and poverty. Essentially, the court is saying that distinctions which rely upon these kinds of differences must be examined very closely and require substantial justification to pass constitutional muster.

Source: Reprinted with permission from W. Murphy, J. Fleming, and S. Barber, *American Constitutional Interpretation,* 2nd ed., pp. 1240–1241, © 1995, Foundation Press, Inc.

However, if the question is not one of fundamental rights or invidious discrimination, then the reasonableness of the restriction is the issue. Reasonableness is determined by examining a number of questions. Is this something the state may validly do? Is it designed to work? And does it work in the least restrictive manner? For example, if you were a training officer or field supervisor, could you establish different criteria for female rookies as opposed to male rookies to assess their probationary periods? There may be some justifications, but the list is very short and the justification would need to be substantial.

A little more difficult is the issue of rule enforcement. Would you strictly apply a regulation to a rookie but permit a veteran officer to "get some slack" on the same question? Prior patterns of rule application can be seen as setting a standard, and changing that standard requires good reason to do so. In other words, it would almost always be unreasonable to arbitrarily treat two people differently.

These standards are difficult for officers to understand without spending a good deal of time studying the field of constitutional law. However, you can use some handy standards to assist you. The one of "arbitrariness" is a good one. For instance, after contemplating a certain action, can you see yourself defending your decision to others who are not connected with law enforcement? If the answer is no, then it is probable that you should not do what you are thinking about doing. The other standard is whether there is a long history of using the same standard and same action. If the department consistently applies a familiar standard, you are better off keeping that standard than making up one of your own.

Also, we must judge our actions not from our own eyes, but from the eyes of the outside observer, detached from the event in question. In most cases, constitutional standards are **objective standards**, not **subjective standards**. An objective standard is one that looks at the actions in question by asking whether a *reasonable person* would have acted in that manner. A subjective standard asks whether the action is justified *from the perspective of the person taking the action*. Self-defense, for example, is a *reasonable person* standard. Similarly, good faith does not mean "I meant no harm," it means you did not know and could not have known that what you were doing was wrong or leading to harm. The idea of *whether you could know* is clearly an objective standard, not from your perspective. Hence, the question usually is "Would a reasonable officer have done this?"

The burden on officers is high. They must assess whether they are acting in a manner that conforms to the standards of due process or equal protection. These standards apply in criminal and non-criminal settings alike. They assist law enforcement as well as restrict it. This set of values most closely resembles Herbert Packer's due process model discussed above. However, the legal model of public management takes more into consideration, since it goes beyond the criminal defendant/suspect application. It also addresses the way in which agencies are administered (including hiring, promotion, and discipline). The most significant difficulty with this set of values is their complex nature and the fact that actions are interpreted by those not connected with law enforcement.

There are three distinct sets (models) of values imposed on law enforcement. Law enforcement can establish other values, and does so, but only to the extent that they are able to fit within the limits of the values set out in the three models above. More importantly, each of these models implies a different set of processes and very different roles for the individual. The problem for patrol and supervisory personnel is to understand that limits imposed by outside forces are part of a democratic system. It is imperative that the values of a law enforcement agency conform to the values imposed from outside. Failure to do so will only cause problems that are not healthy for law enforcement or the delivery of public services. The need is to learn how to balance these interests and values and accept the balance as part of the value system of law enforcement.

SUMMARY

The focus of this chapter has been on values—something for which one has an enduring preference or an enduring belief. Values help guide officer actions and assist in establishing the internal atmosphere and expectations. An examination of the sources of values indicated that they are derived from a number of reference—Packer's models of criminal justice, agency statements, government documents, and professional associations. The chapter also focused on how values are influenced by management pressures for efficiency, politics, and the legal process itself. The balancing of conflicting values is one of the major challenges facing law enforcement officials.

Any law enforcement department must make certain its values are compatible with those of outside sources. It is partly the responsibility of leaders in the organization to instill explicit values imposed by outside forces.

However, the process of instilling values in an organization cannot succeed without the active participation of patrol and supervisory officers. Community policing cannot work, in particular, unless and until the values noted in this chapter are accepted by officers at all levels and practiced as part of what officers do. In effect, law enforcement officers become the vehicles for values in a community. Just as leaders can display acceptance of poor value systems, so law enforcement officers set the tone of value importance in a community. It is often said that "Officers should do the right thing," but the test of what is right must be judged by the standards of values essential in a free society. The organizational process must reflect and reinforce these values in recruitment, hiring, training, promotion, discipline, assignment, leadership, management, structure, and client contact (victim as well as suspect).

QUESTIONS FOR REVIEW

1. What are the similarities and differences between Packer's two models of the criminal justice system?
2. What are the sources of values in law enforcement?
3. Why do agencies develop explicit statements of values?
4. What is the difference between implicit and explicit values?
5. What are differences among the managerial, political, and legal models of managing an agency?
6. What are at least 8 major values that apply to law enforcement?
7. What is a subjective standard as opposed to an objective standard?

SUGGESTED ACTIVITIES

1. Divide into teams of two or three. For each of the scenarios listed below, each team is to prepare a brief assessment of the case including (1) a determination of which aspects of the code of ethics was violated, if any, and (2) the action you would take to address the violation (assume all possibilities apply). Be prepared to debate your position, pro and con.

   (A) Tom is an eight-year veteran of a municipal police department in a medium-sized city in the United States. He has no formal disciplinary history and was an average student at the academy. Assigned to the patrol division, he has discharged his weapon twice in the line of duty, both having been ruled "good shoots." After the second incident, he begins coming to briefing with his gloves on, stroking them and calling them his "killing gloves," referring to his prior shooting incidents. At about the same time, rumors have started among his shift officers concerning his rude and belligerent behavior to them and to civilian women in particular. On patrol one day, you see his vehicle at the side of the road with a young woman in the front seat with him. He is acting in a suspicious manner. Later, the woman reports being molested by Tom and files a complaint. You do not come forward. What should happen to both Tom and you?

   (B) You are one of the officers who responded to a crime scene, took witness statements, and gathered evidence. At trial, you hear on the evening news of some testimony by a fellow officer, your partner, which you know is not true, and the lie is significant. You also know that the defendant is guilty beyond any doubt, and that your partner is a key witness. However, you also know that you were with your partner when events to which he testified occurred (or did not). You are therefore tied to those statements. No one has approached you, most likely assuming you would tell the same story. What do you do? Why?

   (C) You are a Sergeant. A promotional exam is going to be given for the position of Sergeant with four openings. All of the current Sergeants in your agency are white males. Of the 24 applicants for this test, 12 are either female or minority applicants or both. You discover that *all* the other Sergeants are tutoring selected candidates from the line officer applicants for this test. All being tutored are white males. Department rules specifically forbid any assistance to applicants since the oral boards will be composed partially of those current Sergeants.

2. Log on to the World Wide Web and go to: **http://www.ih2000.net/ira/ira.htm**. This site is Ira Wilsker's Home Page; it lists a large number of law enforcement sites on the Web. Browse various police agency sites and review their pages for mission and values statements. Record the three you like best.

CHAPTER GLOSSARY

crime control model: a theory of the criminal justice system (and law enforcement) that suggests that the primary focus of law enforcement should be swift and efficient conviction of the guilty

due process model: an approach to the criminal justice system (and law enforcement) that requires adherence to specific rights and procedures that insure fairness in determining guilt

explicit values: values that are clearly stated

factual guilt: in the crime control model, the mere evidence that the defendant committed the alleged act

hierarchy: a vertical structure of jobs in the workplace where each person reports to only one other person with one person at the top of the "pyramid"

implicit values: values that are "understood" to be true, or are "just known"

legal guilt: the accepted standard of the "due process model" that permits a finding of guilt if and only if there are no factual or procedural errors

legal intervention model: an approach to public management that focuses on legal values and methods of settling administrative disputes

managerial model: an approach to public management produced by the Progressive Reform Movement that focused on "running government more like a business," including hiring by merit, and demanding an end to politics in the administration of government

military model: essentially a hierarchy that employs symbols of military origin to enforce organizational control—including uniforms, rank and orders—coupled with disciplining to enforce it

model: an interpretation of how something in the real world works

objective standard: a method of judgment that depends upon criteria not interpreted by interested parties

political machines: formal political organizations that used the "spoils system" to hire their friends for public office regardless of skill and to get kickbacks in return

political model: an approach to public management that values the input of the various portions of society (sometimes called interest groups)

organizational culture: the basic philosophy and beliefs within the agency, which is passed on to new members when they join

reinventing government: a movement to reduce rules and levels of government, focus on customer service, and eliminate unnecessary regulations

subjective standard: a method of judgment that depends upon criteria interpreted by interested parties (for example, a witness or victim)

total quality management: a modern approach to management that stresses quality in output and customer satisfaction

values: an enduring preference or strong belief

REFERENCES

American Bar Association. 1972. *The Urban Police Function.* Chicago, IL: American Bar Association.

Behan, Cornelius J. 1992. "Values." In *Issues in Policing: New Perspectives,* edited by John W. Bizzack (Lexington, KY: Autumn House Publishing, 37–52).

Franz, V. and D.M. Jones. 1987. Perceptions of Organizational Performance in Suburban Police Departments: A Critique of the Military Model. *Journal of Police Science and Administration* 15(2): 153–161.

Gunther, Gerald. 1991. *Constitutional Law.* 12th ed. Westbury, New York: Foundation Press.

Hensley, Terry. 1988. Civilian Review Boards: A Means to Police Accountability. *The Police Chief* 55(9) (September): 45–46.

Kleinig, John with Yurong Zhang. 1993. *Professional Law Enforcement Codes: A Documentary Collection.* Westport, Connecticut: Greenwood Press.

Knott, Jack H. and Gary J. Miller. 1987. *Reforming Bureaucracy: The Politics of Institutional Choice.* Upper Saddle River, NJ: Prentice Hall.

Murphy, Walter, James Flemming, and Sotirios Barber. 1995. *American Constitutional Interpretation.* 2d ed. Westbury, NY: Foundation Press.

Packer, Herbert L. 1968. *The Limits of the Criminal Sanction.* Palo Alto: Stanford University Press.

Packer, Herbert L. 1964. Two Models of the Criminal Process. *The University of Pennsylvania Law Review* (11): 1–23.

Rokeach, Milton. 1973. *The Nature of Human Values.* New York: Macmillan, Inc.

Rosenbloom, David H. 1993. *Public Administration: Understanding Public Management, Public Management, Politics, and Law in the Public Sector.* 3d ed. New York: McGraw-Hill.

Trojanowicz, Robert and Bonnie Bucqueroux. 1990. *Community Policing: A Contemporary Perspective.* Cincinnati, OH: Anderson Publishing.

U.S. Department of Justice. Community Relations Service. 1987. Principles of Good Policing: Avoiding Violence Between Police and Citizens. In *Critical Issues in Policing: Contemporary*

Readings, 2d ed., by Roger G. Dunham and Geoffrey P. Alpert (Prospect Heights, IL: Waveland Press, 183).

Wasserman, Robert and Mark H. Moore. 1988. Values in Policing. *Perspectives in Policing.* Washington, D.C.: U.S. Department of Justice, No. 8 (November).

Whisenand, Paul M. 1981. *The Effective Police Manager.* Englewood Cliffs, N.J.: Prentice-Hall.

Wilson, Woodrow. 1887. The Study of Administration. *Political Science Quarterly* 2 (June): 197–222.

Zhiyong, Lan and David H. Rosenbloom. 1992. Public Administration in Transition? *Public Administration Review* 52(6) (November/December).

What Is This Noble (and Elusive) Concept We Call Integrity? 1995. *Law Enforcement News* 21(427), 20 July, 8.

New York City's 'Dirty 30' Scandal Nets its First Supervisors. 1994. *Law Enforcement News* 20(411), 15 November, 7.

CHAPTER 7

Policing Roles, Tasks, and Styles

KEY TERMS USED IN THIS CHAPTER

role
role conflict
Project STAR
temporal order maintenance
sustained order maintenance
full neighborhood
   management
police styles
stress

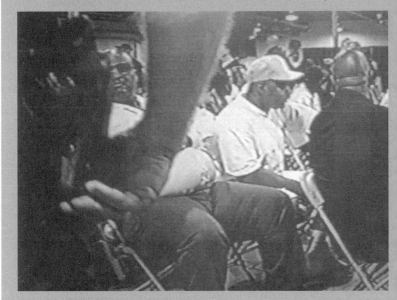

A Boston police officer stands over a group of people during a sting operation in Boston. Police sent out 14,000 letters to local fugitives offering job opportunities. But when over 100 people attended a supposed orientation, they found themselves surrounded by officers. June 1999. (AP/Wide World Photos)

THE POLICE ROLE

The role of the police is one of the most commonly discussed topics in police literature and, unfortunately, one of the most misunderstood. People often take for granted that they understand the role of the police in our society. They know that the police arrest people who allegedly have committed various crimes; the police cite traffic violators, and they respond to calls for assistance to maintain public order. People expect certain action from the police when they are summoned. People expect the police to perform certain functions at vehicular accidents and other situational emergencies. People also observe the police performing a number of duties in a variety of situations and often take for granted that the officers are simply carrying out their role. The purpose of this chapter is to examine what is involved in defining and determining the police role in the United States.

Several questions are related to the problem of defining and examining the police role in American society. What is the role of the police, generally, as an institution? What is the role of the individual law enforcement officer? Does the public have any impact on determining what the police do? What are the different perspectives of this role as seen from the community, the police themselves, and the criminal justice process as a whole?

Like Chapter 6, this chapter contains some conceptual material that may be difficult to grasp at first. Do not become frustrated if you read some sections and need to read the material again and contemplate the points being emphasized. One of the reasons for this chapter is that many officers today do not fully understand their role in society. By understanding one's role in society, one can better reconcile differences of opinions and conflicts that arise about what that role is.

What Is Meant by Role?

Instead of relying on any one perspective of what is meant by **role**, we prefer to define it as *a multidimensional concept consisting of expected behaviors performed by a person in a given situation or position for the purpose of achieving certain objectives or goals.* In other words, role is a blend of behaviors (what one does), expectations and perceptions (what one thinks should be done), and outcomes (what is to be accomplished). Role is difficult to define in concrete terms; it is a concept, and like all concepts, it must be worked out in the mind. It is not a tangible object that simply exists and can be described.

The multidimensional aspects of the concept of role refer to the social, cultural, and psychological elements that influence the determination of expected behavior. Expected behavior generally is defined by the party or parties performing the behavior, which means that the individual normally determines which behaviors are appropriate for a given situation. Sometimes that behavior is determined by several persons reaching a consensus of opinion about appropriate behavior. Another key factor of the concept is that the expected behavior is to achieve certain objectives or goals (outcomes). Not everyone agrees on the values and goals to be achieved by law enforcement, as was mentioned in Chapter 6 in the discussion of the due process and crime control models of criminal justice.

The concept of role is very complex and relational (see Figure 7–1). Role can be viewed from a social (interpersonal) perspective, such as the role of a parent, brother, sister, neighbor, and so on, or from an occupational perspective, such as the role of a doctor, lawyer, judge, teacher, nurse, firefighter, or police officer. But within each of these perspectives, there may be multiple or overlapping roles; for example, a mother also may have roles as a wife, a sister, a daughter, an aunt, and an employee of an agency or company. In her role as an employee, she also may occupy the role of colleague, confidante, supervisor, and so on. The role component in each of these is actually the *behavior* involved and not the status that the person occupies (e.g., mother, sister, employee). What

ROLE is not a concrete object that can be easily defined; it is a blend of social forces, perceptions, and outcomes.

Figure 7–1 The Complexity of a Role

is achieved (outcome) by way of that behavior is a significant determinant in role performance and is the basis of evaluation by others.

The relational aspects of role include the perspectives, personalities, and perceptions of the persons who are in the process of determining their proper role for a given situation. Interpersonal relationships affect how role is interpreted. Therefore, there are sociological and psychological variables at work during the process of role determination. People interpret their role by viewing others, communicating with others, evaluating their surroundings, and gauging their progress toward a desired objective. This process becomes very dynamic, and thus may cause persons to modify their behavior as they interpret situations as they unfold.

Applying the concept of role to policing is very challenging. The common question is "What is the role of the police in a democratic society?" The answer depends on whom is asked. To some, the role of the police is *to enforce the law*; to others, it is *to prevent crime*; still others will say it is *to maintain order*. The point is that all these responses are correct because the role of police in the United States is multifaceted (has may faces) and varies according to place and time and the objective to be accomplished. Notice that these responses are actually all objectives (or outcomes) to be accomplished by the various behaviors of officers. These outcomes are referred to by some writers and groups as "functions," so they speak of the *functions of the police.* Practically speaking, whether one refers to them as functions or outcomes, they are still the goals to be accomplished through the behaviors of officers. The duties of the police have not remained the same over the last 150 years (see Exhibit 7–1). Over the years, the police have acquired or have been assigned many different functions.

What Influences Role?

Before going further in this analysis of role, the question should be asked: What influences the role concept? From the previous paragraphs, as well as the

---

Exhibit 7–1

EARLY POLICE OFFICER DUTIES

The police officer's role has included the following duties:

1820s—Cared for common sewers, vaults, and whatever else affected the health, safety, and comfort of the citizens.

1830s—Emptied privies, conducted cholera checks.

1850s—Removed obstructions from the street, put out fires, tested doors, turned off running water, took drunks home, gathered in stray horses, helped the unemployed find jobs, sheltered the homeless.

1870s—Assisted and advised immigrants and strangers, supervised licenses of all types.

1880s—Called upon and escorted physicians for patients, inspected tenements and lodging houses for sanitary conditions, tested boiler operators for knowledge of equipment.

1910s—Assisted probation officers, were called "welfare" officers, entertained children at Christmas, initiated Junior Police programs, assisted ex-cons to find work, became probation and parole officers.

Source: Reprinted from Law Enforcement Assistance Administration (LEAA), *Two Hundred Years of American Criminal Justice,* 1976, U.S. Department of Justice.

previous chapters, several factors can be identified (see Exhibit 7–2). These factors may overlap and relate to each other as well; they are not totally independent of one another. First, as Samuel Walker has clearly stated, "The most important factor shaping the role of the police is their twenty-four-hour availability." Police are often called upon for various tasks simply because other agencies are not available. Second, role is influenced by the culture of a society—its history, customs, norms, morals, values, and beliefs. A given culture or cultural influences can range from national beliefs and norms (e.g., the "American culture") to local customs and ethnic heritage and values. As a country becomes more "multi-cultured," its national culture is more difficult to describe.

Third, role is influenced by the socialization process. This is related to culture since it is the process by which a person learns about his/her culture. Socialization plays a major role in forming attitudes, both positive and negative, that can have an influence on how situations are interpreted and appropriate behavior determined. Where there is a homogeneous cultural experience, patterns of role behavior become more easily determined and passed on from generation to generation without great fluctuation or debate. In a diverse, multi-

---

Exhibit 7–2

THE MAJOR INFLUENCES UPON POLICE ROLE—A SUMMARY

AVAILABILITY—twenty-four–hour service

CULTURE—a society's history, customs, norms, morals, values, and beliefs

SOCIALIZATION PROCESS—the exchange of culture from one generation to another

LAW—the formal rules, regulations, statutes, ordinances, and court decisions

LOCAL COMMUNITY—its interpretation of what behaviors and goals are desired

EMPLOYERS AND SUPERVISORS—the formal work rules, regulations, policies, and procedures

INDIVIDUAL—perceptions and interpretations of expectations that guide behavior

cultural society, there will be less consensus and more debate as to the proper behavior in a given situation.

A fourth influence on role is the legal provision by which a society lives and prospers. Of course, the legal precepts in the United States are both stable and ever-changing. They are stable in the sense that most of our legal principles are grounded primarily upon British Common Law and the Constitution. The legal provisions are ever-changing, however, in that they are constantly being evaluated, interpreted, expanded, or modified by the legislative and judicial branches of the government.

The fifth influence on role determination is the local community's interpretation of what behaviors are appropriate and what outcomes are sought from that behavior. For example, community leaders, local elected officials, and significant groups in the local environment will have an influence on what is expected in terms of behavior and outcomes of local police agencies (see Exhibit 7–3).

Similarly, a sixth influence will be the employer and supervisors of an officer and the expectations they set for the personnel working for them. In a law enforcement agency, this influence includes the official policies, procedures, and rules of the agency as well as its administrators and supervisors.

Finally, the individual has an influence on role determination and behavior. Individual perception and interpretation of expectations are very significant aspects in determining a person's behavior. An officer, for example, will engage in certain behavior because he believes it to be the appropriate behavior for that given situation. In a 1991 study of statutory law in all 50 states, Burton, Langworthy, and Barker found that only one state (New York) specifically mentions a service function (assist citizens) as part of the formalized role of police officers. Order maintenance and law enforcement were the most prevalent roles indicated in state codes.

Concepts, Dilemmas, and Controversies

The concept of role and its complexities have led to several dilemmas and controversies as far as policing is concerned. One of the major dilemmas is that of definition and context of the concept. For instance, the previous chapter discussed the mission, goals, and values of the police. Are those the same as role? Some researchers refer to the functions of the police, such as to prevent crime, to guarantee constitutional rights, to resolve conflict, or to respond to emergencies. Is it any wonder that students of policing become confused when asked, "What is the police role in the United States?" Does the person asking the question want a "conceptual" response that focuses on the *definition* of role, or does she want a "functional" response that relates to a process of *doing* something (behaviors or duties)? Does she want an "outcome" response in terms of *what* is desired regarding the goal or objective of the role?

Exhibit 7–3

THE COMMUNITY SERVICE ROLE—REFLECTIONS FROM THE PAST

In the course of inquiring into police activities, the Commission encountered many differences of opinion among police administrators as to whether the primary police responsibility of law enforcement is made easier or more difficult by the many duties other than enforcing the law that police ordinarily perform. Police, in large numbers, direct and control traffic. Police watch the polls on election day, escort important visitors in and out of town, license taxicabs and bicycles, and operate animal shelters. Police assist stranded motorists, give directions to travelers, rescue lost children, respond to medical emergencies, help people who have lost their keys unlock their apartments. It is easy to understand why the police traditionally perform such services. These are services that somebody must perform, and police, being ever present and mobile, are logical candidates. Since much of the uniformed patrol officer's time is spent on simply moving around the beat on preventive patrol, it is natural for the public to believe that he has the time to perform services. Moreover, it is natural to interpret the police role of "protection" as meaning protection not only against crime but against other hazards, accidents, or even discomforts of life. . .

The community's study of the role of the police should cover additional ground. It should examine whether it is desirable, or possible, for the police to devote more time than they now generally do to protecting the community against social injustices. Some of these injustices which are criminal, such as loan sharking and consumer frauds, are already police business, although they are more commonly of a sort dealt with by headquarters squads or investigators . . . than by uniformed patrol officers.

Others are not police business, but perhaps should be. Police are uniquely situated to observe what is happening in the community. They are in constant contact with the conditions associated with crime. They see in minute detail situations that need to be and can be corrected. If a park is being badly maintained, if a school playground is locked when it is most needed, if garbage goes uncollected, if a landlord fails to repair or heat his building, perhaps the police could make it their business to inform the municipal authorities of these derelictions. In this way, police would help to represent the community in securing services to which it is entitled.

Source: Reprinted from President's Commission on Law Enforcement and Administration of Justice, *The Challenge of Crime in a Free Society,* pp. 97–98, 1967, U.S. Government Printing Office.

Because of the inconsistent use of terms and phrases such as role, mission, objective, function, and so on, a certain vagueness has resulted in the quest for role definition. In 1931, August Vollmer stated that the "police were organized to suppress crime, protect life and property, and preserve the peace" (National Commission on Law Observance and Enforcement 1931, 17). This should be considered a *functional* statement because of the infinitive verb phrases ("to suppress . . . [to] protect . . . [to] preserve"). A *behavioral* statement (sometimes called "tasks"), on the other hand, would include such phrases as: stops and questions suspects, arrests offenders, issues traffic citations, and conducts investigations. Role statements that focus on *outcomes* usually indicate what is desired as the result of policing, such as crime prevention, crime suppression, protection of property, protection of rights and freedoms, and so on (see Exhibit 7–4).

Therefore, it is very important in any discussion of role to clearly understand the differences in perspectives when one is speaking about the functional, behavioral, and outcome aspects of the job. There are subtle but significant differences in language, and that is part of what leads to confusion over role.

There is a concept that explains the confusion and frustration sometimes encountered by officers who experience competing and sometimes opposite values and expectations. It is referred to as **role conflict** and was explained this way by James S. Campbell in 1970:

> Perhaps the most important source of police frustration, and the most severe limitation under which they operate, is the conflicting roles and demands involved in the order-maintenance, community-service, and crime-fighting responsibilities of the police. Here both the individual officer and the police community as a whole

---

Exhibit 7–4

TYPES OF ROLE STATEMENTS		
FUNCTIONAL	BEHAVIORAL	OUTCOMES
To suppress crime	Stops and questions suspects	Crime suppression
To protect life	Arrests offenders	Protection of life
To protect property	Issues traffic citations	Crime prevention
To preserve the peace	Conducts investigations	Order maintenance
To serve the public	Assists motorists	Public service

find not only inconsistent public expectations and public reactions, but also inner conflict growing out of the interaction of the policeman's values, customs, and traditions with his intimate experience with the criminal element of the population. The policeman lives on the grinding edge of social conflict, without a well-defined, well-understood notion of what he is supposed to be doing there (Campbell *et al.* 1970, 291).

More recently, Carter and Radelet (1999, 118) stated:

. . . the role conflict has been complicated with the addition of quality-of-life issues as a police responsibility. Certainly, this goes beyond the traditional view of the police as either law officer or peace officer. What is more apparent is the police officers in the role of *problem solver*. Officers are being asked to be "proactive," that is, to aggressively look for broad solutions to crime, disorder and quality-of-life problems in the community.

While role conflict has been recognized for decades, it is still very prevalent in some (if not all) agencies. The issue is really how officers deal with it rather than whether it exists. It will probably always exist because the various forces influencing it (Exhibit 7–2 above) will seldom be in total agreement. Role conflict is one factor that influences the level of stress on officers. (Stress is addressed in greater detail later in this chapter.)

Research on Role

The quest to define or determine the appropriate role of police in the United States has been a focus of scholars for many decades. The purpose of this section is to identify several of the major systematic attempts to observe and analyze the role of police officers; it is not to report the many statements that appear in the literature of what the police role is or is not. The role of the police has always been a subject of concern, as evidenced by the pronouncements of voices from the past (see Exhibit 7–5).

We believe that one of the most comprehensive statements regarding the role and expectations of police is that of James Currant (1972, 112):

A simple answer to the question as to what the urban policeman does is that he does everything. Cliches abound concerning the fact that the policeman is a combination psychiatrist, medical doctor, lawyer, marriage counselor and crime-stopper. The truth of the matter is that he is all of these things, yet none of them. . . . In broad general terms, it can be said that police deal with virtually every kind of emergency human problem and, moreover, appear to spend more of their time dealing with problems not related to crime than with crime-related human problems.

Throughout the 1960s and early 1970s, police scholars often attempted to explain the role of the police by examining what they did and how they did it.

Exhibit 7–5

NOTABLE QUOTES ON THE ROLE OF POLICE

"A policeman's duties are numerous, and he is brought in contact with the very best as well as the very worst element of the community. He is called upon to settle family difficulties; arbitrate differences between neighbors; regulate the ubiquitous small boy; act in the capacity of sanitary officer when contagion stalks about, and perform a thousand other offices that are never made public . . ."

—Chief D.S. Gaster, New Orleans, 1900.

"The police were organized to suppress crime, protect life and property, and preserve the peace. Where they have commanded the respect and receive the support of the people they have had little difficulty in carrying out their duties. Under our form of government and, more especially, due to the attitude of the American people generally, law enforcement agencies are usually held in contempt and law enforcement is one of our national jokes. Crime, despite the magnitude of the problem, is but one of the many difficulties confronting the police."

—National Commission on Law
Observance and Enforcement,
Report on Police, Washington, D.C.:
United States Government Printing
Office, 1931: 17.

Source: Reprinted from National Commission on Law Observance and Reinforcement, *Report on Police*, p. 17, 1931, U.S. Government Printing Office.

Some focused on the question of "Why do police behave the way they do?" One text summed up much of these early findings this way:

> If the police are not sure whether their principal function is to prevent crime or serve the public, the researchers are no more consistent in their conclusions. . . . In truth the ambivalence of the police is built into the very structure of law enforcement by the variety of duties imposed upon police practitioners by the law, custom, and ethical requirements of the society they live in (Niederhoffer and Blumberg 1976, 64).

The major research effort of the President's Crime Commission on Law Enforcement and Administration of Justice in the mid-1960s established that the role of the police was not well understood in the United States. Exhibit 7–2, above, clearly depicts a finding that was inconclusive. What is most interesting in those historical sentences is that they appear to coincide with the 1990s explanation of the philosophy of community policing (discussed in more detail in Chapter 9).

One of the most comprehensive research efforts on role was the three-and-one-half-year effort of **Project STAR**, which began in 1971. The project involved agencies in four states and attempted to identify appropriate roles for six key positions (police officer, prosecuting attorney, defense attorney, judge, caseworker, and correctional worker) in the criminal justice system. In this study, role was defined as "the personal characteristics and behavior expected in a specific situation of an individual occupying a position" (Smith *et al.* 1974). Although the project is over twenty-five years old, its findings included excellent discussions and qualitative data related to understanding the concepts associated with the police role.

The project also identified *tasks* and *performance objectives* that were defined respectively as follows (refer to Exhibit 7–6):

Task: an activity to be accomplished within a role that usually involves a sequence of steps and can be measured in relation to time.

Performance objectives: statements of operational behavior required for satisfactory performance of a task, the conditions under which the behavior is usually performed, and the criteria for satisfactory performance.

Within the research, findings indicated that for the position of police officer: (a) each *role* involved the performance of several *tasks* and (b) each *task* involved the performance of more than one *role* (Smith *et al.* 1974, 2). The 13 roles of police officers identified by Project STAR were:

■ Assists criminal justice system and other appropriate agency personnel
■ Builds respect for law and the criminal justice system
■ Provides public assistance
■ Seeks and disseminates knowledge and understanding
■ Analyzes and communicates information
■ Manages cases
■ Assists personal and social development
■ Displays objectivity and professional ethics
■ Protects rights and dignity of individuals
■ Provides humane treatment
■ Enforces law impartially
■ Enforces law situationally
■ Maintains order

Exhibit 7–6

PROJECT STAR'S 33 TASKS PERFORMED BY POLICE OFFICERS IN CARRYING OUT THE ROLES OF THEIR JOB

Advising
Booking and Receiving Inmates
Collecting and Preserving
  Evidence
Communicating
Conferring about Cases
Contacting Families of Suspects
  and Clients
Controlling Crowds
Defending Self and Others
Deterring Crime
Engaging in Legal Research
Engaging in Professional
  Development
Interacting with Other Agencies
Interviewing
Investigating
Making Arrests
Managing Interpersonal Conflict
Moving Inmates
Participating in Community

Relations and Education
  Programs
Participating in Trial Preparation
  Conferences
Patrolling and Observing
Preparing Reports
Preparing Search Warrant
  Requests
Recovering Property
Referring
Regulating Traffic
Responding to Offender
  Requests
Reviewing Case Materials
Searching and Examining
Searching for Fugitives
Testifying as a Witness
Testing for Drug and Alcohol Use
Training
Using and Maintaining
  Equipment

Source: Reprinted from C. P. Smith, D. E. Pehlke, and C .D. Weller, *Role Performance and the Criminal Justice System, Volume II: Detailed Performance Objectives,* Project STAR, pp. 9–12, 1974, National Institute of Justice.

To further illustrate the research of Project STAR and the analysis related to each of the identified roles, Exhibit 7–7 details the finding for the role labeled "provides public assistance."

In 1973, the National Advisory Commission on Criminal Justice Standards and Goals addressed the issue of police role in their "Report on Police." It was Chapter 1 of the Report, which indicated the importance placed on the topic. The report emphasized the concept of "functional police role," which is the idea that an agency must prioritize the expectations placed on its officers in terms of serving the community and that it should be put in writing to guide officers'

Exhibit 7–7

RELATIONSHIP OF TASKS AND PERFORMANCE OBJECTIVES TO ROLE

Roles for police officers can be placed into categories; the roles can be described and performance objectives (or outcomes) identified; roles can involve several tasks and each task can relate to more than one role. The relationship among these aspects is illustrated here for the single role of "Provides Public Assistance."

ROLE

Provides Public Assistance

ROLE DESCRIPTION:

Treating all needs for assistance, requested by the public or observed, in a serious and helpful manner regardless of the appropriateness of the requests. Providing services or appropriate referrals, including any needed arrangements for special assistance, expeditiously and courteously.

PERFORMANCE OBJECTIVES

— To respond courteously and expeditiously to requests for assistance
— To obtain information about public and private community resources for use in helping people
— To make referrals to other public and private agencies
— To take advantage of opportunities to provide assistance based on an assessment that the need exists

TASKS

— Advising
— Communicating
— Interacting with other agencies
— Interviewing
— Patrolling/observing
— Referring
— Using equipment

Source: Adapted from C. P. Smith, D. E. Pehlke, and C. D. Weller, *Role Performance and the Criminal Justice System, Volume II: Detailed Performance Objectives.* Project STAR, 1974, National Institute of Justice.

performance. It was expected that the chief executive officer would develop such a policy in consultation with department employees, the community, and government officials. It was suggested that the policy on role be central to other written policies that guide the department. Other recommendations concerning the police role included the assurance that every officer understand his or her role (Standard 1.5) and that the public as well be informed of the agency's defined police role (Standard 1.6). Other standards relating to the police role addressed the recognition of the use of force and the use of discretion by officers (National Advisory Commission 1973, 12–39).

During the 1970s, several scholars published texts that included discussions about the police role in the U.S. and how it was multifaceted (see Goldstein 1977; Muir 1977; Manning and Van Maanen 1978; Skolnick and Gray 1975; Broderick 1977; and Staufenberger 1980). In essence, most agreed that it was a very complex matter to conceptualize and dissect. The role is heavily influenced by officer perceptions of the job, the demands placed upon them by the public, and by legislative enactments. Coupled with this is the need to occasionally use force, the need to often use discretion, and the expectation that the job be carried out under strict constitutional protection of rights and liberties. One researcher put it this way in describing what makes a good police officer: "Intellectually, he has to grasp the nature of human suffering. Morally, he has to resolve the contradictions of achieving just ends with coercive means" (Muir 1977).

Recent discussions about the police role in the United States have focused on three models of policing (Hoover 1992): the **temporal order maintenance** role mainly associated with crime-specific models of policing, the **sustained order maintenance** role associated with problem-oriented policing, and the **full neighborhood management** role linked with community-oriented policing. As community policing tends to expand in its application, roles will become more committed to long-term relationships (full neighborhood management) with citizens as opposed to the short-term involvement of answering single incident calls (temporal order maintenance) or solving short-lived crime-related problems (sustained order maintenance). These models of policing are more directly associated with the strategies of policing that are discussed in Chapter 9.

Essentially, what the literature describes about the policing role in the United States is that it is unsettled, subject to ongoing societal change, and continually evolving. The role of the police cannot be static; it cannot remain constant because society is always changing. As new problems surface, the police are called to deal with them because there usually is no other agency "out there" to respond.

POLICING STYLES

What is sometimes not distinguished in discussions of role is the difference between police role and **police style**. Simply stated, police style is the manner in which an officer carries out his or her police role. It includes the various techniques, mannerisms, vocabulary, body language, and so on, employed by an officer to achieve an objective. An effective police officer probably will utilize several styles of police behavior to accomplish tasks. Officers' style will reflect their training, role expectation, values, skills, personality, and/or experience. Officers may develop a primary style (the one used most often) and a secondary style or styles (those used as alternatives to the primary style). For example, officers may be very direct and shout out specific commands to a person they are attempting to control. They may be very soft-spoken when addressing children who need comforting, or they may attempt to reason logically and rationally with a couple during a domestic disturbance. So, *regardless of the role and tasks being performed, the officer's style (demeanor and manner) becomes the most observable behavior to the public.*

What Influences Style?

As with role, there are several things that influence an officer's style. In part, style will be dependent on the nature of the complaint, the type of service needed, the environment, the person or persons present, the objective to be achieved, the agency's philosophy and values, and peer pressure. Other elements may influence style as well, such as the quality of training received; the levels of knowledge, education, and skills possessed; backgrounds of the subjects involved in the encounter; the officer's knowledge of available alternatives; and the officer's experience. Exhibit 7–8 identifies many of the sub-elements of these influencing factors. It is evident that style is not a simple concept to analyze.

Research on Police Style

Several scholars in recent decades have started to label various types of police styles. One of the most noted (and most quoted) is the work of James Q. Wilson, *The Varieties of Police Behavior,* published in 1968. Three predominant styles were identified, as follows:

Watchman: Emphasis is on maintaining order by invoking "path of least resistance." Officers often ignore minor violations unless their authority is challenged.

Legalistic: Stresses authority and control mechanisms with emphasis on the letter of the law; generally does not ignore even minor violations.

Service: All calls for service are approached in a serious manner regardless of their nature, and alternatives to formal arrest are emphasized.

Wilson's typologies are widely cited, but the important part of his work is that he developed these styles based upon analysis of eight police departments

Exhibit 7–8

INFLUENCES ON OFFICER STYLES

NATURE OF THE COMPLAINT—Criminal, civil; misdemeanor, felony

TYPE OF SERVICE NEEDED—Emergency, public assistance, investigation

THE ENVIRONMENT—Rural, suburban, urban; house, apartment, outdoors

PERSON OR PERSONS PRESENT—One-on-one contact, crowds, rioters

GOAL/OBJECTIVE OF CONTACT—Identify offender, arrest, referral

AGENCY PHILOSOPHY AND VALUES—Department policies and procedures

PEER PRESSURE—Expectations of other officers

QUALITY OF TRAINING—Depth of training; sensitivity/cultural skills

OFFICER ABILITIES—Communication, evaluation, and empathy skills

EXPERIENCE—Skills and insights learned from doing the job

All of the above factors, and possibly others, can impact an officer's choice of style in handling contacts with citizens and complainants.

---

across the country. In essence, his research was an attempt to show that the ways in which the police perform their tasks are influenced by the nature of the community and political systems of that community. His focus was primarily on the predominant style of the organization and its influence upon the officers.

Several other scholars have contributed to the discussion of style by identifying their own categories of police types. The two scholars mentioned here have developed style typologies for individual officers and not the organization. William Muir categorized four types of officers in his research of coercive power and the policing function (Muir 1977):

Enforcer: Emphasizes legal authority and makes quick decisions as to whether arrest is necessary. Crime control is the major objective.

Reciprocator: Adopts an extreme helping pose trying to reach a solution in all problems. Attempts accommodation with vice operators and undesirables.

Avoider: An officer who attempts to avoid all involvement in situations.

Professional: An officer who understands the complexities of the job and attempts to do the best he or she can, using verbal skills, knowledge, and experience.

Muir's work has influenced others to pursue similar research on types of police officers. Sometimes such research is said to be focused on personality types instead of styles. It should be remembered that to a large degree, an officer's style is a reflection of his or her personality. Such focus is an example of the psychological dimension of role development. John J. Broderick classifies police personalities into four ideal types that reflect officers' values and styles of behavior (Broderick 1987):

Enforcers: A high value is placed on social order and peace and low value on individual rights and due process of law; tend to stress need for authority and respect for law.

Realists: Low value is placed on both social order and individual rights; tend to be less frustrated than other officers, apparently having found a way to come to terms with a difficult job.

Idealists: Individual rights and due process of law receive high value; preservation of social order is viewed as a major role; generally suffers from lack of job satisfaction and frustration.

Optimists: Job is seen as people-oriented, placing a high value on individual rights, less emphasis on crime fighting.

In his book, *Police in a Time of Change* (2d ed.), Broderick presents an excellent discussion of the styles of policing identified by Muir and similar styles developed by other researchers. He mentions that many of the styles developed by researchers are similar and overlap each other's categories (see Table 7–1). A detailed discussion of each of these research efforts is beyond our purpose here; however, the reader is encouraged to review additional material for more in-depth analysis of police styles (see Coates 1972; White 1972; Brown 1968; Hatting *et al.* 1983; Walsh 1984).

ORGANIZATIONAL ROLES OF SELECTED POSITIONS

The police organization consists of many levels (ranks) and positions. Every person working in the organization occupies a position and has certain job functions to perform. These job functions tend to define, within limits, the role of that particular position. Of course, occasionally new job functions (duties) may develop or appear, and they must be assigned to someone to perform. This in-

Table 7–1 A Comparison of Officer Styles from Selected Research

Researcher	*Overlapping or Similar Styles*			
Coats (1972)	Abusive	Community	Task Officer	Service
White (1972)	Tough Cop & Crime Fighter	Problem Solver	Rule Applier	
Muir (1977)	Enforcer	Reciprocator	Avoider	Professional
Broderick (1977)	Enforcers	Idealists	Realists	Optimists
Brown (1981)	Old Style & Clean Beat Crime Fighter	Service Style I Helper	Service Style II Avoider	Professional
Hatting, et al. (1983)	Blue-Collar	True Blue	Jaded Blue	
Walsh (1984)	Medium Arrest	Low Arrest	Zero Arrest	High Arrest

Source: Copyright © 1987, John J. Broderick.

dicates the fluctuating nature of a person's occupational role when working in an agency whose functions and obligations are not static.

Patrol Officers

Patrol officers are so designated because they usually patrol the jurisdiction while in uniform and respond to the immediate needs of the community. They are usually the first responders to most criminal complaints of an emergency nature. They also conduct routine traffic stops while enforcing traffic regulations, in addition to investigating traffic accidents. Patrol officers may be of various rank. Most are of the lower rank of police officer/patrol officer, but some may be sergeants, lieutenants, or even higher rank. Generally, the higher ranking officers are supervisors; therefore, there are fewer of them on patrol than police officers. The patrol force has been called the "eyes and ears" and the "backbone" of the department. These descriptions refer to the fact that these officers are always "out there on the street" and available to call for service. There are usually more officers assigned to the patrol function than any other function. In terms of doing the work for which a police agency generally exists, much, if not most of it, is done by patrol officers.

Detectives (Investigators)

The investigative function of policing is initially carried out at crime scenes by either patrol officers or detectives. Many agencies assign initial investigative duties to patrol officers, who will request the assistance of detectives when the latter are necessary and available. Otherwise, the initial investigative report is forwarded to the detectives of the agency, and they are responsible for the follow-up investigation. Detectives are police officers who have been promoted or assigned to the investigative function on a full-time basis. It should be noted that smaller agencies often do not have full-time investigators, so those duties may be assigned as necessary to a patrol officer. In larger agencies, detectives are either appointed by the chief executive or selected through competitive examination. The role of the detective is to conduct follow-up investigation of assigned cases with the objective of developing a case suitable for prosecution of the alleged offender. This may involve crime scene analysis, evidence collection, photography, interviewing, interrogating, record searches, interpreting crime lab and autopsy reports, preparing reports, preparing affidavits for search and arrest warrants, executing search and arrest warrants, preparing documents for prosecutors, and testifying in court. Investigators spend much time at their desks using the telephone, evaluating reports and records, and writing notes for the various cases they have been assigned. Unlike his or her television counterpart, the detective may pursue a dozen or more active cases simultaneously. One aspect of investigative work is "managing the case," which means keeping things organized and progressing toward the desired objective of identifying a suspect and prosecuting the guilty offender.

In state and federal agencies where uniformed officers do not exist, the personnel are often all investigators (some agencies refer to them as *agents*). Their primary function is to investigate specialized crime such as fraud, embezzlement, liquor violations, counterfeiting, homicides, robberies, kidnapping, computer crime, and so on. These investigators may be assigned their cases hours and days after the incident occurred and may not work on some cases unless local agencies request their assistance. Many local agencies today frequently call in state and/or federal agents as soon as possible, sometimes within an hour of serious incidents.

Supervisors

The organizational role of a supervisor is one of coordinating and managing a group of personnel for which he or she is responsible. This means that supervisors are responsible for leading and guiding the work accomplished by the unit. The role of the supervisor includes general assignment of duties or cases, scheduling personnel, answering questions, making decisions, advising others, evaluating and documenting performance, approving leave and vacation requests, and receiving complaints from the public about unit personnel. Supervisors usually hold the rank of sergeant or above unless they are civilian personnel; in that case, their title could be supervisor, coordinator, manager, or director. Supervisors are assigned throughout the agency in both operational and staff units.

Specialized Functions

Specialty functions within law enforcement agencies include units such as special weapons and tactics (SWAT), crime prevention, public information, internal affairs, training, personnel, fiscal control, identification, detention services, planning and research, vehicle maintenance, parking control, and so on. Usually, the primary functional role of each of these units can be deduced from their titles. It must be remembered that the roles of personnel will vary according to their assigned unit. The priority tasks performed by many specialists do impact the total functioning of the agency; however, these personnel may not be very visible to the public in carrying out the daily policing role of the agency.

The Chief Executive Officer

The primary task and role of the chief executive officer of any law enforcement agency is to lead, coordinate, guide, and manage all the units and personnel employed within the agency. This person is responsible for the agency's operation on a daily basis. Law enforcement officials occupying this position may have various titles besides the common Chief of Police. Titles vary from agency to agency and include Sheriff, Commissioner, Director, Superintendent, Colonel, Marshal, and Chief Constable. The chief executive officer's role usually includes determining the mission and goals of the agency and communicating these to the department personnel and the community. Of course, it has long been recommended that the community, the elected officials, and the officers of the department should be involved in determining the mission and goals of the agency (President's Commission 1968).

Chief executive officials are generally either appointed or promoted to that position (the sheriff is usually an elected position, however). Appointed officials generally have little or no job security or specified term of office. For example, "The average length of time in office for 'big-city' chiefs has dropped to 3.5 years. In Houston the average over the last 25 years has been 2.3 years" (Frankel 1992). The reason for such short periods include politics (the election of different mayors who appoint the chief), scandals or public incidents that forced resignations, mandatory retirement ages, and personal reasons. However, promoted officials often occupy positions where a civil service or promotional exam of some type determines who obtains the job. Often these positions have job security or tenure, meaning that the official cannot be removed except for cause. The job may be theirs for the rest of their working career. Systems vary from state to state and often depend on state law and city charter.

UNDERSTANDING THE ROLE DEBATE

How do the concepts discussed in this chapter relate to policing today? Why are the issues of role and styles of concern? Many officers go about their jobs every day and do not express any problems with their role or the various tasks they perform. Others, however, are vocal about the frustrations they have from the job. They make statements like "I'm a cop, not a social worker!" "I joined this force to enforce the law, not to play games with the neighborhood youth." "I don't have time to worry about overgrown vacant lots, condemned buildings, and abandoned cars." It is statements like these that provide evidence that some officers do not understand their role in a democratic society. Research clearly shows that enforcement of laws or response to crime-related activities consumes between 20 percent and 50 percent of a police officer's time (see Greene and Klockars 1991). Of course, there are exceptions to this figure in some areas within some cities, but that does not negate the fact that the role of today's police officer goes beyond law enforcement. It includes public assistance on many matters, order maintenance, traffic control, and crime prevention.

As discussed in earlier segments of this chapter, the police role in the United States is unsettled, subject to ongoing societal change, and is continually evolving. As new problems surface, the police are called to deal with them because there often is no other agency "out there" to respond. Over time, the police have been caretakers of common sewers, lamplighters, the issuers of licenses, health inspectors, housing inspectors, probation officers, parole officers, employment counselors, animal wardens, child welfare agents, and so on. Other social service agencies came into existence because some of the duties became too time-consuming for officers to continue. In the future, other positions (or agencies) may be created to assume some of the non–law enforcement tasks done by police today. Until that happens, the role of the police is to do whatever society calls upon them to do. It is a simple proposition, but one that is difficult for many to accept. Those who cannot accept this fundamental role of the police in the U.S. should not seek employment in law enforcement agencies.

Those who can accept this responsibility may make excellent police officers. It is the degree of acceptance of this role of ambiguity that impacts the officer's style. Those who accept the changing demands of society, who accept the social service requests from the public, who understand the complexity of social disorder and frustration, and who can acknowledge the rights of all persons should be officers who are accepted by the public. It is this type of officer who exhibits concern for people from all walks of life and learns to treat people with respect and dignity.

So that there is no misunderstanding, an officer can accept this multifaceted police role and still be a law enforcer when necessary. Today's role requires the "wearing of many hats" and being able to adjust one's demeanor and style as necessary for the tasks at hand. The ability of officers to understand the complexity of their role is the challenge facing them today. In 1977, Herman Goldstein discussed the impact of recognizing the multiple functions of the police and he described one ramification this way (Goldstein 1977, 42):

> ... in recruiting personnel to be police officers we need individuals who will not only perform well in dealing with serious crime, but will also be capable in many other areas: resolving conflicts, protecting constitutional guarantees, and handling an incredibly wide range of social and personal problems; and most important who will have the ability to shift with ease from performing one of these functions to performing another.

STRESS AND DISCRETION IN POLICING

Two other concepts are worthy of mention in the overall discussion of the role of policing in today's society. Stress and discretion are factors that influence the daily lives of many professional persons. Both can influence decisions he or she makes and, therefore, both affect behavior. It is not our purpose here to give a detailed analysis of either of these concepts, but we would be remiss not to mention their relationship to issues in this chapter.

Stress

Stress has been broadly defined as "the body's non-specific response to any demand placed on it" (Selye 1994).

Policing is often thought to be a high-stress job compared to other occupations. The conventional wisdom holds that law enforcement officers face perilous conditions, tedious tasks, and hostile work environments, all of which lead to high stress. Stress, it is thought, produces lower productivity, higher levels of physical and mental illness, suicide, and police misconduct. Empirical evidence, however, has been mixed, and there appears to be little evidence that officers are any more stressed than other employees in other occupations, including some with similar job characteristics. Still, there is some evidence to support the idea. One stressor common among occupations is the loss of job discretion, which officers face organizationally (Lennings 1997). Hence, the one stressor that appears to have a significant impact in law enforcement is the organizational restrictions on work, including standard operating procedures and legal rulings. Levels of stress do appear to relate to certain negative health outcomes (Golembiewski *et al.* 1992). Clearly, this is an area of concern and one that will lead to further research.

An excellent treatise and guide for law enforcement managers on the topic of stress, published in 1990, is *Preventing Law Enforcement Stress: The Organiza-*

tion's Role. It divides law enforcement stressors into four categories: (1) those external to the organization, (2) those internal to the organization, (3) those in law enforcement work itself, and (4) those confronting the individual officer. Exhibit 7–9 depicts many of the stressors in each of the four categories.

Exhibit 7–9

SELECTED STRESS FACTORS IN POLICING BY CATEGORY

External Stressors
- Frustration with the American judicial system
- Lack of consideration by the courts in scheduling officers for court appearances
- The public's lack of support and negative attitudes toward law enforcement
- Negative or distorted media coverage of law enforcement

Internal (Agency) Stressors
- Policies and procedures that are offensive to officers
- Poor or inadequate training, career development opportunities
- Poor economic benefits and working conditions
- Excessive paper work
- Inconsistent discipline

Stressors in the Work Itself
- The rigors of shift work, especially rotating shifts
- Role conflicts between enforcing the law and serving the community
- Frequent exposure to life's miseries and brutalities
- Fear and dangers of the job
- Work overload

Stressors Confronting the Individual Officer
- Fears regarding job competence, individual success, and safety
- Necessity to conform
- Necessity to take a second job or to further education
- Altered social status in the community due to attitude changes of others because he or she is now an officer

Source: Reprinted from R. M. Ayres and G. S. Flanagan, *Preventing Law Enforcement Stress: The Organization's Role,* pp. 4–5, 1990, U.S. Department of Justice and the National Sheriffs' Association.

Discretion

Discretion is not a role. Rather, discretion means that law enforcement officers have a wide latitude in choosing which role to assume and which tactics, approaches, or behaviors to employ while acting within a given role. In most respects, officer discretion is an essential component of the job. Most applied law enforcement requires making frequent judgments or choices every day. These choices are normally made without direct supervision due to the decentralized and distributed nature of patrol and investigative work.

Discretion can be defined as "the use of individual judgment by officers in making decisions as to which of several behavioral responses is appropriate in specific situations" (Cox 1996, 46). According to Sykes, Fox, and Clark (1985), "discretion exists whenever an officer is free to choose from two or more task-relevant, alternative interpretations of the events reported, inferred, or observed in a police-civilian encounter." Therefore, discretion is the process of making a choice among believed appropriate alternative courses of action. Although most state codes do not give police officers the specific right to use discretion, it has been professionally and judicially acknowledged. As mentioned in Chapter 1, the police simply cannot enforce every law that has been enacted. Selective enforcement refers to enforcing those laws deemed appropriate to the situation or related to the priorities of the agency and the community. The opposite of selective enforcement is full enforcement, which means enforcing all laws all the time—a condition that most Americans simply do not want.

According to Cox (1996, 47) there are a number of factors influencing discretion, such as the law, department policy, political expectations, pubic expectations, the situation/setting, and the occupational culture in which they operate. The process of making decisions involves the evaluation of all of these factors. In other words, the officer must evaluate the "totality of circumstances." (Review Figure 7–1 again—think of all of the interrelated factors mentioned there and compare them to the ones influencing discretion.)

The lack of guidelines in law enforcement agencies gives individual officers opportunity to inject their own prejudices and legal interpretations into their job performance, which can lead to the abuse of discretion. In making a decision, officers must understand that the decision should be appropriate and defensible. They may be asked to explain their decision in the reporting process or in court. In today's litigious society, decisions made by officers are subject to review by others, and can result in suits for damages. This adds to the levels of stress an officer endures in his or her career.

One study found that in responding to disturbances, officers engaged in 13 distinct contact actions (e.g., request separation, physical restraint, or forced dispersal), 17 processing actions (e.g., follow complainant's request, restrain someone, or admonish disputants), and 17 distinct exit actions (e.g., just leave, arrest, or warn alleged offenders). Similar patterns were observed in traffic stops (Bayley 1986). Discretion is a large part of law enforcement and a major issue in law enforcement reform (Brown 1988). It produces the most significant dilemma in policing. Discretion is essential to job performance, due to the nature of the work and the geographic dispersal of decision-making officers. Indeed, community policing and various related approaches *expect* higher levels of discretion. Yet it is also the case that discretion leads to opportunities for misconduct of all sorts. Hence, standard operating procedures, orders, written directives, skill training, incident reviews, and supervisory approval of reports all operate to restrain discretion, reduce the likelihood of misconduct, and standardize operations. It is worth noting that special operations teams operate with very low levels of discretion in tactical terms, largely due to the high level of inherent danger in such operations.

SUMMARY

This chapter examined the relationships among the concepts of role, tasks, and style. Role was defined as *a multidimensional concept consisting of expected behaviors performed by a person in a given situation or position for the purpose of achieving certain objectives or goals.* Since there are multiple objectives to policing (public safety, law enforcement, protection of constitutional rights, etc.) there are multiple roles. These roles require the performance of different tasks. Style, on the other hand, referred to how these tasks were carried out—the officers' demeanor, approach, and technique. Since these concepts are interrelated, they are difficult to discuss separately. The many factors or influences upon role determination and the development of one's style compounds the issues. Some of the more relevant research was presented regarding role and style. Additionally, organizational roles of selected positions (assignments) were described. The important factors of stress and discretion were briefly discussed in relation to their general impact on role determination.

So what is the role of the police in a democratic society? It is essentially what society says it is (defined by the community, not the officer). Since reaching a consensus is extremely difficult and there are so many different communities across this country, there cannot be just one role for the police to perform. There are many roles for the police in our society. What sets police apart from other occupations in society may be the fact that the state has given them the authority to use force if necessary to carry out their duties (see Klockars 1985 and Bittner 1990). The fact that the police have this authority and power must not be forgotten, since we ask individual officers to come to our rescue when needed and do what has to be done to protect us, but society expects them not to use excessive force even when they have to use force. Likewise, society wants our streets to be safe and free from reckless drivers and others who endanger lives, but we (as individuals) get upset with the police if we are the ones pulled over and given a citation. No one said the job would be easy!

QUESTIONS FOR REVIEW

1. What is the definition of the concept of "role?"
2. List at least five influences upon role determination and briefly state how such factors influence role determination.
3. What is meant by "role conflict"?
4. Compare and contrast the concepts of "police role" and "police style."
5. What are the role differences between the positions of a Patrol Officer and a Detective?

6. Why is it difficult to precisely and definitively answer the question "What is the role of the police in the United States?"

7. What is meant by "stress" and what are the four general categories of law enforcement stressors?

SUGGESTED ACTIVITIES

1. Engage a police officer in a discussion of role and seek his or her interpretation of what roles take priority in the agency that employs him or her.
2. Videotape a 15-minute segment of a police action TV show. Then analyze it for role versus style based on the concepts presented in this chapter. Write a brief report of your findings.
3. Read the mission statements of local police departments or find three or four on the World Wide Web and write down the key phrases that relate to the agency's role. Based on their articulated statements, what are the primary roles of the agencies?
4. Log on to the World Wide Web at **http://www.washington.xtn.net/~jcpd/citizens.htm** and read about the Johnson City, Tennessee Police Department's Citizen's Police Academy. What reason is given for offering this opportunity and what are the requirements to participate?

CHAPTER GLOSSARY

full neighborhood management: a commitment and philosophy of an agency to allow officers to intervene in any problem in a community that requires a response by police officers or other government personnel

police styles: the manner in which officers carry out their police role; it includes the various techniques, procedures, mannerisms, vocabulary, body language, etc. that are available to them

Project STAR: a comprehensive three-and-one-half-year research effort (1971–1974) that involved the federal government and agencies in four states; it attempted to identify appropriate roles for six key positions (police officer, prosecuting attorney, defense attorney, judge, caseworker, and correctional worker) in the criminal justice system

role: a multidimensional concept consisting of expected behaviors performed by a person in a given situation or position for the purpose of achieving certain objectives or goals

role conflict: the confusion and frustration encountered by officers brought on by competing and sometimes opposing values and expectations experienced while performing their job tasks

stress: broadly defined as "the body's non-specific response to any demand placed on it" (Selye 1994)

sustained order maintenance: a phrase referring to intervention by police that requires greater problem-solving analysis and possibly a greater commitment of resources than does short-term intervention

temporal order maintenance: a phrase referring to the short-term intervention by police officers in situations of interpersonal conflict and social disorder

REFERENCES

Ayres, Richard M. and George S. Flanagan. 1990. *Preventing Law Enforcement Stress: The Organization's Role.* Washington, D.C.: U.S. Department of Justice and the National Sheriffs' Association.

Bayley, David H. 1986. The Tactical Choices of Police Patrol Officers. *Journal of Criminal Justice* 14(4): 329–348.

Bittner, Egon. 1990. *Aspects of Police Work.* Boston, MA: Northeastern University Press.

Broderick, John J. 1977. *Police in a Time of Change.* Morristown, NJ: General Learning Press.

Broderick, John J. 1987. *Police in a Time of Change.* 2d ed. Prospect Heights, IL: Waveland.

Brown, Michael K. 1981. *Working the Street: Police Discretion and the Dilemmas of Reform.* New York: Russell Sage Foundation.

Burton, Velmer S., Jr., Robert H. Langworthy, and Troy A. Barker. 1991. *The Prescribed Role of Police in a Free Society: A National Survey of State Legal Codes.* Paper presented at the annual conference of the Midwestern Criminal Justice Association, October 1991, Chicago, IL.

Campbell, James S., Sahid, Joseph R., and Stang, David P. 1970. *Law and Order Reconsidered: Report of the Task Force on Law and Law Enforcement to the National Commission on the Causes and Prevention of Violence.* New York: Bantam Books.

Carter, David L. and Louis A. Radelet. 1999. *The Police and the Community.* 6th ed. Upper Saddle River, NJ: Prentice-Hall, Inc.

Coates, Robert B. 1972. *The Dimensions of Police-Citizen Interaction: A Social Psychological Analysis.* Ph.D. dissertation, University of Maryland.

Cox, Steven M. 1996. *Police: Practices-Perspectives-Problems.* Boston, MA: Allyn and Bacon.

Currant, James, ed. 1972. *Police and Law Enforcement 1973–1974.* Vol. II. New York: AIMS Press, Inc.

Frankel, Bruce. 1992. "Police Chiefs Worry about Job Security." *USA Today* (19 November).

Goldstein, Herman. 1977. *Policing a Free Society.* Cambridge, MA: Ballinger Publishing Company.

Golembiewski, Robert T., Michael Lloyd, Katherine Scherb, Robert F. Munzenrider. 1992. Burnout and Mental Health Among Police Officers. *Journal of Public Administration Research and Theory* 2(4): 424–439.

Greene, Jack R. and Carl B. Klockars. 1985. What Police Do. In *Thinking About Police: Contemporary Readings* (2d ed.) by Carl B. Klockars and Stephen D. Mastrofski (New York: McGraw-Hill).

Hatting, Steven H., Engel, Alan S., and Russo, Phillip A., Jr. 1983. Shades of Blue: Toward an Alternative Typology of Police. *Journal of Police Science and Administration* 11: 54–61.

Hoover, Larry. 1992. *Police Management: Issues and Perspectives.* Washington, D.C.: Police Executive Research Forum.

Klockars, Carl B. 1985. *The Idea of Police.* Newbury Park, CA: Sage Publications, Inc.

Lennings, C. J. 1997. Police and Occupationally Related Violence: A Review. *Policing: An International Journal of Police Strategies and Management* 20(3): 555–566.

Manning, Peter and John Van Maanen, eds. 1978. *Policing: A View from the Street.* Santa Monica, CA: Goodyear Publishing Company, Inc.

Manning, Peter K. 1997. *Police Work: The Social Organization of Policing.* 2d ed. Prospect Heights, IL: Waveland Press.

Muir, William K. 1977. *Police: Streetcorner Politicians.* Chicago: University of Chicago Press.

National Advisory Commission on Criminal Justice Standards and Goals. 1973. *Report on Police.* Washington, D.C.: United States Government Printing Office.

National Commission on Law Observance and Enforcement. 1931. Report on Police. Washington, D.C.: United States Government Printing Office.

Niederhoffer, Arthur and Abraham Blumberg. 1976. *The Ambivalent Force: Perspectives on the Police.* 2d ed. Hinsdale, IL: The Dryden Press.

President's Commission on Law Enforcement and Administration of Justice. 1968. *The Challenge of Crime in a Free Society.* New York: Avon Books.

Selye, Hans. 1974. *Stress Without Distress.* New York, NY: J.B. Lippincott Co.

Skolnick, Jerome and Thomas C. Gray, eds. 1975. *Police in America.* Boston, MA: Little, Brown and Company.

Smith, Charles P., Donald E. Pehlke, and Charles D. Weller. 1974. *Role Performance and the Criminal Justice System, Volume II: Detailed Performance Objectives, Project STAR.* Cincinnati, OH: Anderson Publishing Company and Santa Cruz, CA: Davis Publishing Company.

Staufenberger, Richard, ed. 1980. *Progress in Policing: Essays on Change.* Cambridge, MA: Ballinger Publishing Company.

Sykes, R., J. Fox, and J. Clark. 1985. A Socio-Legal Theory of Police Discretion. In *The Ambivalent Force: Perspectives on the Police* edited by A. Blumberg and E. Niederhoffer. New York, NY: Holt, Rinehart & Winston.

Walker, Samuel. 1992. *The Police in America: An Introduction.* 2d ed. New York: McGraw-Hill.

Organizational Structure

Copies of this flyer were distributed by New Haven (Connecticut) Department of Police Service Recruiters around the city to recruit not just white males, but also minorities and women. April 1999. (AP/Wide World Photos)

This chapter addresses the questions of how organizational structure relates to effectiveness of the police and the ability to meet the challenges from society. By studying and understanding these ideas you will be able to:

1. State why law enforcement agencies are organized in similar ways nationally.
2. Identify the reasons why traditional organizational structure is now questioned.
3. Describe the newer organizational strategies being implemented nationally.
4. Explain the benefits that can be derived from organizational change.
5. Identify the importance of the patrol officer and supervisor in contemporary law enforcement management approaches.
6. Define the benefits and limits of both traditional and contemporary law enforcement organizational designs.

CHAPTER OUTLINE

I. Organization Theory and its Development
II. Classical Organization Theory
   A. Max Weber
   B. Frederick Taylor
   C. Luther Gulick
   D. Classical Theory Applied to Policing
III. Human Relations Theory
   A. Motivation
   B. Leadership
IV. Modern Management Theory
V. Summary

ORGANIZATION THEORY AND ITS DEVELOPMENT

Law enforcement agencies are, above all else, organizations. Yet we give little thought to the necessity of organizing or how we should organize. Recently, despite discussions centered on reducing bureaucracy or downsizing and reinventing government, little attention has been focused on why bureaucracies get large, or what function they were designed to serve. In law enforcement, as in all other areas of government, questions about size, function, and role are directly related to *how* law enforcement agencies are organized and the *reasons* for a particular form of organization. In other words, the role an organization is expected to play dictates, to a very large degree, how it is organized. Similarly, the size of an organization is related to the way it is organized.

This chapter introduces students to law enforcement organizational structure. It proceeds from the assumption that students are prepared to discard preconceived notions of how an organization should be structured. Accordingly, this chapter invites the student to consider multiple options of organization. As this material is read and pondered, memories of organizational experiences should be called upon for examples. Every one of us has been in organizations, even if we did not think of them as such. The Girl Scouts and Boy Scouts, churches, political parties, schools, our employment location, fraternities and sororities, the military, colleges, universities, and even neighborhood watches provide classic examples of organizations. Each is slightly different, and they are different for a reason. The student should examine those differences as we discuss law enforcement organizations, which also differ greatly.

Generally, there are two fields of theory and practice of which law enforcement students should be aware. First is **organization theory**, which is a body of research and practice that looks at organizations from a design perspective. The subjects of organization theory include how an organization should be structured, how tasks should be divided, and how personnel should be assigned to those tasks. The second field of study and practice is **organizational behavior**, which examines how people act within an organization. This field includes motivation, leadership, group dynamics, and organizational change and development. These fields helped give birth to the **human relations** and **human resource movements**. The former addresses the needs of individuals in an organization, while the latter views the individual as an organizational asset. Both are treated here in the context of human relations theory as a single topic. Each of these fields and topics will be examined in turn, together with their importance to law enforcement personnel.

Organizations have been a part of social life from the beginning of recorded history. The Romans, for example, had very complex bureaucracies before the birth of Christ, as the Greeks did before the Romans. Still, very little theory about organization design survived. There is evidence that thought was given to the problem of how to organize. Aristotle, for instance, wrote in 360 B.C. of some organizational issues influenced by culture. Even earlier, the Chinese philosopher Sun Tzu, in his classic work *The Art of War,* discussed the need for hierarchy in organizing armies. One translation (Griffith 1963) indicates that Sun Tzu said:

> The art of war is of vital importance to the state. It is a matter of life and death, a road either to safety or to ruin. Hence under no circumstances can it be neglected. The art of war is governed by five constant factors, all of which need to be taken into account. They are: the Moral Law; Heaven; Earth; the Commander; Method and Discipline. *The Moral Law* causes the people to be in complete accord with their ruler, so that they will follow him regardless of their lives, undismayed by any danger. *Heaven* signifies night and day, cold and heat, times and seasons. *Earth* comprises distances, great and small; danger and security; open ground and narrow passes; the chances of life and death. *The Commander* stands for the virtues of wisdom, sincerity, benevolence, courage, and strictness. By *Method and Discipline* are to be understood the marshaling of the army in it proper subdivisions, the gradation of rank among the officers, the maintenance of roads by

which supplies may reach the army, and the control of military expenditure. These five factors should be familiar to every general. He who knows them will be victorious; he who knows them not will fail.

Writing in approximately 770 A.D., an early Muslim scholar, Abu Yusuf, discussed the administrative problems of Islamic government, including finance and criminal justice (Shafritz and Ott 1996).

What emerged from these early efforts are scattered general ideas about the organization of large entities. Heavy duty, "industrial strength" organization theory really did not arrive until the advent of the industrial revolution.

CLASSICAL ORGANIZATION THEORY

Throughout most of the early history of the United States, the postal department was the largest government organization. Because it was a highly decentralized organization, little thought was paid to its structure. Moreover, from the earliest days of the nation there were few men serving in the regular army or navy. The nation was largely agricultural as well. Accordingly, there was little experience with permanent large-scale organizations anywhere in the United States. However, the development of large scale manufacturing produced problems never before envisioned. It was also at about this time (1880s) that governments became oriented towards social reform. This movement occurred not only in the United States (later expanding with the "New Deal" of the 1930s); it began as early as the 1830s in Prussia (Germany). In the United States, the Interstate Commerce Commission was created in 1886 to regulate railroad fees on behalf of farmers. Between 1880 and 1940, the growth of government agencies and private companies was phenomenal, assisted tremendously by the growth of administrative organizations devoted to social policy, including law enforcement.

The creation of police departments, schools, sanitation districts, fire departments, and prisons required greater attention to the organization and management of large-scale organizations. The models for organizational design were necessarily drawn variously from the military model, the Roman Catholic Church, or the newly emerging economic model (mass production lines). Figure 8–1 illustrates a typical organizational chart for a large agency, and Exhibit 8–1 explains the rationale for "interpreting" the meaning of the lines connecting the boxes and the relationships that can be determined by such charts.

Max Weber

These models were similar enough that several theorists developed highly articulated theories about organization design. Max Weber, writing in the late 1800s (but not published in English before 1922), suggested that organizations

Figure 8–1 Typical Traditional Organizational Chart Design

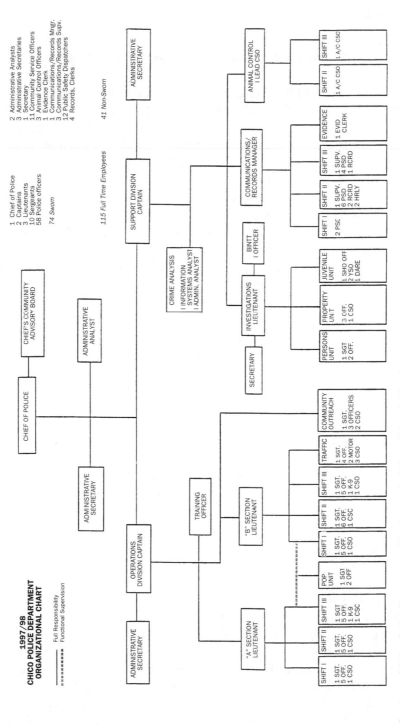

1997/98
CHICO POLICE DEPARTMENT
ORGANIZATIONAL CHART

— Full Responsibility
∎∎∎ Functional Supervision

1 Chief of Police
2 Captains
3 Lieutenants
10 Sergeants
58 Police officers

74 Sworn

2 Administrative Analysts
3 Administrative Secretaries
1 Secretary
11 Community Service Officers
3 Animal Control Officers
1 Evidence Clerk
1 Communications/Records Mngr.
3 Communications/Records Supv.
12 Public Safety Dispatchers
4 Records, Clerks

41 Non-Sworn

115 Full Time Employees

Courtesy of Chico Police Department, City Attorney's Office, Chico, California.

Exhibit 8–1

READING THE TRADITIONAL ORGANIZATIONAL CHART

A table of organization is a chart that shows the positions in an organization and the prescribed interaction between those positions. Each little box on such a chart represents a position or a category of positions. Height on the page is a measure of status. Vertical lines represent the interaction of superiors and subordinates. Horizontal lines represent the interaction of equals.

Any table of organization resembles any other in representing the structure of the organization to consist of positions and interactions. Positions are identified by activity and status. The title of the position on the chart ordinarily identifies its activity. Its distance from the bottom or the top of the chart measures its status. The lines that are drawn between positions indicate prescribed (or occasionally observed) interaction with other positions. Most tables of organization emphasize interaction between superiors and direct subordinates. They minimize or omit interaction between equals and between widely separated positions.

It is sometimes objected that the table of organization does not tell us how an organization works, only how it is *supposed* to work. Informal interaction accounts for part of the discrepancy, but there are other reasons too, such as the tendency for information to lag behind the small social changes that occur continuously and the tendency for desirable conditions to be hopefully included as facts. . . . Nevertheless, the table of organization always tells us a great deal, and it is doubtful whether we can talk sensibly about a particular organization without it.

Source: Adapted with permission from T. Caplow, *Principles of Organization*, pp. 50–62, © 1964, Harcourt, Inc.

---

represented the natural trend in society towards what he called "rationalization." Drawing upon early theory and his observations about world social development, Weber concluded that the essential aspect of organization was **hierarchy** represented by the emergence of **bureaucracy**. This meant a division of labor, clear lines of authority and communication between superior and subordinate, a single unifying authority at the top of the hierarchy producing a clear chain of command, and, most importantly, hiring and promotion based upon merit and productivity, not personality or politics (Gortner *et al.* 1987). In summary, this is the general framework for most organizations in the public sector today, and it represents the design of most law enforcement agencies.

Frederick Taylor

Another theorist of the same time, Frederick Taylor, examined both the way people work (job design) and the way the organization is structured. His **scientific management** theory centered on understanding the work to be done by breaking it down into its smallest parts, which he called "therbligs." By understanding the work better, you could scientifically train a worker to do exactly what the job required. He also developed the organizational idea of a planning staff to give management direction (Fry 1989). These notions, together with those of Weber and others, gave organizations a model for structuring work: Define the job, train to the tasks of that job, hire the best-trained, promote on the same basis, and have a strong and clear hierarchy.

Taylor's purpose was to directly link skill and productivity to pay. He reasoned that if skill was in place and properly applied, productivity should follow. However, he also believed workers were inherently lazy. Consequently, pay was tied directly to the amount of work that *should be performed* in a period of time according to the scientific analysis of each job. If you produced more in that period of time, you received more pay. If you produced less, you received less.

Luther Gulick

In the period of the late 1930s, other organization theorists added to the growing body of work on the topic. The most famous, Luther Gulick, a trusted advisor to then President Franklin Roosevelt, noted that there were limits to the ways work could be divided. He argued that effective communications were essential, and that the **span of control**—the number of employees supervised—should be small. This meant that no single individual should control more than a few people (three to seven). Further, the notion of **unity of command** should apply from the top of an organization to the bottom. This meant that every individual should report to only one individual in the organization, and that the line of authority (or chain of command) would be traceable from any person to the top of the organization.

Most interestingly, he started the debate over whether you should organize by function or by product (both defined later in this chapter), a concept very important to current designs for law enforcement organizations. Finally, he noted that you could also organize either by "dominance of an idea" or by "structuring authority" (Shafritz and Ott 1992). Dominance of an idea meant that a set of values (such as a mission statement or agency goals) could dominate the management of an organization and direct its activities. Structuring by authority was simply the use of hierarchical authority to impose management's desires by orders and supervision.

Classical Theory Applied to Policing

The body of concepts and philosophy from Weber, Taylor, and Gulick, among others, is frequently called **classical organization theory** (see Exhibit 8–2). It took hold in policing for three major reasons. The first was political reform. Prior to the very early 1900s, police forces were quite political, and hiring was politically influenced as positions of rank such as Captain were literally bought and sold (Knott and Miller 1988). The so-called "spoils system" of politics controlled government. The Progressive Reform Movement of the late 1800s and early 1900s sought to end these abuses (see Chapters 3 and 10), in part by advocating reliance on a civil service system. This system employed objective testing for employment and promotion. However, reformers also wanted to maintain some political accountability. In a democracy, there should be some way to control government agencies and maintain political accountability. An organization run much as Weber and Taylor suggested would theoretically achieve these competing goals. Political control would come from carefully designing the jobs to be performed and the manner of performance. A single executive, merit hiring, and promotion would insure that the most qualified would be employed and be responsible to one person. The second reason for the hold that classical theory had on policing was the use of the paramilitary model of command, which fit well in a classic hierarchy. Third, the effort

---

Exhibit 8–2

TENETS OF CLASSICAL ORGANIZATION THEORY

One Executive
Unity of Command
Chain of Command
Short Span of Control
Merit Hire (qualifications)
Scientifically Designed Jobs
Merit Promotion (performance)
Division of Labor and Specialization
Line and Staff Functions Defined by Position

to professionalize law enforcement reinforced the importance of merit and, therefore, hierarchy (see Chapter 15).

Classical writers in organization theory often referred to their observations as the "principles of scientific management." These principles were applied to law enforcement agencies throughout the United States just at the time professionalization and political reform were taking hold. Accordingly, most existing police departments tend to emulate the traditional hierarchical model of an organization. Figure 8–1 (above) is an example of what resulted from the application of traditional organization theory. The trademarks of classic organizations included distinct levels, the differentiation between units (specialization), progressive promotion from within based upon merit, and a single line of authority from top to bottom. The following sections examine some of the ways in which classical principles were applied to policing organizations, and these are followed by a discussion of more contemporary designs.

Organization by Product and Function

When Luther Gulick observed that an enterprise could organize by function or by product, he concluded that the most effective means was to organize by function (Gulick 1937). This was the prevailing belief in most government agencies, and, as Exhibit 8–3 demonstrates, this became the accepted organization method in police agencies. In early application, organization by product was ignored in law enforcement agencies. Organization by product means that *all* officers needed to produce a result, such as drug arrests. This would include patrol, investigation, clerical, non-sworn officers, and other support staff throughout the agency. Organization by function is characterized by grouping employees together according to the major functions that they perform. The number of functions will grow as administrative and service demands grow. A listing of typical functions serviced by police agencies is indicated in Exhibit 8–4.

The most obvious function associated with law enforcement is patrol. In an agency that was organized solely by function, patrol units would be unrelated to other units except by chain of command (see Chapter 9 for a detailed discussion of patrol). In some departments, specialized patrol teams using helicopters, bicycles, motorcycles, boats, or horses may be organized as separate units or deployed as part of the general patrol unit. In larger departments, there may be traffic units that are separate from general patrol. Others may have specialized patrol functions, such as park patrol, harbor or river patrol, or border patrol. In each case, the method or design of organization is related to function. The organization of each department is related to the variety of functions identified by that department. Many functions, such as general patrol, are common to nearly all departments while others, such as harbor patrol or school pa-

Exhibit 8–3

FUNCTIONAL ACTIVITIES

Criminal investigation	Budgetary control
Personnel	Purchasing
Criminal identification	Crime prevention
Communications	Transportation
Traffic regulation and control	Property control
Planning	Follow-up control
Police records	Jail administration
Statistical operations	Public relations
Supply	Intelligence
Criminalistics	Internal affairs
Patrol	Community relations

trol, are employed in only a few places. Exhibit 8–4 identifies the typical line and staff functions within policing agencies.

Similarly, while all law enforcement agencies perform investigations, most have designated investigators or detectives, though the use of these personnel is defined by local circumstances. There is usually a separate detective bureau or investigations unit. In larger agencies, these may be further broken down into heavily specialized investigative units (e.g., burglary, robber, sex crimes, and homicide squads). Sometimes specialized units are given the name "Task Force," though, technically, a task force is really a temporary organizational division that is created for a limited purpose. Examples are organized crime task forces or narcotics task forces, which may be inter-agency units (i.e., comprised of members from several different law enforcement agencies).

Still other departments create permanent units and give them a title that conveys permanency, such as "Organized Crime Unit." The most common of such units specialize in organized crime, narcotics, auto theft, vice (gambling and prostitution), crimes against women (rape and domestic violence), gangs, and white-collar crime. Newer problems have introduced new functional demands, such as environmental crime, computer crime, and growing levels of official corruption. Whether these are given specialized status or not depends solely upon the need and priorities of the agency, thus accounting for the wide variation in organizational applications across the country. For example, white-collar crime is more likely in communities with high concentrations of banking, insurance, or securities activities. Environmental crimes are more likely in communities with industrial facilities using toxic materials.

Exhibit 8–4

COMMON LINE AND STAFF FUNCTIONS
IN LAW ENFORCEMENT AGENCIES

1. Patrol	
2. Criminal investigation	
3. Vice investigation	Line Operations
4. Traffic regulation and control	
5. Crime prevention	
6. Juvenile bureau	

1. Planning
2. Inspection
3. Personnel administration
4. Police records system
5. Statistical operations
6. Follow-up control
7. Identification services
8. Property control
9. Communication system
10. Budgetary control   Staff Functions
11. Purchasing
12. Transportation
13. Jail administration
14. Supply
15. Crime detection laboratory
16. Public relations
17. Intelligence
18. Internal affairs
19. Community relations

Other organizational functions—for instance, records, personnel, and purchasing—are relatively similar from agency to agency. In larger agencies, these are usually separate offices or units. In smaller agencies, functions are frequently combined. For example, criminalistics (or criminal identification) may be part of the investigations unit, while crime prevention, public relations, and community relations may be combined into one unit. The organization principle, however, is generally the same. Departments are organized so that personnel functions determine organizational division.

There are both benefits and limitations to this organizational principle. Beneficially, the organizational chart indicates whom to contact for a given question or problem. Another benefit is the clarity it brings to the organization. Individual duties and responsibilities are more easily defined, making it simpler to train and integrate new personnel. Politically and administratively, this approach produces clear accountability and also encourages an organizational identification or *esprit de corps*. For the administrator and legislative policy maker, it makes budgeting decisions much easier. In short, organization by function is a classical organizational model because divisions are based upon specialization of task.

The classical model, as useful as it is, has its limitations (Franz and Jones 1987). The problems induced by this traditional form of organization are as numerous as the benefits. The impact of benefits and limitations varies according to the environment in which the organization operates. Obviously, a police department in a town of 20,000 people surrounded by farmland operates in a different environment than does one in a city of 800,000 that is itself surrounded by urban sprawl. Similarly, budget and economic conditions, social upheavals, and changing population patterns alter an organization's environment. Issues related to rural crime are discussed in Exhibit 8–5.

In a stable environment, traditional structures are able to predict future needs and demands and rationally plan for those needs. For example, if you can reasonably predict the amount of crime you expect to see in an area over a certain period of time, you can plan patrol and investigation staffing to meet those needs. You can determine your deployment needs by shift, by area, and by day. But in a turbulent and chaotic environment, a condition that organization theorists refer to as a "dynamic environment," the situation is different. It is more difficult to predict adequately the demands that will be placed on an organization. Surprises are more frequent, and in this environment, results are more unpredictable if things are done the way they "always were." Herbert Simon noted that traditional or classical forms of organization reduce the ability of personnel to assess the amount of information needed to plan (Fry 1989). In a set of stable conditions, these limitations are unimportant. But in a period of chaos or rapid change, they pose serious problems for an organization.

Simon also recognized that one of the primary functions of an organization is to make decisions, but he argued that organizations and decision makers are "bounded" by limitations of time, money, knowledge, and other resources. Classical or traditional organizational structures are designed to limit the amount of information that flows to the top decision-making levels. These limitations mean that organizations make decisions with imperfect knowledge. Again, in a stable environment, this is not fatal to organizational decisions, but in a turbulent or dynamic environment, the consequences may be quite negative.

Conditions for law enforcement are changing. Concentrated pockets of violent crime are increasing even while much traditional crime is decreasing. The

Exhibit 8–5

RURAL CRIME AND POLICING

- Compared with urban areas, little is known about rural crime or rural policing. It appears, however, that crime is less frequent in rural areas, and that "community policing," to which many urban departments now aspire, has been a long-standing practice in rural police agencies.

- While the terms "rural" and "urban" are used frequently in everyday language, there are no precise meanings of these terms upon which everyone can agree. Despite this, it is clear that the idea of rural is useful.

- Differences between rural and urban cultures have implications for rural crime and rural policing. For example, both rural and urban areas have pockets of extreme poverty, but the effects of poverty on crime are different in the two areas.

- Differences across rural areas are large and vary by region of the country, across counties within a State, and sometimes even within a county. For example, illegal immigrants may be a concern in the Southwest, vandalism in the Midwest, and the smuggling of tobacco and liquor in areas along the Canadian border. Thus, national policies uniformly covering rural areas may be a mistake, unless those polices can be tailored to fit local needs.

- There are contradictions across studies that need to be explained. For example, some authors report that homicide is higher in rural areas, while others (including UCR data) suggest the opposite. It is unclear whether these differences are the product of sampling, the definitions used, or regional variations.

- Studying these issues across rural areas and between urban and rural areas is useful in the same way that studies of crime across countries tell us much about larger patterns and suggest what works and what does not work in policing and crime prevention.

Source: Reprinted from R. Weisheit, D. Falcone, and L. E. Wells (1994), *Rural Crime and Rural Policing, Research in Action*, 1994, U.S. Department of Justice, National Institute of Justice.

emergence of crack and designer drugs, proliferation of automatic weapons, escalation of drive-by shootings, and increased juvenile violence between 1980 and 1996 have changed the environment for law enforcement. Cities·are growing ever more diverse; many neighborhoods are physically deteriorating and becoming highly transient. Rigid organizations are not well suited to function effectively in these conditions. The major limitations of traditional organization structure, then, relate to the process of decision making and response to environmental change.

Another limitation of classical organization theory is goal displacement. Those who work in the organization learn to focus on rules rather than on service. Similarly, members of the organization are likely to respond to requests for assistance with phrases like "It's not in my job description." This is called **trained incapacity**, because people are trained not only in what *to do*, but also in what *not to do*, even if it makes sense to them to do it. The result of these limitations, called **organizational dysfunction**, is that organizations are not inclined to be imaginative or innovative. They will not use information about the environment properly and are inclined to rigidity. Retreating to "the book" serves to further isolate the organization from its clients, which in the case of policing is the public. Structure and rule rigidity prevent flexibility. All of these problems suggest that law enforcement may need to reassess its current approach to organizational design. This holds important implications for the patrol officer. In classical organizations, patrol officers are at the bottom of the structure. Their role, more or less, is to follow orders within a narrow range and engage in a limited set of predefined tasks. In other organizational formulations, the role of patrol officers would change dramatically.

Many law enforcement agencies recognized some of the limitations of the classical organization structure relatively early in the development of modern policing. Many also realized the limitations built into organizing by function. Minor changes in organizational principles resulted. These were organizing by time and place (or area) (Wilson 1950).

For example, many law enforcement agencies are inherently spread out over large distances that require time to cover. An example is the state highway patrol. Such agencies may be divided into relatively self-contained units called posts, regions, or districts. Figure 8–2 illustrates the geographical distribution of district and county post locations for the Ohio State Highway Patrol. Similarly, municipal police agencies may cover vast amounts of territory and hundreds of thousands or millions of people. Usually, these agencies are divided into "precincts" that may have not only patrol and investigation but other organic specialized units, such as Special Weapons and Tactics (SWAT) teams. The typical arrangement is for each such precinct to include all of the line functions (refer to Figure 8–1) and some of the staff functions (such as records, jail administration, and community relations) in one unit. In this arrangement, a

Ohio State Highway Patrol Post Locations

Courtesy of Ohio State Highway Patrol, Columbus, Ohio.

Figure 8–2 Ohio State Highway Patrol Post Locations

department is organized by area and divided into precincts and each precinct is organized by function.

Another kind of organizational approach is to organize by clientele (Leonard and Moore 1987). A relatively common example of this approach is the creation of juvenile units. Similarly, state highway patrol agencies normally have a special unit assigned to truck safety.

Each of these organizational arrangements can temporarily address some of the limitations of classical hierarchy, but they have their own built-in limitations, since each approach is similar to organization by function. In order to understand the reasons *why* policing is changing and *how* it is changing structurally, it is important to understand its prior forms of organization. The cumulative effects of merit service, professionalization, and specialization. between the 1880s and 1920s, led to a steep hierarchy in most departments. Poor communication, little training, and limited education among officers combined to require close supervision and, thereby adding to the need for a very short span of control. As crime patterns changed in the 1960s, further specialization produced even more complex bureaucracies. Why did these events occur?

Organizations are structured as a response to different task demands made by society and by the environment surrounding the organization (Zhao 1996). If either or both change, then the organization must change. This is why so many private sector organizations are altering their business structures in the 1990s. Not only have market conditions changed, but the environment has changed. Each form of organizational arrangement has certain benefits, but each also has limitations. Organizations that fail to accommodate changes in demands will invariably falter. Attempts at more flexible organizational approaches began to appear as a consequence of the need to adapt to rapidly changing conditions. Hence, law enforcement finds itself hobbled by steep and isolated hierarchies in a turbulent environment. These structures are one of the targets that community policing reformers seek to respond to changing social needs.

HUMAN RELATIONS THEORY

Another set of researchers and practitioners in organizations looked beyond the mere structure of an organization for ways to make organizations more effective. These theorists examined the impact of individuals and small groups on organizations. Experiments in industrial psychology led theorists as early as the 1930s to examine how human beings worked in organizations. The collected body of research and concepts associated with this approach is called the **human relations theory** of management.

Despite more than 60 years of efforts, only the past 30 years produced real change in organization theory and in organizations themselves. For law enforcement agencies, we can generally reduce these to two major areas. **Motivation** is a broad field of study that focuses on *why* people want to work (Conser 1979; Katzell and Thompson 1990). The field of **leadership** is closely related and focuses on *how* management is able to get organizations to follow a defined path. Line and staff employees frequently see both concepts differently than do leaders or managers in an organization. This chapter attempts no detailed analysis of these very complex concepts. We leave that for a course on human resources or organizational behavior. However, it is important for the entry-level officer to be aware of the issues in these areas and how they are developing. The trends hold important implications for patrol-grade officers and supervisors.

Motivation

Researchers addressing motivation focused on human needs and found that while some aspects of work motivate people (motivators), others only prevent dissatisfaction (so-called hygiene factors or maintainers) (Herzberg 1968). These researchers also found that motivation is the product of a calculative process in which individuals arrive at the probabilities of acquiring certain needs (Campbell *et al.* 1970). The central thrust of this theory is that people in organizations have two general drives related to their performance. The first is motivation. People are motivated to perform tasks if three conditions exist: (1) they believe that rewards are tied to performance, (2) they value the rewards, and (3) performance is thought to be achievable. Motivation is enhanced if people are permitted to participate in the setting of organizational goals, are given interesting tasks, and are permitted to participate in deciding how to perform those tasks. Taken together, this means that people can be motivated in an organization if they see clear, achievable goals that they value and to which there is a clear path (Rainey 1993). Exhibit 8–6 summarizes the key elements of the path-goal theory of motivation.

The second distinct drive is satisfaction, or the degree to which employees feel satisfied with their work and with the rewards for that work. Motivation is a response to the expectation of future rewards. Satisfaction is a response to past rewards. They are also distinct in that satisfaction is related to turnover and absenteeism. More importantly, satisfaction improves as participation in

---

Exhibit 8–6

PATH-GOAL THEORY OF MOTIVATION

Clear Goals
Clear Rewards
Valued Goals and Rewards
Participation in Goal Creation
Goals Thought To Be Achievable
Clear Path to Goal Achievement

decision making increases (Wagner 1994; Lawler 1986). These are important factors for both leaders and subordinates to understand. For law enforcement organizations, the known sources of motivation and satisfaction pose a problem. The single most common reward (motivator) is monetary compensation and promotion (Ledford 1995). In civil service systems, these two are tied together in a way they are not in private business. That is, pay for performance is common in business, while pay for longevity (length of tenure) is common in civil service systems such as law enforcement. Moreover, law enforcement agency pay is set by legislative bodies, not by managers, and promotion is largely controlled by civil service rules. Hence, managers in law enforcement are left to find other means to motivate officers, including special training, special assignments, shift assignment, and overtime consideration.

In order to do this, however, they need information. Patrol officers, supervisors, and staff must communicate the level of morale in the agency to managers in order to permit effective decisions. You will recall that traditional hierarchical organization structures restrict effective communication. One solution is to use an alternate organizational structure. An additional solution is for law enforcement managers to adopt leadership approaches that seek out information and participation in decision making.

Alternative motivators are numerous. One is the degree to which leaders listen to subordinates and communicate reasons for actions. Another is job definition, temporary job assignments, general reassignments, and the creation of task forces or teams. Jobs can be redefined to permit subordinates to focus on areas of their own interest. Thus, reassignment of patrol officers to community service programs in the schools, such as DARE, is normally within the authority of managers, but does not involve pay or promotion. Subordinates should be free to make suggestions about such approaches.

Task force and team approaches also address satisfaction. As temporary assignments outside of the normal hierarchy, these approaches overcome the limitations of classical structure and permit employees to take advantage of specialized skills and interests. More importantly, they encourage cooperative decision making. Employees who are given active input into their roles are more motivated and more satisfied.

Issues of motivation and satisfaction are also important due to the high levels of job burnout and stress in law enforcement. Sources of stress are organization practices, criminal justice system practices, public attitudes, and factors intrinsic to the job, including danger, differential social treatment, and unusual working hours. These combine to create personal, social, and family difficulties for officers. Not all stress is negative, of course. It may make officers cautious in dangerous situations or work harder when the stakes are exciting. But it can be negative, and it may cause officers to react to outside stimuli in ways that are not positive (Gaines 1993). Strategies such as exercise can be employed to avoid debilitating stress. Also, officers need to feel free to communicate personal problems to their superiors who, in turn, must reduce the role that the organization plays in creating stress. Participative decision making and the use of **job enlargement** (discussed in detail later in this chapter) to increase levels of motivation and satisfaction will have a beneficial effect. Last, fellow officers must discuss problems and solutions with one another.

Leadership

Theories about leadership demonstrate the close relationship that exists between organizational structure, motivation, and leader behavior. Initially, theories of leadership focused on traits that "good" leaders have. But this is a very limited view, since it implies that certain people are born to be leaders and others are not, which is untrue.

The more likely possibility is that leaders are people who can use certain skills to obtain information in and act in an appropriate way depending upon circumstances. This **contingent leadership** model suggests everyone can learn to be a leader. More importantly, it does not limit leadership to only top positions in an organization. Rather, it implies that patrol officers and supervisors are leaders and can learn skills to become more effective at leading. Research has demonstrated that the most effective leaders were those who employed teams, showed a high level of concern for people as well as a high level of concern for results, and were able to show others in the organization how to achieve goals (Hersey *et al.* 1996; Rainey 1991). This leadership approach produced high performance, high satisfaction, and high levels of motivation.

Clearly, patrol officers are as important as managers in developing good leadership. Indeed, training for leadership roles begins at the patrol level, as the use of task forces, teams, community policing, and similar concepts require leadership at the lowest levels of the organization. Leaders in teams and task forces learn to invite participation and cooperation and discover that every member of the group can lead.

Leadership roles may only be temporary. This is very different from a definition of leadership that is dependent upon the position in the organization. Top managers must be leaders, yes, but all officers must exercise leadership. Because diverse skills, backgrounds, and knowledge increase leadership resources in the organization, patrol officers can contribute dramatically to the leadership of the agency.

The key is seeing leadership not as controlling or commanding, but rather as mentoring, guiding, facilitating, and encouraging others. Traditional "authority" is produced not by demand, but instead by demonstrating an ability to command an organization's resources. Command, therefore, is not obtained merely by giving orders.

MODERN MANAGEMENT THEORY

As the discussion above suggests, the classical paramilitary hierarchy employed in the organization of most law enforcement agencies is not very adaptive to rapidly changing conditions. Further, classical organization structures do not enhance motivation, increase satisfaction, or reduce stress. As is clear from other chapters in this book, the environmental conditions surrounding law enforcement are changing rapidly. Law enforcement organizations are faced with emerging demands from their communities, complex social problems related to crime, shifting crime patterns, shrinking budgets, and slipping morale.

Classical hierarchy is not very adept at satisfying employees. Low employee satisfaction levels produce burnout, stress, and high rates of turnover. Law enforcement officers who are burned out or who are operating under stress are likely to make poor decisions and work with a low degree of effectiveness. Costs to the organization are both financial and performance-related. Turnover is costly because organizations have tremendous investments in employees. The cost of training replacements is significant, and the loss of experienced officers is damaging from a performance perspective. Indeed, the greater the experience of the lost employee, the greater the cost to the organization in terms of performance.

For each of these reasons, law enforcement agencies (like most organizations) find themselves questioning the current practice of organizing by hierarchy (Roberg and Kuykendall 1997). Some approaches to avoiding the limitations of hierarchical structure attempt to employ multiple talents in any one project or assignment.

The first approach to take advantage of multiple talents is the use of **matrix organization** (Figure 8–3) (Swanson *et al.* 1993). Following this approach, a number of personnel are assigned to a given problem regardless of their permanent duty location. The organization is then able to take advantage of the best personnel for a given problem without permanent structuring problems. However, it is very difficult to manage day-to-day operations and achieve accountability in matrix organizations. In many respects, this is not very different from task force operations, though typically a task force takes 100 percent of an employee's time. A matrix assignment, however, involves only part of an employee's time. Hence, an officer could be involved in two or three matrix-based projects at one time.

A variation of this form is problem-oriented policing (POP, discussed in Chapter 9), where efforts are organized around a particular problem (Goldstein 1990). This means that whole operations are mounted against a particular problem. Participant officers may be assigned temporarily or part-time to the problem. This is a form of organization by product, but it may be considered a team design, depending upon the specific situation.

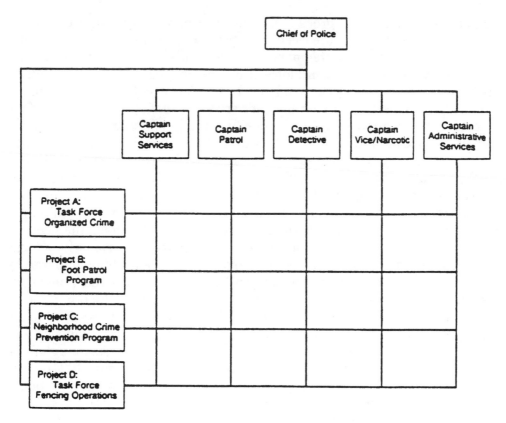

Source: Reprinted from C. R. Swanson, L. Territo, and R. W. Taylor, *Police Administration: Structures, Processes and Behavior*, Third Edition, p. 152, © 1993. Reprinted by permission of Prentice-Hall, Inc., Upper Saddle River, NJ.

Figure 8–3 Matrix Organization Applied to Policing

An organizational form similar to the matrix form is team policing. In this organizational approach, teams are created based upon specific areas, which may be a geographic area, or specific problems (similar to problem-oriented policing, such as, street gangs, prostitution, or drug trafficking). Team members are selected from all, or many, of the line operations and assigned full-time to the team. Teams are fully responsible for the assigned area or problem and typically are given wide discretion.

Each of these approaches (matrix, task force, problem-oriented, and team-oriented policing) are very similar from the perspective of an organization theorist. They differ only in organizational permanence, level of discretion, and complexity of problems assigned. The point of each of these methods is an attempt to overcome some of the serious limitations of classical hierarchy so deeply representative of law enforcement organizations. For patrol officers, each of these methods offers varying degrees of increased responsibility and discretion. In effect, these models give more freedom to patrol officers and supervisors to use a wider variety of skills in attempting a broader variety of solutions than those permitted by traditional organizational structure. Still, each model is essentially based upon the functions that each individual performs in the organization.

In some respects, these determinations are being made independently of the effort to move toward the use of community policing models as a theory or philosophy of policing. But, in practical terms, both the move toward community-oriented policing (COP) and the move away from hierarchy are linked (Bayley 1994). Community policing redefines the roles of officers, the targets of law enforcement activities, and the assignment of resources in the organization (see Chapters 9 and 16). The result is an organization with a very different focus than before. Traditional structures are ill-designed to meet the needs of the new approach. As policing becomes broader in its concerns, with a focus on employees with multiple skills, the narrow design of traditional hierarchy ceases to hold relevance. Hence, law enforcement agencies are redefining management in order to respond to environmental challenges to the organization, to advances in organization and human relations theory, and to respond to the developing theory of community policing (Greene *et al.* 1994). Evidence suggests that COP might improve officer satisfaction and motivation, though there is insufficient evidence to be certain (Wilkinson and Rosenbaum 1994). However, we do know that research generally supports the notion that participation improves performance and satisfaction levels (Wagner 1994).

What should modern law enforcement organizations *look like*, and *how should they work* to meet each of the challenges and satisfy the needs of community policing? In terms of look, modern organizations are developing very "flat" structures (Figure 8–4). These are called flat designs or flat organizations because there are very few levels of hierarchy. Compare Figure 8–1 with Figure 8–4. The most obvious differences between the two designs are, first, the number of levels of organization and, second, the number of units that report to any one person or office above. The so-called span of control is much broader in a flat organizational structure.

This form of organization improves communications within organizations as management obtains information with fewer "filters." That is, information is less likely to be "sanitized," a process by which only good information percolates to the top. Most people hate to be the bearer of bad news, and multiple levels increase the probability that negative information will be blocked. Similarly, orders, instructions, and goals are more easily communicated to lower levels in a flat organization.

In flat organizations, accountability for actions becomes more certain. Previously, it was thought that accountability was best achieved with someone looking over an employee's shoulder at all times. That required a good deal of looking and many people to do it. Hence, large bureaucracies grew to satisfy

Figure 8–4 Department with a "Flat" Organizational Design

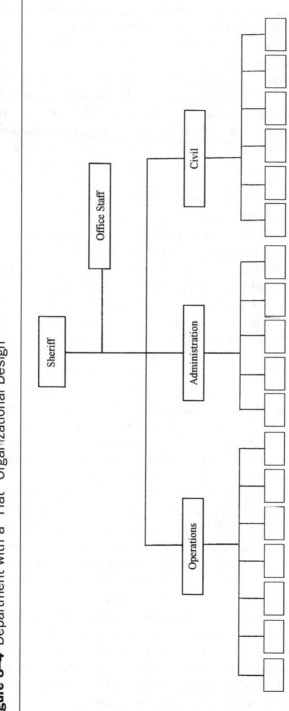

the need for accountability. We now know, however, that bureaucracy actually allows individuals to escape personal accountability. Responsibility can be pushed to lower or higher levels, thereby avoiding it. In flat organizations, however, accountability is very localized and forces individuals to take personal responsibility for performance.

Flat organizations also respond to the need for new ways to motivate and satisfy employees. In flat organizations, the possibility of job enlargement is greater. Job enlargement is a process where employees are given more discretion, flexibility, and authority for performance of assigned duties. Employees are given freedom to determine how best to carry out their tasks. This doesn't mean more work. It means more responsibility for deciding how to do tasks and how to achieve goals set by management. This produces both higher levels of motivation and higher levels of job satisfaction.

Flat forms of organizational design also offer the possibility of organizational flexibility, fluidity, and rapid problem response. More resources are directly under the control of management, and fewer people are required for agreement. Employees are given more choice in how they accomplish tasks. Management is thereby freed to set goals and evaluate performance without a need to "micromanage." As employees are given more responsibility, their skill inventory increases. Coupled with the increase in communications, this leads to greater overall organizational flexibility to respond to rapidly changing conditions.

An agency that is organized in this manner will reduce the costs of its bureaucracy. Previously, one role for mid-level positions was information analysis. In flat organizations, there is less need for organizational positions dedicated to acquiring and analyzing information. These positions will be merged into patrol and other delivery positions, which will become "enlarged." Rapidly improving technology makes this not only possible but necessary. Each employee, from patrol officer to deputy chief, now has access to tremendous amounts of information and the tools for analysis.

The negative aspects of flat organizations are few, but significant. First, this form of organization relies heavily upon a well-trained and educated work force. This includes training in and commitment to basic organizational values (Chapter 6) and goals. Among these would be the mission statement of the organization and the values in the Constitution of the United States and the state in which the agency is located. Training and education (Chapter 11) become the basis for decision making that is decentralized.

A second drawback is the likelihood that divisions or groupings of employees will not be headed by individuals of the same "rank," though they may report to the same superior. In a flat organization, where cooperative decision making at lower levels combines with job enlargement to produce new forms of motivation and satisfaction, rank holds a reduced role. This reduction in rank influence will have negative consequences in the short run, until the correct "rank mix" is established.

Exhibit 8–7

TENETS OF MODERN MANAGEMENT THEORY

Broad Discretion
Value Adherence and Ethics
Open Communications
Participative Decision Making
Cooperative Decision Making
Team and Matrix Assignments
Flat Organizational Structure
Job Enlargement

A third drawback is related to recruitment. Flat designs require the ability to recruit and retain individuals who have the desire and skill to become "self-starters." But the available talent pool is shrinking for every employer in terms of skills and education (Clark 1998).

To summarize the modern perspective, in order to motivate and satisfy employees, avoid burnout, and remain flexible, law enforcement leaders and their organizations must innovate. Law enforcement agencies cannot avoid the imposed hierarchy of civil service, but can employ alternative structures to avoid the limitations of classical structure and gain the benefits of modern managerial approaches. The field must invite job enlargement, cooperative and decentralized decision making, and organizational flattening. Each of these changes is essential to the effective implementation of community policing. To get effective, efficient, satisfied, and motivated employees, organizations must be redesigned. Entry-level officers and veterans alike must accommodate themselves to the implications of these changes and the demands they will make. Exhibit 8–7 summarizes the tenets of modern management theory as described by several authors.

SUMMARY

In this chapter, we looked briefly at the development of organizational theory typical of law enforcement organizations for the better part of the past 100 years. In most respects, we found that traditional or classical structures dominate law enforcement. We looked at the benefits of that organizational approach as well as the problems inherent with that approach. We found that in a rapidly changing world, traditional structures suffer. However, structures that allow lower-level employees to make decisions and participate in leading organizations operate better. (See Appendix 8–1 for additional organizational charts.)

We also looked at some of the ways in which law enforcement organizations may be able to take advantage of this new organizational form, including task groups, teams, and matrix organizations. In each case, the effort increases the span of control, increases individual officer responsibility, and invites innovation and participation in problem solving. We also found that motivation reaches higher levels in this design where management sets clear goals and permits small teams to determine how to achieve those goals. Leadership in such an organization arises from all levels of an organization. Hence, patrol officers must see themselves as leaders *and* followers. Rather than being passive receivers of orders, developing forms of policing theory and organizational principles place patrol officers in the role of leader and decision maker. While adhering to the command structure that is important for political accountability in a democracy, officers must understand the direction of their organizations as we approach the 21st century, even though the police function seemingly has changed little in the past 25 years (Gaines and Cordner 1999).

QUESTIONS FOR REVIEW

1. What were the historical causes of current (traditional) law enforcement organizational designs?
2. What are the limitations and benefits of the traditional or classical organizational structure?
3. What are the benefits and limitations of modern organizational approaches?
4. What motivates employees?
5. What seems to cause stress?
6. What is leadership, and who are leaders?

SUGGESTED ACTIVITIES

1. Ask each student to obtain the organizational chart for a local law enforcement agency. Ask the students to identify the ways in which they are similar and the ways in which they differ.
2. Have each student scan local print media, law enforcement agencies, and community groups for information about how their community has changed in the past 5, 10, and 15 years. When has the most change occurred? What are the challenges that seem to be the most pressing?
3. Develop a list of future challenges that are not yet present but seem likely to happen in the near future that will cause law enforcement problems. These may be variations on current problems or entirely new problems.
4. Most readers of this text have already experimented with tale-telling in circles. Start a story and whisper it to your neighbor. By the time it gets back to you, it will probably not be recognizable. This illustrates how information is slow and inaccurate when it must pass through multiple layers of bureaucracy. Hence, decisions may be based upon faulty or only partial information. In a dynamic environment, it is expected that information will change rapidly.
5. Using your Web browser, search on the term "organizational chart" and locate at least one Web page for a police department. How would you classify it in terms of organizational structure? Why?

CHAPTER GLOSSARY

bureaucracy: the middle of an organization representing the largest portion of the hierarchy; the portion of an organization dedicated to information analysis and communications, including orders

classical organization theory: the body of theory from Weber, Taylor, and Gulick (among others), which relied upon hierarchy, merit hiring, small spans of control, and a single command authority

contingent leadership: a theory of leadership that suggests that everyone can learn to be a leader depending upon the circumstances and a person's abilities in those circumstances

hierarchy: a form of organizational structure that includes a division of labor, clear lines of authority between superior and subordinate, a single unifying authority at the top of the hierarchy, and hiring based upon merit (expertise), not personality or politics

human relations theory: a theory of management that focuses on the needs of the individual and assumes that human needs are related to organizational performance

human resource: a theory of management that looks at individuals as an organizational asset but that ignores the needs of the individual

job enlargement: a process where jobs are given more discretion, flexibility, and authority for performance of assigned duties, so that employees have freedom to determine how best to carry out their tasks; in effect, jobs are made larger

leadership: a field of study, closely related to motivation, that focuses on what makes people able to get organizations to follow a path set by management

matrix organization: an arrangement where a number of personnel are assigned to use a portion of their time for a given problem regardless of their permanent duty location

motivation: a broad field of study that focuses on what makes people want to work

organization theory: the body of research that explores the ways in which people organize themselves to do work

organizational behavior: a body of research that examines organizations in the micro or small group and individual levels

organizational dysfunction: problems inherent in the design of an organization

scientific management: a theory of work organization that held that if you understand and analyze a job by breaking it down into its smallest parts, you can train workers to the exact task without wasting time or effort

span of control: the number of individuals that one person directly supervises or who otherwise directly report to that person

trained incapacity: a behavior that results when employees are trained not only in what to do, but also in what not to do and refuse to go beyond the limited role of their predefined jobs

unity of command: an organizational arrangement where one person is in command of an organization and all other individuals each report to only one person, who can then trace a line of command to the single unifying command at the top

APPENDIX 8–1 SELECTED ORGANIZATIONAL CHARTS

This appendix contains organizational charts for several police departments in the United States. We present them here for comparative purposes and to illustrate that charts tend to be unique and slightly different from each other while maintaining some similarities. Included here are the charts showing the structures for the following departments:

Portland, Oregon
Miami, Florida
Arlington County, Virginia
Lynchburg, Virginia
Santa Maria, California
Orlando, Florida
    —Chief's Staff, with details of composition
    —Patrol Services Bureau, with details of compostion
    —Investigative Services Bureau, with details of composition
    —Special Services Bureau, with details of composition
Ventura, California

PORTLAND POLICE BUREAU
1999 ORGANIZATIONAL CHART

1/22/99

Source: Courtesy of Portland Bureau of Police, Portland, Oregon.

Miami Police Department
Organizational Chart

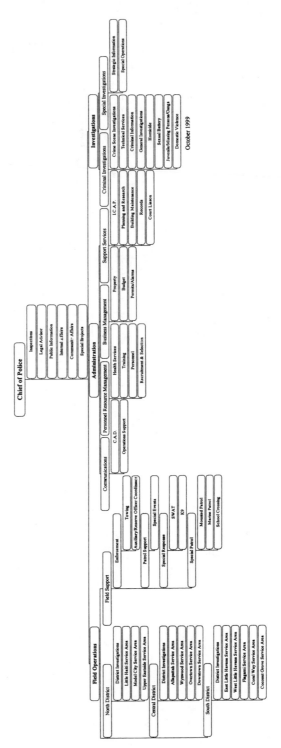

Source: Miami, Florida Police Department

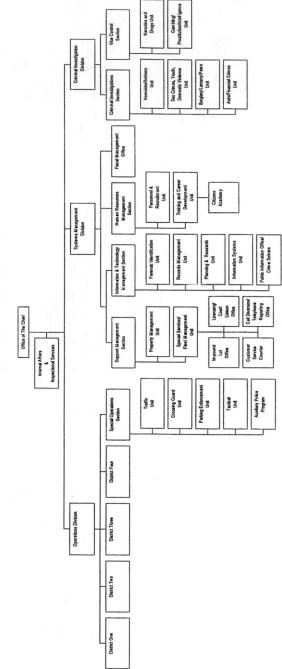

ARLINGTON COUNTY POLICE DEPARTMENT
ORGANIZATIONAL CHART

Courtesy of Arlington County Police Department, Arlington, Virginia

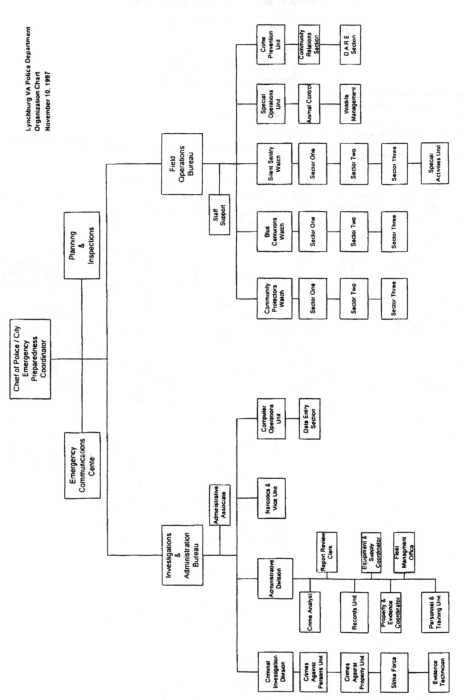

Lynchburg VA Police Department
Organization Chart
November 10, 1997

Courtesy of Lynchburg Police Department, Lynchburg, Virginia.

Santa Maria Police Department
Organizational Chart

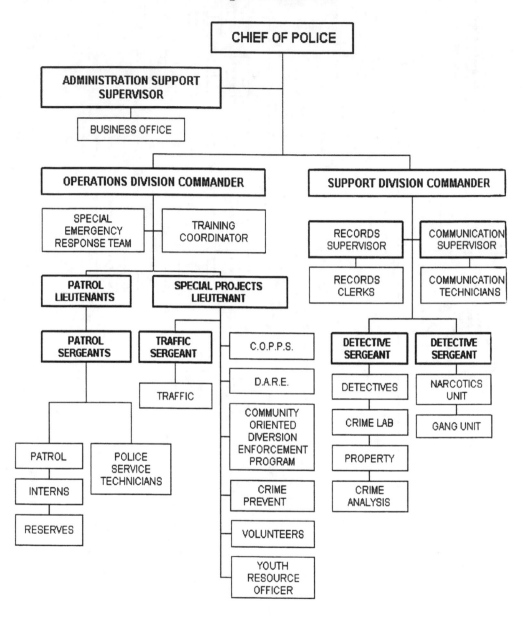

6/13/99

Courtesy of Santa-Maria Police Department, Santa-Maria, California.

ORLANDO POLICE DEPARTMENT
Sworn 614 Civilian 287 Contract 4 Total 905
April 1, 1999

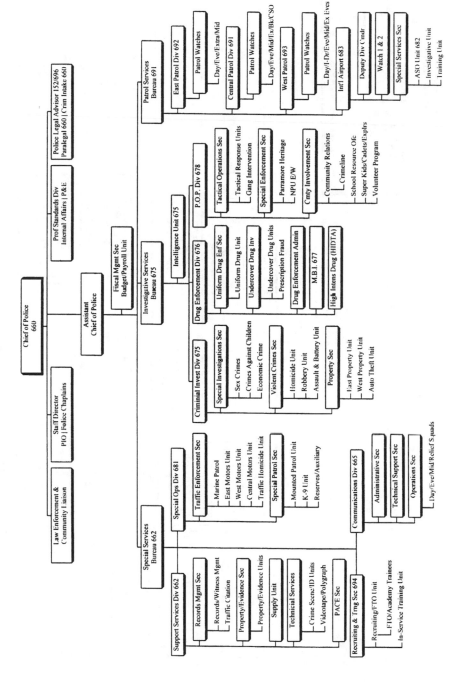

Courtesy of Orlando Police Department, Orlando, Florida.

ORLANDO POLICE DEPARTMENT
April 1, 1999

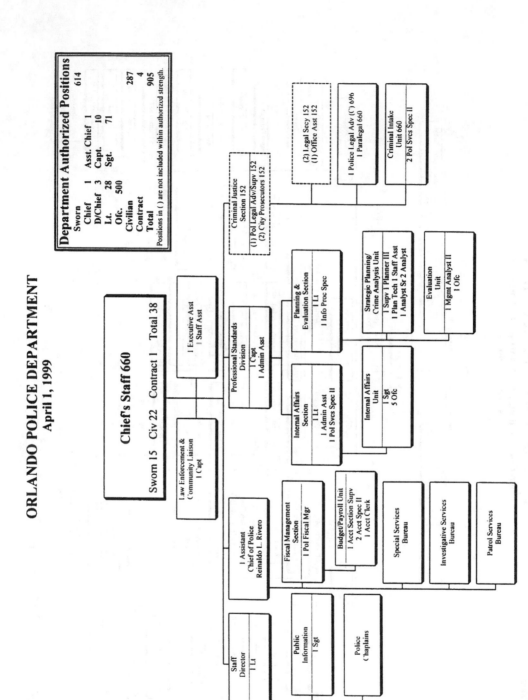

Department Authorized Positions

Sworn			
Chief	1	Asst. Chief	1
D/Chief	3	Capt.	10
Lt.	28	Sgt.	71
Ofc.	500		
Civilian			287
Contract			4
Total			**905**

Positions in ( ) are not included within authorized strength.

Chief's Staff 660

Sworn 15   Civ 22   Contract 1   Total 38

1 Executive Asst
1 Staff Asst

Law Enforcement &
Community Liaison
1 Capt

1 Assistant
Chief of Police
Reinaldo L. Rivero

Staff
Director
1 Lt

Public
Information
1 Sgt

Police
Chaplains

Professional Standards
Division
1 Capt
1 Admin Asst

Fiscal Management
Section
1 Pol Fiscal Mgr

Budget/Payroll Unit
1 Acct Section Supv
2 Acct Spec II
1 Acct Clerk

Special Services
Bureau

Investigative Services
Bureau

Patrol Services
Bureau

Planning &
Evaluation Section
1 Lt
1 Info Proc Spec

Internal Affairs
Section
1 Lt
1 Admin Asst
1 Pol Svcs Spec II

Internal Affairs
Unit
1 Sgt
5 Ofc

Strategic Planning/
Crime Analysis Unit
1 Supv 1 Planner III
1 Plan Tech 1 Staff Asst
1 Analyst Sr 2 Analyst

Evaluation
Unit
1 Mgmt Analyst II
1 Ofc

Criminal Justice
Section 152
(1) Pol Legal Adv/Supv 152
(2) City Prosecutors 152

(2) Legal Secy 152
(1) Office Asst 152

1 Police Legal Adv ((C) 696
1 Paralegal 660

Criminal Intake
Unit 660
2 Pol Svcs Spec II

Courtesy of Orlando Police Department, Orlando, Florida.

CHIEF'S STAFF
April 1, 1999

AUTHORIZED SWORN POSITIONS

1	Chief of Police
1	Assistant Chief of Police
2	Captain
3	Lieutenant
2	Sergeant
6	Officer

15 AUTHORIZED SWORN POSITIONS

AUTHORIZED CIVILIAN POSITIONS

1	Executive Assistant
2	Administrative Assistant
2	Staff Assistant
3	Police Services Specialist II
1	Management Analyst II
1	Planning Supervisor
1	Planner III
1	Planning Technician
1	Information Processing Specialist
1	Crime Analyst Sr
2	Crime Analyst
1	Paralegal
1	Police Fiscal Manager
1	Accounting Section Supervisor
2	Accounting Specialist II
1	Accounting Clerk

22 AUTHORIZED CIVILIAN POSITIONS

CONTRACT POSITION

1	Police Legal Advisor (696)

1 CONTRACT POSITION

TOTAL AUTHORIZED POSITIONS: 38

<u>Note</u>: Positions in parenthesis ( ) on the organizational
chart are not included within authorized strength.

Courtesy of Orlando Police Department, Orlando, Florida.

ORLANDO POLICE DEPARTMENT
April 1, 1999

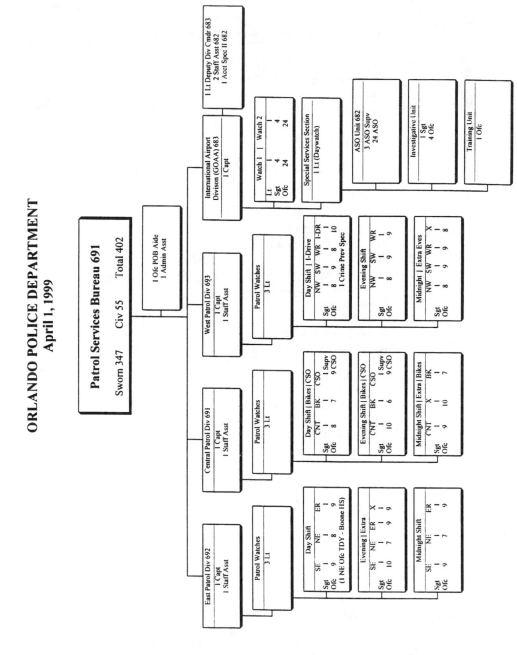

Courtesy of Orlando Police Department, Orlando, Florida.

PATROL SERVICES BUREAU
April, 1999

AUTHORIZED SWORN POSITIONS

1	Deputy Chief
4	Captain
13	Lieutenant
37	Sergeant
292	Officer

347 AUTHORIZED SWORN POSITIONS

AUTHORIZED CIVILIAN POSITIONS

2	CSO Supervisor
18	Community Service Officer
1	Administrative Assistant
5	Staff Assistant
1	Crime Prevention Specialist
1	Accounting Specialist II
3	Airport Safety Officer Supervisor
24	Airport Safety Officer

55 AUTHORIZED CIVILIAN POSITIONS

TOTAL AUTHORIZED POSITIONS: 402

Courtesy of Orlando Police Department, Orlando, Florida.

ORLANDO POLICE DEPARTMENT
April 1, 1999

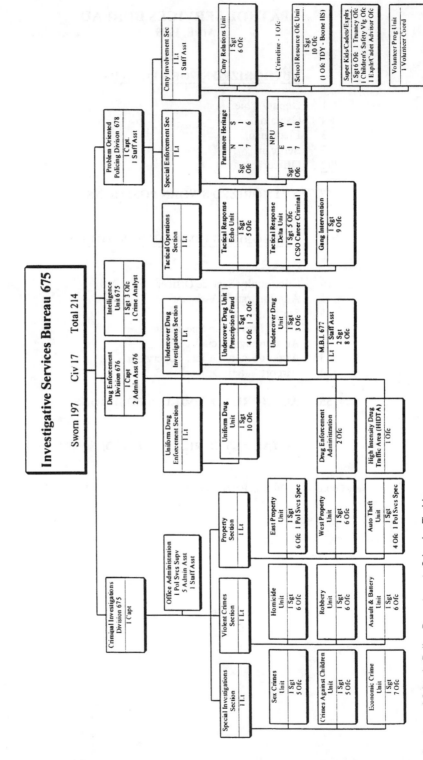

Courtesy of Orlando Police Department, Orlando, Florida.

INVESTIGATIVE SERVICES BUREAU
April 1, 1999

AUTHORIZED SWORN POSITIONS

1	Deputy Chief
3	Captain
9	Lieutenant
25	Sergeant
159	Officer

197 AUTHORIZED SWORN POSITIONS

AUTHORIZED CIVILIAN POSITIONS

1	Police Services Supervisor
1	Community Service Officer
7	Administrative Assistant
4	Staff Assistant
1	Crime Analyst
2	Police Services Specialist I/II
1	Volunteer Coordinator

17 AUTHORIZED CIVILIAN POSITIONS

TOTAL AUTHORIZED POSITIONS: 214

Courtesy of Orlando Police Department, Orlando, Florida.

ORLANDO POLICE DEPARTMENT
April 1, 1999

Special Services Bureau 662
1 Administrative Assistant
Sworn 55   Civ 193   Contract 3   Total 251

Special Operations Division 681
1 Capt
1 Staff Asst
1 CSO

Traffic Enforcement Section
1 Lt

Special Patrol Section
1 Lt

Marine Patrol

Mounted Patrol Unit
1 Sgt 6 Ofc
2 Horse Groom

East Motors Unit
1 Sgt
7 Ofc

K-9 Unit
1 Sgt
7 Ofc

West Motors Unit
1 Sgt
7 Ofc

Reserves

Central Motors (THU)
1 Sgt
5 Ofc | 4 Ofc

Auxiliary

Recruiting & Training Sec 694
1 Lt
1 Pol Career Cnslr
2 Staff Asst

Recruiting/FTO Unit
1 Sgt
4 Ofc
1 CSO Background Inv

FTO Trainees
Academy Trainees

In-Service Training Unit
1 Sgt
3 Ofc
1 Training Spec

Communications Div 665
1 Emer Comm Mgr
1 Staff Asst

Administration Sec
1 Emerg Comm Coord
1 ECS (Validator)
1 Alarm Coord

Technical Support Sec
1 Radio Systems Admin
1 Telecom Spec

Operations Sec
1 Emerg Comm Asst Mgr

Day Squad
2 Emer Comm Shift Supv
15 Emerg Comm Spec

Evening Squad
2 Emerg Comm Shift Supv
16 Emerg Comm Spec

Midnight Squad
3 Emerg Comm Shift Supv
16 Emerg Comm Spec

Relief Squad
2 Emerg Comm Shift Supv
15 Emerg Comm Spec

Support Services Div 662
1 Pol Adm Svcs Mgr
1 Staff Asst

Technical Services Section
1 Pol Tech Svcs Mgr

Crime Scene Unit
3 CST Supv
13 CST
2 Forensic Photographer

Identification Unit
1 ID Supv/Lat Prt Exam Sr
1 Latent Print Exam
2 Fingerprint Techs

Videotape Unit
1 Pol Audiovisual Supv
1 Pol Audiovisual Tech
1 TRAP Camera Aide

Polygraph Unit
1 Polygraph Exam (C) 662

PACE Section
1 Pol Report Svcs Supv
1 Pol Report Svcs Coord

PACE Unit
4 PACE Supv
39 PACE Spec

Records Mgmt Sec
1 Pol Records & ID Supv

Records Unit
1 Pol Svcs Supv
2 Pol Svcs Spec
6 Office Asst

Witness Management Unit
1 Staff Asst

Traffic Citation Unit
1 Pol Svc Spec

Property/Evidence Sec
1 Pol Evidence Supv

Property/Evidence Units
4 Pol Svcs Spec/Prop
2 Pol Svcs Spec I/Prop(C)662
2 Pol Svcs Spec/Evid

Supply Unit
1 Prop Supv 3 Supply Clk
1 Prop Clk Sr 5 Prop Clk
1 Custodian/Lead and 1 Custodian

Courtesy of Orlando Police Department, Orlando, Florida.

SPECIAL SERVICES BUREAU
April 1, 1999

AUTHORIZED SWORN POSITIONS

1	Deputy Chief
1	Captain
3	Lieutenant
7	Sergeant
43	Officer

55 AUTHORIZED SWORN POSITIONS

AUTHORIZED CIVILIAN POSITIONS

1	Police Administrative Services Manager	3	Supply Clerk
1	Emergency Communications Manager	1	Property Supervisor
1	Emergency Communications Asst. Mgr.	1	Property Clerk Sr.
1	Radio Systems Administrator	5	Property Clerk
1	Emergency Communications Coord.	1	Custodian/Lead
1	Alarm Coordinator	1	Custodian
1	Telecommunications Specialist	1	Police Career Counselor
9	Emergency Communications Shift Supv.	2	Community Service Officer
63	Emergency Communications Specialist	1	Training Specialist
1	Police Report Services Supervisor	2	Horse Groom
1	Police Report Services Coordinator	1	Police Technical Services Manager
4	PACE Supervisor	1	Police Audiovisual Supervisor
39	PACE Specialist	1	Police Audiovisual Technician
1	Police Evidence Supervisor	1	TRAP Camera Aide
1	Police Records & ID Supervisor	3	Crime Scene Technician Supervisor
1	Police Services Supervisor	13	Crime Scene Technician
1	Administrative Assistant	2	Forensic Photographer
6	Staff Assistant	1	ID Unit Supv/Latent Print Examiner Sr.
6	Office Assistant	1	Latent Print Examiner
9	Police Services Specialist I/II	2	Fingerprint Technician

193 AUTHORIZED CIVILIAN POSITIONS

CONTRACT POSITIONS

2	Police Services Specialist I (662)
1	Polygraph Examiner

3 CONTRACT POSITIONS

TOTAL AUTHORIZED POSITIONS: 251

Courtesy of Orlando Police Department, Orlando, Florida.

REFERENCES

Bayley, David H. 1994. *Police for the Future.* New York: Oxford University Press.

Campbell, J. P., M. D. Dunnette, E. E. Lawler, and K. Weick. 1970. *Expectancy Theory.* New York: McGraw-Hill.

Caplow, Theodore. 1964. *Principles of Organization.* New York: Harcourt, Brace & World.

Clark, Jacob R. 1998. Is Anybody Out There? Stiff Competition for Recruits Fuels Agencies' Personnel Woes. *Law Enforcement News* 24(488).

Conser, James A. 1979. Motivational Theory Applied to Law Enforcement Agencies. *Journal of Police Science and Administration* 7(3): 285–91.

Franz, V. and D. M. Jones. 1987. Perceptions of Organizational Performance in Suburban Police Departments: A Critique of the Military Model. *Journal of Police Science and Administration* 15(2): 153–61.

Fry, Brian R. 1989. *Mastering Public Administration: From Max Weber to Dwight Waldo.* Chatham, NJ: Chatham House.

Gaines, Larry K. 1993. Coping with the Job: Stress in Police Work. In *Critical Issues in Policing: Contemporary Readings* (2d ed.), edited by Roger G. Dunham and Geoffrey P. Alpert (Prospect Heights, IL: Waveland, 538–50).

Gaines, Larry K. and Gary W. Cordner. 1999. The Function of the Police. In *Policing Perspectives,* edited by Larry K. Gaines and Gary W. Cordner (Los Angeles, CA: Roxbury Publishing Co., 1–2).

Goldstein, Herman. 1990. *Problem-Oriented Policing.* New York: McGraw-Hill.

Gortner, Harold F., Julianne Mahler, and Jeanne Bell Nicholson. 1987. *Organization Theory: A Public Perspective.* Chicago: The Dorsey Press.

Green, Jack R., William T. Bergman, and Edward J. McLaughlin. 1994. Implementing Community Policing: Cultural and Structural Change in Police Organizations. In *The Challenge of Community Policing: Testing the Promises,* edited by Dennis P. Rosenbaum (Thousand Oaks, CA: Sage Publications, 92–109).

Gulick, Luther. 1937. Notes on the Theory of Organizations. In *Papers on the Science of Administration,* edited by Luther Gulick and Lyndall F. Urwick (New York: Institute of Public Administration, 3–13).

Hersey, Paul, Kenneth H. Blanchard, and Dewey E. Johnson. 1996. *Management of Organizational Behavior: Utilizing Human Resources.* 7th ed. Upper Saddle River, NJ: Prentice Hall.

Herzberg, Frederick. 1968. One More Time: How Do You Motivate Employees? *Harvard Business Review* 46(1): 36–44.

House, Robert J. and Terence R. Mitchell. 1974. Path-Goal Theory of Leadership. *Journal of Contemporary Business* (Autumn): 81–97.

Katzell, Raymond A. and Donna E. Thompson. 1990. Work Motivation: Theory and Practice. *American Psychologist* 45(2): 144–153.

Knott, Jack H. and Gary J. Miller. 1987. *Reforming Bureaucracy: The Politics of Institutional Choice.* Englewood Cliffs, NJ: Prentice Hall.

Lawler, Edward E. 1986. *High Involvement Management.* San Francisco: Jossey-Bass.

Ledford, Gerald E., Jr. 1995. Pay as an Organization Development Issue. *Newsletter of the Organizational Development and Change Division, Academy of Management* (Summer).

Leonard, V. A. and Harry W. Moore. 1987. *Police Organization and Management.* 7th ed. Mineola, N.Y.: Foundation Press.

Rainey, Hal G. 1991. *Understanding and Managing Public Organizations.* San Francisco: Jossey-Bass.

Rainey, Hal G. 1993. Work Motivation. In *Handbook of Organization Behavior,* edited by Robert T. Golembiewski (New York: Marcel Dekker, 19–39).

Roberg, Roy R. and Jack Kuykendall. 1997. *Police Management.* 2d ed. Los Angeles, CA: Roxbury Publishing Co.

Shafritz, Jay M. and J. Steven Ott. 1996. *Classics of Organization Theory.* 4th ed. Pacific Grove, CA: Brooks Cole.

Swanson, Charles R., Leonard Territo, and Robert W. Taylor. 1993. *Police Administration: Structures, Processes and Behavior.* 3d ed. New York: Macmillan Publishing Co.

Tzu, Sun. 6th Century B.C. *The Art of War.* Griffith, Samuel B., trans., 1963. Oxford: Clarendon Press.

Wagner, John A. III. 1994. Participation's Effects on Performance and Satisfaction: A Reconsideration of Research Evidence. *Academy of Management Review* 19(2): 312–30.

Weisheit, Ralph, David Falcone, and L. Edward Wells. 1994. Rural Crime and Rural Policing. *Research in Action.* Washington, D.C.: U.S. Department of Justice, National Institute of Justice.

Wilkinson, Deanna L. and Dennis P. Rosenbaum. 1994. The Effects of Organizational Structure on Community Policing: A Comparison of Two Cities. In *The Challenge of Community Policing: Testing the Promises,* edited by Dennis P. Rosenbaum (Thousand Oaks, CA: Sage Publications, 110–26).

Wilson, O. W. 1950. *Police Administration.* New York: McGraw-Hill.

Wilson, Woodrow. 1887. The Study of Administration. *Political Science Quarterly* (June).

Zhao, Jihong. 1996. *Why Police Organizations Change: A Study of Community-Oriented Policing.* Washington, D.C.: Police Executive Research Forum.

CHAPTER 9

The Basic Functions and Strategies of Policing

Indianapolis police officer Lt. Michael Price, center, arrests a suspect for possession of marijuana. Price and his partner were alerted to a suspected drug dealer by a citizen as they patrolled the neighborhood by foot, and were assisted by officers in patrol cars. June 1999. (AP/Wide World Photos)

LEARNING OBJECTIVES

In this chapter, an in-depth discussion of basic law enforcement functions and various strategies to accomplish the goals and objectives of agencies will be described and analyzed. By studying the concepts and principles presented here, you will be able to:

1. Identify and describe the three major functions of police agencies.
2. Describe the evolution of the patrol function from the 1800s to the present.
3. Distinguish preliminary investigation from follow-up investigation in terms of purpose and procedures.
4. Explain the major concepts of crime prevention and CPTED.
5. Compare and contrast the four major strategies of policing.
6. Describe the relationship of role to policing strategy selection.

CHAPTER OUTLINE

THE BASIC FUNCTION OF PATROL

The primary functions of policing agencies vary according to the purpose and authority of the organization. A state highway patrol agency's primary function is to patrol the highways for traffic regulation and enforcement, emergency response to and investigation of vehicular accidents, recovery of stolen autos, apprehension of offenders or wanted persons, and general enforcement of the vehicular registration and licensing laws. An agency with the primary function of investigating criminal offenses and developing cases for prosecution will engage in various information-gathering functions (interviewing, undercover operations, information/intelligence analysis, cultivating informants, and so on) to carry out its responsibilities. A local police agency with general law enforcement authority will have a broader range of functions that encompass uniformed patrol, vehicular accident investigation, case investigation and development, undercover operations, and response to all types of citizen complaints and emergencies. This section describes the basic function of patrol and the various operations associated with it. In the majority of local law enforcement agencies, it is often the number one service priority.

Patrol

The historical evolution and meaning of the word **patrol** is described well in the classic text of Samuel G. Chapman (1964, ix):

> Patrol is a word which stems from the French *patrouille*. The root of *patrouille* is *patte,* the French form of the Latin noun *pes, pedis* which means paw or foot. *Patrouiller,* then means to paddle or puddle in the mud on foot. *The Oxford English Dictionary* discloses that *patrouille* is an altered meaning stemming from the earlier French word *patouiller* which meant "to padle, or dable in with the feet, to stirre up and downe, and trouble, or make foule, by stirring." The etymology of the word *patrol* clearly establishes the function as one which is arduous, tiring, difficult and performed in conditions other than ideal.

The history of the patrol function as a form of protection dates back to the earliest forms of group living when selected individuals "stood guard" or "took up watch" for uninvited persons or wild animals. An early military duty was to survey or patrol the outer perimeters of the encampment to guard against surprise attack and infiltrators. When applied to policing, as stated in Chapter 2, the Roman Vigiles watched over the city and ran to places of disturbance as necessary. The patrol function has existed as long as there have been organized units or groups responsible for social control and the protection of others or the state.

The modern perspective of the patrol function is quite broad and includes more than the act of patrolling. It is considered a primary law enforcement function and includes the following tasks (Commission on Accreditation for Law Enforcement Agencies 1993, Standard 41.1.1):

1. Preventive patrol (including inquiry and inspectional activity) oriented toward prevention of crimes and accidents, maintenance of public order, and the discovery of hazards and delinquency-causing situations,
2. Crime prevention activities,
3. Response to called-for services,
4. Investigation of crimes, offenses, incidents, and conditions including arresting offenders,
5. Traffic direction and control,
6. Regulation of certain businesses or activities as required by law,
7. Maintenance of public order,
8. Provision of emergency services,
9. Development of relationships between citizens and the agency, and
10. Reporting of information to appropriate organizational components.

In early urban policing, *the concept of patrol usually referred to "movement."* In England during the eighteenth century, Henry Fielding advocated roving mounted patrols for crime prevention and "runners" who could respond quickly to trouble situations. Later, in the *First Instructions* to the Metropolitan Police Officers of London in 1829, it was emphasized that officers who patrolled their beat on foot were to be mobile: "He will be able to see every part of his beat, at least once in ten minutes or a quarter of an hour; and this he will be expected to do: so that any person requiring assistance, by remaining in the same spot for that length of time, must certainly meet a constable" (Delane 1829).

The expectations of an American officer on patrol one hundred years ago are echoed by Chief Eldridge of Boston in his address to other law enforcement administrators (see Exhibit 9–1).

Today we might view some of the expectations placed on early **foot patrol** officers (such as knowing contagious persons, knowing who has moved into and out of the beat, and refraining from walking or talking with other officers unless on department business) as a bit extreme or too demanding. Historians generally note that the foot patrol officers of the 1800s and early 1900s were often on their own, lacked any form of communications capability, and were seldom trained or supervised. Most local officers were appointed because of political connections, and this often led to high turnover, little or no job security, abuse of the position, and corruption. It has been argued that the officers of this time period were more like political operatives than professional public servants (Walker 1977; Walker 1984; Hakker 1976; Cordner and Trojanowicz 1992).

Many changes have occurred in twentieth-century policing that have changed certain aspects of the patrol function. Communications technology allows patrol officers to be in constant contact with others—whether it is with the agency's telecommunication operators or directly with the complainant—through the use of cellular phones (see Chapter 13 for more about information technology in policing). Political patronage has been reduced in most jurisdictions (but not all), which impacts the selection of officers (Chapter 10) and the political favors granted on the street. Police officers today are generally better educated and trained (Chapter 11) than their early twentieth-century counterparts and are protected through various employment rights from arbitrary and political dismissal.

One of the major changes in patrol today is that "movement" of the officer takes on many forms other than the traditional foot patrol. The modes of carrying out the patrol function are quite varied today and include horse, bicycle, motorcycle, all-terrain vehicle, boat, automobile, helicopter, and airplane. A closer look at the various modes of patrol is in order.

Foot Patrol

Not only is foot patrol the oldest mode of patrol, it is making a comeback. When radio-equipped patrol cars allowed the police to respond quickly to known events and offenses, foot patrol became the less preferred mode, although most large cities never completely abandoned it. Other social forces such as a growing urban population, development of suburban communities over large geographical areas,

Exhibit 9–1

HOW A BEAT SHOULD BE PATROLLED
by Chief Benjamin P. Eldridge, Boston, 1900*

"The duty of a patrolman is to patrol," said Governor Roosevelt, when Police Commissioner of the City of New York.** To properly patrol his route, the officer, on going out, should immediately proceed to his relieving post, and relieve the officer whose tour of duty has expired. In case the officer to be relieved is not at his post, the relieving officer should report the fact to his station. He should confine his patrol within the limits of his route, except in case of fire, arrest of a prisoner, or other necessary absence from duty. In case he is obliged to leave his route, he will, if practicable, notify his station when he leaves and when he returns.

Patrolmen, properly patrolling their routes, should not walk together, or talk with each other on their routes while on duty, unless it be to communicate information pertaining to the department, or in their line of duty. In patrolling his route, he should note all removals from or into the limits of his route, and acquire such a knowledge of the inhabitants as will enable him to recognize them. He should properly patrol all parts of his route, and make himself perfectly acquainted with the streets, thoroughfares, courts, and houses within it.

If requested, he should direct strangers and others, the nearest and safest way to their places of destination. If he hears the cry of "watch," or other call for assistance, he shall proceed to render aid with all possible dispatch, taking every precaution practicable for the protection of his route when he leaves it for this, or for any other purpose. In properly patrolling his route, he should note all cases of contagious disease, or sudden death, where there is reasonable ground to suspect criminality. He should also watch the conduct of all persons of known bad character, male and female night-walkers, and persons who improperly accost persons of the opposite sex upon the streets, and should do all in his power to protect females from insult and annoyance.

He should see that the laws of the State, or ordinances of the city, are not violated, and should cause the arrest and prosecution of all persons violating them. An officer on his beat should be quiet, civil, and orderly; in the performance of his duty, attentive and zealous; control his temper, and exercise the utmost patience and discretion. He must, at all times, refrain from harsh, violent, coarse, and profane language; and, when

(continues)

Exhibit 9–1 *(continued)*

asked a question, should answer with all possible attention and courtesy. Officers should always remember, and treat every one with courtesy, bearing in mind that honest misfortune and poverty are no disgrace, although often very inconvenient and a source of annoyance. Officers should always conduct themselves as gentlemen, and not allow temper to display itself on any occasion, remembering that he who can control himself is best qualified to control others.

A good officer will also take great pride in his personal appearance. Brass buttons, wreaths, badges, and other equipments should be burnished often enough to keep them in a shining condition. A neat officer on a beat invariably attracts attention, and is the recipient of much merited praise. A neat and tidy appearance indicates that the officer takes a pride in his calling, and desires to reflect credit upon the department of which he is a member. Nothing detracts more from an officer then a slovenly appearance on his beat, and such negligence is, or should be, quickly detected by a superior. The man who brushes his uniform and puts in his leisure shining his buttons is the one who will, in time win promotion.

* Program of the 7th annual convention, National Association of Chiefs of Police of the U.S. and Canada, Cincinnati, May 9–11, 1900, p. 25.

**Theodore Roosevelt was Police Commissioner in New York City for two years (1895–1897). Readers interested in his experiences might refer to *Theodore Roosevelt: An Autobiography* (NY: Macmillan Co., 1913) or *Theodore Roosevelt: A Biography* by Henry F. Pringle (NY, Harcourt, Brace & Co., 1913).

Source: Reprinted with permission from D. C. Dilworth, *The Blue and The Brass: American Policing 1890–1910*, pp. 35–36, © 1976, International Association of Chiefs of Police.

the increasing number of calls for service, and limited agency budgets also impacted the decision to increase the use of mobile patrol. Foot patrol today is gaining in popularity in conjunction with community policing (which is discussed later in this chapter), but not as a total replacement to motorized patrol. It allows officers to make more personal contact with community members on a regular basis. This approach should help strengthen the relationships between officers and the people they serve. By building trust and mutual respect, the agency can maintain positive communication with the community, thus identifying local problems and concerns.

There are several different forms of foot patrol: **fixed post**, **line beat**, or **random** (Adams 1997, 43). Fixed post means that an officer is assigned to a specific, small area such as an intersection, bus station, subway stop, or place where a special problem exits. Line beat foot patrols normally consist of a linear geographical area such as a business district or strip shopping center. Random foot patrol is where an officer is assigned an area consisting of several city blocks, a neighborhood, or a housing district and is allowed to roam over a significant area in no particular pattern of patrol.

Horse Patrol

Surprisingly, there are over 700 horse or mounted patrol units in the United States, according to the National Mounted Service Organization, Incorporated, with about 100 having been formed in the last few years. The interest in community policing efforts has increased the formation of additional units recently. The U.S. Park Police in Washington, D.C., offers a 10-week training school for officers and their horses (Fulton 1993, 34). Most units are used for ceremonial purposes, such as parades, funerals, and special events; other units are used for crowd control at sports events, concerts, demonstrations, riots and civil disorders, and other large gatherings of people. Some units are used in public relations, community policing, and crime prevention programming. Units in larger jurisdictions are used as a regular part of the patrol operation. For example, in 1992, the 27 members of the Los Angeles Police Department's Mounted Unit made over 700 criminal arrests. (See Exhibit 9–2 for more examples of Mounted Patrol Operations.)

Horse patrols were found in 17 percent of the local law enforcement agencies in the 1997 LEMAS survey. Twenty-one percent of the municipalities used them and 7 percent of the county sheriffs used them. Only 2 percent of state agencies used horse patrols (Reaves and Goldberg 1999, xv). The largest contingent of horses, 100, was maintained by the New York City Police Department, but Richland County Sheriff of South Carolina came in second with 66 (Reaves and Goldberg 1999, 127–129).

Non-motorized Wheel Patrol

Where there are wheels, there are officers on patrol. Today's departments are using several forms of non-motorized wheel patrol—bicycles, roller skates, and even skateboards. "Necessity is the mother of invention," so it is possible that we will see even other forms of non-motorized wheel patrol in the future. Bicycle patrol has really become common in the U.S., and is often associated with either a community policing program or a strategic policing method to attack a particular crime or series of offenses. But as Exhibit 9–3 illustrates, the tactic is not new. Many resort communities have used bicycle patrols for years

Exhibit 9–2

MOUNTED PATROL UNITS

Fort Lauderdale Mounted Unit—The unit was started in 1983; its 1998 budget was over $700,000 for one supervisor, seven officers, one attendant, and seven horses. When Hurricane Andrew ripped through Florida, the Fort Lauderdale Mounted Unit went into action to apprehend and care for stray horses until they could be returned to their owners. This Unit also has been used to monitor and control college students during "spring break disturbances."

U.S. Park Police—The 41 mounted officers spend about one-third of their time on patrol, another third on crowd control, and the other third on public relations and education.

Albany, NY—The mounted unit is often called upon to help control crowds and demonstrations at the State Capital buildings, such as the Anti–Ku Klux Klan rally of 1991.

Wyoming—In this state, it is common for citizens using their own horses to join county law enforcement units to conduct searches for missing persons.

Costs—Estimates range between $1,000 and $1,500 to initially outfit a horse and its rider. The cost of feed, bedding, shoes, and veterinarian care range from $1,000 to $5,600 per horse. The cost of a horse ranges up to $2,000; however, in some communities horses are donated by citizens, businesses, and civic groups or are owned by the officers themselves.

Sources: Data from R. V. Fulton, Community Policing on Horseback, *Law Enforcement Technology,* May 1993, pp. 32–34; National Mounted Services Organization; and http://ci.ftlaud.fl.us/police/mounted.html, © 1999, Fort Lauderdale Police Department.

---

to better serve tourists and visitors to beaches, boardwalks, and historical districts. The 1997 LEMAS survey of state and local agencies with 100 or more officers found 13 state agencies and 403 local agencies (out of 651, or 62 percent) utilizing bicycles in their operations (Reaves and Goldberg 1999, 71–80). By contrast, in 1990, only two state agencies and 89 local agencies reported their use.

Exhibit 9–3

EARLY BICYCLE PATROLS

Detroit, Michigan—In 1897, the Police Department added bicycle patrolmen to its operation. Called the "scorcher cops," they were responsible for apprehending speeding cyclists (LEAA, 80).

Lakeland, Florida—In the summer of 1954 to help control and detect nighttime burglaries in the downtown area, the Police Department instituted a bicycle patrol. The innovation here was that the bicycles were equipped with (two-way portable) radios, thus eliminating the need for call boxes. The crime in the target area dropped 75 percent (Leo H. Brooker in Chapman, 114–115).

Sources: Data from Law Enforcement Assistance Administration, *Two Hundred Years of American Criminal Justice*, 1976, U.S. Government Printing Office; and S. G. Chapman, *Police Patrol Readings*, 1964, Charles C. Thomas Publishers.

Motorized Patrol—The Automobile

Motorized patrol is the most common mode of patrol in the United States, but it was not always so . . . "The horse is a natural resource, and men use natural resources only so long as they meet their demands, . . . I am proud to say that the police department of Louisville is in such a line of progress that we feel ourselves beyond the utility of the horse, and can now boast of three power-driven vehicles." This statement was made by Chief J. H. Haager, of Louisville, Kentucky, in 1909 at the 16th annual convention of the International Association of Chiefs of Police (IACP). Previously, in 1907, the Chief had "hired" (rented) fourteen motorized vehicles to assist in successfully controlling the streetcar strike rioting that occurred in November of that year. He used the vehicles to "sneak up on" the rioters—they were not expecting the police to arrive by car! The Chief became a believer in the utility of the automobile and was extolling its benefits to his colleagues during his address at the convention. In 1910, Marshal Farnan of Baltimore, at the 17th annual convention of the IACP, also gave an address describing the use of motorized patrol wagons, which could comfortably carry 16 men—21 during emergencies. He ended his comments on this prophetic note (Dilworth 1976, 176–181):

Fellow members . . . we are living in a very progressive age. There is no such thing as standing still. If we halt in our progressive march, it means that we will go backward. We must utilize every modern invention and facility for assisting us in the work we are sworn to do. . . . It may be the day dream of one who has grown gray in the police service, but I feel that I can almost dip into the future and see still more improved appliances than the motor vehicles being used by the police departments of the world. It does not seem at all improbable that in the years to come, and perhaps not so far away, that the perfection of machines that fly through the air will make them applicable to police service. Be that as it may, let the genius of our inventors assist us in our work to any extent that we may apply it.

The development and refinement of early radio systems in the period from 1926 through the 1930s also greatly influenced the mobilization of American police forces. By 1946, all police vehicles in 88 percent of 858 reporting cities were radio equipped, and by 1964, the use of radio communication in policing was virtually universal (Leonard 1964, 54–56). The ability to maintain communication with headquarters and the ability to be mobile became the new symbol of police efficiency. It was probably the most significant change in policing in 200 years.

Today's squad car is literally an office on wheels. Besides the usual radio equipment, one can find mobile digital terminals (computers), cellular phones, modems, laser radar units, and video cameras. Large motorized vehicles within a department's inventory can include armored vehicles, buses, tow trucks, prisoner transport vehicles, high-performance pursuit cars, mobile emergency command centers, and specially modified show vehicles (often used for crime prevention or DARE programs).

All-Terrain Vehicles (ATVs)

The challenge to respond to emergencies and to pursue wanted persons through all kinds of weather and terrain has led the law enforcement community to adopt other modes of transportation. Such vehicles have proven themselves valuable during and following natural disasters as well. Four-wheel-drive vehicles, four-wheel ATVs, and snowmobiles are becoming standard equipment in many agencies. Where they are not part of the regular inventory, agencies often have made prior arrangements with private vendors or citizens to use them when necessary. The 1997 LEMAS survey found that 20 percent of local agencies and 29 percent of state agencies utilized all-terrain vehicles (Reaves and Goldberg 1999, xvi).

Motorcycles

Police departments were early users of motorcycles. Some began with the Excelsior Autocycle, on which the rider pedaled hard to get moving before a belt drive took over. The Fitchburg, Massachusetts Police Department organized a motorcycle detail as early as 1913. From the 1920s through the 1950s, motorcycles became a popular police mode of transportation and enforcement tool. It was commonly used for traffic enforcement. Some highway patrols began operating with more motorcycles than automobiles. A 1954 survey of 33 agencies, each serving populations over 100,000, revealed that all the departments used motorcycles; 58 percent used them exclusively for traffic law enforcement and the remaining 42 percent used them for various non-traffic duties. In some parts of the police community, there also emerged a debate over whether motorcycles or automobiles should be the vehicle of choice for law enforcement agencies (Chapman 1964, 144–148). The 1997 LEMAS survey of state and local agencies with 100 or more officers found 17 state agencies and 390 (out of 651, or 60 percent) local agencies assigning personnel to motorcycle patrol (Reaves and Goldberg 1999, 71–80, 268).

Helicopters

Since the New York City Police Department's successful experiment with helicopter patrol, which was initiated in October of 1948, helicopters have become a common addition to larger law enforcement agencies. The 1997 LEMAS survey of 651 local agencies and 49 state agencies found 143 local agencies and 34 state agencies utilizing helicopters in their operation (Reaves and Goldberg 1999, 121–130, 273). Helicopters are used for patrol, narcotics interdiction and marijuana field eradication, raids/SWAT team operations, fleeing offender and photo surveillance, general and medical rescue, and miscellaneous transport. The City of Los Angeles has 16 helicopters and a budget of about $5 million for its Air Support Division. Los Angeles City, Los Angeles County, and the Georgia State Patrol were the three largest helicopter units in the 1997 LEMAS study. It costs approximately $300 an hour to operate a helicopter, and each unit can average $600,000 or more for its initial purchase (Ellis 1993, 34–35). The cost and necessity of using helicopters in policing have become somewhat controversial in recent years, especially for departments with constrained budgets. Costs today range from $500,000 to $2 million depending on how the unit is equipped. Other costs include pilot training (up to $4,500) and $75 per hour for fuel (MacDonald *et al.* 1998, 11–12).

Airplanes/Fixed-Wing Aircraft

Although used less frequently than helicopters, small aircraft have been used in law enforcement operations for decades. Today, aircraft are used primarily for traffic enforcement, transport of prisoners, special response team operations, drug interdiction and marijuana plant eradication, and air search and rescue. Forty-two out of 49 state law enforcement agencies utilize aircraft, but only 4 have more than 9 aircraft and 30 had 5 or fewer (Reaves and Goldberg 1999, 273). Of the 651 local agencies surveyed in the 1997 LEMAS study, only 79 utilized airplanes. It is evident from these numbers that state agencies, proportionately, utilize aircraft to a higher degree than local jurisdictions. The obvious reason is that the state agencies' geographical jurisdiction is much greater than local ones, and their budgets also would allow for such expenditures. Aircraft are generally more expensive to operate, require more land space, and are more limited in their utilization than helicopters.

Boats/Watercraft

Marine patrols actually date back centuries to the Egyptians. In more modern times, the Thames Marine Police of London probably was the model for such patrol units. Formed in July of 1789 at the urging of Patrick Colquhoun, it was a joint effort between the English government and the West India Merchants. In 1839, it was incorporated into the Metropolitan Police as the Thames Division.

The LEMAS survey of 1997 found that 260 local agencies (40 percent) and 18 state agencies had boats in their inventory. Interestingly, the state agency reporting the most boats was the Oklahoma Highway Patrol with 112 (Reaves and Goldberg 1999, 273). Some jurisdictions operate regular marine patrols, others have seasonal operations, while others utilize them for emergencies and search/rescue. Of course, their use is largely dependent on the local geography, climate, and flood risk. Most marine craft are found in large cities with inland waterways or harbors and county sheriff's departments (often because of countywide responsibilities for locating drowning victims, which occur at farm ponds or private lakes as well as natural waterways).

Canine (K-9) Units

The use of canines in patrol is reported to have begun in St. Malo, France, in the 1300s, but it was not until the late 1800s that dogs were specifically trained for such work. In April of 1957, the Baltimore City Police Department was the sole police force in the United States that used all-purpose police dogs in law enforcement. There are earlier dates of reported uses of patrol dogs in American cities, but apparently their use was abandoned for a number of reasons. By 1963 about 100 agencies in the U.S. used police dogs for various purposes (Chapman 1964, 410–418).

Today, K-9 units are used for general patrol support, drug and narcotics detection, explosives detection, arson investigation, search and rescue (of lost, injured, trapped, drowned, and buried persons), tracking of suspects, building searches, crowd control, public relations, and poacher detection. Dogs have noses that are a million times more sensitive than humans, and during searches they sniff over 200 times each minute. They are trained to give either "active" or "passive" responses when they have detected that for which they have been trained. For example, a bomb-detecting dog would give a passive response such as sitting down because an active response of scratching or bumping the suspected item could cause it to explode. A dog searching for trapped individuals in a disaster situation (e.g., a building collapse or avalanche) or searching for narcotics would give an active response, possibly scratching (Butterworth 1988, 26).

Some of the largest K-9 units today are maintained by the cities of El Paso, Texas (78 dogs), New York (48 dogs), Washington, D.C. (45 dogs), San Diego (47), Chicago (42), Baltimore County (32), Houston (30), Detroit (28), and Pittsburgh (29). Of the 651 local agencies with 100 or more officers in the U.S., 567 maintain dogs for one or more uses; 43 state agencies do so (Reaves and Goldberg 1999, 120–130, 273). Officers often cite the benefits of using dogs as general crime deterrents since they can outrun humans, and once they begin "zeroing in" on suspects, they cannot be easily dissuaded from their mission. Handlers have to be trained along with the dog assigned to them. In some training programs, potential handlers must successfully pass a psychological examination before being considered suitable for the assignment. They also must be in good physical condition, work well with minimum supervision, be highly motivated, and be committed to the assignment (since a dog's working life can be about 10 years and it usually becomes a member of the officer's "family") (Butterworth 1988, 27). Exhibit 9–4 reports some of the other general factors related to K-9 training and utilization.

THE BASIC FUNCTION OF CRIMINAL INVESTIGATION

The criminal investigation function of law enforcement agencies in the United States also varies considerably according to agencies' size, mission, and jurisdiction. The criminal **investigation process**, however, is one that is universal to all law enforcement agencies because it involves gathering information about reported or suspected criminal activity, determining facts, assessing evidence, and determining whether or not a crime has occurred. As a separate term, "investigate" means "to observe or study closely; to inquire into something systematically, or to search for truthful information." The term is derived from the Latin word *vestigare,* meaning "to track or trace" (Bennett and Hess 1981, 5). The process of investigation occurs whether or not an officer or agent is in uniform. It is carried out by patrol officers, detectives, and agents who can be assisted by civilian personnel. It can be carried out *overtly* (openly, visibly, and directly) or *covertly* (hidden, secretively, and "undercover").

Historically, the criminal investigative function has existed for centuries. The Roman Vigiles had special officials who had inquisition (questioning) responsibilities and were the forerunners of today's detectives. Also from a historical perspective, investigative work has not always enjoyed the favor of the populace. During the time of Napoleon (France, early 1800s), Eugene Francois Vidocq

Exhibit 9–4

THE USE OF CANINES IN POLICING

MAJOR BREEDS: German Shepherds, Dobermans, Golden Labrador Retrievers, Rottweilers, and Weimaraners.

SIZE: Between 70 and 95 pounds.

AGE AT SELECTION: One to three years old.

SCREENING: Complete physical/medical exam, hip x-rays, and urinalysis; must have proper temperament, good with children, friendly; reaction test to unfamiliar conditions such as riding in vehicles, gunfire, slippery floors, quiet surroundings, etc.; ability to concentrate.

TRAINING: Programs can last from 3 weeks to 6 months and range from $3,500 to $5,000. Annual recertification is recommended by some. Many departments deputize their dogs for protection of the department and the dog.

COSTS: Varies, average $6,000–$7,000 per dog; handler's salary during training can range from $1,550 to $6,900; preparing and equipping a cruiser, $2,500; annual food and kennel costs, $600.

OTHER: Often European-bred and require commands in foreign language (which can be beneficial to officers on the street); usually male; white-colored dogs not usually used because they are too visible at night.

Sources: Data from B. Butterworth, Police Forces Go to the Dogs, *Law Enforcement Technology,* November/December 1988, pp. 26–28; P. Meade, Police Ask Public for Donations to Purchase Dog, Train Handler, *Vindicator, B1;* April 1988; and correspondence of May 20, 1998 with the National Association of Police Work Dogs.

commanded a unit of Paris detectives that became known and feared for their methods and extensive network of informers. Vidocq's agents consisted of mostly ex-criminals, since he believed that "it took a thief to catch a thief." Vidocq himself had been in prison at one time. Vidocq's techniques included the establishment of an elaborate record system, extensive intelligence gathering, and use of informants (Holden 1992, 26). The ruthlessness of the French "secret police" at this time caused police reform in some countries to be slowed because of the concern that changes could lead to the creation of forces like those in France (refer to Chapter 2).

The evolution of investigation in the last century has been one of tremendous growth and specialization. Today, many federal and state agencies exist for the sole purpose of conducting criminal investigations. The larger local agencies have specialized assignments and units to conduct the in-depth criminal investigations. However, even with these specialized units, the process at the local level usually begins with a uniformed officer responding to a scene and initiating the investigation of the complaint.

The Preliminary Investigation

Upon receipt of a complaint or action initiated by an officer, the situation in question is investigated. The early stage or phase of this process is known as the **preliminary investigation**. Generally speaking, it is during the preliminary investigation that an investigator (uniformed or plain clothes) determines whether a crime has been committed, what persons (victim, witnesses, suspects) are involved, and what evidence or investigative leads exist. There are a number of basic procedures conducted by investigators during the preliminary phases of an investigation. A training tool developed by the International Association of Chiefs of Police (IACP 1989, 6) and used by many training academies for decades includes a brief action phrase for each letter of the word "preliminary":

P . . . Proceed to the scene promptly and safely

R . . . Render assistance to the injured

E . . . Effect the arrest of the offender

L . . . Locate and identify witnesses

I . . . Interview the complainant and the witnesses

M . . . Maintain the crime scene and protect the evidence

I . . . Interrogate the suspect

N . . . Note all conditions, events, and remarks

A . . . Arrange for collection of evidence

R . . . Report the incident fully and accurately

Y . . . Yield the responsibility to the follow-up investigator

Source: Reprinted with permissioin from *Criminal Investigation*, p. 6, © 1989, International Association of Chiefs of Police.

Of course, it must be fully understood that the above procedures are not meant to be sequential, nor will all of the procedures be performed at every incident. Situations vary, and the order of performing the procedures will vary according to the situation found upon arrival.

Once the preliminary investigation provides sufficient information to determine that a crime has been committed, the investigating officer attempts to answer specific questions that will yield **solvability factors**. These are responses or observations that have a high probability of providing leads for the identification and location of the offender. Solvability factors include such things as the name of a suspect; the availability of witnesses; information about a suspect's description, identification, or location; traceable property; the suspect's vehicular movement; the suspect's *modus operandi* (or method of operation); and the discovery of useful physical evidence (IACP 1989, 5).

During the investigative process, agencies may perform a number of investigative support services, such as fingerprint processing, crime lab services, and ballistics testing. The 1997 LEMAS survey found that the percent of local law enforcement agencies with primary responsibility for such services was 84 percent, 34 percent, and 15 percent respectively. If an agency does not possess the primary responsibility for these investigative support services, it may engage the services of other state or local agencies that do provide such services. Occasionally, agencies contract with privately operated labs for support services.

Follow-up Investigation

The preliminary investigation is often the only investigation necessary to resolve an incident. Suspects can be arrested at the scene or within a few hours after the initial investigation. However, a more detailed, intensive, and prolonged **follow-up investigation** may be necessary. The follow-up investigation often includes these essential procedures (Commission on Accreditation for Law Enforcement Agencies 1999, Standard 42.2.3.):

a. Reviewing and analyzing all previous reports prepared in the preliminary phase, departmental records, and results from laboratory examinations,
b. Conducting additional interviews and interrogations,
c. Seeking additional information (from uniformed officers and informants),
d. Planning, organizing, and conducting searches, and collecting physical evidence,
e. Identifying and apprehending suspects,
f. Determining involvement of suspects in other crimes,
g. Checking suspects' criminal histories, and
h. Preparing cases for court presentation.

THE BASIC FUNCTION OF CRIME PREVENTION

Crime prevention is defined as the "anticipation, recognition and appraisal of a crime risk and the initiation of action to remove or reduce it" (Fennelly

1982, 5). It is an active process, not a passive one. This is an important point since some officers do perceive their role as including a strong crime prevention presence. One could argue, however, that whether officers perceive their role as crime prevention or not, the citizens they serve may. In short, the public expects a certain level of crime prevention from the police, and, according to the above definition, most police are performing crime prevention activities whether they define it as such or not.

The historical foundation for the function of crime prevention by police includes its recognition as a major role in the formation of the London Metropolitan Police of 1829. The second paragraph of the *New Police Instructions* explicitly stated: *"It should be understood at the outset, that the object to be attained is 'the prevention of crime.'"* The instructions gave guidance on how officers were to prevent crime. They included phrases such as "vigilance and activity as may render it impossible for anyone to commit a crime within that portion of the town under their charge" (*New Police Instructions* 1829). By reading the instructions, one concludes that officers were to be committed to their job, serve and reside in the area where assigned, have extensive knowledge of the persons residing in their assigned area, and be held accountable for the crime committed in their districts.

Modern American crime prevention efforts vary greatly from agency to agency depending on the size and governmental level of the law enforcement entity. At the local level of policing, agencies organize crime watch/block watch groups to help prevent crime and for better communication with the citizens. Most agencies offer selected crime prevention programs on topics such as rape prevention, burglary prevention, robbery prevention, how to reduce theft and larceny of personal property (bicycles, auto theft, etc.), anti-shoplifting techniques, computer crime prevention, personal defense/self-protection, and so on. State agencies usually focus crime prevention efforts in a fashion similar to local police departments if their mission covers general police authority or through brochures and poster campaigns for their specific policing authority (e.g., traffic safety and enforcement, alcoholic beverage enforcement, consumer fraud protection, environmental crimes, and so on). Federal agencies do less of the day-to-day, citizen contact–type of crime prevention; their audiences consist of larger groups (often law enforcement officers and business/civic leaders) for purposes of training and information-sharing that may be crime prevention–oriented and could be of subsequent use at the local level.

Officers at the local level (and occasionally at the state level) of policing may be very active in crime prevention associations. Many states have statewide associations, and there are several national associations and training centers as well (see Exhibit 9–5). Insurance companies and local law enforcement agencies also regularly offer crime prevention and fire protection literature to interested individuals and groups.

In the last 20 years, another crime prevention concept has been utilized by some police agencies in conjunction with local architects, building developers,

Exhibit 9–5

CRIME PREVENTION ASSOCIATIONS, TRAINING CENTERS, SOURCES OF INFORMATION

National Crime Prevention Council
1700 K St., NW, Second Floor
Washington, DC 20006

America's Most Wanted
P.O. Box Crime TV
Washington, DC 20016

National Criminal Justice
  Reference Service
Box 6000
Rockville, MD 20849

National Association of Town Watch
7 Wynnewood Road, Suite 215
P.O. Box 303
Wynnewood, PA 19096

Crime Stoppers International
P.O. Box 30413
Albuquerque, NM 87190

Ohio Crime Prevention Association
6543 Commerce Parkway, Suite R
Dublin, OH 43017

International Society of Crime
  Prevention Practitioners
266 Sandy Point Road
Emlenton, PA 16373

International CPTED Association
439 Queen Alexandra Way, S.E.
Calgary, Alberta, Canada T2J3P2

Texas Crime Prevention Association
c/o P.O. Box 163822
Austin, TX 78718

Insurance companies

Local law enforcement agencies

---

and building permit officials. The concept is generally referred to as **CPTED** which means crime prevention through environmental design, a phrase coined by researcher C. Ray Jeffrey in 1971 (National Crime Prevention Council 1997, 7). The concept maintains that the "proper design and effective use of the physical environment can produce behavioral effects that will reduce the incidence and fear of crime, thereby improving the quality of life" (Wright and Thomas 1993, 203). The concept is strongly related to the expression of "defensible space," which was coined by Oscar Newman in 1972. The idea behind CPTED is that residents or occupants of a building can bring the environment under their control through a broad range of mechanisms and procedures that combine to improve safety and prevent criminal behavior. For example, CPTED principles include defining areas within buildings that are considered public, semi-public, or private and encouraging the occupants to report persons who do not belong in the semi-public or private areas. The design of the building or structure facilitates the detection and observation of intruders or strangers, thus improving crime prevention and reducing the fear of crime. CPTED principles can be incorporated into any structure being planned or the remodeling of current facilities. Homes, condominiums, apartments, parks, and even streets can be designed with better crime prevention and detection in mind.

How does CPTED relate to policing? In recent years, the crime prevention units of some police departments and local planning/zoning boards (e.g., Ann Arbor, Michigan; Knoxville, Tennessee; Arlington County, Virginia; Cincinnati, Ohio; Hartford, Connecticut; Tempe, Arizona) have become responsible for studying the architectural diagrams and plans for new facilities to be constructed in their jurisdictions. The analysis of these plans includes a review of crime in the area of the project and a review of proposed features such as traffic/parking patterns, pedestrian patterns, landscaping, alarms, locks, and lighting. Crime prevention specialists can then take their concerns back to the developers for possible modification or clarification. Other considerations such as building and zoning codes may be incorporated into this review process, utilizing the expertise of inspectors from offices specifically assigned that responsibility.

MAJOR STRATEGIES OF POLICING

This portion of Chapter 9 discusses the major strategies of policing as analyzed and developed by the Harvard University John F. Kennedy School of Government's Executive Session on Policing. The phrase **strategies of policing** as used here refers to the agency's definition of what the organization proposes to do and how. It describes the principal products, technologies, and methods used in striving for and achieving the agency's goals and objectives. An agency's strategy of policing helps managers maintain a consistent focus for performance and expectations. It helps identify what the agency values and has established as primary activities.

The following strategies of policing are not meant to be mutually exclusive or exhaustive—elements of more than one strategy may exist in an agency at the same time, and other formal strategies may emerge in the future. At the present time, these categories describe the primary philosophies toward policing utilized by agencies in the U.S. It also must be stated that these strategies co-exist throughout the policing community—no one strategy necessarily dominates the others, and it is not necessarily accurate to claim that one is "better" or "worse" than another.

Professional Crime-Fighting Policing

The **professional crime-fighting** strategy of policing became the dominant approach to policing following the reform movements of the 1920s and 1930s. It is a strategy based on the legal authority of the police coupled with political independence for the purpose of achieving crime control through expert service. Kelling and Moore (1988) stated the following about the professional crime-fighting strategy: "It carried them from a world of amateurism, lawlessness, and political vulnerability to a world of professionalism, integrity, and political independence."

This strategy is carried forth by a disciplined, technically sophisticated, quasi-military, well trained crime-fighting force whose primary tactics are radio-equipped patrol vehicles responding quickly to calls for service, coupled with expert follow-up investigations utilizing modern criminalistic technology and techniques. Underlying this approach is an emphasis on accountability of officer actions, which are impacted by centralized operations, written policies and procedures, and close supervision. One objective served by this strategy is to maintain a highly competent force that is free from corrupting political and criminal influence. This approach embodies the quest for professional status advocated by early and mid-twentieth century reformers.

Major Weaknesses. The professional crime-fighting strategy did much to bring policing into its own right during the fifty years that it dominated policing philosophy; however, it was not without weaknesses. The strategy is primarily reactive-oriented in that quick and competent response to calls for service occurs *after* the incident; crime prevention primarily is premised on **preventive patrol** (the highly visible and random presence of the police).

Another weakness of the professional crime-fighting strategy is that the police become the experts at fighting crime and, therefore, should be allowed to solve the problems with little interaction with or involvement of the community. Incidents are handled according to legal authority and procedure. The community was not expected to get involved with crime fighting and crime control efforts.

A third weakness is that this strategy removes officers from close proximity of citizens. A highly mobilized force runs from one call to the next, not having time to interact with the normal, law-abiding citizen. The majority of an officer's contacts in this strategy involves victims, witnesses, and suspects. This often isolates the officer from knowing the concerns and needs of the citizens and gives the appearance and perception that the officers are less accessible.

A fourth weakness is the fact that this strategy fails to adequately control crime. While the department can be highly efficient with its use of resources, its effectiveness in controlling crime and the underlying social causes of criminal and antisocial behavior is limited at best.

Research Findings. During the 1970s and 1980s, a number of research studies were conducted that tested the effectiveness and perceived benefits of several of the methods or tactics utilized in the professional crime-fighting approach. The concept of preventive patrol and its objectives of deterring crime and intercepting crimes in progress were some of the first tactics scrutinized. Preventive patrol tactics are associated with the uniformed officer's use of "uncommitted time" during a shift (or time between calls for service and other specific assignments). The options available to an officer during this time are varied, as summarized by Cordner and Trojanowicz (1992, 5):

> Patrolling can be stationary or mobile; slow-, medium- or high-speed; and oriented toward residential, commercial, recreational or other kinds of areas. Some patrol officers intervene frequently in peoples' lives by stopping cars and checking out suspicious circumstances; other officers seem more interested in inanimate matters such as parked cars and the security of closed businesses; still other officers rarely interrupt their continuous patrolling. Some officers devote all of their uncommitted time to police-related business, while others devote substantial time to loafing or personal affairs.

While the amount of uncommitted time varies greatly from department to department and from beat to beat within departments, until the 1970s departments rarely questioned the effectiveness of preventive patrol. In the early 1970s, a one-year study of the effects of preventive patrol was undertaken in the Kansas City, Missouri Police Department. A portion of the city was divided into 15 beats, and these beats were grouped according to similar characteristics and demographics. One of three patrolling tactics was used in each beat: (1) no preventive patrol activities—squad cars entered the area only to respond to specific calls for service, (2) customary patrol, including normal preventive patrol tactics, and (3) increased preventive patrol, using additional cars to double and triple the normal levels of preventive patrol. Citizen surveys and interviews were conducted before, during, and after the experiment concerning a number of factors, including reported crime, arrests, fear of crime, citizen satisfaction, and traffic accidents. An analysis of the findings yielded the following:

- The practice of having marked police cars conduct random patrol on preassigned beats does not necessarily prevent crime or reassure the citizens, even if the police strength is increased significantly.
- Police can stop routinely patrolling beats for up to a year without necessarily being missed by the residents, and without a rise in crime rates in the patrol area (Petersilia 1993).

The "Kansas City Preventive Patrol Experiment" neither went unnoticed nor uncriticized; however, it was a landmark study because of its findings and because it ushered in an era of other major studies and experiments that focused on the widely held beliefs about law enforcement tactics. It is not our purpose here to examine these in depth, but a listing of the major ones demonstrates the research efforts directed at police operations since the early 1970s and the various police practices that have been scrutinized:

RESPONSE TIME STUDIES: From 1977 through 1982, beginning with Kansas City (MO) and including the cities of Jacksonville, Florida; San Diego, California; Peoria, Illinois; and Rochester, New York, studies have concluded that police response time was unrelated to the probability of making an arrest or locating a witness. Also, neither dispatch nor travel time was strongly associated with citizen satisfaction. These studies concluded that because of the delay in reporting incidents by citizens, police response time has a negligible impact on crime outcomes (Petersilia 1993; Klockars and Mastrofski 1991).

ALTERNATIVE PATROL STRATEGIES: Following the preventive patrol and response time studies, several projects were undertaken during the mid-1970s to modify the traditional model of patrol. In San Diego, *community-oriented policing* (described in greater detail below) was initiated; it allowed patrol officers greater flexibility to analyze police-related problems and to develop and implement measures to cope with them. In New Haven, Connecticut, the use of *directed deterrent runs* (*D-runs*) were initiated. The patrol activity was directed by detailed crime analysis of the times and places of criminal activity. Tactics such as saturation patrol (increased aggressive patrol of selected areas) were implemented to address the identified problems. In Wilmington, Delaware, the *split patrol program* was developed; it allowed about one-third of the patrol force to engage in directed (or structured) patrol activities designed to increase criminal apprehensions. These various alternatives to traditional preventive patrol clearly demonstrated that other patrol utilization tactics could produce equal or better results (Gay *et al.* 1977; Schell *et al.* 1976; Petersilia 1993).

INVESTIGATIONS RESEARCH: During the mid-1970s, two major studies were undertaken regarding the criminal investigation process in policing. The RAND Corporation study was national in scope while the other, by the Stanford Research Institute, focused on Alameda County, California (Greenberg *et al.* 1975). Both studies plus the follow-up projects that followed yielded several conclusions:

■ Many serious crimes are not and often cannot be solved.
■ Patrol officers are responsible for most arrests because of either making on-scene apprehensions or obtaining identifications from victims or witnesses that lead to apprehensions.
■ Only a small percentage of all Part I arrests results from detective investigations that require special organization, training, or skill.
■ Investigators play a critical role in the post-arrest process, particularly in collecting evidence that will enable the prosecutor to file formal criminal charges (Petersilia 1993, 228).

Strategic Policing

Strategic policing refers to an attempt to expand the professional crime-fighting strategy through more sophisticated, analytical, and targeted crime control applications. In essence, this approach employs directed patrol, decoy and sting operations, drug task forces, violent crimes task forces, and special teams to address specific problems (ranging from street crime to sophisticated white-collar frauds). For example, the 1997 LEMAS study found that 79 percent of local agencies assigned officers on a full-time basis to a special unit for drug enforcement and 76 percent of the agencies participated in a multi-agency task force (Reaves and Goldberg 1999, xvi). This strategy of policing maintains a centralized control of operations and problem identification. It hinges on greater intelligence gathering and information analysis efforts coupled with sophisticated forensic science methods. The principal value of strategic policing is improved crime control through proactive directed methods.

Police "crackdowns," as described by Lawrence Sherman (1990, 2), refer to a "sudden, usually proactive change in activity . . . intended to drastically increase either the communicated threat or actual certainty of apprehension." As such, the tactic of police crackdowns falls within the general sphere of strategic policing. Crackdown targets have included drug trafficking locations, loitering and disorder problems, subway station crimes, prostitution, drunk driving offenders, public housing fears, and street gang activities.

Problem-Solving Policing

Problem-solving policing, also called problem-oriented policing (POP), is a strategy based on the assumption that crime is successfully controlled by discovering the underlying reasons or causes for offenses, which include frustrating relationships and a disorderly environment. Instead of treating criminal activity through the response to "incidents," the police respond to possible underlying causes, the personal and community problems, that foster or promote such activity. The police are trained to engage in the problem-solving approach by utilizing the following four-step process, usually referred to as **SARA** (Goldstein 1990):

Scanning: The identifying and clarifying of what the problem is, its specific location, who is involved, what behavior is occurring, and when it occurs.

Analysis: The obtaining of detailed information specifically about the perceived problem. It is an attempt to answer the appropriate who, what, when, how, and especially why questions that surface regarding the particular problem.

Response: The development of alternative approaches to resolve the problem and selecting from among those alternatives the ones that are likely to significantly impact the problem.

Assessment: The evaluation of the response(s) used in order to determine whether it (or they) worked.

Problem identification in problem-oriented policing often involves more interaction with the community than the professional crime-fighting and strategic approaches. Additionally, data and information gathering takes a broader perspective, since the range of agency responses is not limited to the traditional arrest and prosecution tactics. Since the ideas about the causes of crime and methods for controlling it are substantially widened, the data gathering and response to crime or disorder must be broadened as well. According to Goldstein, the "level of analysis" varies according to the problem being addressed. Some problems require a "top-level analysis," some require "street-level analysis," while others require some "intermediate level of analysis" within the police organizational structure. For example, if a problem exists throughout the city, a top-level analysis would be appropriate. If the problem was very localized to a particular part of the jurisdiction or just a few neighborhoods, a street-level analysis would be appropriate. Goldstein (1990, 69–70) adds that problems ought to be explored as close to the operating (local) level as possible.

In the strategy of problem-solving policing, there is a greater emphasis on crime prevention in that it is hoped that by resolving underlying problems, that specific criminal behavior will not surface or manifest itself again. This approach also attempts to mobilize the community residents to defend themselves and to practice prevention tactics. Additionally, it mobilizes other governmental agencies (such as parks and recreation, public works, housing and building inspection, etc.) when necessary to attack neighborhood problems. The total spectrum of police responses under this strategy is much broader than the previously discussed strategies and includes both formal and informal responses.

Community Policing

It appears as though **community policing** is to the 1990s what the professional crime-fighting strategy was to the 1970s, at least in terms of prevailing thought and advocacy. Students of policing and practitioners have been hearing much about this strategy for the last decade. Community policing (also called community-oriented policing, COP) is the attempt by agencies to form a partnership with the residents of the area to reduce crime victimization and to improve the overall quality of life. It is an extension of problem-oriented policing to a degree. Community policing can utilize the SARA method of defining problems and devising potential responses, but the community residents play a more integral role in the process. Consider the following explanation:

> In community policing, community institutions such as families, schools, neighborhood associations, and merchant groups are seen as key partners to the police in the creation of safe, secure communities. The success of the police depends not only on the development of their own skills and capabilities, but also on the creation of competent communities. Community policing acknowledges

that police cannot succeed in achieving their basic goals without both the operational assistance and political support of the community. Conversely, the community cannot succeed in constructing decent, open, and orderly communities without a professional and responsive police force (Moore and Trojanowicz 1988, 9).

In their acclaimed text, *Community Policing*, Trojanowicz and Bucqueroux (1990, xiii-xv) described the major principles of community policing. The principles should be reviewed for a better understanding of the underlying premises of community policing. Of particular interest are their emphases on police-resident interaction and communication, foot patrol, problem-solving techniques, proactiveness, and commitment to a more comprehensive form of policing. A slightly condensed version of the principles follows:

THE TEN PRINCIPLES OF COMMUNITY POLICING

1. Community Policing is both a philosophy and an organizational strategy that allows the police and community residents to work closely together in new ways to solve the problems of crime, fear of crime, physical and social disorder, and neighborhood decay.
2. Community Policing's organizational strategy first demands that everyone in the department, including both civilian and sworn personnel, must investigate ways to translate the philosophy into practice.
3. To implement true Community Policing, police departments must also create and develop a new breed of line officer, the Community Police Officer (CPO), who acts as the direct link between the police and people in the community.
4. The CPO's broad role demands continuous, sustained contact with the law-abiding people in the community, so that together they can explore creative new solutions to local concerns involving crime, fear of crime, disorder, and decay, with private citizens serving as unpaid volunteers.
5. Community Policing implies a new contract between the police and the citizens they serve, one that offers the hope of overcoming widespread apathy, and at the same time restrains any impulse to vigilantism.
6. Community Policing adds a vital proactive element to the traditional reactive role of the police, resulting in full-spectrum police service.
7. Community Policing stresses exploring new ways to protect and enhance the lives of those who are most vulnerable—juveniles, the elderly, minorities, the poor, the disabled, and the homeless.
8. Community Policing promotes the judicious use of technology, but it also rests on the belief that nothing surpasses what dedicated human beings, talking and working together, can achieve.
9. Community Policing must be a fully integrated approach that involves everyone in the department, with the CPOs as specialists in bridging the gap between the police and the people they serve.

10. Community Policing provides decentralized, personalized police service to the community. It recognizes that the police cannot impose order on the community from outside, but that people must be encouraged to think of the police as a resource they can use in helping to solve contemporary community concerns.

THE RELATIONSHIP OF STRATEGIES TO ROLES

Chapter 7 discussed police roles and styles and explained why it is difficult to examine those concepts in a democratic society. It is not easy to reach a consensus on what the police should emphasize in carrying out their tasks and how they should engage the community. The current discussion of police strategies illustrates the conceptual and philosophical differences in the policing field. Each strategy has its strong advocates; each has its underlying assumptions and goals; and each has its advantages and disadvantages (see Exhibit 9–6 for a comparison of key elements of each strategy). But each strategy should not be viewed as an isolated approach within itself. As one can see, it would be difficult for strategic policing to exist by itself, and the same holds true with problem-solving policing and community policing, to an extent. The real challenge may be a question of "What mix of these strategies will work best in a particular community?"

One could argue that each of the above strategies has its place in policing today. Much will depend on the situation and environment found within a particular community. For example, some departments review the comments and literature on community policing and wonder why others are so excited by it, why some are such strong proponents of it—because some departments have been doing community policing for decades without the fanfare or the notoriety! Small departments always have utilized community policing principles, to some extent, in their daily operations because of their size. As some have tried to explain, community policing is an attempt for some larger communities to bring "small town policing" to their neighborhood or their "corner of the world."

The professional crime-fighting strategy in many larger cities has resulted in the police being isolated from the law-abiding citizenry—patrol officers go from one call to the next, never taking the time to build a more trusting and friendly relationship with the citizens they serve. As some ask, "Talk to citizens in your community; do they know the name of the officers that patrol their area?" Ask that question in a small town whose citizens may have never heard of community policing, and your answer may be "Of course, we know everyone in the department!"

Community expectations as to what the local policing efforts should accomplish vary from place to place. The smaller the community, the greater the likelihood for consensus; the larger the community, the more diverse the opinions (since larger communities usually have more extensive and diverse crime-related problems). All the strategies discussed above are used by agencies of all sizes in an attempt to combat crime and to serve the people—it is largely a matter of priority, commitment, and role expectation that determines which ones are operational at a given time.

The challenge for police managers appears to be: How can the police respond effectively to the crime problem and calls for service within their jurisdiction and do it in such a way that they are sensitive to everyone's needs, responsive to victims, and protective of constitutional rights; and that they instill trust, reduce fear, and encourage self-defense and community vigilance; and do it all cost-efficiently and without partisan-political interference? We do not mean to imply that this challenge is an impossible one. We merely are pointing out that policing does not occur in a vacuum and that many pressures and

---

Exhibit 9–6

CORPORATE STRATEGIES FOR POLICING*

Factor	Professional Crime Fighting	Strategic Policing
AIM:	Create a disciplined, technically sophisticated, quasi-military crime-fighting force	Increased capacity through strategic operations and specialization
PRINCIPAL OPERATING STRATEGIES:	High visibility patrol, rapid response, in-depth investigation; Centralized command	More sophisticated investigations, task forces, raids, use of technology; Centralized command
AUTHORITY:	Based solely on the law	Legalistic, professional, and non-political autonomy
VALUES:	Crime-control Investment in training Enhanced status and autonomy Elimination of corruption and bribery Emphasizes accountability	Strategies and aggressiveness rather than purely reactive; Community can assist the police in crime prevention; Political independence and lawfulness
WEAKNESSES:	Basically reactive Little emphasis on mobilizing the community	Citizens may believe the police are too aggressive and harsh

(continues)

Exhibit 9–6 *(continued)*

CORPORATE STRATEGIES FOR POLICING*

Factor	*Problem-Solving Policing*	*Community Policing*
AIM:	Order maintenance, fear reduction, and crime control through proactiveness and thoughtfulness	Crime control through an effective working partnership between police and the community
PRINCIPAL OPERATING STRATEGIES:	Diagnosing and resolving underlying problems/causes related to crime; Believes crime is caused by particular continuing problems in the community	More interaction with citizens builds trust, improves cooperation and information exchange
	Decentralized operation but specialized	Decentralized geographical distribution and accountability
AUTHORITY:	Based on the law and the obligation to assist the community in resolving recurring problems	Authority of officers is validated through the community in the form of support
VALUES:	Crime-control and prevention through actions other than traditional methods	Community organizations and institutions seen as key partners in creating safe and secure communities
	Broader use of alternatives both civil and criminal; Mobilizes the community when necessary; Mobilizes other agencies	Police need the political support and operational assistance of community; Community views/concerns given high priority
WEAKNESSES:	Community involvement is limited, relies primarily on agency expertise	Increases risks of illegitimate political demands on officers because of closer relationships with community

Source: Adapted from M. H. Moore and R. C. Trojanowicz, Corporate Strategies for Policing, *Perspectives on Policing*, November 1988, National Institute of Justice and Harvard University.

issues interact in the selection of an agency's role and the implementation of a policing strategy. Only when the public and all police officers fully understand these issues can a true dialogue and partnership in policing begin to blossom in a community.

SUMMARY

The purpose of this chapter was to describe the basic functions of law enforcement agencies, primarily at the local level of policing, and how those functions are operationalized into effective policing strategies. It was emphasized that the functions of patrol, investigations, and crime prevention do not operate independently of each other even where specialized units may exist. Each of the three basic functions of policing (patrol, investigation, and crime prevention) were described in some detail.

The major strategies of policing (professional crime fighting, strategic, problem-solving, and community) that have been utilized during the last 30 years were presented and described in terms of underlying philosophies and operational tactics. It was pointed out that these strategies are interrelated to the degree that they can co-exist in the same agency, and each strategy attempts to fulfill particular objectives. The relationship of role to the selection of a department's policing strategy was mentioned as an important factor in understanding the complexities of these issues.

QUESTIONS FOR REVIEW

1. What are the three major functions of police agencies?
2. What is the history of the patrol function from the 1800s to the present?
3. What is the purpose of and what are the procedures used in the preliminary as compared to the follow-up investigation process?
4. What are the beliefs underlying the concept of crime prevention?
5. What does CPTED mean, and what is its basic premise?
6. What are basic tenets of each of the four major strategies of policing?
7. What is the relationship of role to policing strategy selection?

SUGGESTED ACTIVITIES

1. Survey your local police departments and inquire about the number of canines, horses, bicycles, all-terrain vehicles, and aircraft that are part of their inventory. Seek information about any unique programs that have been implemented recently.
2. Interview a local police administrator about his/her department's policing strategy. Does the department utilize more than one strategy of the four discussed in this chapter?
3. Contact local crime prevention units or associations and ask a guest into your classroom for a discussion of their typical activities.
4. Log on to the World Wide Web and go to several of the following URLs and review the concepts and techniques associated with crime prevention:
   http://www.ncpc.org
   http://ncjrs.aspensys.com/
   http://www.weprevent.org

http://www.nationaltownwatch.org/natw.html
http://www.crimepreventcoalition.org/
http://ourworld.compuserve.com/homepages/iscpp/
http://www.tcpa.org/home.htm
http://www.c-s-i.org/index.htm

5. Log on to the World Wide Web and, using a search engine, enter "CPTED" and review the first 10–20 listings. Write a brief three-page concept paper on this approach to crime prevention.

CHAPTER GLOSSARY

community policing (also called community-oriented policing): an attempt by agencies to form a partnership with the residents of the area to reduce crime victimization and to improve the overall quality of life

CPTED (Crime Prevention Through Environmental Design): a concept that maintains that the proper design and effective use of the physical environment can produce behavioral effects that will reduce the incidence and fear of crime, thereby improving the quality of life

fixed post, line beat, or **random foot patrol:** various forms of foot patrol; an officer may be assigned to a fixed or relatively stationary position, such as a "strip" of buildings, or be permitted to roam an assigned area

follow-up investigation: the second level or phase of an investigation; it extends and continues the preliminary investigation and may be conducted by specialists

foot patrol: a type of patrol, conducted by an officer while on foot

investigation process: a major function of most law enforcement agencies that involves the detailed assessment of criminal occurrences for purposes of identifying and prosecuting offenders

modus operandi: phrase meaning "method of operation" and used to assist investigators in developing leads about possible suspects

patrol: a major function of most police agencies that today incorporates elements of general observation and responding to calls for service and emergencies

preliminary investigation: the initial procedures undertaken by an investigator (uni-formed or plain clothes) to determine whether a crime has been committed, what persons (victim, witnesses, suspects) are involved, and what evidence or investigative leads exist

preventive patrol: the highly visible and random presence of the police coupled with the belief that this deters and/or prevents crime from occurring

professional crime-fighting policing: a strategy based on the legal authority of the police coupled with political independence for the purpose of achieving crime control through expert service

problem-solving policing: also called problem-oriented policing, a strategy based on the assumption that crime is successfully controlled by discovering the underlying reasons or causes for offenses which include frustrating relationships and a disorderly environment

SARA: the main problem-solving policing steps or process known as Scanning, Analysis, Response, and Assessment

solvability factors: responses or observations that have a high probability of providing leads for the identifying and locating of an offender

strategies of policing: the phrase used to refer to the agency's definition of what the organization proposes to do and how; it describes the principal products, technologies, and methods used in striving for and achieving the agency's goals and objectives

strategic policing: refers to an attempt to expand the professional crime-fighting strategy through more sophisticated, analytical, and targeted crime control applications

REFERENCES

Adams, Thomas F. 1997. *Police Field Operations.* 4th ed. Upper Saddle River: NJ: Prentice-Hall, Inc.

Bennett, Wayne and Karen M. Hess. 1981. *Criminal Investigation.* St. Paul, MN: West Publishing Company.

Butterworth, Brent. 1988. Police Forces Go to the Dogs. *Law Enforcement Technology* 15(6) (November/December): 26.

Chapman, Samuel G. 1964. *Police Patrol Readings.* Springfield, IL: Charles C. Thomas.

Commission on Accreditation for Law Enforcement Agencies. 1993. *Standards for Law Enforcement Agencies.* 3d ed. Fairfax, VA: Commission on Accreditation for Law Enforcement Agencies.

Commission on Accreditation for Law Enforcement Agencies. 1999. *Standards for Law Enforcement Agencies.* 4th ed. Fairfax, VA: Commission on Accreditation for Law Enforcement Agencies.

Cordner, Gary and Robert C. Trojanowicz. 1992. Patrol. In *What Works in Policing?* edited by Gary W. Cordner and Donna C. Hale (Cincinnati, OH: Anderson Publishing Co.).

Dilworth, Donald C., ed. 1976. *The Blue and The Brass: American Policing 1890–1910.* Gaithersburg, MD: International Association of Chiefs of Police.

Ellis, Tom. 1993. HeliCOPters. *Law Enforcement Technology* 20(9) (September): 34–35.

Fennelly, Lawrence J., ed. 1982. *Handbook of Loss Prevention & Crime Prevention.* Woburn, MA: Butterworth Publishers (citing Arthur Kingsbury, 1976).

Fulton, Roger V. 1993. Community Policing on Horseback. *Law Enforcement Technology* 20(5) (May): 34.

Gay, William G., Theodore H. Schell, and Stephen Schack. 1977. *Improving Patrol Productivity, Volume I, Routine Patrol* and *Improving Patrol Productivity, Volume II, Specialized Patrol.* Washington, D.C.: Law Enforcement Assistance Administration.; and Joan Petersilia, pp. 220–226.

Goldstein, Herman. 1990. *Problem-Oriented Policing.* New York: McGraw-Hill Publishing Company.

Greenberg, Bernard, *et al.* 1975. *Felony Investigation Decision Model—An Analysis of Investigative Elements of Information.* Menlo Park, CA: Stanford Research Institute.

Greenwood, Peter, Joan Petersilia, and Jan Chaiken. 1977. *The Criminal Investigation Process.* Lexington, MA: D. Heath.

Haller, M. 1976. Historical Roots of Police Behavior: Chicago, 1890–1925. *Law and Society Review* 10 (Winter): 303–324.

Holden, Richard N. 1992. *Law Enforcement: An Introduction.* Englewood Cliffs, NJ: Prentice-Hall, Inc.

International Association of Chiefs of Police. 1989. *Criminal Investigation.* Arlington, VA: International Association of Chiefs of Police.

Kelling, George and Mark H. Moore. 1988. The Evolving Strategy of Policing. *Perspectives on Policing.* Washington, D.C.: National Institute of Justice and Harvard University (November).

Leonard, V. A. 1964. *The Police of the 20th Century.* Brooklyn, NY: The Foundation Press, Inc.

MacDonald, John M., Geoffrey P. Alpert, and Angela R. Gover. 1998. The Use of Helicopters in Policing: Necessity or Waste? *Police Forum* 8(2) (April): 9–14.

Mackenzie, Stephen A. 1993. Sniff and Snuff: Dogs Save Time and Money Detecting Bombs. *Police* 17(4) (April): 20–21.

Meade, Patricia. 1998. Police Ask Public for Donations to Purchase Dog, Train Handler. *Vindicator* (April): B1.

Moore, Mark H. and Robert C. Trojanowicz. 1988. Corporate Strategies for Policing. *Perspectives on Policing.* Washington, D.C.: National Institute of Justice and Harvard University (November).

National Crime Prevention Council. 1997. *Designing Safer Communities: A Crime Prevention through Environmental Design Handbook.* Washington, D.C.: National Crime Prevention Council.

Petersilia, Joan. 1993. The Influence of Research on Policing. In *Critical Issues in Policing: Contemporary Readings,* edited by Roger G. Dunham and Geoffrey P. Alpert (Prospect Heights, IL: Waveland Press, Inc.).

Reaves, Brian and Andrew L. Smith. 1999. *Law Enforcement Management and Administrative Statistics, 1997: Data for Individual State and Local Agencies with 100 or More Officers.* Washington, D.C.: U.S. Department of Justice.

Schell, Theodore H., *et al.* 1976. *Traditional Preventive Patrol.* Washington, D.C.: Law Enforcement Assistance Administration.

Sherman, Lawrence W. 1990. Police Crackdowns. *NIJ Reports.* Washington, D.C.: U.S. Department of Justice (March/April).

Spelman, William G. and Dale K. Brown. 1991. Response Time. In *Thinking about Police: Contemporary Readings,* edited by Carl B. Klockars and Stephen D. Mastrofski (2d ed., New York: McGraw-Hill, Inc., 163–169).

Times (London) 1829. New Police Instructions. (25 September): 3–4.

Trojanowicz, Robert and Bonnie Bucqueroux. 1990. *Community Policing: A Contemporary Perspective.* Cincinnati, OH: Anderson Publishing Co.

Walker, Samuel. 1977. *A Critical History of Police Reform: The Emergence of Professionalism.* Lexington, MA: D.C. Heath.

Walker, Samuel. 1984. Broken Windows and Fractured History: The Use and Misuse of History in Recent Police Patrol Analysis. *Justice Quarterly* 1(1): 75–90.

Wright, Jerry L. and Ronald L. Thomas. 1993. Crime Prevention Through Environmental Design (CPTED): The Site Plan Review Process. In *Encyclopedia of Security Management,* edited by John J. Fay (Boston: Butterworth-Heinemann).

CHAPTER 10

Human Resources in Policing

Dallas Assistant Police Chief Terrell Bolton, right, shares a laugh with Chief Ben Click during a news conference announcing Bolton's selection as the new police chief in Dallas, Texas. August 1999. (AP/Wide World Photos)

LEARNING OBJECTIVES

The major tasks of policing are accomplished through the efforts of people—policing is a very labor-intensive service. Personnel policies, procedures, and practices are described in this chapter, and upon its completion you will be able to:

1. Identify and describe the major stages of personnel recruitment and selection functions in police agencies.
2. Describe the legal prerequisites and limitations of personnel functions.
3. Explain at least four different methods utilized in policing for promoting persons to higher rank and responsibility.
4. Distinguish between the concepts of "labor relations" and "collective bargaining."

THE IMPORTANCE OF HUMAN RESOURCE CONSIDERATIONS

Of all the available resources, people are the greatest asset to the policing function. Granted, the United States is a very advanced technological society, but the services provided by law enforcement agencies are performed by humans. It takes many people working together to carry out the functions performed by policing agencies. Although *Robocops* may one day assist in this function, people will continue to be the mainstay for the next several decades. (Issues related to technology in policing are discussed in Chapter 13.)

Individuals preparing to enter the criminal justice field today often are misinformed or have misinterpreted many aspects of personnel selection, promotion, and career development. It is not difficult to meet someone working in the field who may be bitter, frustrated, or disillusioned about his or her job. Others with a criminal justice education may be frustrated because they have not been successful in obtaining employment. In conversations with those employed in the field, negative statements such as the following may be made when asked about job openings and career advancement:

■ "It all depends on who you know—it's all politics."
■ "Merit has little to do with getting ahead in this department."
■ "It doesn't matter how much education or ability you have, you have to play their political games to get ahead."
■ "You'll never make it, you're the wrong color (or sex, or religion, or ethnic group)."

Statements such as these may cause some highly qualified applicants to pursue other careers or agencies. Although there may be some truth to these statements in some agencies, for the most part they are overexaggerated and based on emotion rather than fact and understanding of the personnel process. The motive behind such statements also may be suspect. For example, if I am a police officer who knows that the competition for jobs in my agency is very rigorous, might I *discourage* someone from applying if I am trying to support a friend or relative who is applying also (thus reducing the competitive pool)? Or, am I upset with my employer and trying to keep highly qualified persons from applying? Or maybe I do not want a person to join the department because of the potential competition for promotion slots in the future.

The "bottom line" is *do not believe everything someone tells you about the personnel function of an agency!* The personnel function in policing is highly complex and becoming very legalistic. By understanding the legal, political, and social framework of the personnel function, one has a greater likelihood of successfully passing through its stages. One potential outcome is a highly rewarding career in law enforcement.

Personnel and Expenditures

As mentioned in Chapter 4, the policing function in the United States consists of over 900,000 persons employed in about 18,700 agencies. Sworn officers account for about 650,000 of these persons. Annual expenditures, in payroll, amount to over $41 billion. When reduced to the local level of policing, police personnel is usually one of the largest, if not the largest, units of employees in a jurisdiction. Generally speaking, the public safety function (police and firefighting) is the largest expenditure in jurisdictions regarding personnel costs. Within the individual agencies, personnel costs usually consume 75–95 percent of the budget.

Personnel expenditures include salaries and fringe benefits (health/life/disability/liability insurances, clothing allowances, vacation and holiday pay, etc.). There are also operating costs for agencies, which include furniture, heat, light, communications systems, etc. Exhibit 10–1 depicts the entrance salary and the per-officer operating costs for selected agencies. Agencies were selected to show some of the geographical differences (city versus county, suburban versus rural).

Exhibit 10–1

PERSONNEL COSTS OF EMPLOYING AN OFFICER, SELECTED AGENCIES

AGENCY	ENTRY LEVEL SALARY	ANNUAL OPERATING COST
Pulaski County Sheriff,AK	$18,402	$42,534
Coral Gables PD, FL	$29,793	$115,446
Riverside PD, CA	$35,052	$124,164
Denver PD, CO	$30,300	$78,156
Spokane PD, WA	$28,835	$95,035
Ada County Sheriff, ID	$20,904	$82,961
Topeka PD, KS	$24,523	$64,088
Canton PD, OH	$23,099	$60,428
Philadelphia PD, PA	$27,725	$51,707
Providence PD, RI	$32,540	$44,533
Arlington County PD, VA	$32,639	$93,111
Wake County Sheriff, NC	$23,000	$115,350

Salaries and costs are based on 1997 data. Operating costs include salary and fringe benefits, supplies and contractual services. Capital expenditures such as equipment and construction costs are not included.

Source: B. A. Reaves and A. L. Goldberg, *Law Enforcement Management and Administrative Statistics, 1997: Data for Individual State and Local Agencies with 100 or More Officers*, Tables 6a and 7a, 1999, U.S. Department of Justice, Bureau of Justice Statistics.

Qualities and Attributes

The day-to-day street policing functions have not yet been computerized; it takes thinking people to analyze crime scenes, to interview victims and witnesses, to locate and apprehend suspects, and to prepare cases for prosecution. These aspects of the police function can be assisted with technology, but people carry out these tasks associated with bringing offenders to justice. This is no small point. Do we want a machine to do the police function for us? Think of all the ramifications of this question before answering it, because the technology exists today to almost completely "automate" the criminal justice system. Of course, it would mean transforming our society, our Constitution, and our current sense of privacy. Stop reading for just a moment and answer this question: "What qualities and attributes do you want in the police officers that protect you and your family?" August Vollmer (1969, 222) is credited for making the following statement concerning police officers:

> The citizen expects police officers to have the wisdom of Solomon, the courage of David, the strength of Samson, the patience of Job, the leadership of Moses, the kindness of the Good Samaritan, the strategical training of Alexander, the faith of Daniel, the diplomacy of Lincoln, the tolerance of the Carpenter of Nazareth, and finally, an intimate knowledge of every branch of the natural, biological, and social sciences. If he had all these, he *might* be a good policeman.

As a society and as individuals, we expect a great deal from our law enforcement personnel. We expect integrity, honesty, self-control, tolerance, intelligence, objectiveness, courtesy, courage, concern for others, fairness, maturity, commitment, dedication, a strong character, physical and emotional strength, and insight. Few will argue against such qualities, but take another look at these expectations. How can they be identified in the selection process? How are these measured? How can they be "trained" into an individual? In short, how are such expectations turned into realities? There are no easy solutions to this quest; however, it does take commitment from administrators to strive toward the goal of selecting promising candidates.

THE RECRUITING AND SELECTION PROCESS

Not everyone who wants to become a law enforcement official will become one! Some who enter law school never become attorneys; some who enter medical school never become doctors. It is important to understand that there are many variables that go into the hiring of law enforcement personnel. Everyone simply cannot be hired; there are not enough positions in agencies for that to occur. Of course, "wanting" to be an agent or officer is usually a prerequisite to selection, but it alone is not sufficient.

Recruitment

Recruitment is the development and maintenance of an adequate supply of qualified persons interested in being employed by a specific agency. In reality, there are two types of recruiting efforts: "active" and "passive." Active recruitment occurs when an agency makes a concerted effort to attract candidates to it. This may entail the deployment of existing personnel, either sworn or civilian, as recruiters and sending them into the community to generate interest among potential applicants. This task can be done by personnel specifically assigned to that function or by personnel as part of their regular assignments. Passive recruitment is when the agency has openings and takes applications from those who come to the agency. No outreach or concerted effort is made to attract candidates; it is a "sit back, wait and see" approach.

Some departments spend considerable resources attempting to attract qualified applicants. Recruiting brochures are printed; officers are sent out of town on recruiting trips to colleges, universities, and job fairs; and public announcements are placed in local public media (newspapers, public service announcements on radio, television, and even the Internet). Recruitment material can contain a generous amount of information about the hiring process and the opportunities with the agency or may contain only the basics with telephone numbers and an address to pick up the application. Exhibit 10–2 depicts part of the contents of a recruiting packet from the Columbus (Ohio) Police Department that is distributed by recruiters.

The major objective of the recruiting process is to ensure an adequate supply of interested applicants from which selection will occur. The underlying premise is that the larger the pool of applicants, the greater the likelihood of obtaining enough qualified candidates to process through the selection procedures. Although the recruiting phase is an attempt to increase the number of candidates available for hire, there is a need to attract serious and qualified applicants. Sheer numbers alone are not sufficient; some agencies attract thousands of applicants every time they offer the entrance exam, even if there are no current openings! The recruiting phase should present an accurate portrayal of the job and the responsibilities it carries. Being an officer is not all red lights and sirens, and those who are attracted because of that image may be some of the first to be disqualified. Likewise, some potential and needed candidates, such as women and members of minority groups, may have an image of not being wanted. These groups have not always been treated well by some law enforcement personnel, or the image of abuse or perceptions and reputations of mistreatment may be prevalent in their immediate environments. If the reputation of an agency is a negative one, attempting to recruit highly qualified candidates from any segment of the community may be difficult. An active recruitment program is often the best approach to overcoming negative perceptions. Of course, an agency's administrators must be responsive to any known negative perceptions on the part of the community and should be investigating the source of them.

The Selection Process

The **selection process** includes the various techniques, devices, and procedures used to identify candidates to whom offers of employment may be made. It is often viewed as a series of events linked together and through which an applicant must pass in order to be hired. Most perceive the application form as the beginning of the process and a job offer as the conclusion of the process; however, that is not totally accurate. The selection process actually begins during

Exhibit 10–2

CONTENTS OF A RECRUITING PACKET

The Columbus (Ohio) Police Department's Recruiting Packet is distributed in an attractive blue folder with photos of officers in the specialized units and the city's skyline at night; the one inside pocket contains a number of individual sheets on the following subjects:

"The Selection Process"—describes the eight steps in the process from filing an application to physical and psychological evaluation in step eight. It details the steps so it is clear what happens in each phase of the process.

"Employee Benefits"— describes the fringe benefit package consisting of health insurance, life insurance, paid holidays, paid sick leave, clothing and equipment allowance, prescription drugs, vision care and dental plan, personal liability insurance, prepaid legal plan, retirement, college tuition reimbursement, vacation time, deferred compensation program, credit union membership, and so on.

"About the Columbus Division of Police"—describes the number of personnel, recent innovations, facilities, patrol division, calls for service, special units, and so on.

"Police Officer Salary"—describes the first five pay steps from the training academy through the first 48 months on the job. It shows how the salary climbs from about $28,000 through $47,000 during that period.

"About Columbus, Ohio"—a snapshot description of the city and its demographics, costs of living, community events, and unique aspects. It describes the average weather patterns.

"Let's Hear from You"—a half sheet that contains the phone number and address of the recruiting unit and permits interested parties to mail in their name and address to the agency because of employment interests with the city.

Courtesy of Columbus, Ohio, Department of Public Safety.

the recruiting phase or announcement of job openings. Would-be applicants then begin assessing their true desires and aspirations about applying (some would call this "soul-searching"). Some agencies also require a **pre-application conference** with a ranking field officer. This meeting is for the conveyance of information about the job, the required training, and the agency's expectations of its personnel. It may include watching a videotape and obtaining information about the academy training and probationary periods.

The primary objective of the pre-application conference is to supply accurate, realistic information and to clarify any misperceptions of the future applicant. Some departments encourage possible applicants to meet with officers to discuss the realities of police work before applying. Some departments offer ride-along opportunities with uniformed patrol officers for any member of the public and especially for potential applicants. By obtaining accurate information about the position and agency, future applicants can better assess their desire and willingness to work for that jurisdiction. This is sometimes referred to as **self-selection** in the sense that the applicant is making an informed and more objective decision to continue in the selection process.

Figure 10–1 depicts the typical phases of the selection process for a medium to large agency. The sequence may vary somewhat among agencies, and some agencies may omit certain phases. Smaller agencies may have a somewhat shorter process. Each of the phases is described in this section in an overview manner. It must be understood that detailed information about each phase is beyond the scope of this text, but the reader should consult the references at the end of this chapter for additional information.

The Application. The application form varies greatly from one agency to the next; there is no universally applied standard form. It may be a simple one-page format to a ten-page (or more) document. The information requested may range from basic identification-type inquiries to a complete educational and employment history coupled with questions about drug use. Usually, those agencies that utilize a longer, more detailed application use it as part of the background investigation, whereas the shorter formats are used to contact the applicant and to identify him or her at the next phase of the process.

Written Exam. Written exams are very common in today's selection process. They have changed some over the years because of certain technical and legal requirements (discussed in the next major section of this chapter). Some exams are developed by the local jurisdiction while others may be developed by private companies or public entities that specialize in testing. The examination itself usually consists of several sections, which may include a selected number of the following:

■ English grammar, spelling, punctuation, and sentence structure
■ English comprehension, vocabulary, and word usage
■ Basic mathematics, percentages, and thought problems

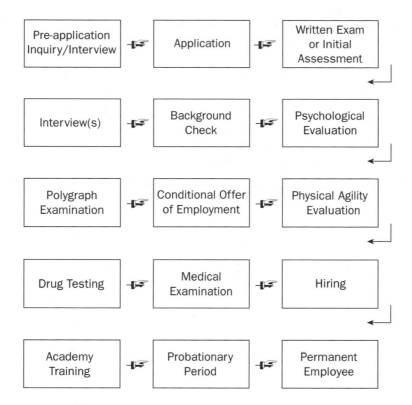

Note: Not all agencies use each stage, and some may use other procedures.

Figure 10–1 Typical Stages in a Selection Process

- Essay or writing samples, printing samplers
- Memorization of facts, numbers, and/or photos and descriptions
- Reasoning/judgment based on scenarios or situational analyses
- Interpretation/application of law/code sections to situations
- Questions about material distributed before the examination that applicants were told to study

Interview(s). Of all the phases of the selection process, the interview is the most universal regardless of the size of the agency. There may be one, two, or even three interviews. They may be conducted by an individual or by a group (sometimes referred to as an interview board or selection board), by civilians (e.g., personnel officials, elected officials), and/or police personnel. They may be conducted at the police department, in the applicant's home, or at another agency location (e.g., personnel office, mayor's office).

There are two types of interviews: **structured** and **unstructured**. The structured interview usually consists of specifically compiled questions that focus on various aspects of the job or the applicant's abilities and background. Some follow-up questions may be asked, many of which are also of a structured nature. The unstructured interview consists of general areas of focus, but the questions are not specifically spelled out. There is greater potential for the unstructured interview to wander off-course during follow-up questions to initial responses, which could be problematic in legal challenges to the selection process.

Candidates for positions sometimes believe that there are right and wrong responses to the questions asked during the interview. In the majority of interviews, it is less a matter of specific responses than it is the reasoning, directness, and appropriateness of what is said as well as the manner in which statements are made; interviewers often are evaluating oral communication skills, poise, composure, responsiveness, and appearance rather than the content or correctness of the specific responses.

Background Check. As the phrase implies, a background check is a formal review and verification of the candidate's formal education, current and previous residences, current and prior employment, traffic and criminal citations and convictions (if any), reported drug history, and credit rating. This usually includes interviews with neighbors, named references, teachers and/or professors, employers, and possibly relatives. In some jurisdictions, background checks are done in person by investigators of the agency to which one has applied; in others they are conducted by mail and over the phone. If an applicant is from out of town, the agency may request certain background information from the police in the candidate's local jurisdiction. An applicant will be required to sign certain release forms that grant the background investigators the authority to gain access to records that would otherwise be confidential.

Polygraph Examination. While sometimes considered part of the background check, polygraph testing should be considered a separate phase of the selection process. The polygraph is a scientifically calibrated instrument that records physiological changes in respiration (pneumograph), electrical resistance of the skin (galvanograph), and changes in blood pressure and pulse rate (cardiosphygmograph). These three measurements are recorded independently of each other by three pen-like devices on graph paper in the instrument. It operates by the existence of a direct relationship between a person's state of mind and his/her physiological condition (Territo 1974, 51). The purpose of polygraph testing is to verify a person's truthfulness or the detection of deception regarding an area of inquiry. The central premises upon which the polygraph is based are that: (a) lying leads to conflict, (b) conflict causes fear and anxiety, and (c) these mental states are the direct cause of measurable physiological changes (Shattuch 1973, 5–6).

Conditional Offer of Employment. Because of certain potential liabilities and allegations, this phase of the selection process has become more common in public agencies. A **conditional offer of employment** means that the candidate is suitable and eligible for hire at that point in the selection process. It means that the candidate will be employed if certain other factors related to physical ability and medical and mental conditions are within job-related limits. Ultimately, if physical, mental, and/or medical conditions are identified that are not within the standards for the position, the offer of employment will be withdrawn.

Psychological Evaluation. The Strawbridge (1990) survey of 72 major police departments in 1990 found that 66 (91.6 percent) agencies included either a **psychometric exam** or **psychological interview** as part of the selection process. This is in stark contrast to surveys done in 1972 and 1976, where the rates were 39 percent and 20 percent respectively for the agencies surveyed (Eisenberg *et al.* 1973; Conser and Thompson 1976). A 1994 survey of 59 departments found 91.5 percent utilizing psychological interviews (Langworthy *et al.* 1995). Generally speaking, the larger the department, the greater the likelihood of having some form of psychological evaluation. Some state regulatory commissions require this type of evaluation as a condition for certification and/or employment of officers throughout the state.

Psychometric examinations, as used here, refer to written instruments used to measure various psychological characteristics such as intelligence, interests/preferences, and personality traits/characteristics. There is a wide variety of such instruments, but the most common to the police selection process include the MMPI (Minnesota Multiphasic Personality Inventory), the CPI (California Personality Inventory), the IPI (Inwald Personality Inventory), Rorschach Psychodiagnostic Inkblots, Human Figure Drawing, and Wonderlic Personnel Test. Some departments utilize more than one test and may combine the process with exams that measure reading levels, attitudes, opinions, and ethnic values. Some of these tests can be machine scored and interpreted while others may require interpretation by a trained psychologist/psychiatrist. The most appropriate approach and use of these tests is when the results are normed against police officer samples. The Law Enforcement Assessment and Development Report (LEADR) and the Minnesota Personnel Interpretive Report (MPIR) are attempts to do just that (Moriarty and Field 1994, 212–215).

Where utilized, psychological interviews are conducted by trained psychologists or psychiatrists. Such interviews may be conducted privately or in group sessions. While many of the psychometric tests have specific, more objective scoring schemes, the psychological interview is considered more subjective and interpretive and, of course, is dependent on the specialist's ability and experience. Both techniques attempt to accomplish the same objective: to select a psychologically stable person who is free of psychopathies (mental illnesses). However, psychological evaluation is not an exact science; the process usually results in "screening-out" candidates with known or suspected unacceptable traits or "selecting-in" candidates with acceptable or predictable traits of what is believed to make a good police officer.

Physical Ability Test. Historically, the physical ability test in selection processes often consisted of completing a specific number of sit-ups, push-ups, and/or chin-ups and performing certain events that included climbing, pushing, running, or crawling. Today, because of adverse court decisions and law-related expectations, the physical ability testing has undergone considerable change. Such testing must be related to job tasks and functions performed by police officers. The test now often consists of some type of obstacle course that simulates what an officer may experience in the field, a 150–170 pound "dummy drag," and a combination of running and sprinting. It may also include other routines, such as dry-firing a service weapon and/or making a simulated arrest. Exhibit 10–3 reports the recommendations of a national conference held on the matter of physical fitness testing in law enforcement by the Major City Chiefs Association, the National Executive Institute Associates, and the Federal Bureau of Investigation (National City Chiefs Association 1993, i-ii).

However, there is still great controversy over physical fitness standards because of the Americans with Disabilities Act (ADA) and the Civil Rights Act of 1991. Litigation continues on these matters and the Supreme Court has yet to rule definitively on physical fitness standards. The issues appear to be whether an agency should establish validated *job-related standards* or *fitness standards.* If they establish job-related standards, the standards must be the same for all ages and for both men and women. If the agency establishes *fitness standards,* they may be gender- and age-normed. The New Hampshire legislature in 1998 enacted statutory law that, beginning on 1 January 2001, will require every full-time police, state corrections, and probation/parole officer who is hired by a state, county, or local law enforcement agency in the state to pass the same medical exam and physical fitness test that the state training council prescribes for new recruits, on an ongoing basis at three-year intervals throughout their careers, as a condition of maintaining their police certification. The tests will be based on the Cooper Aerobics standards at the 35th percentile for the officer's age and sex (Sweeney 1999).

Drug Testing. Employers have the right to prohibit all employees from using or being under the influence of alcohol or illegal drugs at the workplace. Of the 72 major law enforcement agencies surveyed by the Strawbridge in 1990, 55 (76 percent) conducted drug tests as part of the selection process (Strawbridge 1990, 17–24, Table 2). Because law enforcement agencies have the responsibility of enforcing the country's drug laws and because of possible impairment while under the influence of drugs (a safety hazard to others); police agencies are justified in conducting such exams. The major precaution that must be taken is to grant appeals and second tests to those who test positive for drug use when they claim the test is inaccurate and has unfairly disqualified them from employment consideration.

Medical Examination. Medical fitness for police officer candidates is an obvious expectation on the part of an employer. The hiring of an unfit/unhealthy

Exhibit 10–3

RECOMMENDED PHYSICAL ABILITIES TEST

1. The person taking the test must complete a 1/4 mile course consisting of a series of 20–40 yard runs/sprints interspersed with the events listed below.

2. The course includes a 5–6 foot wall climb, 4 foot horizontal jump (may be done while running), a stair climb (six steps up, six steps down), the drag of a 160–170 pound dummy for 50 feet, and another run/sprint in different directions. No specific order or frequency of events was established, but all events should appear at least once.

3. At the conclusion of the course, the applicant must dry fire the service weapon 5 times with both strong and weak hands.

   NOTE: The addition of a 1.5 mile run may be legally defensible for agencies that can demonstrate extended endurance is a needed physical ability that is job-related and consistent with business necessity.

The passing time for completion of this test is to be determined by each agency based on the levels of performance required of its employees. The passing times should not be age or gender adjusted.

Since all physical abilities needed to perform as a law enforcement officer are not tested in this recommended task test, a department may choose to separately test such areas as vision, speech, hearing, reading, writing, manual dexterity, flexibility, sitting, standing, reflexes, and weight/body composition.

Source: Reprinted from Major City Chiefs Association et al., *Physical Fitness Testing in Law Enforcement: An Analysis of the Impact of the Americans with Disabilities Act, The Civil Rights Act of 1991, and the Age Discrimination in Employment Act, A Conference Report*, pp. i–ii, 1993, Federal Bureau of Investigation.

---

candidate could cost the employer (and taxpayer) large sums of money should the person have to retire early on disability or other abnormality that renders them unfit for duty. The focus of concern here is the detection of respiratory, circulatory, or skeletal conditions that are early signs of existing or degenerative diseases or conditions that would interfere with the performance of required tasks and functions. During the late 1980s, some departments were not hiring persons who smoked because of the likelihood of developing respiratory and circulatory diseases (which are covered under some retirement systems). Some agencies still have such restrictions in their hiring process; however, since 1989, at least 29 states and the District of Columbia have enacted legislation prohibiting employers from requiring, as a condition of employment, that employees or prospective employees abstain from the use of tobacco products outside the course of employment (Bureau of National Affairs 1993, 509:501). Today, departments that emphasize greater health consciousness or physical health maintenance in their personnel processes have the added benefit of reducing or slowing the rising cost of health insurance.

Hiring. In every jurisdiction there is an **"appointing authority"** who officially hires the successful applicant according to law. The title of the appointing authority may vary according to the type of jurisdiction. It may be the mayor of a city, the sheriff of a county, a board of supervisors or trustees of a township, the department head of a state agency, a personnel official, or some other official granted such authority by law. It often is believed that the administrative head of the law enforcement agency (the chief, superintendent, commissioner, etc.) is the one who appoints new candidates; however, it is more accurate to say that the chief administrator "recommends" the candidates to the appointing authority.

The hiring process may include the involvement of a central personnel office of a jurisdiction. This office is usually separate from any personnel unit found in the law enforcement agency. For example, some jurisdictions are covered under **civil service** law or regulations. These vary from state to state, so general statements are difficult. Where civil service law exists, strict adherence to the regulations is required. The regulations may relate to written examinations, medical exams, residency, citizenship, bonus points, eligibility lists, appeals, grievances, promotions, layoffs, dismissals, and so on.

A civil service or central personnel agency may actually conduct the initial phases of the selection process and develop a list of qualified candidates; this is known as an **eligibility list** in some jurisdictions. It is from this list of qualified candidates that the law enforcement agency must select its employees. Certain requirements of the law may also apply in considering candidates from such a list. For example, in Ohio, statutory civil service law prior to 1995 required consideration of the top three candidates on a ranked eligibility list for every open entry-level position. This is known as **"the rule of three"** in personnel practices. This allows the appointing (and recommending) authority some discretion in hiring. In 1995, the statutory law was modified to allow the rule of ten, so now the top ten candidates can be considered for the open position.

The ranking of candidates on the eligibility list is based on the raw score of written examinations or assessment procedures and any bonus points awarded for certain factors or job-related criteria such as: (a) previous police experience, (b) state peace officer certification, (c) college education, (d) military experience (veteran), and (e) residency.

Any person interested in employment with a particular agency is encouraged to inquire about the details of its selection process. One needs to develop a full understanding of the process in order to know what to expect and to appreciate the complexity of the process. Some agencies are bound by very rigid civil service or merit system procedures while others offer continuous hiring opportunities.

Academy Training. Once appointed to a law enforcement position, some form of academy training is normally required (unless the person has been a practicing police officer elsewhere, in which case minimal refresher or indoctrination training may be all that is required). Chapter 11 describes this process in detail and is not elaborated upon here. The basic training of a new recruit may take from 6 to 36 weeks and could extend up to a year or more if field training is counted. In medium and larger departments, newly hired persons are paid a regular salary during the basic training period; in smaller departments, officers may have to attend classes on their own time and at their own cost before being considered for the job.

Probationary Period. At the time candidates are hired, they are placed on **probationary status**, which means that their employment is conditional. Not only must their performance meet acceptable standards, their attitudes toward others, willingness to follow orders, ability to be a team player, and so on are also under evaluation. Probationary periods are variable in length with the norm being from six months to 24 months; one year is the average length of probation. During the probationary period in most jurisdictions, the new officer may be dismissed without cause or reason being given. The rights and limitations of probationers are usually controlled by law and department policy. In some agencies, probationers receive lower rates of pay, are not permitted to patrol solo, may not be allowed to join an officer's union, and have limited appeal rights if dismissed.

Permanent Employee Status. Once a candidate has successfully passed through the probationary phase of employment, the officer then achieves **permanent employee status**, which brings with it additional rights and privileges. This status often includes a pay raise; the right to join the union, officer's association, or credit union; additional grievance and appeal rights; and the inclusion of selected personnel benefits such as educational leave and benefits and certain insurances. Once officers reach this phase, the selection process has been completed.

THE LAW AND PERSONNEL PRACTICES

Chapter 3 described the evolution of policing in the United States in broad terms and generalities. It was mentioned that in the early years of policing, particularly in municipalities, the selection and other personnel practices were highly political. Following the passage of the Pendleton Act in 1883, the concepts and procedures of civil service (or merit system) were introduced and adopted in many states throughout the country. Civil service and other personnel-related statutes became the guiding influence upon personnel practices until the 1970s. However, events occurred in the 1960s that set the stage for a decade that would see great challenges to the personnel practices of agencies at all levels across the United States.

The Civil Rights Act of 1964

Although two other major civil rights acts had been enacted by Congress in the 1800s (the Civil Rights Acts of 1866 and 1871), neither had focused its attention specifically on the employment process. In 1964, Congress enacted the **Civil Rights Act of 1964** because of its concern over the reported and documented racial discrimination in employment throughout the country. Specifically, **Title VII** of the Act stated, in part:

> It shall be an unlawful employment practice for an employer . . . to fail or refuse to hire or to discharge any individual, or otherwise to discriminate against any individual with respect to his compensation, terms, conditions, or privileges of employment, because of such individual's race, color, religion, sex, or national origin . . . (Public Law 92–261, § 703).

The concept of **protected classes** can be used to describe one of the outcomes of this legislation. Persons who are discriminated against in employment because of their race, color, religion, sex, or national origin are "protected" by law and may have a right to sue that employer. (The list of who is protected has been extended to other "classes" of persons by other federal and state statutes and now includes the military veteran, persons over age 40, the handicapped, the disabled, pregnant women, and, in some jurisdictions, homosexuals.) One method that is used to determine violations of Title VII is whether the practice in question has an **adverse impact** (also called disparate impact) on a protected class. A procedure or qualification that appears neutral on its face can actually negatively impact one group more than another. For example, a height requirement of 5'9" may appear reasonable, but it excludes about 95 percent of the females in the U.S.; therefore, it has an adverse impact on women. Unless the requirement can be substantiated as being required to do the job (job relatedness), the requirement is discriminatory. The most common method used to allege adverse impact is statistical comparison of hiring rates, promotion rates, and passing rates of protected classes to majority rates (Sauls 1991).

The Civil Rights Act of 1964 also created the **Equal Employment Opportunity Commission** (EEOC) which is authorized to enforce the legislation and to develop guidelines for its implementation. The 1964 Act *did not apply to public employers* and, therefore, had no immediate impact on their practices. However, some agencies did begin a review of their personnel practices to address possible discrimination.

In 1971, the landmark case of **Griggs v. Duke Power Company** (401 U.S. 424) was decided by the U.S. Supreme Court. It was the first interpretation of the Civil Rights Act of 1964 by the Court, and as such its decision became precedent and guiding. The Court said that " . . . good intent or absence of discriminatory intent does not redeem employment procedures or testing mechanisms that operate as 'built-in headwinds' for minority groups and are unrelated to measuring job capability" (*Griggs* 1971, 432). The Court ruled that Griggs and other employees had been discriminated against because the requirements (a high school diploma and passing a standard intelligence test) imposed for promotional opportunities were not adequate measures to determine suitability for the job. The Court concluded (*Griggs* 1971, 431), "If an employment practice which operates to exclude Negroes [a protected class] cannot be shown to be related to job performance, the practice is forbidden" (*clarifying term added*). The Court's decision in *Griggs* essentially established that job qualifications and selection devices must be related to job performance criteria and that artificial, arbitrary, and unnecessary barriers to employment be removed.

The Equal Employment Opportunity Act of 1972

Congress amended the Civil Rights Act of 1964 with the Equal Employment Opportunity Act of 1972, which extended the provisions of the 1964 law to public employers with 25 or more employees. The EEO Act also granted authority to the EEOC to sue public agencies when necessary to redress the effects of discrimination in employment. Following the passage of this Act, public agencies (especially police and fire departments) were sued by members of protected classes, often because their selection processes were inadequate and sometimes indefensible.

The essence of Title VII, as amended (and other anti-discrimination in employment law), is that employers must determine what job skills, knowledge, and abilities (SKAs) are required for proper job performance in a particular position. Determining these SKAs is usually done through a **job analysis** (or task analysis) of the position in question (police officer, supervisor, commander, etc.). The results of the job analysis then are used to develop the criteria that will be used for selection, promotion, transfer, and other personnel actions. The details of conducting job analysis are beyond the scope of this text; however, the intent of it is to determine such things as minimum qualifications for employment, the necessary content for training curriculums, and required criteria for promotion and/or transfer. However, one can observe the outcome of job analysis in the job description and listing of qualifications for an announced opening.

Other Legislative Mandates

Besides the Civil Rights Act of 1964 and the Equal Employment Opportunity Act of 1972, several other pieces of federal legislation have been enacted that impact on the personnel practices of law enforcement agencies. The following is a selected listing with only a brief description of each as to the personnel practices affected.

EQUAL PAY ACT OF 1963: Made applicable to public agencies by 1974 amendments, it provides equal pay for equal positions regardless of one's gender. Bona fide seniority plans are exempted from the act.

AGE DISCRIMINATION IN EMPLOYMENT ACT OF 1967: Amended in 1974 to apply to the public sector, it protects persons over the age of 40 from discrimination based on age.

CIVIL RIGHTS ACT OF 1968: Provides criminal penalties for the interference with any person applying for or enjoying employment or related privileges, or interference with a person's use of hiring halls, labor organizations, or employment agencies.

REHABILITATION ACT OF 1973: Protects individuals from discrimination based on mental or physical disabilities (originally referred to as "handicapped"). State and local governments are impacted if receiving federal assistance.

AMERICANS WITH DISABILITIES ACT OF 1990: This legislation modified and extended aspects of the Rehabilitation Act of 1973 but applies to all public employers with 15 or more employees. Agencies cannot discriminate against otherwise qualified individuals with a disability.

CIVIL RIGHTS ACT OF 1991: Reestablished and reaffirmed some of the provisions and judicial interpretation of earlier legislation. It does prohibit punitive damages in lawsuits against public agencies.

Other state and local legislation in addition to those listed above may impact the personnel practices of law enforcement agencies. The total picture adds up to a very legalistic quagmire with which police administrators must cope every day.

Remedies

One segment of the law is referred to as **remedies**, and it is usually defined in terms of "making a person whole again" who has been wronged. In grievances and lawsuits regarding personnel practices, the following remedies are commonly sought through the legal system:

■ Injunction: A court order prohibiting certain actions by an agency or person.
■ Writ of Mandamus: A petition to a court seeking an order that compels certain actions by an agency or person (orders that it be done).
■ Back pay: If a complaint is found to be justified, the court could order back pay (the amount that would have been earned) to the injured party.
■ Back seniority: The injured party can receive seniority from the time of the original action that injured him or her.
■ Attorney fees: The injured party is awarded monetary fees to cover the expense of the litigation against the party that wronged him or her.
■ Quotas: The setting of fixed ratios of protected group members to receive preference in certain personnel functions. For example, this may lead to an agency hiring two minority members for every majority member hired or the hiring of one woman for every two males hired.
■ Goals/Time Tables: Unlike quotas, this is the setting of percentage or numerical targets to be achieved within certain time limits. It does not require the specific ratios of quotas.

Any one or a combination of these remedies may be ordered by the court or agreed to by the parties to a lawsuit. An out of court agreement is called a **consent decree**, and it often includes conditions (such as quotas, or revisions of personnel policies and practices) that cause hardships or morale problems for law enforcement agencies. Of course, it can also modernize personnel practices and sometimes bring needed resources to the personnel function of an agency or jursidiction.

Affirmative Action and Reverse Discrimination

One concept that has become broadly debated is that of **affirmative action**. The concept itself refers to taking a more aggressive position at recruiting and hiring protected classes that are underrepresented in an agency's workforce. It is sometimes interpreted by many to mean that members of protected classes are given preference in personnel actions. This belief occasionally leads to allegations of **reverse discrimination** by majority members. It is these allegations and beliefs that cause tension and frustration among many officers already employed and many of those who apply for positions and are not hired. The concept of affirmative action is not illegal; however, showing preference during hiring and other personnel practices is. Consider the words of the United States Supreme Court (*Griggs* 1971, 430–431):

> ... In short, the Act does not command that any person be hired simply because he was formerly the subject of discrimination, or because he is a member of a minority group. Discriminatory preference for any group, minority or majority, is precisely and only what Congress has proscribed.

The Court was referring to Section 703 (j) of the Civil Rights Act of 1964, which reads:

> Nothing contained in this title shall be interpreted to require any employer ... subject to this title to grant preferential treatment to any individual or to any group because of the race, color, religion, sex or national origin of such individual or group on account of an imbalance which may exist with respect to the total number or percentage of persons of any race, color, religion, sex, or national origin employed by any employer ... in comparison with the total number or percentage of [such] persons ... in any community, State, section, or other area, or in the available work force. ...

Other court decisions over the years indicate that the anti-discrimination laws apply to all persons, not just minorities. The significance of all this is that agencies must have justifications for their personnel qualifications and practices. They cannot do things simply out of tradition or by intuition and whim. If challenged, they may have to justify their actions to a court or to an investigative agency. In recent years, some jurisdictions (most notably California in its adoption of Proposition 209) have rescinded or modified state affirmative action statutes that permitted preferential treatment of protected groups. The United States Supreme Court refused on November 3, 1997, to interfere with the enforcement of the 1996 ballot initiative prohibiting preferential treatment (Savage 1997).

The U.S. Ninth Circuit Court of Appeals had earlier ruled in the case of *Coalition for Economic Equity v. Wilson* that the referendum was constitutional.

Bona Fide Occupational Qualification

The personnel law enacted to date allows for some discrimination if based on a **bona fide occupational qualification** (BFOQ). This is a form of "legal discrimination" in that it allows the establishment of certain criteria if they are shown to be necessary for the operation of the business (or agency). There are limitations that restrict BFOQs to religion, sex, or national origin, meaning that they cannot discriminate on the basis of race or color. In 1985, the City of Dallas, Texas, successfully defended its college education requirement (45 hours of credit) for police officers by using a BFOQ-based justification (see *Davis v. City of Dallas*, 777 F.2d 205, 1985). Appeal of the case to the U.S. Supreme Court was denied, thus allowing the Appellate decision supporting the requirement to stand. The Appellate Court found that the characteristics of professionalism, unusual degree of risk, and unique public responsibility were part of the position of police officer and were not capable of specific identification and quantification (see Carter *et al.* 1988).

PROMOTION AND CAREER DEVELOPMENT

Persons entering the law enforcement field look forward to a long and satisfying career. Many or most remain with the same agency in which they start. They look forward to promotion and/or career development and growth, which may also include a specialized assignment. Promotion generally refers to a positive change in rank status. A patrol officer is promoted to sergeant; a sergeant is promoted to lieutenant, and so on. Career development refers to a desired change in work assignment that is accompanied by increased responsibility and may involve additional training and/or education. Career development may include a promotion; however, it is not necessary. For example, officers may prefer to continue working in a particular assignment, such as patrol or investigation, and not want promotion into positions that may be more supervisory or managerial in nature. The officers' growth will then be directed at becoming more knowledgeable about patrol work and investigation. Their career development will include skill development and training/education in those areas.

Modern departments recognize the fact that not everyone wants to be promoted in rank and are developing compensation schemes that reward officers who pursue excellence in the critical areas of patrol and investigation. Also, some departments are streamlining their rank structures and eliminating middle management positions. As this movement continues, the opportunities for promotion will decrease. The challenge in such departments is how to increase the incentives of career development in those ranks that continue to exist.

Promotion

There are several methods by which officers are promoted within the law enforcement community. Agency policies differ, and these are often contingent upon the personnel system adopted and state law. The most prevalent models include: (a) political, (b) seniority, (c) past achievements, (d) appointment on merit, (e) testing (under civil service or central personnel office policies), (f) assessment center, and (g) hybrid, or a combination of the above. Each of these is discussed here in an overview manner.

Political. As one would expect, this is the concept of "who you know." It is based on influence and power; it does not necessarily consider merit or ability. Power brokers and political leaders influence the promotion of officers; promotion is a reward for devoted and loyal service to those individuals. Such systems are much less common today, but they still exist in some areas. Modern professional policing rejects this method of promotion.

Seniority. In this type of promotion system, the officer with the longest tenure or length of service with the agency gets the promotion when there is an opening. One is rewarded for "putting in the time" or for "surviving." Promotion is viewed as a reward for years of service. This system, too, is rejected by modern professional departments when used as the sole criterion for promotion.

Past Achievements. Some promotion schemes are rewards for past performance. If officers do an excellent job in one rank, they are promoted to the next rank. The premise here is that if they did well in one position, they will do well in the next, and it is a reward for their efforts to date. Of course, and unfortunately, the premise is faulty as to the belief that the officers will perform well at the next level. Just because one is a good patrol officer, it does not follow that he or she will make a good supervisor.

Appointment on Merit. This system refers to promotion based on ability to perform at the next level. It will involve the evaluation of candidates and the talents, skills, and knowledge needed for the promoted position. All candidates may have been excellent performers in their current rank, but which ones have the leadership, communication, and interaction skills needed in the promoted position? Assessment of candidates focuses on skills and abilities that will be used in the new position; the process is forward-looking and not based merely on past performance. (Of course, it is recognized that some past performance measures may indicate certain skills and abilities needed in the promoted position, but they should be identified as such through job analysis.)

Testing. In order to be more objective (and less political) in the promotion of candidates, many jurisdictions administer written exams for promotion. Some use highly rigid procedures and do not allow for input from supervisors or administrators; the results of the test dictate the promotional rankings. The "rule of one" is used often in such systems, meaning that the person with the highest test score is the next person promoted. While there are benefits to this approach, it relies heavily on "book knowledge" and test-taking ability. It does not necessarily measure interpersonal communications and other leadership qualities. Nor does it adequately simulate field conditions under which this person must make decisions.

Assessment Center. As someone once said, "It is a process or technique, not a place." The **assessment center** approach to promotion involves observation and measurement of what a candidate does and how well it is done in simulated job situations or scenarios that would be encountered in the promoted position. It may involve interviews, oral presentations, psychological testing, writing memos, and role playing. The "assessors" in this approach may be top-level managers/administrators inside the department and/or individuals (with policing expertise) from outside the department. The objective is to analyze the candidate's ability to perform in situations that are common to the promoted position. Elements of stress and confrontation are usually part of this assessment. The entire process may take several days or be conducted intermittently over several weeks.

Hybrid. A hybrid model of promotion may involve two or more of the above approaches. For example, a civil service promotion system may involve a written exam, a supervisory rating, and seniority points. Or an appointment system may involve past performance ratings, promotability ratings of supervisors, and an oral board. Even a primarily political system can involve some assessment of ability and skills so that the appointing authority can defend the choice made.

Whichever system of promotion is used, one must remember that the law of personnel practices discussed above applies, and therefore (if challenged), the agency must be able to show that the criteria for promotion were job-related and relevant. Just as many agencies found themselves in court over selection procedures, many have had their promotional procedures examined and thrown out.

Career Development

Career development is closely associated with various types of training that are discussed in detail in Chapter 11. However, besides the training component, career development involves increasing levels of responsibility and personal growth. Some departments allow for growth within a given rank by establishing sub-ranks or classifications within ranks such as Police Officer I, II, and III, or Sergeant I, II, and III. This allows an officer to remain within a specific rank or job category and still pursue an increase in responsibility and a change of assignment.

Some departments allow for personal growth and assignment change through **lateral entry**. It usually refers to conditions where an officer at the patrol, investigative, or supervisory level can transfer to another agency without any loss of seniority, rank, or salary. Lateral entry is not as common in municipal departments or state agencies as it is in sheriff's departments. Most seniority systems and central personnel system policies protect officers within agencies from the lateral transfer of officers outside the agency (which is a form of protectionism).

LABOR RELATIONS IN LAW ENFORCEMENT

The concept of **labor relations** refers to the sum total of all interactions between the administration of an agency and its employees. Some form of labor relations occurs in all law enforcement agencies; some of these are formal while others are informal. The most formal means of labor relations is referred to as **collective bargaining**, in which a representative of an employee group (often a union) negotiates the terms and conditions of employment with the representative of the employer. The negotiated document that results from this process is usually called "the contract," or "the agreement." In a 1990 survey of 72 major departments in the U.S., 56 (77.7 percent) permitted union membership, 9 compelled it, and 5 forbade it (3 agencies gave no response to the question) (Strawbridge 1990, 11–14, Table 1). In the 1997 LEMAS study of state and local agencies with 100 or more officers, 24 out of the 49 state agencies (48.9 percent) authorized collective bargaining for sworn officers and 408 out of the 651 local agencies (62.6 percent) did so (Reaves and Goldberg 1999, 61–70, 267). Although exact figures are not compiled, it appears that about 70 percent of the major agencies in the United States operate under formal collective bargaining arrangements. However, formal collective bargaining varies from state to state. For example, in the survey of 651 local agencies mentioned above, no agencies in the states of Georgia (local level), Mississippi, Missouri, North Carolina, South Carolina, and Virginia authorized collective bargaining.

History of the Police Union Movement

The unionization movement in the public sector can be traced to the 1830s, when mechanics, carpenters, and other craftsmen employed by the federal government joined existing unions made up of private sector employees. Some of the early issues addressed by public sector employees at that time included the desire for a shorter (10-hour) workday and better wages. But most of the gains made in the public sector up through the 1880s came after such work conditions were considered a standard in the private sector (Public Sector Unionism 1972).

Police officers, too, in the late 1880s began to organize. Initially their organizations were **benevolent associations**, which focused on improving the working conditions and providing assistance (in the form of funeral expenses and widows and orphans funds) to its members who suffered losses. These early associations were often controlled by high-ranking officers, and they did not generally interfere with the operation of the department. In addition to benevolent purposes, these associations often served as fraternal and social aspects of the officers' lives. Although not unions in the formal sense, these associations were early forms of employee organizations.

By the early 1900s, associations were common in most major cities. Some agencies had even encountered more organized officer groups: Ithaca, New York, experienced a walk-out in 1889 because officers' pay had been reduced from $12 to $9 per week, and Cincinnati, Ohio, experienced a strike by 450 officers in 1918 over issues of union organization. By 1919, the American Federation of Labor (AFL) had changed its position on granting formal charters to police locals. It was immediately swamped with 65 applications, which by the end of summer resulted in 37 locals (with a total of over 4,000 officers) being officially recognized (see Smith 1975 and Gammage and Sachs 1977 for details of early police unionism).

The Boston Police Strike of 1919. One of those locals chartered (August 8, 1919) included the Boston Police Social Club. The officers of Boston had been at odds with the city administration for almost a year over a pay raise and working conditions. The pay raise offered by the city had been deemed insufficient by the Social Club, which had acted as a representative of the officers in conferring with the city. Eventually, the city yielded by granting higher wages; however, with the soaring costs and the delayed increase, the amounts were still inadequate. Exhibit 10–4 describes the working conditions found in the Boston Police Department in 1919.

Two days after the Boston Police Social Club received its charter (as the Boston Policemen's Union), Police Commissioner Curtis issued the following order, which in essence prohibited officers from joining a union affiliated with any national organization:

> No member of the force shall join or belong to any organization, club or body composed of present or present and past members of the force which is affiliated with or a part of any organization, club or body outside the department, except that a post of the Grand Army of the Republic, the United Spanish War Veterans,

---

WORKING CONDITIONS IN THE BOSTON P.D. IN 1919

- 78–90 hour workweek depending on assignment
- $21 a week salary
- Officers had to purchase own uniforms
- Political promotion
- Graft at command levels
- Unsanitary, rodent-infested station houses
- Unanswered grievances

Source: Adapted with permission from J. D. Smith, Police Unions: An Historical Perspective of Causes and Organizations, *Police Chief*, November 1975, p. 24, © 1975, International Association of Chiefs of Police.

and the American Legion of World War Veterans may be formed within the department (Spero 1977, 384).

A "war of words" raged for weeks. On August 26, the commissioner filed charges against 8 police officers who had been elected to positions in the union; shortly thereafter, 11 more were charged. Although discussions between the union and members of a select citizens' committee (appointed by Mayor Peters) attempted to resolve the conflict and were making progress, the commissioner insisted on pursuing the charges against the officers. On September 8, after refusing a settlement proposed by the citizen's committee, the commissioner found the officers guilty and suspended them from service.

The reaction of the stunned union came quickly. Later that same day, the union membership voted 1,134 to 2 to strike at 5:45 P.M. on September 9, 1919. For days, Mayor Peters attempted to engage the assistance of Governor Calvin Coolidge, but he refused to become involved; even a meeting of the citizen's committee with the Governor on the night of September 8th proved fruitless. At noon on the 9th, the Governor issued a letter explaining why he would not interfere in the developments in the department. At 5:45 P.M., 1,117 of 1,544 patrol officers left their posts.

Although the commissioner had promised the mayor and the governor that he had planned for continued protection of the city, general rioting, looting, disorder, and individual robberies occurred. By morning, the commissioner said his resources were inadequate and asked the mayor to activate the troops stationed in the city. The mayor did this but also assumed command of the department under statutory authority and restored order to the city. Then, not to be outdone, Governor Coolidge activated the state militia throughout the state and sent it to Boston; he then assumed control of the department. It appeared as though every politician was going to make political points out of the situation. Some reports indicate that 100 people were injured, 7 were killed, and over one million dollars' worth of property damage was done during the four-day strike.

Overnight the opinion of the public had turned against the officers; where sympathy for their cause had once existed, condemnation was universal. Over 1,100 striking officers were dismissed from the Boston police force and the AFL dissolved all charters to police organizations. For the next 20–30 years, the police unionization movement reverted to local fraternal associations.

Governor Coolidge became nationally recognized because of the Boston police strike and his famous statement, "There is no right to strike against the public safety, by anyone, anywhere, anytime." It helped propel him to the vice presidency and then, following the death of President Harding, to the presidency in 1923. Did the strike have any benefits for the Boston police officers? Yes, working conditions improved after the strike, not only in Boston but in other cities as well, but none of the striking officers was rehired.

Labor Legislation & Growth of Public Sector Unionization. From the early 1900s through the 1950s, police associations at the local level increased significantly in number. While the law in many states did not permit formal collective bargaining, it was not prohibited in most. Municipalities at the local level began to recognize local associations as representing the local department's rank and file. This led to formal dialogue (but not necessarily binding negotiated contracts) between the association and the administration of agencies.

The efforts of national associations such as the Fraternal Order of Police; the International Conference of Police Associations; the American Federation of State, County, and Municipal Employees; and other groups kept the issue of formal labor relations and the rights of employees in the forefront of personnel discussions. In 1959, Wisconsin enacted a collective bargaining statute for the public sector; President Kennedy issued Executive Order 10988 in 1962, granting bargaining rights to federal employees; and in 1967, New York State enacted the Tailor Law, which permitted collective bargaining in the public sector. By 1974, there were 35 states with legislation granting collective bargaining rights to public employees (only 27 of these allowed it for police officers, however). By 1985, 40 states had passed some form of legislation dealing with public employees (Gaines *et al.* 1991, 313).

It was the decade of the 1960s that experienced the largest growth in formal unionization efforts. Four general factors have been identified as contributing to that growth during those chaotic years: (1) the perception of increased public hostility, (2) rising crime rates and public demand for "law and order," (3) salaries and benefits that were lower than those for other public employees and the private sector, and (4) poor personnel practices of police agencies (Juris and Feuille 1974). These factors and conditions related to them brought about a police militancy never experienced before in the U.S. Work stoppages, slowdowns, sick-outs (known as the "blue flu"), ticket blitzes, and strikes occurred frequently during labor disputes in the late 1960s and through the mid-1970s. However, because of major strikes in the cities of Albuquerque, New Mexico; Oklahoma City, Oklahoma; and San Francisco, California, in 1975, unions came under heavy criticism by the public, press, and politicians (Ayers 1977, 431).

Contemporary Unionism

Some of the labor dispute practices mentioned above are still used today by employee organizations. For example, during a recent two-year contract dispute, the Los Angeles police utilized blue flu, job slowdown, and massive demonstration tactics to move negotiations forward. Consider the following report:

California—The Los Angeles Police Department was struck this month [June 94] by an outbreak of "blue flu" in a continuous battle with the city over a new contract. Nearly half the department's night shift failed to show up one day this month, forcing day-shift officers to work overtime to fill in. While the next day's overnight shift was normal, half the force again took off during the day shift. The absences could cost the city as much as $1 million a day in overtime costs. A 6-percent raise over two years was rejected by the union earlier in the month (*Around the Nation* 1994, 2).

The union even rented 22 billboards throughout the city showing a masked gunman menacing a young woman as she gets into her car; the signs read, "Warning: This Can Be You Without the Police Department." Following a threat to call a job action during the World Cup soccer tournament in June–July of 1994, Mayor Richard Riordan stepped in to make a new offer, which was accepted by the union ("Members Approve Pact Ending Two-Year Ordeal" 1994, 27). During the late 1990s, many law enforcement bargaining units and their national affiliated associations have been active in obtaining proper compensation for overtime pay, defending the rights of officers during grievances, pushing for broader carrying-concealed-weapons laws, and advocating national legislation for an officers' "bill of rights."

Police unions today are more organized and sophisticated than they have ever been. They have access to excellent legal representation, and they are powerful forces in political lobbying. They have matured greatly in the last two decades. There are many more unionized forces than before, and many departments have to negotiate with more than one union because state laws often allow different unions to represent officers in supervisory ranks. Unions and formal collective bargaining are the norm, which means that personnel practices for the most part are controlled through negotiated agreements. In essence, if an officer believes that he or she has been mistreated by management, the contract is the first document consulted. In many departments, this document (the contract) is as important to the officers as the state criminal code book.

SUMMARY

Personnel are the lifeblood of law enforcement agencies. The quality of service rendered by these persons is dependent on the thoroughness of the selection process, the effectiveness of the training process, the commitment to promote capable people, and the accountability demanded by supervisors and administrators. Human resource operations in police agencies are extremely complex and riddled with legal proscriptions and potential pitfalls. Numerous legislative, administrative, judicial, and contractual issues must be considered in personnel decisions today.

The purpose of this chapter has been to present an overview of the issues impacting the human resource (personnel) function of law enforcement agencies. It reviewed the basic aspects of the recruiting and selections functions, highlighted many of the legal issues related to personnel management, and described the evolution of unionism in American policing. It is hoped that persons committed to a career in policing will achieve an understanding and an appreciation for the matters discussed here.

QUESTIONS FOR REVIEW

1. What are the major stages of the police selection process, and why are they more complex in some departments than in others?

2. Define the concept of "protected class," and describe how it relates to personnel functions such as selection and promotion.

3. What is the significance of the legal concept of "remedies," and what are the typical ones often implemented in cases alleging job discrimination in law enforcement agencies?

4. What are the seven different methods by which an officer can be promoted to higher rank and responsibility?

5. What are the differences between the concepts of "labor relations" and "collective bargaining"?

6. What was the significance of the Boston Police Strike of 1919 in terms of its impact on police unionism?

SUGGESTED ACTIVITIES

1. Contact local law enforcement agencies in your area and ask for a recruitment packet or information about entry positions.

2. At the library, read the landmark U.S. Supreme Court decision of *Griggs v. Duke Power Company*, 401 U.S. 424, 1971; then read the Appellate decision of *Davis v. City of Dallas*, 777 F.2d 205, 1985.

3. Attend a job fair where law enforcement agencies are represented, and talk to recruiters about the stages of the selection process for their agencies.

4. Log on to the World Wide Web and conduct a search on two the following words or phrases: "personnel selection," "job discrimination," "affirmative action," or "police union." Write a brief report of the type of sites found.

5. Log on to the URL **http://www.eeoc.gov** and review the legal information available at this site.

6. Log on to the World Wide Web and search for recent personnel-related statistics and reports; particularly browse the site **http://www.ojp.usdoj.gov/bjs/**.

CHAPTER GLOSSARY

adverse impact: one form of proving job discrimination; the procedure or qualification affects a protected class more negatively than the majority group

affirmative action: the taking of a more aggressive position at recruiting and hiring protected classes that are underrepresented in an agency's workforce

appointing authority: an official who hires a person for a particular job according to established law and procedures

assessment center: a process/procedure involving observation and measurement of a candidate for promotion; it normally includes simulated job situations or scenarios that would be encountered in the promoted position

benevolent associations: one form of employee association; early associations attempted to provide employees with benefits that employers did not, and were also fraternal and social in nature. Today, a police benevolent association (PBA) may also be a union for purposes of collective bargaining.

bona fide occupational qualification: certain criteria deemed required or necessary for the operation of the business (or agency) and which may have an adverse impact on some protected classes

Civil Rights Act of 1964: federal legislation that addressed the equal rights of persons; one part, **Title VII**, prohibited discrimination in employment in the private sector on grounds of race, color, religion, sex, and national origin

civil service: a term referring to non-military government employment or to a specific personnel system established by state or local law

collective bargaining: the most formal means of labor relations, in which a representative of an employee group (often a union) negotiates the terms and conditions of employment with the representative of the employer

conditional offer of employment: the candidate is suitable and eligible for hire at a particular point in the selection process and will be employed if certain other factors related to one's physical ability and medical and mental conditions are within job-related limits

consent decree: an out-of-court settlement by parties to a lawsuit where each agrees to do specified things (remedies) under certain conditions

eligibility list: a list of qualified candidates from which the law enforcement agency must select its employees; usually associated with state and local civil service systems

Equal Employment Opportunity Commission (EEOC): the federal agency authorized to enforce the anti-discrimination in employment legislation and to develop guidelines for employers

Griggs v. Duke Power Company: the landmark decision by the U.S. Supreme Court in 1971 that interpreted the Civil Rights Act of 1964

job analysis: the process of examining and evaluating the required performances of a particular job to determine what job skills, knowledge, and abilities (SKAs) are required

labor relations: the sum total of all interactions between the administration of an agency and its employees

lateral entry: the transferring to another agency without any loss of seniority, rank, or salary

permanent employee status: achieved after successful completion of probation; it grants additional rights and privileges related to position

pre-application conference: usually a meeting with a ranking field officer for the conveyance of information about the job, the required training, and the agency's expectations of its personnel

probationary status: conditional employment during which time the person's performance must meet acceptable standards; their attitudes toward others, willingness to follow orders, ability to be a team player, and so on also are under evaluation

protected classes: individuals and/or groups against which discrimination in employment is prohibited by federal, state, or local law

psychological interview: discussion conducted by trained psychologists or psychiatrists, one-on-one or in group sessions, in an attempt to determine suitability, stability, and any psychopathic diseases or illnesses

pychometric exam: written instruments used to measure various psychological characteristics, such as intelligence, interests/preferences, and personality traits/characteristics

recruitment: the development and maintenance of an adequate supply of qualified persons interested in being employed by a specific agency

remedies: that portion of law consisting of various actions or conditions that can be implemented or ordered "to make a person whole again" when wronged

reverse discrimination: allegation by majority members claiming that their rights have been violated by an employer who is showing unlawful preferences to minorities or women

the rule of three: the practice of considering the top three candidates on a ranked eligibility list for every open entry-level position

the selection process: includes the various techniques, devices, and procedures used to identify candidates to employ; it is often a series of events linked together and through which an applicant must pass in order to be hired

self-selection: the concept of providing accurate, in-depth information to potential applicants so that they can make an informed and more objective decision about entering the selection process

structured interview: usually consists of specifically compiled questions that focus on various aspects of the job or of the applicant's abilities and background; some follow-up questions also may be asked

unstructured interview: consists of general areas of focus, but the questions are not specifically spelled out

REFERENCES

Around the Nation. 1994. *Law Enforcement News* XX (403) (June 15): 2.

Ayres, Richard M. and Thomas L. Wheelen, eds. 1977. *Collective Bargaining in the Public Sector: Selected Readings in Law Enforcement.* Gaithersburg, MD: International Association of Chiefs of Police, Inc.

Ayres, Richard M. 1977. Police Strikes: Are We Treating the Symptom Rather than the Problem? In *Collective Bargaining in the Public Sector: Selected Readings in Law Enforcement,* edited by Richard M. Ayres and Thomas L. Wheelen (Gaithersburg, MD: International Association of Chiefs of Police, Inc.).

Bureau of National Affairs. 1993. *Individual Employment Rights Manual.* Washington, D.C.: Bureau of National Affairs.

Carter, David L., Allen D. Sapp, and Darrel W. Stephens. 1988. Higher Education as a Bona Fide Occupational Qualification (BFOQ) for Police: A Blueprint. *American Journal of Police* VIII (2): 1–27.

Conser, James A. and Roger D. Thompson. 1976. *Police Selection Standards and Processes in Ohio: An Assessment.* Youngstown, Ohio: Youngstown State University.

Davis v. City of Dallas, 777 F.2d 205 (1985).

Elsenberg, Terry, Deborah Kent, and Charles Wall. 1973. *Police Personnel Practices in State and Local Government.* Washington, D.C.: Police Foundation.

Gaines, Larry K., Mittie D. Southerland, and John E. Angell. 1991. *Police Administration.* New York: McGraw-Hill, Inc.

Gammage, Allen Z. and Stanley L. Sachs. 1977. Development of Public Employee/Police Unions. In *Collective Bargaining in the Public Sector: Selected Readings in Law Enforcement,* edited by Richard M. Ayres and Thomas L. Wheelen (Gaithersburg, MD: International Association of Chiefs of Police, Inc.).

Griggs v. Duke Power Company, 401 U.S. 424 (1971).

Juris, Henry A. and Peter Feuille. 1974. Employee Organizations. In *Police Personnel Administration,* edited by O. Glenn Stahl and Richard A. Staufenberger (Washington, D.C.: Police Foundation, 205–206).

Langworthy, R. H., B. anders, and T. Hughes, 1995. *Law Enforcement Recruitment and Selection: A Survey of Major Police Departments in the U.S.* Highland Heights, KY: Academy of Criminal Justice Sciences–Police Section.

Langworthy, R. H. and L. F. Travis, III. 1994. *Policing in America: A Balance of Forces.* New York: Macmillan Publishing Co.

Major City Chiefs Association, National Executive Institute Associates, and Federal Bureau of Investigation. 1993. *Physical Fitness Testing in Law Enforcement: An Analysis of the Impact of the Americans with Disabilities Act, The Civil Rights Act of 1991, and the Age Discrimination in Employment Act, A Conference Report.* Quantico, VA: Federal Bureau of Investigation Academy (August 1993).

Members Approve Pact Ending Two-Year Ordeal. 1994. *American Police Beat* I (4) (July/August): 27.

McEwen, Tom. 1996. *National Data Collection on Police Use of Force.* Washington, D.C.: U.S. Department of Justice and Alexandria, VA: Institute for Law and Justice (April).

Moriarty, Anthony R. and Mark W. Field. 1989. Police Psychological Screening: The Third Generation. *The Police Chief* LVI (2) (February): 36–40.

Moriarty, Anthony R. and Mark W. Field. 1994. *Police Officer Selection: A Handbook for Law Enforcement Administrators.* Springfield, IL: Charles C. Thomas.

Police Protest. 1992. *USA Today* (August 21): 3A.

Public Law 92–261, § 703 (a) (Civil Rights Act of 1964, Title VII).

UCLA Law Review. Public Sector Unionism—Origins and Perspective—Part I: Historical Summary. 1972 19(6) (August): 893–894. In *Collective Bargaining in the Public Sector: Selected Readings in Law Enforcement,* edited by Richard M. Ayres and Thomas L. Wheelen (Gaithersburg, MD: International Association of Chiefs of Police, Inc.).

Reaves, Brian A. and Andrew L. Goldberg. 1999. *Law Enforcement Management and Administrative Statistics, 1997: Data for Individual State and Local Agencies with 100 or More Officers.* Washington, D.C.: U.S. Department of Justice.

Reaves, Brian A. and Pheny Z. Smith. 1995. *Law Enforcement Management and Administrative Statistics, 1993: Data for Individual State and Local Agencies with 100 or More Officers.* Washington, D.C.: U.S. Department of Justice.

Sauls, John Gales. 1991. Employment Discrimination: A Title VII Primer. *FBI Law Enforcement Bulletin* (December): 18–24.

Savage, David G. 1997. High Court Allows Prop 209's Repeal of Affirmative Action. *Los Angeles Times* (4 November): 1.

Shattuch, John. 1973. *The Lie Detector as a Surveillance Device.* New York: American Civil Liberties Union.

Smith, Joseph D. 1975. Police Unions: An Historical Perspective of Causes and Organizations. *The Police Chief* XLII (11) (November): 24.

Spero, Sterling D. 1977. The Boston Police Strike. In *Collective Bargaining in the Public Sector: Selected Readings in Law Enforcement,* edited by Richard M. Ayres and Thomas L. Wheelen (Gaithersburg, MD: International Association of Chiefs of Police, Inc.).

Strawbridge, Peter and Deirdre Strawbridge. 1990. *A Networking Guide to Recruitment, Selection and Probationary Training of Police Officers in Major Police Departments of the United States of America.* New York: John Jay College of Criminal Justice.

Sweeney, Earl M. 1999. New Hampshire's Ongoing Fitness Assessment Program. International Association of Directors of Law Enforcement Standards and Training, Annual Conference Manual, Orlando, FL. 8 June.

Territo, Leonard. 1974. The Use of the Polygraph in the Pre-Employment Screening Process. *The Police Chief* XLI (7) (July): 51.

Vollmer, August. *The Police and Modern Society.* (1939; reprint, Regents of the University of California, 1969).

Winters, Paul A., ed. 1995. *Policing the Police.* San Diego, CA: Greenhaven Press, Inc.

Training, Education, and Socialization

Sgt. Kevin Smith, right, of the New York City Police Department, teaches at class at the Police Academy on cultural diversity. May 1999. (AP/ Wide World Photos)

This chapter addresses the important issues of training, education, and socialization of the police. These issues have a major impact on the culture of policing in the United States. By studying the concepts and principles presented here, you will be able to:

1. Understand the relationship of learning, learning domains, and teaching to the concept of education.
2. List the seven purposes achieved through the training process.
3. Identify and differentiate five types of training commonly found in law enforcement.
4. Describe the evolution of thought since the President's Commission of 1967 on the importance of education for police officers.
5. Explain the influence on law enforcement training and education of three major emerging factors.
6. Define the concept of police subculture.
7. Explain the negative and positive characteristics of the police subculture.
8. Describe the role of training in the socialization of law enforcement officers.

TRAINING CONCEPTS AND PHILOSOPHY

The thought of dressing persons in uniforms and sending them out to enforce the law without training them first is a foreign one to most of us today. However, that was not always the case. Some officers still employed in agencies today experienced just that when they became police officers! A survey of 4,000 police departments, conducted by IACP in 1956, found that 85 percent of all officers received no pre-service training (President's Commission 1967a, 138). For most of American history, law enforcement officials learned their duties and skills through **on-the-job training (OJT)**. OJT included the lessons taught by co-workers and supervisors as well as the experience obtained from doing the daily tasks of the job. Some of these lessons may have been formal, but most were informal in nature and based on the experience of the "teachers." Another term occasionally used to describe this early form of training was "apprenticeship," which has commonly been used in the trade and vocational fields. A true apprenticeship program, however, would be more structured and formal than what OJT actually was.

Today, it is readily apparent that the tasks and responsibilities of law enforcement officials are so complex and burdened with liability that the need for training is unquestioned. However, even though there is consensus on the need for training, there are many issues and controversies about the amount, type, and format of training necessary for the modern officer. There also is great diversity in the level and quality of training across the country. Some academies have access to and utilize the latest technology available, such as interactive computer-assisted learning and virtual reality scenarios, while others are relegated to primarily the lecture and drill format.

As a concept and philosophy, training can mean different things to different people. Some hear the term and immediately think of formal physical exercise and skill development, as in basic military training. Others think of it as a combination of classroom and field-based learning in preparation for a job. Still others perceive it as extensive college preparation followed by an internship and residency, as in medical training. Many discussions of training just presume that students in criminal justice understand what happens at the police academy and have a common understanding of training concepts.

At the outset of this chapter, permit us to state our philosophical position on a number of concepts. We broadly define **education** as what one has learned. **Learning** can be defined as a process that changes a person's knowledge, behavior, or attitude. It refers to changes that are determined primarily by the individual's interaction with his or her environment (Eson 1972, 58). A person's education is achieved by various means: socialization, experience, academics, training, and so on; it is not limited to the classroom or formal setting. Some in the criminal justice field have insisted on making a distinction between "training" and "education," essentially stating that training inculcates the *how* to do something while education focuses on the *why*. Traditionalists argue that training emphasizes skill and ability development while education emphasizes concepts, theory, and critical thinking. Such simple distinctions are unfortunate because, as Saunders (1970, 115) stated, " . . . the best of each will always contain elements of the other." In lieu of distinctions between the concepts, we believe it is more relevant to focus on matters of process and outcomes. The common link between education and training is the process of teaching or instruction, which includes a broad range of activities (Conser 1981, 42, 64). In this perspective, both training and education are considered outcomes, and the "teaching-instruction" process becomes the critical focal point. Various instructional methods can then be utilized to structure the desired outcome. The relationship of these outcomes to the learning process is illustrated in Figure 11–1:

STUDENT ---→ TEACHING-INSTRUCTION PROCESS ---→ LEARNING OUTCOMES

(Learning experiences based
on interaction of subject
matter, teaching methods,
and instructional materials)

Knowledge
Understanding
Thinking Skills
Performance Skills
Communication Skills
Social Skills
Attitudes
Appreciation

LEARNER ---→ WHAT & HOW TAUGHT ---------→ WHAT IS LEARNED
(EDUCATION)

Source: N.E. Gronlund, *Stating Behavioral Objectives for Classroom Instruction*, p. 3, © 1970, Prentice-Hall, Inc. Adapted by permission of Prentice-Hall, Inc., Upper Saddle River, NJ.

Figure 11–1 Relationship of Learning Outcomes to Learning Experiences

Major Purposes of Training

Police training serves a number of organizational purposes. First, it *orients* the person to his or her new job or position. Second, it *indoctrinates* the person to identify with the organization and believe in its goals and objectives. Third, it *transfers the skills and knowledge* necessary to do the job. Fourth, it *standardizes procedures and increases efficiency.* Fifth, it *builds confidence* in the person, since critical tasks can be practiced and mastered in learning situations. Sixth, it *improves safety and helps assure survival.* Finally, it yields other benefits such as *morale* and *discipline.*

It is important to appreciate the complexity of these purposes of training. Often, to a new recruit, it seems that one attends the academy to "learn how to do the job." However, the purposes identified above go beyond that simple notion. Recruits must understand the various objectives of the training experience; otherwise, their focus may be very narrow in terms of what is expected of them. They may miss "the bigger picture" of the learning process.

It also can be argued that training is the foundation for the interrelationship (linking together) of conduct, ethics, and discipline, which is graphically illustrated in Figure 11–2.

These concepts should be presented in a very positive fashion. For example, people often think of discipline as a negative process. Actually, the root of the word comes from the Latin and Greek concepts for training and instruction. We need to think of the term in relation to a "well disciplined" group of officers (or a self-disciplined individual), referring to those who are well trained

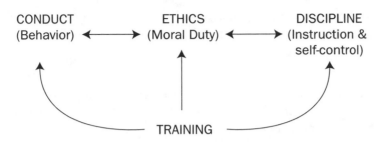

Figure 11–2 Relationship of Training to Conduct, Ethics, and Discipline

and know how to conduct themselves properly and who perform well in critical situations. Training provides the standards by which conduct is measured and judged acceptable. Related to the concepts of conduct and discipline are issues of ethics, morality, societal values, democratic values, and the public interest. These must be discussed and presented in a training context, because they are related to the standards just mentioned. The point being made here is the complexity of the relationship among these concepts—a relationship that is missed or not properly articulated when training and education are presented as two distinct processes.

Learning Domains

There are three generally accepted levels of learning, called the **learning domains** (Bloom 1956):

Cognitive refers to acquiring new knowledge, understanding, and thinking skills. Learning in this domain includes remembering the definitions of crimes, translating legal terms so that others can understand them, and evaluating a situation when given certain facts and making a decision based on the facts and on knowledge of the law. It also would include knowing which methods and techniques to employ in a given situation, such as writing reports or sketching a crime scene.

Psychomotor relates to motor skills and the ability to physically perform a specific behavior. Simple tasks such as learning to walk or ride a bike are examples. Policing examples include properly firing a weapon, conducting a crime scene search, dusting for fingerprints, driving a vehicle at high speeds in a safe manner, and mediating a domestic argument. This domain builds upon the cognitive domain in that one may know "how" to do something but may not be able to actually do it. In law enforcement, skills are learned and practiced so that they become almost automatic (performed without much forethought). Some of the more critical skills relate to self-defense, defensive driving, and radio procedure. It is a general principle of training that during a critical situation, officers revert to the manner in which they learned such skills.

Affective relates to learning that impacts one's values, emotions, and/or attitudes. In policing it relates to "appreciations" and keeping an open, acceptive mind to new knowledge. Persons who are "set in their ways" and are not receptive to new ideas or thinking about things differently are difficult to train. If an officer is to properly benefit from training, he or she must be *willing* to learn; this is a precondition to learning. Examples of the affective domain include listening attentively, accepting differences in race and culture, demonstrating a belief in democratic principles, accepting responsibility for one's own behavior, maintaining good health habits, displaying safety consciousness, and accepting and practicing ethical standards of the law enforcement profession.

Within each domain are different levels of learning; the higher levels become more difficult and complex. For example, in the cognitive domain, six levels are part of the overall taxonomy (Bloom 1956):

1. Knowledge: ability to remember previously learned material.
2. Comprehension: ability to grasp the meaning of words and concepts.
3. Application: ability to use learned material in new situations.
4. Analysis: ability to break down material into its component parts so its structure can be understood.
5. Synthesis: ability to put parts together to form a new whole.
6. Evaluation: ability to judge the value of material for a given purpose.

Notice that "knowledge" and "comprehension" are the lowest levels of cognitive learning whereas "synthesis" and "evaluation" are the higher levels. Often academy training (and even some college-level course work) focuses on the lower levels of these domains; not much time is spent on the higher levels. Students memorize terms, concepts, dates, and events related to a field of study; they may learn to understand the material well enough to pass written exams consisting of multiple choice or other objective-type questions. Unfortunately, success on the street and in complex interpersonal situations often requires using the higher levels of learning in these domains. Learning how to analyze and synthesize the information gathered during incidents and interpersonal contacts is very important in today's society, especially in multicultural and ethnically diverse population centers, which pose new experiences for officers who have different backgrounds.

Methods of Instruction

There are a number of acceptable methods of instruction used in law enforcement training of all types and levels. Exhibit 11–1 identifies these methods according to whether the setting is for individual or group instruction.

Exhibit 11–1

METHODS OF INSTRUCTION

For Groups	*For Individuals*
Lectures	Inquiry
Field Experience	Field Experience/Practice
Field Observation	Field Observation
Case Studies	Case Studies
Field Trips	Field Trips
Demonstrations	Demonstrations
Interviews	Interviews
Role-Playing	Supervised Study
Seminars	Programmed Instruction
Group Exercises	Job Rotation
Discussions	Correspondence Courses
Debates	Computer-Based Instruction
Distance Learning	Distance Learning
Scenarios	Scenarios

Source: Data from A.Z. Gammage, *Police Training in the United States*, p. 206, © 1963, Charles C. Thomas Publishers, Ltd.; and Project STAR, *Police Officer Role Training Program*, p. 75, 1974, National Institute of Justice; with current techniques added.

Of course, this listing of methods does not tell the whole story. We all know that lectures, for example, can be either boring or interesting depending on the instructor's delivery, the content, and the learner's interest. Likewise, computer-aided instruction can be a simple computerized quiz or tutorial program or it can consist of multimedia presentations, interactive decision making, Internet-based assignments, and/or virtual reality scenarios. The method of instruction alone does not ensure successful learning of course objectives. The methods listed in Exhibit 11–1 are not mutually exclusive and some may involve aspects of others mentioned.

Officers must apply learned concepts to field situations. They must analyze behavior and motives of subjects in evaluating truthfulness of statements. They must gather bits and pieces of information and synthesize them for meaning and development of inferences, probable cause, or other conclusions.

TYPES OF TRAINING

In law enforcement, there are many different forms or types of training. The average person watching TV shows or his or her favorite *Police Academy* movie usually is exposed to only one type, the training of recruits. But training is an ongoing process in an officer's career. Laws change, new ones are added, the Supreme Court may modify existing police procedure that does not conform to Constitutional standards, and better ways of accomplishing tasks (possibly through new technology) are developed—all require that new information be conveyed to current officers.

Let us review some fundamental descriptions about the various types of training. It must first be mentioned that there is not a single accepted authority that has defined these different types of training. Nor is there necessarily consensus on the terminology used to differentiate one type from another. For example, what is "in-service" training in one agency could be "advanced" training in another.

Mandatory/Basic/Recruit/Entry-Level Training

The universal training of recruits is a recent development in the United States. Exhibit 11–2 displays a time line summary of early training academies and college involvement in law enforcement training from 1895 through 1974. Although police academies date back to the early 1900s, it was not until the late 1950s and 1960s that most states adopted **mandatory minimum training standards**. In 1959, California and New York established their Commissions on **Peace Officer Standards and Training (POST)** for the purpose of establishing minimum training and selection criteria. All but two states have an office that has legislative authority to establish state minimum standards for law enforcement personnel (Flink 1997, 1). Generally, these offices oversee the certification and/or licensing of peace officers. Although many of these commissions are referred to as POSTs, they may have different agency titles, such as "council" or "board," and they may or may not have the terms "peace officer" and "standards" in their title. For example, in Alaska the agency is known as the Alaska Police Standards Council; in Indiana, it is called the Indiana Law Enforcement Training Board; and in Florida, it is the Florida Department of Law Enforcement. Provisions vary from state to state; however, the International Association of Directors of Law Enforcement Standards and Training has published a "Model Minimum State Standards," which is found in Appendix 11–2 of this text.

The training hours for new recruits vary from jurisdiction to jurisdiction. The state mandatory minimum hours of training is exactly that—a minimum. Appendices 1, 2, and 3 of this chapter illustrate the mandatory minimum hours of training for the states of Colorado, California, and Ohio. Many training academies exceed the state minimums, especially large municipalities and state agencies. Recent data (1997) depicts the variation in the number of "classroom"

Exhibit 11–2

POLICE ACADEMY TRAINING AND COLLEGE PROGRAM TIME LINE

1895—New York City establishes its School of Pistol practice.

1908—First formal training school established in Berkeley, California, by Marshal August Volhner (initially the program was for in-service training).

1909—New York City instituted its police academy (for in-service and recruits).

1911—City of Detroit's first police training school started.

1916—First university-level police training school created at the University of California at Berkeley.

1918—The first school for policewomen was presented at the University of California at Los Angeles.

1919—Louisville, Kentucky Police School organized.

1924–28—University of Southern California sponsored a series of lectures of LAPD command officers that eventually led to a frill police curriculum in the Department of Public Administration.

1930—San Jose State College initiated its police science program. Students could earn an associate arts degree and then a bachelor's degree.

1933—The nation's first baccalaureate degree in criminology was approved at the University of California at Berkeley

1935—The FBI Police Training School, renamed The National Academy, began offering its special course work for state and local officers.

1935—Michigan State College initiated its baccalaureate program and optional 5-year police program.

1936—The Traffic Institute at Northwestern University (Evanston, Illinois) began operation.

1946—The Delinquency Control Institute was established at the University of Southern California.

1951—The Southern Police Institute at the University of Louisville began operation.

1959—The states of New York and California both set up their state minimum standards boards, the Municipal Police Training Council and the Commission on Peace Officer Standards and Training, respectively.
(continues)

Exhibit 11-2 *(continued)*

1963—49 two-year institutions (junior and community colleges) in the U.S. were identified as having crime-related programs.

1968—The passage of the Omnibus Crime Control and Safe Streets Act authorized the finding of new academic and training programs.

1974—The University of Louisville opened the National Crime Prevention Institute.

Source: Adapted with permission from A.Z. Gammage, *Police Training in the United States*, © 1963, Charles C. Thomas Publishers, Ltd.; and G.D. Eastman and J.A. McCain, Education, Professionalism, and Law Enforcement in Historical Perspective, *Journal of Police Science and Administration*, Vol. 9, No. 2, pp. 119–130, © 1981, International Association of Chiefs of Police.

hours required in selected jurisdictions in the U.S. (Reaves and Goldberg 1999):

Albany PD, NY	840	Beaufort County (SC) Sheriff Dept.	400
Atlanta PD, GA	940	Clark County (WA) Sheriff Dept.	600
Baltimore City PD, MD	840	Kent County (MI) Sheriff Dept.	80
Chicago PD, IL	400	New Mexico State Police	1,056
Columbus PD, OH	1,000	South Carolina Highway Patrol	560
Indianapolis PD, IN	752	Texas Dept. Pub. Safety	1,189
Los Angeles PD, CA	1,064	Indiana State Police	784
Miami PD, FL	840	Utah Highway Patrol	336

Source: Reprinted from B.A. Reaves and A.L. Goldberg, *Law Enforcement Management and Administrative Statistics, 1997: Data for Individual and Local Agencies with 100 or More Officers*, 1999, U.S. Department of Justice.

Keep in mind that these are 1997 data; the number of mandated hours could be different today because agencies consistently upgrade the hours. Also, these hours DO NOT include field training hours (discussed below). According to the 1997 LEMAS survey, the median number of training hours for municipal police was 640; for sheriff's departments it was 448, and for primary state agencies it was 823. Median field training hours were 480, 436, and 360 respectively (Reaves and Goldberg 1999). Occasionally (and today, more frequently), the question of training reciprocity between states and/or municipalities arises because of officers seeking employment with or moving to other jurisdictions.

This is a difficult question to answer (as is exemplified in Exhibit 11–3) because of the various regulations and rules within and among the various states.

The topics addressed in a basic training academy are numerous, in some schools numbering over 100 (especially when all the "subtopics" are totaled). Instead of discussing the details of these topics here, the appendices to this chapter contain the condensed listing of subjects and the minimum state mandated hours for selected states. Keep in mind that local agency academies may add topics and hours to the state minimums.

Usually persons attending basic academies have been hired by a law enforcement agency; however, a recent trend in some states allows "students" to pay their own way through the academy whether sponsored by an agency or not. Where this is permitted, the student can attend the academy, graduate, and seek employment with an agency in that state that recognizes the training. Additionally, 23 states permit colleges to conduct some or all of the entry-level law enforcement training (Flink 1997, 113). Although this is a significant number, the

---

Exhibit 11–3

TRAINING RECIPROCITY BETWEEN JURISDICTIONS

Can the police training received in one jurisdiction be transferred to another if an officer changes departments? The answer to this question varies greatly. In some states, departments will not honor or recognize the training hours a person received while working in another jurisdiction, even within the same state. If a current officer decides to change departments, he or she may have to complete the entire academy training at the new agency. On the other hand, a person may be able to change departments, go to another state, and only have to take the hours necessary to learn that state's criminal code—usually 40 to 80 hours.

Some states require a certified officer from another state to take a state exam before receiving a new certification. if you plan a career in law enforcement and intend to start in one agency and move to another (even within the same state), you should learn about any possible reciprocity before you join the first agency; you may have to attend the academy a second time. Other factors enter into the equation, such as moving from a local to state agency, or from a local or state agency to a federal agency. In short, portability of training is not consistent nor guaranteed.

training usually must be regulated or meet the specific guidelines and standards of the state office that certifies the training.

Once a person is employed by an agency, he or she is said to be "on probation," which usually includes one's attendance at the basic academy. The probationary period may extend from 6 to 24 months, but one year is the norm. For most officers, the probationary period represents the only time during which the department can terminate an employee without cause (Gaines and Forester 1983), although that is an overstatement in today's litigious society. (Chapter 10 discussed the probation period as part of the selection process.)

Field Training

Field training consists of "formalized, actual on-the-job instruction by specially selected and trained personnel" called Field Training Officers (FTOs). Field training (generally combined with periodic evaluation of the recruit's performance) usually occurs immediately after the recruit completes the classroom portion of basic training" (McCampbell 1986, 2). A 1997 survey of state regulatory commissions found that only seven states mandated field training for entry-level personnel as part of state standards (Flink 1997, 89). Of course, local agencies are normally responsible for this type of training. One of the most noted formalized field training programs was established in 1972 in the San Jose, California Police Department and has been a model for many departments (see Figure 11–3 for an overview of the San Jose Program, as originally implemented).

Most field training programs commence after the recruit has completed the basic academy (which normally is 10–15 weeks in duration). Then the recruit is assigned to an FTO, or to several of them, for a number of weeks. Some field training programs last up to a year. The FTO is responsible for evaluating the recruit during the field training period. The evaluations usually are formal and very detailed and may occur on a daily or weekly basis. If any weaknesses are found in the recruit's performance, he or she must undergo remedial training. If successful, the recruit can move on to a solo assignment. The officer must continue to perform successfully during this solo phase or else may be assigned for remedial training. During this intensive evaluation period, the department also determines whether the officer should be terminated. Successful completion of the field training leads to permanent employment status. Of course, variations to this sequence may occur since not all jurisdictions are alike in their operation of field training programs. Hughes *et al.* (1996) found that probation officers spent an average of 125 days with an FTO and that the top three typical duties of an FTO were "teaching by example," "mending weaknesses," and "allowing the probationer to take initiative." In California, effective January 1, 1999, every peace officer who is required to complete the

Phase I

Weeks 1–16
  Academy and in-agency classroom
  and range training.

Successful academy performance leads to Phase II. Failure at the Academy leads to dismissal.

Phase II

Weeks 17–18
  Assigned to primary FTO. No evaluations.
Weeks 19–28
  Daily observation reports by FTOs with weekly evaluation reports by supervisors.
Weeks 29–30
  Daily and weekly reports continue, but primary FTO rides in plain clothes with recruit.

During Phase II, recruit is assigned to initial FTO, then to two other FTOs on different shifts, then back to initial FTO. Recruit receives a District Evaluation after completing assignment with each FTO.

At completion of Phase II, successful recruit goes to Phase III. Otherwise, recruit may receive remedial training or be dismissed.

Phase III

Weeks 31–36
  Recruit works a solo beat outside the Training District. Supervisors evaluate biweekly.
Weeks 37–40
  Recruit continues solo beat. Supervisors evaluate monthly.
Weeks 41–44
  Recruit continues solo beat. Ten Month Review Board meets to recommend retention, remedial training, or dismissal.
Weeks 45–52
  Reserved for remedial training if needed. Special board meets to review the performance of recruits with deficiencies.

Recruit begins solo assignment and initial biweekly evaluations followed by monthly ones.

At 10-month review, recruit is certified to continue in Phase III or is recommended for remedial training.

At completion of Phase III, recruit becomes certified as a permanent employee or has Phase III extended. The option of dismissal still exists.

Source: Adapted from M.S. McCampbell, Field Training for Police Officers: State of the Art, *Research in Brief*, 1986, National Institute of Justice.

Figure 11–3   San Jose Academy and Field Training Model

regular basic training course must also complete an approved field training program. The FTO program, at a minimum, must include ten weeks of training; the criteria for structured training, remediation, and evaluation; daily trainee evaluations; and criteria for the selection and training of field training officers and program administrators. As of June 1999, over 400 programs had been approved (O'Brien 1999).

Not all departments have formal FTO programs; however, most departments do have some type of orientation or "break-in" period that involves others. In the Metro Nashville Police Department, after graduation from the academy, rookie officers are oriented and evaluated by "Master Patrol Officers" for a period of six months. They ride with one MPO for two months, then ride with another MPO, in another area of the city, for another two months. Following a rotation to a third MPO, the MPOs and Patrol Supervisors hold a meeting to decide whether to keep the officer, extend probation, or terminate the rookie's employment.

In-Service Training

During a police officer's career, ongoing training is necessary to keep up with changes in criminal law and procedures. **In-service training** (sometimes called "refresher") is the phrase used to refer to training received by officers following their recruit training. It is usually done at the department's facilities, and may be done during regular tours of duty (while on duty). The form of in-service training may vary from "roll-call" training sessions (held just prior to or after a tour of duty) to ones several hours in length. The subject matter of in-service training normally is related to the general assignments of most officers, or officers of a particular unit. Common material covered in such sessions includes legal updates in criminal procedure, new or modifications to standard operating procedures, the proper use of new equipment or weapons, and utilization of new forms or means of incident reporting. Some in-service sessions are used as "refreshers" that include updated material on topics originally covered at recruit school. In the pre-recruit academy years of policing, in-service training served as the primary means of upgrading personnel.

In-service training may be mandated by state law or regulations. By 1997, 33 states required such training for law enforcement personnel (Flink 1997, 77). Such training may include firearms requalification, an additional minimum number of hours, or other types of training. The time frame for such training may be annually or up to 48 months.

Advanced/Specialized Training

Advanced or **specialized training** refers to those sessions that address specialty topics or material that is an extension or a more enhanced version of what was received at basic academies. Such training allows officers to specialize in selected areas of the field. For example, general recruit training covers traffic accident investigation and crime scene processing, but advanced training is available to allow officers to become traffic accident specialists and crime scene technicians. The length of advanced/specialty courses can range from one day to three weeks, although some courses at special institutes may be from one to nine months in length. The following listing is a portion of the 134 courses offered at the Ohio Peace Officer Training Academy in London, Ohio, which is the state's primary advanced training center for local law enforcement personnel:

Advanced Child Abuse Investigation	Dealing with the Suicidal
Introduction to the Occult	Post-Shooting Trauma
Advanced Occult Investigation	Basic Instructor Training
Arson Investigation	Forfeiture Sanctions in Drug Cases
Computer-Related Crime Investigation	Advanced Hostage Negotiations
Death Investigation	Financial Investigative Techniques
Chemical Agents	Surveillance Photography
Trip Wires and Explosive Devices	Traffic Accident Reconstruction

In addition to specialized institutes and periodic training courses offered by professional associations, most states have some type of advanced training facility that offers specialized course work. Colleges and universities also routinely offer specialized courses for police personnel, and many of the courses carry **continuing education credit**. Such credit may be awarded in the form of hours or units, which usually apply to any state or local requirement where training hours are required each year.

Executive and Managerial Training

Another type of training, sometimes called **executive and managerial**, focuses on administrative decision making or supervision issues and skills. Courses in this type of training address subjects such as leadership, motivation, budgeting, first-line supervision, FTO program development and administration, media relations, public speaking, and communication skills. Some states require promoted officers to attend a managerial or supervisor's course as a condition of promotion; however, usually there is no such requirement to do so. Exhibit 11–4 is an illustration of what is taught to new lieutenants in the Los Angeles Police Department.

Another California-based program is unique in the field. It is known as the California Law Enforcement Command College. Originally, it was a 24-month program consisting of 10 workshops and independent study projects. It has evolved into an 18-month, 7-workshop program. Its faculty consists of university

Exhibit 11–4

NEW LIEUTENANT'S COURSE

Los Angeles Police Department uses a bifurcated program of instruction in training new lieutenants in groups of six or eight. One phase of this system is the "Peace Officer Standards and Training (POST) Management Course" mandated by the state of California. The second phase, conducted in-house, is simply called "Lieutenant's School."

The POST course is usually given prior to the LAPD program and includes 75 hours of instruction over ten days. The course is conducted by academic personnel at California State University at Northridge and employs an impressive required reading list that focuses on practical applications of management theories and philosophies, rather than on procedural issues. Each day in the POST program is devoted to a broad topic that, as in the LAPD sergeant's program, is then divided into smaller subtopics. These full day sessions involve such concepts as "Social Change and Managerial Responsibility," "The Evolving Legal Environment," and "The Complexities of Leadership." One full day is also devoted to management analysis and to critiques of filmed case studies. Self-assessment instruments and interactive discussion groups are employed throughout the POST training.

Phase II of this program, LAPD's Lieutenant's School, is a five-day, 40-hour program that covers 26 topics. This part of the program also addresses general management issues (e.g., "Employee Relations," "Values and Principles," "Effective Communication"). In large measure, however, this is a procedurally oriented course of study designed to take up where the POST offering has left off; most of it consists of subjects such as "Divisional Jail Management," "Management of Roll Call Training," "Sick and Injured On-Duty Management," and "Unusual Occurrences Procedures."

Source: Reprinted with permission from V. Henry and S. Grennan, Professionalism Through Police Supervisory Training, in *Police Practice in the '90s: Key Management Issues,* J.J. Fyfe, ed., p. 145 © 1989, International City/County Management Association.

---

professors and consultants who are recognized for their expertise. The Command College curriculum is designed for managers and administrators with high-level command responsibilities. The objectives of the program are to help these individuals develop strategies and methods for managing the complex issues facing law enforcement today and in the future. A "futures research" orientation is a fundamental component to the program. Each participant must com-

WORKSHOPS

1 DEFINING THE FUTURE

1
8

M   2 ENHANCED LEADERSHIP
O
N
T
H   3 FUTURES FORECASTING AND SOCIAL ISSUES
T
S

F   4 TECHNOLOGICAL AND ENVIRONMENTAL ISSUES
O
R

C   5 ECONOMIC AND POLITICAL ISSUES
O
M
P
L   6 FUTURES PLANNING TOOLS
E
T
I
O   7 PRESENTATION OF PAPERS AND CERTIFICATES
N

Source: Reprinted with permission from Command College Executive Leadership Institute Class 25—Session Schedule, *The California Law Enforcement Command College.* ***http://www2.4dcomm.com/comdcoll/***, © 1998, Commission on Peace Office Standards and Training, State of California.

Figure 11–4   CALIFORNIA COMMAND COLLEGE PROGRAM SCHEDULE

plete an independent study project that will be a "contribution to the Command College program, specifically, and to the body of knowledge and practice of law enforcement, generally" (California Commission on POST 1994). Figure 11–4 identifies the workshop sequence of the Command College Program.

Citizen Police Academy

In recent years, **citizen police academies** have begun appearing in many jurisdictions. This academy usually is a means of establishing a liaison and dialogue with the community. The format varies, but such a program can consist of one evening a week for 8–10 weeks. The course is open to residents of the jurisdiction and covers many of the same topics taught in a regular police academy. The sessions are taught by members of the local police department who speak on their areas of expertise. The course is designed to give an overview of the department's policies and procedures. The course also can provide a forum for the participants to offer suggestions and provide input regarding the operations of the agency. Some citizens' academies provide simulations so that participants can learn what it is like to approach suspects, patrol in a cruiser, and fire a weapon. Firearms training is an option in some academies. One of the objectives of the citizen police academy is to achieve a greater public awareness and understanding of the agency's role in the community through the educational aspects of the program. The Metropolitan Nashville (Tennessee) Police Department maintains a citizen police academy on the World Wide Web that includes considerable information about the department. Participants can log on, study the information presented about the department, and take a 25-question test, the successful completion of which allows the participant to print out a certificate of completion.

THE HIGHER EDUCATION AND TRAINING MERGER

Since the early 1900s, professionals in the field of policing have been advocating the benefits of college education for officers (see Exhibit 11–2). However, the standard educational requirement for about 79 percent of all local and 61 percent of state agencies in the U.S. is a high school diploma or GED. The 1997 LEMAS survey of agencies of 100 or more sworn personnel found that 10.3 percent of local agencies required some college, 8.3 percent required an associate's degree, and only 2 percent required a baccalaureate degree. Of the 49 state agencies, 16 percent required some college, 16 percent required an associate degree, and 4 percent required a baccalaureate degree at the time of appointment (Reaves and Goldberg 1999, xiv). Two states, Minnesota and Wisconsin, reported that law enforcement personnel were required by state standards to possess a minimum of an associate degree (however, in Wisconsin, an officer has up to five years to complete the associate degree after appointment).

In 1967, the President's Commission on Law Enforcement and Administration of Justice (1967b, 109–110) recommended that "[t]he ultimate aim of all police departments should be that all personnel with general enforcement powers have baccalaureate degrees," and "[p]olice departments should take immediate steps to establish a minimum requirement of a baccalaureate degree for all supervisory and executive positions." Later, in 1973, the National Advisory Commission on Criminal Justice Standards and Goals stated in Standard 15.1 that every police agency should, no later than:

- 1975, require as a condition of initial employment the completion of at least two years of college education;
- 1978, require as a condition of initial employment the completion of at least three years of college education;
- 1982, require as a condition of initial employment the completion of at least four years of college education.

A study published by the Police Executive Research Forum (PERF) in 1989 reported on the state of education in the police field (Carter *et al.* 1989). It found that 55 percent of all police officers in the study had completed two years of college, as compared to 15 percent in 1970. The study's recommendations included (Ayer's 1990, 17 citing the PERF study):

- All law enforcement agencies should develop long-range plans for requiring a college degree as a minimum criterion for promotion and employment by 1995,
- Effective immediately, all candidates for promotion to management and command ranks should be required to have baccalaureate degrees,
- Effective immediately, all candidates for promotion to first-line and supervisory positions should have a minimum of 60 college credits, and
- The federal government should develop a program to provide financial aid to in-service officers to help further their educations.

Obviously, these time periods have come and gone and the requirement of a college education—even two years of college—has not yet become a requirement in most agencies. In 1967, the President's Commission reported that only 70 percent of the police agencies in the U.S. minimally required a high school diploma as a condition of employment, although the median educational level for all police officers in the country was 12.4 years. By 1988 (in a survey of 531 law enforcement agencies with 100 or more sworn officers or serving a population of 50,000 or more) the average educational level of officers was 13.6 years (Carter and Sapp 1992). Although the mandated minimum educational requirements for entry into the field are not increasing significantly, the competition for the jobs is. Persons possessing only a high school–level education are competing with baccalaureate and master's degree applicants. Colleges and universities are graduating thousands of criminal justice majors annually in the United States, and many are seeking employment in the policing field. By the 2000 census, it is quite likely that the average education level of adults in the U.S. will be higher than the typical minimum education requirement to become a local law enforcement officer. Do citizens want officers whose educational levels are below average?

There are plenty of educational programs at the college level today and there is ample opportunity for interested persons to attend college. That wasn't always the case. By the early 1960s, only about 60 educational programs existed nationally. With the creation of the Law Enforcement Education Program (LEEP) as part of the Law Enforcement Assistance Administration of the late 1960s and early 1970s, by 1977 there were over 750 programs (Hoover 1983). Although exact data are not available, it is estimated that there are about 1,000 criminal justice education programs in the U.S. today. There has been ample debate over the type and quality of educational programming in the United States, and little consensus exists on curricular matters. In 1998, the Academy of Criminal Justice Sciences adopted a set of "Standards for Criminal Justice Education Programs," which are voluntary guidelines and recommendations. They generally address content areas, qualification of faculty, facilities, student-to-faculty ratios, and so on.

Recently, Tulsa, Oklahoma became the largest city in the nation and the only city in that state to require a baccalaureate degree for new recruits, effective January 1998. Prior to that, in 1981 the agency required 108 semester credit hours of college. Chief Palmer stated that officers with college degrees "come to you a little bit more mature, they're a little more aware of diversity issues, and they're more prone to use their minds to problem-solve than one that doesn't have that type of background. . . . What I've seen here is that there's a world of difference between a high school graduate and a college graduate in regard to skill levels and the handling of people" (Men & Women of Letters 1997, 1). Of the city's 794 officers, 73 percent have baccalaureate degrees and another 20 percent have 60 hours or more of college; 40 officers have master's degrees, three have law degrees, and one has a Ph.D.

For the most part, police training and college education still operate "separately and distinctly" from each other. Only recently have the two begun to merge in selected programs or areas in the United States. One of the largest mergers occurred in the state of Minnesota in 1977 with the creation of the Peace Officer Standards and Training Board to replace the older Peace Officer Training Board. It was the first state to establish "licensing" requirements. The "Minnesota Model" was initiated to decentralize the training of recruits by making fuller use of the state's college and vocational school system. Also, requirements for continuing education for license renewal were implemented.

In Minnesota, there is an alternative to the traditional route of securing employment with a police agency first and then attending the recruit training. A person can complete a POST-certified law enforcement program at a two- or four-year academic institution and then sit for the academic portion of the licensing exam. Upon successful completion of the exam, the person can enroll in a law enforcement skills course (of approximately eight weeks in length). Then, after passing the skills training, the person takes the *skills portion* of the licensing exam. If both portions of the licensing exam are successfully completed, the candidate can seek employment anywhere in the state as a police officer. Following a successful one-year probationary period, the new officer is granted a license. The academic portion of the program consists of the following subject areas (Minnesota State Statutes 1998, §§ 626.843 and 626.845):

a. Administration of Justice
b. Minnesota Statutes
c. Criminal Law
d. Human Behavior
e. Juvenile Justice
g. Law Enforcement Operation & Procedures

The skills training consists of the following subject areas:

a. Techniques in Criminal Investigation & Testifying
b. Patrol Functions
c. Traffic Law Enforcement
d. Firearms
e. Defensive Tactics
f. Emergency Vehicle Driving
g. Criminal Justice Information Systems
h. First Aid

Another recent development in the training and education merger is exemplified by the West Virginia State Police Training Program and the Maryland Articulation Agreement. In conjunction with Marshall University's Community and Technical College, the completion of the 960-hour, 28-week training course can lead to an associate degree in addition to certification as a state police officer. This venture began in 1985, was discontinued for a while, and as of 1999 was back in effect. Cadets earn an associate degree in police science by completing the academy and a number of regular college courses taught by Marshall University professors. In Maryland in March of 1999, 18 participating colleges and universities approved an Articulation Agreement that will permit any graduate of a certified recruit program to receive 15 undergraduate credits toward a degree. The process varies somewhat among the colleges, but the credits are fully transferable.

During the late 1980s, developments in Ohio also led to a greater merger of education and training requirements at selected institutions. It is now possible for students to complete the *total requirements* for peace officer certification at state-approved **"college academies"** and then sit for the mandated state exam. Students attending the college academies essentially complete the requirements for training as they complete their college degree program. Originally, most of the college academies "blended" academic material with training curriculum requirements over a two-year course of study. Recently, however, most of the participating college academies in the Ohio system have gone to a "caboose" delivery system—the mandatory training curriculum material is taught at the end of the associate degree program. Examples such as these are common in many states, especially in California and Florida, but most merger arrangements are associated with community colleges. Much of the debate against such programs has come from baccalaureate-granting institutions/programs that emphasize the traditional differences between education and training and criticize narrow vocationally oriented programs. However, it is not uncommon for advanced training academies or programs to affiliate themselves with colleges and universities that allow the granting of limited college credit or continuing education units for advanced or specialty courses. Nevertheless, today's trend is toward a greater merger of training and educational endeavors.

THREE MAJOR EMERGING FORCES

There are two emerging factors that will greatly impact the current aspects of police training and education: the evolving utilization of microcomputers to enhance the learning process and the Violent Crime Control and Law Enforcement Act of 1994. Microcomputer-based police training is "creeping" into the academies in Florida, Illinois, California, Michigan, Ohio, and other states. Programs for basic, in-service, and advanced training are being developed and becoming cost-effective. A 1994 study (Hughes *et al.*) of 64 of the largest agencies in the United States found that 50.9 percent used computers in weapons training, 21.1 percent in police procedure, and 5 percent each in driver training and law. Multimedia and virtual reality programs are emerging in course work beyond firearms training, where many such programs were originally applied. The University of Illinois Police Training Institute has been a leader in the development of computer-based course work for police training programs.

The future of police training will be closely tied to computerization for several reasons: first, because of the sheer volume of information and material that needs to be mastered by police recruits; second, because of the individual attention that a computer can give to (and demand of) the user; third, because of documentation that must be maintained on individual police officers relating to their mastery of concepts and material; and fourth, because of the realism that will be available through virtual reality and artificial intelligence programming. A 1997 survey of state training commissions found 16 respondents indicating that computer-based training was part of their officer training programs. However, only two states had developed their own computer-based training courses. In the opinions of the respondents, the topics considered more useful than others for computer-based presentations were (Flink 1997, 111):

–Report Writing	–First Aid/CPR	–Firearms	–Computer Crime
–Driving	–Legal Areas	–DUI Training	–Narcotics Investigation
–Bloodborne Pathogens	–Cultural Diversity	–Use of Force	–Domestic Violence
–Sexual Assault	–Hazmat	–Radar	–Arrest & Control
–Insurance Fraud	–Traffic Accident Investigation		
–Crime Prevention through Environmental Design			

The second major factor influencing police training and education is the Violent Crime Control and Law Enforcement Act of 1994, signed by President Clinton, containing provisions for several programs. The Act provided for the establishment of the Office on Community Policing, which approves funding to local communities for the hiring of additional officers for community policing activities. This was part of the President's initiative to add 100,000 officers to the policing community nationwide. Another initiative under the Act has been the establishment of "regional community policing institutes" around the country. These institutes have assisted in bringing a wide range of training topics and programs to local and state agencies. These have included state-of-the-art courses that focus on improving training as well as the content of training materials. The Police Corps portion of the Act established the Office of the Police Corps and Law Enforcement Education, which administer scholarships of up to $10,000 per calendar year to participants who agree to work in a state or local police force for at least four years after graduating from an educational institution. Another portion of the Act established law enforcement scholarships for in-service law enforcement personnel to further their education and for college students to work in law enforcement agencies full-time during the summer or part-time for a period not to exceed a year. Both of these programs will attract persons to criminal justice programs across the country if they are fully funded. (Congress has not fully funded either program to date.) One part of the Police Corps legislation also provided scholarships to dependents of law enforcement officers killed on duty. It is expected that the programs developed from the Violent Crime Control and Law Enforcement Act of 1994 will encourage and enhance cooperative working relationships among federal, state, and local agencies.

A third emerging force that will greatly impact law enforcement training is the trend toward problem-oriented training. This trend has several names or derivatives. Some describe it as "problem-based" or "scenario-based" training; others refer to it a "facilitated training." Traditional training methods have emphasized the cognitive knowledge and psychomotor skills of policing. Problem-based training attempts to move learning to the higher domains (refer to "Learning Domains," above) of analysis, synthesis, and application. The method generally flows like this: The cadet is expected to learn the cognitive aspects of policing early in the training process. This is followed by development of psychomotor skills. Then the cadet is immersed in a series of scenarios or problem-based situations where he or she must draw upon learned knowledge and skills and apply them to the situation encountered. Traditionally, this is what has been called role-playing situations. However, instead of just a few role-playing situations, a significant amount of time is spent with these scenarios. Cadets work individually and in groups in responding to these situations. Roles are carefully scripted to achieve maximum learning and the review and evaluation process assists the cadet in developing the critical thinking skills necessary to become decision makers on the street.

The problem-based training method has emerged under several so-called "models." The SARA Problem Solving Model (described in Chapter 9) is the foundation for these models. The Royal Canadian Mounted Police (RCMP) has a community policing model called CAPRA. CAPRA represents a systematic approach to proactive and reactive policing situations based on the principals of community policing: C—Clients, A—Acquiring and analyzing information, P—Partnerships, R—Response, and A—Assessment (Figure 11–5). The Florida Department of Law Enforcement has developed their SECURE Model for basic police officer training: Safety, Ethics, Community, Understanding, Response, Evaluation (FDLE Workshop 1999). Other states, such as Maryland and Kentucky, have adopted a problem-solving approach to basic training as well.

Why is this approach significant as an emerging force in the training arena? We believe that if this trend continues across the U.S., it will enhance the professionalization of the policing function. In part, it will demonstrate the need for recruiting persons who can learn cognitive material quickly and early in the process—this may mean that some college education may become a "de facto" minimum expectation for entry into the academy environment. The trend is also significant because it will better prepare cadets for the critical thinking necessary in today's society.

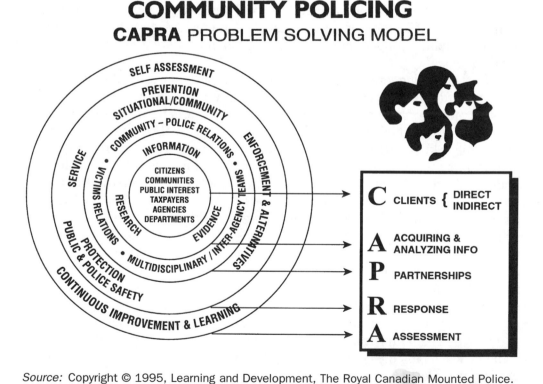

COMMUNITY POLICING
CAPRA PROBLEM SOLVING MODEL

Source: Copyright © 1995, Learning and Development, The Royal Canadian Mounted Police.

Figure 11–5 The Capra Model of The Royal Canadian Mounted Police

SOCIALIZATION INTO THE CULTURE OF LAW ENFORCEMENT

As mentioned in the beginning of this chapter, some of the purposes of police training include job orientation, indoctrination, safety/survival, and morale. As such, training is a key feature in the socialization process. Simply stated, socialization is the process whereby individuals learn and internalize the attitudes, values, and behaviors appropriate to persons functioning as social beings and responsive, participating members of their society. Socialization ensures that the individual will develop an identity, or self-concept, and also the motivation and requisite knowledge to perform adequately in the social roles he is called upon to enact throughout his lifetime (Socialization 1974). Although this topic is often discussed separately from the training process, it includes a learning and internalizing process similar to any training program.

The Police Culture

Socialization plays a vital role in any culture and prepares its people to function in society according to society's norms and values. In an occupational aspect, every employment field has its own unique culture; in law enforcement, it is often referred to as the **police culture** or **subculture**. Goldstein (1977, 10) describes it as "that intricate web of relationships among peers that shapes and perpetuates the pattern of behavior, values, isolation and secrecy that distinguish the police." The police subculture has been referred to by numerous terms in the literature and includes: *police social system, police ethos, occupational personality, the cop personality,* and the *police mystique* (Conser 1980).

James Sterling has discussed the relationship of training to the socialization process in these terms:

> Socialization for the police recruit includes both the adoption of normative modes of police behavior and the extinction of certain other behaviors which were appropriate for his previous civilian roles. In learning the new role, the police recruit undertakes a complex process of learning which includes more than just knowledge and skills. He will also learn a system of attitudes, beliefs, perceptions and values. The most important learning related to perception concerns the identification of role relevant reference groups and a sensitivity to their expectations and evaluations.

Police culture continues to be a topic of lively and vital discussions. Culture, in its broadest sense, is a shared sense of values, goals, and expectations about an organization or profession amongst its members. Police culture, then, is the sum total of the values, goals, and expectations that law enforcement officers share. There are many ways in which police culture has been viewed, and one recent effort attempted to integrate prior perspectives by searching for common themes that tie police together (Crank 1998). Crank argued that police culture reproduces itself in similar ways in different locations. Similarity results from a shared application of practical skills, while facing similar problems and environments, and engaging in similar daily routines. These similarities produce shared themes, which Crank identifies as coercive territorial control, the unknown, solidarity with other officers, death, and a collection of "loosely coupled" themes (e.g., deception, outsiders). Crank's view—that the nature of the work in a particular environment produces culture—conflicts with other recent views of policing organizations as being influenced by external political factors (Zhao 1996) while beat style is influenced by the nature of the beat (Klinger 1997). Recently, conflict between the new chief of police in Spokane, Washington and the police unions in that department was blamed on the different style of policing that the new chief brought from the East coast. If the impression of the patrol officers was true, it is suggestive that cultural differences exist between agencies. Little empirical work has been conducted in this area, partially because of the vagueness of the term "organizational culture," but the notion is intriguing and important for officers and citizens alike to consider.

Conceptually, the police culture can be viewed as containing four dimensions (Goldsmith and Goldsmith 1974). The **occupational dimension** considers the uniquely job-related factors that affect and condition the police to behave in certain ways. The **psychological dimension** focuses on police self-identity and personality development. The **political dimension** considers the relationship between the police community and the policy-making authorities of the agency and society at large. The **social dimension** addresses the police officers' social organization and subculture norms and the nature of police solidarity. It must be noted that although these dimensions permit a non-technical framework for viewing the police subculture, the variables and effects found in each are not isolated to that dimension. The variables are dynamic and can influence the factors or variables in other dimensions.

The Occupational Dimension

Research associated with this dimension focuses on the unique characteristics of the job of policing and how it impacts officers. Studies have concluded that policing often leads to collectively supported secrecy among officers. Such secrecy is considered so important that officers may break the law or their ethical code to support it (Westley 1956). Role conflict, development of police styles, isolationism, and negative perceptions held by police of citizens have been issues discussed in much of the research that reflects occupational variables (Manning 1997; Bayley 1994; Bittner 1990; White 1972; Wilson 1968; Banton 1964; Goldstein 1962).

The work of Jerome Skolnick regarding the "working personality" of police officers has become a classic in the scholarship of policing. His findings state that the variables of danger and authority, when viewed in the context of a prevailing pressure to be efficient, are fundamental to the development of an officer's occupational personality. This preoccupation with potential violence also fosters the development of a **symbolic assailant**, which is a person who uses "gesture, language, and attire that the police have come to recognize as a prelude to violence" (Skolnick 1994, 44). Police are trained to be suspicious, partly because that suspicion may mean the difference between injury and non-injury, between survival and death. Unfortunately, this suspicion may be generalized toward the public at large, which results in increased isolation from citizens and increased police solidarity.

The Psychological Dimension

This dimension emphasizes the self-concept and personality development of officers and attempts to answer the question: "Do officers' personalities change because of the job or independently of the job—or do they change at all?" There is no definitive answer to this question, and studies can be found that are contradictory and inconclusive. The variables that are usually addressed in this dimension concern conservatism, authoritarianism, stereotyping, cynicism, aggressiveness, mental strength and toughness (machoism), and sexism.

Professor William Doerner (1985, 394) has written about his experience of going from professor to police officer and the changes he perceived as a result of the transition: "Changes, which I though were subtle and only partially visible to others, have altered me to such a degree that I am an entirely different person with a completely different set of values, beliefs, and attitudes." Doerner's description of his transition is similar to Professor Kirkham's of the early 1970s. Both reflect the "reality shock" of working the street and how it transformed them. Their accounts and others discuss how personalities of individuals who have become officers appear to turn callous, less trusting, more cold and cynical, and frustrated. Nonetheless, the research is mixed concerning possible personality changes brought on by becoming a police officer.

The Political Dimension

This dimension attempts to analyze policing in light of community power structures and internal/external influences upon the officer. The police have been discussed in terms of political styles, decision-makers, and deviant groups (Wilson 1974; Skolnick 1969). Louis A. Radelet (1973) pointed out four distinguishable types of police-political relationships:

1. *Partisan:* This refers to playing politics in a partisan manner, meaning influenced by the political party in power, the political machine. The history of partisan politics in policing generally has been one of the spoils system and corrupt practices.

2. *Cultural:* Political forms of policing from a cultural perspective occur when the police enforce local mores and expectations even when they may not be lawful. Priorities are given to local parochial interests, and "outsiders" are at a disadvantage.
3. *Fraternalistic:* This occurs where the political power and influence emanates from within the police organization itself, usually through lobbying and/or union efforts.
4. *Administrative:* Here the relationships of the department's chief executive officer to decision makers in government, such as the mayor, city manager, city councils, and so on, are paramount. It relates to influencing public opinion, budget decisions, and department goals. It encompasses the leadership that is integral to effective public administration.

Radelet stated that administrative political policing is the only legitimate form, that the others are questionable at best and often have resulted in improper, sometimes even illegal actions by police. However, contemporary developments involving community policing create a different perspective or set of problems. Consider these comments from Carter (Carter and Radelet 1999, 426):

And now community policing adds yet another dimension to the politics and structure of administration. Traditionally police activities have been dictated by a complete "top-down" approach. That is, police administrators would define programs, the types of crimes that would be addressed, and assorted activities of officers, usually based on a crime analysis that balanced trends with efficiency. Sometimes, this would be even more "top directed" when elected officials asked (or instructed) the police department to focus on specific issues—violent crimes and the illicit drug trade serve as recent examples.

With community policing, officers on the street identify problems, frequently with community input, and thereby determine priorities for problem solving and major police initiatives. The role of police administrators begins to shift toward the responsibility of facilitating resources in order that officers may (it is hoped) accomplish goals and respond to public demands. As officers become increasingly empowered by the community, administrators will increasingly lose influence on departmental policing priorities.

The Social Dimension

The role of the police officer is of major concern here, primarily in terms of role conflict, group behavior, and the socialization process. In many ways, the social dimension is the culmination and integration phase of the entire police subculture. Generally speaking, the operation of police units demands a strong sense of loyalty, comradeship, solidarity, and secrecy. The perceptions of the po-

lice as an occupational group strongly influence their behavior and how they in-
doctrinate (socialize) and accept new members. According to Harris (1973), the
most significant consequence of police training is the cultivation of solidarity—
the subjective feeling of belongingness, moral support, and depersonalization toward other non-officers.

Other aspects of the social dimension have focused on such things as divorce, alcoholism, and suicide rates of police as compared to other groups and
other health issues related to stress. The empirical evidence on these matters
varies from place to place and from study to study. We cannot conclude that
officers suffer from higher rates of divorce, heart disease, ulcers, alcoholism,
and so on because the empirical evidence is mixed.

In the midst of all this confusion, one thing is certain: a police subculture exists, although we may not agree as to its universal characteristics, codes, and
behavior. The police themselves perceive it, and as long as they do, it is real
to them. Barbara Bennett (1978) referred to it as the "police mystique"—"a
body of ideas and attitudes that has become associated with a group of people
or an institution . . . often more imagined than real."

There are, of course, studies that refute the importance of the police subculture and the impact of police socialization on officers. Some of the more recent
developments, such as community policing (Chapter 9) and emphasis on crime
prevention and social service roles (Chapters 9 and 6), may reverse or impede
some of the negative aspects of the police subculture. Also, since more educated persons are being attracted to the field, their backgrounds may modify
the traditional negative impact of some of the socialization process. Students
of policing are being taught about the negative aspects of the police subculture
in academic and even academy programs today. This is often coupled with
greater emphases on ethics and integrity and how the police subculture can
become a positive force for change and integrity maintenance. Conser (1980,
52–53) has suggested the following policy recommendations in order to reduce
or lessen some of the perceived negative aspects of the police subculture and
the socialization process:

1. A commitment to a more open system organization that, in part, reduces
   the secretiveness that often permeates the structure.
2. A greater understanding of the role of the officer in policing the community, particularly regarding norm violations and minor misdemeanors.
3. A greater emphasis at training academies on the police subculture, its
   positive and negative effects—possibly taught by non-police personnel or
   in a cooperative effort with selected non-police trainers.
4. A greater care and emphasis on the selection and training of Field Training Officers in order to overcome aspects of the **detraining syndrome**—
   the process of transforming the highly motivated, idealistic recruit to one
   that is disillusioned and distrustful.

5. A greater commitment and recognition of individual integrity and ethical standards in order to reduce conformity pressures.
6. A commitment to excellence in supervision, developing educated, well-trained and enlightened supervisors who understand principles of leadership, motivation, accountability, and integrity.

If the police subculture is the result of the learning process, then that process can be utilized to reduce the negative attributes usually associated with the subculture.

SUMMARY

Training and education in the law enforcement field have evolved from on-the-job training to a merger of the traditional training academy with an academic curriculum. Variations, of course, do exist because the United States is a very large and diverse country of multiple jurisdictions, and there simply are no nationally accepted standards. Training and education should be viewed as a compound phrase and not two individual and different terms. Education is the more global learning outcome desired for today's officers, who must police a complex world. Training is only one method of acquiring the knowledge and skills necessary for the task.

Although national commissions have recognized the importance of and recommended higher education as a condition of employment for local police officers, few departments require it. The majority of police officers today, however, do have some college education, according to recent surveys. This trend is an important one since most officers can remain on the job for 20–30 years. Departments must ensure that continued education and training occur or their officers will begin to lag behind the average educational levels of society.

The formal training process is considered a major aspect of the socialization of the law enforcement officer. This socialization plays a key role in modifying or developing an officer's attitudes, values, and beliefs. Researchers have been investigating the socialization of police and the resulting occupational subculture. Although studies are sometimes contradictory, the findings have brought a greater understanding of the job and those who perform it.

The issues and controversies related to training and education are diverse and complex. This chapter has addressed only the major ones. Issues related to certification versus licensure, reciprocity of training, the granting of college credit for training (both recruit and advanced), the merger of training and education, mandated continuing education credits/hours, and minimum education requirements as conditions for employment and promotion have been debated for over 25 years, and no consensus or national standard has been reached yet. With the recent interest in national crime legislation, it is possible that an influx of research and programming funds may assist in reaching closure on some of these issues in the near future.

QUESTIONS FOR REVIEW

1. What is the relationship of learning, learning domains, and teaching to the concept of education?
2. What are seven reasons for or purposes of law enforcement training?

3. What are five types of training commonly found in law enforcement? Give examples of each.
4. What did the National Advisory Commission on Criminal Justice Standards and

Goals recommend regarding educational levels as conditions of employment for police officers?

5. What are three major emerging influences on police education and training?

6. What is meant by the police culture?

7. What are the negative and positive characteristics of the police subculture as summarized in this chapter?

8. How does training impact the socialization of law enforcement officers?

SUGGESTED ACTIVITIES

1. Using available library resources, or the World Wide Web, locate the state POST for selected states, then compare and contrast their provisions regarding peace officer training. Focus on the certification and minimum training standards for peace officers. If a law library is available, this would be an excellent source for such research; however, the state codes of most states can be found on the Internet.

2. Contact your local police department and inquire about where and how new recruits are trained; ask a local training academy commander to speak to your class about state rules, regulations, and matters of reciprocity of certification.

3. Have police officers appear as guest speakers in your class and ask them about the police culture. Do they believe they have "changed" since becoming a police officer? If so, how?

4. On the World Wide Web, use the Infoseek search engine and enter the words "peace officer training." Review the results and go visit several of the POST sites.

5. On the World Wide Web, conduct a search of the phrase "citizen police academy." Write a brief report on your findings, including a description of two or three of the most interesting sites located.

CHAPTER GLOSSARY

advanced or **specialized training:** those sessions that address specialty topics or material that is an extension or more enhanced version of what was taught at basic academies

citizen police academy: an informative program containing many of the subjects taught in a basic police academy but meant for members of the local community so that they can learn more about the typical duties, policies, and procedures related to policing in their local communities

college academies: a state-approved recruit training program incorporated into the academic curriculum of an institution of higher education

continuing education credit: formal recognition of additional training received following recruit training; it may be required by state law to remain in your position

detraining syndrome: the process of transforming the highly motivated, idealistic recruit to one who is disillusioned and distrustful

executive and managerial training: focuses on administrative decision making or supervision issues and skills; courses in this type of training address subjects such as leadership, motivation, budgeting, first-line supervision, FTO program development and administration, media relations, public speaking, and communication skills

education: that which one has learned

field training: consists of formalized, on-the-job instruction by specially selected and trained personnel called Field Training Officers (FTOs)

in-service training: training received by officers following their recruit training

learning: a process that changes a person's behavior or attitude

learning domains: various levels of learning that include the cognitive, motor skills, and affective domains

mandatory minimum training standards: the minimum training requirements, usually established by statutory or regulatory mandates

Peace Officer Standards and Training (POST): a general phrase that refers to the state commission, council, board, or agency that is legislatively authorized to regulate law enforcement training throughout a state

occupational dimension: the uniquely job-related factors that affect and condition the police to behave in certain ways

on-the-job training (OJT): the lessons learned by actually doing the job without any pre-service instruction; includes methods and techniques taught by co-workers and supervisors

police culture (or **subculture**): an intricate web of relationships among peers that shapes and perpetuates the pattern of behavior, values, isolation, and secrecy that distinguish the police

political dimension: the relationship between the police community and the policy-making authorities of the agency and society at large

psychological dimension: the self-identity and personality development aspects of the police subculture

social dimension: the police officers' social organization, subculture norms, and the nature of police solidarity

symbolic assailant: a person who uses gesture, language, and attire that the police have come to recognize as a prelude to violence

---

APPENDIX 11–1   Basic Academic Training Program, State of Colorado
(Revised September 1996)

MINIMUM REQUIRED HOURS

Academic: 293
Skills: <u>140</u>
TOTAL: 433

ACADEMIC PORTION:

I. ADMINISTRATION OF JUSTICE   REQUIRED HOURS: 21
    A. Introduction to The Criminal Justice System—3 Hours
    B. Law Enforcement Ethics—6 Hours
    C. Criminal Process—8 Hours
    D. State, Federal, and Local Law Enforcement Agencies—4 Hours

II. BASIC LAW   REQUIRED HOURS: 88
    A. United States Constitution—4 Hours
    B. Arrest, Search and Seizure, Interrogation and Confessions, and
       Rules of Evidence—16 Hours
    C. Colorado Criminal Code—32 Hours
    D. Colorado Children's Code—8 Hours
    E. Victim's Rights—4 Hours
    F. Legal Liability—8 Hours
    G. Liquor Code—2 Hours
    H. Controlled Substances—2 Hours
    I. Ethnic Intimidation—4 Hours
    J. Court Testimony—8 Hours

III. COMMUNITY INTERACTION REQUIRED HOURS: 12
   A. Introduction/Framework for Community Policing—4 Hours
   B. Problem Solving—4 Hours
   C. Community Partnership—2 Hours
   D. Crime Prevention—2 Hours

IV. PATROL PROCEDURES REQUIRED HOURS: 58
   A. Patrol Observation and Perception—3 Hours
   B. Officer Survival—8 Hours
   C. Pedestrian Contacts—2 Hours
   D. Gangs—4 Hours
   E. Vehicle Stops—6 Hours
   F. Vehicle Searches—4 Hours
   G. Building Searches—4 Hours
   H. Handling In-progress Calls—6 Hours
   I. Domestic Violence—4 Hours
   J. Civil Disputes—3 Hours
   K. Crowd Control—6 Hours
   L. Hazardous Materials—8 Hours

V. TRAFFIC CONTROL REQUIRED HOURS: 28
   A. Traffic Code—6 Hours
   B. Traffic Direction—2 Hours
   C. Traffic Accident Investigation—12 Hours
   D. D.U.I.—8 Hours

VI. INVESTIGATIVE PROCEDURES REQUIRED HOURS: 56
   A. Preliminary Investigations—4 Hours
   B. Crime Scene Search—2 Hours
   C. Crime Scene Documentation—12 Hours
   D. Identification and Collection of Evidence—10 Hours
   E. Interview and Interrogation Techniques—6 Hours
   F. Identification of Suspects—4 Hours
   G. Major Case Considerations—18 Hours

VII. COMMUNICATIONS REQUIRED HOURS: 30
   A. Report Writing—16 Hours
   B. Stress Management—4 Hours
   C. Verbal Communication Techniques—8 Hours
   D. Interaction With Special Populations—2 Hours

SKILLS PORTION:

   A. Arrest Control Techniques—56 Hours
   B. Driving—32 Hours
   C. Firearms—52 Hours

Source: Reprinted from *Basic Academic Training Program*, 1996, Colorado Peace Officers Standards and Training Board.

APPENDIX 11–2   Training Subjects and Hours, State of California
(Mandatory Subjects and Minimum Hours)

Functional Training Area   *Required Hours*

1. PROFESSIONAL ORIENTATION   10 hours
   History of law enforcement; ethics; criminal justice components;
   court and corrections systems.
2. POLICE COMMUNITY RELATIONS   15 hours
   Community attitudes and influences; crime prevention;
   psychological stress; citizen evaluations.
3. LAW   45 hours
   Crime elements; an examination of the major crimes in California;
   juvenile law and procedure; local ordinances; penal code.
4. LAWS OF EVIDENCE   15 hours
   Privileged communication; rules of evidence; search and seizure concepts.
5. COMMUNICATIONS   15 hours
   Interpersonal skills; note taking; report writing.
6. VEHICLE OPERATIONS   15 hours
   Pursuit driving; vehicle liability; vehicle control techniques.
7. FORCE AND WEAPONRY   40 hours
   Firearms; use of force; chemical agents; safety procedures.
8. PATROL PROCEDURES   105 hours
   Patrol concepts; interrogation; physical search procedures; prisoner
   transportation; perception and observation techniques; responding to
   crimes and calls for assistance; crowd control; officer survival.
9. TRAFFIC   30 hours
   Vehicle code; traffic control; alcohol violations; accident investigation;
   violator contacts.
10. CRIMINAL INVESTIGATION   45 hours
    Crime scene search; preservation of evidence; interviewing;
    techniques of crime investigation; vice and organized crime;
    courtroom demeanor.
11. CUSTODY 5 hours
    Booking procedures; prisoner rights and responsibilities;
    custody procedures.
12. PHYSICAL FITNESS AND DEFENSE TECHNIQUES   40 hours
    Weight control; weaponless defense; baton techniques.
13. ADMINISTRATION   20 hours
    Includes registration procedures; orientation; equipment issuance;
    drills; academy rules and regulations; diagnostic testing; examinations;
    special training; graduation practice; and other administrative requirements
    relevant to a particular academy.

                                                            Total 400 hours

Source: Reprinted with permission from ***http://www.post.ca.gov/***, © 1998, California Commissiion on Peace Office Standards and Training.

APPENDIX 11–3 Training Subjects and Hours, State of Ohio
(Mandatory Subjects and Minimum Hours)

Functional Training Area	*Required Hours*
I. ADMINISTRATION	21 hours
Basic training, role of peace officer, ethics, criminal justice principles and system, American and Ohio courts, community policing, report writing.	
II. LEGAL	77 hours
Ohio criminal code, rules of evidence, search and seizure, confessions and interrogations, civil liability and use of force, testifying in court.	
III. HUMAN RELATIONS	76 hours
Public relations, handling the mentally ill and disabled, domestic disputes, crisis intervention, child abuse and neglect, missing children, crime prevention cultural sensitivity, victim's rights.	
IV. DRIVING	24 hours
Defensive driving tactics, pursuit, practical exercises.	
V. FIREARMS	60 hours
Safety procedures, handgun/shotgun courses, practical.	
VI. SUBJECT CONTROL	34 hours
Self-defense techniques, intermediate weapons.	
VII. FIRST AID	16 hours
VIII. PATROL	49 hours
Vehicle and foot patrol techniques, crimes in progress, building search procedures, stops and approaches, auto theft and V.I.N. reconstruction, prisoner booking and handling, gangs, communications and radio procedures, report writing.	
IX. CIVIL DISORDERS	17 hours
Control of nonviolent crowds, hostile crowds and riot formations, chemical agents, bombs and explosives, terrorism, hazardous materials response.	
X. TRAFFIC ENFORCEMENT	91 hours
Motor vehicle offenses, direction and control, uniform traffic citations, radar and other traffic technology, D.U.I. and SFST, crash investigation.	
XI. INVESTIGATION	55 hours
Crime scene search, sketching, photography, interviews and interrogations, line-ups, surveillance techniques, search warrants.	
XII. PHYSICAL CONDITIONING	30 hours
	Total: 550 hours

Source: Reprinted with permission from Ohio Peace Officer Training Commission, *Peace Officer Basic Training*, 1999, Attorney General's Office, London, Ohio.

REFERENCES

Ayers, Richard M. 1990. *Preventing Law Enforcement Stress: The Organization's Role.* Alexandria, VA: National Sheriffs' Association.

Banton, Michael. 1964. *The Policeman and the Community.* London: Tavistock.

Bayley, David H. 1994. *Police for the Future.* New York: Oxford University Press, Inc.

Bennett, Barbara. April 1978. The Police Mystique. *The Police Chief* XLV (4): 46.

Bent, Alan Edward. 1974. *The Politics of Law Enforcement: Conflict and Power in Urban Communities.* Lexington, MA: Lexington Books.

Bittner, Egon. 1967. The Police on Skid Row: A Study of Peace-Keeping. *American Sociological Review* 32: 699–715.

Bittner, Egon. 1990. *Aspects of Police Work.* Boston: Northeastern University Press.

Bloom, Benjamin Samuel, ed. 1956. *Taxonomy of Educational Objectives: Cognitive Domain.* New York: David McKay Company, Inc.

State of California. Commission on Peace Officer Standards and Training. 1994. *The California Law Enforcement Command College.* Sacramento, CA: Commission on Peace Officer Standards and Training.

State of California. Commission on Peace Officer Standards and Training. **http://www.post.ca.gov/** and **http://www2.4dcomm.com/comdcoll/** (May 29, 1998).

Carter, David L. and Louis Radelet. 1999. *The Police and the Community.* 6th ed. Upper Saddle River, NJ: Prentice Hall.

Carter, David L. and Allen Sapp. 1992. College Education and Policing: Coming of Age. *FBI Law Enforcement Bulletin* (January): 11.

Carter, David L., Allen Sapp, and Darrel Stephens. 1989. *The State of Police Education.* Washington, D.C.: Police Executive Forum.

State of Colorado. Peace Officers Standards and Training Board. **http://www.state.co.us/gov_dir/dol/post96mv2/96m/pa.htm** (May 29, 1998).

Conser, James A. 1980. A Literary Review of the Police Subculture: Its Characteristics, Impact and Policy Implications. *Police Studies* 2(4) (Winter): 46–54.

Conser, James A. 1981. The Training and Education Cosmos. *The Police Chief* 42 (July): 64.

Crank, John P. 1998. *Understanding Police Culture.* Cincinnati: Anderson Publishing Co.

Doerner, William G. 1985. I'm Not the Man I Used to Be: Reflection on the Transition from Prof to Cop. In *The Ambivalent Force,* edited by Abraham Blumberg and Elaine Niederhoffer. Hinsdale, IL: Dryden Press.

Draves, William A. 1995. *Energizing the Learning Environment.* Manhattan, KS: Learning Resources Network.

Eson, Morris E. 1972. *Psychological Foundations of Education.* 2d ed. New York: Holt, Rinehart and Winston, Inc.

FDLE Workshop. 1999. *Redesigning the Basic Recruit Curriculum.* International Association of Directors of Law Enforcement Standards and Training, Conference Manual, Orlando, FL, June 8, 1999: 253–260.

Flink, William L. and the International Association of Directors of Law Enforcement Standards and Training. 1997. *Sourcebook: Executive Summary.* Richmond VA: CJ Data/Flink & Associates.

Gaines, Larry K. and William Forester. 1983. Recruit Training Processes and Issues. In *The Police Personnel System* by Calvin J. Swank and James A. Conser. New York: John Wiley & Sons, Inc.

Gammage, Allen Z. 1963. *Police Training in the United States.* Springfield, IL: Charles C. Thomas, p. 206; and Project STAR, Police Officer Role Training Program, Santa Cruz, CA: Davis Publishing Company, Inc., 1974: 75.

Goldsmith, Jack and Sharon Goldsmith, eds. 1974. *The Police Community.* Pacific Palisades, CA: Palisades Publishing Company.

Goldstein, Herman. 1963. Police Discretion: The Ideal vs. the Real. *Public Administration Review* 23: 140–148.

Goldstein, Herman. 1977. *Policing a Free Society.* Cambridge, MA: Ballinger Publishing Company.

Gronlund, Norman E. 1970. *Stating Behavioral Objectives for Classroom Instruction.* New York: The Macmillan Company.

Harris, Richard. 1973. *The Police Academy: An Inside View.* New York: John Wiley & Sons, Inc.

Henry, Vincent and Sean Grennan. 1989. Professionalism through Police Supervisory Training. In *Police Practices in the '90s: Key Management Issues,* edited by James J. Fyfe. Washington, D.C.: International City Management Association.

Hoover, Larry T. 1983. The Educational Criteria: Dilemmas and Debate. In *The Police Personnel System,* edited by Calvin Swank and James A. Conser. New York: John Wiley & Sons, Inc.

Hughes, Thomas, Beth Sanders, and Robert Langworthy. 1996. *Police Forum* 6(2) (April): 18–20.

Klinger, David A. 1997. Negotiating Order in Patrol Work: An Ecological Theory of Police Response to Deviance. *Criminology* 35(2): 277–306.

Manning, Peter K. 1997. *Police Work: The Social Organization of Policing.* 2d ed. Prospects Heights, IL: Waveland Press, Inc.

McCampbell, Michael S. 1986. Field Training for Police Officers: State of the Art. *Research in Brief.* November 1986.Washington, D.C.: National Institute of Justice.

Men & Women of Letters. 1997. *Law Enforcement News* XXIII(478) (30 November): 1.

State of Minnesota. 1978. *Minnesota Code of Agency Rules: Peace Officer Standards and Training Board.* St. Paul, MN: Office of the State Register.

Minnesota State Statutes. 1998. §§ 626.843 and 626.845.

National Advisory Commission on Criminal Justice Standards and Goals. 1973. *Report on Police.* Washington, D.C.: U.S. Government Printing Office.

O'Brien, Kenneth. 1999. *Mini Report.* International Association of Directors of Law Enforcement Standards and Training, Conference Manual, Orlando, FL, June 8, 1999, 271.

Ohio Peace Officer Training Council. 1997. *Commander Handbook for Peace Officer Basic Training.* London, OH: Attorney General's Office, Appendix A.

President's Crime Commission Law Enforcement and Administration of Justice. 1967a. *Task Force Report: The Police.* Washington, D.C.: U.S. Government Printing Office.

President's Commission on Law Enforcement and Administration of Justice. 1967b. *The Challenge of Crime in a Free Society.* Washington, D.C.: U.S. Government Printing Office.

Project STAR. 1974. *Police Officer Role Training Program.* Santa Cruz, CA: Davis Publishing Company, Inc.

Radelet, Louis A. 1973. *The Police and the Community.* Beverly Hills, CA: Glencoe Press.

Reaves, Brian and Andrew Goldberg. 1999. *Law Enforcement Management and Administrative Statistics, 1997: Data for Individual State and Local Agencies with 100 or More Officers.* Washington, D.C.: U.S. Department of Justice.

Saunders, Charles B., Jr. 1970. *Upgrading the American Police: Education and Training for Better Law Enforcement.* Washington, D.C.: The Brookings Institution.

Skolnick, Jerome. 1994. *Justice without Trial: Law Enforcement in Democratic Society.* 3d ed. New York: Macmillan College Publishing Company, Inc.

Skolnick, Jerome. 1969. *The Politics of Protest.* New York: Simon and Schuster.

Socialization. 1974. *Encyclopedia of Sociology.* Guilford, CT: The Dushkin Publishing Group.

Stern, Mort. 1962. What Makes a Policeman Go Wrong. *Journal of Criminal Law, Criminology, and Police Science* 59: 97–101.

Westley, William A. 1956. Secrecy and the Police. *Social Forces* 34: 254–257.

White, Susan. 1972. A Perspective on Police Professionalization. *Law and Society Review* 7: 61–85.

Wilson, James Q. 1968. *Varieties of Police Behavior.* Cambridge, MA: Harvard University Press.

Zhao, Jihong. 1996. *Why Police Organizations Change.* Washington, D.C.: Police Executive Research Forum.

Legal Restrictions on Law Enforcement

Detroit police officers during their arraignment in 36th District Court for the beating death of motorist Malice Green. November 1992. (AP/ Wide World Photos)

SOURCES OF AMERICAN LAW

American law is derived from several sources. These sources became more numerous as the nation grew and became more complex, both socially and economically. Police officials must understand the sources of law because they are also the sources of authority for their decisions and actions.

Common Law

The first source of law that traditionally involved law enforcement was the **common law**. Derived from England, this body of legal rules developed over a period of several hundred years. English judges were frequently faced with problems, or cases, for which there were no legal guidelines. Nevertheless, courts needed to reach decisions in an attempt to resolve these problems. Acting under the authority of the King, courts developed legal rules to settle these cases.

These decisions, over time, were relied upon by other judges with similar problems and came to be called **precedent**. Courts would draw upon these older cases to help decide new ones. In effect, the old cases gave the judges guidance. The act of applying and relying upon precedent was called **stare decisis**. This meant that prior decisions should be followed if the facts of the case at issue were similar to the prior case. The courts could construct new rules only if the case to be decided was unlike prior cases. Gradually, this body of law developed and was called the common law.

Criminal and Civil Law

The common law included both **civil law** and **criminal law**. Criminal law and civil law are distinctive areas of the law. Generally speaking, crimes are offenses against the public (or the state), while civil violations are violations against individuals. While individuals are frequently victims in criminal offenses such as assault, rape, or murder, the law considers the public at large to be the victim. The theory is that a society must have order and must protect its members. If the rules of that order are violated and a crime is committed, it is society that is offended. This perspective has governed American Law for over 200 years, but as we see elsewhere in this book, emerging theories of victims' rights and restorative justice are challenging this long-held assumption.

In criminal cases, the state is represented by the prosecutor (or district attorney), who initiates the criminal charge (a process described below). In civil cases, each side is represented by private counsel, and the complaining party (or counsel) must file a complaint alleging a civil violation. A violation of a criminal statute can result in jail or prison time. Civil cases can only result in money damages or orders compelling parties to do or not do something. One does not go to jail or prison for a civil violation (generally speaking); however, if a court order is ignored or violated, one could be jailed for contempt of court. That is not a crime. (Similarly, those who are ordered to pay child support and fail to do so despite the ability to pay may similarly be jailed. In both cases, civil actions could result in being jailed, but only because a court order was ignored or violated. This is different than in a criminal case.)

Civil law includes contracts, torts, property, and civil procedure. A tort is a civil injury of a person or a person's property. Examples of torts include cutting down a tree belonging to another or damaging a person's car by reckless driving. Torts may be intentional or negligent (described below). It is important to understand, however, that an action by someone may create *both* a criminal act and a tort. For example, suppose two people get into an argument and one strikes the other. The person who struck the victim committed an assault and battery. The state could charge that person with assault and battery and, if convicted, jail him or her. That would be a criminal charge.

Additionally, the person who was struck could file a civil complaint alleging the *tort* of assault and battery, an intentional tort, and seek damages from the assailant. In the O.J. Simpson case, the family of Ronald Goldman, one of the two victims Simpson is alleged to have killed, sued O.J. Simpson. While Simpson was tried for murder when the State of California brought criminal charges and was found innocent by a jury, he nevertheless was required to defend a civil action alleging a wrongful death. Eventually, he lost that tort litigation and owed the family of Ron Goldman millions of dollars in damages awarded in the lawsuit. Essentially, a wrongful death alleges that a person (e.g., Ron Goldman) was killed due to the unlawful actions of the defendant (e.g., O.J. Simpson) and that the defendant is liable for damages resulting from the death. Thus, the same act can result in criminal charges and civil complaints.

Common Law courts created the felonies of murder, suicide, manslaughter, burglary, arson, robbery, larceny, rape, sodomy, and mayhem. These offenses generally carried a possible sentence of more than a year in prison. The same courts gradually developed a set of misdemeanor crimes, including assault, battery, false imprisonment, libel, perjury, corrupting morals, and disturbing the peace. These offenses were generally punishable by a sentence of less than a year in prison. Many states in the United States, particularly on the East coast, relied and continue to rely heavily on the common law definitions of these crimes.

Statutory and Code Law

As the nation grew, the complexity of life and changing social norms outstripped the ability of the courts to respond. The creation of common law took centuries and required centuries to evolve, but the changes that came with expansion and industrialization required a more rapid adjustment; so reformers used legislative efforts to create new laws. Legislative bodies, such as the Congress of the United States and state legislatures, passed formal laws that adopted common law definitions of some crimes. These legislatures also created new crimes. Laws that are passed by a legislative body are called *statutes* and are compiled into a coded (numbered) collection of laws (often referred to as the "state code"). When a law is passed by a legislative body, it becomes **statutory law**. It is assigned a number and placed into the state's code. The process of numbering statutes is called codification. All laws of a given type are placed in one section of the code, making them easy to find. For example, each state has a Penal Code or Criminal Code, and all crimes in that state are organized in that section of the code, usually called a "Title" (e.g., Title 29). Also, statutes can be related to one another and cross-referenced by the numbering system. This process of adding new social rules to the criminal law greatly increased the number and kinds of things for which a person could be punished. Today, with state and federal jurisdictions included, every person in the United States is subject to thousands of laws for which they can be criminally prosecuted. It is important to locate statutes and cases for research and reference purposes. Exhibit 12–1 will assist in an initial understanding of how to read statutory and case references.

Many crimes were condensed into the Model Penal Code (MPC), which was adopted by many states. The MPC was written by the American Law Institute, an organization supported by the legal community. Its purpose was (and is) to bring consistency to issues of law common in all states. If each state adopted the same code and each used the same definitions for each crime, confusion and inequity would decrease. Despite these efforts, however, even states adopting the MPC have changed major portions of that code. What is either legal or a minor offense in one state may well be illegal or a very serious offense in another. For example, in Georgia the code prohibits certain kinds of sexual acts, even between two consenting adults (*Hardwick v. Bowers*, 478 U.S. 186, 1986). That same conduct is legal in California. Similarly, possession of a small amount of marijuana may be trivial in one state, such as Ohio or California, but very serious in, for instance, Mississippi. While "common law" crimes are basically illegal in all states, the punishment for any one of them may not be the same in all states. This causes confusion and also makes it very difficult to keep records that communicate useable information on offenders. A computerized "rap sheet," which is a record of an individual's offenses, will usually not describe in detail the nature of a crime in the state from which the conviction was noted. This can cause a problem if, for example, the defendant can be charged with enhanced penalties or a higher level of offense based upon a prior offense. For example, in many states a conviction for petty theft (misdemeanor theft) may elevate a subsequent petty theft to the felony level of grand theft merely on the basis of a prior theft offense. However, unless the title of the prior crime is clear, it could be overlooked. The same is true for registered sex offenders, or morals offenses. In some states, people accused of urinating in public at a party or outside a bar were frequently charged with "indecent exposure." Unfortunately, that offense is now considered a "sex" offense in some states that require offenders to register as "sex offenders," a result that surely was not intended.

The Constitution

Another source of law that significantly influences law enforcement is the Constitution of the United States (see Appendix A). The body of law that has evolved around the Constitution is called, quite simply, **constitutional law**. The Constitution is the "supreme law of the land" (*Marbury v. Madison*, 5 U.S. 137, 2 L. Ed. 60, 1803). This means that no state law may contradict the U.S. Constitution. A constitution plays a specific role in our system of law and politics. Theoretically, it is a grant of power from the people to the government.

Exhibit 12–1

READING CODE AND CASE CITATIONS

Criminal justice students are frequently confronted with footnotes that refer to a case or a statute. How would you find these cases or statutes if you wanted to see the original? The citation attached to each case or statute is the key to finding the original. But what do they mean?

Looking up a Statute   42 USC 1981

The statute noted here is described later in this chapter. Where would you find the original? In citing a statute, common practice requires the *first* number to be the volume or *title* of the code in which this section is found. The second number is the number given to that section of the title. Sections are always in consecutive order (e.g., 1981, 1982, 1983, etc.). The letters in the middle are an abbreviation for the name of the code. The way to read this statute citation is **Title 42, United States Code, section 1981**. Once you know that, all you need to do is find a copy of the Federal Code in the library. Locate the volume labeled 42 (this title may be split into several volumes due to its size). Flip through the pages to section 1981. You will notice that after a code section, there is long list of what are called *annotations.* These are brief summaries of cases (usually short paragraphs) that interpreted that section. This is a good way to see what this code section means.

Looking up a Case   Rizzo v. Goode 423 U.S. 362 (1976)

The case name is assigned by the court issuing the opinion. Case names carry the name of *two* of the parties to the case. There may be more, but this is the official title of the case. The *first* number is the volume of the *reporter* in which the case is found. Reporters literally report cases. In this case, U.S. is read as United States Reports, which is the official reporter for the United States Supreme Court. Volumes are in consecutive order. Every time a case is decided by the Supreme Court, it is placed in the reporter. Cases are placed in consecutive order based upon the date they are decided. Cases appearing in Volume 422, therefore, were announced before this case. The second number is the *page* number of the volume in question. Hence, this case citation is read as **Rizzo versus Goode, volume 423 of the United States Reports, at page 362**. The date, 1976, is used as a reference point only. The volume and page numbers are critical. One set of reference books, called Shepard's Citations, permits you to take the volume and page number of this case (or any case) and look up *the citations of every case that cited this case.* This is how legal research is done. The same process works for statutes and code sections.

That means that the power of government is limited by the terms of the grant (the Constitution).

The Constitution is a contract. Political theorists describe it as a social contract. If you buy a car and you obtain a loan, you agree to pay a certain amount each month. The loan company cannot change the terms of that agreement and make you pay more. In the same way, the Constitution is a limited grant of authority. However, the government (both state and federal) can use every bit of that authority until it is revoked or altered by amending the Constitution. The first portion of the United States Constitution sets out, in very broad terms, the powers of Congress, the President, and the federal judiciary. The Constitution specifically created a Supreme Court, but it left the size of the court to be determined by Congress; the size of the Supreme Court has varied from four members to its current size of nine.

Bill of Rights. While the Constitution itself is a limited grant of authority, there are also specific limitations on the use of that authority. We call these the Bill of Rights (see Appendix A). Generally, people think of these as the first ten amendments to the Constitution. Actually, only the first eight focus on individual rights and privileges. The Ninth and Tenth Amendments attempt to clarify the meaning of limited federal authority and the retention of state roles. The actual meaning of these last two amendments remains the subject of great debate among scholars in constitutional law. The federal Constitution, specifically the Bill of Rights, tends to play more of a restrictive role on law enforcement. The amendments we call the Bill of Rights have been repeatedly interpreted by the Supreme Court of the United States. It is these amendments and their interpretations that have been troublesome for law enforcement, since officers must follow the Court's pronouncements.

Originally, the Bill of Rights did not apply to the states. When the Constitution was reported out from the Constitutional Convention in 1787 for ratification by the 13 former colonies, there was no Bill of Rights. During the debate over approval (ratification) of the Constitution, concern was expressed in many states over the potential power of a centralized government. This concern resulted in the adoption of a Bill of Rights that was attached to the Constitution in 1791. These amendments sought to limit the power of the federal government. They were not intended to apply to the states. The Supreme Court held in 1833 that the Bill of Rights was only a limitation upon the power of the national government (*Barron v. Mayor and City Council of Baltimore*, 32 U.S. 243, 8 L. Ed. 672, 1833). Until the Civil War, this was the understanding of the role of the Bill of Rights.

The Fourteenth Amendment. The Fourteenth Amendment was adopted in 1868, after the Civil War, and was forced on the secessionist states (the Southern states that tried to leave the Union) as part of the terms to end the war. This amendment was designed to restrict the states in their operations and power, an action that seemed necessary after the Civil War. However, that was nearly 80 years before the Fourteenth Amendment was interpreted by the

Supreme Court as protecting individual rights from encroachment by the states. Beginning in the mid-1940s, the Supreme Court held that portions of the Bill of Rights were incorporated into the Fourteenth Amendment (see Exhibit 12–2). This meant that certain rights found in the Bill of Rights were considered to be part of that amendment and, therefore, applicable to the states.

Many restrictions of state power in the area of criminal procedure have resulted from this incorporation approach. For example, a search of one's belongings and a seizure of evidence are restricted by the Fourth Amendment. As a result of the process of the court selecting certain rights for incorporation, restrictions such as these were applied to states and hence to local police. Previously, they applied only to the federal government. The Constitution governs the daily activities of policing officials because it directly limits how officers perform their duties. Because officers take an oath to uphold the Constitution of the United States, they are also restricted by their duty as officers of the Constitution.

Administrative Law

Another source of law that affects the policing function comes from what is known as **administrative law**. This body of law is relatively recent and includes court-made law, agency rules, and statutory law. It had its beginnings with the creation of the civil service and state regulation of the economy in the 1880s. The purpose of administrative law is to guide the process of administrative officers in government agencies and guard against arbitrary decisions. Essentially, the whole of administrative law flows from one central principle, the rule of law, which seeks to remove arbitrariness from decision making (Carter

---

Exhibit 12–2

SECTION 1 OF AMENDMENT XIV TO THE
CONSTITUTION OF THE UNITED STATES

Section 1. All persons born or naturalized in the United States and subject to the jurisdiction thereof, are citizens of the United States and of the State wherein they reside. No State shall make or enforce any law which shall abridge the privileges or immunities of citizens of the United States; nor shall any State deprive any person of life, liberty, or property, without due process of law; nor deny to any person within its jurisdiction the equal protection of the laws.

and Harrington 1991). An arbitrary decision is one that has no clear objective criteria from which to judge each event. If a decision is made without clear criteria, the possibility is very high that the decision will differ from case to case. That is, different standards could be used for different people, which is obviously unfair. This means that decisions of administrative officers must meet, and be based upon, criteria or standards that are applied to each case in the same manner. This area of law impacts law enforcement agencies because, among many other things, it deals with the procedure for hiring, promoting, and disciplining law enforcement officers (see Exhibit 12–3).

Actions of an administrative officer (such as a chief of police) must be based upon statutory authority, but such authority is granted to that administrative officer. This is called *delegation of authority*. It means that a legislative body gave authority to make laws or administrative rules in a certain area to a specific administrative officer or agency. The reasons for establishing administrative law are twofold: (1) Legislatures cannot plan all possible alternative situations within a given law, and (2) Administrative agencies must have some freedom to make rules based upon their experience but guided by the law. Rules must be adopted in a public manner and generally must be supported with some facts. In other words, not only must decisions be free of arbitrariness, but so must rules. For example, a state statute may give chiefs of police authority to make "all necessary rules and regulations for the orderly management" of their department. Relying upon standards of the profession and known training standards, a chief might promulgate (or write) rules that govern procedures for citizen complaints, review of disciplinary actions, job functions, and the like. Usually in agencies these are known as the "Policy and Procedures Manual," but they are not the same from department to department. That is because the chief was given discretion to draw rules, which are merely *guided*

Exhibit 12–3

EXAMPLES OF ADMINISTRATIVE LAW AFFECTING POLICING	
State Training Curriculum	State Labor Relation Procedures
Mandated Selection Criteria	OSHA-type Safety Regulations
Civil Service Testing Procedures	Personnel Appeals Boards
Police Insignia and Uniform Standards	Vehicle/Equipment Bidding Procedures
Promotion Procedures and Criteria	Licensing/Certification Provisions

by some standard principles. However, the rules govern the decisions that fall under them. Hence, the rules are not arbitrary, nor is their application. The rule-making process must produce *written* regulations (oral regulations are not enforceable). A chief executive typically has authority for making rules such as those used in disciplinary procedure. This authority was granted by law. Without clear authority in law, no rule can be made or enforced lawfully.

Additionally, rules must be applied to everyone in the same manner. Exceptions cannot be made. If there are "exceptions," they are based on the rules and, therefore, are not really exceptions. In fact, many administrators, including police, make exceptions. It is important to understand that once exceptions are made, it is difficult to argue that you treat everyone the same. More importantly, because true "exceptions" are outside of the rules, you cannot distinguish between one exception or another. For example, suppose a chief of police has three rookie police officers, each of whom has violated similar, but minor, rules during their field training. Assuming the violations are similar, the chief generally would be required to treat all three similarly (further assuming no other violations existed).

It is clear that each of these sources of law affects law enforcement in many ways. Because law enforcement must respond to all of these areas of law, the environment for law enforcement is growing more and more complex. Law enforcement officers of the past rarely had to worry about such matters. American law continues to evolve, and law enforcement must be alert to these developments.

THE AMERICAN SYSTEM OF JUSTICE

The American system of justice is frequently called a "dual system of justice" because there are two parallel systems of courts. The state court system is typically made up of three levels of courts: trial, appellate, and supreme courts. The federal system is generally designed along the same pattern (see Figure 12–1). Both systems have special types of trial courts, but these courts differ in their jurisdictions (the types of cases a court can hear). Geographical jurisdiction (sometimes called *venue*) means that the courts can hear only cases occurring in their city, county, state, or district. Some federal courts, such as the U.S. Supreme Court, have no geographical limits and theoretically may hear a case originating anywhere in the United State or its territories as long as it is on appeal (the original jurisdiction of the Supreme Court is very limited).* Other jurisdictional factors involve the seriousness of the case. If a case is civil but involves a small amount of money, jurisdiction may be restricted to a municipal court. The same is frequently true for misdemeanor of-

---

*Original jurisdiction means the case can only be filed with the U.S. Supreme Court, for example, if one state sues another over a boundary dispute.

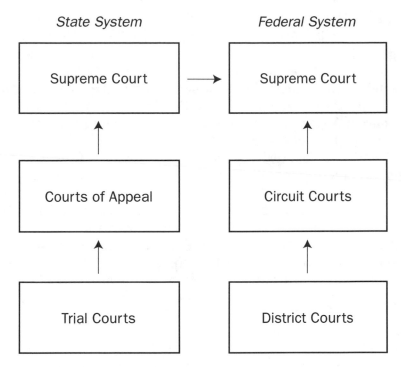

Figure 12–1 The Dual Court System of the United States

fenses in criminal codes, which is an example of jurisdiction based upon the substance of the case.

Federal Courts

Generally speaking (though not always), federal courts cannot hear cases based upon state law, and state courts cannot hear cases based upon federal law. For example, the federal system employs bankruptcy courts for the special function of trying cases of economic bankruptcy. No state court can hear a bankruptcy claim. In the same manner, a federal trial court such as the Federal District Court cannot hear a case based upon a state's criminal law. State courts can interpret the United States Constitution, but the federal judiciary has the final word on this interpretation. State supreme courts have the final say in the interpretation of state law, as long as it does not involve a federal constitutional question. Law enforcement officers at the state and local government level rarely have contact with federal criminal courts, unless working on cases jointly with federal agents.

There are only two ways that a state criminal case can be heard by a federal court. First, a defendant might appeal an issue such as the constitutionality of an ordinance or state law. Initially, a state trial court rules on such a claim. Regardless of the results of such a ruling, the losing side has the right to appeal. Appeals go to the state courts of appeal. Similarly, the court of appeals has the authority to rule on the issue. Again, the losing side may then seek an appeal to that state's highest court. (In most states the highest court is called the Supreme Court. However, in New York, the Supreme Court is the trial court and the Court of Appeals is the highest court. The names of courts usually indicate their level, but not always.)

In most states, the Supreme Court of that state can refuse an appeal at its discretion. Whether refused or heard, however, the losing side may still ask the Supreme Court of the United States to hear the case when it involves a federal question that was heard by the highest court in that state. This is done by petitioning the Supreme Court to issue a **writ of certiorari**, which is an order requiring the lower court to give the Supreme Court the record for review. Taking a case to the U.S. Supreme Court is rare, however. Millions of cases, both criminal and civil, are filed in the United States annually, yet only about 5,000 appeals are filed with the Supreme Court each year, and, in a given year, the Supreme Court generally hears only about 100 of those cases. Because state courts are usually bound by *stare decisis* on constitutional issues, they will rarely contradict a rule that the Supreme Court of the United States previously announced as one that would invite a rebuke from the U.S. Supreme Court.

A second method by which a state criminal case can be heard in a federal court is less rare, but still not very frequent. If a prisoner exhausts all traditional appeals after conviction (as discussed above), there is usually little that can be done. However, if the law upon which he or she was convicted is later challenged or if there is new evidence that was not known at the time of trial, the prisoner may seek a federal writ of habeas corpus. This is an order requiring the person who is holding the prisoner, such as a warden or sheriff, to show cause why the prisoner should not be released. It is not truly a criminal case at this stage, but rather a civil case based upon federal law. If the court issues the writ, the prisoner must be released. The state may appeal to the U.S. Court of Appeals or, if need be, the Supreme Court of the United States.

State Courts

States divide trial responsibility between courts of general jurisdiction and those of limited jurisdiction. The former are generally organized along county boundaries. Some general jurisdiction courts are called *common pleas* or *superior* courts. These courts typically hear serious misdemeanors and all felonies as well as large civil lawsuits. Lower state trial courts such as *municipal* or *county* courts generally have jurisdiction over traffic cases and misdemeanors as well as uncomplicated civil lawsuits such as small claims. Boundaries of courts with limited jurisdiction are usually within one county but encompass only a portion of that county. Some of these lower courts also have the power to hear the beginning of a felony case, called a **preliminary hearing**. This is a hearing to determine if there is sufficient evidence to send the case to the district attorney or grand jury for further prosecution.

Trial Courts. Law enforcement officers who go to court will spend most of their time in state trial courts. When an officer makes an arrest, contact with the local court is initiated. Arrests may be the result of either officer discretion or a warrant for arrest previously issued by a court. Officer discretion arrests occur when an officer determines that **probable cause** exists to arrest. Probable cause is not always easy to define, but one U.S. Supreme Court decision described it this way:

> Probable cause exists where the facts and circumstances within their [arresting officers'] knowledge and of which they had reasonably trustworthy information [are] sufficient in themselves to warrant a [person] of reasonable caution in the belief that an offense has been or is being committed [by the person to be arrested]." *Brinegar v. United States* 338 U.S. 160, 175–176 (1949).

A determination to arrest may be subject to review first by the officer's supervisor. After the officer submits a report justifying the action, a formal approval or disapproval is noted by the supervisor. In practice, many who are arrested are released at the discretion of the officer and his or her supervisors. Written reports reflect the justification for the action.

Those who study the relationship between law enforcement and the courts notice certain behaviors that reflect the experience of working with one another. For example, even though probable cause may exist, an experienced officer, detective, or supervisor may know that there is insufficient evidence to satisfy the judge or district attorney likely to handle the case. Hence, the officers may decide to dispose of the matter at their level. Sometimes officers release a suspect because of assistance the suspect gave with a co-suspect or on another case. It is also possible that on further investigation the case looked different or another suspect emerged. Any number of reasons could produce a release.

In many cases, officer discretion will prevail. However, it is also possible that an assistant district attorney (ADA) or assistant prosecutor will review the reports and initial charges and make an *independent* determination whether or not to proceed with the charge. Frequently, officers confer with an ADA in order to get advice on cases. Once a charge is made, it may also be reviewed by a court in a probable cause hearing (for misdemeanors) or a preliminary hearing (for felonies). In each case, the purpose of the hearing is to determine whether there is sufficient evidence to proceed with the charge. At any stage of the proceedings, a court has the authority to dismiss a case with or without prejudice. If it is dismissed with prejudice, the charge cannot be re-filed at a later date regardless of the evidence then available. If it is dismissed without prejudice, the charge may be re-filed. Less than 1 percent of all felony arrests are dropped due to legal "technicalities," and most of these are drug cases.

Arrest warrants are issued by a court after a probable cause hearing by an officer of the court, or as the result of an **indictment** by a grand jury, or by the issuance of a **prosecutor's information**. In each case, the investigating officers must present testimony to justify issuance. The process varies slightly from state to state, but similar in all. If a charge is formally approved and moves to the warrant stage, the next step is either a dismissal, a plea, or a trial. If there is a plea to the charges, it may involve what is called a *plea bargain.* Typically this involves a discussion involving defense counsel, the prosecutor, and a judge. Law enforcement officers are frequently involved in plea discussions and should be prepared to make their case. It is possible that other participants in plea discussions will include probation officers, psychologists, social workers, and victims.

The process of plea bargaining produces heated debate in nearly every corner of the United States. Some argue that it saves time and money because it eliminates trials. If the plea bargaining incentive were eliminated, defendants might decide to try their case since they could not receive a worse sentence for doing so. In effect, there would be nothing to lose by going to trial. Since only about 9 percent or less of all cases go to trial (see Figure 12–2), even a slight increase in trials would overwhelm the already overburdened justice system. Not only would more officers spend their time waiting in courthouse hallways to testify, we would need to add more clerks and court personnel. Further, more citizens would have their lives disrupted for jury service. The cost in additional judges and prosecutors (who would not be available for other duties) would be tremendous. Others argue that deals should not be made with criminals, and the cost should be absorbed by the current system.

If there is no plea in the case or if it is not dismissed, the case will go to trial. Before a trial begins, and in some states during trial, hearings may occur that determine the admissibility of evidence. These are sometimes called **suppression hearings**. Evidence may be suppressed because of the manner in which it was seized, because it was not presented to the other side during pretrial discovery, or because of some legal restriction on its use (such as forcing a priest to testify about a parishioner).

Appellate Courts. While lower trial courts may rule on matters such as the admission of evidence or the constitutionality of a law, it is the state courts of appeal that settle disputes of law by interpreting state law or the state and federal constitutions. Consequently, these courts have a large impact on law enforcement, though officers rarely attend the oral arguments before such courts. These courts may hear criminal and civil appeals. These same courts hear appeals from lower courts involving civil service issues and related disputes including law enforcement hiring and discipline. Because lower courts are re-

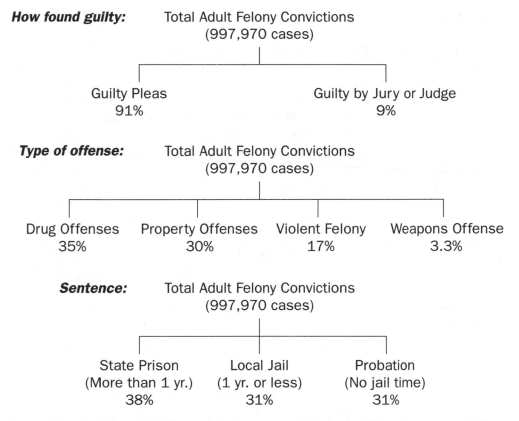

Source: Reprinted from J.M. Brown, P.A. Langan, and D.J. Levin, *Felony Sentences in State Courts, 1996,* May 1999, U.S. Department of Justice, Office of Justice Programs, Bureau of Justice Statistics.

Figure 12–2 State Felony Convictions, 1996

quired to follow the precedents of the appeals courts, appeals decisions shape behavior in the courts below.

THE IMPACT OF COURTS AND THE LAW

In the beginning of this chapter, we examined the sources of law which impact law enforcement. We also reviewed the structure of courts that make the rules that impact law enforcement. Now we are going to examine *how* law enforcement is affected by the various kinds of law. We will also examine *why* law enforcement must consider these issues at the patrol level. The issues in this chapter are of particular interest to patrol officers and their immediate supervisors because most law enforcing takes place at the patrol level.

State Law

One obvious place to begin is the statutory criminal law. In the United States, no act is a crime unless it is defined by a statute. While t many issues in this field must be addressed in a course in criminal law, there are certain aspects that are basic limitations of law enforcement and are briefly discussed here.

Elements of Crimes. First we must acknowledge that each crime defined by statute contains certain **elements**. The elements of a crime are the basic parts of that crime. In determining guilt, *each* element must be proved beyond a reasonable doubt to the trier of fact (a judge or jury). In any trial, only the judge has the authority to decide what law applies to the case. The trier of fact must apply that law and determine whether the facts establish each of the elements of the crime beyond a reasonable doubt. In other words, if you have clear evidence of every element of a crime but one, and on that one you have barely any evidence, you cannot establish guilt. State courts of appeal frequently are asked to examine trials in lower state courts to determine if there was "substantial evidence" for each element. If there *is* substantial evidence, the discretion or judgment of the trier of fact will not be overturned. If the evidence is considered to be less than substantial, courts of appeal may overturn the findings by the trier of fact and reverse the conviction. (Exhibit 12–4 describes the U.S. Supreme Court's interpretation of "beyond a reasonable doubt" in the decision of *In Re: Winship.*)

Actus Reus. Criminal statutes must include, as elements, the actions of the defendant. This also called the **actus reus**. In order for a crime to have happened, there must have been some act. You cannot be prosecuted for merely thinking about things or for being in a particular condition. The *actus reus* may be an affirmative act (doing something) or a negative act (failing to do something). For any act to be called criminal, it must be defined as such by statute. Some of the meanings of the elements may, in some states, rely upon common law definitions. In other states, all terms are defined in the code (Samaha 1990; Reid 1998; Boyce and Perkins 1898).

Mental States. Most criminal statutes require the state to prove that the defendant exhibited a particular mental state. The mental state of a defendant does not refer to the defendant's sanity. Rather, it addresses the degree of culpability (blame) the defendant exhibited. Mental state was known in common law as **mens rea**, or a guilty mind. There are different levels or degrees of culpability. The degree of culpability is merely the degree to which the defendant is responsible for his or her actions. Some crimes specifically include a state of mind, such as *intent* or *purpose* to commit the act charged. Other statutes require a demonstration that the defendant was *reckless* in his or her behavior. Besides purposely and recklessly, other mental states are *knowingly* and *negligently* (see Exhibit 12–5). One who acts intentionally, knowingly, or purposely

Exhibit 12–4

IN RE WINSHIP, 397 U.S. 358 (1970)

The requirement that guilt of a criminal charge be established by proof beyond a reasonable doubt dates at least from our early years as a Nation. The demand for a higher degree of persuasion in criminal cases was recurrently expressed from ancient times, [though] its crystallization into the formula "beyond a reasonable doubt" seems to have occurred as late as 1798. It is now accepted in common law jurisdictions as the measure of persuasion by which the prosecution must convince the trier of all the essential elements of guilt. Although virtually unanimous adherence to the reasonable-doubt standard in common-law jurisdictions may not conclusively establish it as a requirement of due process, such adherence does "reflect a profound judgment about the way in which law should be enforced and justice administered," *Duncan v. Louisiana*, 391 U.S. 145, 155 (1968) . . .

Expressions in many opinions of this Court indicate that it has long been assumed that proof of a criminal charge beyond a reasonable doubt is constitutionally required. . . . The requirement of proof beyond a reasonable doubt has this vital role in our criminal procedure for cogent reasons. The accused during a criminal prosecution has at stake interests of immense importance, both because of the possibility that he may lose his liberty upon conviction and because of the certainty that he would be stigmatized by the conviction. Accordingly, a society that values the good name and freedom of every individual should not condemn a man for commission of a crime when there is reasonable doubt about his guilt.

Moreover, use of the reasonable-doubt standard is indispensable to command the respect and confidence of the community in applications of the criminal law. It is critical that the moral force of the criminal law not be diluted by a standard of proof that leaves people in doubt whether innocent men are being condemned. It is also important in our free society that every individual going about his ordinary affairs have confidence that his government cannot adjudge him guilty of a criminal offense without convincing a proper factfinder of his guilt with utmost certainty.

Exhibit 12–5

SAMPLE STATUTE REGARDING PROOF OF DEFENDANT'S STATE OF MIND

Section 2901.22 Requirements of Culpability.

(A) A person acts **purposely** when it is his specific intention to cause a certain result, or, when the gist of the offense is a prohibition against conduct of a certain nature, regardless of what the offender intends to accomplish thereby, it is his specific intention to engage in conduct of that nature.

(B) A person acts **knowingly**, regardless of his purpose, when he is aware that his conduct will probably cause a certain result or will probably be of a certain nature. A person has knowledge of circumstances when he is aware that such circumstances probably exist.

(C) A person acts **recklessly** when, with heedless indifference to the consequences, he perversely disregards a known risk that his conduct is likely to cause a certain result or is likely to be of a certain nature. A person is reckless with respect to circumstances when, with heedless indifference to the consequences, he perversely disregards a known risk that such circumstances are likely to exist.

(D) A person acts **negligently** when, because of a substantial lapse from due care, he fails to perceive or avoid a risk that his conduct may cause a certain result or may be of a certain nature. A person is negligent with respect to circumstances when, because of a substantial lapse from due care, he fails to perceive or avoid a risk that such circumstances may exist.

---

commits a more serious offense than one who committed the same acts recklessly or negligently. In the first case, the defendant thought about the action before committing it. In the latter case, the defendant ignored a duty or was not careful in thinking about the likely results of his actions. Culpability terminology is usually in the state criminal code sections that officers must interpret for purposes of enforcement. Officers must recognize the differences in the degrees of culpability in order to properly apply the elements of offenses to situations they encounter in society.

For example, suppose two men fired guns in separate incidents. The first man fired at one person, intending to injure or kill that person, but instead hit another standing nearby. The second man, celebrating New Year's Eve, fires his gun in the air not intending to hit the person who is struck with the bullet on its way down. In the first case, it was an intentional act to fire the gun with the intent to hit someone. The fact that he hit the wrong person is irrelevant. In the second case, the defendant was reckless or negligent in his discharge of a weapon. Clearly, these are differences based upon the mental states of the two men.

Crimes that focus on individuals also generally require a showing of harm to that person that was caused by the defendant's acts. But some crimes, such as driving under influence (DUI), require neither a showing of harm nor a particular mental state. These statutes require only what is called **general intent**. This simply means that the individual voluntarily committed an act, and the law "presumes" the defendant intended that act. This presumption is non-rebuttable. This means that the law assumes he meant to take the action, and this assumption is not subject to challenge. For example, in the case of a DUI, it is sufficient to establish that the defendant drove an automobile while under the influence of alcohol. What was in the defendant's mind is not an element of the offense. This is also called **strict liability** and is frequently imposed for such criminal acts as DUI. No evidence regarding intent or mental state is necessary. **Specific intent**, however, is a requirement that the state show the defendant purposely intended to violate the law. This is a higher level of culpability than negligent, reckless, or knowing states of mind. In the example above, the first man had specific intent to fire his gun and injure another person. The second man acted recklessly. In practice, the level of culpability is rarely so clear and is one major justification for plea bargaining, previously discussed.

Defenses. There are a few other aspects in the use of criminal law by law enforcement that deserve mention because they serve to complicate the interpretation of facts in any given case. These restrictions are called **defenses**. A defense to a crime is a means of escaping criminal liability. Essentially, a defense permits defendants to claim that while they did commit the acts charged, they should not be held criminally liable for those actions.

An example is infancy or immaturity. In common law, children under age seven were presumed to be incapable of committing a crime since they could not form the necessary *mens rea*. Those from ages seven through fifteen were treated similarly, but the presumption was rebuttable (Klotter 1994). In our own time, such a rule seems ridiculous, and a trip to the local juvenile court would confirm this. But the age of seven or eight is still used in most statutes as the lower limit of criminal liability. The recent rash of school shootings by teenagers has fueled the debate to abandon such common law distinctions.

Another defense, sometimes called an excuse, does not deny the wrongness of the act. Rather, it asks that the defendant be blameless despite the wrongness of the act charged. An example is insanity, sometimes called diminished capacity or mental impairment. An insane person cannot form the mental states necessary for most crimes (see Exhibit 12–6). Other excuses include duress and **entrapment**. Entrapment occurs when law enforcement officials are found to have enticed a defendant into a criminal act (see Exhibit 12–7). Duress (or compulsion) occurs when someone acts under the imminent threat and apprehension of death or serious bodily harm if they fail to act. This is rarely used.

The reasons for these defenses are important to understand. As we note elsewhere, if someone commits a crime because of peculiar circumstances out of their control, there is little social purpose in punishing them. For example, one justification for punishment is deterrence. An insane person, or one under threat of harm (duress), will not be deterred from committing an act in the future. Moreover, it is questionable whether they have the intent or *mens rea* necessary to deserve blame.

Justifications are defenses that seek to avoid criminal liability by arguing that while the defendant did commit the acts in question, the defendant did the right thing in the circumstances he or she faced. These include **self-defense** and necessity. The justification of self-defense is a typical claim for the use of violence. Self-defense is generally permitted where it is necessary to use violence to protect yourself or another from imminent harm. For the police officer, justification is actually based upon necessity. For example, if an officer uses deadly force, the central question will be whether the use of such force was justified by the circumstances. A ruling that a shooting was "a good shoot" is really a finding that it was justifiable in order to protect human life or execute official duties. As noted below, issues involving deadly force by officers invite much dispute.

Each kind of defense is based upon a history in the common law, and each is ancient in its derivation. However, just as crimes are now defined by statute, so too are defenses. They are interpreted by courts, prosecutors, and (informally) by juries. Therefore, just as conduct may be criminal in one state and not in another, the use and application of any defense also tends to vary across states. What is considered necessary to establish insanity in one state will not suffice in another. In the same manner that the criminal code expresses the accepted norms of society, defenses express the same sorts of norms. Law enforcement officers must understand that these limitations are the expression of the society they serve, even if they disagree with these norms.

Procedural Limitations on Law Enforcement

The substantive criminal law is carefully defined by statute. Unfortunately, the procedural restrictions on law enforcement are not so clear to identify or

Exhibit 12–6

INSANITY AS A DEFENSE

Courts continue to struggle with the idea of insanity. Criminal law attempts to distinguish between the action of human beings based, in part, on the mental state of the defendant. Intentional acts should be punished more harshly than reckless or negligent acts. But if a person is insane, is it possible to act intentionally, or even negligently? Generally, the law suggests it is not possible. But how do we judge when someone is insane? That is the question with which law has struggled for over 150 years.

When Daniel M'Naghten killed the assistant to English Prime Minister Sir Robert Peel in 1843, M'Naghten was acquitted due to insanity, and the court developed a test. Essentially, a defendant was not responsible if (1) the act was the result of a defect of reason, (2) caused by a disease of the mind, and, therefore, (3) could not distinguish between right and wrong.

Other courts had problems applying the **M'Naghten rule** and attempted refinements. The **irresistible impulse rule** excused the conduct when the defendant could not prevent himself or herself from committing the act. The **Durham rule** attempted to simplify the question. It held that a defendant should be held blameless if the act was the product of insanity.

The Model Penal Code attempted to clarify the various approaches. It held that a person is not responsible for a crime if a mental disease or defect produced a lack of substantial capacity either to appreciate the criminality of the conduct or to conform to the law. It also provides that repeated antisocial or criminal behavior is not evidence of a defect or a disease. Some states avoided the entire question by creating the **insane but guilty** standard. If found insane but guilty, the defendant is confined in a mental institution for a period of years *and* until diagnosed well.

---

learn. They are unclear because they are based upon relatively vague constitutional provisions such as due process and *unreasonable searches and seizures.* We will consider only an overview of procedural limitations here, but the restrictions are considerable.

There are many procedural restrictions that impact the functioning of law enforcement agencies, but among the most significant are without question those applying to searches and seizures. For both, law enforcement is bound

Exhibit 12–7

SAMPLE STATUTE PROVIDING ENTRAPMENT AS A DEFENSE

§13–206. Entrapment

A. It is an affirmative defense to a criminal charge that the person was entrapped. To claim entrapment, the person must admit by the person's testimony or other evidence the substantial elements of the offense charged.

B. A person who asserts an entrapment defense has the burden of proving the following by clear and convincing evidence:

1. The idea of committing the offense started with law enforcement officers or their agents rather than with the person.

2. The law enforcement officers or their agents urged and induced the person to commit the offense.

3. The person was not predisposed to commit the type of offense charged before the law enforcement officers or their agents urged and induced the person to commit the offense.

C. A person does not establish entrapment if the person was predisposed to commit the offense and the law enforcement officers or their agents merely provided the person with an opportunity to commit the offense. It is not entrapment for law enforcement officers or their agents merely to use a ruse or to conceal their identity. The conduct of law enforcement officers and their agents may be considered in determining if a person has proven entrapment.

D. If a person raises an entrapment defense, the court shall instruct the jurors that the person has admitted the elements of the offense and that the only issue for their consideration is whether the person has proven the affirmative defense of entrapment by clear and convincing evidence.

---

by the Fourth Amendment to the Constitution of the United States and the interpretations that have been made of its language:

> The right of the people to be secure in their persons, houses, papers, and effects, against unreasonable searches and seizures, shall not be violated, and no warrants shall issue, but upon probable cause, supported by oath or affirmation, and

particularly describing the place to be searched, and the persons or things to be seized.

A **search** is generally defined as the invasion, by an agent of the state, of an area which a person believes is protected or private. That belief will be upheld and a search negated by a court if the "person exhibited an actual (subjective) expectation of privacy, and . . . the expectation is one that society is prepared to recognize as 'reasonable'" (*Katz v. United States*, 389 U.S. 347, 361, 1967).

A **seizure** is generally defined as a "meaningful interference with the possessory interests of the suspect" (*United States v. Jacobsen*, 466 U.S. 109, 113, 1984). The Fourth Amendment applies to searches and seizures of evidence in the same way it applies to arrests. A search or seizure of evidence without a warrant is presumed to be unreasonable. Exhibit 12–8 depicts the standard introductory wording associated with a search warrant and affidavit request used in the County of Butte, California. As stated, an officer would attach the statement of probable cause and submit the affidavit to a magistrate or judge when requesting a search warrant. Such formats and language will vary among states and jurisdictions and may be totally separate documents. Note that on the search warrant portion, detailed information would be entered about the place to be searched and the items for which to search. A search can be of a person or a person's property. Similarly, a seizure may be of property, but it may also be of a person. The latter are called arrests. After arrest, suspects are questioned, and the questioning process is limited by the Fifth and Sixth Amendments.

The general rule of searches and seizures holds that without a warrant, any search or seizure is presumed to be unconstitutional (See *Payton v. New York*, 445 U.S. 573, 1980 and *Chimel v. California,* 395 U.S. 752, 1969). The Fourth Amendment does not require a warrant; it only prohibits a search or seizure that is "unreasonable." The Supreme Court of the United States firmly established the doctrine that absence of a warrant raises the presumption that the search or seizure in question is unreasonable and, therefore, unconstitutional. The court also created many exceptions to this doctrine that serve to rebut the presumption of unreasonableness. In effect, the court made these exceptions statements of reasonableness. If any of the recognized exceptional circumstances apply, the search or seizure is considered reasonable. The ability to understand search and seizure limits on law enforcement, therefore, depends upon one's knowledge of the exceptions to the warrant rule.

Arrest of the Person. The Supreme Court traditionally interpreted arrest to mean any substantial limit upon the ability of a person to freely come and go. Recently that same court revised that principle: "An arrest requires either physical force . . . or, where that is absent, submission to the assertion of authority . . . " (*California v. Hodari D.*, 499 U.S. 621, 1991). When is a warrantless arrest an "unreasonable" seizure under the Fourth Amendment? Generally speaking, the following rules have emerged. An arrest is reasonable if *one* of the following is true:

Exhibit 12–8

STATE OF CALIFORNIA—COUNTY OF BUTTE
SEARCH WARRANT AND AFFIDAVIT

(Affidavit)

_____, being sworn, says that on the basis of the informa-

(Name of Affiant)   tion contained within this Search Warrant and Affi-
davit and the attached and incorporated Statement of Probable Cause, he/she has
probable cause to believe and does believe that the property described below is lawfully seizable pursuant to Penal Code Section 1524, as indicated below, and is now located at the locations set forth below. Wherefore, affiant requests that this Search Warrant be issued.

_____, NIGHT SEARCH REQUESTED: YES [ ]   NO [ ]

(Signature of Affiant)

(SEARCH WARRANT)

THE PEOPLE OF THE STATE OF CALIFORNIA TO ANY SHERIFF, POLICEMAN OR PEACE
OFFICER IN THE COUNTY OF BUTTE: proof by affidavit having been made before me by

_____

(Name of Affiant)

that there is probable cause to believe that the property described herein may be found
at the locations set forth herein and that it is lawfully seizable pursuant to Penal Code
Section 1524 as indicated below by "x" in that it:

_____ was stolen or embezzled.

_____ was used the means of committing a felony

_____ is possessed by a person with the intent to use it as means of committing a
public offense or is possessed by another to whom he or she may have delivered it for the purpose of concealing it or preventing its discovery

_____ tends to show that a felony has been committed or that a particular person
has committed a felony.

_____ tends to show that sexual exploitation of a child, in violation of P.C. Section
311.3 has occurred or is occurring.

YOU ARE THEREFORE COMMANDED TO SEARCH:

FOR THE FOLLOWING PROPERTY:

AND TO SEIZE IT IF FOUND and bring it forthwith before me, or this court, at the courthouse of this court. This Search Warrant and incorporated Affidavit was sworn to and
subscribed before me this _____ day of _____, _____, at _____ A.M./P.M.
Wherefore, I find probable cause for the issuance of this Search Warrant and do issue it.

_____, NIGHT SEARCH APPROVED: YES [ ]   NO [ ]

(Signature of Magistrate)

Courtesy of Sheriff Scott A. Mackenzie, Butte County Sheriff's Office, Oroville, California.

1. The offense was committed in the presence of an officer;
2. The offense is a felony, and the officer has probable cause to be believe the defendant committed it;
3. The offense, though a misdemeanor, is one of violence, and the officer has probable cause to believe that the defendant committed the offense (the test most applicable to domestic violence cases, for example). This applies whether or not the offense was committed in the presence of the officer.

Each of these exceptions relies upon the establishment of probable cause. It is certainly easier to establish probable cause if the officer *sees* the defendant assault someone or commit some other offense. Otherwise, law enforcement officers must rely upon their training, education, and experience to determine if probable cause is present and sufficient to justify a warrantless arrest.

If the case falls outside these exceptions, then law enforcement officials must seek the issuance of an arrest warrant based upon the evidence available. This typically requires a "neutral magistrate" (typically a judge or, in some states, a clerk of courts) to determine whether sufficient evidence exists for a warrant to issue. The same standard of probable cause used for warrantless arrests applies for the issuance of a warrant.

The reason for the general warrant requirement is to reduce the likelihood of arbitrary arrests. The reason for the *exceptions* to the warrant requirement is the belief that in those circumstances set forth above, arrest without a warrant is "reasonable" within the meaning of the Fourth Amendment. For example, it makes sense that if a crime is committed in front of an officer, it would frustrate the meaning of justice in a civil society to delay arrest. Similar rationales are used by courts in the other circumstances. However, it is still good practice to obtain a warrant if there is time to do so. The risk of being wrong is not worth mere convenience.

Search and Seizure. There are also a multitude of circumstances that are clearly law enforcement–initiated stops, but that may or may not reach the status of being full arrests. These require careful study by law enforcement. While the restrictions on the seizure or arrest of an individual are relatively clear, the restrictions that cover a search of a person or his property and seizure of that property are less clear. It is frequently the case that stops, searches, and seizures are closely related in the field.

However, as with arrest, there are various specific exceptions that permit law enforcement officers to engage in searches for evidence, and the seizure thereof, without a warrant to do so. One way to think of these exceptions to the warrant rule is to imagine the expectation of privacy as a cave. The deeper law enforcement seeks to go into the cave, the greater the justification it needs. The exceptions to the warrant rule focus on the question of how reasonable the claimed expectation of privacy may be in the particular circumstances of that search. Some of the most important of these exceptions we address next.

Stop and Frisk. Most of us would expect to have some privacy as we walk along a public street. But our behavior, if not criminal *per se*, may lead others to conclude that we *may* be preparing to commit a crime. In *Terry v. Ohio* (392 U.S. 1, 1968), Chief Justice Earl Warren of the United States Supreme Court contemplated a case in which a Cleveland, Ohio, police detective saw such activity (Exhibit 12–9). In the holding, the Court announced the rule for **"stop and frisk"** cases. While the court permitted a "pat down" of the outer clothing for weapons, a full search of the person was not reasonable in the circumstances. The Court recently revisited this issue and focused on a pat down that

Exhibit 12–9

STOP AND FRISK

We merely hold today that where a police officer observes unusual conduct which leads him reasonably to conclude in light of his experience that criminal activity may be afoot and that the persons with whom he is dealing may be armed and presently dangerous, where in the course of investigating this behavior he identifies himself as a policeman and makes reasonable inquiries, and where nothing in the initial stages of the encounter serves to dispel his reasonable fear for his own or others' safety, he is entitled for the protection of himself and others in the area to conduct a carefully limited search of the outer clothing of such persons in an attempt to discover weapons which might be used to assault him. *Terry v. Ohio*, 392 U.S. 1, (1968).

It remains unclear how many different types of non-arrest detentions might usefully or perhaps must be distinguished for Fourth Amendment purposes. Those detentions of major concern are what is often called "investigatory stops," "investigatory detentions," "field stops," or— memorializing Terry v. Ohio—"*Terry* stops." They are widely assumed to be detentions made in the field for the purposes of gathering further information upon which to base a decision as to whether or not to arrest the suspect. It is similarly assumed that they are and should be effected in situations presenting inadequate grounds for arrest and that they cannot involve either prolonged detention of the suspect or substantial movement of the suspect during the detention.

Source: Reprinted with permission from F.W. Miller et al., *The Police Function*, 5th ed., p. 210, © 1991, Foundation Press, Inc.

found not weapons, but crack cocaine. The Court found that while an officer could seize something other than a weapon after a stop-and-frisk pat down, the nature of the item would need to be clear after a mere pat down. In reversing the conviction in this case, the Court found that the officer had to manipulate the item through the outer clothing to determine what it might be. That, the Court held, was going too far.

Search Incident to Arrest. Another exception, rarely commented upon but the subject of many Supreme Court cases, is the limit of a search incident to arrest. When a person is lawfully arrested (by warrant or otherwise), law enforcement officers may search the immediate vicinity of the person in order to secure any weapons or evidence within the suspect's reach (*Chimel v. California*, 395 U.S. 752, 1969). This does not include an entire house or even an entire car or locked baggage in a car. However, officers may conduct a "protective sweep" of a house to search very briefly for more victims or potential assailants who may pose a threat to the officers if the officers might reasonably expect to find such persons (*Maryland v. Buie*, 494 U.S. 325, 1990). Obviously, people do not hide in cupboards or in drawers, so this is a limited exception, taken by itself.

Automobile Exception. Officers may also conduct a full search of a vehicle at the time of an arrest or stop if there is probable cause to believe the vehicle contains evidence of a crime. This includes any packages or bags in the car (*Carroll v. United States*, 267 U.S. 132, 1925; *California v. Acevedo*, 500 U.S. 565, 1991). The theory behind the automobile exception is, first, that cars are mobile and can carry away the evidence they contain. Second, automobiles are highly regulated and, therefore, offer a low expectation of privacy. Hence, if a reliable informant suggests that a bag in the trunk contains drugs, the car may be stopped and the trunk searched, as may any bag in the trunk. However, this probable cause would not necessarily transfer to a suitcase in the back seat. Absent probable cause to search an automobile, officers may only search for weapons in the areas immediately within the reach of the occupant(s) (*Adams v. Williams*, 407 U.S. 143, 1972). This is the automobile version of a stop and frisk.

Some commentators refer to this as an **exigent circumstances** search. Exigent circumstances refer to the conditions that create a need for immediate action to prevent the destruction of evidence. But the Supreme Court made it clear that the automobile exception to the warrant rule is not that simple. For one thing, *exigent circumstances cannot create probable cause* or even reasonable suspicion. Second, the fact that an automobile is the subject of the search does not create an exigent circumstance. The automobile (or other vehicle) may add to the conditions, but alone it is not enough to create exigent circumstances. The touchstone of the exception is the pre-existence of probable cause. Probable cause may exist before the stop or it may develop in the course of a routine traffic stop. But without probable cause, only a *Terry* type of weapons check is permissible. Exhibit 12–10 illustrates the complexity involved in legal issues surrounding automobile searches.

In April of 1999, the U.S. Supreme Court ruled in *Wyoming v. Houghton* (No. 98–184) that when law enforcement officers have probable cause to search a car, they may inspect passengers' belongings found in the car that are capable

---

Exhibit 12–10

CALIFORNIA v. ACEVEDO, 500 U.S. 565 (1991)

BLACKMUN, J., delivered the opinion of the Court,

Although we have recognized firmly that the doctrine of stare decisis serves profoundly important purposes in our legal system, this Court has overruled a prior case on the comparatively rare occasion when it has bred confusion or been a derelict or led to anomalous results.

In the case before us, *the police had probable cause to believe that the paper bag in the automobile's trunk contained marijuana.* That probable cause now allows a warrantless search of the paper bag. The facts in the record reveal that *the police did not have probable cause to believe that contraband was hidden in any other part of the automobile and a search of the entire vehicle would have been without probable cause and unreasonable under the Fourth Amendment.*

Our holding today neither extends the *Carroll* doctrine nor broadens the scope of the permissible automobile search delineated in *Carroll*, *Chambers*, and *Ross*. It remains a cardinal principle that "searches conducted outside the judicial process, without prior approval by judge or magistrate, are per se unreasonable under the Fourth Amendment— subject only to a few specifically established and well-delineated exceptions." *Mincey v. Arizona*, 437 U.S. 385, 390 (1978), quoting *Katz v. United States*, 389 U.S. 347, 357 (1967).

Until today, this Court has drawn a curious line between the search of an automobile that coincidentally turns up a container and the search of a container that coincidentally turns up in an automobile. The protections of the Fourth Amendment must not turn on such coincidences. We therefore interpret *Carroll* as providing one rule to govern all automobile searches. The police may search an automobile and the containers within it where they have probable cause to believe contraband or evidence is contained. (Emphasis added.)

of concealing the object of the search (see Exhibit 12–11). This decision has triggered additional debate among civil libertarians who believe the law enforcement community will abuse the ruling. The U.S. Supreme Court's opinion stated:

> Whereas the passenger's privacy expectations are, as we have described, considerably diminished, the governmental interests at stake are substantial. Effective law enforcement would be appreciably impaired without the ability to search a passenger's personal belongings when there is reason to believe contraband or evidence of criminal wrongdoing is hidden in the car. As in all car-search cases, the "ready mobility" of an automobile creates a risk that the evidence or contraband will be permanently lost while a warrant is obtained . . .

The Court added that "[w]hen balancing the competing interests, our determinations of 'reasonableness' under the Fourth Amendment must take account of these practical realities. We think they militate in favor of the needs of law enforcement, and against a personal-privacy interest that is ordinarily weak."

Administrative Searches. Officers may seize a vehicle when the driver is arrested or the automobile is evidence in a crime, and they may conduct an impoundment (or inventory) search. If personal belongings or automobiles are routinely seized at arrest as a matter of departmental policy, these may be fully searched in order to protect the property of the defendant and to protect officers from claims of property theft, loss, or damage. There must be some departmental rule or standard practice that supports an impoundment (*South Dakota v. Opperman*, 428 U.S. 364, 1976; *Chambers v. Maloney*, 399 U.S. 42, 1970). Any evidence found in the process of such a search may be seized.

Another type of administrative search is the *sobriety checkpoint*. Automobiles may be stopped and the driver directed to answer questions if certain conditions are met. First, the initial stop at a checkpoint must be directed at all vehicles passing the point. Second, the intrusion must be minimal in order to remain "reasonable" under the standards of the Fourth Amendment. Merely stopping each car briefly in order to make limited inquiries is reasonable. Further inquiries, such as field sobriety testing, could be done if and only if the initial contact produced reasonable suspicion to proceed further (*Michigan Department of State Police v. Sitz*, 496 U.S. 444, 1990). This type of stop is considered reasonable because the expectation of privacy on public highways is very low, and automobiles are highly regulated. However, *random stops* are not permissible (*United States v. Martinez-Fuerte*, 428 U.S. 543, 1976).

Plain View. Another very important exception is the **plain view doctrine**. Essentially, this holds that an officer may seize evidence of a crime or contraband that falls into the plain view of the officer when the officer otherwise has a right to be at that location. If in the process of investigating one crime, an officer sees what is clearly evidence of another crime, it may be seized (*Coolidge*

Exhibit 12–11

WYOMING v. HOUGHTON, __ U.S. __, (1999)

During a routine traffic stop in 1995, a Wyoming Highway Patrol officer noticed a hypodermic syringe in the driver's shirt pocket, which the driver admitted using to take drugs. The officer then searched the passenger compartment for contraband, removing and searching what respondent, a passenger in the car, claimed was her purse. He found drug paraphernalia there and arrested respondent on drug charges. The trial court denied her motion to suppress all evidence from the purse as the fruit of an unlawful search, holding that the officer had probable cause to search the car for contraband, and, by extension, any containers therein that could hold such contraband. The passenger in the vehicle was convicted. The Wyoming Supreme Court reversed the conviction ruling that the officer's search violated the Fourth and Fourteenth Amendments.

This Court has concluded that the Framers would have regarded as reasonable the warrantless search of a car that police had probable cause to believe contained contraband, *Carroll v. United States*, 267 U.S. 132, as well as the warrantless search of containers *within* the automobile, *United States v. Ross*, 456 U.S. 798. Neither *Ross* nor the historical evidence it relied upon admits of a distinction based on ownership. The analytical principle underlying *Ross's* rule is also fully consistent with the balance of this Court's Fourth Amendment jurisprudence. Even if the historical evidence were equivocal, the balancing of the relative interests weighs decidedly in favor of searching a passenger's belongings. Passengers, no less than drivers, possess a reduced expectation of privacy with regard to the property they transport in cars. *See, e.g., Cardwell v. Lewis*, 417 U.S. 583, 590. . . . In contrast to the passenger's reduced privacy expectations, the governmental interest in effective law enforcement would be appreciably impaired without the ability to search the passenger's belongings, since an automobile's ready mobility creates the risk that evidence or contraband will be permanently lost while a warrant is obtained, *California v. Carney*, 471 U.S. 386; since a passenger may have an interest in concealing evidence of wrongdoing in a common enterprise with the driver, *cf. Maryland v. Wilson*, 519 U.S. 408, 413–414; and since a criminal might be able to hide contraband in a passenger's belongings as readily as in other containers in the car, *see, e.g., Rawlings v. Kentucky*, 448 U.S. 98, 102. The Wyoming Supreme Court's "passenger property" rule would be unworkable in practice.

Reversed.

v. New Hampshire, 403 U.S. 443, 1971). However, the officer may not take any action to "discover" additional evidence beyond those actions necessary to carry out the tasks that originally called the officer there (*Arizona v. Hicks,* 480 U.S. 321, 1987). Plain view means plain view, literally right out there for everyone to see.

Consent. One exception, which is more a waiver of rights than a true exception, is that of *consent.* If a person permits a search to occur without a warrant, assuming the consent was freely and intelligently given, he or she cannot later contest the results of the search. The person who gives consent must have some apparent authority to do so.

Consequences of Unlawful Searches

The Exclusionary Rule. There are a number of other exceptions, some so esoteric that their importance is minimal. There are exceptions for abandoned property, open fields, inevitable discovery, airports, and schools. Each plays a particular role in the administration of the Fourth Amendment relative to searches and seizures. However, if no applicable exception exists and no valid warrant was obtained, the search is unreasonable and is therefore unconstitutional. (See Exhibit 12–12 for a case concerning school searches.)

The punishment for conducting an unreasonable search is suppression of the evidence. This generally means the evidence may not be used against the defendant. The notion of suppression comes from the **exclusionary rule** at the federal level, which dates back to 1914. The rule was extended to the states as a result of fairly flagrant abuse of authority by police officers in Cleveland, Ohio, in the case of *Mapp v. Ohio* (367 U.S. 643, 1961). Officers fabricated a story of a fleeing fugitive to burst into a woman's home. When she demanded a warrant, and was shown a piece of paper, she grabbed the paper, placing it inside an article of her clothing. The officers wrestled her to the ground and removed the paper from her blouse. It was not a warrant. Based upon such outrageous conduct the Supreme Court had little trouble suppressing the evidence and applying the exclusionary rule to the states.

Interrogation

The rules that restrict police questioning of a suspect are, in at least one sense, fairly clear. In another, they are not at all clear. However, there are a few basic notions that we can accept. First, a voluntary statement made by a suspect without any questions being asked is always admissible (*Colorado v. Connelly,* 479 U.S. 157, 1986). But it is much more likely that questions *will* be asked by an officer. In order for any responses to be admissible in a court (generally speaking), the suspect must be warned not to say anything. These are the famous *Miranda warnings* (Exhibit 12–13). It is important to remember

Exhibit 12–12

NEW JERSEY v. T. L. O., 469 U.S. 325 (1985)
SCHOOL SEARCHES

To hold that the Fourth Amendment applies to searches conducted by school authorities is only to begin the inquiry into the standards governing such searches. Although the underlying command of the Fourth Amendment is always that searches and seizures be reasonable, what is reasonable depends on the context within which a search takes place. . . . Of course, the Fourth Amendment does not protect subjective expectations of privacy that are unreasonable or otherwise "illegitimate . . . ." To receive the protection of the Fourth Amendment, an expectation of privacy must be one that society is "prepared to recognize as legitimate. . . ."

Although this Court may take notice of the difficulty of maintaining discipline in the public schools today, the situation is not so dire that students in the schools may claim no legitimate expectations of privacy. We have recently recognized that the need to maintain order in a prison is such that prisoners retain no legitimate expectations of privacy in their cells, but it goes almost without saying that "[t]he prisoner and the schoolchild stand in wholly different circumstances, separated by the harsh facts of criminal conviction and incarceration . . . ." Against the child's interest in privacy must be set the substantial interest of teachers and administrators in maintaining discipline in the classroom and on school grounds. Maintaining order in the classroom has never been easy, but in recent years, school disorder has often taken particularly ugly forms: drug use and violent crime in the schools have become major social problems.

How, then, should we strike the balance between the schoolchild's legitimate expectations of privacy and the school's equally legitimate need to maintain an environment in which learning can take place?

The warrant requirement, in particular, is unsuited to the school environment: requiring a teacher to obtain a warrant before searching a child suspected of an infraction of school rules (or of the criminal law) would unduly interfere with the maintenance of the swift and informal disciplinary procedures needed in the schools. Just as we have in other cases dispensed with the warrant requirement when "the burden of obtaining

(continues)

Exhibit 12–12 *(continued)*

a warrant is likely to frustrate the governmental purpose behind the search," we hold today that school officials need not obtain a warrant before searching a student who is under their authority.

The fundamental command of the Fourth Amendment is that searches and seizures be reasonable, and although "both the concept of probable cause and the requirement of a warrant bear on the reasonableness of a search, . . . in certain limited circumstances neither is required."

Under ordinary circumstances, *a search of a student by a teacher or other school official will be "justified at its inception" when there are reasonable grounds for suspecting that the search will turn up evidence that the student has violated or is violating either the law or the rules of the school.* Such a search will be permissible in its scope when the measures adopted are reasonably related to the objectives of the search and not excessively intrusive in light of the age and sex of the student and the nature of the infraction. (Emphasis added.)

that these are warnings, not rights in and of themselves. The warnings were developed because of a long history of abuses by governments using torture to obtain confessions. The history of the Fifth Amendment and its prohibition against self-incrimination is based upon historical lessons. Whenever government has the power to compel confessions, it will use it. If there are no limits, then when is one confession valid and another not? In one case, *Brown v. Mississippi* (297 U.S. 278, 1936), the defendants were beaten and whipped until they confessed. The deputies who presided over the beatings openly admitted their acts (see Exhibit 12–14). It is difficult to imagine how a confession obtained in such a manner can be acceptable in a democracy. Most law enforcement officers today have never seen such behavior. But, at one time it was a too-common practice, even in this republic.

What Is Interrogation? It is important to understand that failure to administer Miranda warnings does not necessarily invalidate statements made by a suspect. The theory of Miranda is based upon possible *coercion* from **custodial interrogation**. Custodial interrogation occurs (1) if words or actions *which call for some verbal response* are (2) made by someone acting on behalf of the state (3) while the suspect is *in custody* (*Pennsylvania v. Muniz*, 496 U.S. 582, 1990). The person asking questions could be an officer or an informant such as a cellmate.

Exhibit 12–13

THE MIRANDA WARNINGS

. . . [W]e hold that when an individual is taken into custody or otherwise deprived of his freedom by the authorities in any significant way and is subjected to questioning, the privilege against self-incrimination is jeopardized. Procedural safeguards must be employed to protect the privilege, and unless other fully effective means are adopted to notify the person of his right of silence and to assure that the exercise of the right will be scrupulously honored, the following measures are required. *He must be warned prior to any questioning that he has the right to remain silent, that anything he says can be used against him in a court of law, that he has the right to the presence of an attorney, and that if he cannot afford an attorney one will be appointed for him prior to any questioning if he so desires. Opportunity to exercise these rights must be afforded to him throughout the interrogation.* . . . [T]he individual may knowingly and intelligently waive these rights and agree to answer questions or make a statement. **Miranda v. Arizona**, 384 U.S. 436 (1966). (Emphasis added.)

In order for custody to exist, a suspect must (1) know she is in custody, or (2) believe her freedom is significantly curtailed. These rules apply at the point that someone *reasonably* becomes a suspect (*Oregon v. Mathiason*, 429 U.S. 492, 1977). Moreover, whether or not Miranda warnings are given, a fully voluntary statement, not in response to questions, is admissible. The courts generally *presume* a statement is involuntary without Miranda warnings. However, this is rebuttable based on circumstances surrounding the statement.

The best practice, of course, is to give Miranda warnings when a person becomes a suspect. But those warnings do not prevent questions or inducements to give statements. Nor do they prevent the suspect from waiving the right against self-incrimination. However, if a suspect requests an attorney, *questioning* must stop.

Fruit of the Poisonous Tree. Sometimes, an officer may make an error and obtain evidence or testimony improperly. What happens if that evidence or testimony leads investigators to other testimony or evidence? That question was addressed by the United States Supreme Court in 1963. The case of *Wong Sun v. United States* (371 U.S. 471, 1963) involved a warrantless invasion of a San

Exhibit 12–14

THE PRIVILEGE AGAINST SELF-INCRIMINATION
BROWN V. MISSISSIPPI, 297 U.S. 278 (1936)

MR. CHIEF JUSTICE HUGHES delivered the opinion of the Court.

The question in this case is whether convictions, which rest solely upon confessions shown to have been extorted by officers of the State by brutality and violence, are consistent with the due process of law required by the Fourteenth Amendment of the Constitution of the United States.

Petitioners were indicted for the murder of one Raymond Stewart, whose death occurred on March 30, 1934. They were indicted on April 4, 1934, and were then arraigned and pleaded not guilty. Counsel were appointed by the court to defend them. Trial was begun the next morning and was concluded on the following day, when they were found guilty and sentenced to death.

Quoting the lower federal court: The crime with which these defendants, all ignorant negroes, are charged, was discovered about one o'clock p.m. on Friday, March 30, 1934. On that night one Dial, a deputy sheriff, accompanied by others, came to the home of Ellington, one of the defendants, and requested him to accompany them to the house of the deceased, and there a number of white men were gathered, who began to accuse the defendant of the crime. Upon his denial they seized him, and with the participation of the deputy they hanged him by a rope to the limb of a tree, and having let him down, they hung him again, and when he was let down the second time, and he still protested his innocence, he was tied to a tree and whipped, and still declining to accede to the demands that he confess, he was finally released and he returned with some difficulty to his home, suffering intense pain and agony. The record of the testimony shows that the signs of the rope on his neck were plainly visible during the so-called trial. A day or two thereafter the said deputy, accompanied by another, returned to the home of the said defendant and arrested him, and departed with the prisoner towards the jail in an adjoining county, but went by a route which led into the State of Alabama; and while on the way, in that State, the deputy stopped and again severely whipped the defendant, declaring that he would continue the whipping until

(continues)

Exhibit 12–14 *(continued)*

he confessed, and the defendant then agreed to confess to such a statement as the deputy would dictate, and he did so, after which he was delivered to jail.

Further details of the brutal treatment to which these helpless prisoners were subjected need not be pursued. It is sufficient to say that in pertinent respects the transcript reads more like pages torn from some medieval account, than a record made within the confines of a modern civilization which aspires to an enlightened constitutional government. . . . But the freedom of the State in establishing its policy is the freedom of constitutional government and is limited by the requirement of due process of law. Because a State may dispense with a jury trial, it does not follow that it be substituted for the witness stand. The State may not permit an accused to be hurried to conviction under mob domination. . . . And the trial equally is a mere pretense where the state authorities have contrived a conviction resting solely upon confessions obtained by violence. The due process clause requires "that state action, whether through one agency or another, shall be consistent with the fundamental principles of liberty and justice which lie at the base of all our civil and political institutions" (*Hebert v. Louisiana*, 272 U.S. 312, 316). It would be difficult to conceive of methods more revolting to the sense of justice than those taken to procure the confessions of these petitioners, and the use of the confessions thus obtained as the basis for conviction and sentence was a clear denial of due process.

Further, if our system is designed to seek justice, coerced confessions work against the system. How can a confession which results from threats or intimidation be trustworthy? If a person confesses but is not guilty, it will permit the truly guilty person to continue victimizing society. We must be certain those whom we punish are the guilty parties. The convenience of law enforcement is not the most important concern. The warnings, therefore, seek to contain government's power and ensure justice. Many in law enforcement do not agree, but the truth is that the mandatory use of the warnings did not cause any loss of effectiveness. In fact, the evidence suggests that law enforcement effectiveness improved after the warnings became mandatory. The warnings themselves are basic and, while the Supreme Court has permitted some deviation from the written warnings, they should be remembered by all law enforcement officers. It would be a mistake to assume that they are no longer important.

Francisco laundry. As a result of information solicited during that illegal search, other potential suspects and locations were identified. The federal officers involved similarly invaded these locations and acquired information and suspects that led to yet another suspect. The question was whether to consider *all* the evidence tainted. The Supreme Court held that some was because it was the "fruit of the poisonous tree." But in some cases, most particularly that of Wong Sun, the evidence was admissible. The test was whether or not conditions intervened to "cut" the connection to the "poisonous tree" of the original invasion. In Wong Sun's case, his home was invaded as a result of evidence obtained at one of the earlier bad searches. But, though he was taken into custody, he was later released without charges. He returned voluntarily and made a statement that resulted in his charges and conviction.

In a more recent case, a suspect kidnapped a 10-year-old girl on Christmas Eve from a community gathering and murdered her. When he was arrested, he was Mirandized, and he *requested counsel*. While officers were transporting the suspect, one of the officers (without asking questions) told the defendant he should tell them where the body could be found. He alluded to the sorrow of the family, the time of year, an approaching snowstorm, and the need for a Christian burial. The defendant relented and showed them the body. That, of course, was compelling evidence against him. It was also taken from a poisonous tree in that the interrogation was unlawful due to the request for counsel. However, the court reasoned that since the body was found in the search zone of a search team, the evidence was going to be discovered *inevitably*. Hence, the inevitable discovery exception to the fruit of the poisonous tree rule was established (*Nix v. Williams*, 467 U.S. 431, 1984; also, see *Oregon v. Elstad*, 470 U.S. 298, 1985).

CIVIL RIGHTS

The most significant liability concern for law enforcement, both patrol and supervision, is undoubtedly that which springs from section 1983 of Title 42 of the United States Federal Code (see Exhibit 12–15). Originally part of the post–Civil War Reconstruction Acts, this section is the basis for horrifying numbers of lawsuits. Whether or not one agrees with the policy of the statute, it is a reality that has been on the books for over 100 years and is not likely to be changed. We will consider briefly the implications of this Act.

Basically, the Act provides that anyone acting under the "color of any statute, ordinance, regulation, custom, or usage" and who subjects someone to the deprivation of their constitutional rights is liable to that person for damages. False arrest, false imprisonment, use of excessive force, conduct that fails to meet training standards, failure to obtain medical aid for a suspect, and a hundred other specific events will trigger this statute. The deprivation of any known constitutional right will produce liability (Antieau 1998).

Exhibit 12–15

FEDERAL CIVIL RIGHTS STATUTE

42 U.S.C. § 1983. Civil action for deprivation of rights.

Every person who, under color of any statute, ordinance, regulation, custom, or usage, of any State or Territory or the District of Columbia, subjects, or causes to be subjected, any citizen of the United States or other person within the jurisdiction thereof to the deprivation of any rights, privileges, or immunities secured by the Constitution and laws, shall be liable to the party injured in an action at law, suit in equity, or other proper proceeding for redress. For the purposes of this section, any Act of Congress applicable exclusively to the District of Columbia shall be considered to be a statute of the District of Columbia.

It is obvious that if there is probable cause to arrest or search someone, there is a privilege to violate related rights. In other words, citizens are free from *unreasonable* searches and seizures, but not from those that are reasonable. Probable cause gives us reasonableness, but the arrest, detention, seizure, or search must be accomplished in a reasonable manner.

Law enforcement officers are limited in the amount of force they may use to effectuate an arrest or search. The amount of force may only be the force reasonably necessary to place a person into custody. Deadly force may be used only if the suspect is threatening the safety of the officer or another person. Any law, custom, or rule to the contrary cannot be relied upon by law enforcement officers. In *Tennessee v. Garner* (471 U.S. 1, 1985) the Supreme Court struck down a state statute that permitted the use of deadly force on any fleeing felon. In doing so, it permitted the parents of a dead teenager to sue a police officer and his department despite the fact that he was trained to fire on unarmed fleeing felons. Improper use of force will result in personal liability.

Of concern to supervisors and managers is the fact that they can be held liable for the civil rights violations of their subordinates. Essentially, liability may be established if it can be shown that a supervisor or manager "knew or should have known" that the event might happen. Liability of superiors for the actions of subordinates has been based upon poor hiring practices, poor training, failure to discipline, improper assignment, and improper retention, among other things (Russell 1994).

Other areas of tort law that we did not examine are destruction or damage to the property of another, slander, libel, false arrest or imprisonment, and conversion of property. These and a number of other torts are important, and deserve discussion at a later date in a separate course. A good policy is to act conservatively, since officers have no way of knowing what interpretation a court may place on his or her behavior. For example, a federal court not long ago ruled that not only may testimony of a suspect not be used if the suspect is not Mirandized, the officer may be liable under Section 1983 for the failure to give the Miranda warning (*Cooper v. Dupnick*, 963 F.2d 1220, 113 S.Ct. 407, 1992; see also Ronzio 1993).

SUMMARY

This chapter illustrates the sources of law and how law enforcement agencies are limited in a number of major and distinct ways by legal restraints. First, law enforcement is limited by how the criminal laws are drawn by legislative authority and interpreted by a multitude of other actors. Second, even though arrests may be made, a prosecutor, grand jury, trial jury, judge, or appeals court may disagree as to the guilt or culpability of the suspect. Third, law enforcement is impacted by constitutional procedural limitations. This covers search and seizure, warrants, arrest, interrogation, and a host of other day-to-day activities. Fourth, agencies are limited by administrative law, which orders and restricts the manner in which agencies may manage their own business. Finally, law enforcement is limited by its potential liability in civil rights violations. For these reasons, aspiring law enforcement officers must take to heart their training and education, which, if followed, will generally protect them.

QUESTIONS FOR REVIEW

1. What are four distinct sources of American law that affect the policing function in the United States?
2. What is the structure of the American system of justice in terms of the relationship between state and federal courts?
3. What is the definition and meaning of the following terms when applied to the criminal law: (a) probable cause, (b) elements of crime, (c) *actus reus*, (d) *mens rea*, and (e) levels of culpability?
4. What is meant by entrapment?
5. What are the basic procedural limitations on law enforcement officers? Explain why these restrictions exist.
6. How does the rule of law both restrict and protect law enforcement officials?
7. What is meant by the allegation that a "violation of Section 1983 of Title 42 of the U.S. Code" has been committed?

SUGGESTED ACTIVITIES

1. Go to your local newspaper and find a story on a local criminal case of significance. In groups of four, apply what you know about mental states and defenses to the case as it is described by the press or the media. Take sides in the group. Construct an argument for conviction, and one for acquittal. The first team of two must take a conviction position first and argue it with the other team of two, who will argue for acquittal. Switch sides. As a group, write an essay that incorporates both positions and comes to some conclusion about the criminal process.
2. What is the difference between right and wrong? Is it merely the act? If so, should all people be punished according to what they have done in their current crime, and not previously

in their lives? Should a three-time felon get the same sentence as a minister with no prior offense history? Write an essay discussing this question, and compare the debate to that surrounding the use of the insanity defense. Is someone who is truly mentally ill to be held to the same standard as someone who is not ill? Why or why not? Defend your answer in class.

3. If you were the chief of police of your local department, what steps would you take to adopt and enforce rules so that you are in compliance with minimum due process requirements?

4. Using your Web browser, search for and go to the home page of the American Bar Association or the United States Courts and locate links to the online versions of case law and code law. Download or print out one case and one statutory code section.

5. Using your Web browser, visit one or both of the following sites:

http://www.lawnewsnetwork.com/   **http://www.findlaw.com/**
http://rominger.org/   **http://www.ncsc.dni.us/**

CHAPTER GLOSSARY

actus reus: the actions of the defendant

civil law: violations against individuals

common law: the body of legal rules developed over a period of several hundred years by judges acting under the authority of the King

criminal law: offenses against the public (or the state)

custodial interrogation: occurs (1) if words or actions *which call for some verbal response* by a suspect are (2) made by someone acting on behalf of the state (3) while the suspect is *in custody*

defenses: permit defendants to claim that while they did commit the acts charged, they should not be held criminally liable for those actions

elements of a crime: the basic parts of a crime

entrapment: a claim that the police enticed a person who is not normally inclined toward crime to commit an offense

exclusionary rule: the doctrine that prohibits the use of illegally seized evidence in court

exigent circumstances: refers to the conditions that create a need for immediate action to protect the general safety of the public, to prevent the destruction of evidence, or to prevent injury to others

fruit of the poisonous tree: evidence that was found solely as a result of an illegal search or seizure

general intent: the individual voluntarily committed an act and the law *presumes* the defendant intended that act

indictment: a ruling by a grand jury that a person should be charged with committing a crime

justifications: a means to avoid criminal liability by arguing that while the defendant did commit the acts in question, the defendant did the right thing in the circumstances he or she faced

mens rea: addresses the degree of intent or recklessness of the defendant

plain view doctrine: the doctrine that allows an officer to seize evidence of a crime or contraband that falls into the plain view of the officer when he or she otherwise has a right to be at that location

precedent: decisions, over time, relied upon by other judges with similar problems

preliminary hearing: a hearing to determine if there is sufficient probable cause to send the case to the district attorney or grand jury for further prosecution

probable cause: exists where "the facts and circumstances within their [arresting officers'] knowledge and of which they had reasonably trustworthy information [are] sufficient in themselves to warrant a man of reasonable caution in the belief that an offense has been or is being committed [by the person to be arrested]"

prosecutor's information: in some states. the procedure by which the district attorney or prosecutor may issue a charge without going before a grand jury; it has the same effect as an indictment

search: generally defined as the invasion, by the state, of an area that a person believes is protected or private; that belief will be upheld by a court if the " . . . person exhibited an actual (subjective) expectation of privacy, and . . . the expectation is one that society is prepared to recognize as 'reasonable'"

seizure: generally defined as a "meaningful interference with the possessory interests of the suspect"

self-defense: generally permitted where it is necessary to use violence to protect yourself or another from imminent harm

specific intent: a requirement that the state show the defendant purposely intended to violate the law

stare decisis: the doctrine that prior decisions should stand if the facts are similar

stop and frisk: in the course of investigating this behavior he identifies himself as a police officer and makes reasonable inquiries, and where nothing in the initial stages of the encounter serves to dispel his reasonable fear for his own or others' safety, he is entitled for the protection of himself and others in the area to conduct a carefully limited search of the outer clothing of such persons in an attempt to discover weapons which might be used to assault him

strict liability: the doctrine under which a defendant will be found guilty regardless of his or her state of mind if the acts in question were committed

suppression hearing: a court order ruling that certain evidence may not be used

writ of certiorari: an order requiring a lower court to give the Supreme Court the record of a case for review

REFERENCES

Antieau, Chester J. 1998. *Federal Civil Rights Acts: Civil Practice.* 2d ed. New York: Lawyers Co-operative Publishing.

Arizona Revised Statutes, §13–206.

Boyce, Ronald N. and Rollin M. Perkins. 1989. *Criminal Law and Procedure: Cases and Materials.* 7th ed. Westbury, NY: Foundation Press.

Carter, Lief H. and Christine B. Harrington. 1991. *Administrative Law and Politics: Cases and Comments.* New York: Harper Collins.

Eisenstein, James, Roy B. Flemming, and Peter F. Nardulli. 1988. *The Contours of Justice: Communities and Their Courts.* Boston: Little, Brown, and Co.

Klotter, John. 1994. *Criminal Law.* 4th ed. Cincinnati, OH: Anderson Publishing.

Magenau, John M. and Raymond G. Hunt. 1993. *Power and the Police Chief: An Institutional and Organizational Analysis.* Newbury Park, CA: Sage Publications.

Nardulli, Peter F., James Eisenstein, and Roy B. Flemming. 1988. *The Tenor of Justice: Criminal Courts and the Guilty Plea Process.* Urbana, IL: University of Illinois Press.

The Ohio Criminal Law Handbook, 1998. Cincinnati, OH: Anderson Publishing Co.

Reid, Sue Titus. 1998. *Criminal Law.* 4th ed. Boston, MA: McGraw-Hill.

Ronzio, Judith A. 1993. Upping the Ante on Miranda. *The Police Chief* (May): 10–11.

Russell, Gregory D. 1994. Liability and Criminal Justice Management: Resolving Dilemmas and Meeting Future Challenges. *American Journal of Criminal Justice* 18 (2) (Spring): 177–98.

Samaha, Joel. 1990. *Criminal Law.* 3rd ed. St. Paul, MN: West Publishing Co.

CASES CITED

Adams v. Williams, 407 U.S. 143, 1972.

Arizona v. Hicks, 480 U.S. 321, 1987.

Barron v. Mayor and City Council of Baltimore, 32 U.S. 243, 8 L. Ed 672 (1833).

Brinegar v. United States, 338 U.S. 160, 175–176, 1949.

Brown v. Mississippi, 297 U.S. 278, 1936.
California v. Acevedo, 500 U.S. 565, 1991.
California v. Hodari D, 499 U.S. 62, 1991.
Carroll v. United States, 267 U.S. 132, 1925.
Chambers v. Maloney, 399 U.S. 42, 1970.
Chimel v. California, 395 U.S. 752, 1969.
Colorado v. Connelly, 479 U.S. 157, 1986.
Coolidge v. New Hampshire, 403 U.S. 443, 1971.
Cooper v. Dupnick, 963 F.2d 1220, 113 S.Ct. 407, 1992.
Hardwick v. Bowers, 478 U.S. 186, 1986.
Katz v. United States, 389 U.S. 347, 361, 1967.
Mapp v. Ohio, 367 U.S. 643, 1961.
Marbury v. Madison, 5 U.S. 137, 2 L. Ed. 60 (1803).
Maryland v. Buie, 494 U.S. 325, 1990.
Michigan Department of State Police v. Sitz, 496 U.S. 444, 1990.
Nix v. Williams, 467 U.S. 431, 1984.
Oregon v. Elstad, 470 U.S. 298, 1985.
Payton v. New York, 445 U.S. 573, 1980.
Pennsylvania v. Muniz, 496 U.S. 582, 1990.
South Dakota v. Opperman, 428 U.S. 364, 1976.
Tennessee v. Garner, 471 U.S. 1, 1985.
Terry v. Ohio, 392 U.S. 1, 1968.
United States v. Martinez-Fuerte, 428 U.S. 543, 1976.
United States v. Jacobsen, 466 U.S. 109, 113, 1984.
Wong Sun v. United States, 371 U.S. 471, 1963.

Technology in Policing

The Director of the Integrated Ballistics Identification System Division in Pennsylvania displays computer technology used to capture, store and compare images of microscopic markings found on the surfaces of bullets and discharged cases. May 1999. (AP/Wide World Photos)

This chapter addresses the use and application of technology in processing law enforcement information. The term *technology* is used in many ways by the average person. To many it is limited to the fields of the physical sciences, such as physics and engineering. Some include the natural sciences (i.e., biology and chemistry) in the discussion of technology. Still others include the methods and techniques developed from the social sciences (e.g., sociology and psychology) when referring to technology. This chapter's primary focus is information technology applied to the gathering, analysis, storage, and retrieval of information. Other technological innovations related to police operations and field techniques are introduced as well. Upon completion of this chapter, you should be able to:

1. Describe the importance and significance of information technology to the field of law enforcement.
2. Understand that many of the developments in computerized information technology have occurred in recent decades.
3. Identify the major applications of information technology in the field of law enforcement.
4. Distinguish between the categories of computers.
5. Describe the inequities that exist among police departments regarding the utilization of information technology.
6. Explain the importance of NCIC and other large databases to law enforcement's mission and operation.
7. Identify the technological innovations that are being applied to field procedures and techniques related to the use of force and investigation.
8. Explain the concerns about potential abuses of technology related to privacy issues.

THE IMPORTANCE OF INFORMATION TECHNOLOGY

When the criminal justice system is officially invoked, one element of the process is universal: information is the basis for action. Today, officers' observations and actions are recorded and may become the foundation for any subsequent initiation of arrest and prosecution. Historically, these actions took place with little documentation. In early years, an officer's word and testimony were sufficient, and little was done to maintain a record base or filing system. Incidents were not that frequent, so one's memory was not cluttered with other cases and field notes. The court system was not "backed up," and jails were not overcrowded. "Justice" was often swift and definite with few appeals. Extensive documentation simply was not necessary.

By the turn of the twentieth century, three influencing factors led to establishing filing systems and the need for more documentation. The first was the increasing level of crime (primarily in urban areas) and the need to keep information about each case in an accurate and detailed manner. One's memory simply could not keep all details readily available. The second influencing factor was the professionalization of policing, which emphasized the increased use of scientific tools and processes (such as fingerprinting, photography, and analysis of crime incidents) and extensive recordkeeping systems to help identify suspects. The third influencing factor was the evolving legal requirements related to the rules of evidence and judicial review of cases. All of these factors led to greater emphasis on processing, storing, and retrieving information.

Today, there probably is not a law enforcement officer alive who goes to work without carrying a pen or pencil and some kind of notepad (unless working undercover). Of course, some carry laptop and notebook computers; handheld computers are finding their way to the street as well. Information gathering and storage also include the use of audio and video technology. The reason for much of this emphasis on information is obvious—it is the basis of operation for the criminal justice process. But one reason for the importance of technology in recording and storing this information is that society and the system itself demand that information be accurate, detailed, and readily accessible. The system has become so complex today that information technology is more important than ever.

THE GENERAL HISTORY OF INFORMATION TECHNOLOGY

One can argue that the history of information technology begins with the first developments in the evolution of communication and writing. The first recordings of pictographic signs and symbols date back to the Sumerian clay tablets of 4000–3500 B.C. Early uses of papyrus and inks have been dated at 2500 B.C. The abacus, a device to assist in the computing of numbers, dates to 3000 B.C. Although scrolls began to be replaced by an early form of "books" around 360 A.D., and the use of lamp-black ink by Chinese artists about 650 A.D. led to the introduction of wood blocks for printing, the printing press was not perfected by Johann Gutenberg until the 1450s. And the use of black-lead pencils was first noted in England in 1500. The more modern societies, therefore, have been recording information routinely for only about 500 years (see Grun 1991; and Augarten 1984 for additional historical information about this evolution).

Recording information was one thing, but using devices to process information has been a more recent endeavor. Appendix 13–1 at the end of this chapter identifies the most significant developments over the last 350–400 years in the ideas and devices related to evolution of computerized information technology. Understanding this evolution leads to an appreciation of where society has been and how rapidly new advancements are occurring. Just as our grandparents and great-grandparents witnessed the transition from the horse and buggy to the automobile and space travel, today's generations are witnessing the transition from playing PacMan on TVs to simulating real situations through virtual reality. The question that remains is "What will our capabilities be in 20–40 years?" Are Star Trek and Star Wars really far-fetched, or will many of us living today actually witness the developments they depict?

The majority of adults today were born before computers became commercially available. Most of today's grade school, high school, and college students, however, have grown up with personal computers and/or other computerized devices at home and school. While young people today may take computing in stride (and for granted), many adults are still hesitant to learn about and use them. This situation also exists in law enforcement agencies; older personnel may resist the increased use of technology while younger officers adapt readily. This gap in backgrounds can keep agencies from moving forward with greater use of technology and cause younger officers to become frustrated at the "lack of progress" in adopting modern technology.

THE HISTORY OF INFORMATION TECHNOLOGY IN POLICING

The evolution of information technology in law enforcement activities is a very interesting one and needs to be placed in context. Today in policing we take many things for granted, such as the telephone and the portable radio. It must be remembered that officers have had the means of communicating with headquarters and other officers for fewer than 100 years. Appendix 13–2 at the end of this chapter presents a time line in order to appreciate the evolution of applications in policing and to illustrate that the next 5–25 years could witness even more far-reaching applications of information technology.

One of the most important milestones for American policing involving the application of information technology occurred in 1967 with the establishment of the FBI's **National Crime Information Center (NCIC)**. It is the national repository for crime-related information and is located in Washington, D.C., at FBI headquarters. It provides computerized information to thousands of criminal justice agencies in the 50 states, the District of Columbia, Puerto Rico, the U.S. Virgin Islands, and Canada on a 24-hour, 7-day-a-week basis (see Exhibit 13–1).

Initially established on January 27, 1967, following lobbying efforts from the law enforcement community at all levels of government, it had 16 terminals, 15 participating agencies, and a database of 23,000 records in five file categories: wanted persons, stolen vehicles, stolen plates, stolen firearms, and identifiable stolen items (FBI 1984; FBI 1996/1997). Over the years, other file cate-

Exhibit 13–1

THE NATIONAL CRIME INFORMATION CENTER (NCIC)

Description: NCIC is the national repository for crime-related information. Located in Washington, D.C. at FBI headquarters, it provides computerized information to over 80 thousand law enforcement and criminal justice agencies in the 50 states, the District of Columbia, Puerto Rico, the U.S. Virgin Islands, and Canada on a 24-hour, seven-day-a-week basis.

History: NCIC went on-line in January of 1967. Initially it had 16 terminals, 15 participating agencies, and a database of 23,000 records in five file categories: Wanted persons, stolen firearms, stolen vehicles, stolen plates, and identifiable stolen items. By the end of 1967, NCIC had handled a total of two million transactions. Some 30 years later, NCIC is still handling almost two million transactions—per day.

Recent Developments: In 1992, the Center became part of the newly structured Criminal Justice Information Service Division within the FBI. Artificial intelligence software capabilities and imaging technology have been incorporated. A recent survey on the benefits of NCIC found that during a one-year period: 81,750 "wanted" persons were found; 113,293 individuals were arrested; 39,268 missing juveniles and 8,549 missing adults were located; and 110,681 cars valued at over $570 million were found.

   NCIC is an important law enforcement tool, and law enforcement officers recognize that—NCIC averages about 20 inquiries a second. And it can be—and has been—used for virtually any type of investigation. One of the most recent well-known cases involving NCIC was the Oklahoma City bombing. Federal investigators, after running Oklahoma City bombing suspect Timothy McVeigh's name through NCIC, discovered that an Oklahoma state trooper had stopped and run an NCIC search on an individual by the name of Timothy McVeigh a little more than an hour after (and about 88 miles away from) the site of the explosion. He was still in custody and was consequently held for further questioning.

The Future: NCIC-2000 will do everything the former NCIC system did, but it will do it better. It will also offer more — including the electronic

(continues)

Exhibit 13–1 *(continued)*

transmission of photographs, mugshots, photographs of stolen property, and fingerprint data. It will have an automated fingerprint matching system that will identify someone based on a right index fingerprint when the subject presents no identification or is suspected of presenting a false I.D. A main feature of NCIC-2000 will be a mobile imaging unit installed inside police squad cars. This unit will consist of a personal computer, a hand-held fingerprint scanner, a hand-held digital camera, and a small printer. The FBI will provide the NCIC-2000 custom-developed software free of charge, but police departments have to obtain their own hardware and some additional commercial software. Other plans include expanded fields that will allow for additional information, improved name search techniques, capability to link all records relating to the same crime, and improved security through encryption, network management, and intrusion detection. NCIC 2000 will be located in Clarksburg, West Virginia and became operational by July 1999.

Sources: Data from W.S. Sessions, Criminal Justice Information Services: Gearing Up for the Future, *FBI Law Enforcement Bulletin,* pp. 1–3, 1993; Federal Bureau of Investigation, *Cooperation: The Backbone of Effective Law Enforcement,* June 1993. U.S. Department of Justice; and Federal Bureau of Investigation, National Crime Information Center: 30 Years on The Beat, *The Investigator,* December 1996/January 1997, Federal Bureau of Investigation.

gories were added. With the recent upgrading of the system, the automated files are organized into 17 databases (FBI National Press Office 1999):

1. Stolen Articles
2. Foreign Fugitives
3. Stolen Guns
4. Criminal History Queries
5. Stolen License Plates
6. Deported Felons
7. Missing Persons
8. Criminal Justice Agency Identifier
9. Stolen Securities
10. Stolen Boats
11. Gang and terrorist members
12. Unidentified Persons
13. U.S. Secret Service Protective File

14. Stolen Vehicles
15. Persons Subject to Protection Orders
16. Wanted Persons
17. Canadian Police Information Center

NCIC 2000 has added the following features to the system (FBI National Press Office 1999):

- Enhanced Name Search (searches all derivatives of names such as Jeff, Geoff, Jeffrey)

- Search of right index finger prints

- Mugshots

- Other identifying images (such as scars, tattoos, and images of vehicles (e.g., 1965 Ford Mustang)

- Sexual Offenders

- Persons on Probation or Parole

- Persons incarcerated in federal prisons

- User manuals available on-line

- Information linking (all information related to a case will be returned on a single inquiry; for example, if stolen guns are in a stolen vehicle, a query on the vehicle will return information on the stolen guns as well)

- Improved data quality

- On-line ad hoc searches to support criminal investigations

- Maintaining five days of system inquiries to allow agencies to be notified if they are looking for information on the same individual or stolen property

NCIC responds to over 1.6 million inquiries daily on the average (over 589 million yearly). The NCIC 2000 system can process greater than 2.4 million transactions per day, with storage of and access to over 39 million records. It provides access to over 80,000 criminal justice users through more than 110,000 terminals and maintains over 24 million criminal and missing person records (not all on-line) (FBI National Press Office 1999; Pilant 1996; Sessions 1993). Any record entered into NCIC must be associated with a document and must contain the identity of the agency entering the record as well as other specific data, depending on the file. Some files can be updated only by specifically authorized agencies. Local agency users must furnish the network system with a specific request and a special NCIC-assigned code that identifies the agency. Various types of requests are entered and then processed. A response is transmitted back to the initiating agency. When an inquiry about a person or property matches data contained in one of the files, it is referred to as a "hit."

In 1992, the Center became part of the newly structured Criminal Justice Information Service Division within the FBI. Artificial intelligence software capabilities are being incorporated into the system in an effort to detect related (linked) criminal activity in its early stages and to detect misuse of information by helping to insure accuracy and reliability of the data. Image technology is being incorporated in order to permit the improved transmission of mug shots and fingerprint images in response to inquiries. In all, over 60 planned upgrades have occurred under a revamped system called **NCIC 2000**. (See **http://www.fbi.gov** for a status report on NCIC 2000). NCIC 2000 began operating on July 15, 1999, at the FBI's new facility in Clarksburg, West Virginia.

During the last two decades, advancements in computer technology have led to great interest and implementation of 911 emergency telephone systems, **computer-aided dispatch systems**, and **automated vehicle locator systems**. More and more agencies have placed their criminal records/incidents and calls for service on-line for quick access and retrieval. Others are heavily involved in **geographic information systems** (GIS; also called computer mapping and **geocoding**) that map crime-related information in order to conduct crime analysis (see Figure 13–1). Some departments now have a "paperless reporting system" because of advancements in radio and computer technology. Artificial intelligence software is now being used to predict burglary patterns and to identify officers with a propensity toward corruption (see Exhibit 13–2).

MAJOR COMPUTER APPLICATIONS IN LAW ENFORCEMENT TODAY

The major uses of computers in law enforcement cover the spectrum from common records storage to automated identity kits. Here is a list of some the current uses of computers (Conser 1988; Conser 1997; Latz 1998; Pilant 1996; Sessions 1993):

Accounting/Financial Management	Master Name Indexing
Arrested Persons Log	Mobile Digital Terminals (MDTs)
Automated Crime Analysis	Parking Citation Management
Automated Criminal Histories	Personnel Files
Automated Criminalistics	Personnel Performance Evaluation
Automated Fingerprint Systems	Property Control/Inventory
Automated Identification Sketches	Records Management (ALL TYPES)
Automated Vehicle Locators (AVL)	Staffing Analysis and Scheduling

Study Area 1 (Beats: 1013,1024,1031,1032,1033,1034)
Two-Six and Latin King Offender Residency Hot Spot Areas*

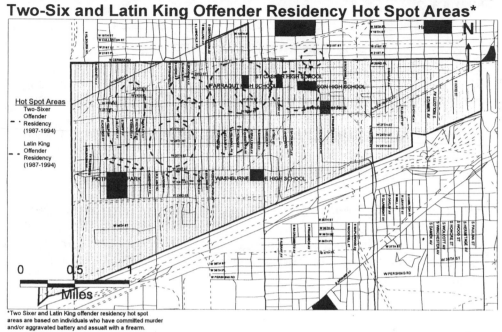

Hot Spot Areas
Two-Sixer
Offender
Residency
(1987-1994)

Latin King
Offender
Residency
(1987-1994)

0   0.5   1

Miles

*Two Sixer and Latin King offender residency hot spot
areas are based on individuals who have committed murder
and/or aggravated battery and assualt with a firearm.

Source: Reprinted with permission from J. Ayad, D. Higgins, and B. Wells, *The STAC/Early Warning System Project: Applying Innovative Technologies to Street Gang Crime in Chicago*, © 1995, Illinois Criminal Justice Information Authority.

Figure 13–1 Example of Geocoding/Geomapping

Automated Lineups

Beat/Patrol/Mapping/Analysis

Budgetary Analysis

Computer Aided Dispatch

Computer Aided Instruction/Training

Mapping/Graphics/Geocoding

Court Docket Scheduling

Employee Characteristics Analysis

Evidence Control/Inventory

Forms Control and Design

Inventory Control

Juvenile Activity Files

Stolen Property Listings

Telecommunications

Traffic Citations

Traffic Accident Analysis

Training Logs

Uniform Crime Reporting

Vehicle Identification Checks

Vehicle Maintenance

Vehicle Registrations

Warrant Management

Weapons Qualification

Word Processing/Report Writing

Exhibit 13–2

ARTIFICIAL INTELLIGENCE SOFTWARE

REBES—The Residential Burglary Expert System is currently operating in Baltimore County, Maryland and Tucson, Arizona. "Rules" are established by experts in the field, based on their knowledge of burglary cases. These rules are then used to process information about known burglaries (locations, dates, modus operandi, etc.) in the hope of identifying possible characteristics and/or names of suspects.

FINCEN—The U.S. Treasury Department's Financial Crimes Enforcement Network database identifies possible money-laundering transactions. It is a neural network used to scan huge volumes of financial information for suspicious patterns in money movement to identify possible laundering operations.

The Chicago Police Department has used an artificial intelligence program, called Brainmaker, as an early warning system to identify traits or behavior patterns shared by officers who have been fired or disciplined. In the first two months of using the program (August/September 1994), 200 at-risk officers were identified. It was planned to be used as a preventive measure although its continued and future use is in doubt because of the potential to have an adverse impact on an officer's career and possible violation of constitutional rights.

The Delaware State Police is using a computer-aided dispatch system that identifies locations where criminal activity is occurring (by translating common landmarks and geographical sites) and where it is likely to occur.

In Alliance, Nebraska, police use an AI application containing 800 rule statements that assist officers in determining solvability of various incidents. It is used to help allocate police resources.

Sources: Data from C. Curtis, The Future of Automation in Law Enforcement, *Police Computer Review*, Vol. 1, No. 4, pp. 1–8; © 1992; Artificial Intelligence Tackles a Very Real Problem—Police Misconduct Control, *Law Enforcement News*, September 30, 1994, p. 1 and 10; T. Newcombe, Artificial Intelligence Fights Crime, *Government Technology*, pp. 1 and 48, November 1993.

The uses and applications of computers in law enforcement are as broad as one's imagination and creativeness. Today, individual officers are developing new applications—the process is no longer one limited to the research and planning or communications section of an agency. The advent of the microcomputer has brought computing power to the individual level and has opened a new realm of applications. A detailed examination of each application listed above is not appropriate here, but current publications (particularly *The Police Chief, Law and Order, Law Enforcement Technology, Law Enforcement News,* and *Government Technology*) contain numerous articles on this ever-changing technology. Selected sites on the World Wide Web, such as **http://www.nlectc.org**, also contain descriptions of the most recent advances and research into technology applied to the law enforcement and corrections fields.

The development of law enforcement databases for a variety of purposes has been extensive. Most larger and medium-sized agencies utilize some type of records management system today. Some are **stand-alone systems** (meaning locally based microcomputer systems not interconnected with other computers) and others are tied to or are part of **regional information systems** (a network of computers linked together on a regional basis and serving many agencies). Exhibit 13–3 contains a listing of some of the electronic databases and communication systems available to selected law enforcement agencies and Exhibit 13–4 identifies the type of technological assistance available through the federally funded regional information sharing system (RISS).

The six RISS centers located throughout the U.S. serve a number of states each:

Middle Atlantic-Great Lakes Organized Crime Law Enforcement Network (MAGLOCLEN) serves Delaware, Indiana, Maryland, Michigan, New Jersey, New York, Ohio, Pennsylvania and the District of Columbia. The center also has member agencies in the Canadian provinces of Ontario and Quebec.

Mid-states Organized Crime Information Center (MOCIC) serves Illinois, Iowa, Kansas, Minnesota, Missouri, Nebraska, North Dakota, South Dakota, and Wisconsin. The center also has member agencies in Canada.

New England State Police Information Network (NESPIN) serves Connecticut, Maine, Massachusetts, New Hampshire, Rhode Island, and Vermont. The center also has member agencies in Canada.

Regional Organized Crime Information Center (ROCIC) serves Alabama, Arkansas, Florida, Georgia, Kentucky, Louisiana, Mississippi, North Carolina, Oklahoma, South Carolina, Tennessee, Texas, Virginia, and West Virginia.

Rocky Mountain Information Network (RMIN) serves Arizona, Colorado, Idaho, Montana, Nevada, New Mexico, Utah, and Wyoming. The center also has member agencies in Canada.

Exhibit 13-3

SELECTED DATABASES IN LAW ENFORCEMENT

ARJIS—Automated Regional Justice Information System is a regional network in the San Diego, California area that contains information on crime cases, arrests, citations, field interviews, traffic accidents, fraudulent documents, and stolen property (which is typical of regional systems).

AUTODIN—The U.S. Defense Department's administrative message system is called the Automatic Digital Network. It connects military installations and other Federal agencies worldwide.

DRUGFIRE—This is a specialized software database that stores and retrieves shell casing images for comparison purposes in attempts to link shooting incidents.

JUST—The Justice Telecommunications System provides the offices of the Department of Justice with worldwide capability to communicate administrative messages within the Department via electronic communications; transmit messages to all other U.S. Government agencies, locations, and individuals worldwide; access selected automated information systems such as NCIC, MIRAC, and state law enforcement agencies via the National Law Enforcement Telecommunications System (NLETS); transmit telegrams to individuals and organizations through commercial systems (TWX, TELEX, MAILGRAM), either domestic or international.

The JUST system is a "store-and-forward" message switching system composed of approximately 500 terminals, located in most headquarters and field offices of the Department. These are connected via private line communications channels to a computer system that controls the network. The computer system provides for the transfer of messages between terminals on the system, from the network to automatic information systems, and for the transfer of messages between the JUST network and other Federal Government networks and agencies as well as to all domestic and international record carriers' networks.

III—Interstate Identification Index is coordinated by the FBI through the NCIC system. It allows access to the criminal history records of the FBI and the individual states. It is being upgraded to include the integrated automated fingerprint identification system with the potential of on-line mug shot files and on-line fingerprint images. *(continues)*

Exhibit 13–3 *(continued)*

MIRAC—The Master Index Remote Access System of the Immigration and Naturalization Service contains information on undocumented immigrants.

NDPIX—The National Drug Pointer Index System became operational in the U.S. in October of 1997. It assists participating agencies in determining whether an active case suspect is under investigation by any other participating agency.

NESPIN—New England State Police Information Network is a regional information system for the states of Connecticut, Massachusetts, Maine, New Hampshire, Rhode Island, and Vermont.

NLETS—The National Law Enforcement Telecommunications System is for administrative messages and it consists of over 64,000 terminals in state and local police departments, courts, correctional facilities, etc. The "system" is comprised of many state and regional "networks" through which queries and responses are transmitted.

RMIN—Rocky Mountain Information Network is a regional information system for the states of Arizona, Colorado, Idaho, Montana, New Mexico, Nevada, Utah, and Wyoming.

SINS—Statewide Integrated Narcotics System (California) is a coordinated effort to reduce conflicts between local, state, and federal agencies working narcotics and other cases. The system can pinpoint locations of critical events; analyze data and trafficking patterns; and access fingerprints, photos, arrest warrants, and criminal record information.

WSIN—Western States Information System is a regional information center of criminal justice data used by the states of Alaska, California, Hawaii, Oregon, and Washington.

Sources: Data from *Law Enforcement Technology*, April 1994, pp. 30–31 and 50, *Regional Information Sharing Systems*, p. 2, 1994, U.S. Justice Department; and T.A. Constantine, The National Drug Pointer Index, *The Police Chief*, pp. 24–30, 1998.

Exhibit 13–4

REGIONAL INFORMATION SHARING SYSTEMS (RISS) PROGRAM

The Regional Information Sharing Systems (RISS) Program is composed of six regional centers that share intelligence and coordinate efforts against criminal networks that operate in many locations across jurisdictional lines. Typical targets of RISS activities are drug trafficking, violent crime and gang activity, and organized criminal activities. Each of the centers, however, selects its own target crimes and the range of services provided to member agencies.

The RISS Program is a federally-funded program administered by the U.S. Department of Justice, Bureau of Justice Assistance. Each RISS center must comply with U.S. Department of Justice Program Guidelines and 28 CFR Part 23, Criminal Intelligence Systems Operating Policies. RISS serves more than 4,900 member law enforcement agencies in 50 states, two Canadian provinces, the District of Columbia, Australia, and Guam.

Each RISS center has from 450 to over 1,000 member agencies. The vast majority of member agencies are at the municipal and county levels, but more than 250 state agencies and 600 federal agencies are also members. The Drug Enforcement Administration; Federal Bureau of Investigation; Internal Revenue Service; Secret Service; Customs; and the Bureau of Alcohol, Tobacco, and Firearms are among the federal agencies participating in the RISS Program. The RISS services available to member law enforcement and criminal justice agencies include:

1. Information Sharing and Communication Network
   Access to timely computerized information on criminal suspects and activities related to Narcotics Trafficking, Violent Crime, Gang Activity, and Firearms Trafficking; Secure Intranet for electronic networking of law enforcement agencies throughout the U.S.; Electronic linking of the six RISS center criminal intelligence databases via the RISS wide area network (RISSNET); and Electronic linking to other systems such as the Southwest Border States Anti-Drug Information System Network

2. Analysis of Multi-jurisdictional Crime
   Analysis of complex case data connecting subjects and criminal events; Analysis of linked RISS databases to identify major criminal

(continues)

Exhibit 13–4 *(continued)*

conspiracies; and information surveys and analysis of gangs, firearms trafficking, and violent crime activities to assist member law enforcement agencies in anti-violence initiatives

3. Information Sharing Conferences With Specialized Training
   Conferences to exchange information on multi-jurisdictional criminal activities, such as: National conference on serial murder; Regional conferences on gang activity, firearms trafficking, and violent crime activity; Regional conferences on methamphetamine labs; and Training to build member agency expertise in investigative techniques, violent crime initiatives, and emerging crime problems

4. Loan of Sophisticated Investigative Equipment Not Otherwise Available or Too Costly for One Agency

5. Funds for Purchase of Evidence, Information, or Other Investigative Expenses to Support Multi-jurisdictional Investigations

Source: Reprinted from **http://www.iir.com/riss/riss.htm**, 11 June 1999, Bureau of Justice Assistance.

Western States Information Network (WSIN) serves Alaska, California, Hawaii, Oregon, and Washington. The center also has member agencies in Canada, Australia, and Guam.

In addition to the RISS centers, the federal government has established the National Law Enforcement and Corrections Technology Center (NLECTC) as a program of the National Institute of Justice's Office of Science and Technology, U.S. Department of Justice. The NLECTC is fully funded from the national level and all of the services to the criminal justice community are at no cost. The Center is not a research and development organization, but an information warehouse that helps law enforcement and corrections agencies to obtain information on appropriate technologies and to voice their needs. It gives the law enforcement and corrections community an opportunity to have their concerns heard and provides manufacturers and suppliers direction for future R&D efforts. The Center has a unique focus to provide information and assistance at the state and local jurisdictions—where most crimes are being committed, investigated, and adjudicated. Specifically, the Center helps these agencies prevent and reduce crime with technology solutions, from software to forensics and beyond. Many high-tech options are open to the law enforcement and corrections agencies. The Center is an impartial resource to help these agencies evaluate a set of solutions. The Center can help the state and local agencies identify problem areas, develop a solution, and implement a new product or technology (NLECTC 1999).

Branches of the Center are titled NLECTC-National, NLECTC-Southeast, NLECTC-Rocky Mountain, NLECTC-West, NLECTC-Northeast, the Border Research and Technology Center, the Office of Law Enforcement Technology Commercialization, and the National Center for Forensic Science. In the last few years, the Center has established effective partnerships between law enforcement, industry, and federal agencies. Its science and technology programs cut across the entire range of criminal justice issues and are aimed at the development of tools that will improve the operational efficiency of all aspects of the criminal justice system. These programs have always had a major focus on enhancing the safety of law enforcement officers, correctional officers, and other officers of the courts as they perform their daily duties of policing and maintaining custodial responsibilities for citizens under confinement by the courts. Technologies that can reduce the risks of injury or death to officers, suspects, and the general public during arrest, transport, and confinement are also of great interest (NLECTC 1999).

The Transition to Microcomputers

The police profession and the world of computer technology are similar, at least in one respect. Each has its own language, well understood and frequently used by people within each respective field, but misunderstood by and confusing to people on the outside. This situation caused few problems up to the 1980s because policing and computer technology intersected in relatively few areas, particularly in small- and medium-sized police agencies. Only large agencies had computers, called **mainframes**, which were very large and very expensive; therefore, computing power was available only to those agencies that could afford to pay large sums of money or share computer time on a large system. In those early days of computer technology, the computer would reside in a large room that was air-conditioned and environmentally controlled. Data that needed to be processed would be brought to the computer, probably in the form of punched cards. Informational printouts would then be produced and delivered to those who needed them. Control of the computer was administered by a small number of computer experts who spoke a strange language, the language of computer science and data processing. This type of environment required that data be **batch processed**. At a predetermined time, a batch of data was entered into the computer (usually on punched cards). Then, reports and listings could be obtained. However, between that time and the time when the next batch of data was processed, information was not available. Unfortunately, in many jurisdictions, the mainframe computer was shared by many agencies or departments within the jurisdiction, so each had to wait its turn for computer time and the processing of its data.

Advances in technology soon made it possible to place data terminals at those locations where the data originated. **Interactive processing** allowed data to be entered and processed as they were generated. The terminals were all connected to the computer, and each terminal could access the data and retrieve the information as necessary. The terminals were connected to the mainframe computer and shared its resources.

Other technological advances reduced the size and cost of computers and produced a generation of computers called **minicomputers**. These computers approach the performance of mainframe computers in many ways, but there are differences. The distinctions are not always clear and definite but are usually related to memory and processing capacity as well as the number of remote terminals that can access the computer at any one time. In most cases, mainframe computers are more expensive than minicomputers.

These two classes of computers, mainframe and minicomputers, are utilized by many law enforcement agencies today; however, mainframes are often being phased out in favor of minicomputers connected to local area networks (LANs) and wide area networks (WANs). These types of systems require people that have some technical knowledge to manage them. If a law enforcement agency is of sufficient size and budget, a mini- or mainframe computer may be appropriate. Also, a small agency may be able to use a portion of a mini- or mainframe computer's resources if the political subdivision has one.

Advances in computer technology in the last decade have produced very capable and powerful **microcomputers** (also called *personal computers*), which are very common in our information society and workplaces today. They have become a primary information processing tool. Not only are microcomputers becoming more powerful, they have also become affordable. It is now possible in many cases to put a microcomputer at the disposal of all persons within an organization, and it is here that the police profession and computer technology intersect and, in some cases, clash.

Police administrators of small- and medium-sized police agencies can afford to purchase a microcomputer system and use it to increase the efficiency of their agency. However, along with the benefits come some problems. As stated earlier, mini- and mainframe computers require a person or persons with extensive technical expertise. Usually, microcomputers do not. Situations often demand that someone within the agency become knowledgeable enough about microcomputers to aid in the decision-making process that is necessary when choosing the appropriate software and hardware, and to deal with other issues such as custom software, policies on access and use of the system, and overall computer security.

Inequities among Agencies

While most law enforcement agencies are connected to the National Crime Information Center through their department's statewide computer system, not all agencies have the same level of internal computer processing capabilities. Many small agencies throughout the country still do not have microcomputers available to their personnel for routine report writing and for database management. Paper and card files exist as the *only* record system in more agencies than we want to admit. This "technological gap" is significant, and in some places is getting larger. Most of the economic resources in small and many medium-sized agencies are applied to personnel costs, and the new technologies are considered frills and luxuries that cannot be afforded. In fact, in some agencies, the officers personally own more computer equipment, and sometimes more advanced computer technology, than the department does.

The level of computer skills within the workforce of law enforcement agencies also varies greatly. While many administrators, high-ranking managers, and supervisors are computer literate, many are not. In some agencies, it is likely that the newly or recently hired officers are more literate and skilled at using microcomputers than the people who supervise them. This imbalance has created problems in some agencies, but it is essential that law enforcement officers of the future be computer literate in order to manage the vast amounts of information that will be involved in daily interactions and to properly use modern equipment. Such knowledge and understanding also will be required in order to investigate the more serious white-collar and computer-related crime of the future. It is reasonable to begin requiring basic computer literacy as an entrance requirement to the field.

OTHER EMERGING TECHNOLOGIES IN POLICING

Chapter 3 of this text highlighted some the early technology applications such as fingerprinting and photography. The discussion above described the impact and evolution of information technology. What other areas of policing have been impacted by improved technology? With regard to firearms, the days of the simple pistol and rifle have given way to automatic weapons and laser-scoped rifles. Nighttime (low-light) goggles and high-tech surveillance equipment (such as **personal video surveillance systems**) are available. Of course, the automobile has continued to be refined, streamlined, and equipped with better lights and sirens. Hand tools such as flashlights, batons, PR-24s, and even handcuffs have undergone redesign and improvements. Radar systems for detecting speeders on the highways have begun using lasers. The next sections of this chapter will review some of the other technologies emerging from the laboratories to be used in policing.

Less-than-Lethal Technologies

In the last ten years, greater scientific inquiry and research have been conducted to subdue individuals in ways that would lessen the chance of serious injury or death. Besides protecting officers from such individuals, one major impetus for such research has been the many lawsuits for wrongful death filed against police departments or allegations of excessive force in making arrests and controlling crowds. The major products being tested for less-than-lethal application include the following (Pilant 1998; Boyd 1995):

Sticky Foam: This is a taffy-colored, gel-like substance that turns into a glue that sticks on contact. It can be dispensed from a shoulder-slung apparatus that contains the material under pressure. When applied, it expands, becomes sticky, and trips-up subjects. At the present time, it takes a large amount of material to be effective, and cleanup is a problem.

Strobe-and-Goggle Technology: The purpose of this technology is to disorient subjects during raids or assaults on barricaded structures. It uses bright flashing light to blind subjects while officers wearing special goggles enter to apprehend subjects. During testing, the limitations have been that the subjects were not disoriented long enough, and the devices generated extreme amounts of light and heat.

Backseat Airbag: As the name implies, this is a backseat version of the airbags used in vehicles to protect occupants during collisions. This version is placed in the backseat to control unruly subjects who often attempt to kick out windows or to damage partitioning screens. The airbag deploys when the backseat occupant gets rowdy.

Remote-Controlled Barrier Strips: In an attempt to limit the dangers of high-speed vehicular pursuits, barrier strips that would pop up and puncture the tires of a vehicle are being researched. The strips would be activated by police as the vehicle being pursued approaches it.

Fleeing Vehicle Tagging System: Also in an attempt to reduce the dangers from high-speed pursuits, officers might one day be able to "tag" a vehicle with a miniature radio transmitter. The police could then track the vehicle at a safe distance without giving immediate chase and endangering the lives of others.

Vehicle Disablers: Another future technological application may be a device that police could aim at a vehicle to disable its internal computer system, which would cause the engine to shut down. The vehicle would be useless, and the occupants could be trapped inside.

People Netting: As with fishnets, people nets could be used to control unruly persons or crowds. This netting would entangle the subjects and make movement difficult.

In 1997, the Pentagon created the Non-Lethal Weapons Program to research and develop new technologies. It is similar to the National Institute of Justice's

(NIJ's) program that began in 1986. In 1994, the NIJ created a working partnership with the Department of Defense. The goal of the NIJ program is the "identification and development of new or improved weapons and other technology that will minimize the risk of death and injury to officers, suspects, prisoners, and the public, and contribute to the reduction of civil and criminal liability suits against police, sheriff, and corrections departments" (Pilant 1998, 55).

Investigative Tools

The ongoing search for better detection equipment and identification technologies continues in both the research lab and the field. A fingerprint visualization system was recently developed by the Alaska Crime Laboratory in cooperation with a nationally known private firm. A device known as the "magic wand" can lift fingerprints from nonporous surfaces at the scene of the crime. When coupled with **automated fingerprint identification systems** (AFIS), such technology increases the chances of identifying suspects and reduces the time to do so. AFIS systems are now in operation in many jurisdictions across the nation.

Some futurists envision other devices that assist police in detecting weapons on subjects. One would be like a hand-held magnatometer but could be used some distance from the subject. It may be possible one day to stand outside a building and detect the person or persons inside through infrared technology. Some "smart-guns" are available today that cannot be fired unless they are held by an authorized person. Subjects who steal such weapons or take guns from officers during a struggle would find them useless when attempting to fire them.

Concealed weapons detection equipment is under development that may be able to prevent random firearm violence and protect criminal justice and military personnel as they perform their tasks. Programs initiated in 1995 are pursuing five technological approaches to detect concealed weapons on individuals: (a) passive millimeter wave (MMW) sensors and infrared (IR) cameras, (b) x-ray sensors, (c) active low-frequency magnetic sensors, (d) magnetometers, and (e) a sensor system combining ultrasound and radar sensors. The hope is to create a portable system that can detect concealed weapons from up to 30 feet (Pennella and Nacci 1997). Such devices could be used in airports, prisons, courts, police stations, and schools, and at large public gatherings. As the devices become more portable, they could become standard equipment on the uniform of officers.

Automated vehicle locator (AVL) systems and global positioning systems (GPS) can allow departments to track the exact location of officers. Other devices permit the monitoring of vital signs for possible stress. Digital imaging systems coupled with wireless technology will permit the sending of crime scene videos, street photos, mug shots, and so on to and from central police stations. Another innovation may include a portable translator that can record and translate voice communications from non-English to English. Agencies already have access to private company services such as the AT&T Language Line, which can connect an agency with interpreters of more than 140 languages any time of the day, every day of the week.

Recent data indicates that the Pentagon spends about $35 billion a year on research and development, and the U.S. Department of Justice spends about $5 million (Komarow 1994). In a 1994 "Memorandum of Understanding," the Department of Defense and the Department of Justice agreed to work more closely in developing and sharing technology that could be applied to civilian law enforcement. The National Law Enforcement and Corrections Technology Center (discussed above) was established in the Justice Department to coordinate and facilitate technological transfer to the civilian law enforcement sector. It is heavily involved in high-technology research to enhance the law enforcement function and to protect officers (see Exhibit 13–5).

Exhibit 13–5

HOW DID SOFT BODY ARMOR ORIGINATE?

The technology used for soft body armor worn by police officers was initially developed for heavy-duty military truck tires that were bullet-resistant. In 1972, a researcher from the U.S. Department of Justice's National Institute of Justice (NIJ) stumbled upon the fiber used in the tires, better known by its trade name Kevlar. Vests were subsequently developed, and NIJ conducted field tests in 15 cities. Since 1975, it is estimated that soft body armor has saved the lives of thousands of police officers.

Development continues today on vests and helmets that would offer greater protection to officers. In the near future, inserts made of titanium and ceramic may be available that offer rifle and bullet protection. The vests are designed to be more concealable and offer greater freedom of movement. Prototypes are being used by the military and the FBI.

Sources: Data from D.G. Boyd, On the Cutting Edge: Law Enforcement Technology, *FBI Law Enforcement Bulletin,* p. 1, 1995; and J.J. Pennella and P.L. Nacci, *Department of Justice and Department of Defense Joint Technology Program: Second Anniversary Report,* February 1997, U.S. Department of Justice.

Policing and Privacy

Since technology is at the heart of many privacy issue debates, and the use and abuse of that technology is often the focal point of debate in policing, it is appropriate to review some of the issues related to technology that reduce privacy and enhance possible detection. Included in this category are technologies that reduce the privacy (liberty) rights of an individual by increasing the ability of others to identify, locate, and follow an individual. Examples are geographic information systems (GIS), global positioning systems (GPS), satellite imagery (SI), remote sensing, telephony interception (including wiretapping, pen registers, and dialed number recorders), concealed weapons detectors, electronic license plate readers, surveillance cameras, and listening devices (Conser 1997).

Curry (1997) authored an excellent article that examines the potential invasion of privacy capabilities of GIS, GPS, SI, and remote sensing technologies when coupled with geodemographics. The combination of satellite surveillance technology and personal demographic information (age, occupation, income, race, education, etc.) can be utilized to track and locate an individual. The potential for abuse is high since the technology and personal information can also be in the hands of private corporations where little or no regulation of invasion of privacy exists. These same technologies, however, can provide additional services to consumers, such as assisting lost motorists, locating stolen vehicles, analyzing business locations, and providing information about real estate that one is interested in purchasing.

Telephony interception capabilities include wiretaps, pen registers, and dialed number recorders (DNRs). The differences among these are: wiretaps refers to the interception of telecommunications conversations, verbal or digital, wire or wireless; pen registers record the phone numbers of incoming phone calls to a target phone; and dialed number recorders capture all numbers dialed from a target phone. Of course, this technology is not just for phone calls; since computer networks and modems operate on phone lines, the same technology is used to monitor and trace those types of communications as well. Congress enacted the Communications Assistance for Law Enforcement Act (CALEA) in 1994. CALEA requires telecommunications companies to protect the privacy and security of communications and call-identifying information unless a court order authorizes interception. It also requires that the companies ensure that law enforcement has the capability to conduct court-ordered surveillance (Anderson 1997b).

Concealed weapons detectors, electronic license plate readers, surveillance cameras, and listening devices all reduce privacy and liberty in that they are used in the detection of criminal behavior. However, they are used usually to screen or observe all individuals in a particular area, which means they reduce the privacy of all who are in that area. Cities such as Redwood City (CA), Baltimore (MD), Camden (NJ), Philadelphia (PA), and Washington, DC, have experimented with or are using surveillance cameras and hidden listening devices to "patrol high-crime areas" (Lewis 1996). In Britain, over 400 city centers have used cameras to monitor public streets where crime was expected, resulting in a 60 percent decrease in crime in some areas (Scanning 1997). In the workplace, it is common practice by many to monitor e-mail, voice mail, and phone calls and to log Internet transactions to detect improper employee behavior. Such monitoring has been upheld by the courts, especially when accompanied by prior stated policy (Sahlberg 1991; Wallace *et al.* 1995; Levin 1995).

On April 16, 1993, the White House announced the future use of the "the Clipper Chip," which would allow law enforcement officials, acting under a court order, to intercept and decrypt information being transmitted in encrypted form. Under this policy, persons using certain networks would have to use Clipper Chip technology to send and receive their transmissions. However, each chip would have two "electronic coded keys" which would be maintained by selected government agencies. When law enforcement agencies suspected criminal activity, a court order could be sought to authorize the utilization of these keys to intercept or monitor digital transmissions. The announcement set off a major privacy debate between computing associations and professionals, and law enforcement officials. Part of the debate concerns how the information superhighway (the National Information Infrastructure) will be secured from fraud and other criminal acts. The Electronic Frontier Foundation (EFF) and the Computer Professionals for Social Responsibility are two groups that have publicly declared their opposition to the Clipper Chip and export controls on encryption technology.

The concept of privacy was addressed by the U.S. Supreme Court recently in a case that involved the police inviting a local news media camera crew to accompany them on a raid. The camera crew filmed the raid and the occupants of the residence as the police subdued them. The occupants were embarrassed by the later broadcast of the film on cable television. The suspect was originally charged with a federal offense but was later convicted of only a misdemeanor. The occupants sued the police, and the U.S. Supreme Court ruled that the inviting of the camera crew was unconstitutional as an unreasonable intrusion. Privacy will become a major issue as our society enters the 21st century. It will likely be the focus of much debate and litigation over the next several years as society gropes for answers to the intrusive nature of much of modern technology and the abuse of information disclosure by both the public and private sectors. Table 13–1 presents one possible paradigm in the debate over privacy and government intrusion.

Table 13–1 presents an initial rendition of what is proposed as a "paradigm of privacy rights." It is premised upon the principles found in the Preamble to the Constitution and the concepts of ordered liberty, citizenship, and responsibility. It has a guiding philosophy of a social compact that attempts to balance

Table 13–1 Proposed Paradigm of Privacy Rights and Government Interests

LEVEL OF INTERACTION	INTERESTS	PROTECTION APPLICATIONS	GOVERNMENT INTRUSION
			Extensive ←——————————————————→ Limited
International	International Sovereignty National Sovereignty	International Law & Treaties Sovereignty Rights	
National	National Security Common Defense/Safety Responsible Citizenship	Constitutional Rights Criminal Law, Administrative Law Civil Rights	
State	Rational State Interests Public Health, Safety, Welfare and Morals Responsible Citizenship	Criminal Law, Victimization Rights Family Law, Civil Law, Civil Rights Confidential Relationships Medical & Fiscal Privacy	
Social	Community Safety Social Compact Social Responsibility	Common Law, Tort Law Customs, Mores, Norms Cultural Privacy	
Companion	Intimate Relationships Personal Choice	Lifestyles and Intimate Relations Joint Property and Effects Marital Privacy Reputation, Public Image	
Self	Personal Thoughts Private Actions Self-Identity Solitude	Personal Property and Effects Personal Bodies Self-protection Personal Privacy & Self-disclosure	

Source: Copyright © 1997, J.A. Conser.

individual rights with the rights of society and an embodiment of the idea of "for the greater good." As a reminder, the Preamble states:

> We the People of the United States, in Order to form a more perfect Union, establish Justice, insure domestic Tranquility, provide for the common Defense, promote the general Welfare, and secure the Blessings of Liberty to ourselves and our Posterity, do ordain and establish this Constitution for the United States of America.

Throughout the Preamble, there is a spirit of cooperation and collective benefit. It is *not* a pronouncement of the sanctity of individualism. The Constitution itself provided a framework within which one could, ideally, prosper in liberty, but it does not place the individual above the common good. The Bill of Rights was later attached for the purpose of protecting individuals from the power of the federal government, with an understanding that state governments were not encompassed by them. It must be noted, however, that several states at the time had provisions similar to the Bill of Rights in their state constitutions protecting the individual at the state level.

The concept of ordered liberty implies the need for respect for law and some regulation of social behavior (social control). Intrinsic rights to privacy coupled with abuse of technology could lead to "unordered liberty" and social chaos. Citizenship and responsibility refer to the obligation owed to others in one's society and culture. Unfortunately, these concepts do not seem to have much popularity today. The duty of obligation seems to have been twisted to mean a societal or governmental obligation to the individual instead of the other way around.

The proposed paradigm is designed to provide the greatest privacy rights to the individual at the personality and intimate relationship levels. As interactions increase with a larger society and begin to involve the type of relationships that are of governmental concerns, privacy rights are more limited and subject to government control and regulation. The use of technology at each level of the paradigm could be determined, through public policy debates, to be appropriate or inappropriate to the privacy rights of individuals. Privacy rights then become socially derivative civil rights. The paradigm is not a panacea for the current privacy controversies and dilemmas facing society, but it is one approach to discussing the limits and parameters of proper government intrusion into our lives. It does require the recognition that the government has the right and authority to regulate morality to certain degrees; the right to protect national security interests; and the right to determine civil rights. The paradigm is a start, and it is not meant to be a finished product. The purpose here is to propose it and to modify or perfect it as it is debated and criticized. Many will not like it since it does not correspond to their advocacy of total self-determination and unfettered behavior.

Does this proposal address the limits of current issues related to technology and its abuse? Maybe there should be no expectation of privacy when in public or logged onto the Internet? Because of advanced technologies, such environments are not totally secure from others. If there are privacy rights in these environments, what price must individuals pay for it? Should privacy rights be based on one's ability to purchase privacy through screening devices, specialized software, and security hardware? Maybe the real issue is that Americans have not learned to respect the privacy rights of others—the same rights so many of us want to claim.

SUMMARY

This chapter has reviewed the tremendous impact that technology is having on policing today. Information and other technology may be one of law enforcement's most important tools in detecting and investigating crime. Information is the greatest asset to the law enforcement function—whether it be from incident reports, crime lab analysis findings, informants, intelligence operations, crime analysis matrices, or modus operandi files. Like any other tool, information technology systems can be used to streamline law enforcement processing of copious amounts of data and factual information. Resources can be better utilized, and the sharing of information should assist in detecting conspiracies, serial incidents, and trends.

With the proper planning, organizing, and control, information technology can become one of the most valuable tools used in law enforcement. As with any tool, abuses are possible, and one of the most controversial aspects of the use of information technology in policing today is the issue of privacy and accuracy of information in the databases and systems used by law enforcement. Information is power in an information-based society. Power can be abused, and with abuses come oversight and restrictions. The greater the restrictions, the less effective the information system becomes, so it is incumbent upon the law enforcement community to insure that progress in information technology does not restrict or impinge on the civil liberties of citizens unlawfully and unreasonably.

Other technologies hold great promise for policing. In the not too distant future, less-than-lethal restraining technology will lessen the need to use deadly force against aggressive subjects in the field. Likewise, improved investigative technologies will assist in evidence gathering and criminal prosecutions. Of course, all of this technology will be useless without adequately qualified and trained personnel to use it. So, in many respects, technology may have an impact on increasing the hiring qualifications needed to enter the field. Future applicants should prepare themselves for this eventuality.

QUESTIONS FOR REVIEW

1. What is the significance of information to the police function, and why is information technology important to the law enforcement community?

2. What are the general dates (in decades) of the evolution of information technology applied to the law enforcement function?

3. What are the major applications of information technology in the police field?

4. What are the differences among mainframe, mini-, and microcomputers in terms of the resources required to operate them?

5. When it comes to the utilization of information technology in policing, there are some inequities . . . What are they, and why do they exist?

6. What is the NCIC, and why is it important? What are the concerns about such large databases in a democratic society?

7. What are the technological innovations that are being applied to field procedures and techniques related to the use of force and crime investigation?

SUGGESTED ACTIVITIES

1. Have members of the class ask their parents (and grandparents, if possible) about their feelings and attitudes toward computers and about the impact of computers on their lives. Discuss their findings in class.
2. Ask the systems administrator or data processing manager of the largest law enforcement agency in your area to speak to your class about the ever-changing technology and what it means for the police occupation.
3. Have each member of the class be responsible for finding one article or detailed advertisement regarding an application of emerging technology in law enforcement. Discuss these in class.
4. Search the World Wide Web for articles and sites on "technology" and "privacy." What are issues associated with policing discussed in some of the material found?
5. Visit several sites on the World Wide Web such as **http://www.nlectc.org** and **http://www.fbi.gov** and view the discussions related to technology research and applications. Be sure to follow some of the links to other sites.
6. Visit agency Web sites such as **http://www.wichitapolice.com/index1.htm** and **http://www.cabq.gov/police**. How is technology changing the way agencies communicate with the public?

CHAPTER GLOSSARY

automated fingerprint identification systems (AFIS): a computerized process that scans a fingerprint and converts it into a digital image that is then analyzed and compared to other known images for matching purposes

automated vehicle location systems: a system used to locate vehicles outfitted with a receiver/transmitter that picks up positioning signals from satellites; the information can be transmitted to a computer-aided dispatch system capable of displaying a map showing the location

batch processing: a data-processing mode that entails computing large amounts of data in groups

computer-aided dispatch systems: an automated system that assists in prioritizing emergency situations and locating and guiding public safety personnel to incidents in the shortest time possible

geographic information systems (GIS; geocoding): a system for displaying and analyzing data that can be used to display location, find patterns and model scenarios

interactive processing: a data-processing mode that is continuous and timely and that allows immediate computation of the data

National Crime Information Center (NCIC): the national database maintained by the FBI that contains the names of missing and wanted persons and various stolen items; accessible to officers throughout the country via a system of computer networks

NCIC 2000: the planning and strategic effort underway by the FBI to upgrade the National Crime Information Center

mainframe computer: the largest of the categories of computers that require specific environmental controls and specially trained personnel to operate

microcomputer: a category of computers that are desktop-sized or smaller

minicomputer: a mid-range category of computer that is smaller than mainframes but larger than microcomputers and is capable of servicing many connected remote terminals

personal video surveillance systems: a system consisting of a small camera and microphone attached to the shirt of an officer and a transmitter attached to his or her duty belt, enabling images and sounds to be sent to a receiver/recorder subsystem located in the officer's vehicle

regional information system: a large computer system that services a regional geographical area and that usually serves as a gateway to NCIC

stand-alone system: a computer system made up of a single microcomputer or a single local network that is not connected to any other system

APPENDIX 13–1   THE EVOLUTION OF INFORMATION TECHNOLOGY

1600s—Galileo Galilei, the Italian mathematician, astronomer, and physicist, who assisted in the renaissance of mathematics as a scientific language. He stated that the "Book of Nature is written in mathematical characters." He influenced many scientists of his time.

1614—The first publication of the discovery of logarithms (the exponent of a base number indicating to what power that base must be raised to produce another given number) by John Napier of Scotland.

1620s—The slide rule was developed by William Oughtred and others to assist in the rapid calculation of numbers.

1640—Blaise Pascal developed an "adding machine" device called the Pascaline that remembered information and executed calculations by the use of wheels and interlocking gears. Its basic principle was used in adding machines for the next 300 years.

1673—Gottfried Wilhelm von Leibniz designed a machine that could process numbers beyond just addition—it was more like an early calculator. Leibniz is better known, however, for his invention of calculus and the perfection of binary arithmetic.

1804—The first fully automated loom was developed by Joseph Marie Jacquard. It was made possible by a memory device controlled by punched holes on a card and could weave very complicated patterns.

1800s—Charles Babbage, an English mathematician, proposed the "Difference Engine" and later the "Analytic Engine," which would have been a true computing device. Neither were ever perfected, and the latter was not completed because of problems in manufacturing the necessary parts. Augusta Ada Byron (daughter of Lord Byron, the poet) later assisted in translating and explaining Babbage's principles and theories.

1840s—George Boole devised a form of algebra (Boolean Algebra) that included the basic operators of AND, OR, and NOT. In 1867, Charles Sanders Pierce brought Boolean Algebra to the United States and continued to modify and extend it.

1890—Building on the punched card principle, Herman Hollerith devised a system of tabulating census forms with a machine that counted the holes on the card. Hollerith went on to form the Tabulating Machine Company, which after several mergers and name changes came to be known as the International Business Machines Corporation (IBM).

1930s—Vannevar Bush, an MIT professor, built a pioneering machine capable of solving differential equations. Bush thought it could be improved. Ultimately, this led to one of his graduate students, Claude Shannon, applying Boolean Algebra to the design of electrical circuits. His work lies at the foundation of modern telephone systems. Other researchers such as John Atanasoff of Iowa State University, George Stibitz of Bell Telephone Laboratories, and Konrad Zuse of Germany were also independently advancing the "computer evolution" with their work in electronics.

1941—Konrad Zuse designed and built (in Germany) the first operational computer, which was program controlled and based on the binary system.

1943—IBM and Howard Aiken succeeded in building the Mark I, a machine using punched paper tape that could "crunch" numbers up to 23 digits long. It was used by the Navy to solve difficult ballistic problems.

1943—The British built an electromechanical machine called COLOSSUS, which was used to decipher German codes and messages. It used vacuum tubes—a breakthrough in the development of the computer.

1945—John W. Mauchly and J. Presper Echert successfully tested the first all-electric digital computer. This Electronic Numerical Integrator And Calculator (ENIAC) was introduced in 1944 at the University of Pennsylvania. It filled an entire room (occupying 3000 cubic feet), weighed 30 tons, had 17,468 vacuum tubes, and consumed 200 kilowatts of electricity (enough to light 70–80 homes).

1947—Howard Aiken advised officials of the National Bureau of Standards that "[t]here will never be enough problems, enough work for more than one or two of these computers. . . ."

1947—The transistor was invented at Bell Telephone Laboratories, but did not appear economically in computer components until 1959. It was initially applied to radio technology.

1948—The Cathode Ray Tube (CRT) was applied to the Mark I by F. C. Williams.

1951—The first commercial computer, UNIVAC (UNIVersal Automatic Computer), was built by Echert and Mauchly. UNIVAC could process words as well as numbers. It was placed on the market by the Remington Rand (Sperry) Corporation. UNIVAC and other subsequent computers were made practical because of two innovations advocated during the mid-to-late-1940s by the collective work of John W. Mauchly, J. Presper Echert, and John von Neumann, who recommended use of (a) a binary number system (1's and 0's coupled with Boolean algebra) and (b) a stored program concept of instructions.

1950s—The cold war with the Soviet Union fueled the government's willingness to invest large sums of money in the development of larger and faster computers.

1953—Jay W. Forrester conceived and first used magnetic core memory successfully in the WHIRLWIND Computer at MIT as part of a massive federally funded project. This project led to others such as SAGE.

1954—The IBM 650 Computer was placed on the market as the first mass-produced computer. During the 1950s and 1960s, there were many advances in the computer industry, such as the development and refinement of various programming languages including FORTRAN, COBOL, ALGO, and BASIC.

1958—Texas Instruments engineer Jack Kilby created the first bone fide integrated circuit, which led to the miniaturization of computer parts.

1961—The first commercially produced electronic chips (silicon chips) containing integrated circuits became available, but were very expensive.

1960s—Many computers were built with integrated instead of transistor circuitry. This opened the era of the minicomputer as well.

1968—The first 256-bit chip was introduced, followed by the 1024-bit chip a few months later.

1970—The first microprocessor chip, the Intel 4004 (4-bit chip), was manufactured after being invented by Ted Hoff.

1972—The first 8-bit microprocessor, the Intel 8008, was introduced, thus opening the microcomputer era.

1974—The Intel 8080 became commercially available.

1975—The first personal computer, the Altair 8800, was sold through Micro Instrumentation and Telemetry Systems of Albuquerque, New Mexico—and the personal computer industry was launched.

1976—The Z-80 microprocessor (an 8-bit chip) was introduced by Zilog Company.

1976—The Intel 8086 (16-bit) chip was introduced.

1977—The Commodore PET, TRS-80 Model I, and Apple I personal computers became commercially available, along with about 28 other brands.

1978—Zilog Z8000 (16-bit) microprocessor was introduced.

1979—Motorola 68000 (16-bit) microprocessor was introduced.

1979—The Osborne I portable with built-in 5–1/4-inch diskette drives was introduced with a 5.5 inch CRT.

1981—IBM entered the personal computer field with the production of the IBM PC.

1981—The 32-bit microprocessor chip was introduced by Hewlett-Packard.

1983—The 80286 microprocessor chips became commercially available.

1983—The Tandy Model 100 laptop was introduced.

1984—The first laptops with a built-in disk drive were marketed.

1985—Handheld and laptop computers began to become economically attractive.

1986—The 80386 microprocessors became commercially available.

1989—The 80486-based microcomputers were marketed.

1993—The first Pentium (80586) microcomputers became available.

1997—The first Pentium II microcomputers became available.

1998—The first Pentium III microprocessor appeared, computing at speeds up to 500 MHZ.

1999—Palmtops and personal organizers become popular and inexpensive.

APPENDIX 13–2 THE EVOLUTION OF INFORMATION TECHNOLOGY IN POLICING

1845—All precinct stations of the New York City Police Department were connected by telegraph.

1867—Telegraph police call boxes were first installed.

1878—The Washington D.C. Police Department installed its first telephone, and by 1880 Chicago had installed telephones in call boxes on officers' beats.

1881—Chicago installed the first emergency police telephone booths.

1900s—Telephotography was employed by several departments, thus permitting the sending of photos from one city to another.

1902—An electric police alarm box system was installed in Kansas City.

1920s—The teletypewriter became a workhorse for communication between departments.

1926—Radio-equipped patrol cars with "receive only" capability were introduced in Berkeley, California.

1928—The Detroit Police Department initiated mobile radio receivers after several years of development. The Police Department of Cleveland, Ohio went on the air in 1929.

1929—The first statewide teletypewriter system was installed by the Pennsylvania State Police.

1933—Two-way police radio communications were initiated in Bayonne, New Jersey, followed by Indianapolis, Indiana.

1940s—Three-way communications capability was introduced.

1960s—Portable radios became less expensive and more popular.

1964—The St. Louis Police Department was the only one in the U.S. to have a computer system. None were in use at the state or national levels.

1967—The FBI's National Crime Information Center (NCIC) began operation in January.

1968—At least 10 states and 50 cities had acquired computerized systems.

1968—Kansas City began operation of ALERT I (Automated Law Enforcement Response Team).

1968—The Ohio Law Enforcement Automated Data System (LEADS) became operational after two-and-a-half years of planning; as a statewide system, it linked Ohio to the Criminal Justice Information System (CJIS), which tied into NCIC and was later connected to NLETS.

1970s—A big push through LEAA grants allowed many other departments to computerize.

1970—New York City's Special Police Radio Inquiry Network (SPRINT) was implemented.

1972—National Law Enforcement Telecommunications System (NLETS) became operational, linking all states except Alaska and Hawaii.

1972—Over 400 systems were in use in criminal justice agencies nationally, 46 percent of which were at the state level and 54 percent at the local level. An LEAA survey identified 39 functions being performed by computer—mostly recordkeeping related to police calls, personnel, and fiscal accounting.

1972—ALERT II in Kansas City expanded and included mobile digital terminals (MDTs) in cruisers.

1976—Computer Aided Dispatch systems were added to several agencies such as Virginia Beach, Virginia, also with mobile digital terminals.

1978—The first Automated Fingerprint and Identification Systems (AFIS) were developed. The large expense for these systems resulted in only a few sales.

1983—Over 800 systems were in use in criminal justice agencies nationally, not counting microcomputer systems.

1983—Renewed interest in AFIS surfaced among larger departments. By 1987, at least 15 states and 20 cities and counties had or were about to acquire AFIS systems.

1984—Notebook-sized computers were incorporated into the daily routine of St. Petersburg, Florida police officers.

1985—The use of microcomputers expanded into every aspect of law enforcement imaginable. Officers began purchasing their own for home and department use.

1986—Cellular telephones were incorporated into the police vehicles in St. Petersburg, Florida.

1987—Optical disk technology is coupled with microcomputers to offer several advantages and new applications.

1990s—Handheld computers appeared in agencies for traffic ticket enforcement; pen-based systems appeared for report-taking tasks; "paperless" and "near-paperless" police departments begin to emerge; vehicle-mounted video cameras were used to document traffic stops; personal video surveillance systems were used to record officer actions.

1999—NCIC 2000 became operational.

REFERENCES

Anderson, Teresa. 1997. Legal Reporter. *Security Management* (May): 86.

Artificial Intelligence Tackles a Very Real Problem—Police Misconduct Control. 1994. *Law Enforcement News* XX (408) (September 30): 1, 10.

Augarten, Stan. 1984. *Bit by Bit: An Illustrated History of Computers.* New York, NY: Ticknor & Fields.

Boyd, David G. 1995. On the Cutting Edge: Law Enforcement Technology. *FBI Law Enforcement Bulletin* (July): 1–6.

Buckler, Marilyn. 1998. NCIC 2000: More Than Just Images. *The Police Chief* (April): 16, 18–19.

Carsone, Louis P. and James A. Conser. 1984. "Silicon Street Blues." *Law and Order* (February): 18–21, 54.

Claude, Lewis. 1996. Will Residents Trade Privacy for Security? *Vindicator* (15 February): A15.

Communications Assistance for Law Enforcement Act. 1994. Public Law 103–414.

Conser, James A., ed. 1988. *Introduction to Microcomputers in Law Enforcement.* Hubbard, OH: Adaptive Systems, Inc.

Conser, James A. 1997. *The Right to Privacy in Digital America.* Paper presented at the Annual Meeting of the Academy of Criminal Justice Sciences, 13 March, Louisville, KY.

Curry, Michael G. 1997. The Digital Individual and Private Realm. *Annals of The Association of American Geographers* 87(4): 681–699.

Curtis, Christine. 1992. The Future of Automation in Law Enforcement. *Police Computer Review* 1(4): 1–8.

Dees, Timothy M. 1994. The Clipper Chip: Who Will Watch the Guardians? *Law Enforcement Technology* (August): 6.

Federal Bureau of Investigation. 1984. *National Crime Information Center: An Investigative Tool.* Washington, D.C.: U.S. Department of Justice (June).

Federal Bureau of Investigation. 1993. *Cooperation: The Backbone of Effective Law Enforcement.* Washington, D.C.: U.S. Department of Justice (June).

Federal Bureau of Investigation. 1996/1997. National Crime Information Center: 30 Years on The Beat. *The Investigator* (December/January). Washington, D.C.: Federal Bureau of Investigation.

FBI National Press Office. 1999. NCIC 2000 Begins Operation. Washington, D.C.: Federal Bureau of Investigation, July 15; **http://www.fbi.gov/pressrm/pressrel/ncic2000.htm.**

Feds Back Away from Clipper Proposal. 1994. *Law Enforcement News* XX (407) (September 15): 5.

Government Security Standards Draw Fire. 1994. *Infosecurity News* (September/October): 10.

Grun, Bernard, ed. 1991. *The Timetables of History.* 3d ed. New York: Simon and Schuster.

Jacob, Ayad, Dan Higgins, and Bill Wells. 1995. *The STAC/Early Warning System Project: Applying Innovative Technologies to Street Gang Crime in Chicago.* Illinois Criminal Justice Information Authority.

Juhl, Ginger M. 1994. SINS Narcotic Network: California Agencies Team Up in High Tech War on Drugs.

Law Enforcement Technology 21(4) (April): 30–31 and 50.

Komarow, Steve. 1994. "Technology Could Tip Scales in Crime War," *USA Today* (23 March).

Law Enforcement Assistance Administration. U.S. Department of Justice. 1976. *Two Hundred Years of American Criminal Justice.* Washington, D.C.: United States Government Printing Office.

Levin, Robert B. 1995. The Virtual Fourth Amendment: Searches and Seizures in Cyberspace. *Maryland Bar Journal* XXVIII(3) (May/June): 2–5.

Lutz, William E. 1998. Computer Mapping Helps Identify Arson Targets. *The Police Chief* (May): 50–52.

Newcombe, Tod. 1993. Artificial Intelligence Fights Crime. *Government Technology* (November): 1, 48.

NLECTC. 1999. *The National Law Enforcement and Corrections Technology Center.* **http://www.nlectc.org**.

Pilant, Lois. 1996. Imaging & Identification Systems. *The Police Chief* (August): 63–68.

Pilant, Lois. 1998. Crime & War: An Analysis of Non-Lethal Technologies and Weapons Development. *The Police Chief* (June): 55–68.

Rich, Thomas F. 1995. The Use of Computerized Mapping in Crime Control and Prevention Programs. *Research in Action.* Washington, D.C.: National Institute of Justice.

Rome Laboratory Law Enforcement Technology Team. 1996. The New Horizon: Transferring Defense Technology to Law Enforcement. *FBI Law Enforcement Bulletin* (April): 10–17.

Sahlberg, John. 1991. *Employee Privacy and Investigations.* Paper presented at American Society for Industrial Security Annual Seminar, 16 September, Washington, D.C.

Samar, Vincent J. 1994. The Right to Privacy Should Be Extensive. In *Civil Liberties: Opposing Viewpoints,* edited by P. Cozic Charles. San Diego, CA: Greenhaven Press, Inc.

Scanning. 1997. *Police Futurist* (Winter): 9.

Schoeman, Ferdinand D. 1983. Bibliographical Essay/Privacy and Criminal Justice Policies. *Criminal Justice Ethics* 2(2): 71–82.

Sessions, William S. 1993. Criminal Justice Information Services: Gearing Up For the Future. *FBI Law Enforcement Bulletin* (February): 1–3.

U.S. Department of Justice. 1994. *Regional Information Sharing Systems.* Washington, D.C.: U.S. Justice Department.

Video Privacy Protection Act of 1988, 102 Stat. 3195.

Wallace, Donald H. and Everett K. Woods. 1995. Surveillance, Eavesdropping and Citizens' Rights. *Journal of Security Administration* (December): 10–17.

Warren, Jim. 1994. Secret Data. *Government Technology* (April): 1, 42–43.

Wiretap Act Moves Ahead—In More Palatable Form. 1994. *Law Enforcement News* (15 September): 5.

Zannes, Estelle. 1976. *Police Communications: Humans and Hardware.* Santa Cruz, CA: Davis Publishing Company.

Future Social Problems

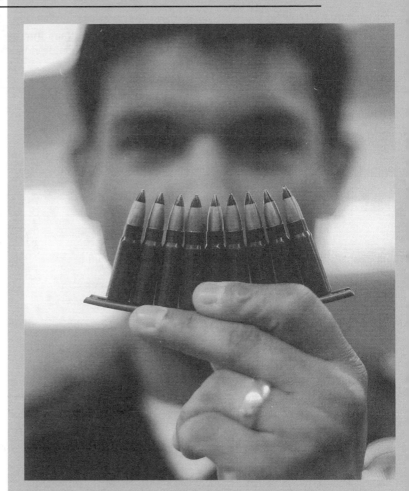

*Los Angeles police officer Robert Quihuis holds body
armor-piercing ammunition seized during early morning
raids across Los Angeles County; five militia members
were arrested and charged with weapons violations.
May 1997. (AP/ Wide World Photos)*

433

This chapter's focus is on changes in the overall environment that patrol officers and supervisors can expect to see in the future and some of the implications of these changes. You are encouraged to speculate on other implications that come to mind as you read and discuss this material with other students. Upon completing the study of this chapter, you should be able to:

1. Identify the major trends in international affairs that can impact law enforcement.
2. Explain the relationship between international trends and national changes.
3. Describe the impacts of immigration, racial, age, and gender changes on law enforcement.
4. Determine the major national trends that impact law enforcement directly.
5. List the major social trends in the nation, and relate them to causes of crime you have learned.

CHAPTER OUTLINE

FUTURE PROBLEMS AFFECTING POLICING

Law enforcement faces the same changes impacting economic, social, and governmental structures of our nation. Law enforcement also must respond to the call for changes from the justice system. In order to assess the nature of those changes, each organization must look to its own environment. This chapter is intended to stimulate the curiosity of the reader and encourage exploration of emerging forces of change. These forces may be global, national, or local in character. In Chapter 16, future challenges peculiar to law enforcement and what they may mean for patrol officers, supervisors, and managers are examined. It reviews the means by which all officers may scan for information, identify challenges, and help develop solutions (or at least accommodations). We say "challenges" because every problem should be viewed as a challenge and opportunity to change.

It is obvious that problems on the horizon are important to managers in law enforcement. Indeed, the nationally acclaimed Command College of the California Commission on Peace Officer Standards and Training is specifically designed as a futures and strategic planning program for managers. But why should patrol officers or supervisors pay attention to such issues? As noted earlier in this text, line officers and their supervisors are the eyes and ears of law enforcement. They will frequently be the first to notice changes in neighborhoods they patrol. They are closer to changes in the environment. Accordingly, they will be aware of information sooner and in greater depth than analysts sitting in either the administration or some distant university. It is not that academic analysts are not important—the authors would never take that position. Rather, both types of analysts are important. Patrol and supervision personnel must learn to analyze changes within their environment. They also must learn to interact with the other type of analysts in order to discuss the implications of such changes and to develop adjustment strategies or countermeasures.

GLOBAL CHALLENGES AND SOCIAL CHANGES

In 1985, then Senator and later Vice President, Albert Gore, Jr. introduced a bill in the U.S. Senate that would have required the United States Government to create a group whose special function would be to focus on world trends and events and project future changes in order to address them in advance (Gore 1990). It is difficult to assess how such a group, if started in 1985, might have helped the nation deal with the changes of the past 15 years. One thing is certain: We were not prepared to deal with these changes, and they have had profound effects on law enforcement as well as all other aspects of American society.

Foreign Terrorist Threats

While problems in international relations may seem very removed from day-to-day concerns of law enforcement, they are not. Take, for example, the collapse of the Soviet Union into various entities, the continuing disputes in the Middle East, open trade with Central and South America, or even increasing illegal immigration rates. Local governments must recognize the threat of international terrorists.

On the issue of security, American communities must now consider themselves more vulnerable as a result of the bombing of the World Trade Center in New York on February 26, 1993. The cause of this event was international political tension, along with a desire to use violence to make a political statement of the most profound sort. The bombing killed six, injured over 1,000, and caused $500 million in damage to the twin towers of the Trade Center. Estimates of damage to local businesses and loss of revenue to local, state, and national government tax coffers push the damage well past the billion-dollar range. The conviction in September 1995 of the ringleaders of the plot to bomb this and other targets led to further threats of terrorist actions. In response, the Federal Aviation Administration declared a "high-level alert," which impacted the operations of airports (and many law enforcement agencies) across the nation.

While few localities expect to see an event of that magnitude, most should anticipate the possibility of something similar happening and should prepare for it. In 1992 there were 1,911 bombings, while in 1995 there were 1,562 (down from 1,916 in 1994) (Maguire and Pastore 1997). These totals are twice that of 1988 figures, and accounted for 45 deaths, 469 injuries, and $22.6 billion in damage (Clark 1994). Some of these bombings are, no doubt, related to traditional crime, but many are drug-related, including some connected with international drug traffic. The domestication of international violence and terrorism presents a serious challenge to local law enforcement.

On April 19, 1995, a federal office building was bombed in Oklahoma City. While the perpetrator (discussed later in this chapter) was a domestic terrorist, he and his conspirators utilized tactics typical of international terrorists. Events such as this have caused the FBI to create a special Weapons of Mass Destruction Unit to address foreign and domestic threats associated with such weapons (FBI 1998b).

For local law enforcement, the difficulties this creates are immense. The language barriers involved where a crime is international in character are significant and prevent adequate intelligence-gathering. Further, the nature of the threat demands multi-agency involvement and increased liaisons between state and federal law enforcement. Managing a relationship between multiple agencies at two levels in the midst of serious threats or disasters requires substantial prior planning and attention *at all levels*. The involvement of foreign nationals makes information gathering difficult. But patrol officers who know the community can interpret patterns of neighborhood events or individual behavior that are out of the norm. Such events are a cause for inquiry and are worthy of note. No officer can assume that information is unimportant merely because there is no crime of which they are aware. Well-kept notes are very important in such conditions, since they may accumulate over a long period of time before patterns emerge. The role of computer-generated databases is significant for gathering this sort of intelligence (Homes and Holmes 1996).

While the bombing of the World Trade Center in New York was the result of Middle East tensions, there are many places in the world equally volatile. China, Ireland, Bosnia, Mexico, and certain areas of the former Soviet Union are only a few of the nations with internal turmoil that has the potential to spread to the United States. Officers should be aware of world and national trends and events. They are frequently linked to local events (Cetron and Davies 1994).

Free Trade and Open Borders

Free trade and open borders are of great concern as well. The notion of free trade will most likely help the general economy in the long run, which can only be good for law enforcement at all levels. However, it also poses interesting and complex problems (Cornish 1990). The increase in truck and other vehicular traffic that followed the **North American Free Trade Agreement (NAFTA)** increased smuggling dramatically. Freedom of travel across borders offers commercial opportunities for transport. Of course, it will not only be drugs, cocaine, and marijuana. Illegal alcohol, drugs that have not yet been approved by the Federal Food and Drug Administration for the treatment of illnesses, and even banned items such as ivory and other products related to endangered species will have new entry points.

These problems are most likely to be apparent in locations with close proximity to seaports or international highway access. However, that includes most of the continental United States. Even the states along the Great Lakes have international seaports. Examine the map of the United States (Figure 14–1). There are 301 ports of entry located throughout the United States. If you are within 500 miles (a one-day drive) from such an entry point, consider your location to be impacted. Obviously, very little of the nation is excluded. The relatively open border with Canada has become the primary entry point for would-be foreign terrorists as well, since the number of Border Patrol agents patrolling it is significantly less than the number patrolling the U.S.-Mexico border (Kasindorf 1998).

Conflicting Cultures

Culture conflict can produce or become related to neighborhood conflict. The disputes of groups throughout the world can easily be carried into America's streets. Shortly after the vicious and outrageous attack by an Israeli settler in March of 1994 on worshiping Muslims in the Middle East, a Muslim in New York City brutally attacked a car of Jewish students with gunfire. Could this have been prevented? There is no reason to believe that it could have been, but vigilant attention and awareness of world events might prevent similar crimes or trigger earlier intervention. One would assume that the potential for conflict could invade any neighborhood populated with emigres from nations currently in conflict over religious or racial differences. Law enforcement will be expected to address the aftermath of these tensions. Policing can also act to reduce tensions using its order maintenance and prevention roles.

Cultural values may conflict with laws in many ways. For example, prohibition of alcohol in the early 20th century was bound to fail where the European populations (such as the Irish and Italians) had integrated alcoholic beverages into daily life. Prohibition, therefore, provided a market for illegal alcohol. In Sicily, the **Mafia** was a family-like structure used to protect the average citizen from corrupt government and landlords. The Mafia and alcohol proved a potent combination, as the well-organized syndicate was able to profit from the sale of liquor and beer during prohibition. Similarly, as new populations emerge in our nation, their primary controlling socialization may be from

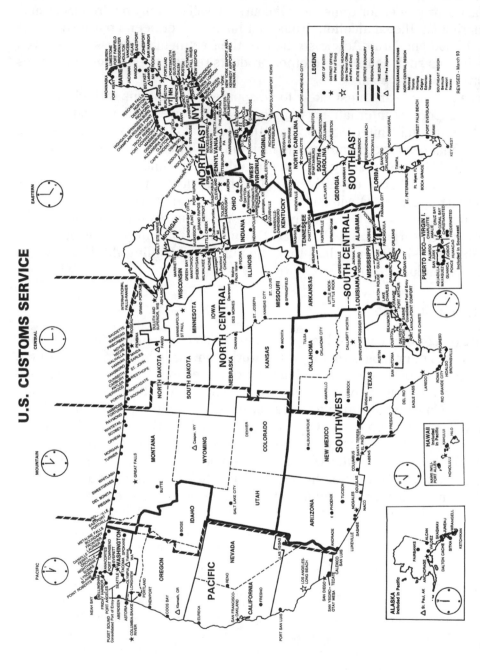

Source: Reprinted from *Importing into the United States,* U.S. Customs Service Publication 5D4A, pp. 48–49, 1994, U.S. Customs Service.

Figure 14–1 U.S. Ports of Entry

their culture. Examination of individual cultures will be necessary in order to assess the challenges. It will be incumbent upon local law enforcement authorities to remain in touch with these changes and assess any implications. Officers may need to identify potential cultural conflicts in their community.

Immigration Patterns

Changes in immigration patterns may impact many things other than just contraband importation or culture conflict. Accelerated immigration (legal and illegal) can be anticipated from a number of sources, including Haiti, Mexico, Cuba, Eastern Europe, Russia, China, and Singapore, to name only a few. As these populations migrate to the United States, they will present challenges similar to those presented by the Irish and Italians when those groups settled in the 19th century. One very recent example is the explosion of the "Russian Mafia" and its activities in the United States. According to the U.S. Bureau of the Census, there will be about 820,000 immigrants per year added to the U.S. population. Of these, 42 percent will be of Hispanic origin, 27 percent will be Asian, 23 percent will be non-Hispanic Whites, and 7 percent will be non-Hispanic Blacks. By 2050, it is expected that 25 percent of the U.S. population—about 80 million people—will be post-1994 immigrants or their descendants. Bouvier and Lindsey (1995) estimate that by the year 2100, 45 percent of the U.S. population will be immigrants or their descendants, using the year 2000 as a baseline. Figure 14–2 illustrates the changing ratio of race/ethnic composition of the U.S. projected through 2050 based on the Bureau of Census's middle series projection figures. By the middle of the next millennium, non-Hispanic Whites will constitute about 53 percent of the total U.S. population; non-Hispanic Blacks, 14 percent; Hispanics, 24 percent; Asians, 8 percent, and American Indian, 1 percent. Table 14–1 shows the percentage of the population by race and ethnic background from 1990 through 2050. Note that for the year 2050, the lowest and highest series projections are included. The middle series is thought to be most likely to occur; however, the others are possibilities.

The collapse of the **iron curtain** and the breakup of the old Soviet Union brought social and economic chaos to Russia and other former Soviet Republics. Obviously, crime can prosper in such an environment. For one thing, the KGB (a Soviet intelligence organization similar to the Central Intelligence Agency in the United States) and secret police were no longer present to keep order. Replacement systems of enforcement were not in place when changes came. In a wholly unregulated economy with no internal restraints, the opportunity was ripe for so-called "black market" transactions. These conditions also produced protection rackets, extortion, robbery, and other forms of random theft and violence. Predictably, the potential profit produced criminal organizations structured solely for economic gain. Members of such organizations are now migrating to the U.S. This prompted the FBI to open a field office in

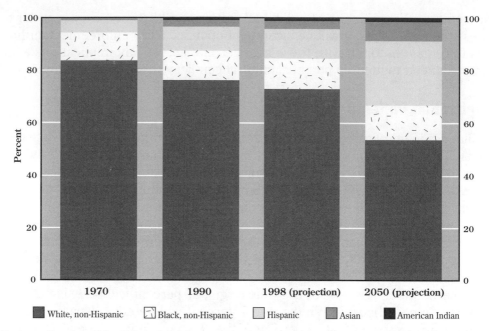

Source: Reprinted from J.C. Day, Population Projections of the United States by Age, Sex, Race, and Hispanic Origin: 1995–2050. U.S. Bureau of Census, *Current Population Reports*, P25–1130, p. 6, 1996, U.S. Government Printing Office.

Figure 14–2 Racial/Ethnic Composition of the U.S. Population, 1970–2050

the U.S. Embassy in Moscow in order to work with Russian law enforcement officials.

Immigration patterns will have other impacts. Tightly knit families with their own language will not be open to law enforcement. To them, American law enforcement may represent the negative governmental forces from which they fled. If their experience taught them that uniformed personnel were not on their side, there is little chance that they will be comfortable calling upon or assisting police officials. Language barriers will pose their own particular difficulty. Departments will need to find new ways to acquire diverse language skills, or they will not be able to do their jobs, even in regard to investigating traffic accidents or reading Miranda warnings. Languages needed by officers include Spanish, Russian, Chinese, Japanese, Vietnamese, Thai, Hmong, Korean, and even French Caribbean, to name but a few.

World Trade and Economic Patterns

World trade and economic patterns will also affect localities. As economic patterns shift, so will the tax base upon which government rests. Rapid changes

Table 14-1 Percent Distribution of the Population by Race and Hispanic Origin: 1990 to 2050

Year	Total	Race					Not of Hispanic origin			
		White	Black	American Indian[1]	Asian[2]	Hispanic origin[3]	White	Black	American Indian[1]	Asian[2]
ESTIMATE										
1990	100.0	83.9	12.3	0.8	3.0	9.0	75.6	11.8	0.7	2.8
PROJECTIONS										
Middle Series										
1995	100.0	83.0	12.6	0.9	3.6	10.2	73.6	12.0	0.7	3.3
2000	100.0	82.1	12.9	0.9	4.1	11.4	71.8	12.2	0.7	3.9
2005	100.0	81.3	13.2	0.9	4.6	12.6	69.9	12.4	0.8	4.4
2010	100.0	80.5	13.5	0.9	5.1	13.8	68.0	12.6	0.8	4.8
2020	100.0	79.0	14.0	1.0	6.1	16.3	64.3	12.9	0.8	5.7
2030	100.0	77.6	14.4	1.0	7.0	18.9	60.5	13.1	0.8	6.6
2040	100.0	76.2	14.9	1.1	7.9	21.7	56.7	13.3	0.9	7.5
2050	100.0	74.8	15.4	1.1	8.7	24.5	52.8	13.6	0.9	8.2
Lowest Series										
2050	100.0	75.7	15.7	1.2	7.4	22.0	55.8	14.2	1.0	7.0
Highest Series										
2050	100.0	73.5	15.8	1.0	9.7	25.7	50.5	13.8	0.8	0.2

[1] American Indian represents American Indian, Eskimo, and Aleut.
[2] Asian represents Asian and Pacific Islander.
[3] Persons of Hispanic origin may be of any race. The information on the total and Hispanic population shown in this report was collected in the 50 States and the District of Columbia and, therefore, does not include residents of Puerto Rico.

Source: Reprinted from J.C. Day, Population Projections of the United States by Age, Sex, Race, and Hispanic Origin: 1995–2050. U.S. Bureau of Census, *Current Population Reports,* P25–1130, p. 13, 1996, U.S. Government Printing Office.

in world trade patterns resulted in American steel and auto industry collapses in the 1970s, which negatively impacted American cities in profound ways. The 1989 movie *Roger and Me* depicted the real impact of these changes on one American city. While the federal government, and many state governments, can shift resources and draw upon a much more diverse tax base for income, local governments have few options. Traditionally, planning in law enforcement was predicated upon reasonably stable municipal and county budgets. In the past two decades, however, stability has given way to widely fluctuating budget resources. Projected budget needs will continue to outpace available resources for some time to come.

Budget impacts may require the reliance upon obsolete equipment, pay cutbacks, reduced training opportunities, and reductions in force (**RIF**, meaning layoffs and terminations). Turnover may increase as officers pursue other career options. Finally, the quality and quantity of recruits will fall precipitously as those with higher skill and knowledge levels seek safety and economic security in another location or career.

As local economic experiences produce change and workers are displaced, unemployment will result in predictable outcomes. The population base will grow increasingly poor. Poverty and social ills related to poverty will increase. These effects are associated with emotional problems, frustration, alcohol and drug abuse, physical assaults, and domestic violence. Consequently, service demands will increase for such things as random low-level violence and drug trafficking. Neighborhoods will fall into disrepair and the general feeling of security and safety will deteriorate, thus generating more crime opportunities (Wilson 1983).

Shifting economic patterns may produce economic *stimulus* in some areas. However, there are problems associated with such a response. Large numbers of new people will pose difficulties. Neighborhoods will grow increasingly transient in nature, which will provide widespread opportunity for household burglaries. Increased income in an area will generate a good deal of new property, and new property generates theft (which is essentially an opportunity crime). These conditions create higher demands for police service as well.

Management, supervisors, and patrol officers all need to be aware of both patterns. Because patterns will vary from location to location, management will need a steady flow of good information from line and supervision in order to assess the implications for their particular agency. Peculiar patterns will develop for each geographical area. Policies and approaches that work in one may not work in another.

NATIONAL CHANGES AND CHALLENGES

Obviously, many of the problems that impact law enforcement have international causes. However, many also have local causes, and many international trends have multiple local implications. These influences affect the kinds of crime that will occur in the future and the processes of hiring, training, and assigning law enforcement personnel. National trends may not be noticed in all locations. They may be more pronounced in some places, and less so in others. However, the idea that they are observable trends implies that *every* area of the nation will eventually be impacted by these changes in some manner.

Domestic Terrorist Threats and Hate Groups

The April 1995 bombing of the Federal Building in Oklahoma City killed 167 people, including several children, and injured many others. The bomb was made of several thousand pounds of fertilizer-based explosives and was packed into a rental truck. Timothy McVeigh, a former member of the U.S. Army and a Gulf War veteran, was charged as one of the conspirators. As the investigation unfolded, national attention turned to the growing influence of so-called **local militias**, as McVeigh was said to be a member of one such group. The isolated location of Oklahoma City, in the so-called heartland of America, and its generally conservative culture combined to add to the shock of the event. Why would anyone pick that location?

While the Oklahoma City bombing was shocking in and of itself, the specter of thousands of armed militia members produced serious concern for law enforcement planners. These groups of loosely organized, poorly disciplined, armed citizens seem to represent a variety of radical anti-government political groups. They are loosely allied nationally and are located in nearly every state in the union. The problem these organizations pose for law enforcement is substantial. They are secretive organizations, train in the use of combat weapons, and espouse anti–law enforcement rhetoric. They use the FBI shootout at Ruby Ridge (Idaho) and the fiasco at the Branch Davidian cult compound in Waco, Texas, as evidence of a great government conspiracy to suppress rights. Law enforcement should expect hostility, suspicion, non-cooperation, and violence from such organizations. Their numbers appear to be growing rapidly, and there is no reason to believe this will not continue. Some have said that the questions raised about Ruby Ridge and Waco have resulted in increased membership in many of these groups, though such allegations are difficult to document (Gwin 1995). In the 1990s, militia-like groups have been involved in bombings and numerous standoffs and shootouts with law enforcement.

The most singularly well known domestic terrorist in contemporary American experience was the unknown individual called the Unabomber, now known as Ted Kaczynski, a former math professor. The name given to this domestic terrorist derives from the tendency of the terrorist in his earliest attacks to target university and airport settings. However, he also attacked non-university individuals. Between 1978 and 1996 he struck 16 times, killing 3 and injuring 23 (Exhibit 14–1). He followed a 1995 bomb threat with a demand that his *manifesto* against technology be published. He threatened to kill more people with more

Exhibit 14–1

THE UNABOMBER'S 17-YEAR ODYSSEY

Northwestern University, Evanston, Illinois, May 25, 1978—A package was found in the Engineering Department parking lot at the Chicago Circle Campus of the University of Illinois. The package was addressed to an Engineering Professor at Rensselaer Polytechnic Institute in Troy, New York. The package had a return address of a Professor at Northwestern's Technological Institute. The package was returned to the addressor, who turned it over to the Northwestern University Police Department because he had not sent the package. On May 26, 1978 the parcel was opened by a police officer who suffered minor injuries when the bomb detonated.

Northwestern University, Evanston, Illinois, May 9, 1979—A disguised explosive device, which had been left in a common area in the University's Technological Institute, slightly injured a graduate student when he attempted to open the box and it exploded.

Chicago, Illinois, November 15, 1979—An explosive device disguised as a parcel was mailed from Chicago for delivery to an unknown location. The bomb detonated in the cargo compartment of an airplane, forcing it to make an emergency landing at Dulles airport. Twelve individuals were treated for smoke inhalation. The explosion destroyed the wrapping and the addressee could not be determined.

Chicago, Illinois, June 10, 1980—A bomb disguised as a parcel postmarked June 8, 1980 was mailed to an airline executive at his home in Lake Forest, Illinois. The airline executive was injured in the explosion.

University of Utah, Salt Lake City, Utah, October 8, 1981—An explosive device was found in the hall of a classroom building and rendered safe by bomb squad personnel.

Vanderbilt University, Nashville, Tennessee, May 5, 1982—A wooden box containing a pipe bomb detonated when opened by a secretary in the Computer Science Department. The secretary suffered minor injuries. The package was initially mailed from Provo, Utah on April 23, 1982, to Pennsylvania State University and then forwarded to Vanderbilt.

(continues)

Exhibit 14–1 *(continued)*

University of California, Berkeley, California, July 2, 1982—A small metal pipe bomb was placed in a coffee break room of Cory Hall at the University's Berkeley Campus. A Professor of Electrical Engineering and Computer Science was injured when he picked up the device.

Auburn, Washington, May 8, 1985—A parcel bomb was mailed on May 8, 1985, to the Boeing Company, Fabrication Division. On June 13, 1985, the explosive device was discovered when employees opened it. The device was rendered safe by bomb squad personnel.

University of California, Berkeley, California, May 15, 1985—A bomb detonated in a computer room at Cory Hall on the Berkeley Campus. A graduate student in Electrical Engineering lost partial vision in his left eye and four fingers from his right hand. The device was believed to have been placed in the room several days prior to detonation.

Ann Arbor, Michigan, November 15, 1985—A textbook-size package was mailed to the home of a University of Michigan Professor in Ann Arbor, Michigan from Salt Lake City. On November 15, 1985, a Research Assistant suffered injuries when he opened the package. The Professor was a few feet away but was not injured.

Sacramento, California, December 11, 1985—Mr. Hugh Scrutton was killed outside his computer rental store when he picked up a device disguised as a road hazard left near the rear entrance to the building. Metal shrapnel from the blast ripped through Scrutton's chest and penetrated his heart.

Salt Lake City, Utah, February 20, 1987—On February 20, 1987, an explosive device disguised as a road hazard was left at the rear entrance to CAAMs, Inc. (computer store). The bomb exploded and injured the owner when he attempted to pick up the device.

Tiburon, California, June 22, 1993—On June 22, 1993, a well-known geneticist received a parcel postmarked June 18, 1993, at his residence. The doctor attempted to open the package, at which time it exploded, severely injuring him. It has been determined that this parcel was mailed from Sacramento, California.

(continues)

Exhibit 14–1 *(continued)*

Yale University, New Haven, Connecticut, June 24, 1993—A professor/Computer Scientist at Yale University attempted to open a parcel that he had received at his office. The parcel exploded, severely injuring him. It has been determined that this parcel was mailed from Sacramento, California on June 18, 1993.

North Caldwell, New Jersey, December 10, 1994—Mr. Thomas Mosser, a New York City advertising executive, was killed in his home when he opened a package addressed to him. The package was mailed from the San Francisco area and bore the return address of a fictitious professor at San Francisco State University.

Sacramento, California, April 24, 1995—Mr. Gilbert Murray, president of the California Forestry Association, was killed at his office when he opened a package addressed to a person who formerly worked at that location. The package had been mailed apparently at the same time as letters sent by the bomber to the **New York Times** and to the Yale University professor who received a bomb on June 24, 1993.

Source: Federal Bureau of Investigation.

---

bombs if the document was not published. It was published in the *Washington Post* in September 1995, and it was generally a rambling denunciation of the role of technology in our society. Partially as a result of that publication, his brother David turned him in, as he became suspicious of Ted Kaczynski's actions and the language used in the manifesto, resulting in an arrest in April of 1996. He also hoped to be able to spare his brother's life. He apparently succeeded, as Ted Kaczynski was sentenced to four consecutive life terms plus 30 years with no option of parole in a federal court in Sacramento, California on May 4, 1998.

The number of hate groups has risen in recent years, according to the Southern Poverty Law Center, which has been tracking the growth and activities of such groups. There were 537 active hate groups identified by the Center in 1998. Of these, 163 were Klan-related organizations, 151 were neo-Nazi, 48 were racist Skinhead, 84 followed a hodge-podge of hate-based doctrines, and 62 were of Christian Identity persuasion (*Intelligence Report* 1999, 7). The Center also monitors "hate-type" Web sites and has identified over 254 of them, up from 163 in 1997. Figure 14–3 depicts the locations of active hate groups in the U.S. according to the Southern Poverty Law Center. Exhibit 14–2 identifies recent hate crime statistics gathered by the FBI.

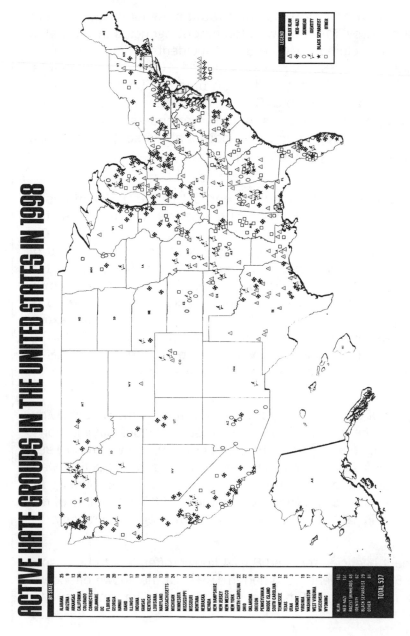

Source: Reprinted with permission from Active Hate Groups in the United States in 1998, *Intelligence Report 93*, Winter 1999, pp. 38–39, © 1999, Southern Poverty Law Center.

Figure 14-3 Hate Groups in the United States, 1998.

Exhibit 14–2

SUMMARY OF HATE CRIME STATISTICS, 1997

During 1997, a total of 8,049 bias-motivated criminal incidents were reported to the FBI by 11,211 law enforcement agencies in 48 states and the District of Columbia. Of the 8,049 incidents, 4,710 were motivated by racial bias; 1,385 by religious bias; 1,102 by sexual-orientation bias; 836 by ethnicity/national origin bias; 12 by disability bias; and 4 by multiple biases. The 8,049 incidents involved 9,861 separate offenses, 10,255 victims, and 8,474 known offenders. Sixty-nine percent of the incidents involved only one individual (person) victim, while 95 percent involved a single offense type.

Offenses
Crimes against persons composed 70 percent of the 9,861 offenses reported. Of all offenses measured, intimidation was the most frequently reported hate crime, accounting for 39 percent of the total. Destruction/damage/vandalism of property accounted for 26 percent of all offenses, while simple assault and aggravated assault accounted for 18 percent and 13 percent, respectively. Eight persons were murdered in 1997 in hate-motivated incidents. Racial bias motivated 5 of the murders, and sexual-orientation bias the remaining 3. When examining offenses associated with racially motivated incidents, 2,336 of the 3,838 anti-black offenses involved white offenders, while 718 of the 1,267 anti-white offenses involved black offenders.

Victims
Eight of every 10 of the 10,255 reported hate crime victims were individuals (people), while the remaining were businesses, religious organizations, or various other targets. Sixty-seven percent of the 10,255 victims in 1997 were targets of crimes against persons. Nearly six of every 10 victims were attacked because of their race, with bias against blacks accounting for 39 percent of the total. Sixty-five percent of the 1,586 total victims of religious bias crimes in 1997 were targets of all crimes against property.

Offenders
Law enforcement agencies reported 8,474 known offenders to be associated with the 8,049 incidents recorded in 1997. Of the known offenders, 63 percent were white and 19 percent were black. Unlike victims and/or

(continues)

Exhibit 14–2 *(continued)*

witnesses of crimes against property, those who witness or are victimized by crimes against persons are frequently able to assist law enforcement with the identification of offenders. Offenders were unknown for 2,791 or 35 percent of the incidents. Of the known offenders in 1997, 37 percent were reported in connection with the offenses of intimidation. Offenders involved in religious-bias crimes are difficult to identify because most of the crimes they commit are against property. Clearance rates are historically low for these types of crimes. Law enforcement identified only 792 offenders in connection with 1,385 religious-bias incidents in 1997.

Locations

In 1997, the majority of reported hate crime incidents, 30 percent, occurred in/on residential properties. Incidents perpetrated on highways/roads/alleys/streets accounted for 21 percent, while 11 percent occurred at schools/colleges. The remaining incidents were widely distributed among various locations.

Source: Reprinted from *Hate Crime Statistics, 1997,* 1998, Federal Bureau of Investigation.

Demographic and Work Force Changes

Between 1999 and 2015, the American labor force is expected to undergo dramatic changes. These changes include the aging of the work force as the average age of workers steadily increases. Other changes will be the continuing rise in the numbers of women and legal immigrants entering professions and the attendant changes in the workplace that must result to accommodate this trend. Finally, the labor force will also experience dramatic changes in racial, cultural, and language diversity.

Age Distribution. One of the major concerns for organizations, both public and private, is the changing nature of the American work force as it relates to the aging population. The members of the **baby boom generation** (those born between 1946 and 1964) now represent nearly one-third of the population. Because of the size of this group of people, the median age of the U.S. population has risen significantly since 1970 (see Figure 14–4). This represents a huge bulge in the middle of the work force (Table 14–2). The next generation after that, the so-called **baby bust generation** or **generation X** (1965–1975) is only half as large. This means that the labor pool will only grow at about 1 percent

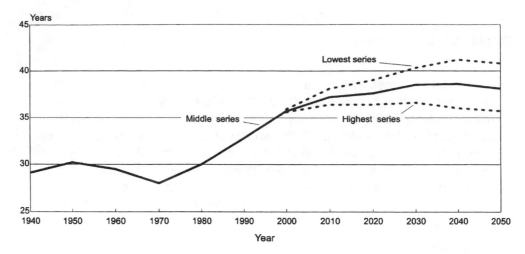

Source: Reprinted from J.C. Day, Population Projections of the United States by Age, Sex, Race, and Hispanic Origin: 1995–2050, U.S. Bureau of Census, *Current Population Reports*, P25–1130, p. 8, 1996, U.S. Government Printing Office.

Figure 14–4 Median Age of the U.S. Population, 1940–2050

per year for the next decade, the slowest rate in nearly 70 years. Hence, there will be many more older workers—and many fewer young workers, traditionally the source of entry-level employees for most organizations, including law enforcement. Calls for service from the elderly population will probably increase as well, because of the number who will be dependent on others (see Figure 14–5).

As the labor force changes, traditional modes of law enforcement recruitment and training will need to address these issues. Recruitment will be affected because older employees seek different job benefits. Training will change because older students learn in different ways than do younger students. Trainers also will need to appreciate the rich and diverse life experience of older students. These differences will enhance actual job performance, but will complicate training, particularly where the age range in class is large. Additionally, promotion will be affected by changing patterns as incoming cohorts of older students will seek promotion sooner and bring broader experience to the promotion competition.

Discipline, too, will change as a result of aging. It will need to become more a teaching tool and less a punishing tool. Law enforcement is faced with more complex, less clear tasks, and a candidate pool less able to respond to increased hiring demands. Accordingly, termination and replacement of officers will be less and less desirable as a disciplinary strategy. The desired strategy will be better training and management, and discipline will figure in this only to the degree it responds to these changes.

Table 14-2 Civilian Labor Force Characteristics, 1976–2006 (Numbers in thousands)

Group	Level				Change			Percent change			Percent distribution				Annual growth rate (percent)		
	1976	1986	1996	2006	1976–86	1986–96	1996–2006	1976–86	1986–96	1996–2006	1976	1986	1996	2006	1986–96	1976–86	1996–2006
Total, 16 years and over	96,158	117,834	133,943	148,847	21,678	16,109	14,904	22.5	13.7	11.1	100.0	100.0	100.0	100.0	2.1	1.3	1.1
Men, 16 years and over	57,174	65,422	72,087	78,226	8,248	6,665	6,139	14.4	10.2	8.5	59.5	55.5	53.8	52.6	1.4	1.0	.8
Women, 16 years and over	38,983	52,413	61,657	70,620	13,430	9,444	8,764	34.5	18.0	14.2	40.5	44.5	46.2	47.4	3.0	1.7	1.3
16 to 24	23,340	23,367	21,183	24,418	27	-2,184	3,236	.1	-9.3	15.3	24.3	19.8	15.8	16.4	.0	-1.0	1.4
25 to 54	58,502	79,583	96,786	101,454	21,061	17,223	4,888	36.0	21.6	4.8	60.8	67.5	72.3	88.2	3.1	2.0	.5
55 and over	14,317	14,904	15,974	22,974	587	1,070	6,999	4.1	7.2	43.8	14.9	12.6	11.9	15.4	.4	.7	3.7
White, 16 years and over	84,787	101,801	113,108	123,581	17,034	11,307	10,473	20.1	11.1	8.3	88.2	86.4	84.4	83.0	1.8	1.1	.9
Black, 16 years and over	9,561	12,654	15,134	17,225	3,093	2,480	2,091	32.4	19.6	13.8	9.9	10.7	11.3	11.6	2.8	1.8	1.3

(continues)

Table 14-2 *(continued)*

Group	Level				Change			Percent change			Percent distribution				Annual growth rate (percent)		
	1976	1986	1996	2006	1976– 86	1986– 96	1996– 2006	1976– 86	1996– 2006	1996– 2006	1976	1986	1996	2006	1986– 96	1976– 86	1996– 2006
Asian and other, 16 years and over[1]	1,822	3,371	5,703	8,041	1,549	2,332	2,338	85.0	69.2	41.0	1.9	2.9	4.3	5.4	6.3	5.4	3.5
Hispanic origin, 18 years and over[2]	—	8,076	12,774	17,401	—	4,698	4,627	—	58.2	36.2	—	6.9	9.5	11.7	—	4.7	3.1
Other than Hispanic origin, 16 years and over[2]	—	109,758	121,169	131,446	—	11,411	10,276	—	10.4	8.5	—	93.1	90.5	88.3	—	1.0	.8
White non-Hispanic[2]	—	94,026	100,915	108,166	—	6,890	7,251	—	7.3	7.2	—	79.8	75.3	72.7	—	.7	.7

[1] The "Asian and other" group includes (1) Asians and Pacific Islanders and (2) American Indians and Alaska Natives. The historical data are derived by subtracting "black" from the "black and other" group; projections are made directly, not by subtraction.
[2] Data by Hispanic origin are not available before 1980.

Source: Reprinted from H.N. Fullerton, Jr., Labor Force 2006: Slowing Down and Changing Composition, *Monthly Labor Review*, p. 24, 1997, U.S. Department of Labor.

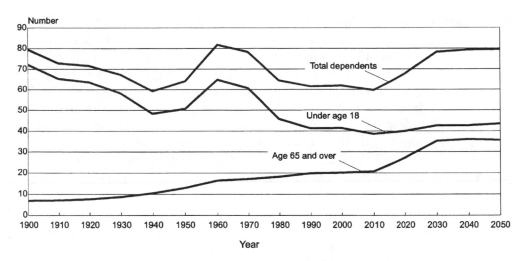

Source: Reprinted from J.C. Day, Population Projections of the United States by Age, Sex, Race, and Hispanic Origin: 1995–2050, U.S. Bureau of Census, *Current Population Reports*, P25–1130, p. 8, 1996, U.S. Government Printing Office.

Figure 14–5 Number of Dependents per 100 Persons, Age 18–64 Years, 1900–2050

Gender and Racial Changes. Other changes in the work force will involve the influx of many more women and minorities. By the year 2006, women will occupy about one-half (47 percent) of the labor force (refer to Table 14–2). Indeed, nearly two-thirds of those who do enter the work force in the next decade will be female. This change will force workplace redesign. Policies for parental leave, child care, and sexual harassment are only a few of the more obvious changes that will result. The way teams work will change, too. Women tend to exhibit different management styles and are more comfortable with collaborative work approaches. Because collaboration and participative management approaches dominate thinking in both public and private management literature and practice, males must learn to adopt these approaches. These are the approaches that will guide management for the next three decades. It is significant to note that Problem-Oriented Policing, Community-Oriented Policing, and Restorative Justice all rely upon collaborative decision-making models.

By the year 2006, minorities will make up nearly 28 percent of the national labor force. This will include many diverse cultures—Asian, Hispanic, Middle Eastern, Caribbean, African, Native American, and African-American, to name only a few in general terms. Again, these changes will force alterations in recruitment, training, and promotion policies.

Educational Changes. Educational differences will also be a problem affecting planning at all levels in law enforcement. Some of these problems arise from apparent contradictions in the landscape of American education. Between 1960 and 1989 the percentage of those 25 to 29 with a high school education increased from about 45 percent to 86 percent. Yet the number of functionally illiterate people increased. More people also attended college, but changes in funding for higher education coupled with a departure from affirmative action in University systems such as California's caused a decline in the number of minorities attending institutions of higher education. This information must be considered in light of increasing demands on the work force for a higher degree of technical skill. One must also consider that more highly educated employees have elevated motivation needs and expect more responsibility and rewards (Jamieson and O'Mara 1991).

Given changes in the labor force and in the public clientele of law enforcement agencies, agencies will be under increased pressure to address training *and* educational needs of employees. Increasingly complex technical crimes, more technical evidentiary demands, emerging technological demands in law enforcement, changing enforcement approaches, and competition with private industry for the same labor pool will combine to force law enforcement to address the training and education issues directly, including the provision of education (as distinguished from training). Many departments are adopting higher educational requirements as hiring criteria. While the number doing so has steadily increased, education does not necessarily solve department problems. Research discloses that educated officers are not necessarily more satisfied and education is unimportant if departments fail to adopt problem solving approaches to crime prevention (Dantzker 1998).

Americans with Disabilities. Another major change facing law enforcement in the coming decade will be the impact of the **Americans with Disabilities Act of 1990 (ADA)**. This act was intended to reduce the obstacles in society that restrict opportunities for the disabled. The forms of discrimination against people with disabilities include barriers in the design of buildings, transportation services, and communication systems, as well as hiring and training standards and job requirements. The purpose of the ADA was not to make organizations hire unqualified applicants, but rather to provide a national mandate for the elimination of barriers unrelated to performance ability and basic social needs. The law defines someone as disabled if there is a mental or physical impairment that substantially limits a major life function (Rubin 1993).

This act will affect law enforcement both externally and internally. External effects will be felt as those with disabilities become more fully integrated into the day-to-day activities of society. First, the disabled will become victims and witnesses more often. Second, their problems will be some that community policing seeks to address. For example, the condition of sidewalks, the safety of bus stops and other public conveyances offer opportunities for officers to improve the quality of life and prevent crime. Third, in cities there will be a new awareness of the need for pedestrian and public transportation safety.

Internally, the largest impact will be in the assessment of hiring and training within each agency. It is important to understand that the ADA is not an affirmative action requirement for those who are classified as disabled. Employers are permitted to hire the most qualified person for a job, but the act safeguards a disabled applicant who is *otherwise qualified*. Two questions must be answered to determine whether the disabled applicant is otherwise qualified: (1) Does this person meet the initial job requirements, such as experience, education, and so on? (2) If so, can he or she perform the **essential functions** of the job, with or without **reasonable accommodation** (Rubin 1993)? The difficulty for law enforcement, as with most employers, will be the determination of essential functions and reasonable accommodations. This should be seen as an opportunity, not a threat. The nature of law enforcement is changing and so too are the skills and demands of the profession. Certainly, many of the tasks traditional to law enforcement will continue. But many new ones are emerging both as a result of new forms of policing and as a result of technology. Stephen Hawking, a brilliant theoretical physicist and author of *A Brief History of Time*, is a quadriplegic, yet he has done more to change our understanding of physics and the universe than anyone since Albert Einstein. Accordingly, the ADA will force law enforcement to examine the way its work is designed. It may well be that tasks can be better described and arranged in order to take advantage of skills that the community, and law enforcement, need. Still, the problem of implementation in law enforcement is large, and no means has been found yet to accomplish easy accommodation, since sworn law enforcement personnel are presumed to be capable of effecting a forcible arrest (Clark and Donohue 1995). Indeed, the sum total of changes facing law enforcement may require a revision of the view that all officers start on the street.

Affirmative Action. Affirmative action looms as an increasingly pernicious problem, not merely for law enforcement but for all of public management. Despite the extensive presence of affirmative action policies in government agencies, a wave of opposition to the continuation of these policies developed in the early 1990s. On the legal front, *some* programs were struck down by courts as unconstitutional. On the political front, affirmative action was a central issue in the 1996 presidential race and all the candidates took clear positions on the issue. Colin Powell, retired general and Chairman of the Joint Chiefs of Staff, and President Bill Clinton represent the two most pronounced supporters of the idea. Most other candidates tended to reject affirmative action. Exhibit 14–3 describes the background and history of affirmative action.

Because the Supreme Court defers to Congress on *federal* policy regarding affirmative action, the impact of litigation has been primarily at the state and local level (Fullilove v. Klutznick, 448 U.S. 448, 1980). However, a major agenda item of the Republican-dominated Congress elected in 1994 was the rollback of affirmative action at the federal level. This suggests the likelihood of major

Exhibit 14-3

WHAT IS AFFIRMATIVE ACTION?

Affirmative action has taken on a life of its own in American politics, but lost in the discussion is the history of and original reason for the policy. Dating to the 1940s and early 1960s, a series of Presidential orders and federal statutes were directed at existing racial discrimination in the United States. Initially, the Presidential orders were directed at the military and related defense industries. Eventually, laws sought to eliminate discrimination in employment, housing, public accommodations, and transportation. In 1954, the Supreme Court declared discrimination in public schools unconstitutional. The fact is that up to the 1960s, African-American citizens could not vote in many places, get loans, or even apply for most jobs. It was obvious that this situation was wrong and needed correction.

The acts and orders that sought to overcome existing racial discrimination tried to achieve equal opportunity. Many people looked to past discrimination and argued that non-whites had been denied opportunity for so long that they deserved a sort of *boost*. In the law, this is called *remedial action* and is no different than the idea of damages in an attempt to make a person whole after a wrong is done. Obviously, on a society-wide basis, remedial action is harder to design. In civil rights, the boost was affirmative action. It argued that some preference should be shown for those who were the targets of past discrimination.

We are now nearly 30 years past the most sweeping of those reforms, the 1964 Civil Rights Act, but we still struggle with *how* to correct past wrongs. Many people who tried to develop systems of providing the boost sought to use quotas as a measure of affirmative action. Hence, if 20% of your city is non-white, then 20% of the police department should be non-white by the formulation. This approach, however, seemingly works a reverse discrimination on whites, and many such allegations are being voiced.

The argument about affirmative action, then, is one about how to implement a system of making up for past discrimination without discriminating more in return. There is no easy method of accomplishing this task. One thing is certain, no one can deny the history and current prevalence of racial discrimination in the United States, and it is an issue with which law enforcement must come to grips.

changes in federal policy. From the perspective of management theorists and consultants, this would likely be a mistake. Organizations tend to make better decisions when *many* people of *diverse* backgrounds participate in decision making (Lawler 1988; Galbraith and Lawler 1993). On the practical law enforcement side, we can speculate whether the O.J. Simpson criminal verdict would have been different if the lead detectives had been African-American in as much as the racial conspiracy argument would not have made any sense to a jury.

In any event, the subject of affirmative action poses major challenges for law enforcement in light of changing patterns in the civilian population, work force, and political landscape. The U.S. Supreme Court decision in a Richmond, Virginia, case addressed the issue of race-conscious construction contract awards; the implications could change the implementation of affirmative action-type programs across the U.S. (see Exhibit 14–4). In this case, the Supreme Court of the United States (1) differentiated Congressional plans that may create racial preferences in federal government policy from those created by states or cities and (2) rejected the use of mere quotas as a remedy for past discrimination in employment or contract cases where special skills are needed.

Disaster and Civil Unrest

Law enforcement must also concern itself with natural disasters and the increasing lethality of social unrest. In the case of natural disasters, the nation has seen several consecutive years of wildfires, floods, hurricanes, and earthquakes that destroyed wide areas of territory and disrupted normal public service. Law enforcement threats emerge from such directions.

There is a wide range of matters that concern law enforcement in such emergencies, and a number of agencies must coordinate their emergency response. Fire services, emergency medical services (EMS), the state and federal Environmental Protection Agency (EPA), search and rescue organizations, law enforcement agencies, National Guard units, corrections agencies, Departments of Transportation, and the **Federal Emergency Management Agency (FEMA)** are all likely to be involved in any major disaster. The coordination of these agencies is critical to success. Coordination requires predefined guidelines and protocols to which each agency agrees. It also requires practice and training in the implementation of emergency protocols. Such disasters also impact public safety personnel's personal lives.

Natural disasters, however, may not be the most likely form of disaster, but rather only the most singularly damaging. Disasters that are the result of human actions are far more likely to cause industrial damage, for example. We can include in this list large vehicle accidents (train derailments and freeway chain-reaction pile-ups, for example), plane crashes, toxic chemical spills, riots, bombings, arsons, and major gas leaks. Each of these represents a unique challenge to law enforcement, and, again, a unique set of predefined response models.

Exhibit 14-4

RICHMOND v. J.A. CROSON CO., 488 U.S. 469 (1989)

Justice Sandra Day O'Connor for the Court

On April 11, 1983, the Richmond City Council adopted the Minority Business Utilization Plan (the Plan). The Plan required prime contractors to whom the city awarded construction contracts to subcontract at least 30% of the dollar amount of the contract to one or more Minority Business Enterprises (MBEs).

While there is no doubt that the sorry history of both private and public discrimination in this country has contributed to a lack of opportunities for black entrepreneurs, this observation, standing alone, cannot justify a rigid racial quota in the awarding of public contracts in Richmond, Virginia. Like the claim that discrimination in primary and secondary schooling justifies a rigid racial preference in medical school admissions, an amorphous claim that there has been past discrimination in a particular industry cannot justify the use of an unyielding racial quota.

In the employment context, we have recognized that for certain entry-level positions or positions requiring minimal training, statistical comparisons of the racial composition of an employer's work force to the racial composition of the relevant population may be probative of a pattern of discrimination. But where special qualifications are necessary, the relevant statistical pool for purposes of demonstrating discriminatory exclusion must be the number of minorities qualified to undertake the particular task.

Given the existence of an individualized procedure, the city's only interest in maintaining a quota system rather than investigating the need for remedial action in particular cases would seem to be simple administrative convenience. But the interest in avoiding the bureaucratic effort necessary to tailor remedial relief to those who truly have suffered the effects of prior discrimination cannot justify a rigid line drawn on the basis of a suspect classification.

However, it is important to remember that contingency plans or standard operating procedures must be flexible enough to adapt to different conditions. Moreover, plans and procedures must be practiced and reviewed on a regular basis in order to insure currency. The purpose of disaster drills is to be able to coordinate the actions of all agencies into an effective response.

While it may seem that disasters are increasing in number and severity, it is more a function of the growth and distribution of the population. The U.S. population is relatively concentrated, and disasters are likely to impact larger numbers of people and create more significant difficulties for officials charged with responding to these problems. In 1998, wildfires in Florida provoked the evacuation of thousands of people and canceled the Daytona 500 auto race. While controversial, evacuations are intended to avoid injury and death to humans, risks that wildfires present.

Medical Issues

Until recently, law enforcement officers needed to concern themselves only with emergency aid to accident victims or getting those in custody to medical facilities if treatment was needed. Now, their environment is more complicated. While medical treatment for custodial individuals is still an issue, the need for adequate training to insure the prompt delivery of treatment is critical. In a 1989 precedent-setting decision, the Supreme Court of the United States held a city liable for not getting proper care to a woman in custody (*Canton v. Harris,* 489 U.S. 378). The failure to do so was traced to the lack of trained personnel present to *assess* the need for medical attention. Liability arose from a failure to observe that need.

Medical issues have arisen in other areas too, of course. Officers need to understand the fragile nature of evidence that requires forensic work. A fatal error in the O.J. Simpson case arose when investigating officers carried a vial of Simpson's blood around Los Angeles for an entire day, exposing it to heat and light, rather than taking it quickly to the crime lab. Preserving evidence in a crime scene where victim assistance is required poses additional problems. While victim treatment is essential, care must be taken not to damage evidence. In some cases, there is a great need to deal directly with emergency personnel and the medical community in general. In rape or driving while intoxicated cases, to name only two, officers must frequently deal directly with medical facility staff. Training is necessary in order to understand the needs and interests of the medical community.

Obviously, one of the largest problems is the threat of AIDS transmission. AIDS (Acquired Immune Deficiency Syndrome) is a complex disease. Essentially, it is a disease that destroys the body's ability to resist other diseases common to mankind. It is transmitted by bodily fluids, generally those such as blood or sexual fluids. Hence, contact with blood or sexual fluids of another person can provide the opportunity for transmission. Accidental exposure to blood or tissue is a major concern for law enforcement. Officers may make contact with either in the process of arresting a suspect or assisting a victim.

It is clear that those in public safety areas share a risk of exposure to AIDS (Woodruff *et al.* 1993). The risk is obvious from the degree to which the disease has spread in the general population (McDonald 1990). The **Centers for**

Disease Control (CDC) estimates that through the year 1996, there were 362,004 deaths from AIDS and another 581,429 cases reported. In 1996 alone, 68,000 new cases were reported. The disease appears to be slightly decreasing overall, but increasing in some populations. Law enforcement personnel would be advised to look frequently at the home page of the Centers for Disease Control for regular updates on the spread of the disease **(http://www.cdc.gov/)**.

It is just this sort of risk that caused the Occupational Safety and Health Administration (OSHA) to issue guidelines on the exposure to *Potentially Infectious Materials* (PIMs). These guidelines are applicable to all employers, including law enforcement agencies. They cover all **blood-borne pathogens**, or pathogenic microorganisms present in human blood. This includes not only the AIDS-causing HIV (human immunodeficiency virus) but also hepatitis B virus (HBV), a very pernicious and highly infectious blood disease. (New strains of hepatitis are now being discovered as well.) There are several very serious illnesses, in fact, that can be contracted by contact with contaminated blood (29 CFR §1910.1030, 1999). The Code of Federal Regulations (C.F.R.) details the diseases covered and the precautions necessary. It is incumbent on every agency to fulfill its mission to train law enforcement officers in the appropriate protective techniques to avoid exposure to blood.

AIDS and HBV are not the only medical problems looming, however. Law enforcement must concern itself with the possible exposure to a far more problematic disease. Tuberculosis (TB) is a disease that attacks all body tissue but primarily the lungs. It is spread primarily by sputum in either airborne droplets (from people spitting or sneezing) or on the ground. This disease was once thought to be conquered, but recently a new strain of the bacteria has emerged that is immune to the drugs previously used to kill the bacteria. There is no known cure for this current strain.

Law enforcement will also need to concern itself with the problem of managing holding facilities and jails in ways that do not expose those in custody to disease. As smoking in the workplace becomes an issue, we would expect that similar issues will invade the domain of law enforcement, not only for employees, but also those in custody.

Gangs and Neighborhood Decay

Another set of related social issues deals with the continuing decay of the cities and the surrounding social fabric. The problem of gang activity was discussed in an earlier chapter and the problem of civil unrest was mentioned above in this chapter. In many ways, these problems are related. Long before James Q. Wilson adopted the metaphor of **"broken windows"** to address the relationship between structural neglect and crime, social scientists noticed that as inhabited areas fell into general disrepair, crime and violence followed. There is no need here to detail why this theory is reasonably correct in suggesting such a relationship. For us, the important aspects deal with what this means for law enforcement.

For many reasons, the overall condition of a neighborhood is related to both general criminal activity and gang activity. Indeed, addressing the issue of improving the way a neighborhood looks is central to combating gangs and crime (California Department of Justice 1993). The importance to law enforcement is obvious. Officers must take a broader view of social conditions. Instead of merely responding to a criminal event, officers must also survey the neighborhood. If there is uncollected garbage, for example, they should call the appropriate authorities. In Marysville, California, officers used a public park cleanup as a "jump start" for reviving an entire neighborhood, rescuing it from drug dealing and prostitution. By organizing citizen groups and inviting businesses to donate materials, the park was revitalized and used as a focal point to attack other criminal activity in the neighborhood. In three years, the turnaround was clear.

Neighborhood deterioration may seem like someone else's problem, but it *becomes* a law enforcement problem if left alone. If an officer sees broken windows in a home that seems inhabited, inquiry should be made as to why they are not fixed. Maybe it is an elderly person too afraid to call for assistance, or someone with a landlord who refuses to act. In the first case, officers can do something directly. In the second case, officers can call the city council or a service club for assistance. Someone will take action and help preserve the neighborhood if the problem is brought to the attention of appropriate agencies and pursued to resolution. If the department is fortunate enough to have community service officers, then this information should be reported to them. Follow-up should always be done. In Santa Rosa, California, all patrol officers serve on two teams. The horizontal team is the "beat/shift" team. However, all beat/shift teams serve together for a COP team for that beat (the vertical team). They report neighborhood problems to their COP supervisor (a different sergeant than their beat sergeant) and collaboratively develop solutions to address the problems. Frequently, they are given time off their shift assignments to work on COP projects.

The conditions to which officers should pay attention include weeds, garbage, abandoned vehicles, trash on lots, buildings seriously in need of repair, buildings that need to be demolished, graffiti, and "broken windows" of all kinds. Perhaps the observant officer can convince the department or local civic groups to have a cleanup and fix-up campaign. The department might, for example, establish a special unit to tow away abandoned vehicles, assist building inspectors and health inspectors, survey neighborhood needs, and create liaisons with community groups that have funds and membership power to use on such projects. But in order for such things to happen, officers need to look for the conditions that imply a need for change. Then they need to take action within the department to address the problems they observed.

Gangs and other outward evidence of decay cannot be addressed merely by dealing directly with those effects. The underlying conditions that give rise to such activity must be the primary focus. Because the interior regions of most cities are old and getting older, and because there are fewer and fewer government dollars for assistance in such projects, law enforcement officers should expect conditions to continue to get worse. Patrol and supervision officers can be the eyes and ears of the *community* as well as the department, and they can coordinate a response.

Gangs are an escalating problem in the United States (see Figure 14–6). In 1992 (the last year for which we have reasonably reliable data), 72 of the 79 largest cities in the United States reported significant gang activity. Overall, 85 percent of 94 jurisdictions in a recent survey reported gang crime problems (see Figure 14–7). In 1995, 21 percent of high school seniors reported at least one event of being in a fight with a group of friends against another group during the previous year (Maguire and Pastore 1997). All indications were that gang activity was increasing, though it must be noted that there is no agreement either in academia or in law enforcement regarding a definition for gang

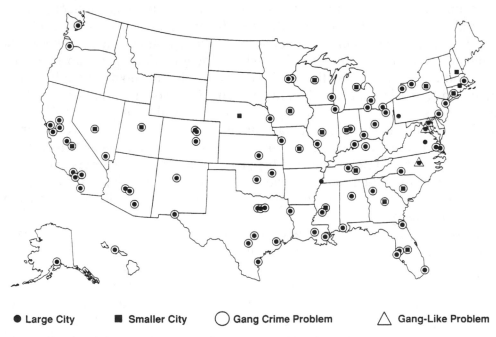

● Large City   ■ Smaller City   ◯ Gang Crime Problem   △ Gang-Like Problem

Source: Reprinted from G. Curry, R.A. Ball, and R.J. Fox, Gang Crime and Law Enforcement Recordkeeping. *Research in Brief*, August 1994, U.S. Department of Justice, National Institute of Justice.

Figure 14–6 Gang Activity in Cities of the United States, 1992

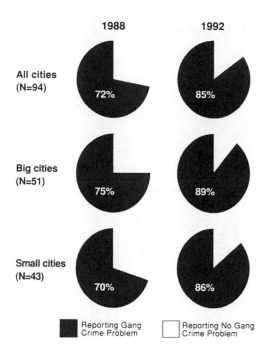

Source: Reprinted from G. Curry, R.A. Ball, and R.J. Fox, Gang Crime and Law Enforcement Recordkeeping, *Research in Brief*, August 1994, U.S. Department of Justice, National Institute of Justice.

Figure 14–7 U.S. Cities Reporting Major Crime Problems, 1988 and 1992

activity. Research suggests that gang members are no more likely to engage in drug trafficking than non–gang members, but they are more likely to engage in violence (Decker and Van Winkle 1994; Esbensen and Huzinga 1993; Klein *et al.* 1991).

The relationship between social conditions, gang activity, and crime is clear. We noted earlier in Chapter 5 that victimization and reported crime were decreasing *overall* in the United States. However, violence in certain areas of our cities is increasing dramatically. Moreover, as Table 14–3 demonstrates, the violent crime rate for those in the 14–25 age range is radically escalating. Males aged 15–24 have the highest homicide victimization rate. Black males have a rate of victimization of 123.1 per 100,000 population followed by Hispanics at 48.9, American Indians at 26.6, Asians at 15.6, and non-Hispanic Whites at 6.4. These figures parallel a worldwide crime increase (Stephens 1994). Law enforcement can address these problems with aggressive responses to criminal events and by aggressively acting against *conditions* that give rise to gangs and violence. The trend line for homicide victimization by age is depicted in Figure 14–8.

Table 14–3 Rates of Violent Crime, and Personal Theft by Sex, Age, Race, and Hispanic Origin, 1997

Victimizations per 1,000 persons age 12 or older

Characteristic of victim	Population	All crimes of violence*	Violent crimes						Personal theft
			Rape/ Sexual assault	Robbery	Total	Assault Aggravated	Simple		
Sex									
Male	106,598,660	45.8	0.3	6.1	39.4	10.9	28.4		1.6
Female	113,240,440	33.0	2.5	2.6	27.9	6.4	21.6		1.7
Age									
12–15	15,701,280	87.9	2.5	8.2	77.1	15.1	62.0		2.8
16–19	15,244,130	96.2	5.6	10.2	80.4	24.6	55.8		3.5
20–24	17,648,850	67.8	2.4	7.4	57.9	17.0	40.9		1.8
25–34	40,162,600	46.9	2.3	4.7	39.9	9.5	30.4		1.1
35–49	62,604,840	32.2	0.6	3.7	27.9	7.4	20.4		1.6
50–64	36,486,320	14.6	0.2	2.2	12.2	2.8	9.4		1.1
65 or older	31,991,100	4.4	0.2	0.9	3.4	0.6	2.8		1.2
Race									
White	184,617,470	38.3	1.4	3.8	33.1	8.2	24.9		1.4
Black	26,683,380	49.0	1.6	7.4	39.9	12.2	27.7		3.3
Other	8,538,250	28.0	1.1	5.0	21.9	6.1	15.8		0.8
Hispanic origin									
Hispanic	21,163,000	43.1	1.5	7.3	34.3	10.4	24.0		2.4
Non-Hispanic	196,323,060	38.3	1.4	3.9	33.0	8.3	24.7		1.5

*The National Crime Victimization Survey includes as violent crime rape/sexual assault, robbery, and assault, but not murder and manslaughter.

Source: Reprinted from M. Rand, Criminal Victimization 1997: Changes 1996–97 with Trends 1993–97, National Crime Victimization Survey, p. 4, 1998, Bureau of Justice Statistics.

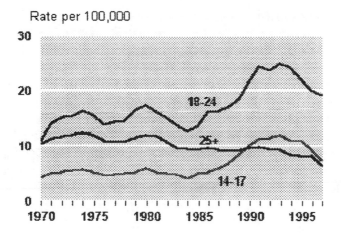

Rate per 100,000

Figure 14–8 Homicide Victimization Rate by Age, 1970–1997

Political Changes and Challenges

Law enforcement agencies are public organizations. They are, therefore, subject to the same limitations and controls that other public agencies experience. This is surely one of the most troubling facts with which policing officials struggle. Political pressure is frequently used in attempts to influence law enforcement agencies. Sometimes political influence is used to stop law enforcement from doing something it seeks to do; on other occasions, it is employed to force law enforcement to do something. At other times, it is used to punish officers for acts that offended some of the wrong people. Finally, it is sometimes employed to honor and reward law enforcement.

The use of such political power may come from state legislatures, Congress, mayors, the courts, governors, or city councils. It may also come from civilian review boards or similar agencies. Two things are important to understand. First, law enforcement agencies have the same reaction to negative political pressure as any agency that views itself as professional. The Departments of Energy and Education and the Environmental Protection Agency all resent political pressure that counters their *professional judgment.*

The second important thing to remember is that, in a democracy, politics *does* rule public policy. Law enforcement has a constitutional duty to respond to the public. Indeed, the notion of community policing is founded on a number of premises, but one of them surely is the idea that law enforcement must be responsive to the community. There may be attempts, of course, to influence law enforcement in illegitimate ways. One of the roles of ethics is to appreciate these differences in order to resist improper influences while heeding the proper political controls of a public agency. Public administration scholars call this the "politics-administration dichotomy," or the attempt (usually in vain) to separate politics from the professional administration of the government's business. The notion is traced to an 1887 article by a young scholar named Woodrow Wilson, long before he became the only President of the United States with a Ph.D. In this article, Wilson laments how politics has infected administration in government agencies. His views paralleled those of the progressive reform movement, which, among other reforms, was responsible for the civil service approach to hiring (Wilson 1887).

Law enforcement should expect political pressure to increase in the coming years. Despite crime rates that are more or less going down, pressure will be placed to do more. Yet budget limitations, also politically determined, will deny any real growth in resources. Law enforcement, therefore, will need to develop local approaches to balancing these pressures against the need to perform and the duty to obey legitimate political authority. This balance will not be easy, but it must be a priority of law enforcement.

Law enforcement will also continue to be investigated when it makes mistakes. Whether the issue is the O.J. Simpson case, racism in the city police departments, the FBI shoot-out at Ruby Ridge, or the ATF/FBI assault at Waco, Texas, law enforcement will be increasingly called upon to justify its actions. With the prevalence of video cameras and Internet connections, hiding from public scrutiny will be exceedingly difficult. Therefore, law enforcement must redouble its efforts at preventing errors or the appearance of error.

SUMMARY

This chapter addressed many of the social changes that will impact law enforcement in the near future. This list, however, barely scratches the surface. Issues that are global or international in scope—such as civil wars in Africa, Bosnia, and the former Soviet Union or NAFTA, immigration, and terrorism—may appear unrelated to local policing, but they are not. National problems such as racism, changing employment trends, juvenile violence, AIDS, poverty, and politics may be visible daily but are difficult to deal with at the local level. It is much easier to recognize the impact or consequences of these forces than it is to know how to change or prevent them.

Your role is to be alert to future social changes and the challenges they present. Such changes will impact the profession of law enforcement in profound ways. The challenges to professionalize the field will be examined in the next chapter. In the final chapter, we will examine how law enforcement officers of every rank can engage in futures studies and look for changes that are coming in order to be able to meet them.

QUESTIONS FOR REVIEW

1. How do social changes and local events in other nations impact law enforcement in the United States?
2. How do economic trade and immigration patterns relate to law enforcement?
3. What is the recent trend in terrorist bombings in the U.S.?
4. How will the American labor force change by the year 2006?
5. What impact will the changes in the labor

force and other population demographics have on law enforcement?

6. Why is it inaccurate to believe that the ADA mandates that law enforcement agencies hire the disabled?

7. What are the historical reasons for affirmative action?

8. What are the major diseases that threaten law enforcement officers on the streets, and why?

SUGGESTED ACTIVITIES

1. In groups of three to five students, discuss how you would project trends in any of the areas covered in this chapter. What evidence would you examine for hints about such trends? What methods would you use to gather evidence?
2. How can law enforcement respond to changes in the labor force? Develop a list of approaches and discuss them in class, along with arguments for and against each approach.
3. Log on to your Internet service provider and look for pages concerning the Unabomber. Does the information available prior to his capture conform to what we now know?

CHAPTER GLOSSARY

ADA: the Americans with Disabilities Act of 1990, which addresses employment and other barriers for those who are disabled

baby boom generation: those born between 1946 and 1964; the largest generation in American history

baby bust generation: those born between 1965 and 1975, a much smaller demographic group than the prior generation

blood-borne pathogens: pathogenic microorganisms present in human blood

"broken windows": the theory attributed to James Q. Wilson claiming that physical evidence of deterioration in a neighborhood leads to or fosters subsequent crime

CDC: the Centers for Disease Control, the major federal agency charged with studying disease and contagious outbreaks in the U.S.

cultural conflict: social conflict that results when a society has several cultures that are intermixed but which have not assimilated one another's values

cultural values: norms or accepted beliefs about the way the world is and the way things should be done; a society or culture comes to "value" these beliefs, and rewards the adherence thereto (and punishes their violation)

essential function: as mandated by the ADA, one of the job requirements—such as experience, skills, education, and so on—determined by an employer to be necessary for an employee to successfully perform the actual job tasks of the position

FEMA: the Federal Emergency Management Agency, charged with responding to major national disasters, if requested by the state affected and approved by the President

iron curtain: the cold war expression that referred to the walls and fences that sealed off the communist countries of Eastern Europe and all of the former Union of Soviet Republics from the rest of the world

local militias: military-type groups of civilians organized locally for the protection of their self-defined civil and constitutional rights; usually heavily armed and may practice defensive military maneuvers

Mafia: organized crime group generally run by Italian-Americans of Sicilian extraction; it takes its name from traditional Sicilian social structure where the *maffia* protected peasants from the Italian central government and landholders

NAFTA: the North American Free Trade Agreement, which attempts to reduce the restriction or tariffs on trade among the countries of Mexico, Canada, and the U.S.

reasonable accommodation: an ADA provision that permits and may require an employer to change certain work-related environments or conditions in order to allow a disabled person to successfully perform the job in question

RIF: reduction in force; a clever name for permanent layoffs

REFERENCES

Bouvier, Leon F. and Lindsey Grant. 1994. *How Many Americans?* San Francisco, CA: Sierra Club Books.

California Department of Justice. 1993. *Gangs 2000: A Call to Action.* Sacramento, CA: California Department of Justice.

Canton v. Harris, 489 U.S. 378, 1989.

Cetron, Marvin J. and Owen Davies. 1994. The Future Face of Terrorism. *The Futurist* 28(9) (November–December): 10–16.

Clark, Jacob. 1994. Crime in the 90's: It's a Blast. *Law Enforcement News* 20(411) (15 March): 1.

Clark, Jacob R. and Stephen Donohue. 1995. Still Wondering After 5 Years: Disabilities Law Continues to Perplex Police Agencies. *Law Enforcement News* 21(429) (15 September): 1, 14.

Cleveland, Harlan. 1995. The Limits of Cultural Diversity. *The Futurist* 29(2) (March–April): 23–26.

Coates, Joseph, Jennifer Jarrat, and John Mahaffie. 1991. Future Work. *The Futurist* 25(3) (May–June).

Cornish, Edward. 1990. Issues of the Nineties. *The Futurist* 24(1) (January–February): 29–36.

Curry, G. David, Richard A. Ball, and Robert J. Fox. 1994. *Gang Crime and Law Enforcement Recordkeeping.* Research Brief. Washington, D.C.: U.S. Department of Justice, National Institute of Justice (August).

Dantzker, M. L. 1998. Police Education and Job Satisfaction: Educational Incentives and Recruit Educational Requirements. *Police Forum* 8(3): 1–4.

Day, Jennifer Cheeseman. 1996. Population Projections of the United States by Age, Sex, Race, and Hispanic Origin: 1995–2050. U.S. Bureau of Census. Current Population Reports, Pub. No. 25–1130.Washington, D.C.: U.S. Government Printing Office.

Decker, Scott and Barrick Van Winkle. 1994. Slinging Dope: The Role of Gangs and Gang Members in Drug Sales. *Justice Quarterly* 11(4): 583–604.

Esbensen, Finn-Aage and David Huizinga. 1993. Gangs, Drugs, and Delinquency in a Survey of Urban Youth. *Criminology* 31(4): 565–86.

Federal Bureau of Investigation. 1998a. *Hate Crime Statistics, 1997.* Washington, D.C.: Department of Justice.

Federal Bureau of Investigation. 1998b. WMD: A Domestic Threat Assessment. *Police Chief* 65(6): 63–67.

Fullerton, Howard N., Jr. 1997. Labor Force 2006: Slowing Down and Changing Composition. *Monthly Labor Review* 120(11): 23–39.

Fullilove v. Klutznick, 448 U.S. 448, 1980.

Galbraith, Jay R. and Edward E. Lawler, III. 1993. *Organizing for the Future: The New Logic of Managing Complex Organizations.* San Francisco: Jossey-Bass.

Gore, Albert, Jr. 1990. The Critical Trends Assessment Act: Futurizing the United States Government. *The Futurist* 24(2) (March): 22–24.

Gwin, Harold. 1995. Recruitment Grows Stronger, Speaker Says. *The Vindicator* (15 September): B4.

Holmes, Ronald M. and Stephen T. Holmes. 1996. *Profiling Violent Crimes: An Investigative Tool.* Thousand Oaks, CA: Sage Publications.

Intelligence Report 93. (Winter 1999). Montgomery, AL: Southern Poverty Law Center.

Kasindorf, Martin. 1998. "Drugs, Terrorists, Smugglers Provoke Calls for Tighter Net." *USA Today* (21 July).

Klein, Malcom W., Cheryl L. Maxson, and Lea C. Cunningham. 1991. Crack, Street Gangs, and Violence. *Criminology* 29(4): 623–50.

Lawler, Edward E. III. 1988. *High Involvement Management.* San Francisco: Jossey-Bass.

Maguire, Kathleen and Ann L. Pastore. 1997 *Sourcebook of Criminal Justice Statistics 1996.* Washington, D.C.: U.S. Department of Justice.

Maieson, David and Julie O'Mara. 1991. *Managing Workforce 2000: Gaining the Diversity Advantage.* San Francisco: Jossey-Bass.

McDonald, Martha. 1990. How to Deal with AIDS in the Work Place. *Business and Health* 8(7) (July): 12–21.

Moore, Michael. 1989. *Roger and Me.* Dog Eat Dog Films.

Rand, Michael. 1998. Criminal Victimization 1997: Changes 1996–97 with Trends 1993–97. *National Crime Victimization Survey.* Washington, D.C.: Bureau of Justice Statistics.

Rubin, Paula N. 1993. *The Americans with Disabilities Act and Criminal Justice: An Overview.* Research in Action. Washington, D.C.: National Institute of Justice.

Stephens, Gene. 1994. The Global Crime Wave: And What We Can Do About It. *The Futurist* 28(4) (July–August): 22–28.

Wilson, James Q. 1983. *Thinking About Crime.* New York, NY: Basic Books.

Wilson, Woodrow. 1887. The Study of Administration. *Political Science Quarterly* 2.

Woodruff, B. A., L. A. Moyer, K. M. O'Rourke, and H. S. Margolis. 1993. Blood Exposure and the Risk of Hepatitis B Virus Infection in Firefighters. *Journal of Occupational Medicine* 35(10): 1048–1054.

Professional Issues
and Problems

Sgt. John Flynn adjusts a video monitor inside a state police vehicle. Civil rights groups called for the cameras after three unarmed minority motorists were shot by two white state troopers during a traffic stop on the Pennsylvania Turnpike in April 1998. (AP/Wide World Photos)

This chapter's focus concerns the professional status and quest for greater recognition of the policing occupation. The issues and problems associated with the quest are diverse, and some are controversial. To some degree, they are multidisciplinary, which makes any resolution or consensus more difficult. Upon completion of this chapter, you should be able to:

1. Distinguish between occupation and profession.
2. Describe the traditional criteria or characteristics of a profession.
3. Identify five benefits of profession status.
4. List and describe seven areas that the policing occupation needs if it hopes to acquire profession status.
5. Define the purpose of a code of ethics and explain the basic tenets of the police code of conduct.
6. Explain the accreditation procedure for law enforcement agencies and list the five steps of the accreditation process.
7. Describe the three basic professional challenges facing the future of the law enforcement community in its quest for profession status.

CHAPTER OUTLINE

I. The Search for Profession Status
  A. Benefits of Profession Status
  B. What Are the Characteristics of a Profession?
  C. Individual versus Collective Status
  D. Policing: Craft or Profession?
  E. Methods for Policing to Achieve Profession Status

II. Ethics
III. Agency Accreditation
IV. The Professional Challenges of the Future
  A. Effective Service
  B. Emerging Crime Problems
  C. Police Misconduct
V. Summary

THE SEARCH FOR PROFESSION STATUS

A profession that has not found itself cannot ask others to do so.
—William Goode

When Goode (1961, 306) wrote those words, he was not addressing them to the law enforcement **occupation**. However, they are very relevant to the challenges facing law enforcement today. Since the late 1800s, various police reform movements in the United States have been identified by practitioners and researchers (see Fogelson 1977; Walker 1977; Kelling and Moore 1988). Some of the reform efforts were directed toward reducing corruption in agencies; some were focused on improved working conditions and economic benefits for officers; some targeted personnel improvement through education and training; others centered on different models of delivering police services. Whether one agrees with the various classifications and categorizations of reform efforts is not the issue. What should be understood is that the motivations for most of the reform efforts included the underlying beliefs that the police occupation should receive higher public status, should not be controlled by politicians, should be more efficient and effective, and should be worthy of the public trust.

Our discussion here focuses on the quest for **profession** status. In order to understand several of the terms and concepts usually associated with this discussion, we present the following definitions:

a. Occupation: any activity or endeavor by which one provides or obtains the means to survive (i.e., "earns a living")
b. Profession: an occupational type based on a special competence with a high degree of intellectual content; a specialty heavily based on or involved with knowledge (see Clark 1966)
c. Professional: a person who masters the standards of a profession as defined by colleagues in the profession; aspects associated with a profession
d. Professionalism: the character trait of affirming the characteristics or standards of a profession; it is a state of mind exhibited through one's conduct
e. Professionalization: the process of achieving or striving toward the goal of professionalism

The idea or concept of professionalism evolves from a sense of pride in one's work and from altruism (a devotion to others and to humanity), as opposed to the underlying selfishness ("What's in it for me?") or greed often associated with corruption. Therefore, any discussion about professionalism must include aspects of values, morality, ethics, standards, criteria, what should be done, and what is right. These terms and concepts often are difficult to define or appreciate because of a lack of consensus among those in the occupation and those in various groups and individuals that make up society. The following will not center on the highly philosophical or intellectual aspects of professionalism but rather on the basic premises underlying the traditional perspective of the search for "profession" status.

Benefits of Profession Status

Several benefits can be identified for the policing field if it achieves profession status. First, there is greater likelihood of public support and cooperation. If citizens perceive the police as professional, they are more apt to interact positively with them, have trust in them, and assist in local policing efforts. Second, the quality of applicants and recruits will improve. Persons seeking employment in the police field usually do not seek employment with departments with negative reputations and internal problems (unless they intend on playing a part in changing that reputation for the better). Agencies with good reputations and public support have little problem hiring highly qualified applicants—the best are attracted to such agencies.

Third, professional departments often enjoy higher compensation. Of course, this is relative to the economic ability of the local community, and comparisons should be made between the agency and local private and public employment rather than to agencies elsewhere. Fourth, personnel in professional agencies tend to have higher morale and *esprit de corps*. Such agencies tend to have better working conditions and internal relationships among officers. Fifth, and maybe most important, the citizens of the community of professional departments should receive efficient and effective police protection and service. In other words, the community benefits from the professionalism of the agency and the officers it employs.

It should be understood that there is interaction among these benefits. It could be argued that money alone could achieve most of the same benefits. It could improve morale, it could attract qualified candidates, and it could ensure higher salaries, all of which could result in good police service that could assure public support and confidence. Money alone could do these things—and may in some places, at least in the short term—but money alone is no guarantee of professionalism. If it were, there would be no doubt about how to achieve professional status. But first let us review the traditional characteristics of a profession.

What Are the Characteristics of a Profession?

The traditionally recognized fields having "profession" status have included medicine and law, with theology and teaching sometimes in the listing. But what made these occupations different from others? What characteristics today are needed to be recognized as a profession? The traditional characteristics of a profession help guide us in understanding the answers to these questions. The following are the typical ones identified in most discussions of traditional criteria of professions:

1. A specific and specialized body of knowledge,
2. Extensive preparation through education and training,
3. A code of ethics,
4. Licensing and regulation boards, associations, or councils,
5. A commitment and obligation to a clientele,
6. Relative autonomy of its members, and
7. Public acknowledgment of profession status.

Often the debate over the inclusion of policing as a profession centers on the above criteria and whether the police "measure up" to them. Exhibit 15–1 outlines the points and counterpoints of the debate.

Exhibit 15–1

THE DEBATE OVER PROFESSION DESIGNATION OF POLICING

Point	*Counterpoint*
1. Policing has a specific body of knowledge associated with crime theory and techniques of handling people.	1. The knowledge of policing is not grounded on extensive research and intellectual exploration.
2. The police field has education and training standards that are rigorous and necessary before one can do the job.	2. Educational standards are rarely beyond high school diplomas and training is counted in hours, not years as in recognized professions.
3. The police field has a code of ethics describing the expectation of behavior.	3. A single code of ethics is not recognized across the field of law enforcement and there are questions about the code's enforcement and the field's commitment to it.
4. Every state has some type of regulating board regarding the certification and/or licensing of officers.	4. Many of the boards and licensing agencies lack enforcement powers, are weak, and merely set minimum standards.
5. The police serve the public and are committed to law, order, and public service. Their obligation is to uphold the law.	5. Are the police truly committed to the public or to themselves? Are they obligated to a clientele or to the law? Are their motivations service-oriented?
6. Officers have considerable discretion and often work alone and make independent decisions.	6. Police officers do not work independently of others; they have supervisors and are employees of agencies, thus their autonomy is very limited.
7. The public recognizes the police field as unique, and understands and appreciates the complexity of public safety services.	7. The public at large still has many concerns about the integrity and honesty of those in policing, albeit this varies greatly from jurisdiction to jurisdiction. The field as a whole does not have public recognition as a profession.

Individual versus Collective Status

R.M. Pavalko once stated that "the distinctions between professions and nonprofessions are differences of degree and not differences of kind." He asserted that as work becomes more complex and technical, claims of professional status are heard with increasing frequency. In the field of law enforcement, such assertions are frequently made. The individual exhibiting professionalism in an occupation not yet a profession is actively engaged in the process of professionalization. Without this process, the nonprofession would not become a profession. On the other hand, once the profession status has been "granted" to an occupational field by the public, the individual can hurt or erode the status by nonprofessional behavior. As such, one can argue that professionalism begins and ends with the individual. Figure 15–1 illustrates the process of professionalization and maintenance of profession status, once it is achieved.

An occupation will not achieve profession status (which must be earned from the public) without its individual members exhibiting professional behavior. Likewise, if an occupation achieves profession status, it cannot maintain it unless the individual members exhibit continued professional conduct. This, in part, explains why the traditional professions of law, medicine, and theology have seen a slight decline in their professional ratings and public acceptance in recent years—because of instances of inappropriate behavior by some members of those professions and the accompanying widespread publicity. Public perceptions about occupations and their degrees of honesty and ethics have been measured by the Gallup Poll for several decades. Exhibit 15–2 displays the trend ratings for selected occupations for the last decade. The ratings for "policemen" have shown improvement over the last three decades: In 1977, it was 37 percent and in 1988, 47 percent.

Exhibit 15–3 displays a selection of questions that have periodically been asked of the public by the Gallup Poll related to confidence, respect, and ability of the police to address crime problems.

Policing: Craft or Profession?

One of the major debates in the quest for profession status is whether policing is a **craft** or an endeavor that is truly based on scientific principles, research

---

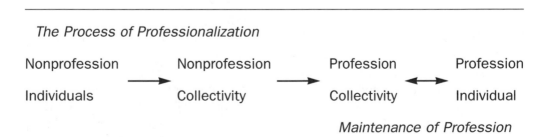

The Process of Professionalization

Nonprofession	Nonprofession	Profession	Profession
Individuals	Collectivity	Collectivity	Individual

Maintenance of Profession

Figure 15–1 Individualism and Professionalism

Exhibit 15–2

PUBLIC RATINGS OF HONESTY AND ETHICS OF SELECTED OCCUPATIONS
Honesty & Ethics—Trend, 1991–1997, 1999*

OCCUPATION	1991	1992	1993	1994	1995	1996	1997	1999
1. Duggists/pharmacists	60%	66%	65%	62%	66%	64%	69%	62%
2. Clergy	57	54	53	54	56	56	59	55
3. Medical doctors	54	52	51	47	54	55	56	52
4. College teachers	45	50	52	50	52	56	55	51
5. Dentists	50	50	50	51	54	53	54	52
6. Policemen	43	42	50	46	41	49	49	49
7. Engineers	45	48	49	49	53	48	49	50
8. Funeral directors	35	35	34	30	35	35	36	39
9. Bankers	30	27	28	27	27	26	34	32
10. Public opinion pollsters	NA	NA	NA	27	25	24	23	NA
11. Journalists	26	27	26	20	23	23	23	30
12. TV reporters/commentators	29	31	28	22	21	23	22	32
13. Business executives	21	18	20	22	19	17	20	25
14. Local officeholders	19	15	19	18	21	19	20	21
15. Building contractors	20	19	20	17	21	23	20	20
16. Newspaper reporters	24	25	22	17	20	17	19	24
17. Stockbrokers	14	13	13	15	16	15	18	14
18. State officeholders	14	11	14	12	15	13	17	17
19. Real estate agents	17	14	15	14	15	15	16	16
20. Lawyers	22	18	16	17	16	17	15	22
21. Labor union leaders	13	14	14	14	14	16	15	15
22. Senators	19	13	18	12	12	15	14	24
23. Advertising practitioners	12	10	8	12	10	11	12	12
24. Congressmen	19	11	14	9	10	14	12	20
25. Insurance salesmen	14	9	10	9	11	11	12	13
26. Car salesmen	8	5	6	6	5	8	8	6

*Based on those saying "high" or "very high" combined with the question, "Please tell me how you would rate the honesty and ethical standards of people in these different fields—very high, high, average, low, or very low?"

Source: Reprinted with permission from Honesty & Ethics Poll; Pharmacists Strengthen Their Position as the Most Highly Rated Occupation, *The Gallup Poll,* © 1999, The Gallup Organization.

Exhibit 15–3

PUBLIC OPINION OF THE POLICE:
RESPECT, CONFIDENCE, AND ABILITY TO DEAL WITH CRIME

How much respect do you have for the police in your area—a great deal, some, or hardly any?

	A Great Deal	Some	Hardly Any	No Opinion
March 5–7, 1999	64%	29%	7%	*%
March 14–17, 1991	60	32	7	1
1967	77	17	4	2
1965	70	22	4	4

How much confidence do you have in the ability of the police to protect you from violent crime—a great deal, quite a lot, not very much, or none at all?

	A Great Deal	Quite A Lot	Not Very Much	None At All	No Opinion
March 5–7, 1999	29%	41%	25%	4%	1%
Oct. 23–25, 1998	19	36	37	8	*
Oct. 23–25, 1998	20	30	39	9	2
Oct. 13–18, 1993	14	31	45	9	1
1989	14	34	42	8	2
1985	15	37	39	6	3
1981	15	34	42	8	1

In general, how would you rate the job the police in your city are doing in dealing with crime—an excellent job, a good job, or only a fair job?

	Excellent Job	Good Job	Only a Fair Job	No Opinion
March 5–7, 1999	30%	48%	21%	1%
Feb. 8–9, 1993	19	52	27	2

*Indicates less than 1% mention by respondents.

For results based on the sample of national adults (N = 1,021) the margin of error is ±3 percentage points.

Source: Reprinted with permission from M. Gillespie, One Third of Americans Believe Police Brutality Exists in Their Area, *The Gallup News Service*, March 22, 1999, © 1999, The Gallup Organization.

(a specific body of knowledge), and rational analysis (see Bayley and Bittner 1993; Roberg and Kuykendall 1993). A craft usually involves the development of skills that are generally learned through experience, rather than in a classroom or training environment. This debate may appear to be a superficial one at first glance, but it raises several questions. Why do many working police officers downgrade academy training and state that real policing can only be learned by doing it (which makes it more like a craft)? Some of these same officers then turn around and want profession designation because their tasks are so complex and difficult to learn. Likewise, if policing is a craft, why worry about entrance standards when one must experience the job in order to learn it? The policing-as-craft belief would negate the need for much of the current entrance testing, screening, or ranking of candidates. Sometimes in the quest for profession status, police officers are their own worst enemies! For example, all of the traditional professions have high educational level requirements and still have extensive "experiential learning" expectations as well.

If the field is a true profession, then it should be guided by specific principles based on research and analysis. And yet, time and time again major research studies have found that police practices did not yield their intended results (see Chapter 9 regarding research into various aspects of patrol and criminal investigation). A major challenge to policing, if it is a profession, is to engage in systematic analysis of all that it does for the purpose of discovering truths about its practices and desired outcomes. It then follows that those practices that are not effective should be changed or discontinued.

We believe that there is another perspective that influences the rise and decline of profession designation and it refers to the *availability* and *access* to specialized and uncommon knowledge and skill. It was mentioned above that a specific and specialized body of knowledge was the first prerequisite for traditional professions. This characteristic of a profession may be more related to the availability of and access to that knowledge than to the actual possession of it. Historically, doctors, attorneys, clergy, and teachers were perceived as professionals because they possessed knowledge that the common person did not. Today, medical information, legal information, theological documents/sacred writings, and information about teaching techniques are all readily available to the masses. Medical databases and books are consulted by individuals today who possess no special training. Standard legal documents can be purchased in printed or electronic form so that the average citizen can write a will or use common legal agreements without engaging an attorney. As the masses have greater access to technical, scientific, legal, and "how to" information, the "mystique" and aura of that field tends to wane and people are less impressed by those in that field. Some police officers have expressed that "everybody thinks they know how our job should be done, so we get no respect and much second-guessing." The public has been exposed to hundreds of hours of "cop shows." People have developed an understanding of much of what officers do. Our contention is that as long as the public, or at least a vocal part of it, thinks that way, policing will not achieve profession status. It will be up to the law enforcement community to make its case by being competent and proficient in what it does—by maintaining a high level of training and being prepared to address an ever-changing society.

Methods for Policing to Achieve Profession Status

There have been several commissions and national studies over the last 30 years that have identified weaknesses in policing, or areas needing improvement. It is difficult to achieve profession status until most publicly acknowledged weaknesses are corrected. To that end, we can identify seven areas that the occupation of policing needs to address in its quest for profession status:

1. Improved Selection Standards: Chapter 10 discussed the need for job-related standards, but these criteria must also take into account the intellectual and mental aspects of policing. Improving educational and psychological standards should become priorities for the entire field.

2. Improved Training Techniques and Standards: In many states, the minimum level of training to become a police officer is less than it is to become a barber. Chapter 11 addressed the issues of training; its importance cannot be overstated. With society becoming so technologically and culturally complex, the importance of better training is obvious.

3. Intensive Evaluation of Performance During Probation: Too many departments treat the probationary period as superficial and automatic. It should contain specific performance criteria and intensive/extensive evaluation of the new officer to determine fitness for the job.

4. Mandatory and More Rigorous In-Service Training/Education: Changes in the law, procedures, and technology demand continuous updating of skills and knowledge, and yet many states and departments still do not mandate in-service training or provide incentives for officers to obtain advanced education. Some departments (and unions) actually make it difficult, if not impossible, for a patrol officer to attend college while off-duty because of rotating schedules or schedules not being synchronized with local colleges and universities.

5. Acceptance of and Commitment to the Practice of a Code of Ethics: While most officers are persons of high integrity and honesty, some appear to have never read, or even heard of, a code of ethics (see the next section). Merely having a code of ethics or calling oneself professional does not make one ethical or a professional. Ethics are exhibited through one's behavior, and professional status is awarded by the persons served.

6. Providing Effective, Efficient, and Courteous Service: The emphasis here is on service and the manner in which it is rendered. All too often the impression left with those served is not a professional one; it can breed distrust and does not move the occupation toward profession status.

7. Systematic Analysis and Research that Guides the Above Activities: A greater amount and more sophisticated levels of research are needed to guide the law enforcement community in effective directions. Research

and commission reports have identified most of the items on this list as deficient or needing attention in the field.

ETHICS

The law enforcement community of the United States does have an established and published code of ethics; in fact, it has more than one. The International Association of Chiefs of Police (IACP) at its 64th Annual Conference in 1957 adopted a code of ethics for the occupation. Along with that code was developed The Canons of Police Ethics containing 11 articles. In 1989, a new Code of Ethics was adopted by the Executive Committee of the IACP during its 96th Annual Conference. At the 98th Annual Conference, the 1989 Code of Ethics was renamed "The Police Code of Conduct" and the 1957 version of the Code of Ethics was resurrected, revised, and adopted as the (1991) Law Enforcement Code of Ethics. In 1998, at the 105th Annual Conference, IACP adopted the Law Enforcement Oath of Honor, which states:

> On my honor, I will never betray my badge, my integrity, my character, or the public trust. I will always have the courage to hold myself and others accountable for our actions. I will always uphold the constitution and community I serve (Higginbotham 1999).

Internationally, countries may substitute the word "constitution" with a monarchy or person or ideal. The IACP, as well as other professional associations, has been very concerned about ethics and integrity in the field. Several key documents such as the IACP's *Law Enforcement Code of Ethics* (Exhibit 15–4), *The Police Code of Conduct* (Exhibit 15–5), and the *Canons of Police Ethics* (Exhibit 15–6) are reprinted here as well as the National Sheriffs' Association's *Code of Ethics for the Office of the Sheriff* (Exhibit 15–7).

But what is a **code of ethics** and why have one? A code of ethics is a basic set of guidelines, or set of standards of behavior, to which one should conform in the performance of one's duty. The word **"ethics"** has several connotations, including the study of human conduct in light of morality; the science dealing with moral duty; and the science of doing the right thing, at the right time, in the right way. **Morality** refers to the conformity to rules of right conduct, and **moral behavior (right conduct)** can be described as representing actions prescribed by the society for the welfare of the people and society as a whole. The interconnectedness of ethics, morality, and right conduct becomes evident upon review of these terms and their meanings. Thus, to act ethically is to act according to certain agreed-upon expectations of proper (right) conduct. The purpose of a code of ethics, then, is to guide the behavior of persons in that particular occupation (or profession). The code becomes the standards against which others will judge the actions of those in the occupation.

Exhibit 15–4

THE LAW ENFORCEMENT CODE OF ETHICS

As a law enforcement officer, my fundamental duty is to serve the community; to safeguard lives and property; to protect the innocent against deception, the weak against oppression or intimidation, and the peaceful against violence or disorder; and to respect the Constitutional rights of all to liberty, equality, and justice.

I will keep my private life unsullied as an example to all and will behave in a manner which does not bring discredit to me or my agency. I will maintain courageous calm in the face of danger, scorn, or ridicule; develop self-restraint; and be constantly mindful of the welfare of others. Honest in thought and deed in both my personal and official life, I will be exemplary in obeying the law and the regulations of my department. Whatever I see or hear of a confidential nature or that is confided to me in my official capacity will be kept ever secret unless revelation is necessary in the performance of my duty.

I will never act officiously or permit personal feelings, prejudices, political beliefs, aspirations, animosities, or friendships to influence my decisions. With no compromise for crime and with relentless prosecution of criminals, I will enforce the law courteously and appropriately without fear or favor, malice or ill will, never employing unnecessary force or violence and never accepting gratuities.

I recognize the badge of my office as a symbol of public faith, and I accept it as a public trust to be held so long as I am true to the ethics of police service. I will never engage in acts of bribery nor will I condone such acts by other police officers. I will cooperate with all legally authorized agencies and their representatives in the pursuit of justice.

I know that I alone am responsible for my own standard of professional performance and will take every opportunity to enhance and improve my level of knowledge and competence. I will constantly strive to achieve these objectives and ideals, dedicating myself before God to my chosen profession . . . law enforcement.

Source: International Association of Chiefs of Police, Adopted by resolution at the 98th Conference, October 1991, (modified version of the original Code of 1957), © 1991, International Association of Chiefs of Police.

Exhibit 15–5 *(continued)*

Cooperation with Other Officers and Agencies

Police officers will cooperate with all legally authorized agencies and their representatives in the pursuit of justice. An officer or agency may be one among many organizations that may provide law enforcement services to a jurisdiction. It is imperative that a police officer assist colleagues fully and completely with respect and consideration at all times.

Personal/Professional Capabilities

Police officers will be responsible for their own standard of professional performance and will take every reasonable opportunity to enhance and improve their level of knowledge and competence. Through study and experience, a police officer can acquire the high level of knowledge and competence that is essential for efficient and effective performance of duty. The acquisition of knowledge is a never-ending process of personal and professional development that should be pursued constantly.

Private Life

Police officers will behave in a manner that does not bring discredit to their agencies or themselves. A police officer's character and conduct while off duty must always be exemplary, thus maintaining a position of respect in the community in which he or she lives and serves. The officer's personal behavior must be beyond reproach.

Source: International Association of Chiefs of Police, Adopted by resolution at the 98th Conference, October 1991, (modified version of the original Code of 1957), © 1991, International Association of Chiefs of Police.

AGENCY ACCREDITATION

One effort to professionalize the police occupation includes the **accreditation** process for law enforcement agencies. In 1979, the **Commission on Accreditation for Law Enforcement Agencies (CALEA)** was established through the combined efforts of four major law enforcement executive associations. (The four associations were the International Association of Chiefs of Police, the National Organization of Black Law Enforcement Executives, the National Sheriffs' Association, and the Police Executive Research Forum.) CALEA was formed to establish a body of standards designed to:

Exhibit 15–6

CANONS OF POLICE ETHICS

ARTICLE I. PRIMARY RESPONSIBILITY OF JOB

The primary responsibility of the police service, and of the individual officer, is the protection of the people of the United States through the upholding of their laws; chief among these is the Constitution of the United States and its amendments. The law enforcement officer always represents the whole of the community and its legally expressed will and is never the arm of any political party or clique.

ARTICLE II. LIMITATIONS OF AUTHORITY

The first duty of a law enforcement officer, as upholder of the law, is to know its bounds upon him in enforcing it. Because he represents the legal will of the community, be it local, state, or federal, he must be aware of the limitations and proscriptions which the people, through the law, have placed upon him. He must recognize the genius of the American system of government which gives to no man, groups of men, or institution, absolute power, and he must insure that he, as a prime defender of that system, does not pervert its character.

ARTICLE III. DUTY TO BE FAMILIAR WITH THE LAW AND WITH RESPONSIBILITIES OF SELF AND OTHER PUBLIC OFFICIALS

The law enforcement officer shall assiduously apply himself to the study of the principles of the laws which he is sworn to uphold. He will make certain of his responsibilities in the particulars of their enforcement, seeking aid from his superiors in matters of technicality or principle when these are not clear to him; he will make special effort to fully understand his relationship to other public officials, including other law enforcement agencies, particularly on matters of jurisdiction, both geographically and substantively.

ARTICLE IV. UTILIZATION OF PROPER MEANS TO GAIN PROPER ENDS

The law enforcement officer shall be mindful of his responsibility to pay strict heed to selection of means in discharging the duties of his office. Violations of law or disregard for public safety and property on the part of an officer are intrinsically wrong; they are self-defeating in that they instill in the public mind a like disposition. The employment of illegal means, no matter how worthy the end, is certain to encourage

(continues)

Exhibit 15–6 *(continued)*

disrespect for the law and its officers. If the law is honored, it must be honored by those who enforce it.

ARTICLE V. COOPERATION WITH PUBLIC OFFICIALS IN THE DISCHARGE
          OF THEIR AUTHORIZED DUTIES

The law enforcement officer shall cooperate fully with other public officials in the discharge of authorized duties, regardless of party affiliation or personal prejudice. He shall be meticulous, however, in assuring himself of the propriety, under the law, of such actions and shall guard against the use of his office or person, whether knowingly or unknowingly, in any improper action. In any situation open to question, he shall seek authority from his superior officer, giving him a full report of the proposed service or action.

ARTICLE VI. PRIVATE CONDUCT

The law enforcement officer shall be mindful of his special identification by the public as an upholder of the law. Laxity of conduct or manner in private life, expressing either disrespect for the law or seeking to gain special privilege, cannot but reflect upon the police officer and the police service. The community and the service require that the law enforcement officer lead the life of a decent and honorable man. Following the career of a policeman gives no man special privileges. It does give the satisfaction and pride of following and furthering an unbroken tradition of safeguarding the American republic. The officer who reflects upon this tradition will not degrade it. Rather, he will so conduct his private life that the public will regard him as an example of stability, fidelity, and morality.

ARTICLE VII. CONDUCT TOWARD THE PUBLIC

The law enforcement officer, mindful of his responsibility to the whole community, shall deal with individuals of the community in a manner calculated to instill respect for its laws and its police service. The law enforcement officer shall conduct his official life in a manner such as will inspire confidence and trust. Thus, he will be neither overbearing nor subservient, as no individual citizen has an obligation to stand in awe of him nor a right to command him. The officer will give service where he can, and require compliance with the law. He will do neither from personal preference or prejudice but rather as a duly appointed officer of the law discharging his sworn obligation.

(continues)

Exhibit 15–6 *(continued)*

ARTICLE VIII. CONDUCT IN ARRESTING AND DEALING WITH LAW VIOLATORS

The law enforcement officer shall use his power of arrest strictly in accordance with the law and with due regard to the rights of the citizen concerned. His office gives him no right to prosecute the violator nor to mete out punishment for the offense. He shall at all times, have a clear appreciation of his responsibilities and limitations regarding detention of the violator; he shall conduct himself in such a manner as will minimize the possibility of having to use force. To this end he shall cultivate a dedication to the service of the people and the equitable upholding of their laws whether in the handling of law violators or in dealing with the law-abiding.

ARTICLE IX. GIFTS AND FAVORS

The law enforcement officer, representing government, bears the heavy responsibility of maintaining, in his conduct, the honor and integrity of all government institutions. He shall, therefore, guard against placing himself in a position in which any person can expect special consideration or in which the public can reasonably assume that special consideration is being given. Thus, he should be firm in refusing gifts, favors, or gratuities, large or small, which can, in the public mind, be interpreted as capable of influencing his judgment in the discharge of his duties.

ARTICLE X. PRESENTATION OF EVIDENCE

The law enforcement officer shall be concerned equally in the prosecution of the wrong-doer and the defense of the innocent. He shall ascertain what constitutes evidence and shall present such evidence impartially and without malice. In so doing, he will ignore social, political, and all other distinctions among the persons involved, strengthening the tradition of the reliability and integrity of an officer's word.

The law enforcement officer shall take special pains to increase his perception and skill of observation, mindful that in many situations his is the sole impartial testimony to the facts of a case.

ARTICLE XI. ATTITUDE TOWARD PROFESSION

The law enforcement officer shall regard the discharge of his duties as a public trust and recognize his responsibility as a public servant. By diligent study and sincere attention to self-improvement he shall

(continues)

Exhibit 15–6 *(continued)*

strive to make the best possible application of science to the solution of crime and, in the field of human relationships, strive for effective leadership and public influence in matters affecting public safety. He shall appreciate the importance and responsibility of his office, hold police work to be an honorable profession rendering valuable service to his community and his country.

Source: Copyright © International Association of Chiefs of Police.

1. increase law enforcement agency capabilities to prevent and control crime;
2. increase agency effectiveness and efficiency in the delivery of law enforcement services;
3. increase cooperation and coordination with other law enforcement agencies and with other agencies of the criminal justice system; and
4. increase citizen and employee confidence in the goals, objectives, policies, and practices of the agency (Commission on Accreditation for Law Enforcement Agencies 1999, xiii).

The standards that initially resulted from this effort consisted of more than 1,012 standards for 48 topical areas. After some modification and field testing, these were reduced to 944 standards, which were adopted and printed in the first accreditation manual in 1983. From the first edition to the current fourth edition (January 1999), the standards underwent periodic review, revisions, deletions, and additions. There are now 439 standards organized into 38 content areas, or chapters (Commission on Accreditation for Law Enforcement Agencies 1999, xiv). Exhibit 15–8 identifies these 38 content areas. By the end of 1998, a total of 510 law enforcement agencies nationwide had been accredited.

The accreditation process is a voluntary one; however, once it is undertaken, standards apply to an agency based on its importance and the size of the agency. For example, there are four agency-size categories based on the total number of authorized full-time sworn and nonsworn personnel: A (1–24), B (25–74), C (75–299), and D (300 or more). Following each stated standard, there appears a series of four codes, in the order of the A-B-C-D categories. These appear in parentheses and indicate whether or not a standard is mandatory (M), other-than-mandatory (O), or non-applicable (N/A), for an agency depending on its category. Exhibit 15–9 illustrates the wording of selected standards and the codes that appear after each standard.

An agency that applies for accreditation will be assessed a fee for the process that is based on agency size. The agency can order other documents (e.g., *Ac-*

Exhibit 15–7

CODE OF ETHICS FOR THE OFFICE OF THE SHERIFF

As a constitutionally elected Sheriff, I recognize and accept that I am given a special trust and confidence by the citizens and employees whom I have been elected to serve, represent and manage. This trust and confidence is my bond to ensure that I shall behave and act according to the highest personal and professional standards. In furtherance of this pledge, I will abide by the following Code of Ethics.

I SHALL ENSURE that I and my employees, in the performance of our duties, will enforce and administer the law according to the standards of the U.S. Constitution and applicable State Constitutions and statutes so that equal protection of the law is guaranteed to everyone. To that end I shall not permit personal opinions, party affiliations, or consideration of the status of others to alter or lessen this standard of treatment of others.

I SHALL ESTABLISH, PROMULGATE AND ENFORCE a set of standards of behavior of my employees which will govern the overall management and operation of the law enforcement functions, court related activities, and corrections operations of my agency.

I SHALL NOT TOLERATE NOR CONDONE brutal or inhumane treatment of others by my employees nor shall I permit or condone inhumane or brutal treatment of inmates in my care and custody.

I STRICTLY ADHERE to standards of fairness and integrity in the conduct of campaigns for election and I shall conform to all applicable statutory standards of election financing and reporting that the Office of the Sheriff is not harmed by the actions of myself or others.

I SHALL ROUTINELY CONDUCT or have conducted an internal and external audit of the public funds entrusted to my care and publish this information so that citizens can be informed about my stewardship of these funds.

I SHALL FOLLOW the accepted principles of efficient and effective administration and management as the principle criteria for my judgments and decisions in the allocation of resources and services in law enforcement, court related and corrections functions of my Office.

(continues)

Exhibit 15–7 *(continued)*

I SHALL HIRE AND PROMOTE only those employees or others who are the very best candidates for a position according to accepted standards of objectivity and merit. I shall not permit other factors to influence hiring or promotion practices.

I SHALL ENSURE that all employees are granted and receive relevant training supervision in the performance of their duties so that competent and excellent service is provided by the Office of the Sheriff.

I SHALL ENSURE that during my tenure as Sheriff, I shall not use the Office of Sheriff for private gain.

I ACCEPT AND WILL ADHERE TO THIS CODE OF ETHICS. In so doing, I accept responsibility for encouraging others in my profession to abide by this Code.

Source: Copyright © National Sheriffs' Association.

---

creditation Program Book, Self-Assessment Manual, Assessor Manual, Accreditation Program Overview, and *Standards for Public Safety Communications Agencies*) to assist it with the process.

An agency seeking accreditation must successfully pass through five phases: application; self-assessment, on-site assessment, commission review and decision, and maintaining compliance and reaccreditation. Each phase is made up of a series of steps. The following is an outline of the major phases involved:

APPLICATION. The accreditation process begins when an agency applies to the Commission for applicant status. Entry into the program is voluntary, and the application form requires the signature of the agency's chief executive officer. Once agency eligibility has been confirmed, the agency and the Commission sign an accreditation agreement that identifies what is expected of each party. The agency completes and returns an Agency Profile Questionnaire (APQ) to staff, thereby providing agency-specific information to facilitate interaction with the accreditation manager to determine applicability of standards, interpreting standards, and providing program-related assistance.

SELF-ASSESSMENT. The return of the APQ triggers the delivery of all necessary materials for the accreditation manager to use in conducting the agency's self-assessment. The manager initiates agency self-assessment, which involves a thorough examination by the agency to determine whether

Exhibit 15–8

CONTENT AREAS OF THE CALEA ACCREDITATION MANUAL

Law Enforcement Role and Authority

Agency Jurisdiction and Mutual Aid

Contractual Agreements for Law Enforcement Services

Organization and Administration

Direction

Crime Analysis

Allocation and Distribution of Personnel and Personnel Alternatives

Fiscal Management and Agency-Owned Property

Classification and Delineation of Duties and Responsibilities

Compensation, Benefits, and Conditions of Work

Collective Bargaining

Grievance Procedures

Disciplinary Procedures

Recruitment

Selection

Training and Career Development

Promotion

Performance Evaluation

Patrol

Criminal Investigation

Vice, Drugs, and Organized Crime

Juvenile Operations

Crime Prevention and Community Involvement

Unusual Occurrences and Special Operations

Criminal Intelligence

Internal Affairs

Inspectional Services

Public Information

Victim/Witness Assistance

Traffic

Prisoner Transportation

Holding Facility

Court Security

Legal Process

Communications

Records

Collection and Preservation of Evidence

Property & Evidence Control

Source: Reprinted with permission from *Standards for Law Enforcement Agencies: The Standards Manual of the Law Enforcement Agency Accreditation Program*, pp. vii–xi, © 1999, Commission on Accreditation for Law Enforcement Agencies, Inc.

Exhibit 15–9

SELECTED CALEA STANDARDS

Standard 1.3.6 *A written report is submitted whenever an employee:*

a. *discharges a firearm, for other than training or recreational purposes;*

b. *takes an action that results in, or is alleged to have resulted in, injury or death of another person;*

c. *applies force through the use of lethal or less-than-lethal weapons; or*

d. *applies weaponless physical force at a level as defined by the agency.*

. . .

Standard 21.1.1 *A written task analysis of every class of sworn employee in the agency is conducted, maintained on file, and includes, at a minimum:*

a. *the work behaviors (duties, responsibilities, functions, tasks, etc.);*

b. *the frequency with which the work behavior occurs; and*

c. *how critical the job-related skills, knowledge, and abilities are.*

. . .

Standard 43.1.5 The agency has written procedures for conducting surveillance, undercover, decoy, and raid operations.

Source: Reprinted with permission from *Standards for Law Enforcement Agencies: The Standards Manual of the Law Enforcement Agency Accreditation Program*, pp. 1–4, 21–1, 43–2 (commentaries omitted), © 1999, Commission on Accreditation for Law Enforcement Agencies, Inc.

---

it complies with all applicable standards. The agency prepares forms and develops "proofs of compliance" for applicable standards (including brief explanations for not complying with other standards) and assembles the forms and "proofs" in a manner that will facilitate a review by Commission assessors. The agency also develops a plan for accomplishing its public information requirements and on-site assessment, which pertain to activities for the next phase. When the agency is satisfied that it has completed all compliance, preparation, and planning tasks, it notifies the Commission that it is ready to become a candidate for accreditation.

ON-SITE ASSESSMENT: The Commission approves the agency's candidate status, selects and trains a team of assessors free of conflict with the candidate agency, and schedules all activities for the assessment team's travel, accommodations, and on-site review of the agency during a period of time mutually agreeable to all parties. During the on-site visit, the assessors, acting as representatives of the Commission, review all standards and, in particular, verify the agency's compliance with all applicable standards. The assessor's relationship with the candidate agency is non-adversarial. Assessors provide the agency with verbal feedback on their progress during, and at the conclusion of, the assessment. Later, the assessors submit a formal, written report of their on-site activities and findings. If the final report reflects compliance with all applicable standards and with required on-site activities, the agency is scheduled for a Commission review. If compliance issues remain unresolved, the agency may return to Step 2 to complete unfinished work, or it may choose other options, for example, appeal or voluntary withdrawal.

COMMISSION REVIEW: The assessors' final report is forwarded to the Commission when all applicable standards and required activities have been complied with. The Commission schedules a hearing at one of its meetings, usually the meeting immediately following the on-site assessment. The agency and its chief executive officer are invited to attend, although attendance is not required. At the hearing, the Commission reviews the final report and receives testimony from agency personnel, assessors, staff, or others. If satisfied that the agency has met all compliance requirements, the Commission awards the agency with accredited status. Accreditation is for a three-year period.

MAINTAINING COMPLIANCE AND REACCREDITATION: To maintain accredited status, the accredited agency must remain in compliance with applicable standards. The agency submits annual reports to the Commission attesting to their continued compliance or reporting any changes or difficulties experienced during the year, including actions taken to resolve noncompliance. If necessary, the Commission reserves the right to schedule interim hearings to consider continuing accredited status if noncompliance becomes a serious issue. At the conclusion of the three-year period, the Commission offers the agency an opportunity to repeat the process and continue their accredited status into the future (Commission on Accreditation for Law Enforcement Agencies, Inc. 1999, xviii–xix).

The most significant aspect of the accreditation process is that it is the only set of national standards for policing that has broad support across various levels of government and types of jurisdictions. It has helped standardize some administrative terminology and principles of operations. It has been recognized by the insurance industry, which often provides lower rates to accredited agencies because the accreditation may provide a more defensible posture in liability claims Also, there is a benefit from the public acknowledgment and recognition that an agency meets national standards. It has been stated that accredited agencies often find that they qualify more easily for grants for innovative police initiatives (Hill 1999, 40).

However, there has been significant debate and controversy over the national accreditation process ever since it started (Eastman 1985). Some state associations (New York, Colorado, and Washington) have gone on record opposing the national accreditation process, instead favoring a state-based one. Efforts to establish law enforcement standards at the state level date to 1976 when the president of the Washington Association of Sheriffs and Police Chiefs (WASPC) was directed by the state legislature to develop such standards. A task force was appointed that was successful in developing standards and goals for the state of Washington. That effort evolved into the present WASPC Law Enforcement Accreditation Program (Washington Association of Sheriffs and Police Chiefs, 1998). The State of Kentucky launched its own program in 1992 and, as of early 1994, eight other states were working on similar processes that provide alternatives to national accreditation (Bizzack and Delacruz 1994). Some of the same benefits identified above are enjoyed as well by states that have their own accreditation standards.

Other complaints about the process have focused on the lack of specific content of policy requirements. Departments may be required to have policies on specific issues, but those policies may vary greatly from agency to agency. Some believe that the standards (which are minimums) set by the Commission will become the level of operations within agencies with few attempting to exceed them; they do not define standards of excellence (Walker 1992). The cost in time and money of becoming accredited also has been an issue of contention ("Proposals for CALEA to Ponder" 1993). Fees have generally ranged from $4,600 to $16,000.

Overall, the accreditation process is a progressive effort because it forces agencies to do a self-assessment and to be reviewed by outsiders. The process requires public input and the attention it receives at the local level should establish a forum for continued interaction. The Commission's activities have fostered greater cooperation among agencies at the national and regional levels. The process may not be perfect but it has accomplished much in its short history. Although the future of accreditation is debatable, there is a need for agencies to recognize and acknowledge certain "standards" in policing if the field is ever going to achieve profession status.

THE PROFESSIONAL CHALLENGES OF THE FUTURE

It is clear from the above discussion that the policing occupation is striving for profession status. But there are three major challenges to which the field must successfully respond in order to achieve that recognition in the eyes of the public. The three challenges are interrelated, and underlying values and attitudes (see Chapter 6) affect all three. First, the police must be able to provide efficient but *effective* service to their constituents, which means being attuned to local conditions and problems and what might be the acceptable alternatives for dealing with them. This largely refers to the whole "quality of life" spectrum of problems that often impact crime (such as education, unemployment, role modeling, and cultural relationships) and is, in part, a major thrust of the community policing movement. With effective service comes a higher level of public support and trust.

Second, the law enforcement community must be able to stay abreast and informed of the *emerging crime problems* (violence, drugs, gangs, white-collar crime, and terrorism) facing the local community and the nation. This means conducting in-depth and multidisciplinary crime analysis; exchanging intelligence information with other federal, state, and local-level agencies; and updating knowledge and techniques through continued education and training. It also means perceiving, evaluating, and anticipating problems within society. It means using community and agency resources wisely and progressively.

Third, the law enforcement community must develop a stronger sense of integrity and reduce *police misconduct.* Maintaining discipline and high morale in law enforcement agencies is not an easy task. As discussed in earlier chapters, the use of discretion often opens an officer or agent to criticism. Officers who use force, including deadly force, are placed under scrutiny not only by the department but also by the news media and public. And, although the officer's use of this discretion and force may have been appropriate and proper, the department must investigate alleged misconduct in order to assure the public that the integrity of the force is intact.

Effective Service

Policing is a service industry; it is heavily dependent upon personnel and technology to address the needs of the community. Providing effective service is not a new idea—it is as old as the function itself. The challenge here is instilling in law enforcement personnel the motivation and orientation of a "service" paradigm that is determined not by the agency alone, but by the community and the agency together. When asked whether an agency provides effective service, whose response should carry the greatest weight when trying to determine levels of professionalism, the community's or the agency's? As discussed above, professional status cannot legitimately be *claimed*, it must be ascribed. In other words, it the community's response that matters most. Public recognition is a key component to gaining profession status.

In order to provide effective service, law enforcement personnel must understand their roles, must understand their community, and must understand themselves. They must be able to act and articulate that understanding. They must "walk the walk and not just talk the talk." That is the complexity of the policing task that is alluded to throughout the chapters of this text. Effective service emerges from competent, well-trained, compassionate, committed law enforcement personnel. That, in part, is the challenge of the community policing movement. Watson, Stone, and DeLuca (1998, 64) state, "An agency that adopts the community policing philosophy does not necessarily provide a different 'menu' of services. Most agencies provide all of the same types of services . . . . The significant differences lie in *how* the services are provided, *by whom*, and *when*." It is interesting to note that, in their text, they point out that a *"police service, . . . means any action performed by the police for the benefit of the public"* (p. 62). One could argue that effective service means adhering to and practicing one's oath of office and code of ethics, and upholding the values of a representative democracy.

The efforts undertaken across the country in the name of community policing are quite varied and not standardized. But to provide effective service, it is necessary to determine what the public wants and needs. According to Watson, Stone, and DeLuca (1998, 74–75), it is the chief executive's role to direct that determination by gathering information from three segments of the community:

1. The parent authority—the elected officials and the appointed managers who have authority over the police agency,
2. The internal community—the personnel of the agency itself, and
3. The external community—the citizens who are served by the agency.

While this activity is easy to list, the process of acquiring and assessing information from each of the three segments is time-consuming and can be uncomfortable. The challenge of providing effective service is not meant to be comfortable—that's why it is a challenge. To assist with this challenge, a number of texts have been published for agency executives and managers. Literature about community policing is available from professional associations, the federal government, other policing agencies, the World Wide Web, and commercial publishers.

Emerging Crime Problems

The second challenge to the police community in reaching profession status relates to its ability to address and respond to the *emerging crime problems* (violence, gangs, white-collar crime, and terrorism) facing the local community and the nation. While the debate rages on regarding policing as an emerging profession, the forces of crime and disorder continue to challenge the field. The words of Alvin and Heidi Toffler (1990, 2–5) are ominous:

> We all know that law enforcement is society's second line of defense. Crime, drug abuse, and sociopathic behavior generally are first held in check by social, disapproval—by family, neighbors, and co-workers. But in change-wracked America, people are less bonded to one another, so that social disapproval loses its power over them.
>
> It is when social disapproval fails that law enforcement must take over. And until the "social glue" is restored to society, we can expect more, not less, violence in the streets, more white-collar crime, more rape and misery—and not just in the inner city.

In just the last decade or two, matters seem to have gotten worse for policing. Although the crime rates have gone down for seven straight years, the level of violence and public fear of it has not. Our country seems to have more serial killers (see Exhibit 15–10), gangs (see Exhibit 15–11), school-related violence, and white-collar and technology-related crime (see Exhibit 15–12) than ever before. At least, the media is giving these issues more attention. The amount of emphasis and level of resources devoted to drug enforcement is enormous, and yet some statistics indicate that the problems may be getting worse. If these problems are not enough, add to them the challenges of environmental crime, hate crime, and terrorism (see Exhibit 15–13). Policing today is not the same as it was a few decades ago.

The challenge to the law enforcement community is how to maintain the capabilities necessary to respond to such emerging problems. Effective response to violence, gang activity, white-collar and computer crime, and terrorism requires large amounts of resources. Costs associated with prevention, intelligence gathering, and responding to incidents related to these issues are enormous. Unfortunately, these problems are not just "big city" or federal problems; they have reached into the local communities. Our purpose here is only to raise the awareness of the reader to the fact that the law enforcement community must be prepared and capable to respond to these issues if it is to be considered a profession.

Police Misconduct

The third challenge to the law enforcement community in achieving profession status is how it responds to police misconduct. As used here, police misconduct is a general phrase to describe various forms of behavior that the public and the police themselves consider inappropriate for officers of the law. In 1999, the Gallup News Service released its findings of a poll related to the public's perception of police brutality (Gillespie 1999):

Exhibit 15–10

SELECTED SERIAL KILLERS IN THE U.S.

Ed Gein—police discovered preserved human heads and chair seats made of human skin on his farm in Wisconsin in 1957; he was committed to psychiatric institution and died in 1984.

Albert DeSalvo—known as the "Boston Strangler" who killed 13 women between 1962–64; convicted of unrelated assaults. He received a life sentence but was killed in prison in 1973.

Dean Corll, Elmer Wayne Henley, and David Owen Brooks—the three killed 27 boys/young men in the Houston, Texas area between 1969–71. Henley, who killed Corll, received six consecutive life terms and Brooks was sentenced to life.

Juan Corona—killed 25 farm workers in 1971 near Yuba City, California; received 25 consecutive life terms.

John Wayne Gacy, Jr.—convicted of killing 33 young men and boys around Chicago; 27 bodies discovered in shallow graves under his home; sentenced to death and executed in 1994.

Patrick Wayne Kearney—confessed to killing 32 men in the Southern California area; he dumped victims along highways. Sentenced to life in prison in 1977.

David Berkowitz—referred to as the "Son of Sam," killed six people in 1976 and 1977; committed to mental institution.

Wayne Williams—sentenced to two life terms for killing two black men but also suspect in 29 deaths of children/young adults in the Atlanta area.

Donald Harvey—sentenced to three consecutive life terms after pleading guilty to 37 murders in hospitals where he worked in the 1980s.

Richard Ramirez—the "Night Stalker," suspected in 14 killings during burglaries in 1984–85 in Southern California; sentenced to death.

Theordore R. Bundy—convicted in three Florida slaying and was a suspect in at least 36; executed in 1990.

(continues)

Exhibit 15–10 *(continued)*

Jeffrey L. Dahmer—confessed to killing and dismembering 17 people since 1978, sentenced in Milwaukee, Wisconsin to 15 consecutive life terms (936 years). Beaten to death in prison by another inmate in 1994.

Donald Leroy Evans—claimed to have killed more than 60 people in 21 state between 1977 and August 1991.

Joel Rifkin—in mid-1993, police stopped his pickup truck after a stop sign violation and found remains of a woman in the back; confessed to killing up to 17 women, mostly prostitutes.

In early November 1998, a man in California walked into a sheriff's office carrying a woman's severed breast in a plastic bag and confessed to killing four women. He was a truck driver who traveled through several western states. Police in those states are trying to connect him to several unsolved slayings.

Sources: Data from Associated Press, U.S. Serial Killer Cases, *The Vindicator*, August 18, 1991, p. A9; D. Howlett, Dahmer: 936 years for "Holocaust," *USA Today*, February 17, 1992, p. 1A; A. Stone, Clues Emerging in Slayings of N.Y. Prostitutes, *USA Today*, July 1, 1993; and M. Puente, Murder Suspect Abused as Child, *USA Today*, August 16, 1991, p. 2A; and Associated Press, Serial Killer Allegations Shock Acquaintances, *The Vindicator*, November 8, 1998, p. A8.

The poll, conducted March 5–7, shows that 38% of Americans believe there have been incidents of police brutality in their area, while 57% disagree. That compares with a similar Gallup poll conducted in March, 1991, in which roughly the same number, 35%, said police brutality existed in their area. The poll also underscores perceptions that minorities feel unfairly targeted by police officers. Fifty-eight percent of nonwhites believe police brutality takes place in their area, compared to only 35% of whites.

When asked, "Have you personally ever felt treated unfairly by the police or by a police officer?" 27% of Americans said yes. Again, the answers differ along racial lines, with 39% of nonwhites saying yes, compared to just 24% of whites. Police brutality is also more likely to be reported in urban areas (57%, compared to 35% in rural areas) and in the West and the South (43% and 41%, respectively).

An extensive study of law enforcement nationwide found seemingly widespread appearance of intentional use of excessive force (Skolnick and Fyfe 1993). According to a special report by Human Rights Watch (1998):

Police abuse remains one of the most serious and divisive human rights violations in the United States. The excessive use of force by police officers, including un-

Exhibit 15–11

GANGS AND RELATED ACTIVITY IN THE U.S.

In a study of 110 jurisdictions in the U.S., the following findings were reported for a 12-month period from 1991–92:

- 249,324 gang members identified
- 4,881 gangs identified
- 46,359 gang-related crimes reported
- 1,072 gang-related homicides reported
- Gang-related crime is a violent crime problem. Homicides and other violent crimes account for about half of all recorded gang-related incidents.
- The overwhelming majority of gang members are black or Hispanic; however, the proportion of white youth involvement is increasing.

In 1997, a survey of 3000 law enforcement agencies provided the following estimates:

- 816,000 gang members
- 30,500 gangs
- 4,824 cities and counties experienced gang activity
- Although there was a slight drop from 1996, the number of gang members rose in small cities and rural counties
- 45% of respondents thought the gang problem was "staying about the same," 35% thought it was "getting worse," and 20% thought it was "getting better"
- 42% of respondents indicated that gangs were involved in the street sale of drugs and 33% were involved in drug distribution for the specific purpose of generating profits.

Sources: Data from G.D. Curry, R.A. Ball, and R.J. Fox, Gang Crime and Law Enforcement Record-keeping, *Research in Brief*, August 1994, U.S. Department of Justice, National Institute of Justice; J.P. Moore and C.P. Terrett, Highlights of the 1997 National Youth Gang Surgery, *OJJDP Fact Sheet*, March 1999, U.S. Department of Justice, Office of Justice Programs.

---

justified shootings, severe beatings, fatal chokings, and rough treatment, persists because overwhelming barriers to accountability make it possible for officers who commit human rights violations to escape due punishment and often to repeat their offenses.

Exhibit 15–12

WHITE-COLLAR & HIGH-TECH CRIME

— The Business Software Alliance announced in early 1999 that it had shut down a software counterfeit operation in Denmark that had produced 125,000 CD-ROMs containing $237 million worth of code.

— An 18-year-old high school dropout was charged with computer tampering. He had altered America Online data and programs that cost the company over $50,000 to repair. In another case, a Cleveland Heights, OH, man, aged 22, was sentenced to 15 months in a federal prison for possessing child pornography—he agreed to plead guilty to that charge in return for dropping 14 counts related to hacking and possession of ESN/MIN pairs used in cellular telephones.

— Between May and mid-August of 1994, German police officials made four seizures of weapons-grade nuclear material being transported by smugglers. The material was believed to be from Russia and/or other former Soviet republics. In July of 1994, the FBI established offices in Moscow and several other Eastern European cities to assist with intelligence sharing and liaison on matters associated with nuclear weapons material smuggling and organized crime activities.

— On September 1, 1998, federal agents raided sites in 32 cities in the U.S. and sites in 11 other countries—cracking the largest, most sophisticated online pornography ring yet, called "Wonderland." More than 100 suspects worldwide were arrested. "Operation Cheshire Cat" the U.S. and "Operation Cathedral" in the UK were coordinated through Interpol. Pornographic images involving children as young as 18 months were confiscated.

— The potential losses for all American industry from computer crime and abuse could amount to as much as $63 billion, according to a study by the American Society for Industrial Security, and according to the FBI, industrial espionage costs U.S. companies anywhere from $24 billion to $100 billion annually. The White House Office of Science and Technology estimates losses to U.S. business from foreign economic espionage at $100 billion a year.

— Less than 1% of the fake money seized nationally in 1995 was computer-generated, but about 40% is today, according to U.S. Secret Service figures. In Los Angeles County, $4.2 million was passed in 1997, compared with $2.7 million four years before; in Orange County, the number more than doubled during that time, from $288,000 to $765,000.

Sources: Data from Why We Hate Software Pirates, *SC Magazine*, May 1999, p. 12; AOL Hacker Charged, *SC Magazine*, May 1999, p. 14; Hacker Gets 15 Months, *SC Magazine*, May 1999, p. 16; Smugglers Try to Sell Bomb Ingredients, and Russia's Nuclear Stockpile Remains a Danger, *The Vindicator*, August 21, 1994, p. A6; Wave of Suicides Follows Raids in World Wide Kid Porn Sweep, *The Vindicator*, November 8, 1998; D. Haldane, Computers Become the Key to Counterfeiting, *Los Angeles Times*, November 5, 1998, p. A3; **http://www/businesswire.com** and **http://www. infowar.com/class_2/class2_.html-ssi, 6.**

Exhibit 15–13

CHRONOLOGICAL SUMMARY OF TERRORIST INCIDENTS IN THE UNITED STATES, 1990–1996

DATE	LOCATION	INCIDENT TYPE	GROUP
1-12-90	Santurce, P.R.	Pipe Bombing	Brigada Internacionalista Eugenio Maria de Hostos de las Fuerzas Revolucionaries Pedro Albizu Campos (Eugenio Maria de Hostos International Brigade of the Pedro Albizu Campos Revolutionary Forces)
1-12-90	Carolina, P.R.	Pipe Bombing	Brigada Internacionalista Eugenio Maria de Hostos de las Fuerzas Revolucionaries Pedro Albizu Campos (Eugenio Maria de Hostos International Brigade of the Pedro Albizu Campos Revolutionary Forces)
2-18-91	Sabana Grande, P.R.	Arson	Popular Liberation Army (PLA)
3-17-91	Carolina, P.R.	Arson	Unknown Puerto Rican Group
4-1-91	Fresno, CA	Bombing	Popular Liberation Army (PLA)
7-6-91	Punta Borinquen, P.R.	Bombing	Popular Liberation Army (PLA)
4-5-92	New York, NY	Hostile Takeover	Mujahedin-E-Khalq (MEK)
11-19-92	Urbana, IL	Attempted Firebombing	Mex. Revolutionary Movement
12-10-92	Chicago, IL	Car Fire and Attempted Firebombing (2 events)	Boricua Revolutionary Front
2-26-93	New York, NY	Car Bombing	International Radical Terrorists
7-20-93	Tacoma, WA	Pipe Bombing	American Front Skinheads
7-22-93	Tacoma, WA	Bombing	American Front Skinheads
1-27/28-93	Chicago, IL	Firebombing (9 events)	Animal Liberation Front

THERE WERE NO INCIDENTS OF TERRORISM IN 1994

4-19-95	Oklahoma City, OK	Truck Bombing	Individuals with Militia contacts
4-1-96	Spokane, WA	Pipe Bombing/Bank Robbery	Phineas Priesthood
7-12-96	Spokane, WA	Pipe Bombing/Bank Robbery	Phineas Priesthood
7-27-96	Atlanta, GA	Pipe Bombing	Pending Investigation

Source: Reprinted from *Terrorism in the United States, 1996*, p. 26, 1997, Federal Bureau of Investigation.

It is beyond the scope of this section, however, to examine this problem in detail. Many scholarly sources have reported on the typical types of behavior associated with police misconduct. Exhibit 15–14 contains a listing of some of the more common terms associated with the various forms of police misconduct.

Recent research into police misconduct by Professors Kappeler, Sluder, and Alpert is reported in their text, *Forces of Deviance* (2d ed., 1998), which examines this issue in detail. They categorize deviant police behaviors into four types: **police crime**, **occupational deviance**, **corruption**, and **abuse of authority**. Police crime includes those acts where the officer's authority and powers as a police officer assisted or facilitated the commission of crime(s). Occupational deviance is akin to police crime, but in these situations the acts (ticket fixing, strip-searching females in custody, abusing a prisoner) probably could not have been committed by anyone not employed in the police occupation. Corruption, as defined in this categorization, "involves the potential for personal gain and the use of police power and authority to further that gain." The emphasis and distinction here is the element of personal gain, and it is usually tied to economic gain. Abuse of authority refers to mistreatment and/or violation of human and legal rights, regardless of motive or intention, by officials possessing police authority. Such abuse may be physical, psychological, or legal (Kappeler et al. 1998, 20–25). Exhibit 15–15 identifies sample behavior of each of the above mentioned categories of police misconduct.

Major Scandals of the Early 1990s. The evolution and history of policing in the United States is fraught with incidents of police misconduct. Media attention to the subject appears to have reached an all-time high. The decade of the 1990s did not start off very favorably for the police occupation. Some of the nation's largest police departments were spotlighted because of police misconduct. In March of 1991, the Rodney King incident occurred; it resulted in over three years of litigation, disturbances at the end of the criminal trial on state charges where officers were found not guilty, two officers being sentenced to prison for violating the civil rights of King, and a civil suit award of $6 million to King. Only a portion of the videotape that captured the incident was shown (over and over again) on all major television networks, but it left an indelible impression in the minds of all who saw it. The findings of the Christopher Commission, which was appointed to investigate the conditions within the L.A. Police Department following the King incident, led some to conclude that "[w]hat emerges from such statistics is a department where the use of force against citizens is not considered a matter of great concern" (Alpert *et al.* 1992, 476).

At the other end of the country, a major drug-related scandal that took years of persistent investigation by a determined internal affairs investigator (Sgt. Joseph Trimboli) began to surface in mid-1992. "The Loser's Club" was a group of rogue cops led by Michael Dowd that engaged in wholesale drug racketeering. (See Exhibit 15–16 for additional details about the Dowd investigation.) By the end of 1992, 101 police officers in the NYPD had been arrested for misconduct in that one year.

Exhibit 15–14

TERMS AND PHRASES ASSOCIATED WITH POLICE MISCONDUCT

Booming doors—the practice of confiscating from drug dealers keys of apartments where drugs and guns are hidden and then going there to steal drugs, guns, and money.

Bribery—payments of cash or gifts for past or future assistance to avoid prosecution; usually higher in value than "mooching."

Chiseling/badging in—police demands for discounts or free admission to entertainment whether on duty or not.

Extortion—demands by officers for advertisements in police magazines or for the purchase of tickets to police-sponsored events through the use of compulsion, force, or fear. Also could involve sums of cash to avoid arrest or for "protection."

Favoritism—granting immunity from traffic arrest or citation or from a summons for minor offenses because of relationship to officer or because of display of window sticker or license plate emblem.

Grass-eaters—officers who take advantage of opportunities for graft that might arise but do not aggressively initiate them.

Meat-eaters—officers who aggressively seek opportunities for graft and other forms of misconduct.

Mooching—receiving free coffee, cigarettes, liquor, food, or other items either as a consequence of being in an underpaid occupation or for future acts of favoritism that might be expected or received by the donor.

Pad—refers to a shadow organization (group) within the department that receives shares of regular bribe payments from citizens; amounts of share depend on rank.

Shakedown—practice of appropriating expensive items for personal use from crime scenes (and may include money, gifts, or favors from citizens).

Shopping—practice of picking up small items (candy, food, etc.) at a store where the door has been accidently left unlocked after business hours.

Testilying—the making of false arrests, tampering with evidence, and then committing perjury on the witness stand.

Source: Data from E. Stoddard, Organizational Norms and Police Discretion: An Observational Study of Police Work with Traffic Violators, *Criminology*, Vol. 17, No. 2, pp. 159–71, © 1979; R.H. Langworthy and F. Travis III, *Policing in America: A Balance of Forces*, p. 341, © 1994, MacMillan Publishing Co.; and NYPD Corruption Woes Bring More Bad News, *Law Enforcement News*, May 15, 1994, p. 13.

Exhibit 15–15

EXAMPLES OF POLICE MISCONDUCT BY CATEGORY

Police Crime	Occupational Deviance	Corruption	Abuse of Authority
Off-duty burglary	Theft of evidence	Accepting bribes	Perjury
Off-duty robbery	Tampering with evidence	Selling drugs	Illegal wire taps
Domestic abuse	Prisoner abuse	Selling "protection"	Forced confessions
Child abuse	Ticket fixing	Accepting sexual favors	Physically beating prisoners
Prostitution	Improper strip searches	Extortion	Humiliating witnesses
Gambling	Driving impounded cars		

Source: Reprinted by permission of Waveland Press, Inc. from Kappeler et al., *Forces of Deviance: Understanding the Dark Side of Policing*, 2nd ed., (Prospect Heights, IL: Waveland Press, Inc., 1998). All rights reserved.

The Mollen Commission was established to hear testimony and to investigate corruption within the NYPD. (The scandal brought back memories of the Knapp Commission of the early 1970s and the testimony of Detective Frank Serpico.) The Mollen Commission heard testimony about robberies, thefts, on-duty drug abuse, excessive use of force, and scams. In 1994 a series of arrests and internal actions occurred:

■ March 15—an officer was arrested and charged with beating a man while off duty in a convenience store, and he pled guilty; he and two other officers who were with him (all had been drinking heavily) were suspended from the department.
■ March 18—three officers were arrested after a police sting videotaped them breaking into an apartment, ransacking it, and beating an undercover officer.
■ March 30—a community police officer was arraigned on 14 counts of grand larceny ("shake downs" of several local merchants).

Exhibit 15–16

COPS GONE BAD IN NEW YORK CITY

In the same auditorium where Frank Serpico testified twenty-one years earlier, Michael Dowd told the Mollen Commission his story. He described his indoctrination into petty crime and brutality by his superiors and how he went from $200-a-week scores of drug money to an $8,000-a-week payoff from a major drug dealer. He spoke of pervasive corruption in the force and how accepted it was.

Former Officer Dowd, of the 75th Precinct, had plead guilty to corruption charges before testifying before the commission. He admitted to sniffing lines of cocaine off the dashboard of his police care in the company of his partner. Dowd was eventually arrested by Suffolk County, NY police for operating a drug ring.

Dowd indicated that he was introduced to corruption at the police academy since it promoted an "us" against "them" (the public) attitude; then drinking on the job helped to continue his illegal activity. He spoke about the "rendezvous at the pool" where virtually the entire 75th would go for drinks, laughs, shooting off their guns, and other immature behavior. He and fellow officers would plan their illicit drug raids there as well. He said his supervisors helped promote a corrupt attitude by implying "do whatever you wish but have an answer if asked."

Source: Data from B. Frankel, Ex-NYC Officer Tells Stark Tale of Cops Gone Bad, *USA Today*, September 28, 1993.

- April 14—fourteen officers (from the 30th Precinct) were arrested on charges of stealing drugs, money, and guns from narcotics dealers and criminals.
- April 15—twelve more officers were arrested on similar charges from the same Precinct.
- May 4—eleven more officers at the 30th had service weapons and badges confiscated and were assigned to "administrative duty"

Source: Data from Bountiful Harvest of Bad Apples, Law Enforcement News, March 31, 1994, p. 4, © 1994, John Jay College of Criminal Justice; and NY Corruption Woes Bring More Bad News, *Law Enforcement News*, May 15, 1994, p. 13, © 1994, John Jay College of Criminal Justice.

New York and Los Angeles were not alone in the problem of controlling police misconduct. Washington, D.C., as of December 1993 had 113 officers under indictment or with charges pending. A group of 12 officers was arrested in mid-December of 1993 after "bragging" about misdeeds to an undercover FBI agent posing as a drug dealer. The Chief of the Department was quoted as saying that during 1989 and 1990, "mistakes" were made in an intensive recruiting effort (most of the officers arrested had been hired during that time) (Fields 1993, 3A). In July of 1995, the City's Civilian Complaint Review Board closed its doors because of a budget cut. The backlog of 770 pending cases of police misconduct were transferred to the Police Department for further action. By the middle of 1998, it was reported that 500 officers were under charges of wrongdoing in the Washington, D.C. police department ("Justice by the Numbers" 1999).

In November of 1992, Malice Green was reportedly pulled from his car and beaten by two Detroit, Michigan officers with their hands and flashlights. A total of seven officers were present before the incident ended. Two of the officers were convicted of murder. In the Atlanta area, three officers were arrested in 1993 for murder, two others for robbery. All were thought to be part of a burglary and robbery ring (Edmonds 1993, 2A; Kappeler 1998, 276). In New Orleans, between 1992 and 1996, 40 officers were arrested on charges including auto theft, robbery, rape, aggravated assault, and even murder (Kappeler 1998, 57). One female officer killed three people as she attempted to rob a restaurant; she's now on death row.

The allegations and revelations of the O.J. Simpson trial of 1995 prompted a number of internal investigations and created an atmosphere of great suspicion of the police in that city and elsewhere. Also during 1995, it was revealed that over 20 officers in the city of Philadelphia were charged with various counts of perjury, civil rights violations, and engaging in drug trafficking. Many of the cases handled by those officers were reopened, and wrongfully convicted subjects were released from prison. The FBI came under great scrutiny during 1995 as well, because of its involvement in the Waco incident, the shooting of a wife and daughter of a Montana fugitive (several years earlier), and allegations that the forensics experts from the crime lab routinely doctored evidence and lied in court.

As the decade of the 1990s closed, the problem of police misconduct and allegations of abuse continued to plague the law enforcement community. Such issues also receive much media attention. New York City again was the site of controversy when, on February 4, 1999, an African immigrant, Amadou Diallo, was hit 19 times by four officers who shot 41 rounds at the 22-year old man. The man was apparently unarmed and the four officers were indicted (NYPD 1999). As this matter was being investigated, another high-profile allegation of police abuse in August of 1997 was going to trial in New York City. The broomstick torture case of Haitian immigrant Abner Louima went to trial in May of 1999. Five officers were indicted for the alleged station house bathroom beating of Louima; two were charged with using a broom handle to sodomize him

(Hays 1999). During the trial, one officer changed his plea to guilty. Of the other four, one was found guilty and three not guilty. Also in May of 1999, the survivors of Tyisha Miller, 19, filed a federal civil rights lawsuit against five officers and the city of Riverside, California. In December of 1998, Miller was found in a locked car by the officers. She appeared unconscious but a handgun was seen on her lap. The officers broke the window and tried to remove the handgun. When they did, Ms. Miller reached for the weapon and the officers shot her 12 times. The District Attorney's investigation cleared the officers of criminal charges, although he criticized their judgment ("Suit Filed" 1999). In each of these incidents, the subject involved was a person of color and most of the officers were white, which heightened the tensions and allegations of racial unrest. Attorney General Janet Reno in April of 1999 called for a national commission to investigate police integrity in light of several incidents involving allegations of police abuse and the high levels of public mistrust of the police, especially among minority segments of the nation (Johnson 1999).

Corruption and scandal do not just hit the large cities, and it would be a serious error to leave that impression. For example, during 1998:

■ The entire command structure of two departments, in Cicero, IL and West New York, NJ, was replaced because of systemic corruption;
■ A Starr County, Texas sheriff was indicted for kickbacks;
■ A three-year corruption scandal in North Carolina resulted in the firing of two Highway Patrol supervisors and the demotion of another;
■ Fifty-five officers in Suffolk County, NY faced dismissal related to fraudulent actions in a hiring entrance exam scandal;
■ Officers in Dallas; Philadelphia; Erie County, NY; and Pioneer Village, KY faced charges in shootings or deaths of others, not related to on-duty incidents;
■ Federal authorities charged 44 persons in a corruption probe, many of them police and corrections officers in the Cleveland, Ohio area;
■ In Mahoning County, Ohio, six officers from local departments and the sheriff's office were indicted on charges ranging from felony theft in office and complicity to commit theft to dereliction of duty; other law enforcement officials were under investigation in a large corrupt practices probe in Northeast Ohio; by early 1999, the Mahoning County Sheriff had been indicted, and three former officers, including the retired chief of police of Campbell, OH, were in prison.
■ A former police captain in Akron, Ohio was sentenced to life for the killing of his ex-wife outside her medical office.

("On the Side of the Law" 1999; "Justice by the Numbers" 1999; Meade and Niquette 1998; Associated Press 1998.)

Departmental Efforts to Control Misconduct. It must be understood that misconduct is not controlled with one simple technique or program. Establishing an internal affairs unit does not ensure control. Control of misconduct (the goal) is achieved through the use of multifaceted control mechanisms (the means). These include professional selection standards, in-depth background investigations, training, corporate values, codes of ethics, written policies and expectations, managerial/supervisory training, citizen complaint procedures, internal investigations systems, complaint monitoring, and civilian review processes. Administrative and elected officials and the public also need to demand accountability. Police errors and intentional wrongdoing can and do lead to substantial penalties from civil litigation. These errors can include everything from the handling of an accident scene to intentional infliction of physical injury (Kappeler 1997). The costs can add another burden to the taxpayers and to government budgets.

A.C. Germann (1993, 6, 10) stated the following regarding traditional policing. The words have a unique relevance to this discussion of misconduct:

> There are far too many police whose values are selfish and individualistic, and who make the position work for them in many ways—free coffee, newspapers, foods, liquor, unnecessary overtime—a plethora of freebies that can lead all the way to theft of property, resale of drugs, . . . Unprofessional police misuse their power and authority against anyone they choose and, particularly, against anyone who does not show deference . . . . Traditional internal discipline is more harsh and punitive with respect to violations of policy and procedure involving facilities and equipment than it is with respect to violations of human rights . . . . The traditional police academy seems to have as its goal the preparation of brutal hit-squad members, rather than community helpers and non-violent conflict resolvers . . . . The traditional police union or employee organization resists any and all attempts to eliminate unsavory customs and traditions . . . . The majority of traditional officers support their colleagues with a code of silence, coverup, and sophisticated political pressure that often results in the dismissal or resignation of professionally oriented administrators.

On the other side of the coin, Germann (1993, 6) recognized that there are

> . . . police administrators, supervisors and officers who are very professional, very honorable, very truthful, and who are truly the unsung heroes of our age. . . . People like these—professional, well educated, highly motivated, with keen minds, social sensitivity, strength of character, and the courage to tell the king that he is naked—are the pride of the American police service. They need to be encouraged, supported, and given the access to the authority and power that are needed for immediate implementation of necessary changes of policy and procedure.

While it is recognized that the negative aspects of the police subculture are prevalent, it can be argued that the subculture itself can be an agent for change in agencies. Not only can enlightened administrators and supervisors encourage proper behavior, but the subculture can be used by professional officers to support and maintain a highly professional atmosphere (Conser 1980). Good, honest, dedicated officers need to take a stand and tell recalcitrant officers that "we won't tolerate that (misconduct) here!"

Because of the attention given to police misconduct in recent years, many jurisdictions have turned to **civilian review** of police misconduct complaints and allegations. In a 1991 study of the nation's 50 largest city police departments, Walker and Bumphus found that 30 had some form of civilian review procedures. (Ten of these had been established just since 1988, indicating an upward trend.) They categorized the review procedures into three types:

Class I: (a) Initial investigation and fact-finding by non-sworn personnel; (b) Review of investigative report and recommendation for action by non-sworn personnel or board consisting of a majority of non-sworn persons.

Class II: (a) Initial investigation and fact-finding by sworn police officers; (b) Review of investigative report and recommendation for action by non-sworn personnel or board which consists of a majority of non-sworn persons.

Class III: (a) Initial investigation and fact-finding by sworn officers; (b) Review of investigative report and recommendation for action by sworn officers; (c) opportunity for the citizen who is dissatisfied with the final disposition of the complaint to appeal to a board which includes non-sworn persons (Walker 1999; Walker and Bumphus 1991, 3).

Of the 30 civilian review programs, 12 were Class I, 14 were Class II, and 4 were Class III. Historically, police officer unions and employee associations have resisted the establishment and operation of civilian review boards because they do not believe that civilians can adequately judge their actions. Officers often have demonstrated over such proposals. In August of 1992, New York City officers demonstrated at City Hall to protest the proposal of an all-civilian review board. It polarized the various groups of police officers, with the Grand Council of Guardians (a Black officers' group) denouncing the protest (Police Protest 1992). By 1991, over 66 percent of the fifty largest cities in the United States had created some form of civilian review (Walker and Bumphus 1992). Kappeler, Sluder, and Alpert (1998, 250) summarize this trend by stating, "The boards are viewed by many as important vehicles for making the police more democratic and accountable. Although some boards have achieved a measure of success, many of the efforts at civilian oversight have met with failure."

SUMMARY

The issues and problems associated with the professionalization movement in policing were the focus of this chapter. There are clear indications that members of the occupation want to be considered professionals because of the status and other benefits that accrue from such a designation. However, there also are a number of problems within the occupation that appears to deter the progress toward being classified as a profession.

The traditional criteria of professions have not yet been vigorously achieved in policing, and the occupation has not committed itself to those criteria. There has been some progress in standardizing some organizational and managerial expectations and procedures through the accreditation process, although it, too, has been an issue of debate. In the final analysis, *wanting* to be classified as a profession is not sufficient, since the premise of our discussion here has been that the recognition is earned and bestowed *by the public* and not by the members of the occupation. There is much yet to be done before the majority of citizens will classify and acknowledge the law enforcement field as a profession.

The challenge of professionalism appears to lie on three fronts: providing effective service, responding to emerging crime problems, and reducing misconduct within the ranks. What policing personnel must understand is that their responses to these three challenges will determine the likelihood of having profession status conferred upon their field.

QUESTIONS FOR REVIEW

1. What are the differences between the concepts of occupation and profession as described in this chapter?
2. What are the seven traditional criteria or characteristics of a profession?
3. What are the five benefits of profession status?
4. What are seven areas that the policing occupation needs to address if it hopes to acquire profession status?
5. What is the purpose or significance of a code of ethics?
6. What is the accreditation process for law enforcement agencies, and how is it implemented?
7. What are the three basic professional challenges that the law enforcement community faces in its quest for profession status?
8. What are four types of police misconduct? Describe each.

SUGGESTED ACTIVITIES

1. Contact a local police department and ask how the code of ethics is explained or distributed to its officers.
2. Set up an in-class debate on whether policing is a profession or occupation.
3. Contact an accredited law enforcement agency close to you and invite the accreditation manager to speak to the class. Ask questions about the process, its cost, and its significance.
4. Log on to the World Wide Web and visit the Gallup organization, **http://www.gallup.com**, for a wealth of opinion information, including several polls related to crime and governmental affairs.
5. Log on to the World Wide Web at **http://www.calea.org/Index.htm** and examine the list of accredited law enforcement agencies. What are the closest agencies to your location? What is the general reputation of those agencies among members of your class and the faculty of the criminal justice program at your location?
6. Log on to the URL **http://www.brasscheck.com/cm/**—what does this site have to do with the public's interest in police corruption and abuse in the city of San Francisco?

CHAPTER GLOSSARY

abuse of authority: the mistreatment and/or violation of human and legal rights, regardless of motive or intention, by officials possessing police authority; may be physical, psychological, or legal

accreditation: a process whereby a law enforcement agency receives national recognition for complying with a certain set of standards

civilian review: the review of police misconduct complaints and allegations by nonpolice persons

code of ethics: a basic set of guidelines, or set of standards of behavior

Commission on Accreditation for Law Enforcement Agencies (CALEA): a governing body established in 1979 that oversees and grants formal accreditation status to law enforcement agencies

corruption: actions that involve the potential for personal gain and the use of police power and authority to further that gain

craft: an occupation that involves the development of skills that are generally learned through experience and not in a classroom

ethics: the study of human conduct in light of morality; the science dealing with moral duty; and the science of doing the right thing, at the right time, in the right way

morality: conformity to rules of right conduct

moral behavior (or **right conduct**): conduct adhering to actions prescribed by the society for the welfare of the people and society as a whole

occupation: any activity or endeavor by which one provides or obtains the means to survive (i.e., "earns a living")

occupational deviance: akin to police crime, but are acts that probably could not have been committed by anyone not employed in the police occupation

police crime: those acts where the officer's authority and powers as a police officer assisted or facilitated the commission of crime(s)

profession: an occupational type based on a special competence with a high degree of intellectual content; a specialty heavily based on or involved with knowledge

REFERENCES

Alpert, G. *et al.* 1992. Implications of the Rodney King Beating. *Criminal Law Bulletin* 28(5): 476.

Associated Press. 1991. U.S. Serial Killer Cases. *The Vindicator* (18 August): A9.

Associated Press. 1994. Smugglers Try to Sell Bomb Ingredients and Russia's Nuclear Stockpile Remains a Danger. *The Vindicator* (21 August): A6.

Associated Press. 1998. Cop Gets Life in Ex-Wife's Killing. *The Vindicator* (24 August): B4.

Associated Press. 1998. Serial Killer Allegations Shock Acquaintances. *The Vindicator* (8 November): A8.

Bayley, David H. and Egon Bittner. 1993. Learning the Skills of Policing. In *Critical Issues in Policing: Contemporary Readings* (2d ed.), by R.G. Dunham and G.P. Alpert (Prospect Heights, IL: Waveland Press, Inc., 106–129).

Bizzack, John W. and Victor Delacruz. 1994. Demystifying Police Accreditation. *Law Enforcement News* XX(400) (30 April): 8, 11.

Bountiful Harvest of Bad Apples. 1994. *Law Enforcement News* XX(398) (31 March): 4.

Clark, B.R. 1966. Organizational Adaptation to Professionals. In *Professionalization*, by H.M. Vollmer and D.L. Mills (Englewood Cliffs, NJ: Prentice-Hall, 282–291).

Coffey, Raymond R. 1994. Drug Prevention Is Best Medicine. *Chicago Sun-Times* (16 September).

Commission on Accreditation for Law Enforcement Agencies. 1998. **http://www.calea.org/** index (27 July).

Commission on Accreditation for Law Enforcement Agencies. 1999. *Standards for Law Enforcement Agencies.* 4th ed. Fairfax, VA: Commission on Accreditation for Law Enforcement Agencies, Inc.

Conser, James A. 1980. A Literary Review of the Police Subculture: Its Characteristics, Impact, and Policy Implications. *Police Studies* 2(4) (Winter): 46–54.

Curry, G. David, Richard A. Ball, and Robert J. Fox. 1994. Gang Crime and Law Enforcement Recordkeeping. *Research in Brief.* Washington, D.C.: U.S. Department of Justice, National Institute of Justice (August).

Eastman, W.E. 1985. National Accreditation: A Costly, Unneeded Make-Work Scheme. In *Police Management Today,* edited by James Fyfe (Washington, D.C.: International City Managers Association, 49–54).

Edmonds, Patricia. 1993. Detroit Calm for Officers' Beating Trial. *USA Today* (2 June).

Fields, Gary. 1993. Indictment: D.C. Cops Bragged about Crimes. *USA Today* (16 December).

Fogelson, Robert M. 1977. *Big-City Police.* Cambridge, MA: Harvard University Press.

Frankel, Bruce. 1993. Ex-NYC Officer Tells Stark Tale of Cops Gone Bad. *USA Today* (28 September).

Germann, A.C. 1993. Changing the Police: An Impossible Dream? *Law Enforcement News* XIX(383) (30 June): 6, 10.

Gillespie, Mark. 1999. One Third of Americans Believe Police Brutality Exists in Their Area. *The Gallup News Service.* Princeton: NJ: The Gallup Organization (22 March).

Goode, William. 1961. The Librarian: From Occupation to Profession? *The Library Quarterly* 31: 306–318.

Hays, Tom. 1999. Brutality Case Testimony: Officer Showed Off Stick Used in Torture. *USA Today* (21 May).

Higginbotham, Charles. 1999. Law Enforcement Oath of Honor. *Resolution adopted 21 October 1998.* Correspondence regarding action taken at the 105th Annual Conference of the International Association of Chiefs of Police, 3 June, at Salt Lake City, Utah.

Hill, Steven J. 1999. The Significance of Police Credentialing. *Police* 23(3) (March): 40–42.

Howlett, Debbie. 1992. Dahmer: 936 Years for "Holocaust." *USA Today* (17 February).

Human Rights Watch. 1998. *Shielded from Justice: Police Brutality and Accountability in the United States.* New York, NY: Human Rights Watch.

Johnson, Kevin. 1999. "Too Many" Believe They Can't Trust Police, Reno Says. *USA Today* (April 16).

Justice by the Numbers. 1998. *Law Enforcement News* XXIV(501, 502) 15/31 December): 19.

Kappeler, Victor E. 1997. Critical Issues in Police Civil Liability. Prospect Heights IL: Waveland Press, Inc.

Kappeler, Victor E., Richard D. Sluder, and Geoffrey P. Alpert. 1998. *Forces of Deviance: Understanding the Dark Side of Policing.* 2d ed. Prospect Heights, IL: Waveland Press, Inc.

Kelling, George L. and Mark H. Moore. 1988. The Evolving Strategy of Policing. *Perspectives on Policing.* Washington, D.C.: U.S. Department of Justice and John F. Kennedy School of Government, Harvard University (November).

Langworthy, R.H. and L.F. Travis III. 1994. *Policing in America: A Balance of Forces.* New York: Macmillan Publishing Co.

Meade, Patricia and Mark Niquette. 1998. Six Charged with Taking Cash, Drugs. *The Vindicator* (2 September): A1.

Milligan, Bernie R. 1994. Gateways to Toll Fraud. *Infosecurity News* 5(4) (July/August): 35–36.

NYPD Corruption Woes Bring More Bad News. 1994. *Law Enforcement News* XX(401) (15 May): 13.

NYPD Under Fire over Killing of Unarmed Man. 1999. *Law Enforcement News* XXV(507) (15 March): 1,10.

On the Side of the Law—Or Are They? 1998. *Law Enforcement News* XXIV(501,502) (15/31 December): 17.

Police Protest. 1992. *USA Today* (21 August): 3A.

Proposals for CALEA To Ponder. 1993. *Law Enforcement News* XIX(376) (15 March): 1, 11.

Puente, Maria. 1991. Murder Suspect Abused as Child. *USA Today* (16 August).

Roberg, R.R. and J. Kuykendall. 1993. *Police and Society.* Belmont, CA: Wadsworth Publishing Co.

Toffler, Alvin and Heidi Toffler. 1990. The Future of Law Enforcement: Dangerous and Different. *FBI Law Enforcement Bulletin* 59(1) (January):2–5.

Skolnick, Jerome H. and James J. Fyfe. 1993. *Above the Law: Police and the Excessive Use of Force.* New York: Free Press.

Stoddard, E. 1979. Organizational Norms and Police Discretion: An Observational Study of Police Work with Traffic Violators. *Criminology* 17(2): 159–71.

Stone, Andrea. 1993. Clues Emerging in Slayings of N.Y. Prostitutes. *USA Today* (1 July).

Suit Filed against Calif. Officers in Fatal Shooting. 1999. *USA Today* (19 May).

Walker, Samuel. 1977. *A Critical History of Police Reform: The Emergence of Professionalism.* Lexington, MA: Lexington Books.

Walker, Samuel. 1992. *The Police in America: An Introduction.* 2d ed. New York: McGraw-Hill.

Walker, Samuel. 1999. *The Police in America: An Introduction.* 3d ed. New York: McGraw-Hill.

Walker, Samuel and Vic W. Bumphus. 1991. *Civilian Review of the Police: A National Survey of the 50 Largest Cities.* Omaha, NE: University of Nebraska at Omaha.

Walker, Samuel and Vic W. Bumphus. 1992. The Effectiveness of Civilian Review: Observations on Recent Trends and New Issues Regarding the Civilian Review of the Police. *American Journal of Police* XI(4): 1–21.

Washington Association of Sheriffs and Police Chiefs. 1998. *Accreditation Program.* Olympia, WA: WASPC.

Winters, Paul A., ed. 1995. *Policing the Police.* San Diego, CA: Greenhaven Press, Inc.

Future Approaches and Strategic Planning

Bensalem, PA community police officer Theresa Nelson has a chat with 8-year-old Victoria McDaniel, near McDaniel's residence. July 1996 (AP/Wide World Photos)

The demands that law enforcement agencies face are undergoing dramatic change, and organized responses must accommodate changing demands. As prior chapters suggested, managing approaches for law enforcement agencies are evolving to meet new demands. In many respects, the role of law enforcement officers and agencies are also changing. This chapter is about planned organizational change and preparing for the future. After studying this material, you should be able to:

1. Identify and list sources of information available to law enforcement.
2. List and explain the major methods of storing information for later use.
3. Develop tools for analyzing information about law enforcement organizations.
4. Explain how to use groups to arrive at problem solutions.
5. List and explain the methods for using and sharing information.

PLANNING TOOLS FOR ALL RANKS

Most members of any organization tend to think in terms of daily routine. Patrol officers and line supervisors in a law enforcement agency can identify with this statement. While the exact nature of daily demands and requests for service are unplanned, there is a certain routine to the work in terms of basic procedures and techniques. Each call can be both different and demanding, but over time the *routine* manner of handling situations becomes clear to new recruits and they settle into this routine. While routines may differ from officer to officer (Bayley 1986), a general similarity prevails. Part of this routine is taking orders, and not making *big decisions* about department policy. Most training programs stress skills and following orders. So why should officers who are not of command rank care about planning or future problems?

Change at every level is essential if law enforcement is to implement and accommodate the societal expectations. In order for law enforcement to meet the challenges of the next century, every officer must participate in decision-making processes. Information-gathering is essential in order to meet these challenges with planning. The function of planning in new models of management demands *participation from all levels of an organization* and that POP and COP incorporate collaborative decision making throughout the department.

Therefore, all levels of an organization must participate in information acquisition and analysis, including patrol and supervision.

Together, the demands for information and participation offer new roles for patrol and supervisory personnel. Each must acquire, evaluate, and share information. The key is being familiar with processes that are available for information acquisition and processing. *Information is power* within an organization. It is both personal power and organizational power. Information permits individuals and organizations to plan and achieve goals.

Information Sources

Generally speaking, information sources are of many types and varieties. Although they commonly take the form of articles, reports, documents, and computer analyses, information sources may also include people, such as victims, witnesses, offenders, and other officers. The focus of this section concerns the types of documents available to law enforcement personnel for planning and analysis purposes. The "human" sources of information, however, should not be neglected and are emphasized below in the group methods section.

Internal Resources.   Planners in any organization begin by finding regularized ways to locate, collect, and store information. In your own organization, you can find valuable information for analyzing trends from several sources. Annual reports to legislative bodies, such as city council, or county supervisors or county commissioners, often provide good summaries of the past year's activities and an overview of plans for the next year. When compared with prior annual reports, these documents offer a window into trends in the agency. These reports rely upon internal data summaries and planning documents prepared by the chief administrative officer or staff officers (a Chief of Police, Sheriff, or their primary support personnel). Reports of interest include the Uniform Crime Reporting forms, which detail reporting, arrest, and clearance data, and budget summaries by month, quarter, and year.

Other internal documents of value might cover past planning for special projects or operations, changes in administrative organization, or even strategic plans if they were constructed in the past. These could include special documents from each division within a department (investigations, traffic, community outreach, etc.) or even planning documents related to wage negotiations with a union or similar labor or professional organization. Key internal documents are identified in Exhibit 16–1.

Information from such sources is organization specific and will give you a good vision of where an organization has been in the past, how it has changed, and trends that seem to be developing. One of the best ways to understand an organization is to read what it says about itself. Additionally, there is no direct data than the numbers it has assembled. Look for budget trends, organizational

Exhibit 16–1

INTERNAL SOURCES OF INFORMATION

- Annual reports to legislative bodies such as city council or county supervisors
- Internal data summaries and planning documents
- Budget reports by quarter and year
- Uniform Crime Reports to the FBI
- Past planning reports on file in the agency
- Division reports from prior years
- Reports to labor organizations, where relevant

---

impacts, staffing trends, equipment needs, and training needs. You must compare data from one reporting year to another in order to determine trends if trend charts are not included. Or you may have to compile your own chart for periods of time not covered in a trend chart. You may find that some data you think is essential is not collected. This is a change you can suggest for planning purposes. Exhibit 16–2 illustrates a data chart and a trend chart; the trend chart for murder was developed from the data chart statistics for the classification of murder. These types of charts are often found in annual reports or presentations made to citizen groups.

External Sources. Information essential to your organization can be obtained from other local government sources. This can be assembled from a broad variety of sources (Exhibit 16–3). Budget reports for your entire jurisdiction (e.g., city, county, township) are useful to project trends in funding for your agency compared to others and even to similar law enforcement agencies. Frequently it is the case that legislative bodies do not see a budget picture as a whole, including the impacts on other agencies in the jurisdiction. Rather, they see a bottom line and try to fit various demands into that bottom line. Lost in discussions on budgets are specific impacts in a given agency that develop over time. One purpose of studying budget documents is to uncover evidence of trends in budgeting that developed years before and that may not be justified now. Reading budgets and evaluating changes may seem imposing tasks, but it is something that comes with practice. Exhibit 16–4 illustrates a sample budget page from a budgeting report.

Exhibit 16–2

DATA CHART AND TREND CHART EXAMPLES

Classification	1990	1991	1992	1993	1994	1995	1996	1997	1998	1999
Murder	22	27	20	26	19	19	59	53	48	54
Rape	55	77	51	77	72	64	82	80	79	55
Robbery	436	393	351	381	386	580	852	831	771	853
Aggravated Assault	696	951	786	1516	348	644	1285	945	1191	1135
Burglary	2498	2314	2356	2424	2617	2442	2919	2245	2041	2121
Arson	300	346	289	326	290	277	406	353	278	312
Auto Theft	1246	1142	1212	950	972	1050	1720	1772	1343	911
Larceny	2393	1739	2315	2786	2767	2876	3048	2753	2637	2453
TOTALS	7646	6989	7380	8486	7471	7952	10371	9032	8388	7894

Exhibit 16–3

EXTERNAL SOURCES OF INFORMATION

- Budget reports for the jurisdiction involved
- Development plans from planning commissions, zoning boards, or development commissions
- Reports from local agencies such as health departments and school boards
- Reports from state agencies such as the department of transportation, fire marshal, and department of public safety
- Reports submitted to jurisdiction boards or commissions by private parties and consultants regarding economic development, agency operations, or strategic planning

Exhibit 16–4

SAMPLE BUDGET PAGES OF AN AGENCY

```
City of Warren, Ohio                      F I N A N C I A L   S Y S T E M                           PAGE    6
DATE 12/02/97          FISCAL YEAR: 1998                                    * * * D E T A I L * * *   BP0251
TIME  9:54:53                             EXPENSE BUDGET WORKSHEET                                    NHUGGIERI

FUND: 100  General Fund          DEPARTMENT: 011  Police - Uniform            SUB DEPARTMENT:
```

ACCOUNT	DESCRIPTION	2 YRS AGO EXPENSE	LAST YEAR EXPENSE	AMENDED BUDGET	CURR YR EXPENSE	DEPARTMENT HEAD	FINANCE AUDITOR	MAYOR	COUNCIL
WAGES									
510 100	Regular Wages	2,543,092	2,630,907	2,814,409	2,593,872	3,127,900	3,127,900	3,155,996	3,155,996
510 200	Overtime	84,843	60,761	70,000	66,584	110,000	110,000	50,000	50,000
510 201	Court Time	77,409	87,212	80,000	69,099	85,000	85,000	85,000	85,000
510 400	Shift Differential	26,630	28,703	30,000	705	41,382	41,382	29,244	29,244
510 500	Roll Call	71,704	80,150	86,500	84,856	110,000	110,000	110,000	110,000
510 600	Stand By Pay	0	0	0	0	0	0	0	
510 710	Education Allowanc	16,987	18,341	18,200	16,672	18,695	18,695	18,383	18,383
510 800	Severance/Separati	39,133	134,719	52,653	53,134	87,000	87,000	87,000	87,000
510 810	Benefit Conversion	0	0	0	0	0	0	12,536	12,536
510 900	Time Coming Payabl	7,612	21,845	15,000	14,812	32,790	32,790	32,790	32,790
510 901	Holiday Time Payab	19,346	77,693	76,000	1,063	66,790	66,790	66,790	66,790
511 000	Longevity	43,930	41,421	45,866	61,206	46,596	46,596	48,372	48,372
511 100	Hazard Pay	38,600	31,500	33,200	24,900	34,000	34,000	33,600	33,600
511 200	Workers' Compensat	50,949	16,649	17,000	19,729	0	0	0	
		3,020,235	3,229,901	3,338,828	2,986,632	3,760,153	3,760,153	3,729,711	3,729,711

```
        510 100  All wages and fringes are based on the current 86 officers.
        510 200  Increase based on wage increase along with court security issues.
                 * Judges have currently determined that two officers are to be
                   stationed in the courtrooms.
                 * Judge Gysegem's court routinely runs over.  With the jail
                   closing, the officers will need to transport prisoners back
                   and forth to the County Jail.  This needs to be done AFTER
                   court is finished.
                 * When the court security officers are on leave, officers must
                   be pulled from other shifts to cover the shortage.  This
                   causes overtime.
                 * At any time, the Judges have warned that they may require as
                   many as four officers in the Courts:  1 each courtroom
                                                          1 assignment office
                                                          1 clerks' office

                 Also includes $30,000 for S.T.E.P. Grant.
        510 800  Retirements of Lt. William Chovan and Ptlm. Ron Massucci.
                 Both will be in the first quarter of the year.
        510 900  Based on applications for payment made in March of 1997.
        510 901  Based on the amount of hours that will be worked by scheduled uniform
                 officers.  Non-scheduled officers were not included.  This figure
                 is based on what will be paid out at the end of 1997 for
                 currently banked holiday hours.  Majority of uniform police
                 officers are not effected in using holidays.  Majority of the
                 officers either work the holiday or are scheduled as a normal
                 day off within their schedule.
```

FRINGE BENEFITS									
520 100	P.E.R.S.	0	264	100	57	0	0	0	
520 200	Police Pension	557,216	614,032	625,503	567,557	664,951	664,951	557,828	657,828
520 500	Hospitalization	390,795	397,023	430,904	406,311	573,282	573,282	521,265	521,265
520 600	Life Insurance	7,608	7,656	7,564	6,928	7,224	7,224	7,140	7,140
520 700	Clothing Allowance	41,925	39,590	41,500	40,814	42,500	42,500	42,000	42,000

```
City of Warren, Ohio                      F I N A N C I A L   S Y S T E M                           PAGE    7
DATE 12/02/97          FISCAL YEAR: 1998                                    * * * D E T A I L * * *   BP0251
TIME  9:54:53                             EXPENSE BUDGET WORKSHEET                                    NHUGGIERI

FUND: 100  General Fund          DEPARTMENT: 011  Police - Uniform            SUB DEPARTMENT:
```

ACCOUNT	DESCRIPTION	2 YRS AGO EXPENSE	LAST YEAR EXPENSE	AMENDED BUDGET	CURR YR EXPENSE	DEPARTMENT HEAD	FINANCE AUDITOR	MAYOR	COUNCIL
FRINGE BENEFITS									
520 800	Workers' Compensat	174,131	185,534	199,127	198,050	158,051	198,051	198,051	198,051
521 000	Uniform Maint. All	30,067	31,344	33,200	32,534	34,000	34,000	33,600	33,600
521 100	Unemployment Compe	0	0	0	0	0	0	0	
521 200	Police Accrued Lia	77,518	77,510	77,520	77,518	77,520	77,520	77,520	77,520
521 400	Medicare (F.I.C.A.	19,673	23,322	25,657	23,444	27,504	27,504	26,561	26,561
		1,298,933	1,376,289	1,460,115	1,354,213	1,625,032	1,625,032	1,564,366	1,564,366

```
                                                                     Actes Phones Dispatch
```

OUTSIDE CONTRACT SERVICES									
530 400	Telephone	253	403	2,064	1,379	2,000	2,000	500	500
530 500	Education	15,580	11,490	15,387	13,154	16,000	16,000	13,000	13,000
531 200	Postage	1,805	1,409	2,117	1,665	2,050	2,050	2,050	2,050
531 300	Vehicle Maint. & B	48,750	67,397	90,326	67,830	70,000	70,000	50,000	50,000
531 400	Equipment Maint.&	9,906	11,243	12,900	12,231	13,000	13,000	13,000	13,000
531 500	Bldg. Maint. & Equ	0	255	425	0	425	425	425	425
531 700	Contracted Labor/S	16,639	18,555	36,525	36,535	32,025	32,025	32,025	32,025
531 702	Canine Services	5,400	212	250	201	1,500	1,500	500	500
532 400	Medical Expenses	4,002	4,604	4,711	3,035	5,000	5,000	4,000	4,000
532 400	Insurance (Fleet)	28,596	16,930	19,000	16,453	30,003	30,000	OK 20,000	20,000
532 500	Insurance (Liabili	50,563	54,146	84,000	68,530	85,500	85,500	85,500	85,500
532 700	Legal Claims	0	2,700	13,605	10,254	10,500	10,500	0	
532 701	Rewards	0	0	500	0	500	500	0	
533 000	Dues	255	470	535	360	550	550	550	550
533 200	Data Processing Se	126,600	126,178	138,000	94,500	135,000	135,000	135,000	135,000
533 400	Travel-Meals-Lodgi	5,754	6,584	5,750	3,212	7,000	7,000	6,000	6,000
533 900	Legal Fees	0	0	0	32	500	500	0	
534 000	Advertising	226	131	500	0	500	500	500	500
		313,769	324,252	417,697	345,991	412,050	412,050	363,050	363,050

```
        530 700  Based upon Lt. Bowers being accepted to PELC and Captain Roberts
                 attending the FBI Academy, above and beyond normal education.
                 Based upon that need to train and certify an additional polygraph
                 operator.  Training is normally a twelve (12) week course
                 for certification.
        531 300  Based on the status of the current fleet of cars without replacements.
                 * Transmissions are being repaired 2 - 3 times @ $600 - 1800 each.
                   Current fleet of cars in need of more maintenance as they get
                   older.
                 * Up-keep for a prisoner transfer van.  Van will be making up to
                   six trips a day between department and jail.
                   (Suggestion: set up separate account in 012 for van up-keep)
        531 702  Based on the assumption that we will be getting a new K9 unit.
        533 200  Based on 45 devices within the department.  Does not include any
                 additional devices required for new communication center.
        533 400  Based on the fact that hotel, meal, and reimbursement cost more than
                 education costs.  Lt. Bowers is expected to attend PELC and Capt.
                 Roberts may be attending the FBI Academy.
                 Based upon the training and certifing of an additional polygraph
```

(continues)

Exhibit 16–4 *(continued)*

```
City of Warren, Ohio                        F I N A N C I A L   S Y S T E M                          PAGE    2
DATE 12/02/97        FISCAL YEAR: 1998                                      * * *  D E T A I L  * * *   BPC251
TIME  9:54:53                                   EXPENSE BUDGET WORKSHEET                                 NBUGGIERI

FUND: 100  General Fund              DEPARTMENT: 011  Police - Uniform          SUB DEPARTMENT:

                                    2 YRS AGO    LAST YEAR    AMENDED      CURR YR     DEPARTMENT    FINANCE
ACCOUNT  DESCRIPTION                 EXPENSE      EXPENSE     BUDGET      EXPENSE       HEAD        AUDITOR      MAYOR      COUNCIL
----------------------------------------------------------------------------------------------------------------------------------
                                      Operator.  Course is normally 12 weeks.

SUPPLIES
540  100  Office Supplies             7,122       7,232       8,005       7,516        9,000        8,000      8,000      8,000
540  200  Tools                           0         100         100          90          200          200        200        200
540  300  Uniforms                      359         360       3,863       1,442        3,800        3,800      2,000      2,000
540  500  Gasoline (Unleaded         40,659      73,532      75,500      58,996       70,000       70,000     70,000     70,000
540  700  Oil & Other Fluids          1,268       1,167       3,000       1,295        2,000        3,000      2,000      2,000
540  900  Operational Mat. &         22,027      27,977      32,021      28,720       35,000       35,000     30,000     30,000
540  901  Canine Supplies               825       1,440       2,000         225        2,600        2,000      1,000      1,000
541  200  Secret Service                500         500       1,500         500        1,500        1,500      1,500      1,500
541  600  Computer Supplies           1,401       2,410       2,105       1,795        3,000        3,000      2,000      2,000
                                    ----------  ----------  ----------  ----------   ----------   ----------  ---------- ----------
                                     74,161     119,718     128,074     100,369      125,500      125,500    116,700    116,700

          540  200   Additional items needed that do not fall within 540 900 accounts.
          540  500   Vehicles are requiring more gasoline as they get older and are less
                     efficient.
          540  700   Based on the fact that the fleet will require more fluids as they
                     get older. Additional invoices have been deducted from
                     531 300 account.
          540  900   Expected additional cost of photo supplies due to jail closing. Will
                     be photographing each prisoner due to County photo imaging system
                     is not compatable and is yet to functioning as they promised.
          540  901   Based upon the expectation of obtaining an additional K9 unit.
          541  200   Detective division is conducting more investigations undercover and
                     with confidential informants.
          541  600   Increase cost of disks and tapes due to new Gateway computer back-up
                     system and the probability of having to obtain County photo
                     images by disk.
INSIDE MAINTENANCE
550  200  Motor Vehicle Main          5,355       6,094       9,800       6,273        7,800        7,800      7,800      7,800
                                    ----------  ----------  ----------  ----------   ----------   ----------  ---------- ----------
                                      5,355       6,094       9,800       6,273        7,800        7,800      7,800      7,800

CAPITAL EXPENDITURES
560  100  Furniture & Fixtur          1,200           0           0           0            0            0          0          0
560  200  Construction                    0           0           0           0            0            0          0          0
560  500  Equipment Purchase         61,729      25,111      11,240       6,240            0            0          0          0
560  600  Vehicle Purchases         188,719      75,276      66,250      45,125            0            0     60,000     60,000
562  100  Major Software Pur              0           0           0           0            0            0          0          0
                                    ----------  ----------  ----------  ----------   ----------   ----------  ---------- ----------
                                    251,648     100,387      77,450      51,365            0            0     60,000     60,000

  * SUB DEPARTMENT TOTALS *         4,868,111   4,913,041   5,437,004   4,645,063    5,930,535    5,930,535  5,841,627  5,841,627

  ** DEPARTMENT TOTALS **           4,964,101   5,156,641   5,432,004   4,645,063    5,930,535    5,930,535  5,841,627  5,841,627
```

Courtesy of City of Warren, Ohio.

Another set of external documents that are invaluable to planning in an agency are development plans from a planning commission, zoning board, development commission, or any agency with a similar role. These detail not only current facilities and buildings in place (residential, commercial, and government), but also those that are planned. Most communities have long-term development plans that signal where development can occur and what sort of construction (single family, multiple unit, commercial, or industrial) may take place. Long-term planning in an agency requires anticipation of coming demands. If the long-term development plan for a county or city projects growth in a given area with multi-family housing, the agency must assess the probable impacts that such development will produce. Reports to these same bodies that were submitted by private parties seeking to develop an area or by consultants hired by the board are also very useful. They tend to be more direct and quite specific in their predictions. For example, those who plan major commercial developments such as a mall or shopping center will usually have marketing data that will predict the traffic in the area and its likely increase. This is usually also addressed in the plan for parking, a central aspect of facility planning. By examining this data compared to current data from your traffic or streets department, you can determine how much traffic will increase in that area and project likely increases in accidents and traffic congestion. In the same respect, reports from state agencies such as the Department of Transportation provide valuable information on major roads that will impact your environment.

Other agencies whose internal documents and reports (often public) will be invaluable include local agencies such as health departments and school boards. Health departments may be required by local ordinance or state law to keep a list of hazardous materials commonly stored within your jurisdiction (some communities require that fire departments keep this data). This data is essential for fire and emergency evacuation planning. You could even combine information. For example, your research may show that a substantial amount of a hazardous chemical is regularly transported in and out of your jurisdiction by standard routes. By examining the location of sewer and water run-off lines under the streets, you could develop a short but effective emergency plan for street closure in the event of a spill. The important point is to be aware that community information is widely available to you. This information is important to planning. Open your mind, learn to ask questions, and keep asking until you find an answer.

In each of the cases noted, valuable information has been collected by other experts for easy use. In the case of development boards, any plans to change the commercial or residential building patterns will produce effects for law enforcement. New commercial risks, changing traffic patterns, criminal opportunities, or population mixes will alter community needs and the demands on law enforcement. For example, evidence developed over time demonstrates that densely concentrated housing such as apartments produces a greater concentration of police service calls, far in excess of their proportion of the population. If 15 percent of the population in a given city was located in dense housing, that area might account for as much as 30 percent of the calls for service. It is generally, the case that population density, regardless of income level, will be predictive of calls for service and crime. Obviously, increased traffic produce a greater opportunity for accidents. But it also produces new demands in patrol and response-time patterns, and may increase the opportunity for more exotic problems like toxic chemical spills that could result in neighborhood disruption or evacuation. Clearly, plans set before such boards and commissions impact law enforcement in the most profound ways.

Other Sources.   Many of these plans will rely upon, or use information from, other sources with which those in law enforcement should be familiar. These include items from the United States Census Bureau, the National Institute of Justice (NIJ), and Department of Justice Bureau of Justice Statistics (BJS). In the case of the NIJ or the BJS, law enforcement officers and departments can receive free regular mailings of materials developed from officially sponsored research in emerging issues. Another source of information is reprints of the Futures Studies written and developed by students in the Command College sponsored by the California Commission on Peace Officer Standards and Training. These are formal studies, conducted over a two-year period of time on specific issues affecting law enforcement. The Command College is the senior executive school of California Law Enforcement.

Other sources of information include daily newspapers from large cities. Large city daily newspapers have the resources to do in-depth analysis and reporting in ways that most smaller papers cannot. In particular, law enforcement officers should pay attention to the papers and magazines noted in Exhibit 16–5. Most of these are available in all larger libraries and some are available online. More importantly, articles published in such sources are included in the *Index to Periodicals* that most libraries carry in their reference section. As you develop a particular interest in one or more fields or issues, you can search for recent articles on those subjects in the index and locate the exact source. Some libraries also have computer-assisted search mechanisms such as Pro-quest™ or Lexis-Nexus™. From these database pools you can extract very specific information on the location of dozens of sources of information on a subject of interest to you. In many cases, you can print out or download whole articles or government documents. Each of these services indexes literally thousands of journals, magazines, and papers.

Exhibit 16–5

MAJOR NEWSPAPERS AND NEWS MAGAZINES IN THE UNITED STATES

Newspapers

- Washington Post
- New York Times
- Chicago Tribune
- Chicago Sun-Times
- Atlanta Constitution
- Atlanta Journal
- Los Angeles Times
- Cleveland Plain Dealer
- USA Today

News Magazines

- Newsweek
- Time
- U.S. News and World Report

Information Storage

Information is not useful unless you can find it. The first thing you need to do with information you gather is find a way to store it. You can store it either in physical file folders or on computer, or both. This section contains techniques that can be helpful in developing a personal reference system

Files. Every time you read a meaningful article you should place a copy of that article in a folder. This folder should be given a name or title that matches the issue or area you are examining (see Exhibit 16–6 for sample folder titles). Over time you will add more issues. You may develop 15 or 20 folders. For example, if your topic of interest was gangs, then your first folder would be entitled "gangs." As your research developed, you might expand this into "gang organization," "gangs and drugs," or any other subtopic. When you go to retrieve the information, you will have either the articles you read or notes on the substance of the article and its location (be sure to record full citations of sources). You can, of course, store the information much more easily on a computer, but you do not need a computer to create a personal reference file.

Computer Storage. Data storage on a computer can be done in a number of different ways. You may have specially designed software for storing information, or may rely upon off-the-shelf products. But each fits into one "niche" or another, for there are only three types of software useful for our discussion. The first is **database** software. In a database program you designate one or more **fields** of information, such as name, address, key word, or any number of identifiers that describe a case (article). You might want to keep a **record** (group of fields) of all the articles you have read. The name of the author, the date, the magazine or journal, the title of the article, the various subjects addressed, and the nature of your interest are all potential fields of information. In a database program, you decide what fields will be used, thereby constructing the database. After defining the fields for each type of information you are going to collect, you enter the information for each field for each case until the information for every case (article) is in the database. Then you can search the database. You might want to find all articles that appeared in *1994* on the subject of *gangs*, for example. Putting those search terms in will return a list of all articles you entered that were published in that year. Obviously you can do this type of storage with information about people, criminal cases, or any group of items with something in common. See Figure 16–1 for a sample screen from a database program.

Another storage method using computer technology is the **spreadsheet**. Spreadsheet software permits you to enter columns and rows of numbers much like an accounting sheet. Spreadsheets are intended for analyzing numerical information. For example, if you wanted to track crime rates in your city over

Exhibit 16–6

FUTURES FOLDER FILES

Drugs
    Transportation
    Sales
    Violence and Drugs
    Alcohol
    Use
Gangs
    Members
    Culture
    Violence
    Guns
    Drugs
    Social Role
Budgets
    Trends
    Fiscal Year
    Projected Demands
    Comparative Agencies
    City
    Department
    County
Training
    State Changes
    New Voluntary Courses
    Interactive
    On-Line
    Liability

Courtesy of Command College, California Peace Officer Standards and Training Board.

---

a period of time and look for trends, each column might be a month and each row a type of crime (robbery, burglary, etc.) or type of criminal (first offender, parolee, probationer, male, or minor, etc.) You could then track the crime or criminal over time. These programs also permit you to *graph* the data for a visual comparison. In short, spreadsheets are a useful storage and analytic tool.

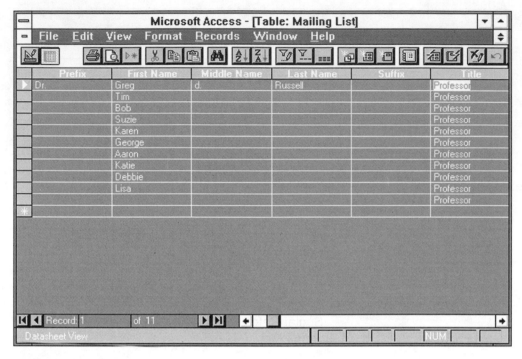

Source: Corel® Paradox®.

Figure 16–1 Sample Screen from a Database Program

See Figure 16–2 for a sample spreadsheet page and Figure 16–3 for a sample chart that can be created from the data stored in a database.

Finally, **word processing** software provides a convenient storage tool (Figure 16–4). Instead of having a "folder" in a physical sense, you can simulate one using a word processing program. Either in a Microsoft Windows™ or a Macintosh™ environment, you can create a "folder." Each of your documents can be created as a separate file. Save each file in your folder of choice. Then, using the word processing program search that directory or folder for any file that has a reference you seek (e.g., gangs, drugs). You can also store all of the information in one file (document) and use the search process to find all references to the subject of interest to you. These are efficient methods of storing text information. Finally, there are utility "add-ons" for word processing software that permit you to create citation databases with long notes regarding the content as well as the citation for the particular article.

What type of information should you keep? Whole articles are useful, but only if they are indexed in some way, either by being filed by subject matter or organized by other method that will help you locate the material. If you have a scanner and a very large hard drive in your computer system, storage of com-

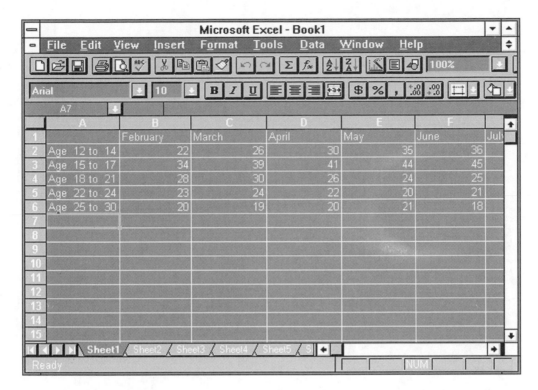

Source: Corel® Quattro® Pro.

Figure 16–2 Sample spreadsheet

plete documents or articles is possible. But most of us will not be able to keep hundreds of full, separate articles on file. Therefore, summary information is useful. First, simply state what the article is about. Second, what is the title? Was there an author? Be certain to note the volume and issue or month of the publication as well as the page number of the article. Did the article mention any experts or other studies in particular? Armed with this information, you can find the article again, and locate similar information.

Collecting information is not an activity that you can do once every three months. Rather, it requires small amounts of time used consistently. If you are consistent about using this approach, you can spend as little as 10 minutes a day and in a year have a very impressive file of usable information. Students should consider these techniques for future research papers. Police officers should consider them for maintaining access to professional knowledge for career advancement, public speaking, specialization, group problem solving, and unique field assignments.

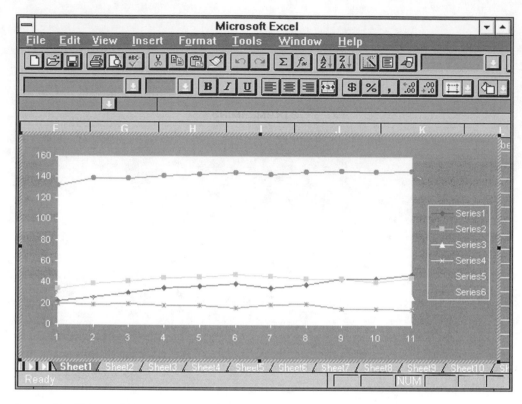

Source: Corel® Quattro® Pro.

Figure 16–3 Sample chart created from data

Sharing and Using Information

Once you have information, what do you do with it? Information is not useful unless you can find it and share it. In any organization, one rule tends to prevail. If a decision is needed, it will be made. The question is never whether enough information is available. The decision will be made on the information that is available, and this is one reason why some decisions fail. Frequently, more information will produce better decisions. Therefore, you need to share your information.

Updated Charts and Tables   Using your spreadsheet abilities, you can enter new data as each month or quarter ends and prepare updated reports on the data of your choosing. Spreadsheets allow you to sum columns or rows, calculate percentages and similar statistics, and develop a regular method of displaying data. As we noted above, they also permit you to graph the data. If the graph is linked to the spreadsheet, the graph will be updated automatically if the spreadsheet is altered. Displaying these on bulletin boards or giving copies

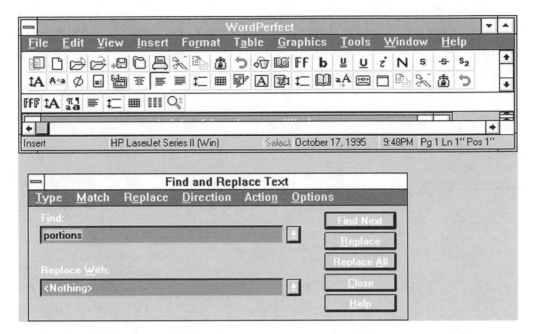

Source: Corel® WordPerfect®.

Figure 16–4 Word processing feature

to fellow officers is a good way to share this information. Use of spreadsheet *presentation* software is extremely valuable for formal meetings, for example.

Mapping. The use of **spatial analysis** or **computer mapping** comes to criminal justice from disciplines such as geography. It holds tremendous promise for law enforcement. Most law enforcement officers have seen the use of pin maps to keep track of criminal events in a given area. Different colored pins are placed on a map for each type of crime committed. The kind of crime, or time of day, or other traits are differentiated by the colors. In this manner, the map gives a general idea of where things are occurring and any patterns that may be evident.

But spatial mapping employs computers to keep track of multiple kinds of information on all the crimes in a given area (see Figures 16–5 and 16–6). This data is then layered over the affected areas. By taking time into consideration, you can design a map that *shows* you the changes in crime patterns over time. It is a useful method for predicting the onset of activity in a given area. This is an emerging process that is taking tremendous leaps and bounds as advances in technology permit new and more powerful approaches to mapping.

Group Methods. When managers or supervisors know that you have information and abilities in certain areas, they will eventually call upon you. Methods

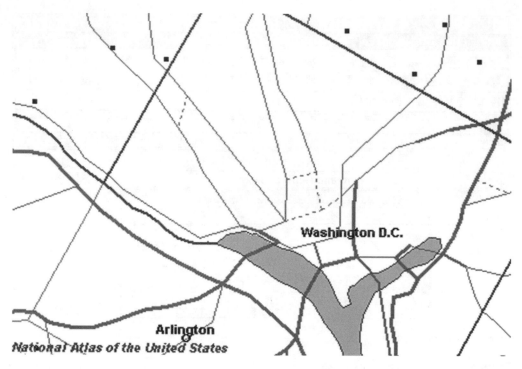

Source: U.S. Geological Survey.

Figure 16–5 Sample Printout of Spacial Mapping

to make your use of information more effective include interaction with others by seeking answers to problems that confront your organization. One very useful and powerful way to encourage effective interaction and information sharing is to employ a method called the **Nominal Group Technique (NGT)**. NGT was developed in 1968 by Andre Delbecq (Delbecq and Van de Ven 1975; Moore 1987). This is a group process for using and sharing information, developing a consensus on problem prioritization, and selecting solutions.

Groups can employ this technique to make formal decision or to merely share information informally with fellow officers. One way to approach informal sharing methods is to have social gatherings structured around this process. Four or five officers might meet at a home, or another place that is comfortable. In advance, each participant receives either a set of questions or one question which they are to answer in writing. Participants bring their answers with them. A sample question might be "What are the five (or ten) most significant problems facing our department in the next five years?" Participants should record their answer *in short phrases.*

One member of the group serves as a recorder and **facilitator**. The process begins with the facilitator recalling the question. Then each person in the group

1997 Gang Related Crimes

Legend:
- ◎ Incidents
- ⋀⋁ Streets
- Police Beat
  - 1
  - 2
  - 3
  - 4
  - 5
  - 6
  - 7
  - 8
  - 9
  - 10
  - 11
  - 12
  - City Boundary

Courtesy of Salinas Police Deptartment, Salinas, California.

Figure 16–6 Sample Printout of Spacial Mapping

takes a turn reading *one* of the answers, in order, and explaining it briefly. *No discussion* of the answers takes place here. The facilitator writes each response on a flip chart sheet. After each person offers their first answer, the procedure is repeated for the second answer. This process continues until each of the answers prepared by each participant is presented. As a flip chart page becomes full, it is torn off and taped to the wall so that all responses are displayed. There may be some repetition or similar statements that need to be combined (there may not be 25 different answers in a group of five members). Next, the group should have open discussion. Again, the recorder should keep notes about the conversations. The order of the discussion can be structured or open. In a structured format, each answer is discussed separately usually with some time limit. The purpose is to force participants into incisive decision making without the influence of worrying about the agendas of others. The intensity of the process is important.

After each answer has been discussed, the group votes. There are two methods of voting. First, each member should list on paper the five answers that they consider to be the most important, ranking them 1 (most important) through 5 (least important of the five). After each member of the group has voted, collect the ballots. Assigning five points for a "1," four for a "2," and so on, score each of the answers for total weighted votes. The top five vote totals will be the group determination of an answer to the question. A sample point tally of an NGT exercise is illustrated in Exhibit 16–7.

A second method is very similar. Rather than ranking the answers, each person constructs a list of the five (or ten) most important answers from all the answers offered by the entire group. The entire list of answers compiled by the group is read one by one. Each participant votes if that answer appears in their new list of the top five (or ten). Each vote is valued equally. Hence, in a group of five the top score is 5. This is an easier method for recordkeeping. At the end, votes are compared and the answer with the most votes is the number one choice. The answer with the second highest total is second, and so on. If there is a tie at the conclusion of voting, participants must choose between alternatives. If two are tied for number four, for example, participants vote to choose which is number four and which is number five. Ties are resolved one tier at a time.

The list of five problems may call for expansion. For example, you might wish to ask a followup question for each of the five. Some suggestions might be: how do we define this problem; what are the top five solutions to parts of this problem; what resources do we need for each solution; what impacts will each problem have on future training policies? One can imagine a wide variety of questions.

The purpose of this process is to produce a new decision approach in organizations. First, decisions on complex questions made by only one person have a greater probability of failing than do decisions made by groups. Many people participating in a decision assures a wider range of information than one person will consider. Over 50 years ago, Herbert Simon identified the tendency of most decision makers to select options from a limited set of predetermined options. He argued that the decision processes of most people are limited by what he called **bounded rationality** (Simon 1947). Our decision process is limited by the amount of information we have, the time we have to assess the

Exhibit 16–7

NOMINAL GROUP TECHNIQUE
"Top 5 Problems Facing Butte County"
2-11-95

ITEM	POINTS
First Place	
Population growth	46
Second Place	
Jurisdictional disputes/Lack of coordination	18
Third Place	
Drug free zones/Campus drug problems	13
Gangs/Graffiti/Guns and drugs in schools	13
Fourth Place	
Increase in violent crime/Firearm possession	7
Education cost increase	7
Lack of programs directed at juveniles	7
Fifth Place	
Staff resources and funding shortages	6
Honorable Mention	
Domestic violence increases/Lack of resources	5
Medical services in relation to expansion	5
Lack of juvenile counseling	5
Expansion of service areas (in size)	4
Community outreach and community integration	3
Drugs	3
Bike-car-train congestion downtown	2
Political coordination	2

Source: Developed in class in senior criminal justice policy seminar, 1995, California State University at Chico.

---

information, and our inability to question ourselves. When faced with complex problems, Simon noted that decision makers search their memory and stop at the first solution that is *good enough* (Simon 1947). This is true in the private sector as well as the public.

We can all understand the first two problems Simon described, but the third deserves more discussion. Each of us holds closely held beliefs (biases, we might call them) and we usually have solutions that we think will work with most any problem. Scholars and practitioners who have studied policy decision making know that our greatest tendency is to attach our favorite solution to nearly every problem we encounter without ever questioning its validity. In debates about crime control, for example, some hold the perspective that if only we punish offenders more severely, crime will go down. Others hold that most offenders are correctable if only we spend enough money on prevention or rehabilitation. The evidence is relatively compelling, of course, that the issue of crime in society is far more complex then *either* solution suggests (see Chapter 6). But rarely do proponents of either approach critically examine their own positions. So it is in administrative agencies of any type, and law enforcement is not immune from this problem

By using a larger group of people to solve a problem, we can overcome these difficulties. When several people lend their efforts to the decision process, diverse perspectives will be reflected. Similarly, the knowledge base will be wider. Lastly, while we cannot create more time, the involvement of several people allows us to consider more options and information in the same amount of time, which, in effect, enlarges the time for decision making. Decisions on complex questions, therefore, should be more effective if several people participate. Most leaders have staff, of course, but the idea of NGT goes far beyond the concept of a staff. It transforms everyone into information gatherers and users.

A second reason for the use of this method is that merely having a group make decisions is not enough. Improperly structured groups will tend to make bad decisions. Groups may tend to operate to prevent dissenting opinions from being heard. Most people like being part of the group (regardless of their backgrounds or beliefs). Individuals will not challenge a generally held view, even if that individual believes that the accepted view is very wrong (Asch 1951).

Sometimes groups are inherently made up of very similar people. Such a group, whose members know one another well and have similar skills and roles, will tend to behave in specific ways. **Group think** syndrome is an example of how small groups can, in a crisis, make horrible decisions. If a group of decision makers are similar in background, have great group cohesion, find themselves under high stress from external pressure, and are insulated from the external environment, they will tend to act in very specific ways. First, the group will seek concurrence and assume that a generally expressed view is unanimous. Second, it will employ stereotypes to bolster to decisions. Third, it will tend to express illusions of invulnerability and morality (Janis 1971). The results of decisions made in such an atmosphere are typically poor. Unfortunately, the preconditions for this mind set are clearly found in law enforcement agencies.

It is interesting to note that rule-based training does not seem to alter group behavior in these conditions. The process of decision making is the source of problems. Therefore, some method of altering the decision process is essential and NGT is one such method. Obviously, in the middle of a crisis it is not possible to write out five possible answers, discuss, vote, and so on until conclusion is reached. However, groups need to consider alternative views and information and prevent group think from occurring. The value of NGT is that it teaches people to not only express differing information and views, but to *expect others to do the same*. It causes decision makers to think openly and to use all their cognitive skills. As group members become more comfortable with sharing information, accepting contradictory information, and listening to differing views, they will develop participative leadership approaches. Outside of a crisis, however, the value of NGT and its related approaches is in long-term planning. With this process you can methodically develop long-term strategic plans with built-in contingency plans for different alternative conditions. Exhibit 16–8 identifies the list of 10 trends that resulted from an NGT project made up of 26 individuals (a combination of students, faculty, city officials, and police practitioners).

AN APPROACH TO PROBLEM SOLVING

Knowing the problems an agency faces is not enough. In order to construct solutions and make long-term plans, there are many factors to take into consideration. One process is to apply NGT to four specific aspects of any agency or department. The preparation of long-term plans, so-called **strategic planning**, requires attention to very specific aspects of not only the outside world but also the agency or department that is doing the planning. These can be characterized as **Weaknesses, Opportunities**, **Threats**, and **Strengths**, or simply "**WOTS**" (Koteen 1991). Very simply, by using the NGT approach you can address four basic questions.

Weaknesses

What are the weaknesses of your organization? There surely are some weaknesses. Most would name lack of money, escalating workloads, insufficient training, and too few computers as typical responses. But your inquiry must go deeper. Maybe you lack certain things because the department fails to prioritize its needs well, thus guaranteeing that a whole set of problems will continue year after year. The real weakness is a lack of planning skill or commitment.

Other weaknesses might be too few contacts with the community, or a lack of good communications for internal information flow. Still others might be outdated personnel systems, departmental regulations that need revision to comply with new laws and needs, or any number of items one might imagine. The key is to open your mind to problems that are more than just too few dollars. Most of us have yet to find a government agency—or, for that matter, a department within a corporation—that is willing to say it has enough money.

Exhibit 16–8

TOP 10 NGT RESULTS TO THE QUESTION "NAME THE TRENDS AFFECTING LAW ENFORCEMENT EXECUTIVES IN THE NEXT TEN YEARS"

Trend 1   Level of Cultural Diversity
The change in the total diversity of the community. Includes all types such as ethnicity, sexual orientation, age, and gender.

Trend 2   Change in Available Resources
Level of funding will be a question. Local, regional, and global economic trends and their effects in law enforcement.

Trend 3   Level of Economic Disparity Between Classes
Collapse of society. Rich become richer and the poor become poorer. Demands of police executive to police both division of the community when one can pay for services and the other cannot.

Trend 4   Court Interference with Management Decision Making
Level of influence courts and judicial system will have on the police executive. How legal will every decision need to be?

Trend 5   Change in Societal Values
Back to the values of the past. The quality of life will become more important. Morals and ethics will play a critical role.

Trend 6   Broader Leadership Responsibilities
Role as a community leader. Consolidation of services under one director. The degree of regionalization.

Trend 7   Technology Changing
Understanding and staying on the edge of technology. Finding the necessary funding.

Trend 8   Level of Public Expectations of Police Accountability
Expectation of perfection. New system of board of review, level of community involvement, and amount of hands-on by city officials.

Trend 9   Level of Ability to Communicate Effectively
Qualification level of police executive candidates.

Trend 10   Level of Public Confidence in Law Enforcement
Public's trust and confidence in law enforcement officers to do the job.

Source: Reprinted with permission from R. Gurrela, California POST Command College Futures Study, Class 21, © 1996, Califnornia Peace Officer Standards and Training Board.

Opportunities

What are the real opportunities that your department faces? Federal and state grants available to most departments are opportunities waiting to be seized. Many grants are also available from private foundations for community-related activities that may have significant law enforcement value. Be inventive. Grants and purposes can be combined, in order to create an entire program. These might involve deploying a special unit for domestic violence cases that would include trained civilian counselors or mediators. This type of project could justify grants from disparate areas like child protection services, dispute resolution, mediation, and spousal abuse, as well as innovative approaches in the delivery of mental health services. The key is to find out which programs are available. This information is available through most libraries, or from online services, government documents, university or college research institutes, and private foundations. Community events, good and bad, can be opportunities with significant benefit to law enforcement's goals of reducing crime and making communities safer. You should see problems as opportunities for growth and achievement. A negative community event, such as a clash between neighboring gangs, could be seen as an opportunity to galvanize others in the community to open a dialogue between the gangs and the community to prevent further problems.

Strengths

What are the real strengths of your department? Maybe it is the training level, education level, or average age. While lack of experience could be seen as a weakness, youthfulness is a strength. Each of these is a different issue with a different impact. Experience is useful only if it is used. Youthful officers may be more inclined to solve problems, while experienced officers might accept certain situations as given and have stopped looking for answers. The two must work together. In some cases, it may be that there is an absence of information-sharing that means experience is not getting translated into a department resource—which is a weakness.

Threats

What threats face the department? These may be politically based, community inspired, or economically centered. Maybe your city or county is about to expand its population base. City annexation or major development within a county poses significant threats for law enforcement. Rapid growth and high-density housing almost always produce higher crime rates. This creates more stress on departments. Typically, however, there is a delay between the onset of problems and increases in budget resources to deal with them. This might require reassignment of patrol areas, shift changes, more overtime, and attention to new community concerns. It may mean changing language and cultural patterns in an area. These are all threats to the department's ability to secure public safety. By "threat," we mean a condition that has the potential to interfere with the mission of law enforcement or that may present increased levels of existing problems or introduce new problems.

By evaluating these four aspects of a department, and employing an approach such as NGT, significant advances can be made in defining problems and solutions to those problems. These solutions, however, are rarely going to be simple because they challenge "the way things have been done for years."

NEW RESPONSES TO TRADITIONAL AND EMERGING PROBLEMS

As law enforcement began to use new tools to gather and assess information, two things resulted. First, law enforcement began to focus on new issues. Second, it became clear that law enforcement needed to change the manner in which agencies were structured, and in how they gathered and used information. The old structure could not respond to the problems of the future.

Community Policing

The most recent model offered for policing reform is *community policing* (which has been discussed throughout this text). The concept is relatively new in modern law enforcement theory, though the notion was initially suggested in the early 1970s (Angell 1971). However, it is not well defined by either its proponents or its detractors. One thing is certain, this is a *philosophy* of policing, not a tactic or project (see Chapter 9). Because it is a philosophy, community policing must address the organizational culture of law enforcement (Trojanowicz and Bucqueroux 1990; Crank and Langworthy 1992; Herbert 1998). Organizational culture is the set of values, principles, and beliefs generally held by members of the organization (refer to Chapter 6). Some researchers suggest that organizational culture is the most important determinant in obtaining subordinate compliance in policing (Brehm and Gates 1993).

What community policing requires in terms of organizational change is not entirely clear. The major proponents hold that it requires police and community members to work closely together. The major focus of this mutual effort should be to find new ways of reducing crime, the fear of crime, and the physical decay of neighborhoods. Police must permit citizens access to and input into policing decisions. Citizens must give support and assistance in return. Further, power and decision making in department management must be decentralized to supervision and line officers. Community policing also requires the placement of Community Policing Officers (CPOs) as outreach specialists in the community (Bayley 1994). Officers must have regular contact with the community to protect those most vulnerable, and forge a working relationship with the community as a whole (Eck and Rosenbaum 1994), though this is a complex goal to achieve (Grinc 1994). The practice of community policing seems to vary by community and region of the nation, even in rural settings (Maguire *et al.* 1997).

Community policing seeks to develop a proactive approach to crime "by intensely involving the same officer in the same community on a long term basis" in order to foster trust (Trojanowicz and Carter 1988). It traces its theoretical lineage through an evolution of modern policing approaches that derived from applied research. The traditional model of police riding in cars until called upon was the result of the cruiser, the radio, and a belief that response time mattered most in crime solving. Research determined, however, that response time was not the most important factor (review Chapter 9). Further, police increasingly became the target of civil rights abuse claims. In response to these and other pressures, policing adopted a *community relations* approach that was essentially public relations and assumed that contact with the community would reduce crime and tensions. This developed into *team policing*. In this approach, a team of officers was targeted at a single area or problem. In this method, team members could be integrated or immersed into that community or neighborhood. As studies demonstrated that police patrol was counterproductive, departments began experimenting with *foot patrol* under the assumption that this would produce closer contact. Eventually, it became clear that a far more dynamic relationship was necessary and that a genuine merging of community and police *interests* was essential. This produced the notion of community policing. Associated with CPO is the notion of Problem Oriented Policing (POP), which suggests that law enforcement should seek out root problems in communities and seek solutions in collaboration with the community (Goldstein 1990).

In a conceptual manner, community policing requires officers to define "communities" by issues or the community of interest that provides the unifying principle for police and community to interact and co-produce safety (Trojanowicz and Moore 1988). Because of its focus on issues, the implementation of community policing tends to vary as widely as its definition. In some departments, it is resisted heavily. Some opponents may make heavy demands on outcomes measurements. The degree and speed of implementation will also vary. Some see the need to address special issues such as juveniles, while others caution against expecting too much too soon, or the use of measures designed for the assessment of reactive policing.

Common Attributes.   Still, the notion of community policing can be reduced to seven commonalities by which it might be measured. First, response time for non-emergency calls will increase, not decrease, as resources are used more in depth in the community. Second, the department should be staffed with specialists in community outreach and designated as CPOs, or all officers will become generalists, practicing community policing as part of their normal duties. Third, there will be multiple contacts with the community at large, including foot patrol, park activities, other organized activities at the neighborhood level, specialized programs for schools, and other organizations. Fourth, increased participation of the community in police affairs will include block watch, training, information sharing, and even the use of civilians in selection and hiring procedures, including assessment centers. Fifth, there will be a heavy use of community research to understand the "issues." Sixth, random car-based patrol will become a very small portion of officers' assignments. Seventh, a greater portion of the time officers spend on duty will be spent identifying community issues. Eighth, law enforcement organizations will decentralize organizational structures and decision making (Russell 1997).

In summary, as threats have mounted, law enforcement has responded with a new formula for policing communities. However, recognition of these problems and their partial solutions also has led to the realization that traditional models of organization needed to be revised (Strecher 1997).

Restorative Justice

A new model of community justice is **restorative justice**. In the broadest sense, restorative justice is a different way of thinking about crime and our response to it. The model focuses on harm caused by offenders; it seeks to repair harm to victims and community, and to reduce future harm by preventing crime. Restorative justice requires offenders to take responsibility for their actions and for the harm they have caused. It seeks reprisal for victims, reparation by offenders, and reintegration of both within the community as communities and government achieve restorative justice through a cooperative effort (Van Ness 1996; Van Ness and Strong 1997; Zehr 1990, 1997). Largely, law enforcement is part of the "community" and has a role to play not only in the role of apprehension and crime prevention suggested by traditional models and community- or problem-oriented policing. In restorative justice it plays a part in assisting community courts, offenders, and victims in reparations *and* offender reintegration. One program in Spokane, Washington seeks to divert certain sorts of non-violent offenders at the point of apprehension to community courts for disposition. The role of law enforcement in this concept is evolving, but certainly holds promise.

SUMMARY

This chapter examined several approaches to addressing the future of law enforcement. First, sources of information were identified. Second, various ways to store this information were described. Third, ways in which this information could be used productively were presented. Specifically examined was the process of Nominal Group Technique and how it might be used to discover the weaknesses, opportunities, threats, and strengths of law enforcement agencies. Fourth, how this type of information may lead to changes in departmental structure, approaches, and outcomes was explained in order to operationalize the emerging standards of community policing.

QUESTIONS FOR REVIEW

1. What are the major internal sources of information in a law enforcement agency?
2. What are the major external sources of information used for planning?
3. What are the major sources of print information?
4. What are the methods of sharing information in printed form?
5. What is the Nominal Group Technique (NGT)?
6. What are the differences between two systems of voting in NGT?
7. What do each of the letters in WOTS analysis stand for?
8. How does planning get utilized in community policing?

SUGGESTED ACTIVITIES

1. Divide the class into groups no smaller than 15 and no larger than 20, if possible. Take an issue or question from this text, from the list of possible trends found in Figure 16–12, or from a list generated by your class or instructor. Assign the class/group to review the question for 24 hours and return with the top 10 answers to the question. Using this question, conduct an NGT in your class.
2. Using the results of the NGT conducted in number 1 above, assess whether further questions need to be resolved. For example, is a WOTS analysis needed? If so, using NGT, conduct a WOTS analysis on a department with which you are familiar or on your school or college.
3. Using the idea of community policing as a starting point, how would you implement it? What are the 10 greatest obstacles to implementation? Use an NGT in your class to assess this question. Follow up with a WOTS analysis. Discuss the results.
4. Find the Internet home page for the National Criminal Justice Reference Service (NCJRS). Explore the links from this page, finding at least 10 sites linked to NCJRS. Download or print out at least two reports, studies, or data sets to employ in analysis.

CHAPTER GLOSSARY

bounded rationality: the limited range of decisions available to an individual because one cannot know all the information necessary to make a perfect decision

computer mapping: the process and technique of plotting information and data onto geographical maps using computer technology

database: in computer terms, a type of applications software that assists the user with the systematic storage of information; it contains multiple records about a subject

facilitator: a person who guides and stimulates the interaction among members of a group; keeps the group focused

field: the smallest element of a database; it refers to one item of information, such as date, name, address, or telephone number

group think: the tendency of groups under stress to make decisions with limited concern for alternatives or options

Nominal Group Technique: a group decision-making approach used to identify multiple problems and multiple solutions

record: a group of related fields that make up a record

restorative juistice: a theory of uniting community, offender, and victim to repair the victim and community and reintegrate the offender; law enforcement plays an active role in all stages of the process

spatial analysis: the process of evaluating the relationship of items within a geographical space; used in computer mapping

strategic planning: a planning process that focuses on the anticipation of events that may shape or have impact on long-range policies

WOTS: an analysis (often using NGT) to diagnose the weaknesses, opportunities, threats, and strengths that affect organizational performance

REFERENCES

Angell, John E. 1971. Toward an Alternative to the Classic Police Organizational Arrangements: A Democratic Model. *Criminology* 9: 185–206.

Asch, Solomon E. 1950. Effects of Group Pressure upon the Modification and Distortion of Judgements. In *Groups, Leadership, and Men*, edited by Harold Guetzkow (Pittsburgh: Carnegie Press, 177–90).

Bayley, David H. 1986. The Tactical Choices of Police Patrol Officers. *Journal of Criminal Justice* 14: 329–48.

Bayley, David H. 1994. *Police for the Future*. New York: Oxford University Press.

Brehm, John and Scott Gates. 1993. Donut Shops and Speed Traps: Evaluating Models of Supervision of Police Behavior. *American Journal of Political Science* 37(2): 555–81.

Crank, John P. and Robert Langworthy. 1992. An Institutional Perspective of Policing. *The Journal of Criminal Law and Criminology* 83(2): 338–63.

Delbecq, A. L., A. H. Van de Ven, and D. H. Gustafson. 1975. *Group Techniques for Program Planning: A Guide to Nominal Group and Delphi Processes*. Glenview, IL: Scott-Foresman.

Eck, John E. and Dennis P. Rosenbaum. 1994. The New Police Order: Effectiveness, Equity and Efficiency in Community Policing. In *The Challenge of Community Policing: Testing the Promises* by Dennis P. Rosenbaum. (Thousand Oaks, CA: Sage Publications, 3–23).

Goldstein, Herman. 1990. *Problem Oriented Policing*. New York: McGraw-Hill.

Grinc, Randolph M. 1994. "Angels in Marble": Problems in Stimulating Community Involvement in Community Policing. *Crime and Delinquency* 40(3): 437–68.

Herbert, Steve. 1998. Police Subculture Reconsidered. *Criminology* 36(2): 343–70.

Janis, Irving. 1971. Group Think. *Psychology Today* 5(6) (November): 43–47, 74–76.

Koteen, Jack. 1991. *Strategic Management in Public and Nonprofit Organizations*. New York: Praeger.

Maguire, Edward R., Joseph B. Kuhns, Craig D. Uchida, and Stephen M. Cox. 1997. Patterns of Community Policing in Nonurban America. *Journal of Research in Crime and Delinquency* 34(3): 368–94.

Moore, Carl M. 1987. *Group Techniques for Idea Building*. Newbury Park, CA: Sage Publications.

Rich, Thomas F. 1995. The Use of Computerized Mapping in Crime Control and Prevention Programs. *Research in Action*. Washington, D.C.: U.S. Department of Justice, National Institute of Justice.

Russell, Gregory D. 1997. The Political Ecology of Police Reform. *Policing: An International Journal of Police Strategies and Management* 20(3): 567–589.

Sanford, Ray. 1993. How to Develop a Tactical Early Warning System on a Small City Budget. *Proceedings: Wordshops on Crime Analysis Through Computer Mapping*. Loyola University: Illinois Criminal Justice Authority.

Simon, Herbert. 1947. *Administrative Behavior*. New York: Macmillan.

Strecher, Victor G. 1997. *Planning Community Policing: Goal Specific Cases and Exercises*. Prospect Heights, IL: Waveland Press.

Trojanowicz, Robert and Bonnie Bucqueroux. 1990. *Community Policing: A Contemporary Perspective*. Cincinnati: Anderson Publishing.

Trojanoqicz, Robert and David Carter. 1988. *The Philosophy and Role of Community Policing*. East Lansing, MI: National Neighborhood Foot Patrol Center, Michigan State University.

Trojanowicz, Robert and Mark Moore. 1988. *The Meaning of Community in Community Policing*. East Lansing, MI: National Neighborhood Foot Patrol Center, Michigan State University.

Van Ness, David. 1996. Restorative Justice and International Human Rights. In *Restorative Justice: An International Perspective*, edited by Burt Galaway and Joe Judson (Monsey, NY: Criminal Justice Press, 17–36).

Van Ness, David and Karen H. Strong. 1997. *Restoring Justice*. Cincinnati: Anderson Publishing Co.

Zehr, Howard. 1990. *Changing Lenses: A New Focus for Crime and Justice*. Scottsdale, PA: Herald Press.

Zehr, Howard. 1997. Restorative Justice: The Concept. *Corrections Today* 59(7) (December): 68–70.

Constitution of the United States

WE THE PEOPLE of the United States, in Order to form a more perfect Union, establish Justice, insure domestic Tranquility, provide for the common defence, promote the general Welfare, and secure the Blessings of Liberty to ourselves and our Posterity, do ordain and establish this Constitution for the United States of America.[a]

ARTICLE. I.

SECTION. 1. All legislative Powers herein granted shall be vested in a Congress of the United States, which shall consist of a Senate and House of Representatives.

SECTION. 2. [1]The House of Representatives shall be composed of Members chosen every second Year by the People of the several States, and the Electors in each State shall have the Qualifications requisite for Electors of the most numerous Branch of the State Legislature.

[2]No person shall be a Representative who shall not have attained to the Age of twenty five Years, and been seven Years a Citizen of the United States, and who shall not, when elected, be an Inhabitant of that State in which he shall be chosen.

[3][Representatives and direct Taxes shall be apportioned among the several States which may be included within this Union, according to their respective Numbers, which shall be determined by adding to the whole Number of free Persons, including those bound to service for a Term of Years, and excluding Indians not taxed, three fifths of all other Persons].[b]

The actual Enumeration shall be made within three years after the first Meeting of the Congress of the United States, and within every subsequent Term of ten Years, in such Manner as they shall by Law direct. The Number of Representatives shall not exceed one for every thirty Thousand, but each State shall have at Least one Representative; and until such enumeration shall be made, the State of New Hampshire shall be entitled to chuse three, Massachusetts eight, Rhode-Island and Providence Plantations one, Connecticut five, New-York six, New Jersey four, Pennsylvania eight, Delaware one, Maryland six, Virginia ten, North Carolina five, South Carolina five, and Georgia three.

[a]This text of the Constitution follows the engrossed copy signed by Gen. Washington and the deputies from the 12 states. The superior number preceding the paragraphs designates the number of the clause; it was not in the original.

[b]The part included in heavy brackets was changed by section 2 of the fourteenth amendment.

[4]When vacancies happen in the Representation from any State, the Executive Authority thereof shall issue Writs of Election to fill such Vacancies.

[5]The House of Representatives shall chuse their Speaker and other Officers; and shall have the sole Power of Impeachment.

SECTION. 3. [1]The Senate of the United States shall be composed of two Senators from each State, [chosen by the Legislature thereof,][c] for six Years; and each Senator shall have one Vote.

[2]Immediately after they shall be assembled in Consequence of the first Election, they shall be divided as equally as may be into three Classes. The Seats of the Senators of the first Class shall be vacated at the Expiration of the second Year, of the second Class at the Expiration of the fourth Year, and of the Third Class at the Expiration of the sixth year, so that one third may be chosen every second Year; [and if Vacancies happen by Resignation, or otherwise, during the Recess of the Legislature of any State, the Executive thereof may make Temporary Appointments until the next Meeting of the Legislature, which shall then fill such Vacancies].[d]

[3]No Person shall be a Senator who shall not have attained to the Age of thirty Years, and been nine Years a Citizen of the United States, and who shall not, when elected, be an Inhabitant of that State for which he shall be chosen.

[4]The Vice President of the United States shall be President of the Senate, but shall have no Vote, unless they be equally divided.

[5]The Senate shall chuse their other Officers, and also a President pro tempore, in the Absence of the Vice President, or when he shall exercise the Office of President of the United States.

[6]The Senate shall have the sole Power to try all Impeachments. When sitting for that Purpose, they shall be on Oath or Affirmation. When the President of the United States is tried, the Chief Justice shall preside: And no Person shall be convicted without the Concurrence of two thirds of the Members present.

[7]Judgment in Cases of Impeachment shall not extend further than to removal from Office, and disqualification to hold and enjoy any Office of honor, Trust or Profit under the United States: but the party convicted shall nevertheless be liable and subject to Indictment, Trial, Judgment and Punishment, according to Law.

SECTION. 4. [1]The Times, Places and Manner of holding Elections for Senators and Representatives, shall be prescribed in each State by the Legislature thereof; but the Congress may at any time by Law make or alter such Regulations, except as to the Places of chusing Senators.

---

[c]The part included in heavy brackets was changed by section 1 of the seventh amendment.
[d]The part included in heavy brackets was changed by clause 2 of the seventeenth amendment.
[e]The part included in heavy brackets was changed by section 2 of the twentieth amendment.

²The Congress shall assemble at least once in every Year, and such Meeting shall [be on the first Monday in December,]ᵉ unless they shall by Law appoint a different Day.

SECTION. 5. ¹Each House shall be the Judge of the Elections, Returns and Qualifications of its own Members, and a Majority of each shall constitute a Quorum to do Business; but a smaller Number may adjourn from day to day, and may be authorized to compel the Attendance of absent members, in such Manner, and under such Penalties as each House may provide.

²Each House may determine the Rules of its Proceedings, punish its Members for disorderly Behaviour, and, with the Concurrence of two thirds, expel a Member.

³Each House shall keep a Journal of its Proceedings, and from time to time publish the same, excepting such Parts as may in their Judgement require Secrecy; and the Yeas and Nays of the Members of either House on any questions shall, at the Desire of one fifth of those Present, be entered on the Journal.

⁴Neither House, during the Session of Congress, shall, without the Consent of the other, adjourn for more than three days, nor to any other Place than that in which the two Houses shall be sitting.

SECTION. 6. ¹The Senators and Representatives shall receive a Compensation for their Services, to be ascertained by Law, and paid out of the Treasury of the United States. They shall in all Cases, except Treason, Felony and Breach of the Peace, be privileged from Arrest during their Attendance at the Session of their respective Houses, and in going to and returning from the same; and for any Speech or Debate in either House, they shall not be questioned in any other Place.

²No Senator or Representative shall, during the Time for which he was elected, be appointed to any civil Office under the Authority of the United States, which shall have been created, or the Emoluments whereof shall have been encreased during such time; and no Person holding any Office under the United States, shall be a Member of either House during his Continuance in Office.

SECTION. 7. ¹All Bills for raising Revenue shall originate in the House of Representatives; but the Senate may propose or concur with Amendments as on other Bills.

²Every Bill which shall have passed the House of Representatives and the Senate, shall, before it become a Law, be presented to the President of the United States; if he approve he shall sign it, but if not he shall return it, with his Objections to that House in which it shall have originated, who shall enter the Objections at large on their Journal, and Proceed to reconsider it. If after such Reconsideration two thirds of that House shall agree to pass the Bill, it

shall be sent, together with the Objections, to the other House, by which it shall likewise be reconsidered, and if approved by two thirds of that House, it shall become a Law. But in all such Cases the Votes of both Houses shall be determined by yeas and Nays, and the Names of the Persons voting for and against the Bill shall be entered on the Journal of each House respectively. If any Bill shall not be returned by the President within ten Days (Sundays excepted) after it shall have been presented to him, the Same shall be a Law, in like Manner as if he had signed it, unless the Congress by their Adjournment prevent its Return, in which Case it shall not be a Law.

[3]Every Order, Resolution, or Vote to which the Concurrence of the Senate and House of Representatives may be necessary (except on a question of Adjournment) shall be presented to the President of the United States; and before the Same shall take Effect, shall be approved by him, or being disapproved by him, shall be repassed by two thirds of the Senate and House of Representatives, according to the Rules and Limitations prescribed in the Case of a Bill.

SECTION. 8. [1]The Congress shall have Power To lay and collect Taxes, Duties, Imposts and Excises, to pay the Debts and provide for the common Defence and general Welfare of the United States; but all Duties, Imposts and Excises shall be uniform throughout the United States;

[2]To borrow Money on the credit of the United States;

[3]To regulate Commerce with foreign Nations, and among the several States, and with the Indian Tribes;

[4]To establish an uniform Rule of Naturalization, and uniform Laws on the subject of Bankruptcies throughout the United States;

[5]To coin Money, regulate the Value thereof, and of foreign Coin, and fix the Standard of Weights and Measures;

[6]To provide for the Punishment of counterfeiting the Securities and current Coin of the United States;

[7]To establish Post Offices and post Roads;

[8]To promote the Progress of Science and useful Arts, by securing for limited Times to Authors and Inventors the exclusive Right to their respective Writings and Discoveries;

[9]To constitute Tribunals inferior to the supreme Court;

[10]To define and punish Piracies and Felonies committed on the high Seas, and Offences against the Law of Nations;

[11]To declare War, grant Letters of Marque and Reprisal, and make Rules concerning Captures on Land and Water;

[12]To raise and support Armies, but no Appropriation of Money to that Use shall be for a longer Term than two Years;

[13]To provide and maintain a Navy;

[14]To make Rules for the Government and Regulation of the land and naval Forces;

[15]To provide for calling forth the Militia to execute the Laws of the Union, suppress Insurrections and repel Invasions;

[16]To provide for organizing, arming, and disciplining, the Militia, and for governing such Part of them as may be employed in the Service of the United States, reserving to the States respectively, the Appointment of the Officers, and the Authority of training the Militia according to the discipline prescribed by Congress;

[17]To exercise exclusive Legislation in all Cases whatsoever, over such District (not exceeding ten Miles square) as may, by Cession of particular States, and the Acceptance of Congress, become the Seat of the Government of the United States, and to exercise like Authority over all Places purchased by the Consent of the Legislature of the State in which the Same shall be, for the Erection of Forts, Magazines, Arsenals, dock-yards, and other needful Buildings; And

[18]To make all Laws which shall be necessary and proper for carrying into Execution the foregoing Powers, and all other Powers vested by this Constitution in the Government of the United States, or in any Department or Officer thereof.

SECTION. 9. [1]The Migration or Importation of such Persons as any of the States now existing shall think proper to admit, shall not be prohibited by the Congress prior to the Year one thousand eight hundred and eight, but a Tax or duty may be imposed on such Importation, not exceeding ten dollars for each Person.

[2]The Privilege of the Writ of Habeas Corpus shall not be suspended, unless when in Cases of Rebellion or Invasion the public Safety may require it.

[3]No Bill of Attainder or ex post facto Law shall be passed.

[4]No Capitation, or other direct, Tax shall be laid, unless in Proportion to the Census or Enumeration herein before directed to be taken.[f]

[5]No Tax or Duty shall be laid on Articles exported from any State.

[6]No Preference shall be given by any Regulation of Commerce or Revenue to the Ports of one State over those of another: nor shall Vessels bound to, or from, one State, be obliged to enter, clear, or pay Duties in another.

[7]No Money shall be drawn from the Treasury, but in Consequence of Appropriations made by Law; and a regular Statement and Account of the Receipts and Expenditures of all public Money shall be published from time to time.

[8]No Title of Nobility shall be granted by the United States: And no Person holding any Office of Profit or Trust under them, shall, without the Consent of the Congress, accept of any present, Emolument, Office, or Title, of any kind whatever, from any King, Prince, or foreign State.

SECTION. 10. [1]No State shall enter into any Treaty, Alliance, or Confederation; grant Letters of Marque and Reprisal; coin Money; emit Bills of Credit; make

[f]See also the sixteenth amendment.

any Thing but gold and silver Coin a Tender in Payment of Debts; pass any Bill of Attainder, ex post facto Law, or Law impairing the Obligation of Contracts, or grant any Title of Nobility.

²No State shall, without the Consent of the Congress, lay any Imposts or Duties on Imports or Exports, except what may be absolutely necessary for executing it's inspection Laws: and the net Produce of all Duties and Imposts, laid by any State on Imports or Exports, shall be for the Use of the Treasury of the United States; and all such Laws shall be subject to the Revision and Controul of the Congress.

³No State shall, without the Consent of Congress, lay any Duty of Tonnage, keep Troops, or Ships of War in time of Peace, enter into any Agreement or Compact with another State, or with a foreign Power, or engage in War, unless actually invaded, or in such imminent Danger as will not admit of delay.

ARTICLE. II.

SECTION. 1. ¹The executive Power shall be vested in a President of the United States of America. He shall hold his Office during the Term of four Years, and, together with the Vice President, chosen for the same Term, be elected, as follows

²Each State shall appoint, in such Manner as the Legislature thereof may direct, a Number of Electors, equal to the whole Number of Senators and Representatives to which the State may be entitled in the Congress: but no Senator or Representative, or Person holding an Office of Trust or Profit under the United States, shall be appointed an Elector.

[The Electors shall meet in their respective States, and vote by Ballot for two Persons, of whom one at least shall not be an Inhabitant of the same State with themselves. And they shall make a List of all the Persons voted for, and of the Number of Votes for each; which List they shall sign and certify, and transmit sealed to the Seat of the Government of the United States, directed to the President of the Senate. The President of the United States shall, in the Presence of the Senate and House of Representatives, open all the Certificates, and the Votes shall then be counted. The Person having the greatest Number of Votes shall be the President, if such Number be a Majority of the whole Number of Electors appointed; and if there be more than one who have such Majority, and have an equal Number of Votes, then the House of Representatives shall immediately chuse by Ballot one of them for President; and if no Person have a Majority, then from the five highest on the List the said House shall in like Manner chuse the President. But in chusing the President, the Votes shall be taken by States, the Representation from each State having one Vote; A quorum for this Purpose shall consist of a Member or Members from two thirds of the States, and a Majority of all the States shall be necessary to a Choice. In every Case, after the Choice of the President, the Person having the greatest

ᵍThis paragraph has been superseded by the twelfth amendment.

Number of Votes of the Electors shall be the Vice President. But if there should remain two or more who have equal Votes, the Senate shall chuse from them by Ballot the Vice President.]ᵍ

³The Congress may determine the Time of Chusing the Electors, and the Day on which they shall give their Votes; which Day shall be the same throughout the United States.

⁴No Person except a natural born Citizen, or a Citizen of the United States, at the time of the Adoption of this Constitution, shall be eligible to the Office of President; neither shall any Person be eligible to that Office who shall not have attained to the Age of thirty five Years, and been fourteen Years a Resident within the United States.

⁵In Case of the Removal of the President from Office, or of his Death, Resignation, or Inability to discharge the Powers and Duties of the said Office,ʰ the Same shall devolve on the Vice President, and the Congress may by Law provide for the Case of Removal, Death, Resignation or Inability, both of the President and Vice President, declaring what Officer shall then act as President, and such Officer shall act accordingly, until the Disability be removed, or a President shall be elected.

⁶The President shall, at stated Times, receive for his Services, a Compensation, which shall neither be encreased nor diminished during the Period for which he shall have been elected, and he shall not receive within that Period any other Emolument from the United States, or any of them.

⁷Before he enter on the Execution of his Office, he shall take the following Oath or Affirmation: "I do solemnly swear (or affirm) that I will faithfully execute the Office of President of the United States, and will to the best of my Ability, preserve, protect and defend the Constitution of the United States."

SECTION. 2. ¹The President shall be Commander in Chief of the Army and Navy of the United States, and of the Militia of the several States, when called into the actual Service of the United States; he may require the Opinion, in writing, of the principal Officer in each of the executive Departments, upon any Subject relating to the Duties of their respective Offices, and he shall have Power to grant Reprieves and Pardons for Offences against the United States, except in Cases of Impeachment.

²He shall have Power, by and with the Advice and Consent of the Senate, to make Treaties, provided two thirds of the Senators present concur; and he shall nominate, and by and with the Advice and Consent of the Senate, shall appoint Ambassadors, other public Ministers and Consuls, Judges of the supreme Court, and all other Officers of the United States, whose Appointments are not herein otherwise provided for, and which shall be established by Law: but the Congress may by Law vest the Appointment of such inferior Officers, as they think proper, in the President alone, in the Courts of Law, or in the Heads of Departments.

ʰThis provision has been affected by the twenty-fifth amendment.

³The President shall have Power to fill up all Vacancies that may happen during the Recess of the Senate, by granting Commissions which shall expire at the End of their next Session.

SECTION. 3. He shall from time to time give to the Congress Information of the State of the Union, and recommend to their Consideration such Measures as he shall judge necessary and expedient; he may, on extraordinary Occasions, convene both Houses, or either of them, and in Case of Disagreement between them, with Respect to the Time of Adjournment, he may adjourn them to such Time as he shall think proper; he shall receive Ambassadors and other public Ministers; he shall take Care that the Laws be faithfully executed, and shall Commission all the Officers of the United States.

SECTION. 4. The President, Vice President and all civil Officers of the United States, shall be removed from Office on Impeachment for, and Conviction of, Treason, Bribery, or other high Crimes and Misdemeanors.

ARTICLE. III.

SECTION. 1. The judicial Power of the United States, shall be vested in one supreme Court, and in such inferior Courts as the Congress may from time to time ordain and establish. The Judges, both of the supreme and inferior Courts, shall hold their Offices during good Behaviour, and shall, at stated Times, receive for their Services, a Compensation, which shall not be diminished during their Continuance in Office.

SECTION. 2. ¹The judicial Power shall extend to all Cases, in Law and Equity, arising under this Constitution, the Laws of the United States, and Treaties made, or which shall be made, under their Authority; to all Cases affecting Ambassadors, other public Ministers and Consuls; to all Cases of admiralty and maritime Jurisdiction; to Controversies to which the United States shall be a Party; to Controversies between two or more States; between a State and Citizens of another State;ⁱ between Citizens of different States, between Citizens of the same State claiming Lands under Grants of different States, and between a State, or the Citizens thereof, and foreign States, Citizens or Subjects.

²In all Cases affecting Ambassadors, other public Ministers and Consuls, and those in which a State shall be Party, the supreme Court shall have original Jurisdiction. In all the other Cases before mentioned, the supreme Court shall have appellate Jurisdiction, both as to Law and Fact, with such Exceptions, and under such Regulations as the Congress shall make.

³The Trial of all Crimes, except in Cases of Impeachment, shall be by Jury; and such Trial shall be held in the State where the said Crimes shall have been

---

ⁱThis clause has been affected by the eleventh amendment.

committed; but when not committed within any State, the Trial shall be at such Place or Places as the Congress may by Law have directed.

SECTION. 3. [1]Treason against the United States, shall consist only in levying War against them, or in adhering to their Enemies, giving them Aid and Comfort. No Person shall be convicted of Treason unless on the Testimony of two Witnesses to the same overt Act, or on confession in open Court.

[2]The Congress shall have Power to declare the Punishment of Treason, but no Attainder of Treason shall work Corruption of Blood, or Forfeiture except during the Life of the Person attainted.

ARTICLE. IV.

SECTION. 1. Full Faith and Credit shall be given in each State to the public Acts, Records, and judicial Proceedings of every other State. And the Congress may by general Laws prescribe the Manner in which such Acts, Records, and Proceedings shall be proved, and the Effect thereof.

SECTION. 2. [1]The Citizens of each State shall be entitled to all Privileges and Immunities of Citizens in the several States.

[2]A Person charged in any State with Treason, Felony, or other Crime, who shall flee from Justice, and be found in another State, shall on Demand of the executive Authority of the State from which he fled, be delivered up, to be removed to the State having Jurisdiction of the Crime.

[3][No Person held to Service or Labour in one State, under the Laws thereof, escaping into another, shall, in Consequence of any Law or Regulation therein, be discharged from such Service or Labour, but shall be delivered up on Claim of the Party to whom such Service or Labour may be due.][j]

SECTION. 3. [1]New States may be admitted by the Congress into this Union; but no new State shall be formed or erected within the Jurisdiction of any other State; nor any State be formed by the Junction of two or more States, or Parts of States, without the Consent of the Legislatures of the States concerned as well as of the Congress.

[2]The Congress shall have Power to dispose of and make all needful Rules and Regulations respecting the Territory or other Property belonging to the United States; and nothing in this Constitution shall be so constructed as to Prejudice any Claims of the United States, or of any particular State.

SECTION. 4. The United States shall guarantee to every State in this Union a Republican Form of Government, and shall protect each of them against Invasion; and on Application of the Legislature, or of the Executive (when the Legislature cannot be convened) against domestic Violence.

[j]This paragraph has been superseded by the thirteenth amendment.

ARTICLE. V.

The Congress, whenever two thirds of both Houses shall deem it necessary, shall propose Amendments to this Constitution, or, on the Application of the Legislatures of two thirds of the several States, shall call a Convention for proposing Amendments, which, in either Case, shall be valid to all Intents and Purposes, as Part of this Constitution, when ratified by the Legislatures of three fourths of the several States, or by Conventions in three fourths thereof, as the one or the other Mode of Ratification may be proposed by the Congress; Provided [that no Amendment which may be made prior to the Year One thousand eight hundred and eight shall in any Manner affect the first and fourth Clauses in the Ninth Section of the first Article; and]k that no State, without its Consent, shall be deprived of its equal Suffrage in the Senate.

ARTICLE. VI.

1All Debts contracted and Engagements entered into, before the Adoption of this Constitution, shall be as valid against the United States under this Constitution, as under the Confederation.

2This Constitution, and the Laws of the United States which shall be made in Pursuance thereof; and all Treaties made, or which shall be made, under the Authority of the United States, shall be the supreme Law of the Land; and the Judges in every State shall be bound thereby, any Thing in the Constitution or Laws of any State to the Contrary notwithstanding.

3The Senators and Representatives before mentioned, and the Members of the several State Legislatures, and all executive and judicial Officers, both of the United States and of the several States, shall be bound by Oath or Affirmation, to support this Constitution; but no religious Test shall ever be required as a Qualification to any Office or public Trust under the United States.

ARTICLE. VII.

The Ratification of the Conventions of nine States, shall be sufficient for the Establishment of this Constitution between the States so ratifying the Same.

DONE in Convention by the Unanimous Consent of the States present the Seventeenth Day of September in the Year of our Lord one thousand seven hundred and Eighty seven and of the Independence of the United States of America the Twelfth IN WITNESS whereof We have hereunto subscribed our Names.

Go WASHINGTON

Presidt. and deputy from Virginia.
JOHN LANGDON, NICHOLAS GILMAN.

kObsolete.

MASSACHUSETTS.
  NATHANIEL GORHAM, RUFUS KING.
CONNECTICUT.
  WM. SAML. JOHNSON, ROGER SHERMAN.
NEW YORK.
  ALEXANDER HAMILTION.
NEW JERSEY.
  WIL: LIVINGSTON, WM. PATERSON,
  DAVID BREARLEY, JONA: DAYTON.
PENNSYLVANIA.
  B FRANKLIN, THOMAS MIFFLIN,
  ROBT MORRIS, GEO. CLYMER,
  THOS. FRITZSIMONS, JARED INGERSOLL,
  JAMES WILSON, GOUV MORRIS.
DELAWARE.
  GEO: READ, GUNNING BEDFORD, jun,
  JOHN DICKINSON, RICHARD BASSETT.
  JACO: BROOM,
MARYLAND.
  JAMES McHENRY, DAN OF ST THOS. JENIFER,
  DANL CARROLL.
VIRGINIA.
  JOHN BLAIR, JAMES MADISON Jr.
NORTH CAROLINA.
  WM. BLOUNT, RICH'D DOBBS SPAIGHT,
  HU WILLIAMSON.
SOUTH CAROLINA.
  J. RUTLEDGE CHARLES COTESWORTH PINCKNEY,
  CHARLES PINCKNEY, PIERCE BUTLER.
GEORGIA.
  WILLIAM FEW, ABR BALDWIN.

Attest:WILLIAM JACKSON, SECRETARY.

RATIFICATION OF THE CONSTITUTION

The Constitution was adopted by a convention of the States on September 17, 1787, and was subsequently ratified by the several States, on the following dates: Delaware, December 7, 1787; Pennsylvania, December 12, 1787; Connecticut, January 9, 1788; Massachusetts, February 6, 1788; Maryland, April 28, 1788; South Carolina, May 23, 1788; New Hampshire, June 21, 1788. Ratification was completed on June 21, 1788.

The Constitution was subsequently ratified by Virginia, June 25, 1788; New York, July 26, 1788; North Carolina, November 21, 1789; Rhode Island, May 29, 1790; and Vermont, January 10, 1791.

AMENDMENTS TO THE CONSTITUTION OF THE UNITED STATES

The ten original amendments—The Bill of Rights—were proposed by Congress on September 25, 1789 and ratified December 15, 1791.

AMENDMENT I

Congress shall make no law respecting an establishment of religion, or prohibiting the free exercise thereof; or abridging the freedom of speech, or of the press; or the right of the people peaceably to assemble, and to petition the Government for a redress of grievances.

AMENDMENT II

A well-regulated militia, being necessary to the security of a free State, the right of the people to keep and bear arms, shall not be infringed.

AMENDMENT III

No soldier shall, in time of peace be quartered in any house, without the consent of the owner, nor in time of war, but in a manner to be prescribed by law.

AMENDMENT IV

The right of the people to be secure in their persons, houses, papers, and effects, against unreasonable searches and seizures, shall not be violated, and no warrants shall issue, but upon probable cause, supported by oath or affirmation, and particularly describing the place to be searched, and the persons or things to be seized.

AMENDMENT V

No person shall be held to answer for a capital, or otherwise infamous crime, unless on a presentment or indictment of a Grand Jury, except in cases arising in the land or naval forces, or in the militia, when in actual service in time of war or public danger; nor shall any person be subject for the same offense to be twice put in jeopardy of life or limb; nor shall be compelled in any criminal case to be a witness against himself, nor be deprived of life, liberty, or property, without due process of law; nor shall private property be taken for public use without just compensation.

AMENDMENT VI

In all criminal prosecutions, the accused shall enjoy the right to a speedy and public trial, by an impartial jury of the State and district wherein the crime shall have been committed, which district shall have been previously ascertained by law, and to be informed of the nature and cause of the accusation; to be confronted with the witnesses against him; to have compulsory process for obtaining witnesses in his favor, and to have the assistance of counsel for his defense.

AMENDMENT VII

In suits at common law, where the value in controversy shall exceed twenty dollars, the right of trial by jury shall be preserved, and no fact tried by a jury shall be otherwise reexamined in any court of the United States, than according to the rules of the common law.

AMENDMENT VIII

Excessive bail shall not be required, nor excessive fines imposed, nor cruel and unusual punishments inflicted.

AMENDMENT IX

The enumeration in the Constitution, of certain rights, shall not be construed to deny or disparage others retained by the people.

AMENDMENT X

The powers not delegated to the United States by the Constitution, nor prohibited by it to the States, are reserved to the States respectively, or to the people.

AMENDMENT XI

The judicial power of the United States shall not be construed to extend to any suit in law or equity, commenced or prosecuted against one of the United States by citizens of another State, or by citizens or subjects of any foreign state [proposed by Congress March 4, 1794, and ratified February 7, 1795].

AMENDMENT XII

The Electors shall meet in their respective States and vote by ballot for President and Vice-President, one of whom, at least, shall not be an inhabitant of the same State with themselves; they shall name in their ballots the person voted for as President, and in distinct ballots the person voted for as Vice-President, and of the number of votes for each, which lists they shall sign and certify, and transmit sealed to the seat of the Government of the United States, directed to the President of the Senate; The President of the Senate shall, in the presence of the Senate and House of Representatives, open all the certificates and the votes shall then be counted; The person having the greatest number of votes for President, shall be the President, if such number be a majority of the whole number of Electors appointed; and if no person have such majority, then from the persons having the highest numbers not exceeding three on the list of those voted for as President, the House of Representatives shall choose immediately, by ballot, the President. But in choosing the President, the votes shall be taken by States, the representation from each State having one vote; a quorum for this purpose shall consist of a member or members from two-thirds of the States, and a majority of all the States shall be necessary to a choice. And if the House of Representatives shall not choose a President whenever the right of choice shall devolve upon them, [before the fourth day of March next following,][1] then the Vice-President shall act as President, as in the case of the death or other constitutional disability of the President. The person having the greatest number of votes as Vice-President, shall be the Vice-President, if such numbers be a majority of the whole number of electors appointed, and if no person have a majority, then from the two highest numbers on the list, the Senate shall choose the Vice-President; a quorum for the purpose shall consist of two-thirds of the whole number of Senators, and a majority of the whole number shall be necessary to a choice. But no person constitutionally ineligible to the office of President shall be eligible to that of Vice-President of the United States [proposed by Congress December 9, 1803, and ratified July 27, 1804].

AMENDMENT XIII

SECTION 1. Neither slavery nor involuntary servitude, except as a punishment for crime whereof the party shall have been duly convicted, shall exist within the United States, or any place subject to their jurisdiction [proposed by Congress January 31, 1865, and ratified December 6, 1865].

SECTION 2. Congress shall have power to enforce this article by appropriate legislation.

AMENDMENT XIV

SECTION 1. All persons born or naturalized in the United States, and subject to the jurisdiction thereof, are citizens of the United States and of the State wherein they reside. No State shall make or enforce any law which shall abridge the privileges or immunities of citizens of the United States; nor shall any State deprive any person of life, liberty, or property, without due process of law; nor to deny to any person within its jurisdiction the equal protection of the laws.

SECTION 2. Representatives shall be apportioned among the several States according to their respective numbers, counting the whole number of persons

[1]Altered by twentieth amendment.

in each State, excluding Indians not taxed. But when the right to vote at any election for the choice of Electors for President and Vice-President of the United States, Representatives in Congress, the executive and judicial officers of a State, or the members of the Legislature thereof, is denied to any of the male inhabitants of such State, being twenty-one years of age, and citizens of the United States, or in any way abridged, except for participation in rebellion, or other crime, the basis of representation therein shall be reduced in the proportion which the number of such male citizens shall bear to the whole number of male citizens twenty-one years of age in such State.

SECTION 3. No person shall be a Senator or Representative in Congress, or Elector of President and Vice-President, or hold any office, civil or military, under the United States, or under any State, who, having previously taken an oath, as a member of Congress, or as an officer of the United States, or as a member of any State Legislature, or as an executive or judicial officer of any State, to support the Constitution of the United States, shall have engaged in insurrection or rebellion against the same, or given aid or comfort to the enemies thereof. But Congress may by a vote of two-thirds of each House, remove such disability.

SECTION 4. The validity of the public debt of the United States, authorized by law, including debts incurred for payment of pensions and bounties for services in suppressing insurrection or rebellion, shall not be questioned. But neither the United States nor any State shall assume or pay any debt or obligation incurred in aid of insurrection or rebellion against the United States, or any claim for the loss or emancipation of any slave; but all such debts, obligations and claims shall be held illegal and void.

SECTION 5. The Congress shall have the power to enforce, by appropriate legislation, the provisions of this article [proposed by Congress June 13, 1866, and ratified July 9, 1868].

AMENDMENT XV

SECTION 1. The right of citizens of the United States to vote shall not be denied or abridged by the United States or by any State on account of race, color, or previous condition of servitude.

SECTION 2. The Congress shall have the power to enforce this article by appropriate legislation [proposed by Congress February 26, 1869, and ratified February 3, 1870].

AMENDMENT XVI

The Congress shall have power to lay and collect taxes on incomes, from whatever sources derived, without apportionment among the several States, and without regard to any census or enumeration [proposed by Congress July 2, 1909, and ratified February 3, 1913].

AMENDMENT XVII

The Senate of the United States shall be composed of two Senators from each State, elected by the people thereof, for six years; and each Senator shall have one vote. The electors in each State shall have the qualifications requisite for electors of the most numerous branch of the State Legislatures.

When vacancies happen in the representation of any State in the Senate, the executive authority of such State shall issue writs of election to fill such vacancies: Provided, That the Legislature of any State may empower the Executive thereof to make temporary appointments until the people fill the vacancies by election as the Legislature may direct.

This amendment shall not be so construed as to affect the election or term of any Senator chosen before it becomes valid as part of the Constitution [proposed by Congress May 13, 1912, and ratified April 8, 1913].

AMENDMENT XVIII

After one year from the ratification of this article the manufacture, sale, or transportation of intoxicating liquors within, the importation thereof into, or the exportation thereof from the United States and all territory subject to the jurisdiction thereof for beverage purposes is hereby prohibited.

The Congress and the several States shall have concurrent power to enforce this article by appropriate legislation.

This article shall be inoperative unless it shall have been ratified as an amendment to the Constitution by the Legislatures of the several States, as provided in the Constitution, within seven years from the date of the submission hereof to the States by the Congress [proposed by Congress December 18, 1917, and ratified January 16, 1919].ᵐ

AMENDMENT XIX

The right of citizens of the United States to vote shall not be denied or abridged by the United States or by any State on account of sex. Congress shall have power to enforce this article by appropriate legislation [proposed by Congress June 4, 1919, and ratified August 18, 1920].

AMENDMENT XX

SECTION 1. The terms of the President and the Vice-President shall end at noon on the 20th day of January, and the terms of Senators and Representa-

ᵐAltered by twenty-first amendment.

tives at noon on the 3rd day of January, of the years in which such terms would have ended if this article had not been ratified; and the terms of their successors shall then begin.

SECTION 2. The Congress shall assemble at least once in every year, and such meeting shall begin at noon on the 3rd day of January, unless they shall by law appoint a different day.

SECTION 3. If, at the time fixed for the beginning of the term of the President, the President elect shall have died, the Vice-President elect shall become President. If a President shall not have been chosen before the time fixed for the beginning of his term, or if the President elect shall have failed to qualify, then the Vice-President elect shall act as President until a President shall have qualified; and the Congress may by law provide for the case wherein neither a President elect nor a Vice-President shall have qualified, declaring who shall then act as President, or the manner in which one who is to act shall be selected, and such person shall act accordingly until a President or Vice-President shall have qualified.

SECTION 4. The Congress may by law provide for the case of the death of any of the persons from whom the House of representatives may choose a President whenever the right of choice shall have devolved upon them, and for the case of the death of any of the persons from whom the Senate may choose a Vice-President whenever the right of choice shall have devolved upon them.

SECTION 5. Sections 1 and 2 shall take effect on the 15th day of October following the ratification of this article (October 1933).

SECTION 6. This article shall be inoperative unless it shall have been ratified as an amendment to the Constitution by the Legislatures of three-fourths of the several States within seven years from the date of its submission.

AMENDMENT XXI

SECTION 1. The Eighteenth article of amendment to the Constitution of the United States is hereby repealed.

SECTION 2. The transportation or importation into any State, Territory, or Possession of the United States for delivery or use therein of intoxicating liquors, in violation of the laws thereof, is hereby prohibited.

SECTION 3. This article shall be inoperative unless it shall have been ratified as an amendment to the Constitution by conventions in the several States, as provided in the Constitution, within seven years from the date of the submission hereof to the States by the Congress [proposed by Congress February 20, 1933, and ratified December 5, 1933].

AMENDMENT XXII

No person shall be elected to the office of the President more than twice, and no person who has held the office of President, or acted as President, for more than two years of a term to which some other person was elected President shall be elected to the office of President more than once.

But this Article shall not apply to any person holding the office of President when this Article was proposed by Congress, and shall not prevent any person who may be holding the office of President, or acting as President, during the term within which this Article becomes operative from holding the office of President or acting as President during the remainder of such term.

This article shall be inoperative unless it shall have been ratified as an amendment to the Constitution by the Legislatures of three-fourths of the several States within seven years from the date of its submission to the States by the Congress [proposed by Congress March 21, 1947, and ratified February 27, 1951].

AMENDMENT XXIII

SECTION 1. The District constituting the seat of Government of the United States shall appoint in such manner as Congress may direct:

A number of electors of President and Vice President equal to the whole number of Senators and Representatives in Congress to which the District would be entitled if it were a State, but in no event more than the least populous State; they shall be in addition to those appointed by the States, but they shall be considered, for the purposes of the election of President and Vice President, to be electors appointed by a State; and they shall meet in the District and perform such duties as provided by the twelfth article of amendment.

SECTION 2. The Congress shall have power to enforce this article by appropriate legislation [proposed by Congress June 16, 1960, and ratified March 29, 1961].

AMENDMENT XXIV

SECTION 1. The right of citizens of the United States to vote in any primary or other election for President or Vice President, for electors for President or Vice President, or for Senator or Representative in Congress, shall not be denied or abridged by the United States or any State by reason of failure to pay poll tax or any other tax.

SECTION 2. Congress shall have power to enforce this article by appropriate legislation [proposed by Congress August 27, 1962, and ratified January 23, 1964].

AMENDMENT XXV

SECTION 1. In case of the removal of the President from office or of his death or resignation, the Vice President shall become President.

SECTION 2. Whenever there is a vacancy in the office of the Vice President, the President shall nominate a Vice President who shall take the office upon confirmation by a majority vote of both houses of Congress.

SECTION 3. Whenever the President transmits to the President Pro tempore of the Senate and the Speaker of the House of Representatives his written declaration that he is unable to discharge the powers and duties of his office, and until he transmits to them a written declaration to the contrary, such powers and duties shall be discharged by the Vice President as Acting President.

SECTION 4. Whenever the Vice President and a majority of either the principal officers of the executive departments or of such other body as Congress may by law provide, transmits to the President Pro tempore of the Senate and the Speaker of the House of Representatives their written declaration that the President is unable to discharge the powers and duties of his office, the Vice President shall immediately assume the powers and duties of the office as Acting President.

Thereafter, when the President transmits to the President Pro tempore of the Senate and the Speaker of the House of Representatives his written declaration that no inability exists, he shall resume the powers and duties of his office unless the Vice President and a majority of either the principal officers of the executive departments or of such other body as Congress may by law provide, transmits within four days to the President Pro tempore of the Senate and the Speaker of the House of Representatives their written declaration that the President is unable to discharge the powers and duties of his office. Thereupon Congress shall decide the issue, assembling within forty-eight hours for that purpose if not in session. If the Congress, within twenty-one days after receipt of the latter written declaration, or, if Congress is not in session within twenty-one days after Congress is required to assemble, determines by two-thirds vote of both houses that the President is unable to discharge the powers and duties of his office, the Vice President shall continue to discharge the same as Acting President; otherwise, the President shall resume the powers and duties of his office [proposed by Congress July 6, 1965, and ratified February 10, 1967].

AMENDMENT XXVI

SECTION 1. The right of citizens of the United States, who are 18 years of age or older, to vote shall not be denied or abridged by the United States or any state on account of age.

SECTION 2. The Congress shall have power to enforce this article by appropriate legislation [proposed by Congress March 23, 1971, and ratified June 30, 1971].

AMENDMENT XXVII

No law, varying the compensation for the services of the Senators and Representatives, shall take effect, until an election of Representatives shall have intervened [proposed by Congress September 25, 1989, and ratified May 8, 1992].

International Association of Directors of Law Enforcement Standards & Training Model Minimum State Standards

PREAMBLE

The idea that those who perform the duties of law enforcement and criminal justice officers should do so with professionalism and a sense of ethics is not really new to western philosophical thinking. In fact, the origins of modern policing are commonly agreed to be found in the teachings of Sir Robert Peel over a century and a half ago. The formation of the International Association of Chiefs of Police in 1893 provided the first nationwide voice for reform and professionalization in policing. In this century, scholars generally agree that the most important early advocacy for professionalism can be found in the writing and actions of Chief August Vollmer, who promoted the notion that the Berkeley Police Department should be composed of competent, trained, and ethical officers.

At the close of the era of prohibition, President Herbert Hoover empowered the Wickersham Commission to look into problems in American policing. This Commission concluded that law enforcement was far too often found to be corrupt, brutal, and composed of unethical and untrained personnel. These shocking conclusions were never manifested in significant public actions, however.

The next major report appears to have been published by the American Bar Association in 1953. In response to a recognition that policing in this country required improved professionalism, the ABA published a "Model Police Training Act." The Act outlined eight broad functions that should ideally be performed by police regulatory agencies.

In 1967 the President's Commission on Law Enforcement and the Administration of Justice published "The Challenge of Crime in a Free Society," and the follow-up task report, "The Police." Contained in both reports were recommendations pertaining to the American system of criminal justice. Major emphasis was focused on the police, and recommendations were offered to affect such areas as community policing, community relations, personnel practices

Source: Reprinted with permission from *Model Minimum State Standards*, International Association of Directors of Law Enforcement Standards & Training.

and procedures, organization and operational policies and structures, and the recommendation that each state establish a Peace Officers Standards and Training (POST) Commission. At that time, 17 states had already established POST bodies. All states had them by 1981.

The National Advisory Commission on Criminal Justice Standards and Goals published its recommendations for improvements in 1973. Specific recommendations for upgrading the quality of police personnel ranged from proposals for improving recruitment and selection to encouraging the imposition of extensive recruit basic and in-service training requirements that would be made mandatory for all police personnel.

California and New York were the first to establish POST commissions in 1959. New Jersey and Oregon created POST commissions shortly thereafter in 1961. The last states to create POST commissions were Tennessee, West Virginia, and Hawaii. The staffs of POST organizations first formed an association in 1969 upon the urging of IACP. In 1987, the name of this association was changed from NASDLET TO IADLEST thereby reflecting a more inclusive Mission and Focus.

No analysis of the development of professionalism in the criminal justice occupations would be complete without a reference to the positive impact of the Law Enforcement Assistance Administration's LEEP program. The Law Enforcement Education Program was the first significant infusion of federal funds designed to improve the education and management skills of police and criminal justice managers. A by-product of that great amount of funds was the establishment and creation of departments of criminal justice in practically every postsecondary institution in the nation. Thus was born the discipline of criminal justice and criminal justice studies that have done so much to advance the knowledge and practice of the criminal justice professions.

To be sure, the public horror and reaction to police brutality and unlawful tactics in response to the general public disobedience of the 1960's led to demands that the quality of police improve. Likewise, a string of important Supreme Court cases recognized that the power of police must be regulated and misuses punished. The extension of the exclusionary rule to the states through *Mapp v. Ohio* (1961) was only the first of the contemporary major decisions to recognize the need to proscribe police unlawfulness. *Mapp* was followed shortly thereafter by *Escobedo v. Illinois* (1964), *Miranda v. Arizona* (1966), *Terry v. Ohio* (1968), and *Chimel v. California* (1989), just to mention some of the more well-known cases. This has been paralleled by the rapid rise of civil liability recourse (42 USC 1983, 1987) against police misconduct. A police officer of the '50s would be confounded by what a professional officer of the '90s considers commonplace.

The POST organizations were created out of the crucible of conflict, change, and the demand for professionalism and ethics in public officers. POST programs exist to assure all citizens that peace officers meet minimum standards of competency and ethical behavior. POST organizations also have an obligation to the officers and agencies that they regulate, to adopt programs that are sensible, effective, and consistent with contemporary notions of what standards should be for all officers.

It is in this spirit of growth and responsiveness that the International Association of Directors of Law Enforcement Standards & Training has resolved to establish a set of MODEL MINIMUM STANDARDS to which all states may aspire.

"Great spirits have always encountered violent opposition from mediocre minds."

—Albert Einstein

MODEL MINIMUM STATE STANDARDS FOR POST ADMINISTRATION

1.0 Concepts, Mission, and Organization

Each State shall have an organization at the state level with adequate authority to set standards for the hiring, training, ethical conduct and retention of police officers, through certification, licensing, or an equivalent methodology.

COMMENTARY
Ever since 1967, when the President's Commission on Law Enforcement and the Administration of Justice issued its landmark report entitled "Task Force Report: The Police," it has been formally acknowledged that the law enforcement task is as great as or greater than that of any other profession, and that the performance of this task requires more than physical prowess and common sense. Law enforcement officers engage in the difficult, important and complex business of helping to regulate human behavior, and their intellectual armament and ethical standards must be no less than their physical prowess. The Commission said in 1967, "The quality of police service will not significantly improve until higher educational requirements are established for its personnel," and that statement is equally true today.

As the Commission pointed out, while all departments are in need of upgraded recruiting efforts, higher minimum standards, better selection procedures and more training, the needs are more pronounced for the smaller police departments, many of whom without mandates at the state level would provide little or no training, use ineffectual selection and screening techniques, and have no organized recruiting programs, resulting in substantial variation in the quality of police service, not only in different areas of the nation, but within the same state.

Therefore, each state should have a commission, council or board on peace officer standards and training to establish, maintain, and update these standards.

1.0.1 Authority to Set Selection Standards

Such a commission should have the authority and responsibility to establish minimum statewide selection standards for all persons having authority to make arrests for violations of the criminal, motor vehicle, fish and game, boating and other laws of the state and for violations of local ordinances, and for all persons having custody of individuals who are incarcerated awaiting arraignment or trial, sentenced to terms in correctional institutions or released on probation or parole by the courts, and persons who hold other related public offices.

1.0.2 Authority to Set Education and Training Standards

Such a commission should have the authority and responsibility to establish minimum educational and training standards for pre-service, in-service and specialized training programs for law enforcement and corrections personnel, and persons who hold other related public offices; determine and approve the length and curricula for such programs; set minimum standards for instructors in such programs; and approve facilities as acceptable for law enforcement and corrections training.

1.0.3 Licensing or Certification

Such a commission should have the authority and responsibility to act as the certification or licensing authority for sworn personnel who perform the duties of law enforcement and corrections officers, and other related public officers, and determine the conditions they must meet for certification or licensing.

1.0.4 Decertification or License Revocation

Such a commission should have the authority and responsibility to decertify or suspend or revoke the licenses of sworn personnel who perform the duties of law enforcement and corrections officers, and other related public officers, for failure to observe training requirements, incompetence or egregious misconduct, and to determine the mechanics and conditions for such decertification.

1.0.5 Conducting Research

Such a commission should have the authority and responsibility to conduct and stimulate research by public and private agencies designed to improve the law enforcement and corrections services.

1.0.6 Compliance Enforcement

Such a commission should have the authority, responsibility and resources to make inspections to assure that its standards are being adhered to, and to sanction persons and agencies who willfully or negligently fail to comply with these standards.

1.0.7 Financial Assistance

Such a commission should have the authority, responsibility and resources to provide financial aid to government units as an incentive to send their officers to training programs.

1.0.8 Representation on the Commission

The majority of the representatives on such a commission should be representatives of local and county law enforcement and correctional agencies, with additional representation from state law enforcement and correctional agencies, the courts, and other appropriate agencies or professions.

COMMENTARY
In some states, standards commissions are separate from training commissions, to avoid any claims of a conflict of interest if the standards setting agency also provides the training. However, in instances where such responsibility is split between two commissions, the participants sometimes indicate that communications and coordination are more difficult and there can be duplication of effort. In some states, the responsibility for corrections training is vested in a separate commission, or some agencies such as State Police or Sheriffs are either exempt from training standards or set their own. However, there are many similarities between police and corrections work at all levels which make it quite logical that the responsibilities for setting standards and delivering training can be vested in a single commission, with adequate resources and division of duties.

1.0.9 Independent Agency

Such a commission should be a separate state agency rather than a division or branch of another agency.

COMMENTARY
Since a standards and training commission should serve the interests of state, local and county criminal justice agencies equally, it is preferable that it maintain its autonomy and avoid any appearance that its actions are dominated by

another criminal justice agency. Since the agency should ideally be funded from a dedicated revenue source, maintaining it as a separate entity will remove the temptation to divert funds to the parent agency.

1.1 Commission, How Constituted and Operated

1.1.1 Terms of Commissioners

The members of the commission should be appointed for staggered terms which are not all coterminous with the term of the appointing authority. The statute should provide that certain members serve by virtue of their office.

COMMENTARY
The commission, while under the control of the politically elected officials of the state, should be set up in such a way as to provide some continuity and expertise in office, so that it will not be used solely as a source of political patronage, and so that it will not be unduly susceptible to political coercion.

1.1.2 Executive Direction

The day-to-day operations of the commission should be under the control of an executive director or other executive head, who is appointed by a majority vote of the commission, and who can only be removed for cause and after a public hearing.

COMMENTARY
The executive director should be a competent professional, chosen because of ability rather than politics, and whose selection should be removed from the partisan political process. He or she should have adequate tenure to develop and implement the goals and objectives of the commission and enforce compliance with commission mandates without fear of political reprisal.

1.1.3 Qualifications of Director

A state statute should set forth minimum qualifications for the executive director, which should include a baccalaureate or graduate degree, considerable experience in the field of law enforcement or corrections, and familiarity with the development and management of training programs.

1.1.4 Funding Source

The commission's operations, including subsidizing the costs of statewide training programs, should be paid out of a dedicated, nonlapsing revenue source independent of the state's general fund and protected within the state constitution, such as a penalty assessment fund or other funding source.

COMMENTARY

A penalty assessment fund, based on a percentage of court fines, has proven to be a worthwhile and constitutionally permissible mechanism for the funding of criminal justice training programs because it involves no tax monies, and because those who contribute to it have a vested interest in being dealt with by competent professionals with high ethical standards and community relations skills.

Where such a fund exists or is enacted, it is important for it to be established as a trust fund within the state constitution, to prevent it from being diverted to other purposes whenever the state experiences a general fund revenue shortfall. It is also important to resist having a variety of other programs funded out of this dedicated revenue source, as the end result is usually that court fines reach the point of diminishing returns, and police and corrections training programs are either inadequately funded or require additional general fund support.

1.1.5 Meetings

State statutes should require the commission to meet at least quarterly, and it should be provided with an adequate budget to employ sufficient full-time staff to carry out its mandated duties, with sufficient equipment, travel, and staff development funds to enable its staff to keep abreast of progressive training methods, maintain appropriate professional certifications, belong to professional organizations and monitor the compliance of criminal justice agencies with its standards.

1.1.6 Subsidies

The state should provide the commission with sufficient funds to enable it to reimburse or subsidize every law enforcement and corrections agency 100 percent of the salary, or underwrite the cost of training programs to be completed by the employees of state, county and local law enforcement and corrections agencies.

1.1.7 Reciprocity

Through reciprocity, the commission should recognize the licensing or certification standards of other states which maintain and enforce equivalent standards, to encourage lateral entry by officers from another state without having to undergo redundant training, either at the academy level or in various specialties.

COMMENTARY

Such reciprocity can be provided through standardized licensing and certification examination programs, supplemented by attendance at programs designed to acquaint officers who move in from another state or whose license or certification has lapsed during a break in service, with updated state laws, tactics and procedures.

1.1.8 Accreditation

The commission should recognize the value of a law enforcement accreditation process in upgrading the police profession, and provide technical assistance and support to departments seeking accreditation.

COMMENTARY

Such support can be provided through commission involvement with state or area-wide PAC's (accreditation coalitions) which provide voluntary assistance to one another in their efforts to achieve national accreditation, or through the establishment of a statewide accreditation program through the commission or another appropriate entity, tailored to the needs of the individual state.

MODEL MINIMUM STATE STANDARDS—PEACE OFFICER SELECTION

2.0 Selection

Each state commission should prescribe minimum statewide standards that must be complied with by hiring authorities who employ law enforcement and corrections officers and other related public officers. These standards should comply with any applicable federal and state equal employment guidelines and relate to the skills and attributes necessary to perform the essential functions of a police or corrections officer.

2.0.1 Drug Screening

State law or regulation should require each candidate for an entry level or lateral entry sworn position, to submit to testing to determine if he or she is currently using an illegal controlled dangerous substance.

COMMENTARY

Peace officers are expected to enforce the law related to the use of controlled dangerous substances, and to prevent prisoners from acquiring such substances. The effectiveness of these officers would be compromised if they were also illegally using these drugs. Therefore, they should receive a valid test to screen for the illegal use of controlled dangerous substances consistent with federal and state laws. The type of test to be utilized would be selected by the agency consistent with their needs and costs, and consistent with minimum requirements set by the commission.

2.0.2 Background Investigation

State law or commission regulation should require each candidate for an entry-level or lateral entry law enforcement or corrections officer position or other related public office, to submit to a thorough background investigation according to protocols developed by the commission, to determine that they have exhibited mature judgment and are of good moral character and reputation.

COMMENTARY
Those called to serve in the criminal justice system are faced with many difficult occupational situations. A documented background investigation is necessary to ensure that all candidates possess the necessary attributes to perform their duties. It is also necessary to screen out undesirable personal characteristics that may adversely affect their performance as officers. This background investigation should include at a minimum interview with previous employers and coworkers, neighbors, past and present family members, character references, school authorities, academic and military records, and a credit record check. Polygraph examinations can be an effective tool to help validate written and oral information, and to detect possible deception by a candidate. They should be used to support, but not as the sole indicator for, employment status decisions.

2.0.3 Fingerprint Check

State law or commission regulation should require the hiring authority to conduct a state and national criminal history check, including fingerprinting, and should prohibit the hiring of any person as a sworn police or corrections officer who has been convicted of a felony, or any other crime or series of crimes which would indicate to a reasonable person that the applicant was potentially dangerous, violent, or had a propensity to break the law.

COMMENTARY
All persons who are expected to enforce the law should be free of a criminal background which would compromise their effectiveness. A criminal history check should be made through the National Crime Information Center and the appropriate local and state criminal history repositories in all communities where the applicant has lived or worked, confirmed by an applicant fingerprint card.

2.0.4 Age Requirements

Each state should set a minimum age requirement for employment as a police or corrections officer, or other related public office, verified by a birth certificate or other appropriate documentation.

COMMENTARY
The minimum age requirement should be established to ensure that candidates will be legally able to perform their duties. This age requirement should be consistent with all federal and state laws, ordinances and regulations related to law enforcement activities, the possession of various types of evidence, and the use of firearms.

2.0.5 Oral Interviews

State law or commission regulation should require all candidates for police and corrections officer positions and other related public offices to be given a personal interview by representatives of the hiring authority to evaluate job-related behaviors, whether by an interview panel or another appropriate assessment process, and should provide guidance to the hiring authority as to any questions which should not be asked during such a process.

COMMENTARY
Personal interviews are a valuable tool to verify and further expand on information provided by a candidate, in order to determine his or her fitness for the job, and to evaluate whether they possess adequate verbal and communications skills for the job.

2.0.6 Citizenship

State law or commission regulation should require all sworn police and corrections officers to be U.S. citizens. In order to encourage the cultural diversity which has enriched our nation over the years, foreign nationals who are becoming citizens should be encouraged to consider law enforcement careers if they can be employed by criminal justice agencies without exercising arrest powers until obtaining full citizenship.

COMMENTARY
Police officers are expected to enforce the laws and constitution of the United States, and are among the few persons who can deprive a U.S. citizen of their freedom. This power should be vested in officers that are loyal citizens, committed to support the laws of the United States and of the state and locality of

their employment. In addition, by being a citizen, an officer will be more familiar with the rights afforded to all citizens.

2.0.7 Driver's License

State law or commission regulation for police officers should require a driver history record that indicates that a candidate is a safe driver who has adequate respect for the traffic laws that they will be enforcing, and has a valid motor vehicle driver's license. A driver's license may not always be a requirement for correctional officers.

COMMENTARY
All police officers will utilize motor vehicles in the performance of their duties at one time or another, and many will drive under emergency conditions. Their driving records should be screened prior to hiring, to determine that they are not poor or unsafe drivers.

2.0.8 Medical Qualifications

Once a conditional offer of employment has been issued, state law or commission regulation should require the hiring agency to provide a job-related pass/fail medical examination to each applicant for a sworn police or corrections officer position and mandate that they are medically fit to complete any necessary training and perform the duties of a police or corrections officer. The commission should provide for a medical review board to consider the cases of any applicant with a disability who feels that it will not prevent them from completing the training or performing the essential functions of the job without endangering others.

COMMENTARY
Such an examination evaluates the candidate's physiological readiness to learn and determines the relative risk that their health will compromise their ability to perform the frequent and critical tasks assigned to them.

2.0.9 Education

State law or commission regulation should require immediately that all persons hired as police or corrections officers possess at a minimum a high school diploma, and should ultimately seek to phase in an entry-level requirement of a baccalaureate degree from a college or university accredited by a regional postsecondary accrediting body. Such college education should include a substantial core of courses in the humanities.

COMMENTARY
Completion of high school insures that candidates will have obtained at least minimal skills in writing, comprehension and analysis required of an officer who must possess superior written and oral communications skills and an ability to read and interpret complex statutes, court decisions, and operational procedures. It will also be an indicator that the candidate can successfully complete a police or corrections academy or entrance-level training program. Although some states allow a G.E.D. in place of a high-school diploma, we are unaware of any other profession that permits entry at the G.E.D. level. As communities move toward community policing, a college education becomes increasingly desirable as an entrance standard.

2.0.10 Physical Fitness Assessment

A valid, job-related physical fitness or agility test based on data obtained from a written job description validated by a job task analysis, should be required on a pass/fail basis for each police and corrections officer candidate, by state law or commission regulation.

COMMENTARY
Each candidate should be tested for physical conditioning, fitness and agility. The results of these tests should be evaluated against established, validated criteria, to determine their ability to complete any necessary training and perform the essential job functions, and reduce the danger to coworkers. Physical fitness or agility standards (muscular strength, muscular endurance, cardiovascular endurance, coordination, flexibility, strength, etc.) must also be validated as job-related to the occupational needs of police and corrections officers. Without validation, such standards may not survive legal challenge, especially if they deny employment to a protected class of people. A decision must be made as to whether candidates must meet certain standards before they can enter an academy, or whether they must achieve certain standards as a requirement for successful completion of the academy. Agility testing, if employed, must be done across the board for all candidates.

2.0.11 Psychological Screening

State law or commission regulation should require hiring authorities to administer a psychological screening to all applicants for sworn police or corrections officer positions, and not to hire applicants who suffer from a current mental illness that would affect their ability to function safely and effectively in the job, or display characteristics such as a tendency toward unnecessary violence or poor impulse control.

COMMENTARY

A psychological assessment is necessary to screen out candidates who may not be able to carry out their responsibilities or endure the uniquely stressful working conditions, or who are not emotionally stable. Only qualified, licensed professionals should interpret these tests, using norm-referenced testing instruments to determine emotional and mental stability, recognizing that an appeal process or second opinion should be afforded to ensure fairness if a candidate is eliminated by this process.

2.1.0 Interstate Training Reciprocity

2.1.1 Reciprocity

Commissions should publish their requirements for reciprocity. They should be designed to notify other commissions as to reciprocity requirements for holding appointment as a police or corrections officer, and the training required or equivalency test needed for lateral entry. The published requirements should specifically address the areas enumerated below.

2.1.2 Prerequisites

Rules should state the prerequisites for holding the position requested by an applicant seeking employment in the state's criminal justice system, prerequisites for attending basic law enforcement training, and a description of the required minimum police or corrections recruit course, including hours of attendance.

2.1.3 Procedures

Rules should describe the procedure to obtain a waiver of basic training requirements, or state that a waiver is not allowed.

2.1.4 Matrix

The commission should develop a matrix to allow the staff to give a preliminary, non-binding opinion regarding the equivalency of training.

2.1.5 Documentation

Rules should prescribe the documentation and the certification of such documents from other educational institutions or training academies that are allowed as proof of completion of courses.

2.1.6 Decertification

Rules should prescribe the charging, hearings, and appeal process for decertification of an officer for infractions of laws, rules, or regulations, and the effect to be given to an out-of-state decertification action or conviction.

2.1.7 Licensing

The commission should publish a listing of any criminal justice position requiring a license or special license, a description of the licensing examination, and the name, address, telephone and FAX numbers of the licensing board or agency.

MODEL MINIMUM STATE STANDARDS—RECRUIT BASIC TRAINING

3.0.0 Basic Training

Commission regulations authorized by state law should establish minimum standards for the accreditation, administration, and delivery of basic training programs required for professional certification or licensing of entry-level police and corrections officers, regardless of whether such programs are delivered by state-run academies, individual law enforcement agencies, institutions of higher learning, or a combination thereof.

NOTE: Due to the difference in national and international police and corrections officer standards and training programs, the following standards may not be totally applicable to some training or educational plans. It is recognized that each commission must abide by its own state, provincial or national standards and regulations.

3.0.1 Purpose

The purpose of basic training should be to provide a supportive and nurturing environment that will encourage officers to be humanistic, compassionate, empathetic, culturally aware and career-oriented, skilled in the use of discretion, able to identify and solve problems in traditional and non-traditional but acceptable ways, and proficient in the use of weapons, the ethical and effective use of both deadly and non-deadly force, and respectful of constitutional limitations on their authority.

3.0.2 Core Competencies

Minimum curriculum requirements for basic training programs should identify a set of core competencies required for satisfactory performance of entry-level tasks. These competencies should include both knowledge and skills identified through job task analysis, and additional abilities in areas such as professional orientation, human relations and the ethical use of discretion that the commission deems consistent with the role of police and corrections officers in a free society.

3.0.3 Matriculation Requirements

Institutions, academies and agencies offering basic training courses should be encouraged to adopt entry standards for their programs that are designed to assure that graduates will meet as closely as possible the minimum professional standards adopted by the commission for occupational certification or licensing as a police or corrections officer.

3.0.4 Medical Examination

Students, as a condition of admission to basic programs, should be required to submit to a medical examination by a licensed physician familiar with the aspects of the curriculum that require physical strength, agility, flexibility and aerobic capacity and who, on a pass/fail basis, certifies that the prospective student can, in the physician's opinion, safely perform the course work required.

3.0.5 Transcripts

Students should be required to present transcripts of all prior education and training as a precondition of admission into a basic police or corrections training program.

3.0.6 Student Records

The items contained in standards 3.0.2 through 3.0.5 above should become a permanent part of the candidate's training records. This record should be available to the commission and on a need-to-know basis to the staff and management of the basic course provider. Medical records should be kept in separate files, or with restricted access. A student's files should be released only to the student's employing or sponsoring law enforcement or corrections agency, if any, or to commission officials, unless the student has given written permission for others to access them, or a valid court order exists. Student records are protected under federal law by the Buckley Amendment. Records should be retained for at least the record retention period required by state law, either in the form of hard copy, computer files, or other court-acceptable media.

3.0.7 Training Course Records

The commission should promulgate standards for the documentation of curriculum and the keeping of historical records for a period of at least twenty years for each basic training class, to include lesson plans, copies of audiovisual aids, tests and examinations, attendance records, student and instructor evaluations, course schedules, and instructor resumes.

3.0.8 Forms and Procedures

Commission administrative regulations should require that each institution have a policy that prescribes the forms and procedures for documenting the candidate's pre-employment or pre-basic requirements. Forms for each requirement should be developed and made available to agencies that will use the services of the training institution. When the candidate arrives for training at the institution, his or her training records should be inclusive and in a manageable format.

3.0.9 Basic Course Administration

Institutions and agencies providing basic training should be required by commission regulation to have a policy manual or course management guide which outlines the procedures to be followed in conducting the basic course. The policies should be directed toward the behavior of employees and staff as well as the students.

3.1.0 Scope

Written policies should describe the rules of the institution as they apply to the students, and each student upon entry should be issued a copy of the rules and acknowledge receipt of them in writing.

3.1.1 Orientation

The commission should require that each agency, institution or academy offering a basic course set aside a block of time at the beginning of the course for verbal orientation of the students and an explanation of the relevant institution rules and the matriculation requirements.

3.1.2 Rules

Written policies should describe the rules of the institution as they apply to the students, and each student upon entry should be issued a copy of the rules and acknowledge receipt of them in writing.

3.1.3 Discipline

The rules should describe the process for charging a student for a rules violation, the penalty for such a violation, and the appeal process.

3.1.4 Records

The rules should describe the records to be maintained for every student who receives any training and the method used to provide a validated transcript of such training. Records maintenance rules should be compatible with state and federal laws concerning student records.

3.1.5 Facility

The rules should prescribe facility requirements commensurate to the curricula to be taught by the institution. Curricula activities such as driver training, firearms training, practical exercises and any other training program mandating special needs should have access to adequate facilities. The facilities should be designed to provide the specific training needed to meet the course objectives.

3.1.6 Grading

Student grading policies should be established in terms of pass/fail, re-testing in regards to a failure (if permitted), appeal of test results, and necessary repeating of a subject area if a failure is substantiated or in case of excessive absence from class. Remedial or re-training should be applied in an equitable manner.

3.1.7 Attendance

Attendance at courses should be mandated. If a percentage of time is allowed for excused absences (for any reason), the percentage of time a student is allowed to be absent and still pass the course should be set by the commission.

3.1.8 Tests

Methods of developing test questions conforming to the performance objectives stated in the course should be explained to each student. The test development process should be stated in procedural format, outlining exactly how the testing program is administered.

3.1.9 Counseling

Training staff advisors and/or counselors should be available to discuss personal or training matters with the students. Remedial study habits should be suggested, along with advice to provide the student with every opportunity to do well in the courses.

3.2.0 Failure

Students failing a training course should be evaluated in terms of attitude, adaptability and retention. Should it be determined that the student can be successfully trained, remedial training should be provided under the guidelines established by the grading policy in 3.1.6 above.

3.2.1 Library

A satisfactory learning resource center should be provided if the student is assigned studies outside of the training handouts or classroom notebook. A library indexed by an acceptable decimal system should be available. The use of interactive video or computer programs is advisable.

3.2.2 Curriculum

The commission should establish minimum curriculum requirements for the basic course, and all institutions and agencies delivering approved basic training should be required to comply with these requirements. Curricula should be based on a valid and reliable job task analysis which is updated at least every five years. Training techniques should be generally accepted as correct and legal. Curricula should be submitted on a standardized form detailing the performance objectives for the course and the training methodology. The curricula should be certified by the commission's executive director upon recommendation of a curricula committee, including legal experts, whose members have examined the content and training methodology for the purpose of validating it. Instructors involved in the delivery of basic training should be credentialed as instructors by the commission.

3.2.3 Safety

Safety rules should be given to all trainees who enter the training facility. The rules, along with rules of conduct, should be discussed during orientation. A form attesting that the rules have been distributed and are understood should be signed by each student, collected by the instructor and filed. High-risk and high-liability curriculum areas should have safety rules posted in a conspicuous manner to remind the students of potential risks. Instructors should be periodically refreshed on the contents of these rules.

3.2.4 Graduation

Diplomas or notices of successful completion of basic courses should be awarded, and should identify the awarding institution, the name of the recipient, statutory mandate for the course (if any), precise name of the course, dates of attendance and graduation, and signature of the agency or institution head.

3.2.5 Insurance

Liability and comprehensive insurance should be provided in accordance with city, county or state laws or regulations. The chief legal counsel for the training agency should be consulted about indemnification.

3.2.6 Hiring

Employment of staff should be done through an established hiring process designed to insure that they possess adequate education, experience, ethical standards and medical condition for the position. The use of guest lecturers should be controlled in a manner that assures their integrity and qualifications to teach.

3.2.7 First Aid

First aid and medical emergency plans should be included in instructor and student orientation materials. If courses include high-risk activities, emergency medical plans should be discussed with students. Every instructor who teaches firearms, driving or other high-risk subjects should be currently certified in first-aid and CPR. First-aid kits and a means of summoning emergency medical assistance should be available at all training sites.

3.2.8 Equipment

Equipment requirements and standards should be established and provided to all agencies or persons participating in the training courses. Standards for weapons and ammunition used on the firing range should be established, as well as vehicles used on the driving range. Other equipment such as uniforms, leather gear, footwear, radar sets, batons, cameras or any other equipment used in training courses should conform to acceptable standards. The standards should be set by the commission or a group of persons having the ability to set such standards in a reliable and expert manner.

MODEL MINIMUM STATE STANDARDS—IN-SERVICE TRAINING

4.0 In-Service Training

IADLEST endorses the concept of additional, commission mandated annual in-service law enforcement training for sworn or commissioned law enforcement officers following basic certification or licensure. We would recommend leaving the number of training hours and the selection and/or approval of subjects to the discretion of local law enforcement administrators, subject to the guidance and minimums set by the commission.

COMMENTARY

As with many professions, and more so than most, law enforcement is an ever-changing occupation. Laws, court decisions, techniques, technology, and indeed the society that we regulate and serve, is in a constant state of flux. For this reason, it is necessary that police and corrections officers keep abreast of their field, so that they can more effectively serve the citizens, help the agencies that employ them avoid civil liability, and develop necessary supervisory and management skills. Unfortunately, in some jurisdictions the continuing education requirement for law enforcement is either non-existent or less than that of some less complex occupations such as barbers or real estate salespersons. This situation must be rectified in order for the criminal justice system to achieve optimal quality and excellence in service.

4.1.1 Statutory Authority; Purpose

Each state legislature should provide its commission with the statutory authority to mandate continuing education requirements for police and corrections officers as a condition of certification or licensure. The purpose of such training should be to ensure continued proficiency in necessary skills, become familiar with new developments and techniques, and achieve a revitalized sense of compassion, professionalism and career interest.

4.1.2 Resources

Each state legislature should provide adequate funding to its commission to assist in the development, presentation and monitoring of in-service training requirements.

4.1.3 Criteria

The criteria for needs assessment, curriculum development, instructor qualifications, research, testing, and student safety should be no less stringent than that which is prescribed for recruit training programs.

MODEL MINIMUM STATE STANDARDS—TRAINING AND INSTRUCTOR STANDARDS

5.0 Task Analysis

Each state commission should conduct a task analysis of the entry level law enforcement position at least once every five years.

COMMENTARY
A task analysis should be conducted statewide to determine the essential functions of the entry level position and the relevant tasks and task steps.

5.0.1 Task Analysis Committee

Each state commission should utilize a committee to assist with the job task analysis (JTA).

COMMENTARY
The committee should be made up of personnel in the criminal justice profession, and assist with the development of the curriculum using results of the JTA. This will assure that the curriculum reflects the actual needs of the basic police officer. The Advisory committee can also be a useful resource to add/modify curriculum during years that the JTA is being upgraded or revised.

5.0.2 Core Curriculum

Each state should develop a minimum standard basic police and corrections training curriculum based upon the results of the job task analysis, plus additional areas such as professional orientation, human relations, and the ethical use of discretion, that the commission deems consistent with the role of police and corrections officers in a free society.

COMMENTARY
Curriculum should be based upon a job task analysis, to assure that the goals and objectives of the course are based upon the current requirements of the position. The job task analysis will identify the most important, most difficult and most frequent tasks required by the essential functions, and further identify those tasks that should be learned at the academy, as opposed to at some other time and place.

5.0.3 Unit Goals

The state standard basic training "core curriculum" should contain a unit goal for each unit of instruction, and performance objectives that are measured by demonstrated performance (written or practical) examinations.

5.0.4 Performance Objective

The curriculum should assign each performance objective a unique alphanumeric identifier.

COMMENTARY
The use of numbered goals and objectives for each unit of instruction assures that the course offers the same curriculum every time it is taught. The alphanumeric identifiers allow the easy tracking and reporting of objectives. This is essential for reports to students or administrators upon completion of a course.

5.0.5 Field Training

Each state commission should establish a field training officers' program of on-the-job training that is also based upon a job task analysis.

COMMENTARY
The basic curriculum and the field training program must both be based upon a task analysis, and complement one another. The field training program should cover the following areas: (1) Knowledge and skills that are unique to the employing agency, but not relevant to the state as a whole. (2) Knowledge and skills that have been determined through a task analysis to be essential to the job, but the local employing agency is better suited as the primary trainer. (3) Demonstrating proficiency in performance objectives that were not met during the academy training process. The final report to the employing administrator should contain the performance objectives that the officer did not achieve while in training at the academy. This report should become a part of the field training program as a remedial loop. The performance objectives should be demonstrated satisfactorily during the field training experience before the officer can be certified. Field training should be an integral part of the "core curriculum" and quantified as to time to be credited.

5.0.6 Written Tests

Each state commission should develop a bank of questions that measure the knowledge required by performance objectives evaluated by written examination.

5.0.7 Performance Demonstration

Each commission should develop a "demonstrated performance" check-off matrix for each performance objective evaluated by demonstrated performance.

COMMENTARY

It is essential that the examination process measure knowledge and skills identified through job task analysis. To do this, questions and demonstrated scenarios should be developed to measure knowledge and skills relative to the course performance objectives. The questions missed or skills not demonstrated are reported to the student so that he or she not only knows the questions they missed, but also the performance objectives not achieved.

5.0.8 Final Examination

Each commission should develop a comprehensive final examination to determine how much knowledge was gained during the basic course, or a basic certification examination to determine that the student has the requisite knowledge to perform the essential job tasks at the entry level.

COMMENTARY

Post-test measurement need not be conducted if careful examination of performance objectives was conducted during the course.

5.0.9 Follow-Up

Each commission should establish a comprehensive post-graduation follow-up survey.

COMMENTARY

The post-graduation follow-up is essential, and ensures that the course and course content remain relevant. The survey should be designed to determine the retention of basic knowledge and skills. Adjustments should be made to course and delivery systems to increase retention and relevancy of the curriculum.

5.0.10 Instructor Training

Each commission should establish an instructor training program for instructors involved in the "basic core" curriculum.

COMMENTARY

A comprehensive instructor training course is essential to a standardized "basic core" curriculum. Unless the instructional staff knows the purpose of performance objectives, how they are measured, and how to write proper test questions and demonstration scenarios, the influence of the goals and objectives on learning and retention will be diminished. Additionally, the instructor should be required to demonstrate the instructional processes he or she will use, before actual use in a teaching role. This requirement may be waived in the case of instructors whose prior education or experience is deemed to be the equivalent of such a course, such as professors or instructors at accredited postsecondary institutions.

5.0.11 Instructor Evaluation

Each state commission should develop an instructor evaluation process. It is important to the instructor to receive feedback on how well he or she does in the classroom. A comprehensive program will not only use the students to evaluate the instructor, but will also utilize feedback from managers, commissioned members, and other designated personnel.

5.0.12 Standardized Lesson Plan Format

Each state commission should develop a standardized format for lesson plans.

COMMENTARY
The lesson plan should meet the standard and contain reference(s) to each performance objective covered during the unit of instruction. The lesson plan should be approved by the course coordinator before the instructor teaches. The lesson plan should be a permanent part of the course record. All multimedia and handouts used during the presentation should be identified on the lesson plan.

5.0.13 Instructor Certification Levels

Each state commission should establish certification levels for persons wishing to be instructors.

COMMENTARY
Different levels of certification should be established for instructors, valid for a set period of time, after which renewal can be requested. A basic level instructor should be required to demonstrate the knowledge and ability to conduct instruction from prepared material. More advanced instructors should also be required to demonstrate the knowledge and ability to determine course objectives, develop lesson plans, coordinate other instructors and utilize results of task analyses. Top-level instructors should be required to demonstrate the ability to develop tests, supervise instructors and support staff, organize goal-setting, assist in developing a budget for training programs and maintain positive public relations. Appropriate instructor designations should recognize certain high-liability areas, such as firearms, defensive tactics, physical fitness, and emergency driving.

5.0.14 Revocation of Certification

Each state commission should have the authority to revoke the certification of instructors.

COMMENTARY
To assure the quality of instruction, the state commission should be authorized to revoke instructor certification of those persons failing to follow commission guidelines or performance objectives.

5.0.15 Annual Instructor Evaluation

Each state commission should conduct evaluations of instructors on a routine basis, at least annually.

COMMENTARY
Commission staff should annually evaluate each instructor conducting mandated training programs. The evaluation will be a useful tool to the instructor and the commission, and ensures that all performance objectives are presented by the instructor, and that high-quality teaching is provided to students.

5.0.16 Instruction and Curriculum Management

Curricula should be carefully documented, validated and updated, as follows:

5.0.17 Documentation

Curricula should have dates of original writing and dates at which time it was updated or revised. A tickler file should trigger automatic review and update consideration. A competent curriculum committee with the appropriate education and background should review and recommend all curriculum. Whenever the commission director is the sole curriculum approving authority, he or she should have the background, education and credentials necessary to make such judgments. The committee or commission director should have statutory authority to approve or deny curricula.

5.0.18 Validation

Validation procedures for curricula should be job task–related, contain performance objectives based upon identified training needs, and test construction should be valid and reliable in testing the performance objectives.

5.0.19 Design

Curriculum design should include full research of the topic(s) or curriculum, source documents written from research, lesson plan(s) developed from the source documents, and the source documents and lesson plan should be kept on file for reference.

5.0.20 Handouts

Handout materials or any reference materials should be serialized, and corresponding numbers placed on lesson plans and curricula to which the handout is related.

5.0.21 Staff Instructors

Staff instructors should be graduates of a recognized college or university with a degree in the appropriate field, or have at least a high school education with a documented background and experience to equate in ratio to years of college or university study.

5.0.22 Background

Instructors should successfully pass a background investigation documenting good moral character and integrity.

5.0.23 Physical Fitness

Instructors should be physically fit and in acceptable health to perform the essential functions of their jobs.

5.0.24 Communications

Instructors should have the ability to communicate with students in a supportive manner and yet be able to render objective judgments in reference to student efforts.

5.0.25 Motivation

Instructors should be able to instruct in a manner that motivates students to learn.

5.0.26 Research Skills

Instructors should be able to research and write training materials such as source documents, lesson plans, and tests.

5.0.27 Testing

Testing, whether pre-test or post-test, should be valid and reliable. If pre-testing is used, it should be done with a specific purpose in mind and result in the ability to measure the instructional results accurately. Otherwise, it will not provide a useable result, but will instead mislead and cause confusion.

5.0.28 Technology

Contemporary information with regard to the use and development of instructional technology should be researched in order to maximize training techniques. The goal should be to correctly apply training technology to enhance the ability of students to learn, and not solely to expedite the training process.

5.0.29 Skills Training

Critical skills areas (vehicle stops, use of deadly force, evidence collection and preservation, etc.) should be tested through the use of graded practical exercises. An acceptable pass/fail criteria should be established for each skills test.

5.0.30 Strategies

Instructional strategies should be utilized when it is determined that a particular strategy is the best technique that could be used to teach a particular attitude, knowledge, or skill.

MODEL MINIMUM STATE STANDARDS—PROFESSIONAL CONDUCT

6.0 Standards of Professional Conduct

Each state should provide its commission with the authority to issue standards for professional conduct of law enforcement and corrections officers which specify occupational professionalism by which the certification or license may be retained by persons holding it, and should be empowered to enforce minimum professional standards through the administrative denial of certification to unqualified applicants, and administrative sanction of officers violating professional standards.

COMMENTARY
Each state has been empowered through its constitution or by legislative authority, to regulate occupations and professions in the public interest, thereby protecting the public health, safety and welfare in the performance of such occupations and professions. A state generally administers this authority through the certification or licensing of persons who have met specific minimum stan-

dards. The authority of a state to grant certification or licensure to persons performing an occupation or profession, also implies that the state may refuse to license, or revoke state certification or licensure. In the case of law enforcement and corrections, these duties should be delegated by the legislature to the appropriate commission or commissions.

6.0.1 Content

Standards of professional conduct should address the commission's authority to provide licensing or certification retention standards, and authority to revoke or decertify law enforcement and corrections officers. This authority and responsibility should parallel minimum standards of certification and training, and include cause for administrative sanction, due process notice, hearing and appeal requirements, and provisions for releasing information to a national data bank of decertified officers, as well as a recertification process.

6.0.2 Certification

Each commission should establish procedures and regulate, monitor and certify that persons employed as law enforcement and corrections officers have met the minimum standards for employment, training, and retention.

COMMENTARY
These standards should offer public notice regarding the high ethical, character, training and competency standards required by the state for the employment of law enforcement and corrections officers.

6.0.3 Uniformity

A set of uniform certification or licensing standards should apply to all officer applicants in the state.

6.0.4 Compliance

Prior to issuance of certification or licensure, the commission should verify the compliance of the applicant with minimum standards, by collecting, verifying and maintaining all documentation establishing compliance, and assuring that a proper background investigation and criminal history check have been completed, and requiring the training institution or hiring authority to provide assurance of completion of all pre-hiring requirements, subject to verification by commission audit.

6.0.5 Ongoing Compliance

The commission should be authorized to monitor and enforce ongoing compliance with criteria for the retention of certified or licensed law enforcement or corrections officers.

COMMENTARY
In order to provide a means to identify officers in possession of commission certificates or licenses who involve themselves in unethical or unlawful conduct which would be considered outrageous, contemptible, inhumane, cruel, immoral, indecent, improper, flagrant, excessive, notorious, wanton, intolerable or shocking to the conscience, each state should maintain a professional certification or licensing compliance system. The creation of such a system will assist in preserving minimum standards of conduct and public trust in persons holding commission certification or licensure. It will also provide means for notice to future law enforcement or corrections employers of those applicants who have violated professional standards and have been sanctioned by the commission.

6.0.6 Application, Certification and Denial

Each commission should require a formal application for certification, with specified criteria. If minimum standards are met, the applicant should be certified. If the applicant does not appear to meet minimum standards, the commission should formally notify the applicant of its intention to reject the application and allow a hearing, pursuant to the state administrative procedure act or other applicable law, if the applicant files a timely request for such a hearing.

6.0.7 Reporting Misconduct

Commission regulations should mandate that employing agencies notify the commission when an officer leaves employment, whether terminated, laid off, resigned, or retired. The facts and circumstances leading to the separation should be required to be disclosed where officer misconduct would give rise to possible sanction by the commission. Instances of such misconduct substantiated by an officer's employing agency should also be disclosed to the commission. All law enforcement agencies in the state should be required to report to the commission, the arrest of any person known or identified to them as a police or corrections officer.

COMMENTARY
Public respect for the law is linked to public respect for those who enforce it. When the public becomes aware of unethical, illegal or unconstitutional conduct,

on- or off-duty, by those who are sworn to uphold the law and preserve the peace, public confidence is shaken and all criminal justice professionals and agencies suffer diminished effectiveness through diminished public respect, cooperation, and confidence.

6.0.8 Investigation of Misconduct

The commission should evaluate, and may inquire into, all allegations reported to them of officers violating commission standards. The commission should cooperate with employing agencies in this regard. If the information obtained by inquiry indicates that an officer is in violation of commission standards which could result in the imposition of sanctions, the matter should be presented to the commission or executive director for determination. If the investigation results in a conclusion that no cause for action exists, the employing agency and officer should be so notified. If cause is found, the commission should issue a formal administrative complaint, specifying the charges upon which the sanctions may be imposed.

6.0.9 Grounds for Action

A set of uniform professional standards applicable to all officers certified or licensed by the commission should be established and published. The commission should have the authority to sanction misconduct including any act or conduct which raises substantial doubts about the officer's honesty, fairness, or respect for the rights of others, regardless of whether the misconduct constitutes or is prosecuted as a crime, including but not limited to a plea of guilty, nolo contendere or a finding of guilt as to one or more of a specified series of misdemeanor charges, regardless of withheld adjudication or suspended sentence; a plea of guilty, nolo contendere or a finding of guilt as to a felony or similar offense, regardless of withheld adjudication or suspended sentence; unlawful sale, possession or use of a controlled dangerous substance, or failure to meet mandatory commission standards. State law should permit the commission to consider the existence of an annulled record in making certification and decertification decisions.

6.1.0 Possible Sanctions

Depending on the type of violation, the facts and circumstances of the case, and the prior record of the officer, the commission should impose the most appropriate administrative sanction, to include suspension or revocation of the license or certificate, probation, which may include remedial retraining, or formal reprimand or censure.

6.1.1 Sanction Procedure

In accordance with the state administrative procedure act or other applicable law, the officer should be given notice of the proposed administrative sanction and be provided an opportunity to be heard in the administrative hearing upon request, and to be represented by counsel at his or her own expense. If the hearing results in a finding that the standard of professional conduct was not violated or a conclusion that the conduct in question does not warrant administrative sanction, the case should be dismissed. In the event a violation of professional standards is found, the commission should impose sanctions as appropriate.

6.1.2 National Repository

It is recommended that, upon the establishment of a national repository of information regarding decertified officers, each state commission contribute toward this repository.

COMMENTARY
Each state's society is highly mobile. The number of law enforcement and corrections officers certified or licensed who have been sanctioned by state commissions, continues to expand. There are many accounts of officers with histories of violating professional standards attempting to or becoming employed in the criminal justice professions in states outside the jurisdictions where the violations occurred. To protect criminal justice agencies from employing a person who has been decertified in another state, each state should have the authority to release information on decertified officers upon an official request, and within authorized release guidelines.

6.1.3 Dissemination

Each state should have an authorized state agency that can establish policy and procedures for the dissemination of information to a national repository regarding officers whose commission certificate or license has been suspended, revoked or decertified for punitive reasons. Information to be released should include the name, date of birth and social security number of the officer, the name and address of the commission, and the name and telephone number of a contact person at the state commission who can answer inquiries into the nature of the sustained grounds for decertification.

6.1.4 Recertification

Each commission should adopt a process whereby law enforcement and corrections officers whose commission certificates or licenses have lapsed or been suspended, revoked or decertified, may apply to have them restored, reinstated or re-issued. Officers should first be required to demonstrate compliance with minimum state certification or licensing standards before recertification will be considered. Application to the commission as provided in the initial certification or licensing process should be made. Any denial of certification should be in writing, listing the reasons therefore, and describing any appeals process.

Index